A TEXTUAL COMMENTARY ON THE GREEK NEW TESTAMENT

Second Edition

A Companion Volume to the

UNITED BIBLE SOCIETIES'
GREEK NEW TESTAMENT

(Fourth Revised Edition)

by

BRUCE M. METZGER

on behalf of and in cooperation with the Editorial Committee
of the United Bible Societies' Greek New Testament

DEUTSCHE BIBELGESELLSCHAFT
UNITED BIBLE SOCIETIES

This volume is intended to be used with the fourth revised edition of the United Bible Societies' Greek New Testament.

Orders may be placed with the

	in the USA
German Bible Society	American Bible Society
P.O. Box 81 03 40	1865 Broadway
D–70520 Stuttgart	New York, NY 10023

First Edition
© 1971 United Bible Societies, U.S.A.
Second Edition
© 1994 Deutsche Bibelgesellschaft, D–Stuttgart
Second Edition, 2nd printing
© 1998 Deutsche Bibelgesellschaft, D–Stuttgart

ISBN 3-438-06010-8

CONTENTS

PREFACE TO THE SECOND EDITION

The present edition of this Textual Commentary has been adapted to the fourth revised edition of *The Greek New Testament,* published by the German Bible Society on behalf of the United Bible Societies early in 1993. This means that each of the 284 additional sets of variant readings that were included by Committee decision in the apparatus of the fourth edition has now a corresponding entry in the Commentary. On the other hand, the comments on almost all of the 273 sets of variant readings that the Committee removed from the apparatus, because the variants were of less significance for translators and other readers, are no longer retained in the Commentary.

Other adjustments have also been made. For example, the implications of recent discussions concerning the so-called Caesarean text are reflected at various places in the Commentary. Further bibliographical items have been added here and there, particularly in connection with the expanded discussion of problems relating to the two main types of text in the book of Acts.

As was true in the earlier edition of the Commentary, textual discussions are usually supplied with the citation of only the more important manuscript witnesses. In some cases this information differs slightly from the citation given in the apparatus for those passages in the fourth edition of the Greek text. For example, certain later Greek uncial manuscripts as well as evidence from the Gothic version, which are no longer cited in the fourth edition of the text volume, continue to be cited here. On the other hand, additional minuscule manuscripts as well as evidence from the Old Church Slavonic version, which are now included in the apparatus of the fourth edition, are not repeated here. For a statement of the different principles followed in selecting witnesses to be cited in the third and the fourth editions, see the Introduction to each edition.

Special thanks are due to Irene Berman, who prepared the

typescript from the writer's handwritten copy; Harold P. Scanlin, who developed the Greek uncial characters that are used here and there in discussions of palaeography; and Karen Munson, who read the page proofs with meticulous care.

BRUCE M. METZGER
Princeton Theological Seminary
September 30, 1993

PREFACE TO THE FIRST EDITION

The present volume is designed to serve as a companion to the third edition of the United Bible Societies' Greek New Testament, edited by Kurt Aland, Matthew Black, Carlo M. Martini, Bruce M. Metzger, and Allen Wikgren.

One of the chief purposes of the commentary is to set forth the reasons that led the Committee, or a majority of the members of the Committee, to adopt certain variant readings for inclusion in the text and to relegate certain other readings to the apparatus. On the basis of a record of the voting of the Committee, as well as, for most sessions, more or less full notes of the discussions that preceded the voting, the present writer has sought to frame and express concisely (a) the main problem or problems involved in each set of variants and (b) the Committee's evaluation and resolution of those problems. In writing the commentary it was necessary not only to review what the Committee had done, but also to consult once again the several commentaries, concordances, synopses, lexicons, grammars, and similar reference works that had been utilized by members of the Committee during their discussions. More than once the record of the discussion proved to be incomplete because, amid the lively exchange of opinions, the Committee had come to a decision without the formal enunciation of those reasons that appeared at the time to be obvious or self-evident. In such cases it was necessary for the present writer to supplement, or even to reconstruct, the tenor of the Committee's discussions.

The general Introduction to the commentary includes an outline of the chief kinds of considerations that the Committee took into account in choosing among variant readings. By becoming acquainted with these criteria (pp. 10*–14*) the reader will be able to understand more readily the presuppositions that underlie the Committee's evaluations of the divergent readings.

In addition to the 1440 sets of variant readings supplied in the apparatus of the Bible Societies' edition, the selection of which was made chiefly on the basis of their exegetical importance to the translator and student, the Committee suggested that certain other readings also deserved discussion in the supplementary volume. The author has therefore included comments on about 600 additional sets of variant readings, scattered throughout the New Testament; the majority of them, it will be noted, occur in the book of Acts, which, because of its peculiar textual problems, seemed to demand special attention (see the Introduction to the book of Acts).

In the comments on the variant readings for which the text-volume supplies an apparatus, it was considered sufficient to cite merely the more important manuscript witnesses; the reader of the commentary will be able to supplement the partial citation of evidence by consulting the fuller apparatus in the text-volume. On the other hand, occasionally the discussion in the commentary supplements the apparatus in the text-volume by the citation of additional witnesses, a few of which were not known at the time of the Committee's work, and others of which had been deemed unimportant for citation in the apparatus. Since the present volume is designed to assist translators and students who may not have available an extensive library, the comments on the 600 additional sets of variant readings are accompanied by a more or less full citation of evidence, drawn from such standard *apparatus critici* as those of Tischendorf, von Soden, Nestle, Merk, Bover, Souter, Hoskier (for Revelation), and Wordsworth and White, as well as from editions of individual manuscripts.

The writing of the commentary was begun during 1964, when the author, on sabbatical leave from his usual academic duties, was a member of the Institute for Advanced Study in Princeton. During the following years, as the first draft of each major section was completed, it was circulated among the other members of the Committee to make certain that the comments reflected adequately the Committee's deliberations. Frequently it had happened that the members of the Committee differed in their evaluation of the textual evidence, and thus many readings were adopted on the basis of a majority vote. In special cases, when a member holding a minority opinion had strong feelings that the majority had seriously gone astray, opportunity was given for him to express his own point of view. Such occasional comments, identified by the writer's initials and enclosed within square brackets, are appended to the main discussion of the textual problem in question.

The author is grateful to Professors Black, Martini, and Wikgren who, having read the typescript of the commentary, made several suggestions, corrections, and additions which have been incorporated into the volume; for the errors that remain he alone, of course, is responsible. Appreciation must also be expressed to Dr. Robert P. Markham for his capable and courteous assistance given at all stages of the work. The formidable task of typing the handwritten copy of the manuscript was executed with exceptional accuracy by Mrs. Richard E. Munson. Similarly the craftsmen of the firm of Maurice Jacobs, Inc., deserve commendation for the high quality of their work, which included the preparation of a special font of Greek type to represent the script used in uncial manuscripts. Assistance in the onerous task of proofreading was given by Dr. Markham, Mr. Stanley L. Morris, Mrs. Munson, Dr. Erroll Rhodes, and Professor Wikgren. Finally, I wish to express my sincere thanks to Dr. Eugene A. Nida of the American Bible Society for having invited me to prepare this companion to our Greek text. Although the writing of the volume proved to be a far greater and much more exacting task than it appeared when I accepted the invitation, now that it is completed I am grateful to him for having given me the opportunity of enlarging, as one may hope, the usefulness of the United Bible Societies' edition of the Greek New Testament.

BRUCE M. METZGER

Princeton Theological Seminary
September 30, 1970

ABBREVIATIONS

1. MODERN AUTHORS AND EDITORS

Aland-Aland = *The Text of the New Testament, An Introduction to the Critical Editions and to the Theory and Practice of Modern Textual Criticism*, by Kurt Aland and Barbara Aland (Grand Rapids, 1987; 2nd ed., 1989).

Bauer-Arndt-Gingrich-Danker = *A Greek-English Lexicon of the New Testament and Other Early Christian Literature;* A Translation and Adaptation of Walter Bauer's *Griechisch-deutsches Wörterbuch zu den Schriften des Neuen Testaments und der übrigen urchristlichen Literatur,* 4te Aufl., 1952, by William F. Arndt and F. Wilbur Gingrich, 2nd ed., revised and augmented by F. Wilbur Gingrich and Frederick W. Danker from Walter Bauer's 5th ed., 1958 (Chicago and Cambridge, 1969).

Black, *Aramaic Approach* = *An Aramaic Approach to the Gospels and Acts,* by Matthew Black (Oxford, 1946; 3rd ed., 1967).

Blass-Debrunner-Funk = *A Greek Grammar of the New Testament and Other Early Christian Literature;* A Translation and Revision of F. Blass and A. Debrunner's ninth-tenth German edition … by Robert W. Funk (Chicago, 1961).

Bruce = *The Acts of the Apostles; the Greek Text with Introduction and Commentary,* by F. F. Bruce (London, 1951); 3rd ed., 1990.

Clark = *The Acts of the Apostles; A Critical Edition with Introduction and Notes on Selected Passages,* by Albert C. Clark (Oxford, 1933).

Haenchen = *Die Apostelgeschichte,* neu übersetzt und erklärt von Ernst Haenchen, 5te Aufl. (*Kritisch-exegetischer Kommentar über das Neue Testament,* begründet von H. A. W. Meyer; Göttingen, 1965); English trans. (Philadelphia, 1971).

Harris = *Codex Bezae, a Study of the So-Called Western Text of the New Testament,* by J. Rendel Harris (*Texts and Studies,* vol. II; Cambridge, 1891).

Hort = F. J. A. Hort's "Notes on Select Readings," in *The New Testa-*

ment in the Original Greek, the Text Revised by Brooke Foss Westcott and Fenton John Anthony Hort; [vol. II] *Introduction [and] Appendix* (Cambridge and London, 1881; 2nd ed., 1896).

Lake and Cadbury = *The Beginnings of Christianity;* Part I, *The Acts of the Apostles,* ed. by F. J. Foakes Jackson and Kirsopp Lake; vol. IV, *English Translation and Commentary,* by Kirsopp Lake and Henry J. Cadbury (London, 1933).

Metzger = *The Text of the New Testament, Its Transmission, Corruption, and Restoration,* by Bruce M. Metzger (Oxford, 1964; 3rd ed., 1992).

Moulton, *Prolegomena* = *A Grammar of New Testament Greek,* by James Hope Moulton; vol. I, *Prolegomena* (Edinburgh, 1906; 3rd ed., 1908).

Moulton-Howard, *Grammar* = *A Grammar of New Testament Greek,* by James Hope Moulton and Wilbert Francis Howard; vol. II, *Accidence and Word-Formation* (Edinburgh, 1929).

Moulton and Milligan = *The Vocabulary of the Greek Testament Illustrated from the Papyri and Other Non-Literary Sources,* by James Hope Moulton and George Milligan (London, 1930).

Moulton-Turner = *A Grammar of New Testament Greek,* by James Hope Moulton; vol. III, *Syntax,* by Nigel Turner (Edinburgh, 1963).

Ropes = *The Text of Acts,* by James Hardy Ropes, being vol. III of *The Beginnings of Christianity;* Part I, *The Acts of the Apostles,* ed. by F. J. Foakes Jackson and Kirsopp Lake (London, 1926).

Torrey = *The Composition and Date of Acts,* by C. C. Torrey (*Harvard Theological Studies,* vol. I; Cambridge, Massachusetts, 1916).

Turner (see Moulton-Turner).

Weiss, *Der Codex D* = *Der Codex D in der Apostelgeschichte; Textkritische Untersuchungen,* by Bernhard Weiss (*Texte und Untersuchungen,* Neue Folge, II. Band; Leipzig, 1899).

Westcott and Hort, *Introduction* = *The New Testament in the Original Greek,* the Text Revised by Brooke Foss Westcott and Fenton John Anthony Hort; [vol. II] *Introduction [and] Appendix* (Cambridge and London, 1881; 2nd ed., 1896).

Zuntz = *The Text of the Epistles; a Disquisition upon the* Corpus Paulinum, by G. Zuntz (London, 1953).

2. OTHER ABBREVIATIONS

ad loc. = *ad locum* (at the passage)
al = *alia* (other witnesses)
ASV = American Standard Version (1901)
AV = Authorized or King James Version (1611)
bis = twice
cf. = *confer* (compare)
e. g. = *exempli gratia* (for example)
hiat = is lacking (used of a passage in a fragmentary manuscript)
i. e. = *id est* (that is)
NEB = New English Bible (New Testament, 1961)
NRSV = New Revised Standard Version (1990)
REB = Revised English Bible (1989)
RSV = Revised Standard Version (New Testament, 1946)
s.v. = *sub voce* (under the word)
ter = three times
vid = *videtur* (it seems; used to indicate that the reading is not certain, especially in a damaged manuscript)

For the abbreviations of the titles of the books of the Bible, and the sigla of manuscripts and early versions of the New Testament, see the Introduction in *The Greek New Testament* (fourth revised edition), supplemented by the sigla of witnesses listed in the Appendix at the close of the present volume. For further information concerning individual Greek manuscripts cited in the apparatus, see Caspar René Gregory, *Textkritik des Neuen Testamentes,* 3 vols. (Leipzig, 1900–09); Kurt Aland, *Kurzgefasste Liste der griechischen Handschriften des Neuen Testaments: I. Gesamtübersicht* (Berlin, 1963); and Kurt Aland and Barbara Aland, *The Text of the New Testament; An Introduction to the Critical Editions and to the Theory and Practice of Modern Textual Criticism,* translated by Erroll F. Rhodes, 2nd ed., revised and enlarged (Grand Rapids – Leiden, 1989).

N. B.: When the siglum of a manuscript is enclosed within parentheses, this means that the manuscript supports the reading in most respects but differs in some unimportant detail or details.

It should be observed that, in accord with the theory that members of f^1 and f^{13} were subject to progressive accommodation to the later Byzantine text, scholars have established the text of these families by adopting readings of family witnesses that differ from the Textus Receptus. Therefore the citation of the siglum f^1 or f^{13} may, in any given instance, signify a minority of manuscripts (or even only one) that belong to the family.

INTRODUCTION

Most commentaries on the Bible seek to explain the meaning of words, phrases, and ideas of the scriptural text in their nearer and wider context; a textual commentary, however, is concerned with the prior question, What is the original text of the passage? That such a question must be asked – and answered! – before one explains the meaning of the text arises from two circumstances: (*a*) none of the original documents of the Bible is extant today, and (*b*) the existing copies differ from one another.

Despite the large number of general and specialized commentaries on the books of the New Testament, very few deal adequately with textual problems. In fact, there is none that deals comprehensively with the entire New Testament, and those that supply the fullest discussions were written during the past century and are, of course, seriously out of date today. Among nineteenth century works devoted exclusively to textual problems are Rinck's commentary on the Acts of the Apostles and the Epistles,[1] and Reiche's three volumes on the Pauline and Catholic Epistles.[2] Not nearly so extensive but much

---

[1] Wilhelm Friedrich Rinck, *Lucubratio critica in Acta Apostolorum, Epistolas Catholicas et Paulinas,* in qua de classibus librorum manu scriptum quaestio instituitur, descriptio et varia lectio septem codicum Marcionarum exhibitur, atque observationes ad plurima loca cum Apostoli tum Evangeliorum dijudicanda et emendanda proponuntur (Basel, 1830).

Prior to Rinck, J. J. Griesbach began a comprehensive textual commentary on the New Testament, but finished only the portions on Matthew and Mark (*Commentarius criticus in textum Graecum Novi Testamenti,* particula I [Jena, 1798]; particula II [Jena, 1811]). It may also be mentioned that in 1844 J. I. Doedes commented at considerable length on nearly fifty passages that involve major textual problems in the New Testament in his *Verhandeling over de tekstkritiek des Nieuwen Verbonds* (= Teyler's Godgeleerd Genootschap, vol. XXXIV; Haarlem, 1844), pp. 387–481.

[2] Johann Georg Reiche, *Commentarius criticus in N[ovum] T[estamentum], quo loca graviora et difficiliora lectionis dubiae accurate recensentur et explicantur;* Tomus I, *Epistolas Pauli ad Romanos et ad Corinthios datas continens* (Göttingen, 1853); Tomus II, *Epistolas Apostoli Pauli minores continens* (1859); Tomus III, *Epistolam ad Hebraeos et Epistolas Catholicas continens* (1862).

more widely known are the "Notes on Select Readings" that are included in the second volume, entitled *Introduction [and] Appendix,*
of B. F. Westcott and F. J. A. Hort's *The New Testament in the Original Greek* (Cambridge and London, 1881).[3] Approximately 425 passages are considered in these Notes, some of which involve lengthy
discussions that remain permanently valuable, while others provide
merely the citation of evidence without comment. The second edition
of the volume (1896) contains nearly 50 additional Notes, prepared
by F. C. Burkitt and dealing with the newly discovered Sinaitic
Syriac manuscript of the Gospels. At the close of the century Edward
Miller, a disciple of Dean J. W. Burgon, issued Part I of his *Textual
Commentary upon the Holy Gospels* (London, 1899), covering the
first fourteen chapters of the Gospel according to Matthew. This
work, however, is misnamed, for instead of being a commentary in
the usual sense of the word, it comprises nothing more than a critical
apparatus of variant readings.

The twentieth century saw the publication of de Zwaan's doctoral
dissertation devoted to the textual problems of 2 Peter and Jude,[4]
and Turner's elaborate analyses of Markan usage, culminating in "A
Textual Commentary on Mark I."[5] More recently R. V. G. Tasker
has provided about 270 brief "Notes on Variant Readings" in the
Appendix to his edition of *The Greek New Testament* (Oxford and
Cambridge, 1964), the text of which is to be regarded as lying
behind *The New English Bible* (1961).

In the following pages the reader will find a succinct statement of

---

[3] In the two volumes entitled *The Revisers' Greek Text* (Boston, 1892), which are
in commentary-format, S. W. Whitney discusses about 700 passages in the Revised
Version of 1881, which was translated basically from Westcott and Hort's Greek text;
in almost all cases Whitney prefers the Textus Receptus, represented in the King James
or so-called Authorized Version.

[4] Johannes de Zwaan, *II Petrus en Judas; textuitgave met inleidende studiën en
textueelen commentaar* (Leiden, 1909).

[5] C. H. Turner, "Marcan Usage: Notes, Critical and Exegetical, on the Second
Gospel," *Journal of Theological Studies,* XXV (1923–24), pp. 377–386; XXVI
(1924–25), pp. 12–20, 145–156, 225–240, 337–346; XXVII (1925–26), pp. 58–62;
XXVIII (1926–27), pp. 9–30, 349–362. The textual commentary was published in
Journal of Theological Studies, XXVIII (1926–27), pp. 145–158.

(1) the history of the transmission of the New Testament text, (2) the principal criteria used in choosing among conflicting witnesses to the text, and (3) the chief witnesses to the New Testament listed according to types of text.

I. History of the Transmission of the New Testament Text

In the earliest days of the Christian church, after an apostolic letter was sent to a congregation or an individual, or after a gospel was written to meet the needs of a particular reading public, copies would be made in order to extend its influence and to enable others to profit from it as well. It was inevitable that such handwritten copies would contain a greater or lesser number of differences in wording from the original. Most of the divergencies arose from quite accidental causes, such as mistaking a letter or a word for another that looked like it. If two neighboring lines of a manuscript began or ended with the same group of letters or if two similar words stood near each other in the same line, it was easy for the eye of the copyist to jump from the first group of letters to the second, and so for a portion of the text to be omitted (called homoeoarcton or homoeoteleuton, depending upon whether the similarity of letters occurred at the beginning or the ending of the words). Conversely the scribe might go back from the second to the first group and unwittingly copy one or more words twice (called dittography). Letters that were pronounced alike were sometimes confused (called itacism). Such accidental errors are almost unavoidable whenever lengthy passages are copied by hand, and would be especially likely to occur if the scribe had defective eyesight, or was interrupted while copying, or, because of fatigue, was less attentive to his task than he should have been.

Other divergencies in wording arose from deliberate attempts to smooth out grammatical or stylistic harshness, or to eliminate real or imagined obscurities of meaning in the text. Sometimes a copyist would substitute or would add what seemed to him to be a more appropriate word or form, perhaps derived from a parallel passage (called harmonization or assimilation). Thus, during the years imme-diately following the composition of the several documents that eventually were collected to form the New Testament, hundreds if not thousands of variant readings arose.

Still other kinds of divergencies originated when the New Testament documents were translated from Greek into other languages. During the second and third centuries, after Christianity had been introduced into Syria, into North Africa and Italy, into central and southern Egypt, both congregations and individual believers would naturally desire copies of the Scriptures in their own languages. And so versions in Syriac, in Latin, and in the several dialects of Coptic used in Egypt were produced. They were followed in the fourth and succeeding centuries by other versions in Armenian, Georgian, Ethiopic, Arabic, and Nubian in the East, and in Gothic, Old Church Slavonic, and (much later) Anglo-Saxon in the West.

The accuracy of such translations was directly related to two factors: (*a*) the degree of familiarity possessed by the translator of both Greek and the language into which the translation was made, and (*b*) the amount of care he devoted to the task of making the translation. It is not surprising that very considerable divergencies in early versions developed, first, when different persons made different translations from what may have been slightly different forms of Greek text; and, second, when these renderings in one or another language were transmitted in handwritten copies by scribes who, familiar with a slightly different form of text (either a divergent Greek text or a divergent versional rendering), adjusted the new copies so as to accord with what they considered the preferable wording.

During the early centuries of the expansion of the Christian church, what are called "local texts" of the New Testament gradually developed. Newly established congregations in and near a large city, such as Alexandria, Antioch, Constantinople, Carthage, or Rome, were provided with copies of the Scriptures in the form that was current in that area. As additional copies were made, the number of special readings and renderings would be both conserved and, to some extent, increased, so that eventually a type of text grew up that was more or less peculiar to that locality. Today it is possible to identify the type of text preserved in New Testament manuscripts by comparing their characteristic readings with the quotations of those passages in the writings of Church Fathers who lived in or near the chief ecclesiastical centers.

At the same time the distinctiveness of a local text tended to become diluted and mixed with other types of text. A manuscript of the Gospel of Mark copied in Alexandria, for example, and taken later to Rome would doubtless influence to some extent copyists transcribing the form of the text of Mark heretofore current at Rome. On the whole, however, during the earliest centuries the tendencies to develop and preserve a particular type of text prevailed over the tendencies leading to a mixture of texts. Thus there grew up several distinctive kinds of New Testament text, the most important of which are the following.

The *Alexandrian text,* which Westcott and Hort called the *Neutral text* (a question-begging title), is usually considered to be the best text and the most faithful in preserving the original. Characteristics of the Alexandrian text are brevity and austerity. That is, it is generally shorter than the text of other forms, and it does not exhibit the degree of grammatical and stylistic polishing that is characteristic of the Byzantine type of text. Until recently the two chief witnesses to the Alexandrian text were codex Vaticanus (B) and codex Sinaiticus (ℵ), parchment manuscripts dating from about the middle of the fourth century. With the acquisition, however, of the Bodmer Papyri, particularly $\mathfrak{P}^{66}$ and $\mathfrak{P}^{75}$, both copied about the end of the second or the beginning of the third century, evidence is now available that the Alexandrian type of text goes back to an archetype that must be dated early in the second century. The Sahidic and Bohairic versions frequently contain typically Alexandrian readings.

The so-called *Western text,* which was widely current in Italy and Gaul as well as in North Africa and elsewhere (including Egypt), can also be traced back to the second century. It was used by Marcion, Tatian, Irenaeus, Tertullian, and Cyprian. Its presence in Egypt is shown by the testimony of $\mathfrak{P}^{38}$ (about A.D. 300) and $\mathfrak{P}^{48}$ (about the end of the third century). The most important Greek manuscripts that present a Western type of text are codex Bezae (D) of the fifth century (containing the Gospels and Acts), codex Claromontanus (D) of the sixth century (containing the Pauline epistles), and, for Mark 1.1 to 5.30, codex Washingtonianus (W) of the fifth century. Likewise the Old Latin versions are noteworthy witnesses to a Western type of text; these fall into three main groups, the African, Italian, and Hispanic forms of Old Latin texts.

The chief characteristic of Western readings is fondness for paraphrase. Words, clauses, and even whole sentences are freely changed, omitted, or inserted. Sometimes the motive appears to have been harmonization, while at other times it was the enrichment of the narrative by the inclusion of traditional or apocryphal material. Some readings involve quite trivial alterations for which no special reason can be assigned. One of the puzzling features of the Western text (which generally is longer than the other forms of text) is that at the end of Luke and in a few other places in the New Testament certain Western witnesses omit words and passages that are present in other forms of text, including the Alexandrian. Although at the close of the last century certain scholars were disposed to regard these shorter readings as original (Westcott and Hort called them "Western non-interpolations"), since the acquisition of the Bodmer Papyri many scholars today are inclined to regard them as aberrant readings (see the Note on Western Non-Interpolations, pp. 164–166).

In the book of Acts the problems raised by the Western text become most acute, for the Western text of Acts is nearly ten percent longer than the form that is commonly regarded to be the original text of that book. For this reason the present volume devotes proportionately more space to variant readings in Acts than to those in any other New Testament book, and a special Introduction to the textual phenomena in Acts is provided (see pp. 222–236).

An Eastern form of text, which was formerly called the *Caesarean* text,[6] is preserved, to a greater or lesser extent, in several Greek manuscripts (including Θ, 565, 700) and in the Armenian and Georgian versions. The text of these witnesses is characterized by a mixture of Western and Alexandrian readings. Although recent

---

[6] For a summary of the chief research on the so-called Caesarean text, see Metzger, "The Caesarean Text of the Gospels," *Journal of Biblical Literature,* LXIV (1945), pp. 457–489, reprinted with additions in Metzger's *Chapters in the History of New Testament Textual Criticism* (Leiden and Grand Rapids, 1963), pp. 42–72.

research has tended to question the existence of a specifically Caesarean text-type,[7] the individual manuscripts formerly considered to be members of the group remain important witnesses in their own right.

Another Eastern type of text, current in and near Antioch, is preserved today chiefly in Old Syriac witnesses, namely the Sinaitic and the Curetonian manuscripts of the Gospels and in the quotations of Scripture contained in the works of Aphraates and Ephraem.

The *Byzantine text,* otherwise called the *Syrian text* (so Westcott and Hort), the *Koine text* (so von Soden), the *Ecclesiastical text* (so Lake), and the *Antiochian text* (so Ropes), is, on the whole, the latest of the several distinctive types of text of the New Testament. It is characterized chiefly by lucidity and completeness. The framers of this text sought to smooth away any harshness of language, to combine two or more divergent readings into one expanded reading (called conflation), and to harmonize divergent parallel passages. This conflated text, produced perhaps at Antioch in Syria, was taken to Constantinople, whence it was distributed widely throughout the Byzantine Empire. It is best represented today by codex Alexandrinus (in the Gospels; not in Acts, the Epistles, or Revelation), the later uncial manuscripts, and the great mass of minuscule manuscripts. Thus, except for an occasional manuscript that happened to preserve an earlier form of text, during the period from about the sixth or seventh century down to the invention of printing with moveable type (A.D. 1450–56), the Byzantine form of text was generally regarded as *the* authoritative form of text and was the one most widely circulated and accepted.

After Gutenberg's press made the production of books more rapid and therefore cheaper than was possible through copying by hand, it was the debased Byzantine text that became the standard form of the New Testament in printed editions. This unfortunate situation was not altogether unexpected, for the Greek manuscripts of the New Testament that were most readily available to early editors and printers were those that contained the corrupt Byzantine text.

---

[7] Cf. E. J. Epp in *Journal of Biblical Literature,* XC (1974), 393–396, and K. Aland and B. Aland, *The Text of the New Testament,* 2nd ed. (1989), p. 66 and p. 172.

The first published edition of the printed Greek Testament, issued at Basel in 1516, was prepared by Desiderius Erasmus, the Dutch humanist scholar. Since Erasmus could find no manuscript that contained the entire Greek Testament, he utilized several for the various divisions of the New Testament. For the greater part of his text he relied on two rather inferior manuscripts now in the university library at Basel, one of the Gospels and one of the Acts and Epistles, both dating from about the twelfth century. Erasmus compared them with two or three others, and entered occasional corrections in the margins or between the lines of the copy given to the printer. For the book of Revelation he had but one manuscript, dating from the twelfth century, which he had borrowed from his friend Reuchlin. As it happened, this copy lacked the final leaf, which had contained the last six verses of the book. For these verses Erasmus depended upon Jerome's Latin Vulgate, translating this version into Greek. As would be expected from such a procedure, here and there in Erasmus's reconstruction of these verses there are several readings that have never been found in any Greek manuscript – but which are still perpetuated today in printings of the so-called Textus Receptus of the Greek New Testament (see the comment on Rev. 22.19). In other parts of the New Testament Erasmus also occasionally introduced into his Greek text material derived from the current form of the Latin Vulgate (see the comment on Acts 9.5-6).

So much in demand was Erasmus's Greek Testament that the first edition was soon exhausted and a second was called for. It was this second edition of 1519, in which some (but not nearly all) of the many typographical blunders of the first edition had been corrected, that Martin Luther and William Tyndale used as the basis of their translations of the New Testament into German (1522) and into English (1525).

In the years following many other editors and printers issued a variety of editions of the Greek Testament, all of which reproduced more or less the same type of text, namely that preserved in the later Byzantine manuscripts. Even when it happened that an editor had access to older manuscripts – as when Theodore Beza, the friend and successor of Calvin at Geneva, acquired the fifth-century manuscript that goes under his name today, as well as the sixth-century codex

Claromontanus – he made relatively little use of them, for they deviated too far from the form of text that had become standard in the later copies.

Noteworthy early editions of the Greek New Testament include two issued by Robert Etienne (commonly known under the Latin form of his name, Stephanus), the famous Parisian printer who later moved to Geneva and threw in his lot with the Protestants of that city. In 1550 Stephanus published at Paris his third edition, the *editio Regia,* a magnificent folio edition. It is the first printed Greek Testament to contain a critical apparatus; on the inner margins of its pages Stephanus entered variant readings from fourteen Greek manuscripts, as well as readings from another printed edition, the Complutensian Polyglot. Stephanus's fourth edition (Geneva, 1551), which contains two Latin versions (the Vulgate and that of Erasmus), is noteworthy because in it for the first time the text of the New Testament was divided into numbered verses.

Theodore Beza published no fewer than nine editions of the Greek Testament between 1565 and 1604, and a tenth edition appeared posthumously in 1611. The importance of Beza's work lies in the extent to which his editions tended to popularize and stereotype what came to be called the Textus Receptus. The translators of the Authorized or King James Bible of 1611 made large use of Beza's editions of 1588–89 and 1598.

The term *Textus Receptus,* as applied to the text of the New Testament, originated in an expression used by Bonaventura and Abraham Elzevir (Elzevier), who were printers in Leiden. The preface to their second edition of the Greek Testament (1633) contains the sentence: *Textum ergo habes, nunc ab omnibus receptum, in quo nihil immutatum aut corruptum damus* ("Therefore you [dear reader] have the text now received by all, in which we give nothing changed or corrupted"). In one sense this proud claim of the Elzevirs on behalf of their edition seemed to be justified, for their edition was, in most respects, not different from the approximately 160 other editions of the printed Greek Testament that had been issued since Erasmus's first published edition of 1516. In a more precise sense, however, the Byzantine form of the Greek text, reproduced in all early printed editions, was disfigured, as was mentioned above, by the accumulation over the centuries of myriads of scribal alterations, many of minor significance but some of considerable consequence.

It was the corrupt Byzantine form of text that provided the basis for almost all translations of the New Testament into modern languages down to the nineteenth century. During the eighteenth century scholars assembled a great amount of information from many Greek manuscripts, as well as from versional and patristic witnesses. But, except for three or four editors who timidly corrected some of the more blatant errors of the Textus Receptus, this debased form of the New Testament text was reprinted in edition after edition. It was only in the first part of the nineteenth century (1831) that a German classical scholar, Karl Lachmann, ventured to apply to the New Testament the criteria that he had used in editing texts of the classics. Subsequently other critical editions appeared, including those prepared by Constantin von Tischendorf, whose eighth edition (1869–72) remains a monumental thesaurus of variant readings, and the influential edition prepared by two Cambridge scholars, B. F. Westcott and F. J. A. Hort (1881). It is the latter edition that was taken as the basis for the present United Bible Societies' edition. During the twentieth century, with the discovery of several New Testament manuscripts much older than any that had hitherto been available, it has become possible to produce editions of the New Testament that approximate ever more closely to what is regarded as the wording of the original documents.

II. CRITERIA USED IN CHOOSING AMONG CONFLICTING READINGS IN NEW TESTAMENT WITNESSES

In the preceding section the reader will have seen how, during about fourteen centuries when the New Testament was transmitted in handwritten copies, numerous changes and accretions came into the text. Of the approximately five thousand Greek manuscripts of all or part of the New Testament that are known today, no two agree exactly in all particulars. Confronted by a mass of conflicting readings, editors must decide which variants deserve to be included in the text and which should be relegated to the apparatus. Although at first it may seem to be a hopeless task amid so many thousands of variant readings to sort out those that should be regarded as original, textual scholars have developed certain generally acknowledged criteria of evaluation. These considerations depend, it will be seen, upon probabilities, and sometimes the textual critic must weigh one set of probabilities against another. Furthermore, the reader should be advised at the outset that, although the following criteria have been drawn up in a more or less tidy outline form, their application can never be undertaken in a merely mechanical or stereotyped manner. The range and complexity of textual data are so great that no neatly arranged or mechanically contrived set of rules can be applied with mathematical precision. Each and every variant reading needs to be considered in itself, and not judged merely according to a rule of thumb. With these cautionary comments in mind, the reader will appreciate that the following outline of criteria is meant only as a convenient description of the more important considerations that the Committee took into account when choosing among variant readings.

The chief categories or kinds of criteria and considerations that assist one in evaluating the relative worth of variant readings are those which involve (I) External Evidence, having to do with the manuscripts themselves, and (II) Internal Evidence, having to do with two kinds of considerations, (A) those concerned with Transcriptional Probabilities (i. e. relating to the habits of scribes) and (B) those concerned with Intrinsic Probabilities (i. e. relating to the style of the author).[8]

OUTLINE OF CRITERIA

I. EXTERNAL EVIDENCE, involving considerations bearing upon:

A. The date and character of the witnesses. In general, earlier manuscripts are more likely to be free from those errors that arise from repeated copying. Of even greater importance, however, than the age of the document itself are the date and character of the type

---

[8] The table of criteria has been adapted from the present writer's volume, *The Text of the New Testament, its Transmission, Corruption, and Restoration* (Oxford, 1964; third edition, 1992), which may be consulted for a fuller account of the science and art of textual criticism.

of text that it embodies, as well as the degree of care taken by the copyist while producing the manuscript.

B. The geographical distribution of the witnesses that support a variant. The concurrence of witnesses, for example, from Antioch, Alexandria, and Gaul in support of a given variant is, other things being equal, more significant than the testimony of witnesses representing but one locality or one ecclesiastical see. On the other hand, however, one must be certain that geographically remote witnesses are really independent of one another. Agreements, for example, between Old Latin and Old Syriac witnesses may sometimes be due to common influence from Tatian's Diatessaron.

C. The genealogical relationship of texts and families of witnesses. Mere numbers of witnesses supporting a given variant reading do not necessarily prove the superiority of that reading. For example, if in a given sentence reading x is supported by twenty manuscripts and reading y by only one manuscript, the relative numerical support favoring x counts for nothing if all twenty manuscripts should be discovered to be copies made from a single manuscript, no longer extant, whose scribe first introduced that particular variant reading. The comparison, in that case, ought to be made between the one manuscript containing reading y and the single ancestor of the twenty manuscripts containing reading x.

D. Witnesses are to be weighed rather than counted. That is, the principle enunciated in the previous paragraph needs to be elaborated: those witnesses that are found to be generally trustworthy in clear-cut cases deserve to be accorded predominant weight in cases when the textual problems are ambiguous and their resolution is uncertain. At the same time, however, since the relative weight of the several kinds of evidence differs in different kinds of variants, there should be no merely mechanical evaluation of the evidence.

II. INTERNAL EVIDENCE, involving two kinds of probabilities:

A. Transcriptional Probabilities depend upon considerations of the habits of scribes and upon palaeographical features in the manuscripts.

1. In general, the more difficult reading is to be preferred, particularly when the sense appears on the surface to be erroneous but on

more mature consideration proves itself to be correct. (Here "more difficult" means "more difficult to the scribe," who would be tempted to make an emendation. The characteristic of most scribal emendations is their superficiality, often combining "the appearance of improvement with the absence of its reality."[9] Obviously the category "more difficult reading" is relative, and sometimes a point is reached when a reading must be judged to be so difficult that it can have arisen only by accident in transcription.)

2. In general the shorter reading is to be preferred, except where

(a) Parablepsis arising from homoeoarcton or homoeoteleuton may have occurred (i. e., where the eye of the copyist may have inadvertently passed from one word to another having a similar sequence of letters); or where

(b) The scribe may have omitted material that was deemed to be (i) superfluous, (ii) harsh, or (iii) contrary to pious belief, liturgical usage, or ascetical practice.

3. Since scribes would frequently bring divergent passages into harmony with one another, in parallel passages (whether quotations from the Old Testament or different accounts in the Gospels of the same event or narrative) that reading which involves verbal dissidence is usually to be preferred to one which is verbally concordant.

4. Scribes would sometimes

(a) Replace an unfamiliar word with a more familiar synonym;

(b) Alter a less refined grammatical form or less elegant lexical expression, in accord with contemporary Atticizing preferences; or

(c) Add pronouns, conjunctions, and expletives to make a smoother text.

B. Intrinsic Probabilities depend upon considerations of what the author was more likely to have written. The textual critic takes into account

1. In general:

---

[9] Westcott and Hort, *op. cit.,* vol. II, p. 27.

> (*a*) The style and vocabulary of the author throughout the book:
>
> (*b*) The immediate context; and
>
> (*c*) Harmony with the usage of the author elsewhere; and,
>
> 2. In the Gospels:
>
> (*a*) The Aramaic background of the teaching of Jesus;
>
> (*b*) The priority of the Gospel according to Mark; and
>
> (*c*) The influence of the Christian community upon the formulation and transmission of the passage in question.

It is obvious that not all of these criteria are applicable in every case. The textual critic must know when it is appropriate to give greater consideration to one kind of evidence and less to another. Since textual criticsim is an art as well as a science, it is inevitable that in some cases different scholars will come to different evaluations of the significance of the evidence. This divergence is almost inevitable when, as sometimes happens, the evidence is so divided that, for example, the more difficult reading is found only in the later witnesses, or the longer reading is found only in the earlier witnesses.

In order to indicate the relative degree of certainty in the mind of the Committee for the reading adopted as the text,[10] an identifying letter is included within braces at the beginning of each set of textual variants. The letter {A} signifies that the text is certain, while {B} indicates that the text is almost certain. The letter {C}, however, indicates that the Committee had difficulty in deciding which variant to place in the text. The letter {D}, which occurs only rarely, indicates that the Committee had great difficulty in arriving at a decision. In fact, among the {D} decisions sometimes none of the variant readings commended itself as original, and therefore the only recourse was to print the least unsatisfactory reading.

III. Lists of Witnesses According to Type of Text

The following are some of the more important witnesses to the text of the New Testament arranged in lists according to the predominant

---

[10] It will be noted that this system is similar in principle but different in application from that followed by Johann Albrecht Bengel in his edition of the Greek New Testament (Tübingen, 1734).

type of text exhibited by each witness. It will be observed that in some cases different sections of the New Testament within the same witness belong to different text-types.

Alexandrian Witnesses

(1) Primary Alexandrian:

$\mathfrak{P}^{45}$ (in Acts) $\mathfrak{P}^{46}$ $\mathfrak{P}^{66}$ $\mathfrak{P}^{75}$ ℵ B Sahidic (in part), Clement of Alexandria, Origen (in part), and most of the papyrus fragments with Pauline text.

(2) Secondary Alexandrian:

Gospels: (C)[11] L T W (in Luke 1.1 to 8.12 and John) (X) Z Δ (in Mark) Ξ Ψ (in Mark; partially in Luke and John) 33 579 892 1241 Bohairic.

Acts: $\mathfrak{P}^{50}$ A (C) Ψ 33 (11.26–28.31) 81 104 326.

Pauline Epistles: A (C) H I Ψ 33 81 104 326 1739.

Catholic Epistles: $\mathfrak{P}^{20}$ $\mathfrak{P}^{23}$ A (C) Ψ 33 81 104 326 1739.

Revelation: A (C) 1006 1611 1854 2053 2344; less good, $\mathfrak{P}^{47}$ ℵ.

Western Witnesses

Gospels: $\mathfrak{P}^{69}$ ℵ (in John 1.1–8.38) D W (in Mark 1.1–5.30) 0171, the Old Latin, (syr^s and syr^c in part), early Latin Fathers.

Acts: $\mathfrak{P}^{29}$ $\mathfrak{P}^{38}$ $\mathfrak{P}^{48}$ D E 383 614 1739 syr^{hmg} syr^{palms} cop^{G67} early Latin Fathers, Ephraem.

Epistles: the Greek-Latin bilinguals D F G, Greek Fathers to the end of the third century, Old Latin mss. and early Latin Fathers.

It will be observed that for the book of Revelation no specifically Western witnesses have been identified.

Byzantine Witnesses[12]

Gospels: A E F G H K P S V W (in Matt. and Luke 8.13–24.53) Π Ψ (partially in Luke and John) Ω and most minuscules.

---

[11] In this list parentheses indicate that the text of the manuscript thus designated is mixed in character.

[12] As was mentioned earlier, these have been variously designated by other writers as Antiochian, Syrian, Ecclesiastical, or Koine witnesses.

Acts: H L P 049 and most minuscules.
Epistles: L 049 and most minuscules.
Revelation: 046 051 052 and most minuscules.

In assessing the preceding lists of witnesses two comments are appropriate. (*a*) The tables include only those witnesses that are more or less generally acknowledged to be the chief representatives of the several textual types. Additional witnesses have at times been assigned to one or another category.

(*b*) While the reader is encouraged to refer from time to time from the commentary to the above lists of witnesses, it must never be supposed that parity of external support for two separate sets of variant readings requires identical judgments concerning the original text. Although the external evidence for two sets of variant readings may be exactly the same, considerations of transcriptional and/or intrinsic probabilities of readings may lead to quite diverse judgments concerning the original text. This is, of course, only another way of saying that textual criticism is an art as well as a science, and demands that each set of variants be evaluated in the light of the fullest consideration of both external evidence and internal probabilities.

THE GOSPEL ACCORDING TO MATTHEW

1.7-8   Ἀσάφ, Ἀσάφ {B}

It is clear that the name "Asaph" is the earliest form of text preserved in the manuscripts, for the agreement of Alexandrian (ℵ B) and other witnesses (*f*¹ *f*¹³ 700 1071) with Eastern versions (cop arm eth geo) and representatives of the Western text (Old Latin mss. and D in Luke [D is lacking for this part of Matthew]) makes a strong combination. Furthermore, the tendency of scribes, observing that the name of the psalmist Asaph (cf. the titles of Pss 50 and 73 to 83) was confused with that of Asa the king of Judah (1 Kgs 15.9 ff.), would have been to correct the error, thus accounting for the prevalence of Ἀσά in the later Ecclesiastical text and its inclusion in the Textus Receptus.[1]

Although most scholars are impressed by the overwhelming weight of textual evidence supporting Ἀσάφ, Lagrange demurs and in his commentary prints Ἀσά as the text of Matthew. He declares (p. 5) that "literary criticism is not able to admit that the author, who could not have drawn up this list without consulting the Old Testament, would have taken the name of a psalmist in place of a king of Judah. It is necessary, therefore, to suppose that Ἀσάφ is a very ancient [scribal] error." Since, however, the evangelist may have derived material for the genealogy, not from the Old Testament directly, but from subsequent genealogical lists, in which the erroneous spelling occurred, the Committee saw no reason to adopt what appears to be a scribal emendation in the text of Matthew.

1.10   Ἀμώς, Ἀμώς {B}

The textual evidence for the reading "Amos," an error for "Amon," the name of the king of Judah, is nearly the same as that which reads Ἀσάφ in verses 7 and 8.

---

[1] In the genealogy in 1 Chr 3.10 most Greek manuscripts read Ἀσά, though ms. 60 reads Ἀσάβ. In *Antiq.* VIII.xi.3–xii.6 Josephus uses Ἄσανος, though in the Latin translation *Asaph* appears.

In 1 Chr 3.14 most manuscripts present the correct Ἀμών (or its near equivalent Ἀμμών), but Ἀμώς is read by A B^c (B* and one minuscule read Ἀμνών). In the narrative account concerning King Amon in 2 Kgs 21.18-19, 23-25; 2 Chr 33.20-25 several Greek witnesses erroneously read Ἀμώς.

Despite Lagrange's preference for Ἀμών (see his argument quoted above on verses 7-8), the Committee was impressed by the weight of the external evidence that attests Ἀμώς.

1.11 ἐγέννησεν {A}

In order to bring the text of Matthew into harmony with the genealogy in 1 Chr 3.15-16, several of the later uncial manuscripts (M U Θ Σ), as well as a variety of other witnesses (including f¹ 33 209 258 478 661 954 1354 1604 syr^h with *, pal geo), have added τὸν Ἰωακίμ, Ἰωακὶμ δὲ ἐγέννησεν. Although it is possible to argue that the clause had accidentally fallen out during transcription, the external evidence in its favor is not as weighty as that which supports the shorter text (ℵ B C E K L S V W Γ Δ Π most minuscules it vg syr^c, s, p cop^sa, bo arm eth). It should be noted also that when the clause is present there are fifteen generations in the second tesseradecade (compare ver. 17).

1.16 τὸν ἄνδρα Μαρίας, ἐξ ἧς ἐγεννήθη Ἰησοῦς ὁ λεγόμενος Χριστός {A}

There are three principal variant readings: (1) "and Jacob begot Joseph *the husband of Mary, of whom Jesus was born, who is called Christ*," is supported by a wide representation of textual families in early Greek and versional witnesses, including 𝔓¹ ℵ B C W vg syr^p, h, pal cop^sa, (bo) geo.

(2) "and Jacob begot Joseph, *to whom being betrothed the virgin Mary bore Jesus, who is called Christ*," is supported by several Greek and Old Latin witnesses (Θ f¹³ l 547 it^a, (b), c, (d), g1, (k), q). Similar to this are the readings of the Curetonian Syriac manuscript, "Jacob begot Joseph, *him to whom was betrothed Mary the virgin, she who bore Jesus the Christ*," and of the Armenian version, "Jacob begot

Joseph *the husband of Mary, to whom was betrothed Mary the virgin, from whom was born Jesus who was called Christ.*" In the more complete form of the *Liber generationis* incorporated by Hippolytus in his *Chronicle* (completed about A.D. 234), the genealogy from Adam to Christ closes with the words *Ioseph, cui disponsata fuit uirgo Maria, quae genuit Iesum Christum ex spiritu sancto* (ed. by Rudolf Helm, 1955, p. 126; "Joseph, to whom was betrothed the virgin Mary, who [fem.] bore Jesus Christ from the Holy Spirit").

(3) "Jacob begot Joseph; *Joseph, to whom was betrothed Mary the virgin, begot Jesus who is called the Christ,*" is attested by the Sinaitic Syriac manuscript.

Other witnesses have sometimes been supposed to support reading (3). Thus, in the *Dialogue of Timothy and Aquila,* an anonymous treatise (dating perhaps from the fifth century)[2] that presents a debate between a Christian and a Jew, Mt 1.16 is referred to three times. The third of these is a loose quotation of the commonly received text, Ἰακὼβ δὲ ἐγέννησεν τὸν Ἰωσὴφ τὸν μνηστευσάμενον Μαριάμ, ἐξ ἧς ἐγεννήθη ὁ Χριστὸς ὁ υἱὸς τοῦ θεοῦ ("And Jacob begot Joseph, who was betrothed to Mary, from whom was born the Christ the Son of God").[3] The second quotation, which stands at the close of a rapid recapitulation of the genealogy, is Ἰακὼβ δὲ τὸν Ἰωσήφ, ᾧ μνηστευθεῖσα Μαρία· ἐξ ἧς ἐγεννήθη Ἰησοῦς ὁ λεγόμενος Χριστός ("And Jacob [begot] Joseph, to whom was betrothed Mary, from whom was born Jesus who is called Christ").[4] The first time that Mt 1.16 occurs in the Dialogue, the Jew quotes it in exactly the form given in (1) above and then follows it with his own inference, namely καὶ Ἰωσὴφ ἐγέννησεν τὸν Ἰησοῦν τὸν λεγόμενον Χριστόν, περὶ οὗ νῦν ὁ λόγος, φησίν, ἐγέννησεν ἐκ τῆς Μαρίας ("And [so] Joseph begot Jesus who is called

---

[2] For the text see F. C. Conybeare, *The Dialogues of Athanasius and Zacchaeus and of Timothy and Aquila* (Oxford, 1898), pp. 65–104, and E. J. Goodspeed, *Journal of Biblical Literature,* XXV (1905), pp. 58–78. A. Lukyn Williams (*Adversus Judaeos* [Cambridge, 1935], pp. 67–78) thinks that the main section of the treatise dates from about A.D. 200.

[3] *Op. cit.,* p. 88.

[4] *Op. cit.,* p. 76.

Christ, about whom we are talking, it says, he begot [him] from Mary").[5] Despite the protestations of Conybeare to the contrary,[6] it seems clear that these words are not a second citation added to the first, but are a Jewish interpretation of the commonly received text of Mt 1.16.[7]

Another witness that is sometimes thought to support the reading of the Sinaitic Syriac is a twelfth century Jacobite Syrian writer, Dionysius Barsalibi, bishop of Amida. Hermann von Soden, for example, cites in his apparatus for Mt 1.16 the name of Barsalibi as patristic attestation entirely parallel with that of syr[s]. The evidence, however, is far from being so clear-cut, as the following account of the principal points will make obvious.

In his Commentary on the Gospels Barsalibi discusses the syntactical difference between the ways in which the Greek and Syriac languages express "from whom" in Mt 1.16, but both the Greek and the Syriac, he declares, explicitly attest that Jesus was born of Mary and not from Joseph.[8] The critical point concerns Barsalibi's comment on Mt 1.18, which reads as follows: "Here the manner of his [Jesus'] corporeal birth [the evangelist] teaches. When therefore you hear [the word] 'husband' [i. e., in ver. 19], do not think that he was born according to the law of nature – he who had constituted the law of nature. And when it comes to Joseph ܐܡܪ ܕܡܟܝܪܐ ܠܗ ܠܒܬܘܠܬܐ, and therefore afterwards it says, 'Now the birth of Jesus the Messiah was thus,' that is, not as the rest of men was he born, but a new thing is the manner of his birth, and higher than the nature of those who are

---

[5] Ibid.

[6] F. C. Conybeare, "Three Early Doctrinal Modifications of the Text of the Gospels," Hibbert Journal, I (1902–03), pp. 96–102.

[7] See also F. Crawford Burkitt, Evangelion da-Mepharreshe, II (Cambridge, 1904), p. 265, and Theodor Zahn, Introduction to the New Testament, II (Edinburgh, 1909), p. 565, who agree in taking the words as a Jewish interpretation, and not as a Greek witness supporting the text of the Sinaitic Syriac.

[8] Dionysius Bar Ṣalībī, Commentarii in Evangelia, ed. by Sedláček and Chabot in Corpus Scriptorum Christianorum Orientalium, Series Secunda, Tom. XCVIII (Paris, 1906), p. 46, lines 23 ff. (of the Syriac text), and pp. 35 ff. (of the Latin translation). For a discussion of the passage, see Wm. P. Armstrong, "Critical Note (Matt. 1.16)," Princeton Theological Review, XIII (1915), pp. 461–468.

born."[9] The words cited in Syriac can be translated either (a) "it says, 'Who begot the Messiah,'" or (b) "it says that he begot the Messiah." According to rendering (a), Barsalibi appears to be quoting from some manuscript or author, not identified here or elsewhere, whose text of Mt 1.16 paralleled the reading of the Sinaitic Syriac. On the other hand, according to rendering (b), Barsalibi is making his own summary exposition of Matthew's account of Joseph's relation to the Messiah. In either case, however, it is obvious that so far as Barsalibi is concerned he intends his quotation (if it be a quotation) or his summary exposition to be perfectly in accord with his earlier discussion of ver. 16 and his immediately following declaration that Jesus' birth was unique. In other words, it appears that Barsalibi fully accepted the Peshitta text of ver. 16 (i. e. the reading designated (1) above).

A third witness that has been thought to support the Sinaitic Syriac reading is one manuscript of the Arabic Diatessaron. Although Theodoret explicitly states that Tatian did not utilize the Matthean and Lukan genealogies in his Diatessaron, the mediaeval Arabic Diatessaron does contain them (ms. A includes the Matthean genealogy after I,81, and the Lukan genealogy after IV,29, but mss. B and E give them as an appendix after the close of the Diatessaron). At Mt 1.16 ms. A, which dates from the twelfth century, reads يعقوب ولد يوسف رجل مريم الذي منها ولد ايسوع المسيح "Jacob begot Joseph, the husband of Mary, who [masc.] of her begot Jesus the Messiah."[10] (The other two manuscripts employ the correct feminine form, التي.) That ms. A should in its special reading somehow reflect the text of a Greek manuscript of Mt 1.16 is, as Burkitt declares,[11] most unlikely. On the contrary it is altogether likely that the use of the masculine who is either a blunder of a careless copyist or the dialectal usage of the masculine relative for the feminine.[12] If then the relative is corrected, who of her will become of whom (fem.),

---

[9] Ibid., p. 70, lines 9 ff. (of the Syriac text), and p. 53 (of the Latin translation).
[10] A.-S. Marmardji, Diatessaron de Tatien (Beyrouth, 1935), p. 532.
[11] Op. cit., II, p. 265.
[12] So Marmardji, op. cit., p. 533, note.

and the second instance of the verb ܘܠܕ will be construed as a passive *(was born),* agreeing with the reading of the Peshitta version.[13]

There appears to be, therefore, no substantial evidence to add in support of the singular reading of the Sinaitic Syriac (reading (3) above).

What now are the relative merits of the three principal readings?

The external evidence in support of (1) is extremely good: it is read by all known Greek uncial manuscripts except Θ, and by all other manuscripts and versions except the limited number that support (2) and (3). Transcriptional probabilities suggest that reading (2) arose (perhaps at Caesarea) because the expression "the husband of Mary" was thought to be misleading in a genealogical context. Lest the hasty reader assume that Jesus was the physical son of Mary and her husband Joseph, the text was altered to bring it into conformity with ver. 18 where the verb μνηστεύεσθαι is used to describe the relationship of Mary to Joseph. On the other hand, if reading (2) be supposed to be original, it is exceedingly difficult to imagine why any scribe would have substituted reading (1) for such a clear and unambiguous declaration of the virginity of Mary.

There is no evidence that reading (3) ever existed in a Greek manuscript of the first Gospel. The Committee judged that it arose either as a paraphrase of reading (2) – this was Burkitt's view – or as a purely mechanical imitation of the preceding pattern in the genealogy. Since every name in the genealogy up to Joseph is written twice in succession, it may be that the scribe of the Sinaitic Syriac (or an ancestor of this manuscript) carelessly followed the stereotyped pattern and in ver. 16, having made the initial mistake of repeating the word "Joseph," went on to produce reading (3).

1.18   Ἰησοῦ Χριστοῦ {B}

It is difficult to decide which is the original reading. On the one hand, the prevailing tendency of scribes was to expand either

---

[13] For a fuller discussion of the readings, see B. M. Metzger's contribution to *Studies in New Testament and Early Christian Literature,* ed. by David E. Aune (Leiden, 1972), pp. 16–24.

Ἰησοῦς or Χριστός by the addition of the other word. The Western reading Χριστοῦ in Old Latin and Old Syriac witnesses seems to have a certain appropriateness, but it may be an assimilation to ἕως τοῦ Χριστοῦ of the preceding sentence. It can also be argued that in the narrative of his birth one would expect to find the personal name "Jesus," yet Ἰησοῦ in W may have been conformed to the following command by the angel (ver. 21).

On the other hand, though the external evidence in support of Ἰησοῦ Χριστοῦ appears to be overwhelming, the reading is intrinsically improbable, for in the New Testament the definite article is very rarely prefixed to the expression Ἰησοῦς Χριστός (only in inferior manuscripts in Ac 8.37; 1 Jn 4.3; and Re 12.17).

In the face of such conflicting considerations, the Committee judged that the least unsatisfactory course was to adopt the reading that was current in many parts of the early church.

1.18 γένεσις {B}

Both γένεσις and γέννησις mean "birth," but the former also means "creation," "generation," and "genealogy" (compare 1.1), whereas the latter means more strictly "engendering" and therefore became the customary word used in patristic literature to refer to the Nativity. At the same time it is understandable that scribes very often confused these two words, which orthographically and phonetically are so similar.

In the present passage not only do the earlier representatives of several text-types support γένεσις, but the tendency of copyists would have been to substitute a word of more specialized meaning for one that had been used in a different sense in ver. 1, particularly since γέννησις corresponds more nearly with the verb γεννᾶν used so frequently in the previous genealogy.

1.22 τοῦ προφήτου

Before τοῦ προφήτου a variety of witnesses (including D 267 954 1582*[vid] it[a? b, c, d] vg[mss] syr[c, s, h, pal] arm Irenaeus[1/2]) insert Ἡσαΐου. The name is clearly a scribal explanation, for if it had been present originally there is no adequate reason that would account for its absence from the mass of Greek witnesses.

1.25 υἱόν {A}

The Textus Receptus, following C D* K W Δ Π most minuscules *al*, inserts τόν before υἱόν and adds αὐτῆς τὸν πρωτότοκον ("*her firstborn* son") from Lk 2.7.

The reading of the Sinaitic Syriac ("she bore *to him* [to Joseph] a son") is in conformity with the singular reading of this manuscript in ver. 16 (see the discussion above) and its reading (shared with syr^c) in ver. 21 ("shall bear *to thee* a son").

2.5 διὰ τοῦ προφήτου

Not content with merely the mention of τοῦ προφήτου several witnesses (4 syr^{hmg (ms)} cop^{boms}) add Μιχαίου, and it^a reads *per Esiam prophetam dicentem* ("through Isaiah the prophet saying").

2.18 κλαυθμός {B}

The longer reading, θρῆνος καὶ κλαυθμός, appears to be a scribal assimilation to the Septuagint text of Jr 31.15 (LXX 38.15). It entered the Textus Receptus and lies behind the rendering of the AV, "lamentation, and weeping, and great mourning."

3.15 αὐτόν (2)

Between verses 15 and 16 two Latin manuscripts (it^a vg^{ms}) describe the baptism of Jesus as follows: *Et cum baptizaretur Iesus* (om. *Iesus* it^a), *lumen magnum fulgebat* (*lumen ingens circumfulsit* it^a) *de aqua, ita ut timerant omnes qui congregati erant* (*advenerant* it^a) ("And when Jesus was being baptized a great light flashed (a tremendous light flashed around) from the water, so that all who had gathered there were afraid"). According to Isho'dad of Merv (ninth century) and Dionysius Barsalibi (twelfth century), Tatian's Diatessaron also contained a reference to the light. The passage from Isho'dad's *Commentary on the Gospels* is as follows:

"And straightway, as the Diatessaron testifies, a great light shown, and the Jordan was surrounded by white clouds, and many troops of spiritual beings were seen singing praises in the air; and the Jordan stood still quietly from its course, its waters not being troubled, and a scent of perfumes was wafted from thence; for the Heavens were opened" (M. D. Gibson's translation, p. 27).

How much of this extract should be regarded as Tatianic, and how much may have been taken from other sources (perhaps an early hymn), is not known, but it is thought that, in view of Ephraem's remark about "the shining of the light upon the waters" (*Com.* iv.5), at least the reference to the light on the Jordan was present in the Diatessaron.

Several other writers refer to the tradition of the light, including Justin Martyr, who says that after Jesus had gone down into the water "a fire was kindled in the Jordan" (πῦρ ἀνήφθη ἐν τῷ Ἰορδάνῃ, *Dial. c. Tryph.* 88), and Epiphanius, after the voice came from heaven, "immediately a great light shone around the place" (εὐθὺς περιέλαμψε τὸν τόπον φῶς μέγα, *Panarion haer.* xxx, xiii, 7).

3.16 [αὐτῷ] {C}

The joining of ℵ* B, the Old Syriac, and Irenaeus[lat] in support of the shorter reading makes a very strong combination, which might well be regarded as the original text. On the other hand, however, it is possible that copyists, not understanding the force of αὐτῷ, omitted the word as unnecessary. In order to show this balance of possibilities the Committee enclosed αὐτῷ within square brackets.

3.16 [καὶ] ἐρχόμενον {C}

No transcriptional or dogmatic considerations seem to have been at work here, and the parallels offer no assistance in deciding between the readings with or without καί. On the strength of the diversity of textual groups that support καὶ ἐρχόμενον, the Committee retained the words in the text, but, in order to reflect the possibility that καί, being absent from early representatives of both Alexandrian and Western text-types (ℵ* B it^a, b, c, h Irenaeus^lat *al*), may not have been part of the text originally, enclosed it within square brackets.

4.10 ὕπαγε {A}

If the words ὀπίσω μου were originally in the text, no satisfactory reason can be found to account for their omission. On the other hand, if they were originally absent, copyists who recalled the words of Jesus to Peter, ὕπαγε ὀπίσω μου, Σατανᾶ (Mt 16.23, where there is no variation of reading), would have been likely to supply them here.

4.17 μετανοεῖτε, ἤγγικεν γάρ {A}

Despite the absence of μετανοεῖτε and γάρ in the Old Syriac and one manuscript of the Old Latin, and although it could be argued that the words are a later assimilation of the text to 3.2, the unanimity of the Greek evidence, as well as the overwhelming testimony of the rest of the versional and patristic witnesses, seemed to the Committee to require that the words be retained in the text.

5.4-5 μακάριοι ... παρακληθήσονται. (5) μακάριοι ... τὴν γῆν. {B}

If verses 3 and 5 had originally stood together, with their rhetorical antithesis of heaven and earth, it is unlikely that any scribe would have thrust ver. 4 between them. On the other hand, as early as the second century copyists reversed the order of the two beatitudes so as to produce such an antithesis and to bring πτωχοί and πραεῖς into closer connection.

5.11 [ψευδόμενοι] {C}

It is uncertain whether ψευδόμενοι should be included or omitted from the text. On the one hand, the absence of the word in the Western tradition (D it^b, c, d, h, k syr^s geo Tertullian *al*) can be accounted for as the result of scribal accommodation of the passage to the Lukan form of the beatitude (Lk 6.22). On the other hand, more than one scribe would have been tempted to insert the word in order to limit the wide generalization in Jesus' teaching, and to express specifically what was felt to be implied by the very nature of the case (compare 1 Pe 4.15 f.). In order to represent the balance of transcriptional probabilities, the Committee decided to include the word in the text, but to enclose it within square brackets.

5.22 αὐτοῦ {B}

Although the reading with εἰκῇ is widespread from the second century onwards, it is much more likely that the word was added by copyists in order to soften the rigor of the precept, than omitted as unnecessary.

5.32 καὶ ὃς ἐὰν ἀπολελυμένην γαμήσῃ, μοιχᾶται {B}

The reading of B (ὁ ... γαμήσας) seems to have been substituted for the reading of the other uncials (ὃς ἐὰν ... γαμήσῃ) in order to make the construction parallel to the preceding participial clause (ὁ ἀπολύων). The omission of the words καὶ ... μοιχᾶται (D it^a, b, d, k Greek and Latin mss^acc. to Augustine) may be due to pedantic scribes who regarded them as superfluous, reasoning that if "everyone who divorces his wife, except on the ground of unchastity, makes her an adulteress [when she remarries]," then it would go without saying that "whoever marries a divorced woman [also] commits adultery."

5.44 (bis) ὑμῶν καὶ προσεύχεσθε ὑπὲρ τῶν διωκόντων ὑμᾶς {A}

Later witnesses enrich the text by incorporating clauses from the parallel account in Lk 6.27-28. If the clauses were originally present in Matthew's account of the Sermon on the Mount, their omission in early representatives of the Alexandrian (ℵ B), Western (it^k Irenaeus^lat Cyprian), Eastern (syr^c, s), and Egyptian (cop^sa, bo) witnesses would be entirely unaccountable. The divergence of readings among the added clauses likewise speaks against their originality.

5.47 ἐθνικοί {B}

In later witnesses, followed by the Textus Receptus, the reading τελῶναι appears to have been substituted for ἐθνικοί in order to bring the statement into closer parallelism with the preceding sentence. The Armenian version conflates the reading with the Lukan form of the saying (Lk 6.32-34).

6.4 ἀποδώσει

The Textus Receptus, following D E M S W X^vid Δ Π Σ Φ 28 565 1241 *al*, introduces αὐτός ("himself") before ἀποδώσει, and other witnesses (700 1223) add the word after σοι. These readings are obvious expansions designed to heighten the impressiveness of the saying; the shorter text, supported by all other known witnesses, is clearly to be preferred.

6.4 σοι {B}

The phrase ἐν τῷ φανερῷ, which is absent from the earliest witnesses of the Alexandrian, Western, and Egyptian types of texts, appears to have been added by copyists in order to make more explicit an antithetical parallelism with the preceding phrase ἐν τῷ κρυπτῷ. The point in the whole section, however, is not so much the openness of the Father's reward as its superiority to mere human approval (compare verses 6 and 18).

6.6 σοι {B}

See the comment on ver. 4.

6.8 ὁ πατὴρ ὑμῶν {A}

The expanded reading ὁ θεὸς ὁ πατὴρ ὑμῶν (ℵ^a B cop^sa Origen) occurs nowhere else in Matthew, and is a scribal intrusion reflecting a characteristically Pauline collocation of θεός and πατήρ (Ro 1.7;

1 Cor 1.3; 2 Cor 1.2; Ga 1.3; Eph 1.2; 6.23; Php 1.2; 2.11; Col 3.17; 1 Th 1.1; 2 Th 1.1,2; 2.16; 1 Tm 1.2; 2 Tm 1.2; Tt 1.4; Phm 3). The reading ὁ πατὴρ ὑμῶν ὁ οὐράνιος, found in several later witnesses, is obviously conformed to the text of ver. 9. The occurrence of ἡμῶν instead of ὑμῶν in several witnesses is due to scribal inadvertence, since in later Greek η and υ were pronounced alike.

6.8 πρὸ τοῦ ὑμᾶς αἰτῆσαι αὐτόν

Instead of the customary reading, "Your Father knows what you need *before you ask him,*" two Western witnesses (D^gr it^h [it^d *hiat*]) have the vigorous and almost colloquial substitute, "… before you open your mouth" (πρὸ τοῦ ἀνοῖξαι τὸ στόμα).

6.12 ἀφήκαμεν

Is the second verb in the fifth petition "as we forgive" (AV) or "as we have forgiven" (RSV)? The latter translates the aorist form of the verb (ἀφήκαμεν), read by ℵ* B Z 1 22 124^mg 1365 1582, five manuscripts of the Latin Vulgate, syr^p. h with * cop^fay. On the other hand the present tense (ἀφίεμεν or ἀφίομεν) is supported by all other Greek witnesses as well as by most ancient versions, namely the Old Latin, the majority of the Vulgate manuscripts, both the Sahidic and Bohairic forms of the Coptic, the Curetonian Syriac (syr^s *hiat*), the Gothic, the Armenian, the oldest manuscript of the Georgian, and the Ethiopic. Except for the Syriac Peshitta the parallel in Luke (11.4) reads the present tense (ἀφίομεν or ἀφίεμεν).

If the original form of the Lord's Prayer in Aramaic had a verb in the perfect tense used as a present, the aorist tense in Greek would represent a mechanical translation less idiomatic than the present tense. On the basis of the weight of the external evidence, as well as considering the non-parallel reading, a majority of the Committee preferred ἀφήκαμεν.

6.13 πονηροῦ. {A}

The ascription at the close of the Lord's Prayer occurs in several forms. In K L W Δ Θ Π f^13 *al* it is the familiar triple strophic form, whereas the Sahidic and Fayyumic (like the form quoted in the Didache) lack ἡ βασιλεία καί, the Curetonian Syriac lacks ἡ δύναμις καί, and the Old Latin k reads simply "for thine is the power for ever and ever." Some Greek manuscripts expand "for ever" into "for ever and ever," and most of them add "amen." Several late manuscripts (157 225 418) append a trinitarian ascription, "for thine is the kingdom and the power and the glory of the Father and of the Son and of the Holy Spirit for ever. Amen." The same expansion occurs also at the close of the Lord's Prayer in the liturgy that is traditionally ascribed to St. John Chrysostom.

The absence of any ascription in early and important representatives of the Alexandrian (ℵ B), the Western (D and most of the Old Latin), and other (f¹) types of text, as well as early patristic commentaries on the Lord's Prayer (those of Tertullian, Origen, Cyprian), suggests that an ascription, usually in a threefold form, was composed (perhaps on the basis of 1 Chr 29.11-13) in order to adapt the Prayer for liturgical use in the early church. Still later scribes added "of the Father and of the Son and of the Holy Spirit."[1]

6.15   ἀνθρώποις {C}

It is problematic whether an original reading τὰ παραπτώματα αὐτῶν was omitted by copyists as unnecessary, in view of the presence of the same words in ver. 14 and τὰ παραπτώματα ὑμῶν later in ver. 15, or whether the words were introduced in the interests of producing a balanced, liturgical style. The Committee judged that, in view of the absence of the words from the parallel statement added in some witnesses after Mk 11.25, they should be regarded as an intrusion into the text of Matthew, especially since they disturb the chiastic structure of verses 14 and 15.

6.18   σοι {A}

See the comment on ver. 4.

---

[1] See Joël Delobel, "The Lord's Prayer in the Textual Tradition," *The New Testament in Early Christianity,* ed. by Jean-Marie Sevrin (Louvain, 1989), pp. 293–309.

6.25 *[ἢ τί πίητε]* {C}

In favor of the shorter reading, lacking ἢ τί πίητε, is the possibility that the text was assimilated to ver. 31. The variation between καί and ἤ can also be taken as an indication of the secondary nature of the addition. On the other hand, the similarity of the ending of φάγητε and πίητε may have occasioned a transcriptional oversight on the part of one or more copyists. To represent the balance of probabilities the Committee retained the words but enclosed them within square brackets.

6.28 αὐξάνουσιν· οὐ κοπιῶσιν οὐδὲ νήθουσιν {B}

The reading of K L W Δ Π f^{13} 28 565 700 892 *al,* giving the verbs in the singular number, appears to be a scribal correction introduced because the plural subject is neuter gender (compare also Lk 12.27).

The original reading of codex Sinaiticus, which was detected when the manuscript was examined under an ultra-violet ray lamp, is οὐ ξένουσιν (= ξαίνουσιν) οὐδὲ νήθουσιν οὐδὲ κοπιῶσιν, "they do not card neither do they spin nor toil." This reading, though regarded as original by some scholars, doubtless arose as a scribal idiosyncrasy that was almost immediately corrected.[2] Codex Koridethi, supported by the Curetonian Syriac, reverses the order of verbs, placing the specific word ("spin") before the general word ("toil").

6.33 τὴν βασιλείαν *[τοῦ θεοῦ]* καὶ τὴν δικαιοσύνην αὐτοῦ {C}

The textual data are susceptible of quite diverse evaluations. On the one hand, according to the opinion of a minority of the Committee, the reading that best explains the rise of the other readings is that supported by ℵ (B) it[1] *al,* inasmuch as the addition of τοῦ θεοῦ (or τῶν οὐρανῶν) after βασιλείαν seems to be an altogether natural

---

[2] On the variant, see T. C. Skeat, *Zeitschrift für die neutestamentliche Wissenschaft,* XXXVII (1938), pp. 211–214; Peter Katz, *Journal of Theological Studies,* New Series, V (1954), pp. 207–209; and T. F. Glasson, *ib.,* XIII (1962), pp. 331–332.

supplement, which, if present originally, would not have been deleted. (The transposition of δικαιοσύνην and βασιλείαν in B is perhaps the result of the desire to suggest that righteousness is prerequisite to participation in the kingdom; compare 5.20.)

On the other hand, a majority of the Committee was impressed by the prevailing usage of Matthew, who almost never employs βασιλεία without a modifier (the instances in 8.12; 13.38; 24.7,14 were regarded as special exceptions), and explained the absence of a modifier in several witnesses as due to accidental scribal omission. In view of these conflicting interpretations, it was thought best to include the words in the text but to enclose them within square brackets.

7.13   πλατεῖα ἡ πύλη {B}

The words ἡ πύλη are absent (in ver. 13) from ℵ* 1646 it[a, b, c, h, k] and many patristic quotations of the saying, and (in ver. 14) from 113 182* 482 544 it[a, h, k] and many patristic quotations. Although some have argued that the word was originally present in ver. 14, and has been introduced into most witnesses in ver. 13, the Committee regarded such an explanation as inadequate to account for the absence of the word from witnesses in ver. 14. On the whole it seemed best to follow the reading of the overwhelming weight of the external evidence, and to account for the absence of the word in one or both verses as a deliberate excision made by copyists who failed to understand that the intended picture is that of a roadway leading to a gate.

7.14   τί {B}

Besides having wide external support the reading τί also has strong internal probabilities in its favor. There is no reason why the familiar ὅτι, if original, should have been altered to τί, used here to represent the Semitic exclamation מָה ("how!" compare Ps 139.17).[1] On the other hand, copyists who did not perceive the underlying

---

[1] Cf. Black, *Aramaic Approach*, p. 89; 3rd ed., p. 123. For a parallel in Modern Greek, see Blass-Debrunner-Funk, § 299 (4).

Semitism would have been tempted to assimilate τί to the preceding ὅτι of ver. 13.

7.14 ἡ πύλη {A}

See the comment on ver. 13.

7.24 ὁμοιωθήσεται {B}

In view of the quality and diversity of the external attestation, the Committee preferred ὁμοιωθήσεται. Likewise the passive verb, "shall be compared," is more likely to have been altered to the active form, "I shall compare him," than vice versa, especially if the copyist recalled the Lukan form of the saying ("I will show you what he is like," Lk 6.47).

8.10 παρ᾽ οὐδενὶ τοσαύτην πίστιν ἐν τῷ Ἰσραὴλ εὗρον {B}

The reading οὐδὲ ἐν τῷ Ἰσραὴλ τοσαύτην πίστιν εὗρον, besides being clearer and easier than the text, is doubtless an assimilation to the parallel in Lk 7.9. The other two readings probably arose through inadvertence on the part of copyists.

8.18 ὄχλον {C}

After repeated discussions a majority of the Committee finally decided that, despite its slender attestation, the reading of B and cop[sa] is to be preferred, and that the other readings are to be explained as amplifications made in order to emphasize the size of the crowd around Jesus.

8.21 τῶν μαθητῶν [αὐτοῦ] {C}

Although the support of ℵ B 33 it[a] cop[sa] for the omission of αὐτοῦ would usually be regarded as exceptionally strong evidence, in this case a majority of the Committee was impressed by the possibility that αὐτοῦ may have been deleted in order to prevent the reader from inferring that the γραμματεύς of ver. 19 was one of Jesus' disciples.

On the other hand, it can be argued that it is because of the word ἕτερος, not αὐτοῦ, that a reader might infer that γραμματεύς of ver. 19 was a disciple of Jesus. Actually the absence of αὐτοῦ does not improve the sense, but rather makes the text more ambiguous. In order to represent these two opposing arguments the Committee decided to retain αὐτοῦ enclosed within square brackets.

8.25 προσελθόντες {B}

Although it could be argued that the shorter reading of ℵ B 892 is the result of Alexandrian pruning of the text of superfluous details (Jesus' disciples are mentioned in ver. 23), the agreement of Western witnesses (it[a, c, k, l] vg Jerome) makes it probable that the shorter reading is original and that the several variant readings represent stages of a growing text.

8.25 σῶσον {B}

Since σώζειν in the New Testament seldom stands without an object, the addition of a supplementary ἡμᾶς was made early in a wide variety of witnesses. That it would have been deleted, if present in the original text, appears to be unlikely.

8.28 Γαδαρηνῶν {C}

The healing of the demoniacs is recounted by all three Synoptic Gospels, and in each account there are three principal variant readings referring to the place at which the miracle occurred: Γαδαρηνῶν, Γερασηνῶν, and Γεργεσηνῶν. The evidence of the chief witnesses for the three accounts is as follows:

	Γαδαρηνῶν	Γερασηνῶν	Γεργεσηνῶν
Mt 8.28	(ℵ*) B C[txt] (Δ) Θ syr[s, p, h]	it vg cop[sa] syr[hmg 2]	ℵ[c] C[mg] K L W f[1] f[13] cop[bo]
Mk 5.1	A C K f[13] syr[p, h]	ℵ* B D it vg cop[sa]	ℵ[c] L Δ Θ f[1] syr[s, hmg] cop[bo]
Lk 8.26	A K W Δ[gr] Ψ f[13] syr[c, s, p, h]	𝔓[75] B D it vg cop[sa]	ℵ L X Θ f[1] cop[bo]

Gerasa was a city of the Decapolis (modern Jerash in Transjordan) located more than thirty miles to the southeast of the Sea of Galilee and, as Origen perceived (*Commentary on John*, v, 41 (24)), is the least likely of the three places. Another Decapolitan city was Gadara, about five miles southeast of the Sea of Galilee (modern Um Qeis). Although Origen also objected to Gadara (which, he says, was read by a few manuscripts) because neither lake nor overhanging banks were there, Josephus (*Life*, IX, 42) refers to Gadara as possessing territory "which lay on the frontiers of Tiberias" (= the Sea of Galilee). That this territory reached to the Sea may be inferred from the fact that ancient coins bearing the name Gadara often portray a ship. Origen prefers Gergesa, not because it occurs in manuscripts – he is silent about this – but on the dubious basis of local tradition (it is the place "from which, it is pointed out, the swine were cast down by the demons") and of the still more dubious basis of etymology ("the meaning of Gergesa is 'dwelling of those that have driven away,'" and thus the name "contains a prophetic reference to the conduct shown the Savior by the citizens of those places, who 'besought him to depart out of their territory'").

Of the several variant readings the Committee preferred Γαδα-ρηνῶν on the basis of (*a*) what was taken to be superior external attestation ((ℵ*) B C^txt (Δ) Θ syr^s, p, h geo^1 mss known to Origen *al*), and (*b*) the probability that Γεργεσηνῶν is a correction, perhaps proposed originally by Origen,[1] and that Γερασηνῶν (which is supported only by versional evidence) is a scribal assimilation to the prevailing text of Mark (5.1) and/or Luke (8.26, 37).

9.4   καὶ ἰδών {B}

A majority of the Committee preferred the reading ἰδών to εἰδώς because (*a*) the latter appears to be a correction of the former ("seeing" another's thoughts seems to be a less appropriate expres-

---

[1] For the part that Origen may have had in disseminating the reading Γεργεσηνῶν, see Tj. Baarda, "Gadarenes, Gerasenes, Gergesenes and the 'Diatessaron' Traditions," in *Neotestamentica et Semitica, Studies in Honour of Matthew Black*, ed. by E. Earle Ellis [and] Max Wilcox (Edinburgh, 1969), pp. 181–197, especially 185 ff.

sion than "knowing" them), and (*b*) ἰδών, which corresponds to the statement in ver. 2, was more likely to be altered to εἰδώς through recollection of ἐπιγνούς in the parallel accounts (Mk 2.8 and Lk 5.22) than vice versa. The weight of the combined testimony supporting καί greatly predominates over that supporting δέ.

9.8   ἐφοβήθησαν {A}

Superficial readers and copyists, failing to see the deep meaning of "were afraid" (i. e., people felt a profound sense of awe and alarm in the presence of One who had the right to forgive sins), substituted for ἐφοβήθησαν what seemed to be a more appropriate word, ἐθαύμασαν ("marvelled," or "were astonished"). The external evidence supporting the more difficult reading is not only early but it includes representatives of both the Alexandrian and the Western text-types.

9.14   νηστεύομεν [πολλά] {C}

The reading of ℵ^a is obviously a scribal assimilation to the parallel in Lk 5.33, where πυκνά is read without variation. It is more difficult to decide whether πολλά, which is absent from the Markan account (Mk 2.18), was added originally by Matthew or by subsequent copyists. The Committee decided that, on balance, the non-parallel reading should be preferred; yet, in view of the absence of the word from several important witnesses (ℵ* B *al*), a majority thought it best to enclose πολλά within square brackets.

9.34   *include verse* {B}

It is difficult to decide whether this verse should be included in the text or placed in the apparatus. According to several commentators (e. g. Allen, Klostermann, Zahn) the words are an intrusion here from 12.24 or from Lk 11.15. On the other hand, the evidence for the shorter text is exclusively Western and relatively meager. Moreover, the passage seems to be needed to prepare the reader for 10.25. A majority of the Committee was impressed by the preponderant weight of the witnesses that include the verse.

10.3 Θαδδαῖος {B}

Although it is easy to explain the origin of the conflate readings "Thaddaeus who was called Lebbaeus" and "Lebbaeus who was called Thaddaeus," it is more difficult to decide whether Θαδδαῖος or Λεββαῖος is the original reading. On the basis, however, of the agreement of early representatives of Alexandrian, Western, and Egyptian witnesses, the Committee judged that Θαδδαῖος is to be preferred. The reading *Judas son of James* in syrˢ may have been introduced from Lk 6.16 (= Ac 1.13). The name *Judas Zelotes* in several Old Latin manuscripts (compare also the same name in the fifth century mosaic in the great Baptistry at Ravenna [Battistero degli Ortodossi]) may be a further assimilation to the previous name in Luke's list, "Simon who was called the Zealot."[1]

10.4 Ἰσκαριώτης

The textual problems of the name Iscariot are connected with its meaning. According to most scholars Ἰσκαριώτης (Ἰσκαριώθ) is derived from the Hebrew קְרִיּוֹת אִישׁ, "a man from Kerioth." In support of this derivation is the variant reading ἀπὸ Καρυώτου (Jn 6.71 ℵ* Θ f¹³ syrʰᵐᵍ· ᵍʳ; 12.4 D; 13.2 D itᵉ; 14.22 D). Other scholars, starting with the form Σκαριώτης (which is the reading of D here; 26.14; Mk 14.10), have proposed a wide variety of possible (and impossible) derivations, including words meaning a leathern girdle or apron, a bandit or assassin, a liar or traitor, and a man of ruddy complexion.[2] The problem is further complicated by variant

---

[1] For further information see Eb. Nestle in Hastings' *Dictionary of the Bible*, IV, pp. 741 f.; W. C. Allen in *Encyclopædia Biblica*, III, cols. 5031 f.; and Barnabas Lindars in *New Testament Studies*, IV (1958), pp. 220–223.

[2] For information concerning these theories see, e. g., Roman B. Halas, *Judas Iscariot, a Scriptural and Theological Study of his Person, his Deeds and his Eternal Lot* (Washington, 1946), pp. 10–38, Harald Ingholt, "The Surname of Judas Iscariot,"

readings in Jn 6.71 and 13.26, where several good witnesses attach the epithet to the father of Judas.

In the present passage the Committee was impressed by the age and diversity of text-type of the Greek witnesses supporting a form of the name with initial iota, and preferred Ἰσκαριώτης, which is supported by the preponderant weight of evidence.

10.8 νεκροὺς ἐγείρετε

The clause νεκροὺς ἐγείρετε involves five variant readings. (1) The words are absent from a considerable number of (mostly later) witnesses, including C³ L X Y Γ Θ Π, about one hundred fifty minuscule manuscripts, syr^p. pal cop^sa arm eth^2 mss geo^1. B Eusebius Basil. (2) In other witnesses the clause stands after καθαρίζετε (16 348 372 1093 1579, followed by the Textus Receptus), or (3) after ἐκβάλλετε (P W Δ 566 1573 2145 syr^h), or (4) before ἀσθενοῦντας (vg^ms). Finally, (5) the reading adopted as the text is supported by a wide variety of witnesses, including ℵ* B C* D N Σ Φ f¹ f¹³ 22 33 157 349 399 543 565 it^a, b, c, h, k, l, q vg syr^s cop^bo eth geo^A arab Cyril Hilary.

Although variation in position of a word or phrase sometimes arouses suspicion of interpolation, in this case the divergence of order seems to have arisen either accidentally (owing to similarity of endings of successive clauses), or deliberately (in order to produce what was regarded as a more appropriate or a more emphatic sequence of the four clauses). While it is true that Matthew is fond of grouping items in threes – and therefore it may be argued that the fourth item here was added by scribes – it is unlikely that they would have introduced an ambiguous command (is it the physically or the spiritually dead?). On balance, a majority of the Committee regarded the shorter reading as due to accidental omission and preferred the reading attested by representatives of the Alexandrian, the Western, and other types of text.

---

in *Studia Orientalia Ioanni Pedersen ... dicata* (Copenhagen, 1953), pp. 152–162, and Lawrence Besserman, "Judas Iscariot," *Dictionary of Biblical Tradition in English Literature*, ed. by D. L. Jeffrey (1992), pp. 418–420.

10.23 ἑτέραν {C}

Although it is possible that the additional clause (perhaps in the form preserved in D, ἄλλην ἐὰν δὲ ἐν τῇ ἀλλῇ διώκουσιν ὑμᾶς, φεύγετε εἰς τὴν ἄλλην, "… and if in the other they persecute you, flee to the next") may have dropped out accidentally because of homoeoteleuton (ἄλλην … ἄλλην), the Committee preferred to regard the words as a natural continuation, inserted in order to explain the following statement, οὐ μὴ τελέσητε τὰς πόλεις τοῦ Ἰσραὴλ ἕως [ἂν] ἔλθῃ ὁ υἱὸς τοῦ ἀνθρώπου (which was taken to mean, "You will not exhaust the cities of Israel [as cities of refuge], before the Son of Man comes"). In deciding between the two short readings ἑτέραν and ἄλλην, the Committee preferred the former because of the general excellence of the Alexandrian text.

11.2 διὰ τῶν μαθητῶν {B}

Instead of "through (διά) his disciples," a reading that is widely supported by ancient witnesses of different types of text (ℵ B C* D P W Z Δ Θ Σ f¹³ 33 *al*), the Majority text incorporates a harmonistic assimilation to the parallel account in Luke (7.19) and reads "two (δύο) of his disciples."

11.9 ἰδεῖν; προφήτην {B}

The textual problem is complicated by the possibility of taking τί as meaning either "what?" or "why?" The printed text of verses 7 and 8 may be translated either (*a*) "What did you go out into the wilderness to behold? A reed shaken by the wind? (8) What then did you go out to see? A man dressed in soft clothing?" or (*b*) "Why did you go out into the wilderness? To behold a reed shaken by the wind? (8) But why did you go out? To see a man dressed in soft clothing?" (The second interpretation is represented in the Gospel of Thomas, Logion 78.)

In ver. 9 the Committee decided that the reading ἰδεῖν προφήτην, which involves the previously mentioned ambiguity, is more likely to be original than the reading προφήτην ἰδεῖν, which, in the context, has to be taken in only one way, namely, "Why then did you go out? To see a prophet?"

11.15 ὦτα {B}

In view of the frequent occurrence elsewhere of the fuller expression ὦτα ἀκούειν (Mk 4.9, 23; 7.16; Lk 8.8; 14.35), it was to be expected that copyists would add the infinitive here (and in 13.9 and 43). If the word had been present in the original text, there is no reason why it should have been deleted in such important witnesses as B D 700 *al.*

11.17 ἐθρηνήσαμεν {B}

After repeated discussion the Committee decided that copyists were more likely to insert ὑμῖν for the sake of parallelism with the preceding strophe than to delete it as unnecessary. Furthermore, the shorter text is supported by representatives of widely diversified text-types.

11.19 ἀπὸ τῶν ἔργων {B}

The Committee regarded the reading τέκνων (widely supported by B^2 C D K L X Δ Θ Π and most minuscules) as having originated in scribal harmonization with the Lukan parallel (7.35).[1] The readings with πάντων represent further assimilation to the passage in Luke.

11.23 μὴ ἕως οὐρανοῦ ὑψωθήσῃ {B}

Palaeographically it is easy to see how the reading preserved in the earliest witnesses, which represent all the pre-Byzantine types of text,

---

[1] Some scholars (e. g., Lagarde, *Abhandlungen der Gesellschaft der Wissenschaften zu Göttingen,* Philol.-hist. Kl., xxxv (1888), p. 128 Anm., Zahn, Klostermann) have thought that the Matthean ἔργων and the Lukan τέκνων arose from the ambiguity of the unpointed Aramaic עבדיה, which may be pronounced *ābādeh,* "her works," or *ăbdeh,* "her servants." Others (e. g., Eb. Nestle and Lagrange), however, point out that it is still to be shown that τέκνον (rather than παῖς) is ever used as the equivalent of עֲבְדָא.

was accidentally modified. After Καφαρναούμ the first letter of μή was accidentally dropped, with the consequent alteration of the verb to either ὑψωθεῖσα or ὑψώθης depending on whether Η was taken as the article ἡ or the relative ἥ. The strong external attestation for the presence of μή is supported also by intrinsic and transcriptional probability. The unexpected turn of expression, "And you, Capernaum, will you be exalted to heaven?" is a sharp and startling interrogation, entirely in the manner of Jesus' use of vivid language. On the other hand, most copyists were likely to prefer the more commonplace statement, "And you, Capernaum, that are exalted to heaven...."

11.23 καταβήσῃ {C}

Whether the verb should read "you shall go down" or "you shall be brought down" is a difficult question to answer. Considerations of transcriptional probabilities – such as the heightening of the sense and the replacement of the rare verb with the more usual verb – are inconclusive (see also the comments on Lk 10.15). Despite the possibility of assimilation to the text of Is 14.15 (which reads καταβήσῃ), a majority of the Committee preferred this verb, supported as it is by the earliest representative of both the Alexandrian and the Western types of text.

11.27 τὸν υἱόν ... ὁ υἱός {A}

It is perhaps not surprising to find witnesses that modify the wording of this verse, chiefly by way of rearrangement. Following οὐδεὶς ἐπιγνώσκει, several witnesses (including N Diatessaron[(syr), arm] and a variety of church fathers, some with slight modifications[2]) read "[no one knows] the Father except the Son, and no one knows the Son except the Father." The transposition, which may have been occasioned by the presence of πατρός immediately preceding,

---

[2] For a list of such modifications, see B. F. Westcott, *A General Survey of the History of the Canon of the New Testament,* 6th ed. (Cambridge and London, 1889), pp. 135 f.

results in an awkward sequence with the following, "and anyone to whom the Son chooses to reveal him."

12.4   ἔφαγον {C}

Although ἔφαγον is supported by only ℵ B and 481, as the non-parallel reading it is more likely to have been altered to ἔφαγεν than vice versa. The text implies that David, having gone into the sanctuary, brought out the bread of the Presence which he and those who were with him ate.

12.15   [ὄχλοι] πολλοί {C}

While it is possible that through homoeoteleuton ὄχλοι may have accidentally fallen out, it is slightly more probable that scribes, influenced by the familiar phrase "many crowds" or "great crowds" (e. g. 4.25; 8.1; 13.2; 15.30; 19.2), strengthened the simple πολλοί (a reading that is supported by early Alexandrian and Western witnesses) by adding ὄχλοι, either before or after πολλοί.

12.25   εἰδὼς δέ {C}

The subject ὁ Ἰησοῦς was a natural addition, introduced by copyists who thought the words necessary for the sake of clarity. Had they been present originally, no one would have deliberately omitted them. The reading εἰδώς, whether with or without ὁ Ἰησοῦς, is supported by the overwhelming weight of external evidence. (See also the comment on 9.4.)

12.47   [include verse] {C}

The sentence, which seems to be necessary for the sense of the following verses, apparently was accidentally omitted because of homoeoteleuton (λαλῆσαι ... λαλῆσαι). In view, however, of the age and weight of the diverse text-types that omit the words, the Committee enclosed the words within square brackets in order to indicate a certain amount of doubt concerning their right to stand in the text.

13.9 ὦτα {B}

See the comment on the same variant reading at 11.15.

13.13 ὅτι βλέποντες οὐ βλέπουσιν καὶ ἀκούοντες οὐκ ἀκούουσιν οὐδὲ συνίουσιν {B}

Several representatives of the Western and of other types of text, influenced by the parallel passages in Mk 4.12 and Lk 8.10, altered the construction to ἵνα with the subjunctive mood of the verb. The references to seeing and hearing come from Is 6.9-10, but in reverse order. Several witnesses add from Mark (or Isaiah) καὶ μὴ συνιῶσιν ("and not perceive").

13.35 διά {C}

On the one hand, the reading "through Isaiah the prophet" is supported by codex Sinaiticus (first hand), several important minuscule manuscripts, one Ethiopic manuscript, and copies of the Gospel known to Eusebius and Jerome. The latter also states that Porphyry cited it as showing the ignorance of Matthew (*tam imperitus fuit*). Transcriptional probabilities at once favor this as the more difficult reading, for it is easy to suppose that so obvious an error would have been corrected by copyists (compare 27.9; Mk 1.2).

On the other hand, if no prophet were originally named, more than one scribe might have been prompted to insert the name of the best known prophet – something which has, in fact, happened elsewhere more than once (see comments on 1.22; 2.5; 21.4; Ac 7.48). It is also possible that some reader, observing the actual source of the quotation (Ps 78.2), might have inserted "Asaph," and subsequently – as Jerome suggests – other readers, not having heard of such a prophet (cf. 2 Chr 29.30), changed it to the much more familiar "Isaiah." No extant document is known to read Ἀσάφ.

In the face of such conflicting transcriptional probabilities, the Committee preferred to follow the preponderance of external evidence.

13.35   ἀπὸ καταβολῆς [κόσμου] {C}

It can be argued that the shorter reading, attested by representative witnesses of the Alexandrian, Western, and Eastern types of text, was original, and that κόσμου was added by scribes from 25.34, where the text is firm.

On the other hand, since the preponderance of the external evidence was taken to support the inclusion of κόσμου, a majority of the Committee was reluctant to drop the word from the text entirely and therefore decided to retain it enclosed within square brackets.

13.43   ὦτα {B}

See the comment on the same variant reading at 11.15.

13.55   Ἰωσήφ {B}

The name Ἰωσῆς (or Ἰωσῆ), which represents the Galilean pronunciation (יוֹסֵי) of the correct Hebrew (יוֹסֵף), appears to be an intrusion from Mk 6.3 into the text of Matthew. The substitution of Ἰωάννης is the result of scribal inadvertence, arising from the frequency elsewhere of references to James and John, the sons of Zebedee. The reading Ἰωάννης καὶ Ἰωσῆς is a manifest conflation, farthest removed from the original.

14.1   τετραάρχης

See the comment on Ac 13.1.

14.3   Φιλίππου {A}

According to Josephus (see his *Antiquities*, XVIII.v.4) the first husband of Herodias was named Herod (being the son of Herod the Great and Mariamne, Simon's daughter), whereas it was [Herod] Philip the tetrarch (Lk 3.1) who married Salome, the daughter of Herodias. In Mk 6.17 all manuscripts except two name Philip as Herodias's first husband ($\mathfrak{P}^{45}$ and ms. 47 omit the name Philip). It appears, therefore, that either Josephus failed to give the full name of Herodias's first husband (Herod Philip), or Mark confused Herodias's husband and son-in-law. In Lk 3.19 several witnesses (including A C K W 33 565 syr^p cop$^{sa^{pt}, bo}$) insert $\Phi\iota\lambda\acute{\iota}\pi\pi\sigma\upsilon$ before $\tau\sigma\hat{\upsilon}$ $\dot{\alpha}\delta\epsilon\lambda\phi\sigma\hat{\upsilon}$ $\alpha\dot{\upsilon}\tau\sigma\hat{\upsilon}$, though it is absent from the better witnesses (including ℵ B D L Γ Δ Λ Ξ Old Latin Vulgate Gothic).

It appears, therefore, that in 14.3 Matthew followed the original text of Mark and read $\Phi\iota\lambda\acute{\iota}\pi\pi\sigma\upsilon$, whereas several Western witnesses were assimilated to the shorter text of Lk 3.19 and thus brought Matthew's account into harmony with that of Josephus.

14.9 $\lambda\upsilon\pi\eta\theta\epsilon\grave{\iota}\varsigma$ $\acute{o}$ $\beta\alpha\sigma\iota\lambda\epsilon\grave{\upsilon}\varsigma$ $\delta\iota\acute{\alpha}$ {B}

The reading supported by the chief representatives of the Alexandrian and the Western types of text involves a certain ambiguity (i. e. does the phrase with $\delta\iota\acute{\alpha}$ qualify $\lambda\upsilon\pi\eta\theta\epsilon\grave{\iota}\varsigma$ or $\dot{\epsilon}\kappa\acute{\epsilon}\lambda\epsilon\upsilon\sigma\epsilon\nu$?). In order to resolve the ambiguity copyists inserted $\delta\acute{\epsilon}$, thus altering the hypotactic construction ("And being grieved, the king, because of his oaths and because of those who sat with him, commanded [it] to be given") to the more colloquial paratactic construction ("And the king was grieved; but because of his oaths and because of those who sat with him, he commanded …").

14.12 $\alpha\dot{\upsilon}\tau\acute{o}[\nu]$

On the one hand, the predominant external evidence attests $\alpha\dot{\upsilon}\tau\acute{o}$ (or its phonetic near-equivalent, $\alpha\dot{\upsilon}\tau\hat{\omega}$), with only ℵ* B 0106 it^a syr$^{c, s}$ eth attesting $\alpha\dot{\upsilon}\tau\acute{o}\nu$. On the other hand, however, it is much more likely that copyists would conform the personal pronoun to the impersonal for the sake of grammatical concord with $\pi\tau\hat{\omega}\mu\alpha$ (or $\sigma\hat{\omega}\mu\alpha$), than vice versa. In order to represent the opposition between external evidence and transcriptional probability, it was decided to print $\alpha\dot{\upsilon}\tau\acute{o}[\nu]$.

14.24 σταδίους πολλοὺς ἀπὸ τῆς γῆς ἀπεῖχεν {C}

The question is whether Matthew was here assimilated by copyists to John (σταδίους εἴκοσι πέντε ἢ τριάκοντα, Jn 6.19) or to Mark (ἦν τὸ πλοῖον ἐν μέσῳ τῆς θαλάσσης, Mk 6.47). Since the process of harmonization more often took place among the Synoptic Gospels than between the Fourth Gospel and one of the Synoptics, and since the Johannine parallel is very slight (involving among Greek witnesses only the word σταδίους),[1] it appears that the reading of B *f*[13] *al* best accounts for the rise of the others.

14.29 καὶ ἦλθεν {B}

The reading καὶ ἦλθεν ("Peter walked upon the water *and came* to Jesus") seemed to say too much, and therefore was altered to ἐλθεῖν ("Peter walked upon the water *to come* to Jesus"). Although the reading of א* has the appearance of being a conflation, it may be merely an exegetical expansion introduced by the scribe. The reading of eth^ro is a translational error.

14.30 ἄνεμον [ἰσχυρόν] {C}

From the standpoint of external evidence, although the combination of א B* 073 33 cop^sa, bo, fay is impressive attestation, a majority of the Committee considered it too exclusively Egyptian to be followed here, where the shorter text may have arisen by accidental omission in the ancestor of one text-type. From the standpoint of internal considerations, although it can be argued that ἰσχυρόν was added by scribes in order to heighten the dramatic effect (as σφόδρα was added in W), a majority was inclined to regard its presence as intrinsically required in order to explain Peter's increasing fear. In order to represent these conflicting considerations the Committee decided to retain ἰσχυρόν in the text, but to enclose it within square brackets.

---

[1] The Bohairic version has been partially conformed to the Johannine account; it reads "the ship was at a distance from the land about twenty-five stadia."

15.4 εἶπεν {B}

The presence of τὴν ἐντολὴν τοῦ θεοῦ in ver. 3 probably prompted copyists to change the statement, "For God said …" to "For God commanded, saying …," whereas, if the reading ἐνετείλατο λέγων had been original, it is difficult to account for the substitution of the more colorless εἶπεν (in Mk 7.10, where the text is firm, the subject of εἶπεν is Μωϋσῆς).

15.6 τὸν πατέρα αὐτοῦ {C}

On the one hand, it can be argued that the addition of the phrase "or his mother" doubtless seemed necessary to scribes who observed the references to both father and mother in the preceding verses. On the other hand, the absence of ἢ [or καὶ] τὴν μητέρα αὐτοῦ may be accounted for either as accidental omission (owing to similarity with the preceding τὸν πατέρα αὐτοῦ) or as deliberate stylistic suppression of one element in a frequently repeated phrase. In view of the balance of such transcriptional considerations, the Committee made its decision on the basis of what was judged to be superior external attestation.

15.6 τὸν λόγον {B}

It is clear that τὴν ἐντολήν was introduced to suit ver. 3, but whether it supplanted τὸν λόγον or τὸν νόμον is more difficult to decide. Although it is tempting to regard νόμον as original and λόγον as the result of harmonization to Mk 7.13, a majority of the Committee was impressed by the weight of the external evidence supporting λόγον. Furthermore, since a specific commandment is cited, there would have been a tendency to replace λόγον with either ἐντολήν or νόμον.

15.14 τυφλοί εἰσιν ὁδηγοί [τυφλῶν] {C}

Although from the standpoint of external evidence the reading τυφλοί εἰσιν ὁδηγοί, supported by B and D, may seem to be preferable, the readings that most adequately account for the emergence of the others (as emendations of the arrangement, or mistakes arising from palaeographical similarities) are τυφλοί εἰσιν ὁδηγοὶ τυφλῶν and ὁδηγοί εἰσιν τυφλοὶ τυφλῶν. Of these two readings, the Committee preferred the former on the basis of superior attestation; at the same time, however, in deference to the weight of B and D, it was decided to retain τυφλῶν enclosed within square brackets.

15.15 τὴν παραβολὴν [ταύτην] {C}

A majority of the Committee preferred to adopt the reading attested by a wide variety of witnesses and to explain the absence of ταύτην in other witnesses as the result of deliberate excision by scribes who thought it inappropriate (the "parable" does not immediately precede). Nevertheless, in view of the weight of the witnesses that omit ταύτην (ℵ B f¹ 700 892 cop^sa geo^B Origen), it was thought best to enclose the word within square brackets.

15.31 λαλοῦντας, κυλλοὺς ὑγιεῖς {C}

The manuscripts of this verse reflect a variety of changes, some accidental and some deliberate. Although it can be argued that the words κυλλοὺς ὑγιεῖς were added in order to make a series of four items corresponding to the number (though not to the sequence) in ver. 30, it is more likely that they were omitted, perhaps because it seemed superfluous to say that the crippled became well and that the lame were walking. The twofold meaning of κωφός ("dumb" and "deaf") accounts for the variation between λαλοῦντας in most witnesses, and ἀκούοντας in B and a few other witnesses (N O Σ conflate both participles). The reading of most Greek lectionaries shows the influence of the parallel account in Mk 7.37 (ἀλάλους λαλεῖν). The reading adopted for the text is supported by a broad spectrum of attestation.

15.39 Μαγαδάν {C}

The best external evidence supports Μαγαδάν, yet not only the site, but even the existence of such a place-name is uncertain. The parallel passage in Mk 8.10 has "the districts of Dalmanutha" *(τὰ μέρη Δαλμανουθά)*, an equally unknown site and name. The well-known Semitic word for tower,[1] in Greek *Μαγδαλά(ν)*, is read in many manuscripts in place of *Μαγαδάν* or *Δαλμανουθά*. (See also the comment on Mk 8.10.)

16.2-3   *[ὀψίας γενομένης ... οὐ δύνασθε:]* {C}

The external evidence for the absence of these words is impressive, including ℵ B *f*[13] 157 *al* syr[c, s] cop[sa, bo mss] arm Origen and, according to Jerome, most manuscripts known to him (though he included the passage in the Vulgate). The question is how one ought to interpret this evidence. Most scholars regard the passage as a later insertion from a source similar to Lk 12.54-56, or from the Lukan passage itself, with an adjustment concerning the particular signs of the weather. On the other hand, it can be argued (as Scrivener and Lagrange do) that the words were omitted by copyists in climates (e. g. Egypt) where red sky in the morning does not announce rain.

In view of the balance of these considerations it was thought best to retain the passage enclosed within square brackets.

16.12   *τῶν ἄρτων* {C}

In view of the use of the expression "the leaven of the Pharisees and Sadducees" in verses 6 and 11, it was perhaps natural that a few witnesses should repeat one or both of the words "Pharisees" "Sadducees" after *ζύμης* in ver. 12. Although the reading of D Θ *f*[13] *al* without any qualifying genitive ("Then they understood that he did not tell them to beware of leaven, but of the teaching of the Pharisees and Sadducees") might be thought original and each of the other readings an expansion, it is also possible that copyists considered the presence of *τῶν ἄρτων* or *τοῦ ἄρτου* to be unnecessary to the sense and therefore omitted the words as superfluous. In view of the balance of transcriptional possibilities, the Committee decided to adopt the reading supported by ℵ[c] B L 892 and several early versions.

---

[1] Hebrew מִגְדָּל, Aramaic מִגְדְּלָא, Arabic مجدل.

16.13   *Τίνα λέγουσιν οἱ ἄνθρωποι εἶναι* {B}

Both the variety of positions of *με* in the witnesses that include it and the fact that in the parallel passages the word is firm indicate that it was originally absent from Matthew's account.

16.20   *ὁ Χριστός* {B}

To the shorter reading, which is supported by widely diversified ancient witnesses (ℵ* B L Δ Θ *f*¹ *f*¹³ 28 565 700 1010 1424 it syrᶜ, ᵖ copˢᵃ Origen *al*), inattentive scribes added *Ἰησοῦς* either before *ὁ Χριστός* (ℵ² C W lat syrʰ *al*) or after *ὁ Χριστός* (Dᵍʳ itᶜ). But since others knew and acknowledged Jesus' personal name, it would have been useless to deny or affirm that he was Jesus; the point under discussion was whether he was the Messiah *(ὁ Χριστός)*.

16.27   *τὴν πρᾶξιν* {B}

The reading *τὴν πρᾶξιν,* which is supported by the weight of diversified witnesses, focuses attention on a person's work or course of life considered as a whole. The scribes of a scattering of Greek witnesses (ℵ* *f*¹ 28 1424 *al*), supported by several early versions, preferred the more usual plural expression *(τὰ ἔργα),* which has been taken over by the Textus Receptus.

17.2   *τὸ φῶς* {A}

Instead of *τὸ φῶς,* which is strongly supported by witnesses representing all types of text, several Western witnesses, recollecting what is said in 28.3, make the comparison in terms of the clothing being "white as snow" *(χιών).*

17.4   *ποιήσω ὧδε* {B}

Instead of the reading that speaks of Peter's volunteering to make the three *σκηνάς* (the singular number *ποιήσω* accords with the self-assured forwardness of the apostle), the scribes of most witnesses assimilated the verb to the plural number (ποιήσωμεν), a reading found in the parallel accounts at Mk 9.5 and Lk 9.33.

17.20 ὀλιγοπιστίαν {A}

It is more likely that the evangelist used ὀλιγοπιστίαν, a rare word that occurs nowhere else in the New Testament (though ὀλιγόπιστος is used four times in Matthew), and that, in view of ἄπιστος in ver. 17, copyists substituted the more frequently used word ἀπιστία (which occurs eleven times in the New Testament), than that the reverse process took place.

17.21 *omit verse* {A}

Since there is no satisfactory reason why the passage, if originally present in Matthew, should have been omitted in a wide variety of witnesses, and since copyists frequently inserted material derived from another Gospel, it appears that most manuscripts have been assimilated to the parallel in Mk 9.29.

17.22 συστρεφομένων {B}

It is probable that the reading συστρεφομένων (taken to mean "were gathering together") would strike copyists as strange, and therefore would be changed into what seemed more appropriate (ἀναστρεφομένων, "were staying"). The verb συστρέφειν, which occurs only twice in the New Testament, apparently means here "while they were crowding (around Jesus)."

17.26 εἰπόντος δέ {B}

The reading εἰπόντος δέ, lacking a substantive, was deemed to be the reading that best explains the origin of the other readings.

After Ἄρα ... υἱοί, which may be taken as a question, a note-worthy expansion appears in minuscule manuscript 713, dating from the twelfth century: ἔφη Σίμων, Ναί. λέγει ὁ Ἰησοῦς, Δὸς οὖν καὶ σύ, ὡς ἀλλότριος αὐτῶν ("Simon said 'Yes.' Jesus says, 'Then you

also give, as being an alien to them'"). The same expansion occurs
also in the Arabic form of the Diatessaron (25.6). The nucleus of this
occurs in Ephraem's Commentary on Tatian's Diatessaron, where the
Syriac text (14.17) reads, "Give to them therefore as an alien," and
the Armenian reads, "Go; you also give as one of the aliens."

18.11 *omit verse* {B}

There can be little doubt that the words ἦλθεν γὰρ ὁ υἱὸς
τοῦ ἀνθρώπου (ζητῆσαι καὶ) σῶσαι τὸ ἀπολωλός are spurious
here, being absent from the earliest witnesses representing several
textual types (Alexandrian, Egyptian, Antiochian), and manifestly
borrowed by copyists from Lk 19.10. The reason for the interpolation was apparently to provide a connection between ver. 10 and
verses 12-14.

18.14 ὑμῶν {C}

Between the readings "your Father" and "my Father" it is difficult
to decide.[1] The latter, though strongly attested, probably reflects the
influence of τοῦ πατρός μου in ver. 10 (compare also ver. 35). The
reading ἡμῶν (D* and a few other witnesses) is probably itacism for
ὑμῶν.

18.15 ἁμαρτήσῃ [εἰς σέ] {C}

It is possible that the words εἰς σέ are an early interpolation into
the original text, perhaps derived by copyists from the use of εἰς ἐμέ
in ver. 21. On the other hand, it is also possible to regard their omission as either deliberate (in order to render the passage applicable to
sin in general) or accidental (for in later Greek the pronunciation of
η, ῃ, and εἰ was similar). In order to reflect this balance of possibilities, the Committee decided to retain the words enclosed within
square brackets.

---

[1] Matthew has 19 instances of the expression "my Father," and 18 instances of
"your Father" (σοῦ or ὑμῶν).

18.19 πάλιν *[ἀμὴν]* λέγω {C}

It is difficult to decide whether the presence of ἀμὴν λέγω in the preceding sentence may have prompted scribes to add ἀμὴν before λέγω at the beginning of this sentence, or whether they may have deleted the word as redundant. Faced with this quandary, the Committee decided to include the word but to enclose it within square brackets.

18.26 λέγων {A}

Although κύριε may have been omitted in order to conform the passage to ver. 29, it is more likely that the word was inserted in order to adapt the expression to a spiritual interpretation. The combination of B D Θ 700 vg syr^(c, s) arm geo *al* is a significant constellation of witnesses supporting the shorter reading.

18.29 αὐτοῦ

Although it is possible that the phrase εἰς τοὺς πόδας αὐτοῦ (C² E F H K M S U V Γ Δ Π most minuscules, followed by the Textus Receptus) was accidentally omitted in transcription, the eye of the scribe passing from αὐτοῦ to αὐτοῦ, the Committee preferred the shorter text (ℵ B C* D G L Θ 1 71 124 700 892 1396 1424 1573 1579 1582, most of the Old Latin, vg syr^(c, s, pal) cop^(sa, bo) eth geo) and regarded the longer reading as a natural expansion introduced by scribes in order to explain πεσών.

18.35 ὑμῶν

The words τὰ παραπτώματα αὐτῶν, which the Textus Receptus, following the later witnesses, adds at the close of the sentence, are a natural expansion, derived perhaps from 6.14. The Committee preferred the shorter reading supported by the chief representatives of the Alexandrian, Western, and other types of text (ℵ B D L Θ 1 22* 700 892 1582 it^(a, b, c, d, e, ff2, l, q, rl) vg syr^(c, s) cop^(sa, bo) geo eth Speculum).

19.4 κτίσας {B}

It is easier to suppose that copyists changed the word κτίσας (which is supported by several excellent witnesses) to ποιήσας, thus harmonizing it with the Septuagint text of Gn 1.27 (which is quoted in the immediate context), than to suppose that ποιήσας was altered to suit the Hebrew word used in Gn 1.27 (ברא, which means "created").

19.7 ἀπολῦσαι [αὐτήν] {C}

It is difficult to decide whether αὐτήν is an addition (as τὴν γυναῖκα undoubtedly is) to a concisely stated expression, or whether the word was deleted in order to assimilate the passage to the near-parallel in Mk 10.4. Since the external evidence is likewise so nearly balanced, the Committee decided to retain the word enclosed within square brackets.

19.9 μὴ ἐπὶ πορνείᾳ καὶ γαμήσῃ ἄλλην μοιχᾶται {B}

The "excepting clause" in the Matthean account of Jesus' teaching on divorce occurs in two forms: παρεκτὸς λόγου πορνείας ("except on the ground of unchastity") and μὴ ἐπὶ πορνείᾳ ("except for unchastity"). It is probable that the witnesses (including B D f^1 f^{13} 33) that have the former reading have been assimilated to 5.32, where the text is firm. Likewise the phrase ποιεῖ αὐτὴν μοιχευθῆναι ("makes her commit adultery" [i. e. when she remarries]) has come into several witnesses (including B C* f^1) from 5.32, where it is firm. The short reading of 1574, καὶ γαμήσῃ ἄλλην, has been conformed to the prevailing text of Mk 10.11.

19.9 μοιχᾶται {B}

After μοιχᾶται several witnesses (including K W Δ Θ Π f^{13}) add καὶ ὁ ἀπολελυμένην γαμῶν (or γαμήσας) μοιχᾶται ("and he who marries a divorced woman commits adultery"). Although it could be argued that homoeoteleuton (μοιχᾶται … μοιχᾶται) accounts for its accidental omission from ℵ D L 1241 al, the fact that B C* f^1 *al* read μοιχᾶται only once (at the conclusion of the combined clauses) makes it more probable that the text was expanded by copyists who accommodated the saying to the prevailing text of 5.32.

19.10 μαθηταὶ *[αὐτοῦ]* {C}

Although the combination of ℵ B Θ it^e cop^{sams} in support of the shorter reading is noteworthy, the Committee was impressed by the possibility that the presence of αὐτῷ before μαθηταί prompted some copyists to delete αὐτοῦ. It was thought best, therefore, to retain the word enclosed within square brackets.

19.11 τὸν λόγον *[τοῦτον]* {C}

On the one hand, since the general tendency of scribes is to make the text more explicit, e. g. by adding the demonstrative pronoun, the shorter reading, supported by B f^1 and several early versions, has a certain presumption in its favor. On the other hand, however, the ambiguity of the reference of τοῦτον in the context – does it refer to the deduction made by the disciples (ver. 11), or to the preceding exposition of Jesus (verses 4-9)? – may have prompted some scribes to delete the word. In order to reflect the balance of possibilities, the Committee decided to retain the word enclosed within square brackets. The reading of Θ is obviously secondary.

19.16 διδάσκαλε {A}

The word ἀγαθέ, which is absent from early and good representatives of the Alexandrian and the Western texts, was manifestly brought in by copyists from the parallel accounts in Mark (10.17) and Luke (18.18). (See also the comment on the following variant reading.)

19.17 τί με ἐρωτᾷς περὶ τοῦ ἀγαθοῦ; εἷς ἐστιν ὁ ἀγαθός {A}

Many of the witnesses (but not Θ 700 *al*) that interpolate ἀγαθέ in ver. 16 also modify ver. 17 by substituting for Matthew's distinctive account the words from the parallel accounts, *τί με λέγεις ἀγαθόν; οὐδεὶς ἀγαθὸς εἰ μὴ εἷς ὁ θεός* ("Why do you call me good? No one is good but God alone," Mk 10.18; Lk 18.19). If the latter reading were original in Matthew, it is hard to imagine why copyists would have altered it to a more obscure one, whereas scribal assimilation to Synoptic parallels occurs frequently.

19.20 *ἐφύλαξα* {A}

Despite Matthew's identification of the speaker as *νεανίσκος* (verses 20 and 22), the scribes of many witnesses assimilated the account to the Synoptic parallels by adding *ἐκ νεότητός μου* (Mk 10.20) or *ἐκ νεότητος* (Lk 18.21).

19.24 *κάμηλον* {A}

Instead of *κάμηλον*, a few of the later Greek manuscripts read *κάμιλον*, meaning "a rope, ship's cable." The two Greek words had come to be pronounced alike.

19.29 *πατέρα ἢ μητέρα* {C}

The presence of *γυναῖκα* in many witnesses seems to be the result of scribal assimilation to the Lukan parallel (Lk 18.29), and the replacement of *πατέρα ἢ μητέρα* by *γονεῖς* in other witnesses may either reflect influence from the same parallel or be a substitution arising independently. The absence of *πατέρα ἢ* in D and several Old Latin witnesses appears to be the result of homoeoteleuton.

19.29 *ἑκατονταπλασίονα* {B}

The several readings are reflected in the parallel passages: the text of Mark (10.30) reads *ἑκατονταπλασίονα* ("a hundredfold"); most of the manuscripts of Luke (18.30) read *πολλαπλασίονα* ("manifold"); and the Western text of Luke (D Old Latin syr[hmg]) reads *ἑπταπλασίονα* ("sevenfold"). What was judged to be predominant external support, as well as considerations involving the dependence

of Matthew upon Mark, led the Committee to prefer ἑκατονταπλασίονα.

20.10 *[τὸ]* ἀνὰ δηνάριον καὶ αὐτοί {C}

In the interest of heightening the emphasis, scribes moved καὶ
αὐτοί to follow ἔλαβον. Although τό might have been omitted by
scribes as superfluous, yet because of the weight of the combination
of B and D, the Committee decided to retain the word enclosed within
square brackets.

20.15 *[ἤ]* (1) {C}

External support for the presence or absence of ἤ at the beginning
of ver. 15 is rather evenly divided, with representative witnesses of
the Alexandrian (B and ℵ), the Western (D and Old Latin), and other
(Θ and *f*¹ *f*¹³) texts on opposite sides. From a transcriptional point
of view it is more likely that scribes would have dropped the word
after σοι (in later Greek both η and οι were pronounced "ee") than
inserted it. On balance the Committee thought it best to retain the
word, but to enclose it within square brackets.

20.16 ἔσχατοι. {A}

Although it is possible that the words πολλοὶ … ἐκλετοί had
been accidentally omitted from an ancestor of ℵ B L Z 085 *al* owing
to homoeoteleuton, the Committee regarded it as much more likely
that they were added here by copyists who recollected the close of
another parable (22.14, where there is no significant variation of
reading).

20.17 τοὺς δώδεκα *[μαθητάς]* {C}

Although copyists often add the word μαθηταί to the more primitive expression οἱ δώδεκα (see Tischendorf's note *in loc.* and 26.20
below), a majority of the Committee judged that the present passage
was assimilated to the text of Mark (10.32) or Luke (18.31). In order

to represent both possibilities it was decided to employ square brackets.

The reading with αὐτοῦ in several minuscules and versions is clearly a secondary expansion.

20.22   πίνειν. {A}

The clause ἢ τὸ βάπτισμα ... βαπτισθῆναι, which is absent from important early witnesses representing several types of text (א D L Z Θ f¹³ al), was added by scribes in order to assimilate the passage to the parallel in Mk 10.38 f.

20.23   οὐκ ἔστιν ἐμὸν [τοῦτο] δοῦναι {C}

Because the word τοῦτο, which is absent from early and good witnesses, occurs at various places in various witnesses, it would be tempting to regard it as a scribal enhancement of the text. Nevertheless, since the word does not appear in the parallel account in Mark, the Committee decided to retain it in Matthew, but to enclose it within square brackets in order to indicate doubt as to its proper position in the text.

20.23   πίεσθε

The majority of the manuscripts have filled out the sentence by adding from the parallel in Mk 10.39 the clause καὶ τὸ βάπτισμα ὃ ἐγὼ βαπτίζομαι βαπτισθήσεσθε. The shorter text is decisively supported by the same witnesses that read the shorter text in ver. 22.

20.26   ἔσται {B}

Although the combination of B and D in support of ἐστίν is not insignificant, the Committee judged that the preponderant weight of the external evidence supports the future tense. The same variation occurs also in the parallel at Mk 10.43.

20.28 πολλῶν

After πολλῶν several Western witnesses (D and, with minor variations, Φ it syr^{c, hmg}) add Ὑμεῖς δὲ ζητεῖτε ἐκ μικροῦ αὐξῆσαι καὶ ἐκ μείζονος ἔλαττον εἶναι. Εἰσερχόμενοι δὲ καὶ παρα-κληθέντες δειπνῆσαι μὴ ἀνακλίνεσθε εἰς τοὺς ἐξέχοντας τόπους, μήποτε ἐνδοξότερός σου ἐπέλθῃ καὶ προσελθὼν ὁ δειπνοκλήτωρ εἴπῃ σοι, Ἔτι κάτω χώρει, καὶ καταισχυνθήσῃ. Ἐὰν δὲ ἀναπέσῃς εἰς τὸν ἥττονα τόπον καὶ ἐπέλθῃ σου ἥττων, ἐρεῖ σοι ὁ δειπνοκλήτωρ, Σύναγε ἔτι ἄνω, καὶ ἔσται σοι τοῦτο χρήσιμον ("But seek to increase from that which is small, and from the greater to become less. When you enter into a house and are invited to dine, do not recline in the prominent places, lest perchance one more honorable than you come in, and the host come and say to you, 'Go farther down'; and you will be put to shame. But if you recline in the lower place and one inferior to you comes in, the host will say to you, 'Go farther up'; and this will be advantageous to you"). This interpolation is a piece of floating tradition, an expanded but inferior version of Lk 14.8-10.

20.30 Ἐλέησον ἡμᾶς, [κύριε,] {C}

Influenced by the recollection of similar passages elsewhere, copyists have introduced many variations. Since the parallels in Mk 10.47 and Lk 18.38 both contain Ἰησοῦ, it is probable that the Matthean readings involving this word are secondary. Although it can be argued that the shortest reading (ἐλέησον ἡμᾶς, υἱὲ Δαυίδ) is original and all the other readings are scribal expansions, it is more likely that copyists, influenced by Matthew's earlier account of the healing of the blind men, produced by assimilation an exact parallel to 9.27. Furthermore, it appears that readings with υἱέ reflect a more elegant Greek style than the more Semitic usage of the nominative (cf. Blass-Debrunner-Funk, § 147 (3)). As the least unsatisfactory resolution of all the diverse problems a majority of the Committee decided to adopt the reading of 𝔓^{45vid} C W Δ 1 28 al, but, in view of the variation in position of κύριε, to enclose this word within square brackets.

20.31 Ἐλέησον ἡμᾶς, κύριε {C}

The sequence κύριε, ἐλέησον ἡμᾶς is well attested by ℵ B D L Z Θ *f*[13] 543 892 1010 1293 it[a, b, c, d, h, l, n, rl] vg syr[p, pal] cop[sa, bo] arm geo[1], whereas the sequence ἐλέησον ἡμᾶς, κύριε is attested by 𝔓[45vid] C N O W X Γ Δ Π Σ Φ most minuscules it[ff2, q] syr[h] geo[2] (κύριε is omitted by 118 209 700 1675 vg[ms] syr[pms]). Despite the somewhat poorer quality of the external evidence supporting the second sequence, this reading was preferred by a majority of the Committee because it is the non-liturgical order of words and so would have been likely to be altered in transcription to the more familiar sequence.

21.4 προφήτου

Several witnesses (M[mg] 42 it[a, c, h] cop[boms] Hilary) add Ζαχαρίου before or after προφήτου; other witnesses (vg[4 mss] cop[boms] eth) prefix "Isaiah."

21.12 ἱερόν {B}

The addition of τοῦ θεοῦ appears to be a natural expansion, made in order to emphasize the profanation of the holy place. The fact that the parallel passages (Mk 11.15 and Lk 19.45; cf. Jn 2.14) lack τοῦ θεοῦ would not be an occasion for copyists, if they observed the fact, to delete the words from copies of Matthew, but rather for inserting the words in copies of the other Gospels. Although the Jews had little use for such a phrase (since for them "the temple" could mean only one thing), the longer expression would not be intrinsically objectionable to anyone, and therefore its omission cannot be accounted for on that ground. It appears, therefore, that internal considerations join with strong external evidence in support of the reading ἱερόν.

21.29-31 οὐ θέλω, ὕστερον δὲ μεταμεληθεὶς ἀπῆλθεν … ἑτέρῳ … ἐγώ, κύριε· καὶ οὐκ ἀπῆλθεν … ὁ πρῶτος {C}

The textual transmission of the parable of the two sons is very much confused (see also the comment on 21.32). Is the recusant but subsequently obedient son mentioned first or second (ver. 29)? Which of the two sons did the Jews intend to assert had done the father's bidding (ver. 31), and what word did they use in their reply to Jesus' question (πρῶτος or ἔσχατος or ὕστερος or δεύτερος)? There are three principal forms of text:

(a) According to ℵ C* K W Δ Π it^{c, q} vg syr^{c, p, h} *al,* the first son says "No" but afterwards repents. The second son says "Yes" but does nothing. Which one did the will of the father? Answer: ὁ πρῶτος.

(b) According to D it^{a, b, d, e, ff2, h, l} syr^s *al,* the first son says "No" but afterwards repents. The second son says "Yes" but does nothing. Which one did the will of the father? Answer: ὁ ἔσχατος.

(c) According to B Θ f^{13} 700 syr^{pal} arm geo *al,* the first son says "Yes" but does nothing. The second says "No" but afterwards repents. Which one did the will of the father? Answer: ὁ ὕστερος (B), or ὁ ἔσχατος (Θ f^{13} 700 arm), or ὁ δεύτερος (4 273), or ὁ πρῶτος (geo^A).

Because (b) is the most difficult of the three forms of text, several scholars (Lachmann, Merx, Wellhausen, Hirsch) have thought that it must be preferred as readily accounting for the rise of the other two as improvements of it. But (b) is not only difficult, it is nonsensical – the son who said "Yes" but does nothing obeys his father's will! Jerome, who knew of manuscripts in his day that read the nonsensical answer, suggested that through perversity the Jews intentionally gave an absurd reply in order to spoil the point of the parable. But this explanation requires the further supposition that the Jews not only recognized that the parable was directed against themselves but chose to make a nonsensical reply rather than merely remain silent. Because such explanations attribute to the Jews, or to Matthew, far-fetched psychological or overly-subtle literary motives, the Committee judged that the origin of reading (b) is due to copyists who either committed a transcriptional blunder or who were motivated by anti-Pharisaic bias (i. e., since Jesus had characterized the Pharisees as those that say but do not practice (cf. Mt 23.3), they must be represented as approving the son who said "I go," but did not go).

As between forms (a) and (c) the former is more probably the original. Not only are the witnesses that support (a) slightly better than those that read (*c*), but there would be a natural tendency to transpose the order of (*a*) to that of (*c*) because:

(1) it could be argued that if the first son obeyed, there was no reason to summon the second; and

(2) it was natural to identify the disobedient son with either the Jews in general or with the chief priests and elders (ver. 23) and the obedient son with either the Gentiles or the tax collectors and the prostitutes (ver. 31) – and in accord with either line of interpretation, the obedient son should come last in chronological sequence. It may also be remarked that the inferiority of form (*c*) is shown by the wide diversity of readings at the close of the parable.[1]

21.32   οὐδέ

The confusion that marks the transmission of 21.29-31 seems to have affected also the text of the final clause of this verse. Instead of οὐδέ (which is read by B O Θ Σ Φ 0138 1 *f*[13] 22 33 157 543 565 700 892 1579 1582 most of the Old Latin vg cop[bo] eth) other witnesses (including ℵ C L W X Π 28 118 209 the Byzantine text and cop[sa]) read οὐ. D and syr[s] omit the negative; it[c, e, h] alter its position (*quod non credidistis*). Δ omits the entire clause (from ὑμεῖς δέ to the end of the verse), perhaps by homoeoteleuton.

The omission of the negative is probably accidental, for the resulting sense ("but you, when you saw it, at last repented [i. e. changed

---

[1] For other discussions of this perplexing passage see Josef Schmid (who concludes that form (*c*) is original), "Das textgeschichtliche Problem der Parabel von den zwei Söhnen," in *Vom Wort des Lebens, Festschrift für Max Meinertz*, ed. Nikolaus Adler (= *Neutestamentliche Abhandlungen;* 1. *Ergänzungsband;* Münster/Westf., 1951), pp. 68–84, and J. Ramsey Michaels (who argues that forms (*a*) and (*c*) were derived from (*b*)), "The Parable of the Regretful Son," *Harvard Theological Review*, LXI (1968), pp. 15–26.

Lachmann's suggestion (*Novum Testamentum Graece*, II, p. v) that the words between πατρός and Ἀμήν are an early interpolation has met with no general approval, though in Westcott's opinion "it seems not unlikely that Lachmann is substantially right" ("Notes on Select Readings," p. 17). Westcott and Hort mark the passage with an obelus, indicating that in their judgment the text contains a primitive error lying behind all extant witnesses.

your minds] so as to believe in him") seems to be an extremely inappropriate conclusion of Jesus' saying; likewise the transfer of the negative to the final verb is no less infelicitous ("... repented later because you did not believe on him"). The reading οὐδέ, supported by early and widely diversified witnesses, seems to have been altered to οὐ by copyists who did not see the force of the argument ("and you, seeing this, did not even feel remorse afterwards so as to believe him").

21.39 αὐτὸν ἐξέβαλον ἔξω τοῦ ἀμπελῶνος καὶ ἀπέκτειναν {A}

The Western text (D Θ it[a, b, c, d, e, ff2, h, r1] geo Irenaeus Lucifer Juvencus) has been assimilated to the sequence in Mark, where the son is killed and then cast out of the vineyard (Mk 12.8). Matthew and Luke (20.15), reflecting that Jesus had been crucified outside the city (Jn 19.17, 20; He 13.12 f.), reverse the order and put the casting out before the killing.

21.44 [Καὶ ... αὐτόν.] {C}

Many modern scholars regard the verse as an early interpolation (from Lk 20.18) into most manuscripts of Matthew. On the other hand, however, the words are not the same, and a more appropriate place for its insertion would have been after ver. 42. Its omission can perhaps be accounted for when the eye of the copyist passed from αὐτῆς (ver. 43) to αὐτόν. While considering the verse to be an accretion to the text, yet because of the antiquity of the reading and its importance in the textual tradition, the Committee decided to retain it in the text, enclosed within square brackets.

22.10 ὁ γάμος {B}

The Committee considered the reading ὁ νυμφών (here meaning "the wedding hall") to be an Alexandrian correction introduced in the place of ὁ γάμος, which may have seemed to be somewhat inappropriate with the verb "filled."

22.23 Σαδδουκαῖοι, λέγοντες {B}

Although the definite article after Σαδδουκαῖοι could have dropped out because of confusion with the termination of the noun, the Committee considered it to be much more likely that copyists added the article by assimilation to the parallel passages (Mk 12.18; Lk 20.27). Without the article the participle means that the Sadducees advanced their negative opinion at the beginning of their conversation with Jesus; with the article the passage states the Sadducean creed ("Sadducees, who say that …"). Since this would be the only place where Matthew has provided an explanation of this sort concerning Jewish affairs, the reading without the article is to be preferred.

22.30 ἄγγελοι {B}

While the evidence for ἄγγελοι is limited in extent, it nevertheless includes the leading representatives of the Alexandrian and the Western types of text. The addition of *(τοῦ) θεοῦ* is a natural expansion, which, if present in the text originally, would not have been likely to be omitted.

22.32 ἔστιν [ὁ] θεός {C}

In the interest of greater precision, the later form of the text inserted a second θεός ("For God is not a God of dead people, but of living"). In order to reflect the difficulty of deciding whether ὁ was omitted by assimilation to the parallel in Mk 12.27, or whether it was added under the influence of the four instances of ὁ θεός immediately preceding, the Committee retained ὁ within square brackets.

22.35 [νομικός] {C}

Despite what seems to be an overwhelming preponderance of evidence supporting the word νομικός, its absence from family 1 as well as from widely scattered versional and patristic witnesses takes on additional significance when it is observed that, apart from this passage, Matthew nowhere else uses the word. It is not unlikely, therefore, that copyists have introduced the word here from the parallel passage in Lk 10.25. At the same time, in view of the widespread testimony supporting its presence in the text, the Committee was reluctant to omit the word altogether, preferring to retain it enclosed within square brackets.

23.4 βαρέα [καὶ δυσβάστακτα] {C}

Impressed by the weight of the external evidence supporting the longer text, a majority of the Committee explained the absence of καὶ δυσβάστακτα in L f^1 892 al as perhaps due to stylistic refinement or to accidental oversight (the eye of the copyist passing from one καὶ to the other). Nevertheless, because it is possible that the words may be an interpolation from Lk 11.46, it was decided to enclose them within square brackets.

[The words καὶ δυσβάστακτα should not stand in the text, for (a) if they were present originally, no good reason can account for their absence from such a wide variety of witnesses, and (b) the tendency of copyists to enhance the solemnity of Jesus' words accounts for the prefixing of μεγάλα before βαρέα in א, and for the interpolation after βαρέα of the synonymous expression καὶ δυσβάστακτα from Lk 11.46. B.M.M.]

23.7 ῥαββί

The geminated form ῥαββί, ῥαββί (D E F G H K M S U V W Y Γ Ω al) is more solemn and formal, and is probably the result of heightening by copyists. The Committee preferred to follow the shorter reading, which is strongly supported by א B L Δ Θ Σ 0107 0138 f^1 it vg syr[p] cop[sa, bo] arm eth geo[1, A] arab pers.

23.9 μὴ καλέσητε ὑμῶν {B}

Instead of the first ὑμῶν in this verse, several Western witnesses (D Θ vg al) replace it with ὑμῖν, and a few late Greek manuscripts omit it as superfluous.

23.13 Οὐαὶ δὲ ὑμῖν ... εἰσελθεῖν. {A}

That ver. 14 is an interpolation derived from the parallel in Mk 12.40 or Lk 20.47 is clear (*a*) from its absence in the earliest and best authorities of the Alexandrian and the Western types of text, and (*b*) from the fact that the witnesses that include the passage have it in different places, either after ver. 13 (so the Textus Receptus) or before ver. 13.

23.19 τυφλοί {B}

Apparently the words μωροὶ καί were inserted by copyists from ver. 17, inasmuch as no satisfactory reason can be found to account for their deletion if they had been original.

23.23 ἀφιέναι {C}

The Committee regarded the second aorist ἀφεῖναι (ℵ B L 892) as an Alexandrian refinement of the present tense ἀφιέναι.

23.25 ἀκρασίας {A}

Since ἀκρασίας, which is strongly supported by early and good witnesses, seemed to be inappropriate with ἁρπαγῆς (yet, as Bauer-Arndt-Gingrich-Danker point out, "intemperance" corresponds to the "cup"), various scribes replaced it with one or another gloss, ἀδικίας, ἀκαθαρσίας, or πονηρίας.

23.26 τοῦ ποτηρίου ... τὸ ἐκτὸς αὐτοῦ {D}

The weight of the external evidence appears to support the longer text. At the same time the presence of αὐτοῦ (instead of αὐτῶν) in B* f^{13} 28 *al* seems to be a hint that the archetype lacked καὶ τῆς παροψίδος. On balance, there is a slight probability that the words were inserted by copyists from ver. 25.

23.38 ὑμῶν ἔρημος {B}

On the one hand, it can be argued that copyists added ἔρημος in order to conform the quotation to the text of Jr 22.5. On the other hand, however, in view of what was taken to be the preponderant weight of external evidence a majority of the Committee preferred to include ἔρημος, explaining its absence in some witnesses as the result of deletion by copyists who thought the word superfluous after ἀφίεται.

24.6 γενέσθαι {B}

The shortest reading is supported by a wide variety of early witnesses. It is probable that copyists expanded the saying by adding such natural expressions as "*all things* must take place," or "*these things* must take place," or "*all these things* must take place." If any of these had been the original reading, there is no satisfactory reason that would account for its deletion.

24.7 λιμοὶ καὶ σεισμοί {B}

Although the words καὶ λοιμοί may have been accidentally omitted because of the similarity of ending, it is more likely that they were added at various places by scribes who recollected Lk 21.11.

24.31 σάλπιγγος {B}

Although it is possible that copyists may have omitted φωνῆς as unnecessary, it is much more probable that they would have made the expression more explicit by adding φωνῆς or καὶ φωνῆς (being influenced perhaps by the account of the theophany in Ex 19.16). It should be observed that, though the expression φωνὴ μεγάλη occurs many times in the New Testament, σάλπιγξ μεγάλη occurs only here.

24.36 οὐδὲ ὁ υἱός {B}

The words "neither the Son" are lacking in the majority of the witnesses of Matthew, including the later Byzantine text. On the other hand, the best representatives of the Alexandrian and the Western types of text contain the phrase. The omission of the words because of the doctrinal difficulty they present is more probable than their addition by assimilation to Mk 13.32. Furthermore, the presence of μόνος and the cast of the sentence as a whole *(οὐδὲ ... οὐδέ ...* belong together as a parenthesis, for εἰ μὴ ὁ πατὴρ μόνος goes with οὐδεὶς οἶδεν) suggest the originality of the phrase.

24.38 *[ἐκείναις]* {C}

While it is possible that ἐκείναις was accidentally omitted in some witnesses because of the similarity in the terminations of words, yet because of the weight of the witnesses that support its inclusion, the Committee concluded that the word should be retained, but enclosed within square brackets.

24.42 ἡμέρα {B}

Instead of ἡμέρα, which is strongly supported by ℵ B D W Δ Θ Σ *f*[13] *al*, the Textus Receptus, following E F G H L *al*, reads ὥρα, taken from verse 44 as a more exact term.

25.1 τοῦ νυμφίου {B}

It can be argued that the words καὶ τῆς νύμφης ("and the bride"), which are supported by a rather strong combination of witnesses, were omitted because they were felt to be incompatible with the widely held view that Christ, the bridegroom, would come to fetch his bride, the church. But it is doubtful whether copyists would have been so sensitive to the logic of the allegory. Furthermore, those who omitted the words envisaged the wedding as taking place in the home of the fiancée; those who added the words envisaged the bringing of the bride by the bridegroom to his home (or the home of his parents) where the wedding takes place. Since the latter custom was more common in the ancient world,[1] it is probable that the words are an

---

[1] Cf. Hilma Granqvist, *Marriage Conditions in a Palestinian Village*, II (Helsingfors, 1935), pp. 79 ff.; Joachim Jeremias, *The Parables of Jesus* (New York, 1963), p. 173; and *idem*, in Kittel's *Theological Dictionary of the New Testament*, IV, p. 1100.

interpolation by copyists who did not notice that the mention of the bride would disturb the allegorical interpretation of the parable. Only the bridegroom is mentioned in what follows.

25.13 ὥραν {A}

The clause ἐν ᾗ ὁ υἱὸς τοῦ ἀνθρώπου ἔρχεται (C³ Γ Π³ Φ *f*¹³ 28 157 543 700 1241 syrᵖᵃˡᵐᵍ) is a pendantic addition made by well-meaning copyists who recollected the similar clause in 24.44. In reality, the warning is more energetic without it, and is amply perspicuous to one who has read what precedes, from 24.36 onward. The Committee preferred the shorter text, which is decisively supported by 𝔓³⁵ ℵ A B C* D L W X Y* Δ Θ Π* Σ Φ 047 *f*¹ 33 565 892 1219 1424* 1604 2145* it vg syrˢ, ᵖ, ʰ, ᵖᵃˡᵗˣᵗ copˢᵃ, ᵇᵒ arm eth.

25.15-16 ἀπεδήμησεν. εὐθέως πορευθείς {B}

Although the external evidence supporting the reading adopted for the text is limited in extent, it is good in quality. More important, this reading best explains the origin of the other readings, which arose when copyists sought to eliminate the asyndeton as well as the ambiguity of where εὐθέως belongs, by inserting δέ before or after πορευθείς.

The punctuation adopted for the text is in accord with the usage elsewhere in Matthew (where εὐθέως or εὐθύς invariably belongs to what follows) and with the sense of the parable (there is no point in the master's departing immediately; there is much point in the servant's immediately setting to work).

26.14 Ἰσκαριώτης

See the comment on 10.4.

26.20 μετὰ τῶν δώδεκα {C}

As is the case in 20.17, the reading μαθηταί after οἱ δώδεκα is doubtful. In the present verse the weight of the external evidence seems to favor the shorter reading.

26.27 ποτήριον {B}

The tendency of copyists would probably have been to add rather than to delete the definite article.

26.28 διαθήκης {B}

The word καινῆς has apparently come from the parallel passage in Luke (22.20); if it had been present originally, there is no good reason why anyone would have deleted it.

26.39

At the close of ver. 39 several secondary witnesses (C³ᵐᵍ f¹³ 124 230 348 543 713 788 826 828 983) add from Lk 22.43-44 the words ὤφθη δὲ αὐτῷ ἄγγελος ἀπ' (ἀπὸ τοῦ 543 826 983) οὐρανοῦ ἐνισχύων αὐτὸν καὶ γενόμενος ἐν ἀγωνίᾳ ἐκτενέστερον προσηύχετο· ἐγένετο δὲ (om. 124) ὁ ἱδρὼς αὐτοῦ ὡσεὶ θρόμβοι αἵματος καταβαίνοντες ἐπὶ τὴν γῆν.

26.71 οὗτος {B}

The reading καὶ οὗτος appears to have come into the text from the Lukan parallel (Lk 22.59). The concurrence of the best representatives of the Alexandrian, the Western, and the early Syriac texts in support of the shorter reading constitutes strong external support.

27.2 Πιλάτῳ {B}

If Ποντίῳ had been present originally, there is no good reason why it should have been deleted. On the other hand, its insertion by copyists is natural at the first passage where Pilate's name occurs in the Gospels. The two names also appear in Lk 3.1; Ac 4.27; 1 Tm 6.13. In the post-apostolic church the double name was common (cf. Ignatius, *Trall.* 9, *Magn.* 11, *Smyr.* 1, and many passages in Justin

Martyr). In Josephus's *Antiquities*, XVIII.ii, Πιλᾶτος occurs frequently, with Πόντιος Πιλᾶτος at the first occurrence.

27.4   ἀθῷον {A}

The Greek Old Testament has αἷμα ἀθῷον ("innocent blood") fifteen times; αἷμα δίκαιον ("righteous blood") four times; and αἷμα ἀναίτιον ("blameless blood") four times. Thus it could be argued that αἷμα δίκαιον, being a rare expression, was more likely to have been altered to the more common αἷμα ἀθῷον than contrariwise. On the other hand, however, it may be that δίκαιον was introduced by copyists from 23.35. In any case, the weight of the external evidence here is strongly in support of ἀθῷον.

27.9   Ἰερεμίου {A}

The reading Ἰερεμίου is firmly established, being supported by ℵ A B C L X W Γ Δ Θ Π and most minuscules, most of the Old Latin, vg syr[htxt, pal] cop[sa, bo] goth arm eth geo. Since, however, the passage quoted by the evangelist is not to be found in Jeremiah, but seems to come from Zechariah (11.12-13), it is not surprising that several witnesses (22 syr[hmg] arm[mss]) substitute Ζαχαρίου, while others (Φ 33 157 1579 it[a, b] vg[ms] syr[s, p, pal] cop[boms] pers[p] Diatessaron[a, l] mss[acc. to Augustine]) omit the name entirely. Curiously, two witnesses (21 it[l]) read "Isaiah" – perhaps because, as the most prominent of the prophets, his name is met with most frequently in the New Testament (see the comment on διά in 13.35).

27.10   ἔδωκαν {B}

It is difficult to decide whether the final *nu* came into the text in order to avoid hiatus with the following vowel, or whether it was deleted under the influence of μοι. On the strength of the diversity of external evidence a majority of the Committee preferred the plural form.

27.16 *['Ιησοῦν] Βαραββᾶν* {C}
27.17 *['Ιησοῦν τὸν] Βαραββᾶν* {C}

The reading preserved today in several Greek manuscripts and early versions was known to Origen, who declares in his commentary on the passage, "In many copies it is not stated that Barabbas was also called *Jesus,* and perhaps [the omission is] right." (Origen discloses in what follows his reason for disapproving of the reading *Jesus Barabbas*; it cannot be right, he implies, because "in the whole range of the scriptures we know that no one who is a sinner [is called] Jesus.")

In a tenth century uncial manuscript (S) and in about twenty minuscule manuscripts a marginal comment states: "In many ancient copies which I have met with I found Barabbas himself likewise called 'Jesus'; that is, the question of Pilate stood there as follows, *Τίνα θέλετε ἀπὸ τῶν δύο ἀπολύσω ὑμῖν, 'Ιησοῦν τὸν Βαραββᾶν ἢ 'Ιησοῦν τὸν λεγόμενον Χριστόν*; for apparently the paternal name of the robber was 'Barabbas,' which is interpreted 'Son of the teacher.'" This scholium, which is usually assigned in the manuscripts either to Anastasius bishop of Antioch (perhaps latter part of the sixth century) or to Chrysostom, is in one manuscript attributed to Origen, who may indeed be its ultimate source.

In ver. 17 the word *'Ιησοῦν* could have been accidentally added or deleted by transcribers owing to the presence of *ὑμῖν* before it (ΥΜΙΝΙΝ). Furthermore, the reading of B 1010 *(τὸν Βαραββᾶν)* appears to presuppose in an ancestor the presence of *'Ιησοῦν.*

A majority of the Committee was of the opinion that the original text of Matthew had the double name in both verses and that *'Ιησοῦν* was deliberately suppressed in most witnesses for reverential considerations. In view of the relatively slender external support for *'Ιησοῦν,* however, it was deemed fitting to enclose the word within square brackets.

27.24 *τούτου* {B}

The words *τοῦ δικαίου* (compare the variant reading in ver. 4), which occur at different places in a variety of manuscripts (but not in the best representatives of the Alexandrian and Western texts), appear to be an accretion intended to accentuate Pilate's protestation of Jesus' innocence.

27.28 ἐκδύσαντες αὐτόν {B}

The reading ἐνδύσαντες seems to be a correction suggested by the nudity at the time of the flagellation. The sequence of stripping (ἐκδύσαντες) and clothing again is paralleled by ver. 31.

27.29 ἐνέπαιξαν {B}

The imperfect tense may be the result of conformation to ἔτυπτον (ver. 30). In any case, however, the combination of ℵ B D L 33 892 *al* supporting the aorist seemed to the Committee to be the superior attestation.

27.35 κλῆρον {A}

After κλῆρον the Textus Receptus, following Δ Θ 0250 *f*¹ *f*¹³ 1424 *al*, adds ἵνα πληρωθῇ τὸ ῥηθὲν ὑπὸ τοῦ προφήτου· Διεμερί-σαντο τὰ ἱμάτιά μου ἑαυτοῖς, καὶ ἐπὶ τὸν ἱματισμόν μου ἔβαλον κλῆρον (Ps 22.18). Although it could be argued that the passage fell out by reason of homoeoteleuton, the eye of the copyist passing from κλῆρον to κλῆρον, the Committee was impressed by the absence of the passage from early witnesses of the Alexandrian and the Western types of text (ℵ A B D L W Γ Π 33 71 157 565 700 892ᶜ itff2, 1 vgmss syrs, p, hmg, pal eth persp) and the likelihood that copyists were influenced by the parallel passage in Jn 19.24, with the phrase τὸ ῥηθὲν ὑπὸ (or διὰ) τοῦ προφήτου assimilated to Matthew's usual formula of citation.

27.38

After the words "one on the right" and "one on the left" the Old Latin codex Colbertinus (itᶜ) supplies names for the two robbers who were crucified with Jesus: *nomine Zoatham* and *nomine Camma* respectively.[1] (See also the comment on Lk 23.32.)

27.40 *[καί]* (3) {C}

On the one hand, καί may have been omitted due to confusion with the first syllable of the following word; on the other hand, it may have been inserted by those who took the conditional clause *(εἰ ... θεοῦ)* with what precedes. To indicate the balance of considerations, a majority of the Committee thought it best to retain the word, but to enclose it within square brackets.

27.42 βασιλεύς {B}

Not understanding the irony implied by the statement, "He is the King of Israel," copyists, influenced by ver. 40, inserted εἰ. If originally present, there would have been no good reason to omit the word.

27.46 ηλι ηλι λεμα σαβαχθανι

Instead of ηλι (or ηλει), representing the Hebrew אֵלִי ("my God"), the text of several witnesses, including א B 33 cop^sa, bo eth, was assimilated to the reading ελωι of Mk 15.34, representing the Aramaic אֱלָהִי ("my God"), the ω for the α sound being due to the influence of the Hebrew אֱלֹהַי.

The spelling λεμα (א B 33 700 998 *al*) represents the Aramaic לְמָא ("why?"), which is also probably to be understood as lying behind λιμα (A K U Γ Δ Π 090 *al*) and λειμα (E F G H M S V *al*), whereas λαμα (D Θ 1 22 565 1582 *al*) represents the Hebrew לְמָה ("why?").

As in Mk 15.34, most witnesses read σαβαχθανι or something

---

[1] For other names that have been given to the two robbers, see the present writer's article, "Names for the Nameless in the New Testament; a Study in the Growth of Christian Tradition," in *Kyriakon: Festschrift Johannes Quasten,* edited by Patrick Granfield and Josef A. Jungmann (Münster/W., 1970), pp. 89 ff., reprinted (with additions) in Metzger, *New Testament Studies* (Leiden, 1980), pp. 33 ff.

similar (σαβαχθανει, ℵ A Δ 1 69; σαβακτανει, B 22 713 1402), which represents the Aramaic שְׁבַקְתַּנִי ("thou hast forsaken me"). Codex Bezae, however (as also in the Markan parallel), reads ζαφθανει, representing the Hebrew עֲזַבְתַּנִי ("thou hast forsaken me"; for the spelling, see the comment on Mk 15.34), and thus this manuscript in both Matthew and Mark is consistent in giving a transliteration representing a Hebrew original throughout, instead of part Hebrew (the first words) and part Aramaic (the last word). (See also the comment on Mk 15.34.)

27.49 αὐτόν. {B}

Although attested by ℵ B C L *al* the words ἄλλος δὲ λαβὼν λόγχην ἔνυξεν αὐτοῦ τὴν πλευράν, καὶ ἐξῆλθεν ὕδωρ καὶ αἷμα must be regarded as an early intrusion derived from a similar account in Jn 19.34. It might be thought that the words were omitted because they represent the piercing as preceding Jesus' death, whereas John makes it follow; but that difference would have only been a reason for moving the passage to a later position (perhaps at the close of ver. 50 or 54 or 56), or else there would have been some tampering with the passage in John, which is not the case. It is probable that the Johannine passage was written by some reader in the margin of Matthew from memory (there are several minor differences, such as the sequence of "water and blood"), and a later copyist awkwardly introduced it into the text.

28.6 ἔκειτο

Providing a subject for ἔκειτο was a quite natural addition for copyists to make; if present originally, there is no reason why it should have been deleted. In Matthew the word κύριος is never applied to Jesus except in his reported sayings.

28.7 ἀπὸ τῶν νεκρῶν

While recognizing the difficulty of accounting for the absence of the words ἀπὸ τῶν νεκρῶν from D 565 and several early versions, a majority of the Committee judged that the preponderance of external evidence favors their inclusion. Their omission may have been due to an oversight in transcription, perhaps prompted by the circumstance that in the preceding sentence (ver. 6) ἠγέρθη stands without such an addition.

28.8 ἀπελθοῦσαι {B}

The reading ἀπελθοῦσαι, which is strongly supported by a wide range of witnesses, was assimilated by copyists to the parallel in Mk 16.8, where ἐξελθοῦσαι is firm.

28.9 καὶ ἰδού {A}

Although it is possible that the words ὡς δὲ ἐπορεύοντο ἀπαγγεῖλαι τοῖς μαθηταῖς αὐτοῦ καὶ ἰδού fell out of the text due to homoeoteleuton, their absence from the earliest and best representatives of both early types of text (the Alexandrian and the Western) led the Committee to regard them as a natural expansion derived from the sense of the preceding verse.

28.11 ἀπήγγειλαν {B}

In view of the weight of evidence, the Committee preferred ἀπήγγειλαν to ἀνήγγειλαν, a verb that occurs nowhere else in Matthew.

28.15 [ἡμέρας] {C}

On the one hand, there is strong and diversified external evidence in support of the presence of ἡμέρας. On the other hand, in similar expressions elsewhere (11.23; 27.8) Matthew does not add ἡμέρας to σήμερον. The Committee therefore decided to represent this balance of considerations by including the word enclosed within square brackets.

28.20 αἰῶνος. {A}

After αἰῶνος most manuscripts, followed by the Textus Receptus, terminate the Gospel with ἀμήν, reflecting the liturgical usage of the text. If the word had been present originally, no good reason can be found to account for its absence from the better representatives of the Alexandrian and the Western text-types.

THE GOSPEL ACCORDING TO MARK

1.1 Χριστοῦ [υἱοῦ θεοῦ] {C}

The absence of υἱοῦ θεοῦ in ℵ* Θ 28ᶜ *al* may be due to an oversight in copying, occasioned by the similarity of the endings of the *nomina sacra*. On the other hand, however, there was always a temptation (to which copyists often succumbed)[1] to expand titles and quasi-titles of books. Since the combination of B D W *al* in support of υἱοῦ θεοῦ is extremely strong, it was not thought advisable to omit the words altogether, yet because of the antiquity of the shorter reading and the possibility of scribal expansion, it was decided to enclose the words within square brackets.

1.2 ἐν τῷ Ἠσαΐᾳ τῷ προφήτῃ {A}

The quotation in verses 2 and 3 is composite, the first part being from Mal 3.1 and the second part from Is 40.3. It is easy to see, therefore, why copyists would have altered the words "in Isaiah the prophet" (a reading found in the earliest representative witnesses of the Alexandrian and the Western types of text) to the more comprehensive introductory formula "in the prophets."

1.4 [ὁ] βαπτίζων ἐν τῇ ἐρήμῳ καί {C}

In view of the predominant usage in the Synoptic Gospels of referring to John as "the Baptist" (ὁ βαπτιστής occurs in Mk 6.25 and 8.28, as well as seven times in Matthew and three times in Luke), it is easier to account for the addition than for the deletion of the definite article before βαπτίζων. The omission of καί in a few Alexandrian witnesses is the result of taking ὁ βαπτίζων as a title.

---

[1] See, for example, the expansions introduced into the title of the book of Revelation (Metzger, *The Text of the New Testament*, 3rd ed., p. 205).

1.6 τρίχας {A}

Instead of reading, as do all other witnesses, that John the Baptist was clothed with "camel's hair" *(τρίχας καμήλου)*, D and it[a] read "camel's skin" *(δέρριν καμήλου)*. Although Turner[2] considered the latter to be the original text of Mark, Lagrange[3] pointed out that camel's skin is much too thick and hard for Bedouins to think of using it as clothing. Consequently, it appears that scribes who exchanged δέρριν for τρίχας did so without any firsthand knowledge of Near Eastern customs. It may be, as Moulton and Milligan[4] suggested, that the word is a corruption derived from Zch 13.4. The argument[5] that the absence of the following words ("and had a leather belt around his waist" *(καὶ ζώνην ... αὐτοῦ)* lacking in D and several Old Latin witnesses) means that the original text of Mark (assumed to have been δέρριν) was accommodated to and expanded from Mt 3.4 is less probable than that through scribal inadvertence a line of text fell out between καὶ ... καί or between καμήλ<u>ου</u> ... αὐτ<u>οῦ</u>.

1.8 ὕδατι {B}

The tendency of scribes would have been to add ἐν before ὕδατι (compare the parallels in Mt 3.11 and Jn 1.26, which read ἐν ὕδατι).

1.11 ἐγένετο ἐκ τῶν οὐρανῶν {B}

The omission of the verb appears to be either accidental or in partial imitation of Matthew's καὶ ἰδοὺ φωνὴ ἐκ τῶν οὐρανῶν λέγουσα (Mt 3.17). The reading with ἠκούσθη (Θ 28 565 *al*) is clearly a scribal improvement of either of the other two readings.

---

[2] C. H. Turner, *Journal of Theological Studies*, XXVIII (1926-27), p. 151.

[3] M.-J. Lagrange, *Évangile selon saint Marc*, 5th ed. (Paris, 1929), in loc.

[4] *The Vocabulary of the Greek Testament* (London, 1930), p. 142.

[5] So Ernst von Dobschütz in *Eberhard Nestle's Einführung in das Griechische Neue Testament*, 4th ed. (Göttingen, 1923), p. 7.

1.14   εὐαγγέλιον {A}

The insertion of τῆς βασιλείας was obviously made by copyists in order to bring the unusual Markan phrase into conformity with the much more frequently used expression "the kingdom of God" (cf. ver. 15).

1.27   τί ἐστιν τοῦτο; διδαχὴ καινὴ κατ᾽ ἐξουσίαν· καί {B}

Among the welter of variant readings, that preserved in ℵ B L 33 seems to account best for the rise of the others. Its abruptness invited modification, and more than one copyist accommodated the phraseology in one way or another to the parallel in Lk 4.36. The text can also be punctuated διδαχὴ καινή· κατ᾽ ἐξουσίαν καὶ ..., but in view of ver. 22 it seems preferable to take κατ᾽ ἐξουσίαν with διδαχὴ καινή.

1.29   ἐκ τῆς συναγωγῆς ἐξελθόντες ἦλθον {B}

Although the singular number of the participle and verb is supported by strong external evidence (including B D Θ f¹ f¹³ al), and although the reading "they came ... with James and John" appeared strange to some members of the Committee, a majority was inclined to favor the plural because copyists would tend to change the plural to the singular in order (a) to focus attention on Jesus, (b) to conform the reading to the parallels in Mt 8.14 and Lk 4.38, and (c) to provide a nearer antecedent for αὐτῷ of ver. 30.

1.34   αὐτόν {A}

It is clear that Mark terminated the sentence with αὐτόν and that copyists made various additions, derived probably from the parallel in Lk 4.41 (ὅτι ᾔδεισαν τὸν Χριστὸν αὐτὸν εἶναι). If any one of the longer readings had been original in Mark, there is no reason why it should have been altered or eliminated entirely.

1.39   ἦλθεν {B}

Although the periphrastic imperfect is typically Markan, a majority of the Committee decided that in the present passage ἦλθεν is needed to carry on the idea of ἐξῆλθον in the previous sentence, and that ἦν was introduced by copyists from the parallel in Lk 4.44.

1.40 [καὶ γονυπετῶν] {C}

On the one hand, the combination of B D W *al* in support of the shorter text is extremely strong. On the other hand, if καὶ γονυπετῶν αὐτόν were the original reading, homoeoteleuton could account for its accidental omission. On the whole, since in the parallel passages Matthew's use of προσεκύνει (Mt 8.2) and, still more, Luke's πεσὼν ἐπὶ πρόσωπον (Lk 5.12) seem to support the originality of the idea of kneeling in Mark's account, the Committee decided to retain καὶ γονυπετῶν with ℵ L Θ f¹ 565 *al* but to enclose the expression within square brackets.

1.41 σπλαγχνισθείς {B}

It is difficult to come to a firm decision concerning the original text. On the one hand, it is easy to see why ὀργισθείς ("being angry") would have prompted over-scrupulous copyists to alter it to σπλαγχνισθείς ("being filled with compassion"), but not easy to account for the opposite change. On the other hand, a majority of the Committee was impressed by the following considerations. (1) The character of the external evidence in support of ὀργισθείς is less impressive than the diversity and character of evidence that supports σπλαγχνισθείς. (2) At least two other passages in Mark, which represent Jesus as angry (3.5) or indignant (10.14), have not prompted over-scrupulous copyists to make corrections. (3) It is possible that the reading ὀργισθείς either (*a*) was suggested by ἐμβριμησάμενος of ver. 43, or (*b*) arose from confusion between similar words in Aramaic (compare Syriac *ethraḥam*, "he had pity," with *ethra'em*, "he was enraged").⁶

---

⁶ For a discussion of the possibility of confusion in Aramaic, see Eberhard Nestle, *Introduction to the Textual Criticism of the Greek New Testament* (London, 1901), pp. 262 f.

2.1 ἐν οἴκῳ

Although part of the Committee preferred εἰς οἶκον (A C Γ Δ Π Φ 090 *f*¹ *f*¹³ 22 28 157 330 543 565 579 *al*) as less literary and in the Markan style, a majority was impressed by the widespread and diversified attestation supporting ἐν οἴκῳ (‭א‬ B D L W Θ Σ 33 571 892 1071 *al*).

2.4 προσενέγκαι {B}

The absence of a direct object *(αὐτόν)* may have led to the substitution of προσεγγίσαι ("to come near") or προσελθεῖν ("to come to") for προσενέγκαι ("to bring to").

2.4 διὰ τὸν ὄχλον

Here D and W unite with two manuscripts of the Armenian version to read ἀπὸ τοῦ ὄχλου. One member of the Committee considered this reading to be much more in accord with Markan style than διὰ τὸν ὄχλον (which is also the reading of the parallel in Lk 5.19), and suggested that it may reflect a primitive Aramaic מִן.

2.5 ἀφίενται {B}

Although strongly supported in the manuscripts, the perfect tense *(ἀφέωνται)* appears to be secondary, having been introduced by copyists from Luke's account (Lk 5.20). Mark's use of the present tense *(ἀφίενται)* was followed by Matthew (Mt 9.2).

2.9 ἀφίενται {B}

See the comment on ver. 5.

2.14 Λευίν {A}

The reading Ἰάκωβον in Western witnesses shows the influence of 3.18, where Ἰάκωβον τὸν τοῦ Ἀλφαίου is included among the twelve.

2.15-16 αὐτῷ. **(16)** καὶ οἱ γραμματεῖς τῶν Φαρισαίων ἰδόντες {C}

The more unusual expression οἱ γραμματεῖς τῶν Φαρισαίων is to be preferred, since the tendency of scribes would have been to insert καί after οἱ γραμματεῖς under the influence of the common expression "the scribes and the Pharisees." Since in the Gospels the verb ἀκολουθεῖν is used of Jesus' disciples, never of those who were hostile to him, a full stop should follow αὐτῷ. Unmindful of this usage, copyists transferred the stop to follow πολλοί and inserted καί before ἰδόντες.

2.16 ἐσθίει {B}

The addition of καὶ πίνει is a natural accretion inserted by copyists, perhaps under the influence of the parallel passage in Lk 5.30. The shorter reading, which is strongly supported by B D W *al,* was followed by Matthew, who added ὁ διδάσκαλος ὑμῶν (Mt 9.11), an expression that, in turn, was adopted in Mk 2.16 by the scribes of C L Δ *f*[13] *al.*

2.22 ἀπόλλυται καὶ οἱ ἀσκοί {C}

The reading which best explains the origin of the others is that preserved in B 892 cop[bo]. Since the pendant καὶ οἱ ἀσκοί seems to require a verb, most witnesses moved ἀπόλλυται (making it plural) after οἱ ἀσκοί. Furthermore, under the influence of the parallels in Mt 9.17 and Lk 5.37, copyists introduced the verb ἐκχεῖται as more appropriate than ἀπόλλυται to describe what happens to wine.

2.22 ἀλλὰ οἶνον νέον εἰς ἀσκοὺς καινούς {C}

Not observing that εἰ … ἀσκοί is parenthetical and therefore that the force of βάλλει carries over to the words after ἀλλά, copyists inserted βλητέον (from Lk 5.38) or βάλλουσιν (from Mt 9.17). The omission of the words ἀλλὰ … καινούς in D and it[a, b, d, ff2, i, r1, t] may have been either deliberate (when the copyist, not observing their regimen with βάλλει, could make no sense of them), or, more probably, accidental (occasioned by the repetition of the words οἶνος and ἀσκός in close succession).

2.26 ἐπὶ Ἀβιαθὰρ ἀρχιερέως

According to 1 Sm 21 it was Ahimelech, not Abiathar, who was high priest when David ate the bread of the Presence. In order to avoid the historical difficulty, D W *al* omit ἐπὶ Ἀβιαθὰρ ἀρχιερέως, thereby conforming the text to Mt 12.4 and Lk 6.4. Other witnesses, reluctant to go so far as to delete the phrase, inserted τοῦ before ἀρχιερέως (or ἱερέως) in order to permit the interpretation that the event happened in the time of (but not necessarily during the high-priesthood of) Abiathar (who, was afterward) the high priest.

3.7-8 [ἠκολούθησεν], καὶ ἀπὸ τῆς Ἰουδαίας καὶ ἀπὸ Ἱεροσολύμων {C}

This nest of variant readings probably arose from the prolix style of Mark's summary statement. The Committee regarded the reading of B L 565 as the least unsatisfactory text, and the one that accounts best for the origin of most of the other readings. Thus, the change from the singular number to the plural ἠκολούθησαν, the addition of αὐτῷ after such a verb, and the modification of word order are not surprising. The absence of the verb from Western and other witnesses (D W *f*[13] 28 Old Latin *al*) may be due either to an accident of transcription, or, more probably, to deliberate editorial revision. In view, however, of a residuum of uncertainty involving ἠκολούθησεν, it was thought best to enclose the word within square brackets.

3.8 πλῆθος πολύ {A}

The absence of πλῆθος πολύ in a few witnesses (W it[a, b, c] syr[s] cop[sa]) is probably to be accounted for as a stylistic improvement of Markan redundancy (cf. πολὺ πλῆθος in ver. 7).

3.14 δώδεκα, [οὓς καὶ ἀποστόλους ὠνόμασεν,] ἵνα ὦσιν μετ' αὐτοῦ {C}

Although the words οὓς ... ὠνόμασεν may be regarded as an interpolation from Luke (6.13), the Committee was of the opinion that the external evidence is too strong in their favor to warrant their ejection from the text. In order to reflect the balance of probabilities, the words were retained but enclosed within square brackets.

3.16 [καὶ ἐποίησεν τοὺς δώδεκα,] καί {C}

On the one hand, it can be argued that the words καὶ ... δώδεκα have come into the text as the result of scribal oversight (dittography with opening words of ver. 14); on the other hand, the clause seems to be needed in order to pick up the thread of ver. 14 after the parenthesis ἵνα ... δαιμόνια. In order to reflect the balance of both external evidence and internal considerations, the Committee decided to retain the words within square brackets.

The reading of W, καὶ περιάγοντας κηρύσσειν τὸ εὐαγγέλιον καί, is suspect, for this manuscript also inserts τὸ εὐαγγέλιον after κηρύσσειν in ver. 14. The reading of f[13] cop[sa], πρῶτον Σίμωνα καί ("*First is Simon, and* he gave a surname to Simon, Peter"), though attractive, appears to be an assimilation to Mt 10.2, introduced in order to smooth an awkward construction.

3.18 καὶ Θαδδαῖον {A}

The substitution of Λεββαῖον for Θαδδαῖον occurs in Western witnesses also at Mt 10.3, where many witnesses conflate both readings (see the comment on Mt 10.3). The omission of Θαδδαῖον from W must be accidental, for only eleven persons are mentioned; it[e], which also omits Thaddaeus, adds *Iudas* after Bartholomew.

3.19 Ἰσκαριώθ

See the comment on Mt 10.4.

3.20 ἔρχεται {B}

The singular number, read by early witnesses of the Alexandrian and the Western types of text, was altered in most witnesses to the plural, which is the easier reading following upon verses 17-19.

3.21 ἀκούσαντες οἱ παρ' αὐτοῦ {A}

The original reading οἱ παρ' αὐτοῦ ("his friends" or "his relatives") apparently proved to be so embarrassing that D W *al* altered it to read, "When *the scribes and the others* had heard about him, they went out to seize him, for they said, 'He is beside himself.'"

3.29 ἀμαρτήματος {B}

Either κρίσεως ("judgment") or κολάσεως ("torment") was introduced by copyists in order to relieve the difficulty of the unusual expression in the text, and ἀμαρτίας was substituted by others as being more familiar than ἀμαρτήματος (which occurs in the four Gospels only here and in ver. 28; elsewhere in the New Testament it occurs three times).

3.32 σου [καὶ αἱ ἀδελφαί σου] {C}

A majority of the Committee considered it probable that the words καὶ αἱ ἀδελφαί σου were omitted from most witnesses either (*a*) accidentally through an oversight in transcription (the eye of the scribe passing from σου to σου), or (*b*) deliberately because neither in ver. 31 nor ver. 34 (nor in the parallel passages) are the sisters mentioned. Had the words been interpolated, the addition would probably have been made already in ver. 31. Nevertheless, in view of the weight of attestation for the shorter text, it was thought best to enclose the disputed words within square brackets.

[The shorter text should be adopted; the longer reading, perhaps of Western origin, crept into the text through mechanical expansion. From a historical point of view, it is extremely unlikely that Jesus' sisters would have joined in publicly seeking to check him in his ministry. B.M.M.]

4.8 καὶ αὐξανόμενα {C}

The reading that best explains the origin of the others is αὐξανό-μενα (‭א‬ B 1071 *al*), which is nominative neuter plural agreeing with the subject ἄλλα ("Other [seeds] fell into the good ground, and while growing up and increasing they yielded fruit; and brought forth ..."). Under the influence of ἀναβαίνοντα, which can be (wrongly) construed with καρπόν, there was a strong tendency to alter αὐξανόμενα to αὐξανόμενον or αὐξάνοντα. Another factor that contributed to altering the participle was the assimilation of ἄλλα to ἄλλο in verses 5 and 7 (the singular number is read by ‭א‬ᶜ A D Δ Π Σ Φ *f*¹ *f*¹³ 22 157 543 565 700 1071 *al*).

4.8 ἕν ... ἕν ... ἕν {C}

The reading that predominates in the manuscripts is εν, whether accented ἐν or ἕν. In favor of the latter is the probability that under-lying the variants was the Aramaic sign of multiplication ("-times" or "-fold"), חד, which also is the numeral "one."

4.15 εἰς αὐτούς {C}

Instead of εἰς αὐτούς (B W *f*¹ *f*¹³ 28 *al*), several witnesses (‭א‬ C L Δ 892 *al*) smooth the expression by reading ἐν αὐτοῖς, while other witnesses (D Θ 33 and the Majority Text) assimilate the text to Matthew's wording ἐν τῇ καρδίᾳ αὐτοῦ (Mt 13.19), and a few other witnesses (A it¹ eth) assimilate to Luke's wording ἀπὸ τῆς καρδίας αὐτῶν (Lk 8.12).

4.20 ἕν ... ἕν ... ἕν {C}

See the comment on ver. 8.

4.24 καὶ προστεθήσεται ὑμῖν {A}

The omission of καὶ προστεθήσεται ὑμῖν seems to have been accidental, owing to homoeoteleuton. The words τοῖς ἀκούουσιν appear to be a gloss inserted to explain the connection of the saying with βλέπετε τί ἀκούετε. One Latin manuscript and the Gothic version read "shall be added to you *who believe.*"

4.28 πλήρη[ς] σῖτον {C}

Among the several variant readings, the reading πλήρη σῖτον (ℵ A C² L Δ *f*¹ *f*¹³) is the most classical, with σῖτον in apposition to the preceding accusatives, while in colloquial Hellenistic Greek πλήρης is frequently used as an indeclinable adjective (so Bauer-Arndt-Gingrich-Danker, *A Greek-English Lexicon, s.v.*). In view of the strange confusion of readings among the manuscripts, the Committee considered πλήρης (C*vid Σ 28 *al*) as probably the true reading, but decided to enclose the final sigma within square brackets in deference to the weight of the witnesses that support πλήρη.

4.40 δειλοί ἐστε; οὔπω {A}

The reading adopted as the text has by far the best external support. The reading ... πῶς οὐκ (A C K Π 33 *al*) seems to have arisen from a desire to soften somewhat Jesus' reproach spoken to the disciples.

5.1 Γερασηνῶν {C}

Of the several variant readings, a majority of the Committee preferred Γερασηνῶν on the basis of (*a*) superior external evidence (early representatives of both the Alexandrian and Western types of text), and (*b*) the probability that Γαδαρηνῶν is a scribal assimilation to the prevailing text of Matthew (8.28), and that Γεργεσηνῶν is a correction, perhaps originally proposed by Origen (see the comment on Mt 8.28). The reading of W *(Γεργυστήνων)* reflects a scribal idiosyncrasy.

5.21 τοῦ Ἰησοῦ [ἐν τῷ πλοίῳ] {C}

Although a minority of the Committee regarded the phrase ἐν τῷ πλοίῳ as an early scribal insertion, added before τοῦ Ἰησοῦ in W and after τοῦ Ἰησοῦ in a great number of witnesses (including ℵ A (B) C L Δ f¹³ 33 1079 1241 *al*), the majority preferred the reading witnessed by the Alexandrian and other text-types, and explained the absence of the phrase as either accidental or by assimilation to the parallel in Luke (8.40). The change of position of the phrase in W is due to the desire to achieve a better sequence. In view, however, of the conflict of transcriptional probabilities, it was thought best to enclose the words within square brackets.

5.22   ὀνόματι Ἰάϊρος

It has sometimes been argued (e. g. by Vincent Taylor, *The Gospel According to St. Mark*, p. 287) that the words ὀνόματι Ἰάϊρος are an early interpolation, because (1) they are absent from several Western witnesses (D it[a, e, ff2, i]); (2) the parallel account in Matthew does not identify Jairus by name; (3) the only other person mentioned by Mark outside the Passion Narrative, apart from the disciples, is Bartimaeus (10.46), and the name Jairus is not mentioned in 5.35 ff.; and (4) the use of ὀνόματι is Lukan rather than Markan; elsewhere Mark uses ὄνομα with the dative (3.16 f.; 5.9).

When these arguments are analyzed, their weight is greatly diminished. Considered in reverse order:

(*a*) The three instances of ὄνομα with the dative are scarcely sufficient to establish Mark's preferred usage, especially since two of the instances report the conferring of a name upon a person, when the dative is to be expected (ἐπιτιθέναι, 3.16 f.). That Luke generally prefers ὀνόματι is true but irrelevant, for the Lukan parallel (8.41) to the passage under consideration reads ἀνὴρ ᾧ ὄνομα Ἰάϊρος (which accounts for the Markan variant ᾧ ὄνομα Ἰάϊρος in W Θ 565 700).

(*b*) Whether it is fair to exclude from one's consideration the many names in Mark's Passion Narrative is open to question. In any case, however, Taylor has unaccountably overlooked the presence, in addition to Bartimaeus, of Mark's references by name to John the Baptist (1.4, 6, 9, 14; 6.14, 16-18, 24 f.). The absence of the name Jairus in 5.35 ff. surely cannot prove that it is an interpolation in 5.22. (Jairus occurs only once in the Lukan narrative (8.41); is it also an interpolation there?)

(*c*) The absence of the name in Matthew's account would be explained if, as has been sometimes argued on the basis of other instances, Matthew utilized a copy of a Western text of Mark.[1] In any case, however, it must be observed that Matthew has very much condensed Mark's whole account, and omits much more than merely the name of Jairus.

(*d*) The external evidence supporting the presence of ὀνόματι Ἰάϊρος is far more impressive (including 𝔓⁴⁵ ℵ A B C L N Δ Π Σ Φ almost all minuscules it[b, c, l, q] vg syr[c, s, p, h, pal] cop[sa, bo, fay] arm geo) than the testimony supporting the absence of these words (D it[a, e, ff2, i]). Put another way, from a text-critical point of view it is more probable that the name Jairus was accidentally dropped during the transmission of part of the Western text (represented by one Greek manuscript and several Old Latin witnesses) than that it was added, at the same point in the narrative, in all the other textual groups. See also the Note on Western non-interpolations, following Lk 24.53.

5.36 παρακούσας {B}

The ambiguity of παρακούσας ("ignoring" or "overhearing") led to its replacement in ℵ[a] A C D K Θ Π *al* by the Lukan parallel ἀκούσας (Lk 8.50).

5.41 Ταλιθα κουμ

The reading Ταβιθα (without κουμ) in W 28 245 349 and several Old Latin and Vulgate manuscripts is due to scribal confusion with the proper name in Ac 9.40. The curious reading of codex Bezae ῥαββει θαβιτα κουμι seems to be a corruption of ραβιθα, the transliteration of רְבִיתָא, an Aramaic dialectal form meaning "girl." The variation between κουμ (ℵ B C L M N Σ *f*¹ 33 892) and κουμι (A D Δ Θ Π Φ *f*¹³ 22 28 124 543 565 579 700 1071 most minuscules

---

[1] See T. F. Glasson, "Did Matthew and Luke use a 'Western' Text of Mark?" *Expository Times,* 55 (1943–44), pp. 180–184; and 77 (1965–66), pp. 120–121.

it[a, e] vg syr[p, h, hgr] arm eth) reflects the difference in gender of the forms of the Aramaic imperative singular (קוּם is masculine, sometimes used without reference to sex; קוּמִי is feminine). According to Dalman both forms came to be pronounced alike,[2] the final *i* of the feminine imperative falling away after the stressed penult.[3] The expansion in it[e] *tabea acultha cumhi* has not been satisfactorily explained.[4]

6.2 καὶ αἱ δυνάμεις ... γινόμεναι {C}

A majority of the Committee preferred the grammatically difficult reading of the Alexandrian text (ℵ* B 33 892 *al*) as best accounting for the origin of the other readings; thus, some witnesses added αἱ after τοιαῦται (ℵ[c] L Δ), while many others eliminated the article before δυνάμεις and changed the participle into a finite verb, either γίνονται or γίνωνται (introduced by ἵνα). The latest reading, which was incorporated into the Textus Receptus, prefixes ὅτι to the indicative clause.

6.3 τέκτων, ὁ υἱός {A}

All uncials, many minuscules, and important early versions read, "Is not this the carpenter, the son of Mary ...?" Objection was very early felt to this description of Jesus as carpenter,[1] and several witnesses (including 𝔓[45]) assimilate the text to Mt 13.55 and read,

---

[2] M.-J. Lagrange, however, disagrees with this commonly accepted view (*Evangile selon saint Marc, ad loc.*).

[3] G. A. Dalman, *Grammatik des jüdisch-palästinischen Aramäisch*, 2te Aufl. (Leipzig, 1905), p. 266, n. 1.

[4] F. H. Chase thought that *acultha* "is a relic of the Syriac word ܪ ܐܠ ܐ ܟ (macultha = food)" (*The Syro-Latin Text of the Gospels* [London, 1895], pp. 110 f.).

[1] For example, Celsus, the second-century antagonist of Christianity, sneeringly remarked that the founder of the new religion was nothing but "a carpenter by trade" – a jibe that Origen sought to rebut by declaring, "In none of the Gospels current in the churches is Jesus himself ever described as a carpenter" (*contra Celsum*, VI.34 and 36). Either Origen did not recall Mk 6.3, or the text of this verse in copies known to him had already been assimilated to the Matthean parallel.

"Is not this *the son of* the carpenter, the son of Mary …?" The Palestinian Syriac achieves the same result by omitting ὁ τέκτων.

6.3 καὶ Ἰωσῆτος {B}

The combination of Alexandrian and Western witnesses, along with Θ *f*[13] 33 565 700 *al*, provides considerable support for the reading Ἰωσῆτος. Codex Sinaiticus and several other witnesses have assimilated the name to Ἰωσήφ in Mt 13.55. According to Lagrange (commentary *in loc.*), the name Ἰωσῆ (A C W *f*[1] *al*) is a transcription of יוסי, the Galilean form of יוסף.

6.14 καὶ ἔλεγον {B}

The plural ἔλεγον, read by B W it[a, b, d, ff2] and supported by the intention of D[gr] (ἐλέγοσαν), seems to be the original reading. Copyists altered it to ἔλεγεν in agreement with ἤκουσεν, not observing that after the words καὶ ἤκουσεν ὁ βασιλεὺς Ἡρῴδης the sentence is suspended, in order to introduce parenthetically three specimens of the opinions held about Jesus *(καὶ ἔλεγον … ἄλλοι δὲ ἔλεγον … ἄλλοι δὲ ἔλεγον)*, and is taken up again at ver. 16, ἀκούσας δὲ ὁ Ἡρῴδης…

6.20 ἠπόρει, καί {C}

On the one hand, the reading ἐποίει, which has been thought to reflect a Semitic original,[2] is supported by a broad spectrum of Greek and versional witnesses. On the other hand, the reading ἠπόρει, though sometimes suspected of having arisen by scribal assimilation to the Lukan statement concerning Herod's being "much perplexed" (διηπόρει, Lk 9.7) on another occasion, was preferred by a majority of the Committee on the grounds of (*a*) strong external support (ℵ B L (W) Θ cop[sa, bo]); (*b*) the usage, in this case, of πολλά as an adverb, in keeping with Markan style; and (*c*) the intrinsic superiority

---

[2] Cf. C. C. Torrey, *Our Translated Gospels* (New York, 1936), p. 155; Blass-Debrunner-Funk, § 414 (5).

of meaning in contrast to the banality of the clause when ἐποίει is read.

6.22 θυγατρὸς αὐτοῦ Ἡρῳδιάδος {C}

It is very difficult to decide which reading is the least unsatisfactory. According to the reading with αὐτοῦ the girl is named Herodias and is described as Herod's daughter. But in ver. 24 she is Herodias's daughter, who, according to other sources, was named Salome, a grand-niece of Herod. The reading with αὐτῆς τῆς must mean something like "the daughter of Herodias herself," unless αὐτῆς be taken as the redundant pronoun anticipating a noun (an Aramaism). The reading with τῆς, read by f¹ and (presumably) Greek witnesses lying behind several early versions, is the easiest and seems to have arisen from an accidental omission of αὐτῆς.

A majority of the Committee decided, somewhat reluctantly, that the reading with αὐτοῦ, despite the historical and contextual difficulties, must be adopted on the strength of its external attestation.

6.23 αὐτῇ [πολλά] {C}

Since the use of πολλά in an adverbial sense (= "much, vehemently") is a characteristic of Markan style (1.45; 3.12; 5.10, 23, 38, 43; 6.20; 9.26; 15.3), it may be suspected that the word, occurring here originally, was dropped accidentally in the course of transcription. On the other hand, however, the general excellence of the witnesses that lack the word (א A B L Δ Π f¹ f¹³ al) makes it advisable to enclose the word within square brackets.

6.23 ὅ τι {C}

It is likely that ὅ was inserted by copyists who, coming upon the letters οτι, took them as ὅτι (rather than ὅ τι) and thus felt need of a relative pronoun to introduce the subsequent clause. The other readings represent scribal idiosyncrasies.

6.33   ἐκεῖ καὶ προῆλθον αὐτούς {B}

Amid the wide variety of readings, it is obvious that the Textus Receptus, which follows E F G H and many minuscules, is conflate,[3] being made up of ἐκεῖ καὶ προῆλθον αὐτούς and συνῆλθον πρὸς αὐτόν, each of which is witnessed separately. Of the two component readings, the former is supported by ℵ B 892 *al* as well as, indirectly, by L Δ Θ 1241 *al* (προσῆλθον and προῆλθον are easily confused palaeographically). It is probable that προῆλθον was altered to either προσῆλθον or συνῆλθον by copyists who thought it unlikely that the crowd on the land could have outstripped the boat (it is beside the point to observe, as Lagrange does, that the wind may have been contrary). Thus, both external evidence and internal considerations converge in making it probable that the reading with προῆλθον is the original.

6.41   μαθηταῖς [αὐτοῦ] {C}

The weight of the external evidence is rather evenly divided between the readings with and without αὐτοῦ. Normally Mark speaks of "his disciples," more rarely "the disciples." The former expression is an archaic trait reflecting a stage in the transmission of the Gospel tradition when the disciples of Jesus were not yet "*the* disciples" (compare the parallels in Mt 14.19 and Lk 9.16). On the one hand, therefore, it appears that αὐτοῦ should be read. On the other hand, however, since shorter readings in the Alexandrian text are generally to be preferred, the Committee thought it best to enclose αὐτοῦ within square brackets.

6.44   [τοὺς ἄρτους] {C}

External evidence is evenly divided between the witnesses that include the words τοὺς ἄρτους and those that omit them. Moreover, several witnesses (such as D W syr^s) that frequently have the longer

---

[3] For a lengthy discussion of this conflate reading, see Westcott and Hort, *Introduction,* pp. 95–99.

reading, here have the shorter reading. From the point of view of transcriptional probabilities, it is more likely that copyists were tempted to delete than to add τοὺς ἄρτους, for the presence of these words raises awkward questions why "loaves" should be singled out with no mention of the fish (the Old Latin ms. c reads both). In view of these conflicting considerations the Committee thought it best to retain the words but to enclose them within square brackets.

6.45 εἰς τὸ πέραν {A}

The phrase εἰς τὸ πέραν is omitted by several witnesses (𝔓⁴⁵ᵛⁱᵈ W f¹ syrˢ), no doubt because of the difficulties involved in the geography (Bethsaida was in the domain of Philip the tetrarch, and consequently was east of the Jordan River).

6.47 ἦν {B}

Several important witnesses (𝔓⁴⁵ D f¹ 28 al) add the expressive word πάλαι ("already," "for a long time," "just now"). While it can be argued that Matthew (who reads τὸ δὲ πλοῖον ἤδη ... 14.24) may have known a copy of Mark that included πάλαι, if the word had been present in the original form of the Gospel of Mark, in the opinion of a majority of the Committee it is difficult to account for its absence from such a wide variety of witnesses.

6.51 λίαν [ἐκ περισσοῦ] ἐν ἑαυτοῖς {C}

The Committee recognized that the double superlative, λίαν ἐκ περισσοῦ, is altogether in the style of Mark and is supported by a variety of witnesses that represent a broad geographical spread. At the same time, however, because ἐκ περισσοῦ is lacking in important witnesses (ℵ B L Δ 892 al), it was judged appropriate to enclose the phrase within square brackets.

6.51 ἐξίσταντο {B}

The shorter reading is to be preferred, for the expanded reading ἐξίσταντο καὶ ἐθαύμαζον appears to be a heightening of the narrative by copyists who recalled the account in Ac 2.7, where the same pair of verbs appears.

7.3   πυγμῇ {A}

The difficulty of understanding the significance of πυγμῇ (literally "with a [the] fist") in a context explaining Jewish ceremonial washings prompted some copyists to omit it (Δ syrˢ copˢᵃ) and others to replace it with a word that gives better sense, such as πυκνά ("often" or "thoroughly," ℵ W itᵇ· ¹ vg *al*), or *momento* ("in a moment," itᵃ), or *primo* ("first," itᵈ).

7.4   ἀγορᾶς {A}

The abruptness of καὶ ἀπ᾽ ἀγορᾶς ἐὰν μὴ βαπτίσωνται οὐκ ἐσθίουσιν was relieved by the addition in several witnesses (D W *al*) of ὅταν ἔλθωσιν ("*when they come* from the market place, they do not eat unless they wash themselves").

7.4   βαπτίσωνται {B}

Although it can be argued that the less familiar word (ῥαντίσωνται) was replaced by the more familiar one (βαπτίσωνται), it is far more likely that Alexandrian copyists, either wishing to keep βαπτίζειν for the Christian rite, or, more probably, taking ἀπ᾽ ἀγορᾶς as involving a partitive construction, introduced ῥαντίσωνται as more appropriate to express the meaning, "except they sprinkle [what is] from the market place, they do not eat [it]."

7.4   καὶ χαλκίων [καὶ κλινῶν] {C}

It is difficult to decide whether the words καὶ κλινῶν were added by copyists who were influenced by the legislation of Lv 15, or whether the words were omitted (*a*) accidentally because of homoeoteleuton or (*b*) deliberately because the idea of washing or sprinkling beds seemed to be quite incongruous. In view of the balance of probabilities, as well as the strong witnesses that support each reading, a majority of the Committee preferred to retain the words, but to enclose them within square brackets.

7.7-8 ἀνθρώπων. ἀφέντες ... ἀνθρώπων. {A}

The Greek text that lies behind the AV, "as the washing of pots and cups: and many other such like things ye do," which is absent from the oldest and best witnesses, is doubtless a scribal addition, derived from ver. 4. The fact that the longer reading is found at two different places – at the beginning of ver. 8 (D Θ *al*) and at the end of ver. 8 (K X Π *f*[13] 33 700 892 *al*) – likewise indicates its secondary nature.

7.9 στήσητε {D}

It is most difficult to decide whether scribes deliberately substituted στήσητε ("establish") for τηρήσητε ("keep"), as being the more appropriate verb in the context, or whether, through inadvertence in copying and perhaps influenced subconsciously by the preceding phrase τὴν ἐντολὴν τοῦ θεοῦ, they replaced στήσητε with τηρήσητε. The Committee judged that, on the whole, the latter possibility was slightly more probable.

7.16 *omit verse* {A}

This verse, though present in the majority of witnesses, is absent from important Alexandrian witnesses (ℵ B L Δ* *al*). It appears to be a scribal gloss (derived perhaps from 4.9 or 4.23), introduced as an appropriate sequel to ver. 14.

7.19 καθαρίζων {A}

The overwhelming weight of manuscript evidence supports the reading καθαρίζων. The difficulty of construing this word in the sentence[1] prompted copyists to attempt various corrections and ameliorations.

---

[1] Many modern scholars, following the interpretation suggested by Origen and Chrysostom, regard καθαρίζων as connected grammatically with λέγει in ver. 18,

7.24   Τύρου {B}

The words καὶ Σιδῶνος seem to be an assimilation to Mt 15.21 and Mk 7.31. If they had been present originally, there is no reason why they should have been deleted. The witnesses in support of the shorter text include representatives of the Western and other types of text.

7.28   κύριε {B}

Similar considerations apply in evaluating the evidence for this variant reading as those that were mentioned in discussing the variant in ver. 24. Apparently the word ναί (which occurs eight times in Matthew, four times in Luke, and nowhere else in Mark) was introduced here from the parallel passage in Mt 15.27.

7.31   ἦλθεν διὰ Σιδῶνος {A}

According to the reading supported by the best representatives of the Alexandrian and the Western texts, as well as by other noteworthy witnesses, Jesus took a circuitous route, passing north from Tyre through Sidon and thence southeast across the Leontes, continuing south past Caesarea Philippi to the east of the Jordan and thus approached the lake of Galilee on its east side, within the territory of the Decapolis.

The reading καὶ Σιδῶνος ἦλθεν is a modification that copyists introduced either accidentally (being influenced by the familiar expression "Tyre and Sidon") or deliberately (because Jesus' itinerary appeared to be extraordinarily roundabout).

7.35   καὶ [εὐθέως] {C}

Mark's fondness for εὐθύς (which sometimes appears as εὐθέως in various manuscripts) makes it probable that the adverb was employed either here or before ἐλύθη. The external support, how-

---

and take it as the evangelist's comment on the implications of Jesus' words concerning Jewish dietary laws.

ever, for εὐθύς before ἐλύθη is extremely weak, whereas it is relatively strong for including εὐθέως here. At the same time, the combination of witnesses that lack εὐθέως (ℵ B D L Δ *al*) is so impressive that a majority of the Committee considered it advisable to enclose εὐθέως within square brackets.

8.7 εὐλογήσας αὐτά {B}

The reading εὐχαριστήσας (D 1009 it^d, q) appears to be a scribal assimilation to ver. 6. Of the other readings the one chosen for the text has the best external support. Several witnesses omit the pronoun either as superfluous (in view of the following ταῦτα) or perhaps as inappropriate (Jesus blessed God's name, not the fishes).

8.10 τὰ μέρη Δαλμανουθά {B}

Two sets of variant readings are involved. The reading τὰ μέρη, supported by almost all the uncials and by many important minuscules (ℵ A B C K L X Δ Θ Π *f*^1 *f*^13 33 565 700 *al*), is clearly to be preferred; its synonym τὰ ὅρια (which occurs in the parallel passage in Mt 15.39) and the readings derivative from τὰ ὅρια (τὰ ὅρη and τὸ ὅρος) lack adequate support.

Dalmanutha (read by all uncials except D) is a place of uncertain location. Puzzled by the word, which occurs nowhere else,[1] copyists replaced it by Μαγεδά(ν) or Μαγδαλά, readings that occur in the parallel passage in Matthew (15.39).

8.15 Ἡρῴδου {A}

The reading τῶν Ἡρῳδιανῶν, which was current as early as the third and fourth centuries (𝔓^45 W cop^sa), is clearly a scribal alteration influenced by 3.6 and 12.13.

---

[1] Many attempts have been made to account linguistically or palaeographically for the origin of the word Dalmanutha (see Eb. Nestle in Hastings' *Dictionary of Christ and the Gospels*, i, pp. 406 f., and the literature mentioned in Bauer-Arndt-Gingrich-Danker, *s.v.*).

8.26 μηδὲ εἰς τὴν κώμην εἰσέλθῃς {B}

The development of the principal variant readings seems to have proceeded as follows:

(1) μηδὲ εἰς τὴν κώμην εἰσέλθῃς (ℵ^c B L *f*¹ syr^s cop^{sa, bo, fay})

(2) μηδενὶ εἴπῃς ἐν τῇ κώμῃ (it^k)

(3) μηδὲ εἰς τὴν κώμην εἰσέλθῃς μηδὲ εἴπῃς τινὶ ἐν τῇ κώμῃ (A C ... *al*)

(4) ὕπαγε εἰς τὸν οἶκόν σου καὶ μηδενὶ εἴπῃς (parent of the following)

    (4*a*) καί + ἐὰν εἰς τὴν κώμην εἰσέλθῃς (Θ it^{b.1} vg)

    (4*b*) εἴπῃς + εἰς τὴν κώμην (D)

    (4*c*) εἴπῃς + ἐν τῇ κώμῃ (Θ 565)

    (4*d*) καί + μηδὲ εἰς τὴν κώμην εἰσέλθῃς μηδὲ εἴπῃς τινὶ ἐν τῇ κώμῃ (124)

Reading (1), which is supported by early representatives of the Alexandrian, Eastern, and Egyptian text-types, appears to be the earliest form of text. Reading (2) arose in the interest of clarifying the import of (1), and reading (3) is obviously a conflation of (1) and (2). Reading (4), which is an elaboration of (2) with the help of an introductory phrase, appears to be the parent of several further modifications that are attested by Western and other witnesses.

8.38 λόγους {B}

Although the reading without the word λόγους gives good sense ("whoever is ashamed of me and of my [followers]"), it is easier to account for the origin of the shorter reading as due to accidental omission, facilitated by the similarity of the ending of the words ἐμοὺς λόγους, than to account for the insertion of the word in a wide variety of different types of text.

8.38 μετά {A}

The reading with καί instead of μετά appears to have arisen from scribal inattentiveness, or from assimilation to the parallel in Lk 9.26.

9.14 ἐλθόντες ... εἶδον {B}

The reading that involves the singular number focuses attention upon Jesus, whereas the plural requires the reader to distinguish between "they" (i. e., Jesus, Peter, James, and John, returning from the Mount of Transfiguration) and "the disciples" (i. e., the other nine who had been left on the plain). Both these internal considerations led the Committee to prefer the reading strongly supported by ℵ B L W Δ Ψ 892 al.

9.23 τὸ εἰ δύνῃ {B}

The extreme compression of the sentence has given trouble to copyists. Not seeing that in τὸ εἰ δύνῃ Jesus is repeating the words of the father in order to challenge them,[1] a variety of witnesses have inserted πιστεῦσαι, which has the effect of changing the subject of the verb "can" from Jesus to the father. As a result the τό now seemed more awkward than ever, and many of these witnesses omit it.

9.24 παιδίου {A}

The presence of the words μετὰ δακρύων in the later manuscripts reflects a natural heightening of the narrative introduced by copyists and correctors (cf. corrections in A and C). Certainly if the phrase were present originally in the text, no adequate reason can be found to account for its deletion.

9.29 προσευχῇ {A}

In light of the increasing emphasis in the early church on the necessity of fasting, it is understandable that καὶ νηστείᾳ is a gloss that found its way into most witnesses. Among the witnesses that resisted such an accretion are important representatives of the Alexandrian and the Western types of text.

---

[1] Ver. 22 "... if you can do anything, have pity on us and help us." (23) And Jesus said to him, "'If you can!' All things are possible for the one who believes."

9.38 καὶ ἐκωλύομεν αὐτόν, ὅτι οὐκ ἠκολούθει ἡμῖν {B}

Among many minor variations, there are three principal readings:
(1) "and we forbade him, because he was not following us"; (2) "who
does not follow us, and we forbade him"; and (3) "who does not
follow us, and we forbade him, because he does not follow us." The
last is a conflate reading that presupposes the existence of the other
two. Reading (1) is preferred because of superior witnesses (ℵ B Δ Θ
Ψ syr^{s, p, pal} *al*) and because in reading (2) there has been a transposition of the last clause to bring it into proximity to its subject (with the
change also of ὅτι to ὅς).

9.41 ἐν ὀνόματι {A}

The expression ἐν ὀνόματι ὅτι ("under the category that" or "on
the ground that"; hence, "because"), though perfectly acceptable
Greek, appears to have struck some copyists as strange; they therefore modified it in various ways.

9.42 πιστευόντων [εἰς ἐμέ] {C}

The presence of εἰς ἐμέ is very strongly attested (A B L W Θ Ψ
f^1 f^{13} syr^s cop^{sa} *al*). At the same time, however, the absence of the
words from ℵ D and Δ, as well as the possibility that they may have
come into the Markan text from the Matthean parallel (18.6), casts
substantial doubt upon their right to a firm place in the second
Gospel. The Committee therefore decided to enclose the phrase
within square brackets.

9.44 *omit verse* {A}

The words ὅπου ὁ σκώληξ ... οὐ σβέννυται, which are lacking
in important early witnesses (including ℵ B C W it^k syr^s cop^{sa}), were
added by copyists from ver. 48.

9.45 εἰς τὴν γέενναν {A}

Influenced by the parallel passage in ver. 43, copyists tended to
add one or another modifier to the reading that is decisively supported

by representatives of the Alexandrian, the Western, the Eastern, and the Egyptian types of text.

9.46 *omit verse* {A}

See the comment on ver. 44.

9.49 πᾶς γὰρ πυρὶ ἁλισθήσεται {B}

The opening words of this verse have been transmitted in three principal forms: (1) πᾶς γὰρ πυρὶ ἁλισθήσεται (B L Δ f^1 f^{13} syrˢ copˢᵃ *al*, "For every one will be salted with fire"); (2) πᾶσα γὰρ θυσία ἁλὶ ἁλισθήσεται (D itᵇ· ᶜ· ᵈ· ᶠᶠ2· ⁱ, "For every sacrifice will be salted with salt"); and (3) πᾶς γὰρ πυρὶ ἁλισθήσεται καὶ πᾶσα θυσία ἁλὶ ἁλισθήσεται (A K Π *al*, "For every one will be salted with fire, and every sacrifice will be salted with salt"). The history of the text seems to have been as follows. At a very early period a scribe, having found in Lv 2.13 a clue to the meaning of Jesus' enigmatic statement, wrote the Old Testament passage in the margin of his copy of Mark. In subsequent copyings the marginal gloss was either substituted for the words of the text, thus creating reading (2), or was added to the text, thus creating reading (3). Other modifications include πυρὶ ἀναλωθήσεται (Θ, "… will be consumed with fire …"), θυσία ἀναλωθήσεται (Ψ, "… sacrifice will be consumed …"), ἐν πυρὶ δοκιμασθήσεται (1195, "… will be tested by fire …"), and πᾶσα δὲ οὐσία ἀναλωθήσεται (implied by itᵏ, "and all [their] substance will be destroyed," ο being read for Θ, and ΑΝΑΛΩ for ΑΛΙΑΛΙϹ).

10.1 [καὶ] πέραν {C}

The reading διὰ τοῦ πέραν (A K X Π most minuscules, followed by the Textus Receptus; cf. the AV rendering "into the coast of Judaea by the farther side of Jordan") is manifestly an explanatory correction introduced by copyists who were perplexed by the geographical difficulties involved in the earlier readings. In choosing between καὶ πέραν (Alexandrian text) and πέραν (Western and

Antiochian texts), the Committee was impressed by the diversity of external support for the second reading, but considered that the absence of the καί may be due to assimilation to the parallel in Matthew (19.1). In order to reflect the balance of external witnesses and internal probabilities, it was decided to retain καί but to enclose it within square brackets.

10.2 καὶ προσελθόντες Φαρισαῖοι {B}

The chief problem presented by the variant readings involves the presence or absence of the words προσελθόντες (οἱ) Φαρισαῖοι. Did the original text read merely ἐπηρώτων, an impersonal plural ("people asked him" or "he was asked"), and has the reference to the Pharisees come into many witnesses by assimilation to the parallel passage in Matthew (19.3)? Despite the plausibility of such a possibility, the fact that the Matthean passage is not absolutely parallel (προσῆλθον αὐτῷ Φαρισαῖοι) and the widespread and impressive support for the longer reading led a majority of the Committee to retain the words in the text.

[Inasmuch as the impersonal plural is a feature of Markan style, the words προσελθόντες Φαρισαῖοι are probably an intrusion from Matthew; if retained at all, they should be enclosed within square brackets. B.M.M. and A.W.]

10.6 αὐτούς {B}

The insertion of ὁ θεός as the subject of ἐποίησεν must have seemed to copyists to be necessary lest the uninstructed reader imagine that the previously mentioned subject (Moses) should be carried on. Several witnesses (D W it[b, d, ff2, k, r1] *al*) omit αὐτούς as superfluous.

10.7 μητέρα [καὶ προσκολληθήσεται πρὸς τὴν γυναῖκα αὐτοῦ] {C}

Have the words καὶ προσκολληθήσεται πρὸς τὴν γυναῖκα (or τῇ γυναῖκι) αὐτοῦ been added in most copies in order to assimilate the quotation to the fuller form of text found in Mt 19.5 (and Gn 2.24), or were they inadvertently omitted in transcription (the eye of the scribe passing from καί to καί)? In order to represent the very close balance of probabilities, a majority of the Committee decided to include the clause in the text (where it seems to be necessary for the sense, otherwise οἱ δύο in ver. 8 could be taken to refer to the father and the mother!), but to enclose it within square brackets. As between πρὸς τὴν γυναῖκα and τῇ γυναῖκι, the former was preferred because the dative construction is obviously a stylistic correction.

10.13 ἐπετίμησαν αὐτοῖς {A}

In order to avoid possible ambiguity as to who it was that the disciples were rebuking, the scribes of A D W Θ f^1 f^{13} al replaced αὐτοῖς with τοῖς προσφέρουσιν or τοῖς φέρουσιν. The shorter reading is strongly supported by ℵ B C L Δ Ψ 579 892 1342 al.

10.19 μὴ ἀποστερήσῃς {A}

Since the command, "Do not defraud" (a reminiscence of Ex 20.17 or Dt 24.14 [Septuagint mss. A F] or Sir 4.1), may have seemed to be inappropriate in a list of several of the Ten Commandments, many copyists – as well as Matthew (19.18) and Luke (18.20) – omitted it.

10.21 δεῦρο ἀκολούθει μοι {A}

The Textus Receptus, following A and many minuscules, adds a gloss from 8.34, ἄρας τὸν σταυρόν. The shorter text is strongly supported by ℵ B C D Δ Θ Ψ al.

10.23 εἰσελεύσονται

The Western text (D it$^{a, b, d, ff2}$) has moved ver. 25 so as to follow εἰσελεύσονται (reading verses 23, 25, 24, 26). The transposition appears to be the work of the Western redactor who sought to improve the sense by making a more gradual sequence (first, it is difficult for rich people to enter the kingdom; then, it is difficult for those who trust in riches [for this addition, see the comment on ver. 24] to enter). Although some have preferred the transposed sequence, it is precisely (as Lagrange points out *ad loc.*) the too-logical order of the Western text that renders it suspect as a secondary modification of the more primitive text. The minuscule 235 includes ver. 25 twice (reading verses 23, 25, 24, 25, 26).

10.24   ἐστιν {B}

The rigor of Jesus' saying was softened by the insertion of one or another qualification that limited its generality and brought it into closer connection with the context. Thus, A C D Θ *f*¹ *f*¹³ *al* read ἐστιν τοὺς πεποιθότας ἐπὶ χρήμασιν ("for those who trust in riches"); W and it^c insert πλούσιον ("a rich man"); and 1241 reads οἱ τὰ χρήματα ἔχοντες ("those who have possessions").

10.25   κάμηλον {A}

See the comment on Mt 19.24.

10.26   πρὸς ἐαυτούς {B}

The reading πρὸς αὐτόν appears to be an Alexandrian correction, taking the place of πρὸς ἑαυτούς, which is preserved in A D W Θ *f*¹ *f*¹³ it vg goth arm eth *al*, and refined in M* it^k syr^p geo (πρὸς ἀλλήλους).

10.31   [οἱ] {C}

On the one hand, the weight of evidence supporting the presence of οἱ is not impressive, but, on the other hand, scribes, recollecting the parallel in Mt 19.30 (which lacks the article), may have omitted it here. In order to reflect the balance of considerations, the Committee chose to include the word but to enclose it within square brackets to indicate a considerable degree of doubt whether it belongs in the text.

10.34 μετὰ τρεῖς ἡμέρας {A}

The typically Markan reading, μετὰ τρεῖς ἡμέρας (which occurs also in 8.31 and 9.31; elsewhere of Jesus' resurrection, only Mt 27.63), has been conformed by copyists to the much more frequently used expression, τῇ τρίτῃ ἡμέρᾳ (compare the parallels in Mt 20.19 and Lk 18.33).

10.36 τί θέλετέ [με] ποιήσω {C}

The reading that seems best to account for the emergence of the other readings is that of ℵ¹ B Ψ, where the accusative με is followed, not, as one would expect, by the infinitive (ποιῆσαι, as in many of the later manuscripts), but by the deliberative subjunctive, ποιήσω. There may also have been interference from the recollection of the text of ver. 51.

10.40 ἀλλ' οἷς {A}

Several early versions (itᵃ, ᵇ, ᵈ, ff², ᵏ syrˢ cpoˢᵃ eth) read the Greek ΑΛΛΟΙϹ as ἄλλοις, despite the lack of syntactical concord with the preceding part of the sentence.

10.40 ἡτοίμασται {A}

The presence of the phrase ὑπὸ (or παρὰ) τοῦ πατρός μου in several witnesses, some of them early (as ℵ* itᵃ, ʳˡᵛⁱᵈ), is clearly an intrusion from the parallel in Mt 20.23.

10.43 ἐστιν {A}

The future tense, which is supported by A C³ K X Π and most minuscules (followed by the Textus Receptus), appears to be a scribal amelioration designed to soften the peremptory tone of the present ἔστιν. It is also possible that the future may have arisen from assimilation to ἔσται in the next line.

11.3   αὐτὸν ἀποστέλλει πάλιν {B}

The interpretation of this passage is obscure. Are the words καὶ
εὐθὺς αὐτὸν ἀποστέλλει πάλιν ὧδε part of the message, or a
statement of what will happen? Matthew (21.3) evidently took the
words in the latter sense. The presence, however, of πάλιν in most
witnesses suggests that the words, as part of the message, give
assurance that the animal is to be returned after Jesus has used it.
Although it may be argued that copyists, moved by considerations of
what would become of the animal, inserted πάλιν before or after the
verb, the fact that similar considerations did not operate in the case of
the Matthean parallel, as well as the strength of the testimony of ℵ
Dᵍʳ L 892 al, suggests that the original text was αὐτὸν ἀποστέλλει
πάλιν, which was subsequently modified either under the influence
of the parallel or because it was no longer interpreted as part of the
message. The future tense, which is smoother than the present,
appears to be a scribal correction.

11.19   ἐξεπορεύοντο ἔξω τῆς πόλεως {C}

Although it is possible that the singular verb (ἐξεπορεύετο) was
altered to the plural in order to suit the next verse, the weight of the
evidence tends to support the plural. The omission of the verb in L is
the result of an accident in transcription.

11.22   Ἔχετε {B}

Inasmuch as elsewhere the solemn expression ἀμὴν λέγω ὑμῖν is
always introductory and is never preceded by a protasis,[1] it appears
that the original reading is the exhortation Ἔχετε πίστιν θεοῦ, and
that the reading introduced by εἰ (ℵ D Θ f¹³ 28 al) arose by assimilation to the saying in Lk 17.6 (cf. also Mt 21.21).

---

[1] It should be observed that here εἰ may not only be taken as the ordinary conditional particle ("If you have faith in God, …"), but can also be construed as an interrogative particle introducing (like Hebrew אִם) a direct question ("Do you have faith
in God?"; see Blass-Debrunner-Funk, § 440 (3)).

11.24 ἐλάβετε {A}

The aorist tense, representing the Semitic usage of the prophetic perfect (which expresses the certainty of a future action), seemed too bold and was altered either to the present tense (λαμβάνετε) or, under the influence of the parallel in Mt 21.22, to the future tense (λήμψεσθε).

11.26 *omit verse* {A}

Although it might be thought that the sentence was accidentally omitted because of homoeoteleuton, its absence from early witnesses that represent all text-types makes it highly probable that the words were inserted by copyists in imitation of Mt 6.15.

12.23 ἐν τῇ ἀναστάσει [ὅταν ἀναστῶσιν] {C}

The absence of ὅταν ἀναστῶσιν from ℵ B C* D L W Δ Ψ *al* is probably deliberate, having been omitted by copyists as superfluous (Matthew and Luke also omitted the words, probably for the same reason). It is hard to imagine that a copyist would have been tempted to gloss ἐν τῇ ἀναστάσει, and the pleonasm is in accord with Mark's style (cf. 13.19 f.). At the same time, however, in deference to the generally high reputation of the witnesses that attest the omission, the Committee thought it right to enclose the words within square brackets.

In order to suggest more clearly that ver. 23 constitutes the nub of the query, copyists inserted οὖν at various places in various witnesses.

12.26 [ὁ] θεὸς ... [ὁ] θεός {C}

It is difficult to decide whether the weight of B D W, supporting the absence of the second and third instances of ὁ, is sufficient to counterbalance the weight of almost all other witnesses that include the article in all three instances. In order to represent the considerable doubt as to the original reading, the Committee decided to include ὁ all three times but, in the second and third instances, to enclose the word within square brackets.

12.34 *[αὐτόν]* {C}

Since the pronoun αὐτόν forestalls the subject of the dependent clause (literally, "Jesus seeing him, that he answered wisely"), it is not surprising to find that it has been omitted by many copyists. On the other hand, in view of the weight of witnesses that lack the word, the Committee decided to indicate the balance of evidence by retaining the word but enclosing it within square brackets.

12.36 *ὑποκάτω* {C}

The parallel in the preferred text of Matthew (22.44) supports Mark's substitution of ὑποκάτω (B Dᵍʳ Ψ 28 syrˢ copˢᵃ, ᵇᵒ *al*) for the Septuagint's ὑποπόδιον. Since the latter reading is quoted in Lk 20.43 and Ac 2.35, copyists would have tended to replace Mark's modification with the "correct" reading.

12.41 *καθίσας κατέναντι τοῦ γαζοφυλακίου* {B}

The reading that best explains the origin of the others is preserved in א L Δ 892 itᵃ, ᵏ *al*. Copyists were more likely to insert the words ὁ Ἰησοῦς in order to identify the subject than to delete them. Elsewhere Mark uses κατέναντι (11.2; 13.3), but never ἀπέναντι. Those responsible for W Θ *f*¹ *f*¹³ 28 565 *al* obviously thought that it was more appropriate for Jesus to stand (ἑστώς) than to sit in the temple.

13.2 *ὧδε λίθος ἐπὶ λίθον* {B}

On the basis of preponderant manuscript evidence (א B L W Δ Θ Ψ *f*¹ *f*¹³ 28 33 700 *al*) the Committee preferred the reading ὧδε λίθος ἐπὶ λίθον. The reading of A and a number of minuscules (λίθος ἐπὶ λίθῳ) reflects the influence of Lk 21.6.

13.8 ἔσονται λιμοί {B}

Although it is possible that the words καὶ ταραχαί may have
fallen out in transcription because of some similarity to the following
word ἀρχή, it is more probable that here we have an example of a
growing text, expanded by various copyists in various ways.

13.33 ἀγρυπνεῖτε {B}

The Committee regarded the reading καὶ προσεύχεσθε as a
natural addition (derived perhaps from 14.38) that many copyists
were likely to make independently of one another. If the words had
been present originally, it is difficult to account for their omission in
B D 2427 it[a, c, d, k] cop[fay].

14.5 ἐπάνω {A}

It has been argued that ἐπάνω is a second-century addition that
reflects the depreciation of currency after the time of Nero. If that
were the case, however, one would expect early rather than late
Greek evidence in support of the shorter reading. It is more probable
that several copyists and/or translators omitted ἐπάνω either because
they objected to its colloquial usage (see Blass-Debrunner-Funk,
§ 185) or because they were influenced by the parallel account in Jn
12.5, where the word is not used.

14.24 τῆς διαθήκης {A}

It is much more likely that καινῆς is a scribal addition, derived
from the parallel accounts in Lk 22.20 and 1 Cor 11.25, than that,
being present originally, it was omitted from ℵ B C L Θ Ψ 565 it[k]
cop[sams, bo] geo[1].

14.25 οὐκέτι οὐ μὴ πίω {C}

The absence of οὐκέτι from ℵ C L W *al* is probably to be accounted for as the result of scribal assimilation to the parallel passage
in Matthew (26.29). Although the use of the verb προστιθέναι in D

Θ 565 suggests Semitic influence (in the Septuagint προσέθετο with an infinitive frequently renders הוֹסִיף with an infinitive), none of the three readings is strongly enough supported to be accepted as the original.

14.30 ἢ δὶς ἀλέκτορα φωνῆσαι {C}

It appears that scribes either preferred to move δίς closer to the verb or to omit it by assimilation to a parallel account (Mt 26.34; Lk 22.34; Jn 13.36).

14.39 τὸν αὐτὸν λόγον εἰπών {A}

Although some have thought that these words are a gloss which entered all types of text except the Western, it is far more likely that a copyist accidentally omitted them in transcription (perhaps they constituted a sense line in an ancestor of codex Bezae).

14.41 ἀπέχει· ἦλθεν {B}

The difficulty of interpreting the impersonal use of ἀπέχει in the context led copyists to introduce ameliorations. Several Western and other witnesses (including D W Θ f¹³) add τὸ τέλος (meaning perhaps, "the end has fully come"), a gloss that may have been suggested by Lk 22.37; a few witnesses (including Ψ 892 al) omit ἀπέχει; and itᵏ rewrites the passage as follows: *et venit tertio et ubi adoravit dicit illis: dormite jam nunc, ecce appropinquavit qui me tradit. Et post pusillum excitavit illos et dixit: jam hora est, ecce traditur filius hominis* ... ("and he came the third time and when he had prayed he says to them, 'Sleep on now; behold, he who betrays me has come near.' And after a little he aroused them and said, 'Now is the hour; behold, the Son of Man is betrayed ...'").

14.65 αὐτῷ {A}

Several witnesses (Θ 565 700 itᶠ syrᵖ), no doubt influenced by the parallel account in Mt 26.67, have replaced αὐτῷ with αὐτοῦ τῷ προσώπῳ (D reads τῷ προσώπῳ αὐτοῦ). See also the following set of variant readings.

14.65 προφήτευσον {B}

The longer reading involving the addition of the question τίς ἐστιν ὁ παίσας σε; ("Who is it that has struck you?"), with or without the introductory Χριστέ, appears to be an assimilation to the text of Matthew (26.68) or Luke (22.64). The shortest reading, προφήτευσον, supported as it is by the Alexandrian text and several early versions, best accounts for the rise of the other readings.

14.68 [καὶ ἀλέκτωρ ἐφώνησεν] {C}

It is difficult to decide whether these words were added or omitted from the original text. It is easy to explain their addition: copyists would have been tempted to insert the words in order to emphasize the literal fulfillment of Jesus' prophecy in ver. 30 (perhaps copyists would also have reasoned that Peter could not have known that a crowing of the cock was the second if he had not heard the first). It is also easy to explain the omission of the words: copyists wished to bring the Markan account of two cock-crowings into harmony with the narratives of the other three Gospels, which mention only one cock-crowing (perhaps copyists also asked themselves why, if Peter had heard the cock, he did not at once repent).

In the face of such conflicting possibilities, and with each reading supported by impressive external evidence, the Committee decided that the least unsatisfactory solution was to include the words in the text, but to enclose them within square brackets.

14.72 ἐκ δευτέρου {B}

Several witnesses omit ἐκ δευτέρου (ℵ C*vid L itc Diatessaroni, s), probably in order to harmonize Mark with the account in the other Gospels (Mt 26.74; Lk 22.60; Jn 18.27); see also the comment on 14.68.

14.72 ὅτι Πρὶν ἀλέκτορα φωνῆσαι δὶς τρίς με ἀπαρνήσῃ {B}

The reading that seems to account best for the origin of the others is the one supported by C² L Ψ 892 *al,* in which δίς and τρίς stand side by side. Copyists moved one or the other of the adverbs in order to improve the style and euphony, or omitted δίς in accord with the same considerations that appear to have operated at verses 30 and 68 concerning the second cock-crowing (see the comments on these passages).

14.72 καὶ ἐπιβαλὼν ἔκλαιεν {B}

The difficulty of interpreting the meaning of ἐπιβαλών led copyists to replace it with ἤρξατο in several Western and other witnesses, including D Θ 565 Old Latin *al.* In a few witnesses (ℵ* A*ᵛⁱᵈ C) the imperfect tense *(ἔκλαιεν)* was assimilated to the aorist *(ἔκλαυσεν)* of the parallel passages (Mt 26.75 and Lk 22.62).

15.8 ἀναβὰς ὁ ὄχλος {B}

The verbs ἀναβοᾶν and ἀναβῆναι were liable to be confused in manuscripts (cf. the Septuagint of 2 Sm 23.9; 2 Kgs 3.21; Ho 8.9). There is no other occurrence of ἀναβοᾶν in Mark, but ἀναβαίνειν occurs nine times. The external evidence in support of ἀναβάς (a verb that is particularly appropriate if Pilate's quarters were in the Tower of Antonia) is strong (ℵ* B D 892 most of the Old Latin vg copˢᵃ, ᵇᵒ goth).

The insertion of ὅλος in a few witnesses was made in the interest of dramatic heightening of the narrative.

15.12 *[θέλετε]* ποιήσω {C}

It is difficult to decide whether the shorter reading (supported by ℵ B C W Δ Ψ *f¹ f¹³ al*) is secondary, having been conformed to Mt 27.22, or whether θέλετε has been inserted by assimilation to ver. 9 or Mt 27.21 or Lk 23.20 (compare also Mk 10.36). On the whole the Committee thought it best to include θέλετε in the text but to enclose it within square brackets.

15.12 *[ὅν λέγετε]* {C}

Although there is strong external attestation for the omission of ὅν λέγετε, Matthew's reading τὸν λεγόμενον Χριστόν (Mt 27.22) seems to presuppose the originality of ὅν λέγετε in Mark. On the other hand, however, the insertion of the clause may be regarded as a scribal amelioration, introduced in order to throw the onus for the use of the title "The King of the Jews" upon the high priests. The unique reading of B is probably to be explained as the result of accidental omission of ὅν. On balance the Committee judged that the least unsatisfactory solution was to include the words in the text, but to enclose them within square brackets to indicate doubt that they have a right to stand there.

15.25 *τρίτη*

In the interest of harmonization with Jn 19.14, instead of τρίτη a few witnesses read ἕκτη (Θ 478** syr^hmg eth). According to the suggestion of several patristic writers, τρίτη has arisen out of a confusion between Ϝ (= 6) and Γ (= 3). (See also the comment on Jn 19.14.)

15.28 *omit verse* {A}

The earliest and best witnesses of the Alexandrian and the Western types of text lack ver. 28. It is understandable that copyists could have added the sentence in the margin from Lk 22.37, whence it came into the text itself; there is no reason why, if the sentence were present originally, it should have been deleted. It is also significant that Mark very seldom expressly quotes the Old Testament.

15.34 *ελωι ελωι λεμα σαβαχθανι*

The reading ηλει ηλει of D Θ (059 ελει) 0192 (131 ηλι) 565 *al* represents the Hebrew אֵלִי ("my God"), and has been assimilated to the parallel in Matthew (27.46). The great majority of uncials and minuscule manuscripts read ελωι ελωι, which represents the

Aramaic אֱלָהִי ("my God"), the ω for the *a* sound being due to the influence of the Hebrew אֱלֹהִי.

The spelling λεμα (א C L Δ Ψ 72 495 517 579 1342 1675 *al*) represents the Aramaic לְמָא ("why?"), which is also probably to be understood as lying behind λιμα (A K M P U X Γ Π *f*¹³ 33 106 118 131 209 543 697 700 1270 *al*), whereas λαμα (B D N Θ Σ 1 22 565 1295 1582 *al*) represents the Hebrew לָמָה ("why?").

All Greek manuscripts except codex Bezae read σαβαχθανι or something similar (σιβακθανει, A; ζαβαφθανει, B; σαβαχθανει, C *al*), which represents the Aramaic שְׁבַקְתַּנִי ("thou hast forsaken me"). The reading ζαφθανι of D (it^d reads *zapthani;* it^k *zaphani;* it^ff2 *sapthani;* it^i* *izpthani*) is a scholarly correction representing the Hebrew of Ps 22.1 עֲזַבְתָּנִי ("thou hast forsaken me").[1]

Thus, in the text preferred by the Committee the entire saying represents an Aramaic original, whereas the Matthean parallel is partly Hebrew and partly Aramaic (see the comment on Mt 27.46).

15.34 ἐγκατέλιπές με {B}

It is perhaps more likely that copyists should have altered ἐγκα-τέλιπές με to agree with the Matthean reading με ἐγκατέλιπες (Mt 27.46), than that they should have changed με ἐγκατέλιπες to ἐγκατέλιπές με to agree with the Septuagint of Ps 22.2.

The reading of D^gr (supported by a few other Western witnesses[2]) ὠνείδισάς με ("[Why] hast thou reproached [or, taunted] me?") may have been substituted for the usual reading by someone who could not understand how God would have forsaken Jesus on the cross.

15.39 ὅτι οὕτως ἐξέπνευσεν {C}

Although the witnesses that include κράξας or its equivalent are diversified and widespread, while those that lack it are chiefly of one

---

[1] It is perhaps not surprising that most witnesses have dropped the initial *a*-sound (with the ʿain), coming as it does immediately after the terminal vowel of λαμα.

[2] Three Old Latin manuscripts support, each in its own way, the reading of D^gr: *exprobasti me* it^c, *me in opprobrium dedisti* it^i, and *me maledixisti* it^k*.

textual type (Alexandrian), a majority of the Committee preferred the shorter reading and regarded the participle as an early interpolation from Mt 27.50.

15.44 *εἰ πάλαι* {B}

Although the reading *πάλαι* may perhaps have arisen through a desire to avoid the repetition of *ἤδη* in the sentence, it is more probable that copyists, feeling that *πάλαι* was somehow inappropriate in the context, sought to ameliorate the passage by replacing it with *ἤδη*. Several manuscripts that read *ἤδη* (including D W Θ) also alter *ἀπέθανεν* to the perfect tense.

16.1 *διαγενομένου τοῦ σαββάτου … καὶ Σαλώμη* {A}

The omission by D it[k] of the names of the two women (who are identified in the previous sentence) is clearly in the interest of simplification, and the omission by D it[d, n] of mention of the passing of the sabbath allows the purchase of the spices to take place on Friday (as similarly Lk 23.56). The overwhelming preponderance of attestation of all other witnesses supports the text adopted by the Committee.

16.2 *ἀνατείλαντος* {A}

Because of the lack of harmony with the parallel accounts in Mt 28.1; Lk 24.1; and Jn 20.1 (and even with Mark's own *λίαν πρωΐ*), several Western witnesses (D it[c, n, q] Tyconius Augustine) have sought to alleviate the difficulty by replacing the aorist with the present tense (*ἀνατέλλοντος*).

16.4

At the beginning of ver. 4 the Old Latin codex Bobiensis (it[k]) introduces a description of the actual resurrection of Jesus Christ. At one or two places the text of the gloss does not appear to be sound, and various emendations have been proposed:

Subito autem ad horam tertiam tenebrae diei factae sunt per totam orbem terrae, et descenderunt de caelis angeli et surgent [surgentes?, surgente eo?, surgit?] *in claritate vivi Dei* [viri duo? + et?] *simul ascenderunt cum eo; et continuo lux facta est. Tunc illae accesserunt ad monimentum* ... ("But suddenly at the third hour of the day there was darkness over the whole circle of the earth, and angels descended from the heavens, and as he [the Lord] was rising [reading *surgente eo*] in the glory of the living God, at the same time they ascended with him; and immediately it was light. Then the women went to the tomb ...)." The emendation *viri duo,* which in the context appears to be unnecessary, has been proposed in view of the account in the Gospel of Peter of two men who, having descended from heaven in a great brightness, brought Jesus out of the tomb, and "the heads of the two reached to heaven, but the head of him who was being led by them overpassed the heavens" (§§ 35–40).

16.9-20   *The Ending(s) of Mark*

Four endings of the Gospel according to Mark are current in the manuscripts. (1) The last twelve verses of the commonly received text of Mark are absent from the two oldest Greek manuscripts (א and B),[1] from the Old Latin codex Bobiensis (it^k), the Sinaitic Syriac manuscript, about one hundred Armenian manuscripts,[2] and the two oldest Georgian manuscripts (written A.D. 897 and A.D. 913).[3]

---

[1] Two other Greek manuscripts, both of the twelfth century, also lack verses 9-20, namely 304 and 2386. The latter, however, is only an apparent witness for the omission, for although the last page of Mark closes with ἐφοβοῦντο γάρ, the next leaf of the manuscript is missing, and following 16.8 is the sign indicating the close of an ecclesiastical lection *(τλ = τέλος),* a clear implication that the manuscript originally continued with additional material from Mark (see Kurt Aland, "Bemerkungen zum Schluss des Markusevangeliums," in *Neotestamentica et Semitica, Studies in Honour of Matthew Black,* ed. by E. Earle Ellis [and] Max Wilcox [Edinburgh, 1969], pp. 157–180, especially pp. 159 f., and *idem,* "Der wiedergefundene Markusschluss?" *Zeitschrift für Theologie und Kirche,* LXVII [1970], pp. 3–13, especially pp. 8 f.).

[2] For their identity see Ernest C. Colwell in *Journal of Biblical Literature,* LV (1937), pp. 369–386.

[3] It has often been stated that three Ethiopic manuscripts, now in the British Museum, lack the last twelve verses of Mark. This statement, made originally by D. S. Margoliouth and reported by William Sanday in his *Appendices ad Novum Testamentum Stephanicum* (Oxford, 1889), p. 195, is erroneous; for details see the present

Clement of Alexandria and Origen show no knowledge of the existence of these verses; furthermore Eusebius and Jerome attest that the passage was absent from almost all Greek copies of Mark known to them. The original form of the Eusebian sections (drawn up by Ammonius) makes no provision for numbering sections of the text after 16.8. Not a few manuscripts that contain the passage have scribal notes stating that older Greek copies lack it, and in other witnesses the passage is marked with asterisks or obeli, the conventional signs used by copyists to indicate a spurious addition to a document.

(2) Several witnesses, including four uncial Greek manuscripts of the seventh, eighth, and ninth centuries (L Ψ 099 0112 *al*), as well as Old Latin k, the margin of the Harclean Syriac, several Sahidic and Bohairic manuscripts,[4] and not a few Ethiopic manuscripts,[5] continue after verse 8 as follows (with trifling variations): "But they reported briefly to Peter and those with him all that they had been told. And after these things Jesus himself sent out through them, from east to west, the sacred and imperishable proclamation of eternal salvation." All of these witnesses except it[k] also continue with verses 9-20.

(3) The traditional ending of Mark, so familiar through the AV and other translations of the Textus Receptus, is present in the vast number of witnesses, including A C D K W X Δ Θ Π Ψ 099 0112 *f*[13] 28 33 *al.* The earliest patristic witnesses to part or all of the long ending are Irenaeus and the Diatessaron. It is not certain whether

---

writer's article, "The Ending of the Gospel according to Mark in Ethiopic Manuscripts," contributed to the Festschrift for Morton Scott Enslin (*Understanding the Sacred Text,* ed. by John Reumann *et al.* [Valley Forge, Pa., c. 1972]), and reprinted, with additions, in Metzger, *New Testament Studies* (Leiden, 1980), pp. 127–147.

The Arabic manuscript, Rom. Vat. Arab. 13, has sometimes been cited (e. g. by Tischendorf and Tregelles) as a witness for the form of the Gospel that ends at ver. 8. Since, however, through an accidental loss of leaves the original hand of the manuscript breaks off just before the end of Mk 16.8, its testimony is without significance in discussing the textual problem. See F. C. Burkitt, "Arabic Versions," Hastings' *Dictionary of the Bible,* I, p. 136, foot of col. *a,* and C. R. Williams, *The Appendices to the Gospel according to Mark* (= *Transactions of the Connecticut Academy of Arts and Sciences,* XVIII; New Haven, 1915), pp. 398–399.

[4] See P. E. Kahle, "The End of St. Mark's Gospel. The Witness of the Coptic Versions," *Journal of Theological Studies,* n.s. II (1951), pp. 49–57.

[5] See the article mentioned in footnote 3 above.

Justin Martyr was acquainted with the passage; in his *Apology* (I.45) he includes five words that occur, in a different sequence, in ver. 20 (*τοῦ λόγου τοῦ ἰσχυροῦ ὃν ἀπὸ Ἰερουσαλὴμ οἱ ἀπόστολοι αὐτοῦ ἐξελθόντες πανταχοῦ ἐκήρυξαν*).

(4) In the fourth century the traditional ending also circulated, according to testimony preserved by Jerome, in an expanded form, preserved today in one Greek manuscript. Codex Washingtonianus includes the following after ver. 14: "And they excused themselves, saying, 'This age of lawlessness and unbelief is under Satan, who does not allow the truth and power of God to prevail over the unclean things of the spirits [*or*, does not allow what lies under the unclean spirits to understand the truth and power of God]. Therefore reveal your righteousness now' – thus they spoke to Christ. And Christ replied to them, 'The term of years of Satan's power has been fulfilled, but other terrible things draw near. And for those who have sinned I was handed over to death, that they may return to the truth and sin no more, in order that they may inherit the spiritual and incorruptible glory of righteousness that is in heaven.'"

How should the evidence of each of these endings be evaluated? It is obvious that the expanded form of the long ending (4) has no claim to be original. Not only is the external evidence extremely limited, but the expansion contains several non-Markan words and expressions (including *ὁ αἰὼν οὗτος, ἁμαρτάνω, ἀπολογέω, ἀληθινός, ὑποστρέφω*) as well as several that occur nowhere else in the New Testament (*δεινός, ὅρος, προσλέγω*). The whole expansion has about it an unmistakable apocryphal flavor. It probably is the work of a second or third century scribe who wished to soften the severe condemnation of the Eleven in 16.14.

The longer ending (3), though current in a variety of witnesses, some of them ancient, must also be judged by internal evidence to be secondary. (*a*) The vocabulary and style of verses 9-20 are non-Markan (e. g. *ἀπιστέω, βλάπτω, βεβαιόω, ἐπακολουθέω, θεάομαι, μετὰ ταῦτα, πορεύομαι, συνεργέω, ὕστερον* are found nowhere else in Mark; and *θανάσιμον* and *τοῖς μετ' αὐτοῦ γενομένοις*, as designations of the disciples, occur only here in the New Testament). (*b*) The connection between ver. 8 and verses 9-20 is so awkward that it is difficult to believe that the evangelist intended the section to be a continuation of the Gospel. Thus, the subject of ver. 8 is the women, whereas Jesus is the presumed subject in ver. 9; in ver. 9 Mary Magdalene is identified even though she has been mentioned only a few lines before (15.47 and 16.1); the other women of verses 1-8 are now forgotten; the use of $\dot{\alpha}\nu\alpha\sigma\tau\dot{\alpha}\varsigma$ $\delta\acute{\epsilon}$ and the position of $\pi\rho\hat{\omega}\tau o\nu$ are appropriate at the beginning of a comprehensive narrative, but they are ill-suited in a continuation of verses 1-8. In short, all these features indicate that the section was added by someone who knew a form of Mark that ended abruptly with ver. 8 and who wished to supply a more appropriate conclusion. In view of the inconcinnities between verses 1-8 and 9-20, it is unlikely that the long ending was composed *ad hoc* to fill up an obvious gap; it is more likely that the section was excerpted from another document, dating perhaps from the first half of the second century.

The internal evidence for the shorter ending (2) is decidedly against its being genuine.[6] Besides containing a high percentage of non-Markan words, its rhetorical tone differs totally from the simple style of Mark's Gospel.

Finally it should be observed that the external evidence for the shorter ending (2) resolves itself into additional testimony supporting the omission of verses 9-20. No one who had available as the conclusion of the Second Gospel the twelve verses 9-20, so rich in interesting material, would have deliberately replaced them with a few lines of a colorless and generalized summary. Therefore, the documentary evidence supporting (2) should be added to that supporting (1). Thus, on the basis of good external evidence and strong internal considerations it appears that the earliest ascertainable form of the Gospel of Mark ended with 16.8.[7] At the same time, however, out of deference to the evident antiquity of the longer ending and its importance in the textual tradition of the Gospel, the Committee decided to include verses 9-20 as part of the text, but to enclose them

---

[6] For a full discussion of the Greek and Latin evidence for the endings of Mark, with a more favorable estimate of the originality of the shorter ending, see the article by Aland in the Festschrift for Matthew Black, referred to in footnote 1 of p. 102 above.

[7] Three possibilities are open: (*a*) the evangelist intended to close his Gospel at this place; or (*b*) the Gospel was never finished; or, as seems most probable, (*c*) the Gospel accidentally lost its last leaf before it was multiplied by transcription.

within double square brackets in order to indicate that they are the work of an author other than the evangelist.[8]

SHORTER ENDING

For a discussion of the shorter ending, see the section (2) in the comments on verses 9-20 above. The reading Ἰησοῦς is to be preferred to the others, which are natural expansions. It is probable that from the beginning the shorter ending was provided with a concluding ἀμήν, and that its absence from several witnesses (L cop^boms eth^most mss) is due either to transcriptional oversight or, more probably, to the feeling that ἀμήν is inappropriate when verses 9-20 follow.

VARIANT READINGS WITHIN [MARK] 16.9-20

Since the passage 16.9-20 is lacking in the earlier and better manuscripts that normally serve to identify types of text, it is not always easy to make decisions among alternative readings. In any case it will be understood that the several levels of certainty ({A}, {B}, {C}) are within the framework of the initial decision relating to verses 9 to 20 as a whole.

16.14-15 ἐπίστευσαν. καὶ εἶπεν αὐτοῖς {A}

For the addition preserved in W, see section (4) in the comments on verses 9-20 above.

---

[8] For a discussion of W. R. Farmer's *The Last Twelve Verses of Mark* (Cambridge, 1974) and of J. Hug's *La Finale de l'Évangile de Marc* (Paris, 1978), see Metzger, *The Text of the New Testament*, 3rd ed. (Oxford, 1992), pp. 296 f.

16.17 λαλήσουσιν καιναῖς {B}

Although it is possible that καιναῖς may have been added in imitation of καινὴ διαθήκη and καινὸς ἄνθρωπος, it is more probable that it dropped out of several witnesses through homoeoteleuton with the following καὶ ἐν ταῖς [i. e. κἄν ταῖς].

16.18 [καὶ ἐν ταῖς χερσὶν] ὄφεις {C}

Although it is possible that the expression καὶ ἐν ταῖς χερσίν was added in imitation of the account in Ac 28.3-6, a majority of the Committee preferred to follow the Alexandrian group of witnesses. At the same time, in view of the absence of any good reason to account for the omission of the words from such witnesses as A D[supp] W Θ Π f[13] 28 700 it[c, dsupp, l, o, q] vg syr[p, pal] al, it was thought appropriate to enclose them within square brackets.

16.19 κύριος Ἰησοῦς {C}

Among the several titles applied to Jesus by the Church, the use of κύριος standing alone appears to be a later development, more solemn than κύριος Ἰησοῦς.

16.20 σημείων. {B}

On the addition of ἀμήν in most witnesses, see the comment on Mt 28.20.

THE GOSPEL ACCORDING TO LUKE

1.3 *κἀμοί*

Several copyists, dissatisfied that Luke makes no explicit mention of inspiration in connection with his writing the Gospel, added the words "it seemed good to me *and to the Holy Spirit* ... to write an orderly account" (it[b, q] vg[3 mss] goth). The supplement comes from Ac 15.28 ("it seemed good to the Holy Spirit and to us").

1.28 *σοῦ* {A}

Although many witnesses (including A C D Θ and most minuscules, followed by the Textus Receptus) read after *σοῦ* the words *εὐλογημένη σὺ ἐν γυναιξίν,* it is probable that copyists inserted them here from ver. 42, where they are firmly attested. If the clause had been original in the present verse, there is no adequate reason why it should have been omitted from a wide diversity of early witnesses (including ℵ B L W Ψ *f*[1] 565 700 1241 syr[pal] cop[sa, bo] arm geo *al*).

1.35 *γεννώμενον* {A}

The words *ἐκ σοῦ* are apparently an early addition prompted by a desire for greater symmetry after the two preceding instances of the second person pronoun. The expanded reading gained wide currency in the early church through Tatian's Diatessaron. The reading ܒܟܝ (literally "in thee"), for which Dionysius Barsalibi (died A.D. 1171) argues vigorously in his commentary on Luke,[1] is read by the earliest manuscripts of the Peshitta (the Curetonian and Sinaitic Syriac manuscripts are not extant here) and is adopted as the text in Pusey and Gwilliam's critical edition.

---

[1] See Tj. Baarda, "Dionysios bar Ṣalībī and the Text of Luke 1.35," *Vigiliae Christianae,* XVII (1963), pp. 225–229.

1.46 Μαριάμ {A}

Who is represented as the speaker of the Magnificat? According to the overwhelming preponderance of evidence, comprising all Greek witnesses and almost all versional and patristic witnesses, it was spoken by Mary. On the other hand, according to half a dozen witnesses, chiefly Latin, it was spoken by Elizabeth. These latter witnesses are three Old Latin manuscripts (namely ms. a of the fourth century *[Elisabet]*, ms. b of the fifth century *[Elisabel]*, and ms. l* of the seventh or eighth century *[Elisabeth]*), and three patristic writers (Irenaeus in his *Against Heresies* IV.vii.1 according to the Armenian translation and certain manuscripts of the Latin translation [but in III.x.1 all manuscripts read Mary]; Niceta, bishop of Remesiana in Dacia [Yugoslavia]; and Jerome's translation of Origen's remark that some [Greek?] manuscripts of Luke read Elizabeth instead of Mary).

How shall this evidence be interpreted?[2] There are three possibilities: (1) The original text read simply Καὶ εἶπεν, Μεγαλύνει ..., and some copyists supplied Mary, and others Elizabeth. (2) The name Elizabeth was present originally, but, because of doctrinal considerations related to the veneration of the Virgin, most copyists changed it to Mary. (3) The name Mary was present originally, but several copyists, assuming that the Magnificat was included in the subject of ἐπλήσθη πνεύματος ἁγίου (ver. 41), and noticing the use of αὐτῇ in ver. 56, changed Mary to Elizabeth.

Although sympathetic to the supposition that perhaps neither name was present in the original text, the Committee was impressed by the overwhelming weight of external evidence, as well as by the balance of internal probabilities, and therefore preferred to read Μαριάμ as the subject of εἶπεν.

1.66 χεὶρ κυρίου ἦν {A}

Not noticing that the last clause of the verse is an observation made by the evangelist (such occasional remarks are characteristic of

---

[2] For a bibliographical survey of the chief arguments, see R. Laurentin in *Biblica*, XXXVIII (1957), pp. 15–23.

Luke; cf. 2.50; 3.15; 7.39; 16.14; 20.20; 23.12), several Western witnesses (D it[d, ff2, l, q, 26] syr[s]) omit ἦν, thus bringing the clause within the question of those who had heard about Zechariah ("What then will this child be, for the hand of the Lord is with him?").

1.74 ἐκ χειρὸς ἐχθρῶν {B}

The addition of ἡμῶν is a natural expansion, particularly in view of ἐξ ἐχθρῶν ἡμῶν in ver. 71. The readings with τῶν or πάντων are obviously secondary.

1.78 ἐπισκέψεται {B}

The future tense ἐπισκέψεται, supported by a variety of early witnesses, was probably altered to the aorist in conformity with ver. 68, thus beginning and closing the canticle with ἐπεσκέψατο.

2.9 καί (1) {B}

On the one hand, the reading καὶ ἰδού is in harmony with the solemn style of Luke in chaps. 1 and 2 (where ἰδού occurs ten times). On the other hand, however, it is difficult to imagine why, if ἰδού were present originally, copyists would have omitted it. The Committee preferred the shorter reading, attested as it is by a variety of good authorities.

2.11 Χριστὸς κύριος {A}

The combination Χριστὸς κύριος, which occurs nowhere else in the New Testament,[1] seems to have been quite deliberately used by Luke instead of the much more frequent Χριστὸς κυρίου. It was to be expected that copyists, struck by the unusual collocation, should have introduced various modifications, none of which has significant external attestation.

---

[1] The combination occurs by error (instead of Χριστὸς κυρίου) in the Septuagint translation of Lm 4.20 and in Ps Sol 17.32.

2.14 ἐν ἀνθρώποις εὐδοκίας {A}

The difference between the AV, "Glory to God in the highest, and on earth peace, good will toward men," and the RSV,

"Glory to God in the highest,
      and on earth peace among men with whom he is pleased!"
is not merely a matter of exegesis of the meaning of the Greek, but is first of all one of text criticism. Does the Angelic Hymn close with εὐδοκία or εὐδοκίας?

The genitive case, which is the more difficult reading, is supported by the oldest representatives of the Alexandrian and the Western groups of witnesses. The rise of the nominative reading can be explained either as an amelioration of the sense or as a palaeographical oversight (at the end of a line εὐδοκίας would differ from εὐδοκία only by the presence of the smallest possible lunar sigma, little more than a point, for which it might have been taken – thus ΕΥΔΟΚΙΑᶜ).

The meaning seems to be, not that divine peace can be bestowed only where human good will is already present, but that at the birth of the Saviour God's peace rests on those whom he has chosen in accord with his good pleasure.[2] Prior to the discovery of the Dead Sea Scrolls it was sometimes argued that "men of [God's] good pleasure" is an unusual, if not impossible, expression in Hebrew. Now, however, that equivalent expressions have turned up in Hebrew[3] in several Qumran Hymns ("the sons of his [God's] good pleasure," 1 QH iv.32 f.; xi.9; and "the elect of his [God's] good pleasure," viii.6), it can be regarded as a genuinely Semitic construction in a section of Luke (chaps. 1 and 2) characterized by Semitizing constructions.

2.33 ὁ πατὴρ αὐτοῦ καὶ ἡ μήτηρ {B}

In order to safeguard the doctrine of the virgin birth of Jesus, ὁ πατήρ was replaced by Ἰωσήφ in a variety of witnesses, some of

---

[2] It should be noted that the Sahidic version employs the possessive pronoun, "And peace upon earth among men of his desire [pleasure]."

[3] According to J. A. Fitzmyer, S.J. (*Theological Studies,* XIX [1958], pp. 225-227) the expression "among men of [his] good pleasure" has been found also in an Aramaic fragment from Qumran.

them ancient (Old Latin, Gothic, and the Diatessaron). Other witnesses added αὐτοῦ after μήτηρ, either for stylistic balance with ὁ
πατὴρ αὐτοῦ (as ℵ* L 157 *al*), or by transfer when ὁ πατήρ was
replaced by Ἰωσήφ. Besides a number of singular readings, Ἰωσὴφ
ὁ πατὴρ αὐτοῦ καὶ ἡ μήτηρ αὐτοῦ (157 eth) is an obvious conflation.

2.38 Ἱερουσαλήμ {A}

The reading Ἱερουσαλήμ best explains the rise of the other
readings: the insertion of ἐν relieves the grammatical ambiguity, and
the substitution of Ἰσραήλ enhances the theological implications of
the passage.

2.41 οἱ γονεῖς αὐτοῦ

In the interest of safeguarding the doctrine of the virgin birth a few
copyists and translators replaced οἱ γονεῖς αὐτοῦ with the proper
names ὅ τε Ἰωσὴφ καὶ ἡ Μαριάμ (1012 it[a, b, l] [it[c, ff2] add *mater eius*]
Diatessaron[l, t]). (See also the comments on verses 33 and 43.)

2.43 οἱ γονεῖς

As in verses 33 and 41, in order to safeguard the doctrine of the
virgin birth copyists replaced οἱ γονεῖς (ℵ B D L Θ 1 13 33 157 1241
al) with Ἰωσὴφ καὶ ἡ μητήρ (A C X Γ Δ Λ Π Ψ 28 543 565 892
1071 1424).

3.1 τετρααρχοῦντος *(ter)*

See the comment on Ac 13.1.

3.19 τετραάρχης

See the comment on Ac 13.1.

3.22 Σὺ εἶ ὁ υἱός μου ὁ ἀγαπητός, ἐν σοὶ εὐδόκησα {B}

The Western reading, "This day I have begotten thee," which
was widely current during the first three centuries, appears to be

secondary, derived from Ps 2.7. The use of the third person ("This is … in whom …") in a few witnesses is an obvious assimilation to the Matthean form of the saying (Mt 3.17).

3.32 Σαλά {B}

The original reading appears to be Σαλά (𝔓⁴ ℵ* B syrˢ· ᵖᵃˡ copˢᵃ· ᵇᵒᵐˢˢ eth), which copyists later assimilated to Σαλμών, the reading of both the Matthean parallel (Mt 1.4-5) and the Septuagint of 1 Chr 2.11, or to Σαλμάν, the reading of ms. B at Ru 4.20 f. (Σαλμών, ms. A). In view of the early tradition that Luke was a Syrian of Antioch it is perhaps significant that the form Σαλά appears to embody a Syriac tradition (the Peshitta version of Ru 4.20 f. reads ܐܠܣ).

3.33 τοῦ Ἀμιναδάβ τοῦ Ἀδμὶν τοῦ Ἀρνί {C}

Faced with a bewildering variety of readings, the Committee adopted what seems to be the least unsatisfactory form of text, a reading that was current in the Alexandrian church at an early period.[1]

4.4 ἄνθρωπος {B}

The shortest reading, which has good and early support, must be original; the longer forms of text have been assimilated by copyists to the Matthean parallel (Mt 4.4) or to the Septuagint of Dt 8.3, either verbatim or according to the general sense. If any of the longer forms of text had been original, its omission from ℵ B L W 1241 syrˢ copˢᵃ· ᵇᵒ would be unaccountable.

---

[1] Although the reading τοῦ Ἀμιναδάβ τοῦ Ἀράμ is supported by an impressive range of witnesses (A D 33 565 1079 many versions), with a reading that involves three names (such as that adopted by the Committee) Luke's entire genealogy of Jesus falls into an artistically planned pattern, even more elaborate than Matthew's (cf. Mt 1.17); thus, from Adam to Abraham, 3 x 7 generations; from Isaac to David, 2 x 7 generations; from Nathan to Salathiel (pre-exilic), 3 x 7 generations; from Zerubbabel (post-exilic) to Jesus, 3 x 7 generations, making a total of 11 x 7, or 77 generations from Adam to Jesus.

4.5-12

In order to bring Luke's account of the Temptation into harmony with the sequence of temptations in Matthew (4.5-11), several Old Latin witnesses (it[b, c, l, q, r1]), at least one Vulgate manuscript (G), and Ambrose in his Commentary on the Gospel According to Luke,[1] transpose verses 5-8 to follow verses 9-12.

4.17 ἀναπτύξας {B}

Since the synagogal copies of Old Testament books were in scroll form, the use of the verb "to unroll" is highly appropriate. Although copyists may have introduced ἀναπτύξας as a pedantic correlative to πτύξας in ver. 20, it is more probable that, being accustomed to books in codex (or leaf) form, they introduced the frequently used verb ἀνοίγειν, "to open," as an explanatory substitution for ἀναπτύσσειν (which occurs only here in the New Testament).

4.18 με (2) {A}

Following ἀπέσταλκέν με, a number of witnesses continue with the words ἰάσασθαι τοὺς συντετριμμένους τὴν καρδίαν. This is an obvious scribal supplement introduced in order to bring the quotation more completely in accord with the Septuagint text of Is 61.1.

4.44 εἰς τὰς συναγωγὰς τῆς Ἰουδαίας {B}

In view of Luke's earlier reference (in ver. 14) to the beginning of Jesus' Galilean ministry, the reading τῆς Ἰουδαίας ($\mathfrak{P}$[75] ℵ B C L f[1] 892 *Lect* syr[s, h] *al*) is obviously the more difficult, and copyists have corrected it to τῆς Γαλιλαίας in accord with the parallels in Mt 4.23 and Mk 1.39. Another attempt to avoid the difficulty was the substitution of τῶν Ἰουδαίων (W l[18]). As for the variation in prepositions,

---

[1] *Expositio Evangelii secundum Lucan,* ed. by C. Schenkl in *Corpus Scriptorum Ecclesiasticorum Latinorum,* XXXII, pars iv [= iii] (Vienna, 1902), pp. 149–156.

the use here of εἰς is pregnant ("Jesus went *into* and preached *in*") and is to be preferred to the more commonplace ἐν.

5.17 οἳ ἦσαν ἐληλυθότες {B}

The difficulty of the reading supported by the overwhelming mass of witnesses (according to which the enemies of Jesus had come from every village of Galilee, Judea, and Jerusalem) prompted some copyists to omit οἳ altogether (ℵ* 33) and others to replace it with δέ (D it^{d, e} syr^s), so that it is the sick who have come from all parts to be healed.

5.17 αὐτόν {A}

The failure to see that αὐτόν is the subject, not the object, of τὸ ἰᾶσθαι led copyists to replace it with a plural form, as αὐτούς (A C D *al*), πάντας (K Cyril), αὐτοὺς πάντας (syr^{pal}), or τοὺς ἀσθενοῦντας (*l*^{11}).

5.33 οἱ (2) {B}

Copyists who remembered the parallel account in Mk 2.18 transformed the statement into a question.

5.38 βλητέον {B}

The gerundive (the only verbal adjective in -τέος that occurs in the New Testament) was replaced in a few witnesses by βάλλουσιν of the Matthean parallel (9.17), from which also was derived the widespread interpolation καὶ ἀμφότεροι συντηροῦνται (or τηροῦνται).

5.39 *include verse* {A}

The external attestation for the inclusion of the verse is almost overwhelming; its omission from several Western witnesses may be due to the influence of Marcion, who rejected the statement because it seemed to give authority to the Old Testament.

5.39 *[καί]* {C}

The evidence for and against the inclusion of *καί* is so evenly balanced as to call for the use of square brackets.

5.39 *χρηστός* {A}

The comparative degree of the adjective is probably a scribal emendation introduced in order to make the comparison more apparent. Actually, however, the point is that the prejudiced person does not even wish to try what is new (the gospel), being satisfied that the old (the Law) is good.

6.1 *σαββάτῳ* {C}

The word *δευτεροπρῶτος* occurs nowhere else, and appears to be a *vox nulla* that arose accidentally through a transcriptional blunder. Perhaps some copyist introduced *πρώτῳ* as a correlative to *ἐν ἑτέρῳ σαββάτῳ* in ver. 6, and a second copyist, in view of 4.31, wrote *δευτέρῳ*, deleting *πρώτῳ* by using dots over the letters – which was the customary way of cancelling a word. A subsequent transcriber, not noticing the dots, mistakenly combined the two words into one, which he introduced into the text. Alternatively, as Skeat has suggested,[1] by dittography the letters *βατω* were added to *σαββάτῳ*. A later copyist interpreted the *β* as *δευτέρῳ* and the *α* as *πρώτῳ*, and took *τῳ* as an indication that the adjective was to agree with *σαββάτῳ*.

6.4 *καὶ ἔδωκεν τοῖς μετ' αὐτοῦ* {A}

The addition of *καί* after *ἔδωκεν*, which enhances the point of the argument, seems to be secondary, the work of copyists who may or

---

[1] T. C. Skeat in *Novum Testamentum*, xxx (1988), pp. 103–106.

may not have been following the Markan parallel (2.26). No good reason can be found to account for its omission if it had been in the text originally.

6.4 μόνους τοὺς ἱερεῖς; {A}

Codex Bezae transfers ver. 5 after ver. 10, and in its place reads the following: τῇ αὐτῇ ἡμέρᾳ θεασάμενός τινα ἐργαζόμενον τῷ σαββάτῳ εἶπεν αὐτῷ, Ἄνθρωπε, εἰ μὲν οἶδας τί ποιεῖς, μακάριος εἶ· εἰ δὲ μὴ οἶδας, ἐπικατάρατος καὶ παραβάτης εἶ τοῦ νόμου ("On the same day he saw a man working on the sabbath and said to him, 'Man, if you know what you are doing, you are blessed; but if you do not know, you are accursed and a transgressor of the law'"). The scribe (or editor) of D thus makes Luke enumerate three incidents concerning Jesus and the sabbath, and climaxes the series with the pronouncement concerning the sovereignty of the Son of Man over the sabbath.

6.5 κύριός ἐστιν τοῦ σαββάτου ὁ υἱὸς τοῦ ἀνθρώπου {B}

It is rather more probable that copyists inserted καί before τοῦ σαββάτου, thus giving more point to the saying (and assimilating it to the parallel in Mk 2.28), than that καί should have been deleted from early representatives of several text-types. The non-Markan word order is likewise to be preferred.

6.10 εἶπεν {A}

Several groups of witnesses assimilate the account to the Markan parallel (Mk 3.5) by adding ἐν ὀργῇ (or μετ᾽ ὀργῆς), a phrase which, in the opinion of a majority of the Committee, Luke is not likely to have used (from a sense of reverence).

6.16 Ἰσκαριώθ

See the comment on Mt 10.4.

6.31 ποιεῖτε {B}

The shorter reading, supported by a diversity of early witnesses, is preferable to the longer readings, which appear to be, in various ways, scribal assimilations to the wording of the Matthean parallel (Mt 7.12).

6.35 μηδέν {B}

The reading μηδένα ἀπελπίζοντες ("despairing of no one"), which introduces into the context an alien motive, appears to have arisen in transcription, the result of dittography.

6.48 διὰ τὸ καλῶς οἰκοδομῆσθαι αὐτήν {A}

The distinctively Lukan clause assigning the reason for the permanence of the house ("because it had been well built"), which corresponds to the earlier statement concerning the builder's industry ("dug deep, and laid the foundation upon rock"), was supplanted by copyists who preferred the reason given by Matthew ("for it was founded upon the rock," Mt 7.25). The omission of the clause in several witnesses ($\mathfrak{P}^{45\text{vid}}$ 700 syr^s) is the result of accidental oversight occasioned by homoeoteleuton (αὐτὴν ... αὐτήν).

7.7 ἰαθήτω {B}

The more peremptory tone of the imperative ἰαθήτω was softened by scribal assimilation to the Matthean ἰαθήσεται (Mt 8.8).

7.10 δοῦλον {A}

It is difficult to decide whether ἀσθενοῦντα was added, in story-telling fashion, to identify the servant, or whether it was deleted as either superfluous or contradictory with ὑγιαίνοντα. Faced with this balance of considerations, the Committee gave primary consideration to external evidence and adopted the reading supported by $\mathfrak{P}^{75}$ ℵ B L W f^1 700 al.

7.11 ἐν τῷ ἑξῆς {B}

With ἐν τῇ ἑξῆς the reader is to supply ἡμέρᾳ ("on the next day"); with ἐν τῷ ἑξῆς one supplies χρόνῳ ("[soon] afterward"). Elsewhere, however, when Luke writes τῇ ἑξῆς he does not prefix ἐν (Lk 9.37; Ac 21.1; 25.17; 27.18); on the other hand, when χρόνῳ is to be understood, Luke uses ἐν τῷ καθεξῆς (Lk 8.1). On the whole, it is more probable that the less definite expression of time would be altered to the more definite than vice versa. Furthermore, the evidence supporting τῷ ἑξῆς is more weighty than that supporting τῇ ἑξῆς.

7.11 αὐτοῦ {B}

Considerations of transcriptional and intrinsic probabilities seem to suggest the originality of ἱκανοί. The word may have been omitted by copyists either deliberately (the expression οἱ μαθηταὶ αὐτοῦ ἱκανοί is unusual and occurs nowhere else in the New Testament) or accidentally (in view of the following ΚΑΙΟ). Furthermore, the word is a favorite of Luke (it occurs 27 times in Luke-Acts out of a total of 40 occurrences in the New Testament). On the other hand, however, since the external evidence in support of αὐτοῦ without ἱκανοί is excellent in respect of age and diversity of text-type, a majority of the Committee decided to adopt the shorter reading.

7.19 κύριον {C}

Since it is not likely that copyists would have deleted the name Ἰησοῦν, and since κύριος is in accord with Lukan style, the Committee preferred the reading κύριον.

7.28 γυναικῶν Ἰωάννου {B}

The shortest reading, which is also supported by the earliest manuscripts, best accounts for the rise of the other readings. It appears that προφήτης was inserted by pedantic copyists who wished thereby to exclude Christ from the comparison, while others added τοῦ βαπτιστοῦ, assimilating the text to Mt 11.11.

7.32 ἐθρηνήσαμεν {B}

In order to make a better balance of clauses, A Δ Ψ *f*¹ *al*, followed by the Textus Receptus, insert ὑμῖν following ἐθρηνήσαμεν. The shorter text is supported by a wide variety of types of text (ℵ B D L W Θ Ξ *f*¹³ *al*).

7.35 πάντων τῶν τέκνων αὐτῆς {B}

Some witnesses (D L Θ Ψ 28 700 *al*) omit the word πάντων, thus not only conforming the text in this respect to Mt 11.19, but also permitting an easier interpretation. The presence of the word, supported by most other witnesses, is in accord with Luke's fondness for πᾶς (6.17, 30; 9.43; 11.4). As regards the position of πάντων, the Committee preferred to follow the reading of B W *f*¹³ 892 and to explain the origin of the reading of A Δ Ξ and most minuscules as having arisen when the word, having been omitted in order to conform the text in this respect to that of Matthew, was restored at the wrong place. The reading of ℵ* and of manuscripts known to Ambrose is totally conformed to the text of Mt 11.19.

7.39 προφήτης {A}

The insertion of the article before προφήτης (in B* Ξ 205) is an exegetical allusion to "the Prophet" predicted in Dt 18.15; compare Jn 1.21; 6.14; 7.40.

7.45 εἰσῆλθον {A}

Instead of εἰσῆλθον, a few witnesses (L* *f*¹³ 157 1071 *al*) read εἰσῆλθεν ("[from the time] she came in"), which appears to be an attempt to avoid the suggestion of an exaggeration in "[from the time] I came in."

8.3 αὐτοῖς {B}

The plural is supported by good representatives of the Alexandrian and the Western text-types; the singular (compare Mt 27.55; Mk

15.41) appears to be a Christocentric correction, due perhaps to Marcion.

8.26   Γερασηνῶν   {C}

Of the several variant readings, a majority of the Committee preferred Γερασηνῶν on the basis of (a) superior external attestation (early representatives of both the Alexandrian and Western types of text), and (b) the probability that Γαδαρηνῶν is a scribal assimilation to the prevailing text of Matthew (8.28), and that Γεργεσηνῶν is a correction, perhaps proposed originally by Origen (see the comments on Mt 8.28).

8.37   Γερασηνῶν   {C}

See the comment on ver. 26.

8.43   ἥτις [ἰατροῖς προσαναλώσασα ὅλον τὸν βίον]   {C}

The clause ἰατροῖς προσαναλώσασα ὅλον τὸν βίον looks like a digest of Mk 5.26. The question is whether anyone except Luke himself would rewrite Mark in this way – with skillful condensation and the substitution of προσαναλώσασα (a hapax legomenon in the New Testament for δαπανήσασα). On the other hand, the early and diversified evidence for the shorter text (𝔓75 B (D) (itᵈ) syrˢ· ᵖᵃˡᵐˢˢ copˢᵃ arm geo) is well-nigh compelling. As a resolution of these conflicting considerations a majority of the Committee decided to retain the words in the text but to enclose them within square brackets, indicating doubt whether they have a right to stand there.

8.44   ὄπισθεν ἥψατο τοῦ κρασπέδου   {B}

The words τοῦ κρασπέδου constitute one of the so-called minor agreements of Matthew and Luke against Mark. The Committee regarded this as accidental and decided to follow the overwhelming weight of the external evidence supporting the inclusion of the words.

8.45 *Πέτρος* {B}

The addition of "and those with him" may be due to scribal harmonizing with Mark's *καὶ ἔλεγον αὐτῷ οἱ μαθηταὶ αὐτοῦ,* or to
an attempt to have Peter share the blame of rebuking Jesus. In any
case, the weight of the testimony of 𝔓⁷⁵ B syrᶜˑ ˢˑ ᵖᵃˡ copˢᵃ supporting
the shorter reading is too strong to be set aside.

8.45 *καὶ ἀποθλίβουσιν* {B}

Although it may be held that the omission of the clause "And you
say, 'Who touched me?'" was due to stylistic pruning by Alexandrian
copyists, the diversity of wording in the several forms of the addition
makes it probable that they represent scribal efforts at assimilation to
the parallel account in Mk 5.31.

8.49 *μηκέτι* {B}

The Committee preferred to follow the preponderant weight of the
combination of 𝔓⁷⁵ ℵ B D syrʰ ʷⁱᵗʰ * copˢᵃ *al,* which attests the less
frequently used word *μηκέτι* (it occurs nowhere else in Luke).

9.1 *δώδεκα* {B}

Luke apparently took over from Mark (6.7) the primitive appellation *τοὺς δώδεκα,* preserved in early representatives of the Alexandrian and the Western text-types. Later copyists either added or
substituted *μαθητάς* (compare the parallel in Mt 10.1), or added
ἀποστόλους, with or without *αὐτοῦ.*

9.2 *ἰᾶσθαι [τοὺς ἀσθενεῖς]* {C}

Impressed by the concurrence of B and syrᶜˑ ˢ in supporting the
shorter text, the Committee was somewhat inclined to regard the
other forms of text as scribal expansions introduced in order to
relieve the abruptness of the simple verb. At the same time, however,
the evidence of the Old Syriac is weakened by its reading "the infirm"

as the object of "heal" at the close of ver. 1. Likewise, in Luke ἰάομαι, except when passive, always has a direct object. Faced with these conflicting data, the Committee decided that the least unsatisfactory solution was to include the words τοὺς ἀσθενεῖς (supported by ℵ A D L Ξ Ψ *f*¹ *al*) in the text, but to enclose them within square brackets indicating doubt that they have a right to stand there.

9.3   *[ἀνὰ] δύο* {C}

The reading with ἀνά appears to be an elucidation of the meaning implicit in the context (i. e. not simply that the Twelve but that no individual should have two coats); but was this an addition made originally by Luke or by later copyists? Or did Alexandrian scribes, taking for granted that readers would correctly understand the passage, delete ἀνά in accord with the parallels (Mt 10.10; Mk 6.9)? To reflect these alternative possibilities, the Committee decided to include the word in the text but to enclose it within square brackets. (Among the versions only it^d syr^h and goth express the force of ἀνά, but whether the others simply omit to render the word or whether they rest upon a Greek text that lacked it, it is difficult to say. Syr^s reads "and not even two coats.")

9.7   *τετραάρχης*

See the comment on Ac 13.1.

9.10   *εἰς πόλιν καλουμένην Βηθσαϊδά* {B}

Amid the diversity of readings, the Committee preferred to adopt the Alexandrian reading (supported by (𝔓⁷⁵) ℵ¹ B L Ξ* 33 cop) and to explain the other readings as attempts to alleviate difficulties arising from the reference in ver. 12 to "a lonely place." The phrase εἰς τόπον ἔρημον, derived from parallels in Mt 14.13 and Mk 6.32, was either added to the text (A C W Θ Ξ^mg *al*) or substituted for πόλιν (ℵ* Ψ). "Village" replaces "city" in D and Θ, and neither word occurs in Ψ *al*.

9.26 λόγους {A}

See the comment on Mk 8.38.

9.35 ἐκλελεγμένος {B}

The original Lukan reading is undoubtedly ἐκλελεγμένος, which occurs in a quasi-technical sense only here in the New Testament. The other readings, involving more usual expressions, are due to scribal assimilation (ἐκλεκτός, 23.35; ἀγαπητός, Mk 9.7; Lk 3.22; ἀγαπητός, ἐν ᾧ εὐδόκησα, Mt 17.5).

9.47 εἰδώς {C}

Although it is difficult to make a confident decision between εἰδώς ("knowing") and ἰδών ("seeing"), a majority of the Committee preferred the reading attested by both early Alexandrian (א B) and Antiochian (syr^c, s) witnesses. (See also the comment on Mt 9.4.)

9.49 ἐκωλύομεν {B}

Although the reading ἐκωλύομεν might be regarded as having arisen from assimilation to the parallel in Mk 9.38, the Committee preferred it to the reading ἐκωλύσαμεν, being supported, as it seems, by the earliest manuscript (𝔓^75vid) and by other weighty Alexandrian witnesses (א B L Ξ).

9.54 αὐτούς {B}

The reading ὡς καὶ Ἡλίας ἐποίησεν, as well as the longer readings in verses 55 and 56, had fairly wide circulation in parts of the ancient church. The absence of the clauses, however, from such early witnesses as 𝔓^45, 75 א B L Ξ 1241 it^l syr^s cop^sa, bo suggests that they are glosses derived from some extraneous source, written or oral.

9.55-56   αὐτοῖς {A}

The additions to ver. 55 *(καὶ εἶπεν, Οὐκ οἴδατε ποίου πνεύματός ἐστε)* and to ver. 56 *(ὁ γὰρ υἱὸς τοῦ ἀνθρώπου οὐκ ἦλθεν
ψυχὰς ἀνθρώπων ἀπολέσαι ἀλλὰ σῶσαι)* are somewhat less well
attested than the addition to ver. 54 (see the comment on ver. 54). The
addition to ver. 56 echoes Lk 19.10 (cf. Jn 3.17).

9.59   *[Κύριε,]* {C}

The omission of *κύριε* from B* D syr⁵ *al* is puzzling; what motive
would have prompted copyists to delete it? On the other hand, the
word might well have been added, either from ver. 61 or from the
parallel in Mt 8.21. Since, however, the absence of *κύριε* may have
been due to a transcriptional blunder (ειπε κε επιτρεφον), it
was thought safer to retain the word in the text, but to enclose it
within square brackets indicating doubt that it has a right to stand
there.

9.62   *εἶπεν δὲ [πρὸς αὐτὸν]* ὁ Ἰησοῦς {C}

It is difficult to decide which reading best explains the rise of the
others. The phrase *πρὸς αὐτόν* is lacking in 𝔓⁴⁵, ⁷⁵ B 0181 700
cop^(samss); it is placed after ὁ Ἰησοῦς in A C W Θ Ψ *f*¹³ *al*; D reads ὁ
δὲ Ἰησοῦς εἶπεν αὐτῷ; and Δ omits ὁ Ἰησοῦς. The Committee
judged that the least unsatisfactory interpretation of the data was to
adopt the reading supported by ℵ L Ξ *f*¹ 33 157 1241, but out of
deference to the evidence of B and 𝔓⁴⁵, ⁷⁵ to enclose *πρὸς αὐτόν*
within square brackets.

9.62   *ἐπιβαλὼν τὴν χεῖρα ἐπ' ἄροτρον καὶ βλέπων εἰς τὰ
ὀπίσω* {C}

The curious variation in the order of the participles *(εἰς τὰ ὀπίσω
βλέπων καὶ ἐπιβάλλων τὴν χεῖρα αὐτοῦ ἐπ' ἄροτρον)* in several
witnesses (𝔓⁴⁵vid D it^((a), (b), c, d, e, (l), (q)) *al*) is probably due to scribal inad-

vertence; in any case, the reading scarcely makes sense. Although it may be argued that αὐτοῦ was deleted by scribes for stylistic reasons (as not needed with parts of the body), a majority of the Committee was impressed by the weight of the witnesses ($\mathfrak{P}^{75}$ B 0181 f^1 al) that attest to its absence.

10.1   [δύο] (1) {C}

Was it seventy or seventy-two whom Jesus appointed and sent on ahead of him? The external evidence is almost evenly divided. On the one hand, the chief representatives of the Alexandrian and the Western groups, with most of the Old Latin and the Sinaitic Syriac, support the numeral "seventy-two." On the other hand, other Alexandrian witnesses of relatively great weight (‫א‬ L Δ Λ Ξ), as well as other noteworthy evidence (f^1 and f^{13}), join in support of the numeral "seventy."

The factors that bear on the evaluation of internal evidence are singularly elusive. Does the account of the sending of 70 or 72 disciples have a symbolic import, and, if so, which number seems to be better suited to express that symbolism? The answers to this question are almost without number, depending upon what one assumes to be the symbolism intended by Jesus and/or the evangelist and/or those who transmitted the account.[1] In order to represent the balance of external evidence and the indecisiveness of internal considerations, a majority of the Committee decided to include the word δύο in the text, but to enclose it within square brackets to indicate a certain doubt that it has a right to stand there.[2]

---

[1] It is often assumed, for example, that the symbolism is intended to allude to the future proclamation of the gospel to all of the countries of the world. But even in this case there is uncertainty, for in the Hebrew text of Genesis 11 the several nations of earth total seventy, whereas in the Greek Septuagint the enumeration comes to seventy-two.

[2] For a fuller discussion of the external evidence and internal probabilities, as well as a list of about twenty instances from ancient Jewish literature involving either 70 or 72, see the chapter entitled, "Seventy or Seventy-two Disciples?" in Metzger's *Historical and Literary Studies, Pagan, Jewish, and Christian* (Leiden and Grand Rapids, 1968), pp. 67–76.

[The concept of "70" is an established entity in the Septuagint and in Christian tradition. The number of examples of "70" in the Old Testament is overwhelming: there are always 70 souls in the house of Jacob, 70 elders, sons, priests, and 70 years that are mentioned in chronological references to important events. The number 72 appears only once, where, amid many other numbers, 72 cattle are set aside for a sacrificial offering (Nu 31.38). If 72 occurs in the Letter of Aristeas (as the number of translators of the Septuagint) as well as in III Enoch, these sporadic instances are not to be compared in significance with the tradition involving 70.

Consequently it is astonishing that the reading ἑβδομήκοντα δύο occurs at all in 10.1 and 17, and that it has such strong support. A reading that in the Gospels has in its support 𝔓⁷⁵ B D, the Old Syriac, the Old Latin, etc., etc. is ordinarily regarded at once as the original reading. If in addition the opposing reading lies under the suspicion of ecclesiastical "normalizing," the testimony becomes irrefutable. The opposing witnesses represent entirely an ecclesiastical normalizing. That they are in the majority is altogether understandable; if they are ancient, this only proves how early the normalizing process began to operate. For these reasons ἑβδομήκοντα δύο should be printed without square brackets. K.A.]

10.15 καταβήσῃ {C}

It is difficult to decide between the merits of καταβήσῃ and καταβιβασθήσῃ. Did copyists heighten the sense of the saying by replacing the former word with the latter; or did they replace the more rare verb (καταβιβάζεσθαι) with the much more usual verb (καταβαίνειν), thus also assimilating the quotation to the text of the Septuagint? A majority of the Committee, impressed by the superior external testimony of 𝔓⁷⁵ B D *al*, adopted καταβήσῃ. (See also the comment on Mt 11.23.)

10.17 [δύο] {C}

See the comment on ver. 1.

10.21　*[ἐν] τῷ πνεύματι τῷ ἁγίῳ* {C}

The strangeness of the expression "exulted in the Holy Spirit" (for which there is no parallel in the Scriptures) may have led to the omission of *τῷ ἁγίῳ* from 𝔓⁴⁵ A W Δ Ψ *f*¹³ itᑫ goth Clement *al.* The varying positions of *ὁ Ἰησοῦς,* as well as the absence of the words from the earliest witnesses, condemn them as secondary. Since the Septuagint frequently construes *ἀγαλλιᾶσθαι* with a preposition *(ἐν* or *ἐπί),* the Committee decided to retain the *ἐν* but, in view of its absence from such witnesses as 𝔓⁷⁵ A B C W Δ Θ Ψ *f*¹ *f*¹³ 28 565 700 *al,* to enclose it within square brackets.

10.22　*πάντα* {A}

The reading *καὶ στραφεὶς πρὸς τοὺς μαθητὰς εἶπεν* (A C K W X Δ Θ Ψ 28 565 itᶠᶠ², ⁱ, ¹ syrᵖ, ʰ goth *al*) is doubtless secondary, derived from ver. 23 and introduced by copyists in order to smooth the abrupt transition from Jesus' prayer (ver. 21) to his statement to the disciples (ver. 22). Not only is such a mechanical repetition foreign to Luke's style, but one does not turn to the same persons twice (the presence of *κατ' ἰδίαν* in ver. 23 makes no significant difference to the meaning of *στραφείς,* for the prepositional phrase is probably to be taken with *εἶπεν).*

10.32　*[γενόμενος] κατὰ τὸν τόπον ἐλθών*

The participle *γενόμενος,* read by 𝔓⁴⁵ A C D E G H K M S U V W Γ Δ Θ Λ and most minuscules, is absent from 𝔓⁷⁵ ℵᶜ [owing to homoeoteleuton ℵ* omits the entire verse] B L X Ξ 0190 *f*¹ 28 33 700 *al.* The participle *ἐλθών,* read by 𝔓⁷⁵ ℵᶜ B C E G H K M S U V W Γ Δ Θ Λ Ξ and many minuscules, is absent from 𝔓⁴⁵ D Π 63 68 114 243 253 265 270 482 489 726 990 1200 1219 1375 *al.* It is difficult to decide whether the longer text, being redundant, was shortened by copyists, some of whom deleted *γενόμενος* and others *ἐλθών,* or whether the longer text is the result of conflation. In view of the collocation *γενόμενοι κατά* in Ac 27.7, a minority of the Committee preferred the reading *γενόμενος κατά* as a Lukan expression; at the same time, in view of the divided attestation for and against ἐλθών, they preferred to enclose that word within square brackets. The majority of the Committee, however, impressed by what was taken as superior manuscript support, preferred to retain ἐλθών in the text without brackets; and, being reluctant to identify γενέσθαι κατά as a special Lukan collocation, thought it necessary, in view of the weight of the witnesses that omit γενόμενος, to enclose this word within square brackets.

10.38   αὐτόν {B}

No motive is apparent for the deletion of the phrase "[received him] *into her house*" if it were present in the text originally. On the other hand, the bold and bare ὑπεδέξατο αὐτόν seems to call for some appropriate addition, which copyists supplied in various forms, some introducing οἰκίαν, others οἶκον, and each with or without αὐτῆς, ἑαυτῆς, or αὐτοῖς.

10.41-42   μεριμνᾷς καὶ θορυβάζῃ περὶ πολλά, ἑνὸς δέ ἐστιν χρεία {C}

The rare verb θορυβάζεσθαι (𝔓³, ⁴⁵, ⁷⁵ ℵ B C D L W Θ *f*¹ *al*) seems to have given trouble to copyists, who replaced it with the more frequently used verb τυρβάζειν (A K P Δ Π Ψ *f*¹³ *al*). Most of the other variations seem to have arisen from understanding ἑνός to refer merely to the provisions that Martha was then preparing for the meal; the absoluteness of ἑνός was softened by replacing it with ὀλίγων (preserved today only in 38 and several versions); and finally in some witnesses (including 𝔓³ ℵ B L *f*¹ 33) the two were combined, though with disastrous results as to sense. The omission of both clauses (as well as γάρ after Μαριάμ) from itᵃ, ᵇ, ᵉ, ff2, i, l, rl syrˢ (D retains only θορυβάζῃ) probably represents a deliberate excision of an incomprehensible passage, if it is not a sheer accident, perhaps occasioned by homoeoarcton (*Μάρθα … Μαριάμ*).

11.2   λέγετε

After λέγετε codex Bezae continues with an obvious interpolation, derived from Mt 6.7: μὴ βαττολογεῖτε ὡς οἱ λοιποί, δοκοῦσιν γάρ τινες ὅτι ἐν τῇ πολυλογίᾳ αὐτῶν εἰσακουσθήσονται, ἀλλὰ προσευχόμενοι λέγετε.

11.2 πάτερ {A}

In view of the liturgical usage of the Matthean form of the Lord's Prayer, it is remarkable that such a variety of early witnesses managed to resist what must have been an exceedingly strong temptation to assimilate the Lukan text to the much more familiar Matthean form. It is not surprising, therefore, that the great majority of witnesses read Πάτερ ἡμῶν ὁ ἐν τοῖς οὐρανοῖς, as in Mt 6.9.

11.2 ἐλθέτω ἡ βασιλεία σου {A}

The most interesting variant reading in the Lukan form of the Lord's Prayer is the petition, "Thy holy Spirit come upon us and cleanse us," preserved in substantially the same wording in two minuscule manuscripts (ἐλθέτω τὸ πνεῦμα σου τὸ ἅγιον ἐφ' ἡμᾶς καὶ καθαρισάτω ἡμᾶς, ms. 700 of the eleventh century; ms. 162, dated A.D. 1153, agrees except for the sequence σου τὸ πνεῦμα and the omission of ἐφ' ἡμᾶς). That the same reading was current in copies of Luke's Gospel during the fourth and fifth centuries is proved by quotations of the petition in the writings of Gregory of Nyssa in Cappadocia and Maximus-Confessor. The former, in one of his homilies on the Lord's Prayer, declares expressly that, instead of the petition concerning the coming of the kingdom, Luke has ἐλθέτω τὸ ἅγιον πνεῦμα σου ἐφ' ἡμᾶς καὶ καθαρισάτω ἡμᾶς. Gregory's testimony is confirmed by Maximus who, in commenting on Mt 6.10, remarks that what Matthew speaks of as "kingdom," another of the evangelists has called "Holy Spirit." In proof of such equivalence Maximus quotes (perhaps from Gregory) ἐλθέτω σου τὸ πνεῦμα τὸ ἅγιον καὶ καθαρισάτω ἡμᾶς.

The earliest trace of such a petition is preserved by Tertullian who, in commenting rapidly on five of the petitions of the Lord's Prayer in Luke (whether according to his own text, or Marcion's, or both is uncertain), places first after the invocation to the Father a petition for the Holy Spirit, followed by a petition for God's kingdom. An early

Western text (Marcion's and/or Tertullian's) must therefore have had the reading quoted by Gregory (or at least the first part of it), but it must have stood in place of ἀγιασθήτω τὸ ὄνομά σου. Finally, codex Bezae has been thought to preserve a remnant of the petition for the Spirit, for in this manuscript the petition ἀγιασθήτω ὄνομά σου (sic) is followed by ἐφ᾽ ἡμᾶς ἐλθέτω σου ἡ βασιλεία.

How shall this testimony be evaluated? First, it is by no means certain that ἐφ᾽ ἡμᾶς in codex Bezae should be taken as evidence of an earlier petition for the Holy Spirit; to pray that God's name may be hallowed "upon us" is entirely congruent with Old Testament references to causing the divine "name to dwell there" (e. g. Dt 12.11; 14.23; 16.6, 11, where the Septuagint renders "for my name to be invoked there"). Furthermore, the evidence from Tertullian comes from a treatise written during his Montanist period, when he had a special fondness for texts pertaining to the Holy Spirit; in his earlier exposition of the Lord's Prayer he betrays no knowledge of the existence of such a petition.

Apparently, therefore, the variant reading is a liturgical adaptation[1] of the original form of the Lord's Prayer, used perhaps when celebrating the rite of baptism or the laying on of hands. The cleansing descent of the Holy Spirit is so definitely a Christian, ecclesiastical concept that one cannot understand why, if it were original in the prayer, it should have been supplanted in the overwhelming majority of the witnesses by a concept originally much more Jewish in its piety.

11.2   σου· (2) {A}

After σου (2) the great majority of witnesses interpolate γενηθήτω τὸ θέλημά σου, ὡς ἐν οὐρανῷ καὶ ἐπὶ τῆς γῆς from Mt 6.10. If the Lukan text had originally contained these words, no good

---

[1] Compare the similar prayer in the Greek form of the Acts of Thomas, 27, ἐλθὲ τὸ ἅγιον πνεῦμα καὶ καθάρισον τοὺς νεφροὺς αὐτῶν καὶ τὴν καρδίαν αὐτῶν (Bonnet's ed., p. 143, line 2). See also Joël Delobel, "The Lord's Prayer in the Textual Tradition," The New Testament in Early Christianity, ed. by Jean-Marie Sevrin (Louvain, 1989), pp. 293–309.

reason can be suggested that accounts for their absence from such varied witnesses as 𝔓⁷⁵ B L *f*¹ vg syrᶜ, ˢ arm *al.*

11.4 *μὴ εἰσενέγκης ἡμᾶς*

Marcion apparently read *μὴ ἀφῆς ἡμᾶς εἰσενεχθῆναι* ("*Do not allow us to be led* into temptation"), a theological amelioration of the usual form of the petition.

11.4 *πειρασμόν* {A}

A variety of excellent witnesses (𝔓⁷⁵ ℵ*, ᵃ B L *f*¹ 700 vg syrˢ copˢᵃ, ᵇᵒ arm geo *al*) resisted the temptation to conform the text to the prevailing Matthean form of the Lord's Prayer (Mt 6.13).

11.10 *ἀνοιγ[ήσ]εται* {C}

It is difficult to decide between *ἀνοιγήσεται* and *ἀνοίγεται*. On the one hand, the former reading may have arisen as the result of scribal assimilation to the future tense at the end of ver. 9; on the other hand, the latter reading may be the result of assimilation to the present tense of ver. 10. In order to represent the balance of probabilities, a majority of the Committee decided to print *ἀνοιγ[ήσ]εται*.

11.11 *ἰχθύν* {B}

It is difficult to decide (*a*) whether, like the Matthean account (7.9), Luke originally had two pairs of terms (but not the same two pairs as Matthew), and a third pair was incorporated from Matthew (bread and stone); or (*b*) whether Luke originally had three pairs and, through an accident in transcription, one of the pairs was omitted. A majority of the Committee, considering the longer readings to be the result of scribal assimilation to Matthew, preferred the shorter reading, which is attested by 𝔓⁴⁵ (𝔓⁷⁵) B 1241 and several early versional and patristic witnesses.

11.11   καὶ ἀντὶ ἰχθύος {C}

The reading with καί ($\mathfrak{P}$[45, 75] B cop[sa] *al*) preserves a Semitism that most copyists replaced with μή, the usual Greek interrogative particle.

11.12   ἐπιδώσει {C}

It is easy to see why most copyists would have inserted μή, thus alerting the reader that the following words are to be taken as a question.

11.13   [ὁ] ἐξ οὐρανοῦ {C}

In view of the Matthean parallel (7.11) ὁ πατὴρ ὑμῶν ὁ ἐν τοῖς οὐρανοῖς δώσει, it is easy to account for the rise of the variant readings ὑμῶν ὁ ἐξ οὐρανοῦ and ὁ οὐράνιος. It is much more difficult to decide between ἐξ οὐρανοῦ ("the Father will give *from heaven* the Holy Spirit to those who ask him") and ὁ ἐξ οὐρανοῦ, which seems to be a pregnant construction for ὁ ἐν οὐρανῷ ἐξ οὐρανοῦ. So evenly is the external evidence divided and so unconvincing are the arguments based on internal considerations that a majority of the Committee finally decided to include ὁ in the text, but to enclose it within square brackets, indicating doubt that it has a right to stand there.

11.13   πνεῦμα ἄγιον {B}

Not only is the external evidence that supports πνεῦμα ἄγιον excellent, but assimilation with the first half of the verse as well as with Matthew's ἀγαθά (7.11) accounts for the origin of the other readings.

11.14   [καὶ αὐτὸ ἦν] {C}

On the one hand, the expression καὶ αὐτὸ ἦν κωφόν appears to be a Semitism in the Lukan style. On the other hand, the external evidence in support of the shorter reading is exceedingly weighty. In order to reflect these conflicting considerations, the Committee decided to include the words in the text, but to enclose them within square brackets.

11.23 σκορπίζει {A}

The addition of με after σκορπίζει, which is so difficult as to be almost meaningless, must be a scribal blunder.

11.24 [τότε] λέγει {C}

On the basis of external evidence, a majority of the Committee preferred to include τότε, but, in view of the possibility that it may be a scribal assimilation to the parallel in Mt 12.44, decided to enclose the word within square brackets.

11.25 σεσαρωμένον {B}

The original Lukan form of the account is clearly that preserved in 𝔓⁷⁵ ℵ* D Θ 700 most of the Old Latin, the Old Syriac, al. Copyists could not resist introducing from the Matthean parallel (12.44) the word σχολάζοντα before or after σεσαρωμένον, with or without καί.

11.33 [οὐδὲ ὑπὸ τὸν μόδιον] {C}

Since Luke preferred not to use μόδιον in 8.16, a word that is present in the parallel in Mark (and Matthew), it may well be that the word, with its clause, was absent from the original form of the present passage also. On the other hand, since the clause is attested by weighty and diversified external evidence, a majority of the Committee was unwilling to drop it altogether and compromised by enclosing the words within square brackets.

11.42 ταῦτα δὲ ἔδει ποιῆσαι κἀκεῖνα μὴ παρεῖναι {B}

Marcion, finding these words entirely unacceptable, omitted them from his edition of Luke's Gospel; their absence from codex Bezae may be due to scribal oversight, or, more probably, to influence from the Marcionite form of text.

11.48 οἰκοδομεῖτε {C}

Since οἰκοδομεῖν is usually transitive, most scribes added a suitable object, drawn from ver. 47.

12.14 κριτὴν ἢ μεριστήν {B}

The multiplicity of variant readings has arisen from the rarity of μεριστής (which occurs nowhere else in the Greek Bible), from the recollection of Ex 2.14 τίς σε κατέστησεν ἄρχοντα καὶ δικαστήν; (quoted in Acts 7.27 and 35), and from the possibility that the second of the terms was omitted accidentally (through homoeoteleuton) or deliberately (as inappropriate to describe Christ). The reading that best accounts for the rise of the others is preserved in 𝔓⁷⁵ ℵ B L f¹ f¹³ al.

12.21 include verse {A}

The omission of ver. 21 from D it[a, b, d] must be accidental, for the weight of external evidence attesting its inclusion is overwhelming. Furthermore, a careful author such as Luke would not be likely to pass directly from εἶπεν of ver. 20 to εἶπεν of ver. 22 (different speaker).

At the close of the verse several of the later manuscripts include (perhaps from 8.8 or Mt 11.15) the stereotyped expression ταῦτα λέγων ἐφώνει· ὁ ἔχων ὦτα ἀκούειν ἀκουέτω.

12.22 μαθητὰς [αὐτοῦ] {C}

In accordance with Lukan usage, a majority of the Committee preferred to adopt αὐτοῦ, supported as it is by the overwhelming preponderance of external evidence, but to enclose it within square brackets in view of its absence from several important early witnesses (𝔓⁴⁵vid, ⁷⁵ B).

12.27   αὐξάνει· οὐ κοπιᾷ οὐδὲ νήθει {B}

After some hesitation a majority of the Committee rejected the reading of D it[d] syr[c, s] *al, οὔτε νήθει οὔτε ὑφαίνει* ("they neither spin nor weave"), as a stylistic refinement introduced by copyists in view of the following reference to Solomon's clothing. (See also the comment on Mt 6.28.)

12.31   αὐτοῦ {B}

It is more likely that αὐτοῦ was replaced by τοῦ θεοῦ (as has in fact happened in codex Bezae) than vice versa. The reading τοῦ θεοῦ καὶ τὴν δικαιοσύνην αὐτοῦ is an intrusion from the parallel in Mt 6.33. One of the idiosyncrasies of the scribe of 𝔓[75] is his tendency to omit personal pronouns.[1]

12.39   οὐκ {B}

The original Lukan text seems to have lacked ἐγρηγόρησεν ἂν καί. Scribes would have been almost certain to assimilate the shorter reading (preserved in 𝔓[75] ℵ* *al*) to the longer reading found in the parallel passage (Mt 24.43), whereas there is no good reason that would account for the deletion of the words had they been present originally.

12.56   πῶς οὐκ οἴδατε δοκιμάζειν {B}

Although it is possible that copyists inserted οἴδατε in conformity with the preceding clause, it is more probable that they omitted the word in order to heighten Jesus' condemnation ("Why do you not know how to interpret …?" implies a lack of knowledge; "Why do you not interpret …?" implies an unwillingness to use one's knowledge).

---

[1] So Ernest C. Colwell, "Scribal Habits in Early Papyri: A Study in the Corruption of the Text," in *The Bible in Modern Scholarship,* ed. by J. Philip Hyatt (Nashville, 1965), p. 385, who states that the scribe of 𝔓[75] "drops more than a dozen [personal pronouns], and adds one."

13.7 ἔκκοψον [οὖν] {C}

In order to reflect the balance of external evidence for and against the inclusion of οὖν, as well as the absence of any compelling consideration relating to transcriptional and intrinsic probabilities, the Committee felt obliged to retain the word in the text, but to enclose it within square brackets, indicating a measure of doubt that it has a right to stand there.

13.9 εἰς τὸ μέλλον· εἰ δὲ μή γε {B}

The more difficult reading (attested by $\mathfrak{P}^{75}$ ℵ B L *al*), which involves aposiopesis (a sudden breaking off in the middle of a sentence), was ameliorated in most witnesses by transposing so as to read εἰ δὲ μή γε, εἰς τὸ μέλλον.

13.19 εἰς δένδρον {B}

Although copyists may have deleted μέγα to harmonize Luke with the prevailing text of Matthew (13.32), it is much more probable that, in the interests of heightening the contrast between a mustard seed and a tree, μέγα was added – as it was added also in a few witnesses in the Matthean parallel (syr$^{p(1\ msc)}$ cop^{sa} eth geo^B).

13.27 ἐρεῖ λέγων ὑμῖν {C}

The reading adopted by the Committee, though narrowly attested, seems to account best for the origin of the other readings. The awkwardness of the participle λέγων (which probably represents the construction of the Hebrew infinitive absolute: "he will *indeed* say to you") would have prompted copyists either to alter it to the indicative (λέγω) or to omit it as superfluous.

13.27 οὐκ οἶδα [ὑμᾶς] πόθεν ἐστέ {C}

The multiplicity of variant readings of these words in ver. 27 contrasts with the fidelity with which they have been transmitted in ver. 25 (where only Marcion seems to have omitted ὑμᾶς). The reading οὐδέποτε εἶδον ὑμᾶς of D arose because of influence from the Matthean parallel (οὐδέποτε ἔγνων ὑμᾶς, 7.23). The absence of πόθεν ἐστέ in several minuscules (56 61 71 291 692) appears to be the result of scribal oversight arising from homoeoteleuton with the following ἀπόστητε. Since both external evidence and internal probabilities concerning the presence or absence of ὑμᾶς are so evenly balanced, the Committee decided to retain the word in the text, but to enclose it within square brackets.

13.35 ὑμῶν {B}

The Committee judged that the presence of ἔρημος in D N Δ Θ Ψ f[13] al is the result of assimilation to the text of Jr 22.5 or to the prevailing text of Mt 23.38; its absence is strongly supported by 𝔓[45vid, 75] ℵ A B L W f[1] al.

13.35 ἕως [ἥξει ὅτε] εἴπητε {C}

The rarity of construing ὅτε with the subjunctive (Blass-Debrunner-Funk, § 382 (2)), as well as the temptation to assimilate to the Matthean parallel (23.39), seems to have prompted many copyists to omit ἥξει ὅτε, and, in some cases (Θ 1241 al), to prefix ἀπ' ἄρτι (Δ conflates the Matthean and Lukan readings). Apart from the subsidiary problem involving variation in the presence or absence of ἄν after ἕως (with the corresponding change of ἥξει to ἥξῃ in Ψ f[1] 565 700 al), the manuscript basis for the reading "until the time [or, the day] comes when you will say …" includes A D W Ψ f[1] 28 it[a, b, (c), d, ff2, l, q, r1] vg syr[c, s, h with *] Marcion al.

14.5 υἱὸς ἢ βοῦς {B}

The oldest reading preserved in the manuscripts[1] seems to be υἱὸς ἢ βοῦς. Because the collocation of the two words appeared to be

---

[1] It has been conjectured that υἱός is a corruption of the old Greek word ὄϊς ("a sheep"); see John Mill, *Novum Testamentum Graecum*, 2nd ed. (Leipzig, 1723), p. 44, § 423.

somewhat incongruous, copyists altered υἱός either to ὄνος (cf. 13.15) or to πρόβατον (cf. Mt 12.11). Several witnesses (Θ 2174 syrᶜ) conflate all three words.

14.17 ἕτοιμά ἐστιν {C}

In view of the expression πάντα ἕτοιμα in the Matthean parallel (Mt 22.4), it is natural that many copyists should have added πάντα, either after ἐστίν or before ἕτοιμα. As between ἐστίν and εἰσίν, the preponderant weight of witnesses supports the former.

14.27

Through homoeoteleuton the entire verse has been accidentally omitted in M* R Γ 29 47 57 60 69 71 213 245 482 544 659 692 1279 1574 syrˢ copᵇᵒᵐˢ *.

15.1 πάντες {A}

The absence of πάντες (a word that Luke is fond of using; see the comment on 7.35) from several witnesses (W itᵃᵘʳ, ᵇ, ᶜ, ˡ, q syrˢ, ᶜ, ᵖ copˢᵃᵐˢˢ), if not an accident, may be the decision of scribes who were unhappy with the hyperbole.

15.16 χορτασθῆναι ἐκ {B}

On the basis of age and diversity of text-type of witnesses, the Committee preferred the reading χορτασθῆναι ἐκ.

15.21 υἱός σου {A}

While recognizing that several good manuscripts (ℵ B D 700 *al*) combine to support the reading ποίησόν με ὡς ἕνα τῶν μισθίων σου, the Committee thought it far more probable that the words were added (from ver. 19) by punctilious scribes than omitted, either accidentally or deliberately.

16.12 ὑμέτερον {A}

The reading ἡμέτερον (B L *al*) has the appearance of being a later theological refinement (= "belonging to the Father and the Son"), expressing the divine origin of the true riches (ver. 11) – as is also expressed by the Marcionite reading ἐμόν. It is more likely, however, that, owing to the constant scribal confusion between υ and η (in later Greek the two vowels came to be pronounced alike), copyists who wrote ἡμέτερον intended ὑμέτερον – for in the context the correct antithesis to "another's" is "yours."

16.19 πλούσιος

It was probably *horror vacui* that prompted more than one copyist to provide a name for the anonymous Rich Man. In Egypt the tradition that his name was Nineveh is incorporated in the Sahidic version, and seems to be reflected also in 𝔓⁷⁵, which reads πλούσιος ὀνό-ματι Νευης (probably a scribal error for Νινευης). During the third and fourth centuries a tradition was current in the West that the Rich Man's name was Phineas. The pseudo-Cyprianic treatise *De pascha computus,* which was written in the year 242/3 in Africa or in Rome, declares (ch. 17): *Omnibus peccatoribus a deo ignis est praeparatus, in cuius flamma uri ille Finaeus dives ab ipso dei filio est demonstratus* ("Fire has been prepared by God for all sinners, in the flame of which, as was indicated by the Son of God himself, that rich man Phineas is burned"). The same tradition is repeated toward the close of the fourth century in the last of the eleven anonymous treatises that are customarily assigned to Priscillian, a wealthy, highly educated layman who became the founder of a gnosticizing sect in southern Spain. Here the name is spelled Finees (in the only manuscript extant of *Tract* ix the name is spelled *Fineet* with the *t* stroked out and surmounted by *s*). The reason that the name Phineas was given to the Rich Man may be because in the Old Testament (Nu 25.7, 11) Eleazar [compare Lazarus] and Phinehas are associated. A note in the margin of a thirteenth century manuscript of the poem "Aurora," a versified Bible written in the twelfth century by Peter of Riga, states *Amonofis dicitur esse nomen divitis* ("The name of the Rich Man is said to be Amonofis [i. e. Amenophis]").[1]

16.21   τῶν πιπτόντων {B}

The more picturesque expression τῶν ψιχίων ("the crumbs") was introduced by copyists from Mt 15.27.

16.21   πλουσίου {A}

The presence of καὶ οὐδεὶς ἐδίδου αὐτῷ in a few witnesses (*f*[13] 1071 it[1] vg[cl] *al*) is a scribal expansion derived from 15.16.

16.23   καὶ ἐν τῷ ᾅδῃ {A}

Several witnesses, chiefly Western (ℵ* lat Marcion), lack καί and join the prepositional phrase with ἐτάφη in ver. 22. Considering the weight of the evidence supporting καί, as well as the style of Luke who generally avoids asyndeton, the presence of καί before ἐν seems to be assured.

17.3   ἁμάρτῃ {A}

In order to harmonize with ver. 4 (cf. a similar passage at Mt 18.15), the phrase εἰς σέ was introduced in several witnesses. Here the shorter text is strongly supported by ℵ A B L W Θ *f*[1] 892 *al*.

17.9   διαταχθέντα {B}

There is no adequate reason that could account for the omission of αὐτῷ or οὐ δοκῶ, if either had been present originally; whereas the retort οὐ δοκῶ has the appearance of being a marginal comment that found its way into the Western text, and more than one scribe would have been likely to attach αὐτῷ to τὰ διαταχθέντα, which seems to cry out for such a complement.

---

[1] So M. R. James, *Journal of Theological Studies,* IV (1902–03), p. 243.

17.23 ἰδοὺ ἐκεῖ, [ἤ,] ἰδοὺ ὧδε {C}

The great variety of readings has arisen partly from the circumstance that in later Greek ει, η, and ι came to be pronounced alike,
thus facilitating alteration of the text, and partly from confusion
arising from inattention on the part of copyists. Furthermore, recollection of the Markan sequence (ὧδε … ἐκεῖ, 13.21) may also
have exerted an influence on copyists. The Committee preferred the
reading attested by 𝔓⁷⁵ and B as the earliest reading preserved in the
extant witnesses, but in view of the absence of ἤ from such varied
witnesses as Dᵍʳ K W X Π 28 33 700 892 itᵇ, ff2, i, rl, s vg syrᶜ, ˢ, ᵖ, ʰ ʷⁱᵗʰ *,
it was thought appropriate to enclose the word within square
brackets.

17.24 ὁ υἱὸς τοῦ ἀνθρώπου [ἐν τῇ ἡμέρᾳ αὐτοῦ] {C}

Although copyists may have inadvertently omitted the phrase ἐν
τῇ ἡμέρᾳ αὐτοῦ because of homoeoteleuton (-που … -του), the
Committee was impressed by the combination of evidence for the
shorter text in the best representatives of the Alexandrian and the
Western types of text (𝔓⁷⁵ B D itᵃ, ᵇ, ᵈ, ᵉ, ⁱ). The readings with
παρουσία, a word that occurs nowhere else in the Gospel according
to Luke, are the result of scribal assimilation to the parallel passage in
Mt 24.27.

17.33 ἐὰν ζητήσῃ τὴν ψυχὴν αὐτοῦ περιποιήσασθαι {B}

The verb περιποιεῖσθαι, which occurs only here in the Gospels,
was altered by some copyists to the much more familiar word σώζειν
(compare 9.24), and by other copyists (in the Western tradition) to
ζωογονεῖν, which occurs elsewhere in the Gospels only in the
second half of this verse.

17.36 *omit verse* {A}

Although it is possible that ver. 36, δύο ἐν ἀγρῷ· εἷς παρα-
λημφθήσεται καὶ ὁ ἕτερος ἀφεθήσεται, may have been acci-

dentally omitted through homoeoteleuton (an accident that happened to ver. 35 in ℵ* and a few other witnesses), in view of the weighty manuscript authority supporting the shorter text ($\mathfrak{P}^{75}$ ℵ A B L W Δ Θ Ψ f^1 28 33 565) it is more probable that copyists assimilated the passage to Mt 24.40.

18.11   πρὸς ἑαυτὸν ταῦτα {C}

External evidence ($\mathfrak{P}^{75}$ B Θ Ψ f^1 892 Origen) favors the reading ταῦτα πρὸς ἑαυτόν, but internally the more difficult sequence seems to be πρὸς ἑαυτὸν ταῦτα. The latter was ameliorated to read καθ᾽ ἑαυτὸν ταῦτα (D it^d geo²), "[standing] by himself..." Because of the difficulty of construing πρὸς ἑαυτόν (especially when the words stood next to σταθείς),[1] several witnesses (ℵ* l^{1761} it$^{b, c, ff2, i, l, q, r1}$ cop$^{sa, ach}$ eth geo¹ Diatessaron$^{n, t}$) omit the phrase entirely.

18.24   αὐτὸν ὁ Ἰησοῦς [περίλυπον γενόμενον] εἶπεν {C}

On the one hand, the excellent attestation for the shorter text (ℵ B L f^1 1241 al) and the variety of positions of περίλυπον γενόμενον suggest that the words were introduced by copyists, perhaps from ver. 23 (περίλυπος ἐγενήθη). On the other hand, since Luke's penchant of repeating a word or phrase in adjacent passages[2] may have operated here, a majority of the Committee did not feel at liberty to omit the phrase entirely, but enclosed it within square brackets.

18.25   κάμηλον {A}

See the comment on Mt 19.24.

---

[1] According to C. C. Torrey, *Our Translated Gospels,* p. 79, and M. Black, *Aramaic Approach,* 3rd ed., p. 103, the words πρὸς ἑαυτόν immediately after σταθείς are to be understood as the Aramaic ethic dative, meaning, "The Pharisee, taking his stand, prayed...."

[2] See H. J. Cadbury, "Four Features of Lucan Style," *Studies in Luke-Acts,* ed. by Leander E. Keck and J. Louis Martyn (New York, 1966), pp. 87–102.

19.15 *τί διεπραγματεύσαντο* {B}

The reading *τίς τί διεπραγματεύσατο* (A K Θ Π 063 *f*¹ *f*¹³ most minuscules, followed by the Textus Receptus [AV "how much every man had gained by trading"]) seems to be the result of scribal efforts to make the narrative more precise. The reading of W Δ *al,* involving the simple form of the verb *(ἐπραγματεύσατο),* comes from ver. 13.

19.25 *include verse* {A}

Although it could be argued that ver. 25 was a marginal comment subsequently inserted by copyists into the text (but in that case the subject of *εἶπαν* would probably not have been left ambiguous – are they the bystanders of ver. 24, or those to whom Jesus was telling the parable?), a majority of the Committee considered it to be more probable that the words were omitted in several Western witnesses (D W 565 it^{b, d, e, ff2} syr^{c, s} cop^{bo} *al*) either (*a*) by assimilation to the Matthean parallel (25.28-29) or (*b*) for stylistic reasons, thereby providing a closer connection between verses 24 and 26. A majority of the Committee considered that, on balance, both external attestation and transcriptional probabilities favor the retention of the words in the text.

19.38 *ὁ ἐρχόμενος ὁ βασιλεύς* {C}

The transmission of the Lukan form of salutation is complex. The majority of witnesses (ℵ^c A K L Δ Ψ *f*¹ *f*¹³ *al*) read *ὁ ἐρχόμενος βασιλεύς* ("Blessed be *he who comes as king* in the name of the Lord"). Others (W 1216 *al*) omit *ὁ βασιλεύς,* thus bringing the quotation into harmony with its Old Testament original (Ps 118.26) as well as with the Synoptic parallels (Mt 21.9; Mk 11.10). The omission of *ὁ ἐρχόμενος* (ℵ* Origen *al*) is probably to be accounted for as a transcriptional oversight, occasioned by homoeoteleuton *(-μενος … -μενος).* The Western text (D it^{a, c, d, ff2, i, r1, s}), perhaps under the influence of Mk 11.10 and Jn 12.13, repeats *εὐλογημένος* and transposes *ὁ βασιλεύς* so as to read quite smoothly *εὐλογημένος ὁ ἐρχόμενος ἐν ὀνόματι κυρίου, εὐλογημένος ὁ βασιλεύς.* The reading ὁ ἐρχόμενος ὁ βασιλεύς (B arm^(mss)), being the most diffi-cult, accounts best for the origin of the others.

19.42 ἐν τῇ ἡμέρᾳ ταύτῃ καὶ σύ {B}

The insertion of καί γε before ἐν τῇ ἡμέρᾳ gives the phrase a special force, which the Committee regarded as probably a secondary development (elsewhere in the New Testament καί γε occurs only at Ac 2.18 in a quotation). The reading καὶ σὺ ἐν τῇ ἡμέρᾳ ταύτῃ (D Θ al) seems to be a colloquial adaptation of ἐν τῇ ἡμέρᾳ ταύτῃ καὶ σύ (ℵ B L 892 Origen).

19.42 εἰρήνην {B}

It seemed to the Committee more likely that copyists would have inserted σου (or σοι) than deleted it.

20.9 ἄνθρωπός [τις] ἐφύτευσεν ἀμπελῶνα {C}

Of the four variant readings, those of C (ἀμπελῶνα ἄνθρωπος ἐφύτευσεν) and D (ἀμπελῶνα ἐφύτευσεν ἄνθρωπος) agree in placing first the noun that describes the setting of the parable (agreeing in this respect with the chief readings of the Markan parallel, 12.1). The only difference between the other two Lukan readings, which are supported by the overwhelming weight of the ex-ternal testimony, is the presence or absence of τις. On the one hand, Luke commonly writes ἄνθρωπός τις (10.30; 12.16; 14.16; 15.11; 16.1, 19; 19.12); on the other hand, many of the same witnesses that insert τις here also insert τις in the clearly secondary reading in Mark (W Θ f^13 syr^p arm geo^2). In order to reflect the conflict between these two considerations, the Committee decided to print τις enclosed within square brackets.

20.27 οἱ [ἀντι]λέγοντες {C}

On the one hand, the external attestation for the reading οἱ λέγοντες is very strong, including, as it does, good representatives of the Alexandrian and the Western types of text. On the other hand, however, this reading may have arisen from scribal assimilation to the Matthean parallel (22.23); it is, furthermore, the easier reading, for it avoids the double negative involved in ἀντιλέγοντες ... μή. On the basis, therefore, of transcriptional probabilities the Committee preferred ἀντιλέγοντες, but out of deference to the very much superior external attestation supporting λέγοντες, it was thought best to enclose ἀντι within square brackets. The reading οἵτινες λέγουσιν is an obvious scribal correction for the pendant nominative participle.

20.34 τούτου {A}

Following τούτου, several Western witnesses (D with some support from Old Latin and Old Syriac) insert a characteristic expansion, γεννῶνται καὶ γεννῶσιν ("[those of this age] are begotten and beget").

20.36 δύνανται {B}

Instead of saying flatly, "they cannot die anymore," several witnesses (chiefly Western) soften the statement by using μέλλουσιν ("they will not die anymore").

20.45 τοῖς μαθηταῖς [αὐτοῦ] {C}

The general tendency seems to have been to drop αὐτοῦ after readers had come to regard οἱ μαθηταί as needing no identifying possessive pronoun; in the present instance, however, what on this basis appears to be the later reading is supported by the weighty combination of B and D. In order to reflect these conflicting considerations the Committee decided to include αὐτοῦ in the text, but to enclose it within square brackets.

21.4 δῶρα {B}

The words τοῦ θεοῦ seem to be a scribal explanation appended to δῶρα for the benefit of Gentile readers who had never seen the γαζοφυλάκιον (ver. 1) in the Temple at Jerusalem.

21.11 καὶ ἀπ' οὐρανοῦ σημεῖα μεγάλα ἔσται {C}

Amid the variety of readings that have very little internal probability to commend one above another, the Committee was content to follow the text of B, the order of which may have provoked copyists to rearrange the words in other sequences.

21.19 κτήσασθε {C}

The aorist imperative, which is attested by ℵ D K L W X Δ Ψ *f*¹ *al,* seems to be slightly preferable, for copyists would have perhaps been likely to conform it to the future tense, used several times in the preceding context.

21.35 ὡς παγίς· ἐπεισελεύσεται γάρ {B}

Does ὡς παγίς belong at the close of the preceding clause, or at the beginning of the following clause? The former alternative appears to be preferable in view of (*a*) the strong combination of Alexandrian and Western evidence (ℵ B D Old Latin) in support of the sequence of γάρ following the verb, and (*b*) the greater likelihood that copyists, recollecting Is 24.17, would have transposed γάρ so as to attach ὡς παγίς with what follows, than vice versa.

21.38 αὐτοῦ. {A}

After αὐτοῦ eight manuscripts that belong to family 13 (namely, 13, 69, 124, 346, 543, 788, 826, 983) add the account of the woman taken in adultery (Jn 7.53–8.11). The insertion was no doubt suggested by the parallel between the situation implied in Jn 8.1-2 and that described here. (See also the comments on Jn 7.53–8.11.)

22.16 ὅτι οὐ μὴ φάγω {B}

It appears that copyists inserted οὐκέτι in order to alleviate an otherwise abrupt saying (cf. the preferred text of Mk 14.25). If the word were present originally, there is no satisfactory explanation to account for its absence from 𝔓⁷⁵ᵛⁱᵈ ℵ A B L Θ *f*¹ itᵃ copˢᵃ, ᵇᵒ *al.*

22.17-20 {B}

The Lukan account of the Last Supper has been transmitted in two principal forms: (1) the longer, or traditional, text of cup-bread-cup is read by all Greek manuscripts except D and by most of the ancient versions and Fathers; (2) the shorter, or Western, text (read by D it[a, d, ff2, i, l]) omits verses 19b and 20 (τὸ ὑπὲρ ὑμῶν ... ἐκχυννόμενον), thereby presenting the sequence of cup-bread.[1] Four intermediate forms of text, which appear to be compromises between the two principal forms, are the following: (*a*) two Old Latin manuscripts (it[b, e]) modify the shorter text by placing ver. 19a before ver. 17, thus securing the customary order of bread-cup; (*b*) the Curetonian Syriac reads the same, but is enlarged with the wording of 1 Cor 11.24 added to ver. 19a; (*c*) the Sinaitic Syriac is still further expanded, chiefly by the insertion of "after they had supped" at the beginning of ver. 17 and "this is my blood, the new covenant" (ver. 20b) between verses 17 and 18; and (*d*) the Peshitta Syriac lacks (perhaps due to homoeoteleuton) verses 17 and 18, as do also *l*[32], two Sahidic manuscripts, and one Bohairic manuscript. For convenience of comparison the six forms of the text are set forth in parallel columns on p. 149.

It is obvious that the chief problem is concerned with the merits of the two principal forms of text, since each of the others can be accounted for more or less satisfactorily as modifications of either the shorter or the longer form.

Considerations in favor of the originality of the longer text include the following: (*a*) The external evidence supporting the shorter reading represents only part of the Western type of text, whereas the other representatives of the Western text join with witnesses belonging to all the other ancient text-types in support of the longer reading. (*b*) It is easier to suppose that the Bezan editor, puzzled by the sequence of cup-bread-cup, eliminated the second mention of the cup without being concerned about the inverted order of institution thus produced, than that the editor of the longer version, to rectify the inverted order, brought in from Paul the second mention of the cup, while letting the first mention stand. (*c*) The rise of the shorter version can be accounted for in terms of the theory of *disciplina arcana*, i. e. in order

---

[1] The same sequence also occurs in the *Didache*, ix, 2–3; cf. also 1 Cor 10.16.

Majority Text	D it^{a.d.ff2.i.l}	it^{b.e}	syr^c	syr^s	syr^p
17. καὶ δεξάμενος τὸ ποτήριον εὐχαριστήσας εἶπεν, Λάβετε τοῦτο καὶ διαμερίσατε εἰς ἑαυτούς.	17. καὶ δεξάμενος τὸ ποτήριον εὐχαριστήσας εἶπεν, Λάβετε τοῦτο, διαμερίσατε ἑαυτοῖς.	19. καὶ λαβὼν ἄρτον εὐχαριστήσας ἔκλασεν καὶ ἔδωκεν αὐτοῖς λέγων, Τοῦτό ἐστιν τὸ σῶμά μου.	19. καὶ λαβὼν ἄρτον εὐχαριστήσας ἔκλασεν καὶ ἔδωκεν αὐτοῖς καὶ ἔλεγεν, Τοῦτο ἐστιν τὸ σῶμά μου τὸ ὑπὲρ ὑμῶν· τοῦτο ποιεῖτε εἰς τὴν ἐμὴν ἀνάμνησιν.	19. καὶ λαβὼν ἄρτον ἔκλασεν καὶ ἔδωκεν αὐτοῖς καὶ ἔλεγεν, Τοῦτό ἐστιν τὸ σῶμά μου τὸ ὑπὲρ ὑμῶν διδόμενον· τοῦτο ποιεῖτε εἰς τὴν ἐμὴν ἀνάμνησιν.	19. καὶ λαβὼν ἄρτον εὐχαριστήσας ἔκλασεν καὶ ἔδωκεν αὐτοῖς καὶ ἔλεγεν, Τοῦτό ἐστιν τὸ σῶμά μου τὸ ὑπὲρ ὑμῶν διδόμενον· τοῦτο ποιεῖτε εἰς τὴν ἐμὴν ἀνάμνησιν.
18. λέγω γὰρ ὑμῖν, [ὅτι] οὐ μὴ πίω ἀπὸ τοῦ γενήματος τῆς ἀμπέλου ἕως οὗ ἔλθη ἡ βασιλεία τοῦ θεοῦ ἔλθη.	18. λέγω γὰρ ὑμῖν, ἀπὸ τοῦ νῦν οὐ μὴ πίω ἀπὸ τοῦ γενήματος τῆς ἀμπέλου ἕως οὗ ἔλθη ἡ βασιλεία τοῦ θεοῦ.	17. καὶ δεξάμενος τὸ ποτήριον εὐχαρι- στήσας εἶπεν, Λάβετε (τοῦτο, om. e) διαμε- ρίσατε εἰς ἑαυτούς.	17. καὶ δεξάμενος τὸ ποτήριον εὐχαρι- στήσας εἶπεν, Λάβετε τοῦτο, διαμερίσατε εἰς ἑαυτούς.	20ᵃ. καὶ μετὰ τὸ δειπνῆσαι,	20. καὶ ὡσαύτως καὶ τὸ ποτήριον μετὰ τὸ δειπνῆσαι, λέγων, Τοῦτο τὸ ποτήριον ἡ καινὴ διαθήκη ἐν τῷ αἵματί μου τὸ ὑπὲρ ὑμῶν ἐκχυννόμενον.
19. καὶ λαβὼν ἄρτον εὐχαριστήσας ἔκλα- σεν καὶ ἔδωκεν αὐτοῖς λέγων, Τοῦτό ἐστιν τὸ σῶμά μου τὸ ὑπὲρ ὑμῶν διδόμενον· τοῦτο ποιεῖτε εἰς τὴν ἐμὴν ἀνάμνησιν.	19. καὶ λαβὼν ἄρτον εὐχαριστήσας ἔκλα- σεν καὶ ἔδωκεν αὐτοῖς λέγων, Τοῦτό ἐστιν τὸ σῶμά μου.	18. λέγω γὰρ ὑμῖν (ὅτι, om. e) ἀπὸ τοῦ νῦν οὐ μὴ πίω ἀπὸ τοῦ γενήματος (+ τούτου b) τῆς ἀμπέλου (+ ταύτης b) ἕως οὗ ἔλθη ἡ βασι- λεία τοῦ θεοῦ.	18. λέγω ὑμῖν ὅτι ἀπὸ τοῦ νῦν οὐ μὴ πίω ἀπὸ τοῦ γενήματος τούτου τῆς ἀμπέλου ἕως οὗ ἔλθη ἡ βασι- λεία τοῦ θεοῦ.	17. δεξάμενος τὸ ποτήριον εὐχαριστήσας εἶπεν, Λάβετε τοῦτο, διαμερίσατε εἰς ἑαυ- τούς·	20. καὶ ὡσαύτως καὶ τὸ ποτήριον μετὰ τὸ δειπνῆσαι, λέγων, Τοῦτο τὸ ποτήριον ἡ καινὴ διαθήκη ἐν τῷ αἵματί μου τὸ ὑπὲρ ὑμῶν ἐκχυννόμενον.
20. καὶ τὸ ποτήριον ὡσαύτως μετὰ τὸ δειπ- νῆσαι, λέγων, Τοῦτο τὸ ποτήριον ἡ καινὴ δια- θήκη ἐν τῷ αἵματί μου, τὸ ὑπὲρ ὑμῶν ἐκχυν- νόμενον.				20ᵇ. τοῦτό ἐστιν τὸ αἷμά μου ἡ διαθήκη ἡ καινή.	
				18. λέγω γὰρ ὑμῖν ὅτι ἀπὸ τοῦ νῦν οὐ μὴ πίω ἀπὸ τοῦ γενήματος τούτου ἕως οὗ ἔλθη ἡ βασιλεία τοῦ θεοῦ.	

Table of six forms of the text of Lk 22.17-20, reproduced (with a few minor modifications) from the chapter, "The Textual Data," by Sir Frederick G. Kenyon and S. C. E. Legg, in *The Ministry and the Sacraments*, ed. by Roderic Dunkerley (London, 1937), pp. 284 f. By "Majority Text" at the head of the first column is meant the consensus of 𝔓^75 ℵ A B C K L T^vid W X Δ Θ Π Ψ 063 f¹ f¹³ apparently all minuscules it^{c.q.r1} vg syr^pal cop^{sa.bo} arm geo. It will be understood that the Greek form given to the versions is in some details uncertain.

to protect the Eucharist from profanation, one or more copies of the Gospel according to Luke, prepared for circulation among non-Christian readers, omitted the sacramental formula after the beginning words.

Considerations in favor of the originality of the shorter text include the following: (*a*) Generally in New Testament textual criticism the shorter reading is to be preferred. (*b*) Since the words in verses 19b and 20 are suspiciously similar to Paul's words in 1 Cor 11.24b-25, it appears that the latter passage was the source of their interpolation into the longer text. (*c*) Verses 19b-20 contain several linguistic features that are non-Lukan.

The weight of these considerations was estimated differently by different members of the Committee. A minority preferred the shorter text as a Western non-interpolation (see the Note following 24.53). The majority, on the other hand, impressed by the overwhelming preponderance of external evidence supporting the longer form, explained the origin of the shorter form as due to some scribal accident or misunderstanding.[2] The similarity between verses 19b-20 and 1 Cor 11.24b-25 arises from the familiarity of the evangelist with the liturgical practice among Pauline churches, a circumstance that accounts also for the presence of non-Lukan expressions in verses 19b-20.

22.31 Σίμων (1) {B}

The Textus Receptus, following a considerable number of witnesses, inserts εἶπεν δὲ ὁ κύριος as if to mark the beginning of a new

---

[2] Kenyon and Legg, who prefer the longer form of text, explain the origin of the other readings as follows: "The whole difficulty arose, in our opinion, from a misunderstanding of the longer version. The first cup given to the disciples to divide among themselves should be taken in connection with the previous verse (ver. 16) as referring to the eating of the Passover with them at the reunion in Heaven. This is followed by the institution of the Sacrament, to be repeated continually on earth in memory of Him. This gives an intelligible meaning to the whole, while at the same time it is easy to see that it would occasion difficulties of interpretation, which would give rise to the attempts at revision that appear in various forms of the shorter version" (Sir Frederick G. Kenyon and S. C. E. Legg in *The Ministry and the Sacraments*, ed. by Roderic Dunkerley [London, 1937], pp. 285 f.).

subject. On the strength of $\mathfrak{P}^{75}$ B L T 1241 syr^s *al,* the Committee preferred the shorter text, considering that it would have been natural for an identifying phrase to be added whenever the reading of the Scripture lesson was begun at this point.

22.43-44 ⟦*omit verses*⟧ {A}

The absence of these verses in such ancient and widely diversified witnesses as $\mathfrak{P}^{(69\text{vid}),\ 75}$ ℵ^a A B T W syr^s cop$^{sa,\ bo}$ arm^{mss} geo Marcion Clement Origen *al,* as well as their being marked with asterisks or obeli (signifying spuriousness) in other witnesses (Δ^c Π^c 892$^{c\ mg}$ 1079 1195 1216 cop^{bomss}) and their transferral to Matthew's Gospel (after 26.39) by family 13 and several lectionaries (the latter also transfer ver. 45a), strongly suggests that they are no part of the original text of Luke. Their presence in many manuscripts, some ancient, as well as their citation by Justin, Irenaeus, Hippolytus, Eusebius, and many other Fathers, is proof of the antiquity of the account. On grounds of transcriptional probability it is less likely that the verses were deleted in several different areas of the church by those who felt that the account of Jesus being overwhelmed with human weakness was in-compatible with his sharing the divine omnipotence of the Father, than that they were added from an early source, oral or written, of extra-canonical traditions concerning the life and passion of Jesus. Nevertheless, while acknowledging that the passage is a later addi-tion to the text, in view of its evident antiquity and its importance in the textual tradition, a majority of the Committee decided to retain the words in the text but to enclose them within double square brackets.

22.62 *include verse* {A}

Although it is possible that the verse has come into the Lukan text from the parallel passage in Mt 26.75, a majority of the Committee regarded it as more probable that the words were accidentally omitted from several witnesses (0171^{vid} it$^{a,\ b,\ e,\ ff2,\ i,\ l^*,\ r1}$) than added without sub-stantial variation (only ὁ Πέτρος is added in several witnesses after ἔξω) in all other witnesses.

22.68   ἀποκριθῆτε {B}

While it might be argued that the words μοι ἢ ἀπολύσητε have
fallen out accidentally owing to homoeoteleuton (-ητε ... -ητε) in
the ancestor(s) of 𝔓⁷⁵ ℵ B L T 1241 *al,* such an explanation cannot
account for the absence of the words ἢ ἀπολύσητε from Θ *f*¹ 1365
al. The Committee therefore was inclined to regard both μοι and ἢ
ἀπολύσητε as early glosses.

23.2   ἡμῶν

According to Epiphanius (*c. Marc.* 316) after διαστρέφοντα τὸ
ἔθνος ἡμῶν Marcion added καὶ καταλύοντα τὸν νόμον καὶ τοὺς
προφήτας ("and abolishing the law and the prophets," compare
Mt 5.17), an interpolation that has survived in seven Old Latin
manuscripts (it^{b, c, e, ff2, i, l, q}) as well as in several manuscripts of the
Vulgate. (See also the comment on ver. 5.)

23.5   ὧδε

According to Epiphanius (*c. Marc.* 316) after ὧδε Marcion added
καὶ ἀποστρέφοντα τὰς γυναῖκας καὶ τὰ τέκνα, a reading that is
preserved in expanded form in two Old Latin manuscripts: codex
Colbertinus (it^c) reads *et filios nostros et uxores avertit a nobis, non
enim baptizatur sicut nos* ("and he alienates our sons and wives from
us, for he is not baptized as we are"); codex Palatinus (it^e) has the
same down to *nobis,* and continues *non enim baptizantur sicut et nos,
nec se mundant* ("for they are not baptized as also we are, nor do they
purify themselves"). (See also the comment on ver. 2.)

23.11   [καὶ] ὁ Ἡρῴδης {C}

On the basis of the age of 𝔓⁷⁵ and the difficulty of understanding
the force of καί in the context, the reading καὶ ὁ Ἡρῴδης appears to
be preferred. At the same time, because of the combination of B D^{gr} Θ
and most of the Old Latin in support of the reading ὁ Ἡρῴδης, a

majority of the Committee thought it right to place καί within square brackets.

23.15   ἀνέπεμψεν γὰρ αὐτὸν πρὸς ἡμᾶς {A}

In the transmission of this clause copyists became hopelessly confused, producing statements either utterly banal, as ἀνέπεμψα γὰρ ὑμᾶς πρὸς αὐτόν (A D W X Δ Ψ *f*¹, followed by the Textus Receptus), or totally nonsensical, as ἀνέπεμψα γὰρ αὐτὸν [= Herod!] πρὸς ὑμᾶς (71 248 788 *al*). The best attested reading (𝔓⁷⁵ ℵ B K L T Θ *al*) is also the most appropriate in the context.

23.17   *omit verse* {A}

The secondary character of the verse is disclosed not only by its omission from such early witnesses as 𝔓⁷⁵ A B L T 070 892* 1241 itᵃ copˢᵃ *al,* but also by its insertion, in slightly different forms, either here or after ver. 19 (where codex Bezae agrees in wording with the reading of Θ Ψ). Although homoeoarcton (ANAΓKHN … ANEKPAΓON) might account for the omission in one family of witnesses, such a theory is unable to explain its widespread omission and its presence at two different places. The verse is a gloss, apparently based on Mt 27.15 and Mk 15.6.

23.23   αὐτῶν {B}

The Committee judged that the omission of the words καὶ τῶν ἀρχιερέων by homoeoteleuton was less likely than their addition by copyists who wished to specify more particularly the identity of those who called for the crucifixion of Jesus.

23.32   σὺν αὐτῷ

Codex Rehdigeranus (itˡ) gives the names of the two robbers as *Ioathas et Maggatras* ("Joathas and Maggatras"). The fragmentary codex Usserianus (itʳ¹) reads … *et Capnatas* ("… and Capnatas"). (See also the comments on Mt 27.38 and Mk 15.27.)

23.34 *omit verse* **34a** ⟦ὁ δὲ Ἰησοῦς ἔλεγεν, Πάτερ, ἄφες αὐτοῖς, οὐ γὰρ οἴδασιν τί ποιοῦσιν.⟧ {A}

The absence of these words from such early and diverse witnesses as 𝔓[75] B D* W Θ it[a, d] syr[s] cop[sa, bomss] *al* is most impressive and can scarcely be explained as a deliberate excision by copyists who, considering the fall of Jerusalem to be proof that God had not forgiven the Jews, could not allow it to appear that the prayer of Jesus had remained unanswered. At the same time, the logion, though probably not a part of the original Gospel of Luke, bears self-evident tokens of its dominical origin, and was retained, within double square brackets, in its traditional place where it had been incorporated by unknown copyists relatively early in the transmission of the Third Gospel.

23.38 ἐπ᾽ αὐτῷ {A}

The mention here of the three languages in which the inscription on the cross was written is almost certainly a gloss, probably taken from the text of Jn 19.20. Every consideration weighs against it: (*a*) it is absent from several of the earliest and best witnesses (𝔓[75] B C* it[a] syr[c, s] cop[sa, bo] *al*); (*b*) the authorities that insert the words differ among themselves (as to the order of the languages, as to the introductory word, γεγραμμένη or ἐπιγεγραμμένη, and as to the order of participle and ἐπ᾽ αὐτῷ); and (*c*) there is no satisfactory explanation for the omission of the statement, if it were originally present in the text. See also the comment on Jn 19.20.

23.42 εἰς τὴν βασιλείαν {B}

Although the reading of 𝔓[75] B L *al* has, from one point of view, the appearance of being a scribal correction (εἰς being considered more appropriate than ἐν with ἔλθῃς), a majority of the Committee preferred it as more consonant with Lukan theology (compare 24.26) than either of the other readings. The reading of most witnesses, ὅταν ἔλθῃς ἐν τῇ βασιλείᾳ σου ("when you come in your kingly power"), and still more the reading of codex Bezae, ἐν τῇ ἡμέρᾳ τῆς ἐλεύσεώς σου ("in the day of your [second] coming"), reflect a developed interest in the eschatological kingdom.

23.43 αὐτῷ

Pious fancy was especially active concerning the story of the penitent robber. In order to make certain that the reader may know to which of the two robbers the words of Jesus were addressed, codex Bezae inserts after αὐτῷ the words τῷ επλησοντι [which is to be corrected to ἐπιπλήσσοντι] ("said to him *who reproved*"). The same manuscript continues by substituting Θάρσει ("Have courage!") for Ἀμήν σοι λέγω. Codex Colbertinus (it^c) has the homiletic insertion of *credis* before *amen* (probably to be understood as a question, "*Do you believe*? Truly I say to you ..."). Instead of ἐν τῷ παραδείσῳ the Curetonian Syriac and the Arabic Diatessaron have "in the Garden of Eden." The Curetonian Syriac rearranges the order of words, joining σήμερον, not with μετ' ἐμοῦ ἔσῃ, but with Ἀμήν σοι λέγω ("Truly I say to you today that with me you will be ...").

23.45 τοῦ ἡλίου ἐκλιπόντος {B}

The words καὶ ἐσκοτίσθη ὁ ἥλιος ("the sun was darkened") appear to be the easier reading, substituted by copyists for τοῦ ἡλίου ἐκλιπόντος [or ἐκλείποντος], which may mean either "the sun's light failed" or "the sun was eclipsed."

23.48 ὑπέστρεφον

In order to heighten the account, several witnesses include various interpolations. After τὰ στήθη codex Bezae adds καὶ τὰ μέτωπα ("beating their breasts *and their foreheads*"). The Old Syriac (syr^{c, s}) reads, "All they who *happened to be there and* saw that which came to pass were beating on their breasts and saying, '*Woe to us! What has befallen us? Woe to us for our sins!*'" One manuscript of the Old Latin (it^g) adds at the close of the verse, *dicentes vae vobis* (to be corrected to *nobis*) *quae facta sunt hodie propter peccata nostra; adpropinquavit enim desolatio Hierusalem* ("saying, 'Woe to us on account of our sins that we have committed this day! For the desolation of Jerusalem has drawn near'").

Similar references to grief expressed at the death of Jesus are quoted in Ephraem's Commentary on the Diatessaron (xx,28 of the Armenian version, ed. Leloir), "Woe was it, woe was it to us; this was the Son of God" ... "Behold, they have come, the judgments of the desolation of Jerusalem have arrived!" Cf. also the apocryphal Gospel of Peter, § 7 (25), ἤρξαντο κόπτεσθαι καὶ λέγειν, Οὐαὶ ταῖς ἁμαρτίαις ἡμῶν· ἤγγισεν ἡ κρίσις καὶ τὸ τέλος Ἱερουσαλήμ ("They began to lament and to say, 'Woe unto our sins; the judgment and the end of Jerusalem has drawn near'").

23.53 κείμενος

Several witnesses (including U 13 69 124 348 1043 1194 1355 1689) add from the parallels in Mt 27.60 and Mk 15.46 the statement καὶ προσεκύλισεν λίθον μέγαν ἐπὶ τὴν θύραν τοῦ μνημείου. Furthermore, codex Bezae expands the text with a characteristic interpolation: καὶ θέντος αὐτοῦ ἐπέθηκεν τῷ μνημείῳ λίθον ὃν μόγις εἴκοσι ἐκύλιον ("and after he had been laid [there] he [Joseph of Arimathea] placed over the tomb a stone which twenty men could scarcely roll"). The same or a similar expansion is found in it^c (et cum positus esset in monumento, posuerunt lapidem quem vix viginti volvebant) and in the Sahidic version ("and when they had put him, they set a stone against the mouth of the sepulchre; this which hardly will twenty men be able to roll").

24.1-2 ἀρώματα. εὗρον δέ

Between verses 1 and 2 codex Bezae, joined by 0124 it^c and cop^sa, expands the narrative with an interpolation partly derived from the parallel account in Mark (16.3): ἐλογίζοντο δὲ ἐν ἑαυταῖς, Τίς ἄρα ἀποκυλίσει τὸν λίθον. ἐλθοῦσαι δὲ εὗρον ... ("And they [the women] were pondering in themselves, 'Who will roll away the stone.' And when they had come they found ...").

24.3 τοῦ κυρίου Ἰησοῦ {B}

A minority of the Committee preferred the shortest reading, supported by D it^a, b, d, e, ff2, l, r1 (see the Note on Western non-interpolations following 24.53). The majority, on the other hand, impressed by the weight of 𝔓⁷⁵ ℵ A B C W Θ f¹ f¹³ 33 565 700 *al*, regarded the reading of D as influenced by ver. 23, and the omission of κυρίου in a few witnesses as due to assimilation to Mt 27.58 or Mk 15.43. The expression "the Lord Jesus" is used of the risen Lord in Ac 1.21; 4.33; 8.16.

24.6 οὐκ ἔστιν ὧδε, ἀλλὰ ἠγέρθη {B}

A minority of the Committee preferred to follow the evidence of D it^(a, b, d, e, ff2, l, rl) geo^B and to omit the words οὐκ ἔστιν ὧδε, ἀλλὰ ἠγέρθη as an interpolation (see the Note following 24.53), derived from Mt 28.6 and/or Mk 16.6, and cast into antithetic form (… ἀλλά …). The majority of the Committee, on the other hand, interpreted the antithesis as evidence of independence of the Lukan formulation from that of Matthew and Mark (which lack ἀλλά). In any case, the reading of C* *al* is obviously a scribal assimilation to the Synoptic parallels.

24.9 ἀπὸ τοῦ μνημείου

A majority of the Committee, considering the absence of the words ἀπὸ τοῦ μνημείου from D it^(a, b, c, d, e, ff2, l, rl) arm geo to be due to an accident in transcription, was impressed by the overwhelming external attestation, beginning with 𝔓⁷⁵, that supports the inclusion of the words in the text.

24.10 ἦσαν δέ {B}

The omission of ἦσαν δέ (A D W it^(d, e) syr^(c, s, h with *) *al*) seems to be an attempt to improve the syntax. The reading ἦν δέ, preserved in K Π Ψ f¹ *al*, singles out Mary Magdalene for special mention.

24.12 *include verse* {B}

Although ver. 12 is sometimes thought to be an interpolation (see the Note following 24.53) derived from Jn 20.3, 5, 6, 10, a majority

of the Committee regarded the passage as a natural antecedent to
ver. 24, and was inclined to explain the similarity with the verses in
John as due to the likelihood that both evangelists had drawn upon a
common tradition.

24.13 ἑξήκοντα {B}

The variant reading ἑκατὸν ἑξήκοντα (ℵ K* Θ Π syr^pal arm)
seems to have arisen in connection with patristic identification of
Emmaus with 'Amwâs (mod. Nicopolis), about twenty-two Roman
miles (176 stadia) from Jerusalem (thus Eusebius, Jerome, Sozomen,
though they do not mention the distance). This, however, is too far for
the travelers to have re-traversed that same evening (ver. 33). The
"seven" of it^e is undoubtedly due to a scribal blunder.

24.17 καὶ ἐστάθησαν {B}

On the strength of a variety of evidence, some of it early (𝔓^75 ℵ A*
B 0124 579 it^e cop^sa, bo syr^pal), the Committee preferred ἐσταθήσα-
μεν rather than ἐστε, which is supported by most other witnesses.
According to this reading, the question ends with περιπατοῦντες,
and the two travelers stand still for a moment in silence, displeased on
being interrupted in their conversation by a stranger; then the silence
is broken by the reply of Cleopas.

24.18 Κλεοπᾶς

A gloss in the margin of codex S (which dates from A.D. 949)
states ὁ μετὰ τοῦ Κλεωπᾶ πορευόμενος Σίμων ἦν, οὐχ ὁ Πέτρος,
ἀλλ' ὁ ἕτερος ("The one journeying with Cleopas was Simon, not
Peter but the other [Simon]"). Codex V (which dates from the ninth
century) has the marginal note: ὁ μετὰ Κλεοπᾶ Ναθαναὴλ ἦν, ὡς
ἐν Παναρίοις ὁ μέγας ἔφη Ἐπιφάνιος. Κλεοπᾶς ἀνέψιος ἦν τοῦ
σωτῆρος, δεύτερος ἐπίσκοπος Ἱεροσολύμων ("The one with
Cleopas was Nathanael, as the great Epiphanius says in his *Panarion*
[xxiii.6]. Cleopas was a cousin of the Saviour, the second bishop of
Jerusalem").

24.19 Ναζαρηνοῦ {B}

It is probable that scribes replaced the less frequently used word Ναζαρηνός (six times in the New Testament, including one other time in Luke [nowhere in Acts]) by the more frequently used Ναζωραῖος (thirteen times in the New Testament, including eight times in Luke and Acts).

24.32 ἡμῶν καιομένη ἦν

The word καιομένη seems to have given trouble to copyists. The reading of D^gr ἦν ἡμῶν κεκαλυμμένη ("Was not our heart veiled ...?") may have been derived from 2 Cor 3.14-16. The early versions offer a wide variety of readings: among the Old Latin manuscripts *excaecatum* (it^c) and *optusum* (it^l) seem to imply πεπηρωμένη or πεπωρωμένη ("blinded" or "hardened"); less obvious as to its origin is the reading of it^e *exterminatum* ("destroyed"), though this may be a scribal blunder for *exterritum* ("terrified").

The Old Syriac (Sinaitic and Curetonian) manuscripts and the Peshitta version read "Was not our heart *heavy* ...?"[1] as do also the Armenian version, the Arabic and Persian Harmonies, and one manuscript of the Sahidic version; this reading seems to imply βραδεῖα in Greek, probably from ver. 25, ὦ ἀνόητοι καὶ βραδεῖς τῇ καρδίᾳ τοῦ πιστεύειν.... The other Sahidic manuscripts read, "Is not then our heart *being covered* for us ...?"

"Burning," which is attested by the overwhelming preponderance of witnesses, best suits the context.

24.32 [ἐν ἡμῖν] ὡς ἐλάλει ἡμῖν {C}

Although 𝔓^75 B D geo Origen unite in support of the shorter reading, the Committee was reluctant to omit the words ἐν ἡμῖν entirely, in view of the possibility that copyists may have deleted them as superfluous in the context. It was thought best, therefore, to retain

---

[1] In Syriac the difference between the words for "heavy" and "burning" is only the position of a dot; the former is spelled ܝܩܝܪ and the latter ܝܩܝܕ.

them in the text, but enclosed within square brackets indicating doubt that they have a right to stand there.

24.36 καὶ λέγει αὐτοῖς, Εἰρήνη ὑμῖν {B}

The words ἐγώ εἰμι, μὴ φοβεῖσθε, either before εἰρήνη ὑμῖν (as in W 579) or after (as in G P it^c vg syr^{p, h, pal} cop^{bomss} arm eth geo Diatessaron^{a, i, n}), are undoubtedly a gloss, derived perhaps from Jn 6.20. The Committee was less sure concerning the origin of the words καὶ λέγει αὐτοῖς, Εἰρήνη ὑμῖν, which, as the regular form of Semitic greeting, might well be expected on this occasion. When the passage is compared with Jn 20.19 ff. the question arises: have the two evangelists depended upon a common tradition, or have copyists expanded Luke's account by adding the salutation from John's account? A majority of the Committee, impressed by the presence of numerous points of contact between Luke and John in their Passion and Easter accounts, preferred to follow the preponderance of external attestation and to retain the words in the text. (See also the Note on Western non-interpolations, following 24.53.)

24.37 πνεῦμα

Instead of πνεῦμα, which is read by the overwhelming majority of witnesses, Codex Bezae reads φάντασμα ("they thought they saw *a ghost*"), a reading which, according to Tertullian, was in Marcion's New Testament.

24.40 *include verse* {B}

Was ver. 40 omitted by certain Western witnesses (D it^{a, b, d, e, ff2, l, rl} syr^{c, s}) because it seemed superfluous after ver. 39? Or is it a gloss introduced by copyists in all other witnesses from Jn 20.20, with a necessary adaptation (the passage in John refers to Jesus' hands and side; this passage refers to his hands and feet)? A minority of the Committee preferred to omit the verse as an interpolation (see the Note following 24.53); the majority, however, was of the opinion that, had the passage been interpolated from the Johannine account, copyists would probably have left some trace of its origin by retaining τὴν πλευράν in place of τοὺς πόδας (either here only, or in ver. 39 also).

24.42 μέρος {B}

The words καὶ ἀπὸ μελισσίου κηρίου (or κήριον) ("and from a honeycomb") in many of the later manuscripts (followed by the Textus Receptus) are an obvious interpolation, for it is not likely that they would have fallen out of so many of the best representatives of the earlier text-types. Since in parts of the ancient church honey was used in the celebration of the Eucharist and in the baptismal liturgy, copyists may have added the reference here in order to provide scriptural sanction for liturgical practice.

24.47 εἰς (1) {B}

On internal grounds it is difficult to decide between the two readings, for both are in accord with Lukan usage (e. g. Lk 3.3 βάπτισμα μετανοίας εἰς ἄφεσιν, and Ac 5.31 δοῦναι μετάνοιαν τῷ Ἰσραὴλ καὶ ἄφεσιν ἁμαρτιῶν). On the basis of (a) what was taken to be slightly superior external attestation, and (b) the probability that, in view of the following εἰς, copyists would have been more likely to alter the first εἰς to καί, rather than vice versa, a majority of the Committee preferred the reading εἰς.

24.47 ἀρξάμενοι {B}

The reading that best accounts for the origin of the others seems to be the *nominativus pendens,* ἀρξάμενοι, supported by ℵ B C* L X 33 *al.* In attempting to improve the syntax, some copyists preferred the accusative absolute, ἀρξάμενον (𝔓⁷⁵ A C³ K W Δ* f¹ f¹³ *al.*), and others the genitive absolute, ἀρξαμένων (with ὑμῶν understood; D Δ² *al.*). The nominative singular, ἀρξάμενος (Θ Ψ 565 1071 *al.*), probably arose through assimilation to εἶπεν (ver. 46).

24.49 καὶ [ἰδοὺ] ἐγώ {C}

On the one hand, the agreement of 𝔓[75] and D, along with ℵ L 33 it[a, b, c, d, e, ff2, l, r1] vg syr[s, p] cop[sa, bo], provides strong support for the shorter text. Likewise there is no reason why the solemn emphatic wording καὶ ἰδοὺ ἐγώ, which seems especially suitable for the last words of Jesus, should have been altered by copyists. On the other hand, however, the Committee, being impressed by the weight of the attestation supporting the reading καὶ ἰδοὺ ἐγώ, preferred to retain the word ἰδού, but to enclose it within square brackets, indicating doubt that it belongs in the text.

24.51 καὶ ἀνεφέρετο εἰς τὸν οὐρανόν {B}

Here ℵ* and geo[1] join D and it[a, b, d, e, ff2, j, l] in supporting the shorter text. (The Sinaitic Syriac condenses ver. 51 by omitting διέστη and εἰς τὸν οὐρανόν, reading ܪ‍ܝܐ‍ܪ ܐ‍ܘ‍ܪ ܝ‍ܝ‍ܕ ܪ‍ܬ‍ܘ

ܐ‍ܘ‍ܡ‍ܝ‍ܟ "And while he blessed them, he was lifted up from them"; thus, though shortened, syr[s] still alludes to the ascension.) A minority of the Committee preferred the shorter reading, regarding the longer as a Western non-interpolation (see the Note following 24.53).

The majority of the Committee, however, favored the longer reading for the following reasons. (1) The rhythm of the sentence seems to require the presence of such a clause (compare the two coordinate clauses joined with καί in ver. 50 and in verses 52-53). (2) Luke's opening statement in Acts ("In the first book, O Theophilus, I have dealt with all that Jesus began to do and teach, until the day when he was taken up [ἀνελήμφθη]") implies that he considered that he had made some reference, however brief, to the ascension at the close of his first book. (3) If the shorter text were original, it is difficult to account for the presence of καὶ ἀνεφέρετο εἰς τὸν οὐρανόν in so many and such diversified witnesses, beginning with 𝔓[75] about A.D. 200. (4) If the clause were a copyist's addition, prompted by his noticing the implications of Ac 1.1-2 (see point (2) above), one would have expected him to adopt some form of the verb

ἀναλαμβάνειν, used in Ac 1.2 and other passages referring to the
ascension, rather than the less appropriate ἀναφέρειν, which in the
New Testament ordinarily has the specialized meaning "to offer up."
Finally, (5) the omission of the clause in a few witnesses can be accounted for either (*a*) through accidental scribal oversight occasioned
by homoeoarcton (ΚΑΙΑ ... ΚΑΙΑ ...) or (*b*) by deliberate excision,
either (i) in order to relieve the apparent contradiction between this
account (which seemingly places the ascension late Easter night) and
the account in Ac 1.3-11 (which dates the ascension forty days after
Easter), or (ii) in order to introduce a subtle theological differentia-
tion between the Gospel and the Acts (i. e., the Western redactor, not
approving of Luke's mentioning the ascension twice, first to conclude
the earthly ministry of Jesus, and again, in Acts, to inaugurate the
church age, preferred to push all doxological representations of Jesus
to a time after the ascension in Acts, and therefore deleted the clause
in question as well as the words προσκυνήσαντες αὐτόν from
ver. 52 – for when the account of the ascension has been eliminated,
the mention of Jesus being worshipped seems less appropriate).[2]

24.52   προσκυνήσαντες αὐτόν {B}

Although a minority of the Committee preferred the shorter reading, regarding the others as interpolations (see the Note following
24.53), the majority considered it more probable that the words
προσκυνήσαντες αὐτόν had been omitted either accidentally (the
eye of the copyist passing from ΑΥΤΟΙ ... to ΑΥΤΟΝ) or, perhaps,
deliberately (so as to accord better with the shorter reading in ver. 51;
see the concluding comments on the previous variant reading).

24.53   εὐλογοῦντες {B}

The readings αἰνοῦντες καὶ εὐλογοῦντες (A C² K W X Δ Θ Ψ
*f*¹ *f*¹³ 33) and εὐλογοῦντες καὶ αἰνοῦντες (eth) are undoubtedly

---

[2] For other instances of what appear to be doctrinal alterations introduced by the
Western reviser, see the comments on Ac 1.2 and 9 as well as the references mentioned
in Group *D* in footnote 12, p. 226 below. Cf. also Eldon J. Epp, *The Theological
Tendency of Codex Bezae Cantabrigiensis in Acts* (Cambridge, 1966).

conflations, arising from combinations of εὐλογοῦντες ($\mathfrak{P}^{75}$ ℵ B C* L syr$^{s, pal}$ cop$^{sa, bo}$ geo) and αἰνοῦντες (D it$^{a, b, d, e, ff2, l, r1}$ Augustine). It is more difficult to decide between the two earlier readings. On the one hand, since εὐλογεῖν is a favorite word with Luke (it occurs twelve other times in the Third Gospel, whereas αἰνεῖν occurs in only three other passages), one can argue that it was probably original here. On the other hand, since in patristic Greek εὐλογεῖν comes to be a distinctively Christian term used in praising God (in contrast with the pagan usage of αἰνεῖν), copyists would have tended to replace instances of the latter verb with the former. Considerations relating to the context are similarly indecisive. It can be argued that the presence of εὐλογεῖν in verses 50 and 51 prompted copyists to introduce the same verb in ver. 53; or, thinking it more appropriate that the activity of the disciples should be differentiated from that of their risen Lord, out of reverence copyists may have altered εὐλο-γοῦντες to αἰνοῦντες. Faced with these conflicting considerations, a majority of the Committee preferred to make a decision on the basis of external attestation, and therefore chose εὐλογοῦντες, supported as it is by early and diversified witnesses.

24.53 θεόν. {A}

The word ἀμήν, which is absent from the earliest and best representatives of both the Alexandrian and the Western types of text, is a liturgical addition introduced by copyists. (See also the comment on Mt 28.20.)

Note on Western Non-Interpolations

One of the features of the Western text is the occasional omission of words and passages that are present in other types of text, including the Alexandrian. How should one evaluate such omissions from a form of text which is generally much fuller than other text-types? According to one theory, popularized at the close of the last

century by Westcott and Hort,[1] such readings, despite their being
supported by the generally inferior Western witnesses, ought to be
preferred rather than the longer readings, though the latter are attested
by the generally superior manuscripts, B and ℵ. Nine such readings
were designated by Westcott and Hort as "Western non-interpolations,"[2] on the assumption that all extant witnesses except the
Western (or, in some cases, some of the Western witnesses) have in
these passages suffered interpolation.

In recent decades this theory has been coming under more and
more criticism. With the acquisition of the Bodmer Papyri, testimony
for the Alexandrian type of text has been carried back from the fourth
to the second century, and one can now observe how faithfully that
text was copied and recopied between the stage represented by $\mathfrak{P}^{75}$
and the stage represented by codex Vaticanus. Furthermore, scholars
have been critical of the apparently arbitrary way in which Westcott
and Hort isolated nine passages for special treatment (enclosing them
within double square brackets), whereas they did not give similar
treatment to other readings that also are absent from Western witnesses.[3]

With the rise of what is called Redaktionsgeschichte (the analysis
of the theological and literary presuppositions and tendencies that
controlled the formation and transmission of Gospel materials),
scholars have begun to give renewed attention to the possibility that
special theological interests on the part of scribes may account for the
deletion of certain passages in Western witnesses. In any case, the
Bible Societies' Committee did not consider it wise to make, as it
were, a mechanical or doctrinaire judgment concerning the group of
nine Western non-interpolations, but sought to evaluate each one
separately on its own merits and in the light of fuller attestation and
newer methodologies.

---

[1] B. F. Westcott and J. F. A. Hort, *The New Testament in the Original Greek,*
[vol. II] *Introduction [and] Appendix* (Cambridge and London, 1881; 2nd ed., 1896),
pp. 175–177.

[2] The nine passages are Mt 27.49; Lk 22.19b-20; 24.3, 6, 12, 36, 40, 51, and 52.

[3] E. g. Mt 9.34; Mk 2.22; 10.2; 14.39; Lk 5.39; 10.41-42; 12.21; 22.62; 24.9; Jn 4.9.
In all these passages the consensus of textual opinion (including that of Westcott and
Hort) is almost unanimous that the Western text, though shorter, is secondary.

During the discussions a sharp difference of opinion emerged. According to the view of a minority of the Committee, apart from other arguments there is discernible in these passages a Christological-theological motivation that accounts for their having been added, while there is no clear reason that accounts for their having been omitted. Accordingly, if the passages are retained in the text at all, it was held that they should be enclosed within square brackets. On the other hand, the majority of the Committee, having evaluated the weight of the evidence differently, regarded the longer readings as part of the original text. For an account of the reasons that the majority felt to be cogent in explaining the origin of the shorter text, see the comments on the several passages.

THE GOSPEL ACCORDING TO JOHN

1.3-4 οὐδὲ ἕν. ὃ γέγονεν ἐν {B}

Should the words ὃ γέγονεν be joined with what goes before or with what follows? The oldest manuscripts (𝔓⁶⁶, ⁷⁵* ℵ* A B) have no punctuation here, and in any case the presence of punctuation in Greek manuscripts, as well as in versional and patristic sources, cannot be regarded as more than the reflection of current exegetical understanding of the meaning of the passage.

A majority of the Committee was impressed by the consensus of ante-Nicene writers (orthodox and heretical alike) who took ὃ γέγονεν with what follows. When, however, in the fourth century Arians and the Macedonian heretics began to appeal to the passage to prove that the Holy Spirit is to be regarded as one of the created things, orthodox writers preferred to take ὃ γέγονεν with the preceding sentence, thus removing the possibility of heretical use of the passage.

The punctuation adopted for the text is in accord with what a majority regarded as the rhythmical balance of the opening verses of the Prologue, where the climactic or "staircase" parallelism seems to demand that the end of one line should match the beginning of the next.[1]

[On the other hand, however, none of these arguments is conclusive and other considerations favor taking ὃ γέγονεν with the preceding sentence. Thus, against the consideration of the so-called

---

[1] For discussions in support of taking ὃ γέγονεν with what follows, see K. Aland, "Über die Bedeutung eines Punktes. (Eine Untersuchung zu Joh. 1, 3 4)," in *Studies in the History and Text of the New Testament in Honor of Kenneth Willis Clark,* ed. by Boyd L. Daniels and M. Jack Suggs (= *Studies and Documents,* XXIX; Salt Lake City, 1967), pp. 161–187 (an expanded form of the study appeared in *Zeitschrift für die neutestamentliche Wissenschaft,* LIX [1968], pp. 174–209), and Ed. L. Miller, *Salvation-History in the Prologue of John. The Significance of John 1:3/4* (Leiden, 1989), pp. 17–44.

rhythmical balance (which after all is present in only a portion of the Prologue, and may not necessarily involve ὃ γέγονεν) must be set John's fondness for beginning a sentence or clause with ἐν and a demonstrative pronoun (cf. 13.35; 15.8; 16.26; 1 Jn 2.3, 4, 5; 3.10, 16, 19, 24; 4.2, etc.). It was natural for Gnostics, who sought support from the Fourth Gospel for their doctrine of the origin of the Ogdoad, to take ὃ γέγονεν with the following sentence ("That which has been made in him was life" – whatever that may be supposed to mean).[2] It is more consistent with the Johannine repetitive style, as well as with Johannine doctrine (cf. 5.26, 39; 6.53), to say nothing concerning the sense of the passage, to punctuate with a full stop after ὃ γέγονεν. B.M.M.]

1.4 ἦν {A}

In order to relieve the difficulty of meaning when ὃ γέγονεν (ver. 3) is taken as the subject of ἦν ("that-which-has-come-into-being in him *was* life"), the tense of the verb was changed from imperfect to present *(ἐστιν)* in ℵ D Old Latin syr[c] cop[sa, fay] and many early ecclesiastical writers. The presence, however, of the second ἦν (in the clause ἡ ζωὴ ἦν τὸ φῶς) seems to require the first.

1.13 οἳ οὐκ ... ἐγεννήθησαν {A}

Several ancient witnesses, chiefly Latin (it[b] Irenaeus[lat] Tertullian Origen[lat] Ambrose Augustine Ps-Athanasius), read the singular number, "[He] who was born, not of blood nor of the will of the flesh nor of the will of man, but of God" (the Curetonian Syriac and six manuscripts of the Peshitta Syriac read the plural "those who" and the singular verb "was born").

All Greek manuscripts, as well as the other versional and patristic

---

[2] Despite valiant attempts of commentators to bring sense out of taking ὃ γέγονεν with what follows, the passage remains intolerably clumsy and opaque. One of the difficulties that stands in the way of ranging the clause with ἐν αὐτῷ ζωὴ ἦν is that the perfect tense of γέγονεν would require ἐστιν instead of ἦν (see also the comment on 1.4).

witnesses, attest the plural number. (Several minor variant readings occur within the verse: D* and itᵃ omit οἵ, thus leaving the verse without grammatical connection with the preceding sentence; other variants in the verse are mentioned in the following entry.)

Although a number of modern scholars (including Zahn, Resch, Blass, Loisy, R. Seeburg, Burney, Büchsel, Boismard, Dupont, and F. M. Braun)[3] have argued for the originality of the singular number, it appeared to the Committee that, on the basis of the overwhelming consensus of all Greek manuscripts, the plural must be adopted, a reading, moreover, that is in accord with the characteristic teaching of John. The singular number may have arisen either from a desire to make the Fourth Gospel allude explicitly to the virgin birth or from the influence of the singular number of the immediately preceding αὐτοῦ.

1.13 οὐδὲ ἐκ θελήματος ἀνδρός {A}

The presence of similar beginnings (οὐδέ ... οὐδέ) and similar endings (σαρκός ... ἀνδρός) of the second and third clauses has occasioned the accidental omission of one or the other clause. The clause οὐδὲ ... σαρκός was omitted in E* and several minuscule manuscripts, and the clause οὐδὲ ... ἀνδρός was omitted in B* al.

1.18 μονογενὴς θεός {B}

With the acquisition of 𝔓⁶⁶ and 𝔓⁷⁵, both of which read θεός, the external support of this reading has been notably strengthened. A majority of the Committee regarded the reading μονογενὴς υἱός, which undoubtedly is easier than μονογενὴς θεός, to be the result of scribal assimilation to Jn 3.16, 18; 1 Jn 4.9. The anarthrous use of θεός (cf. 1.1) appears to be more primitive. There is no reason why the article should have been deleted, and when υἱός supplanted θεός it would certainly have been added. The shortest reading, ὁ μονο-

---

[3] For literature, see Josef Schmid in *Biblische Zeitschrift*, N. F., ɪ (1957), pp. 118 f. The singular number is adopted in the Jerusalem Bible (1966), but not in the New Jerusalem Bible (1985).

γενής, while attractive because of internal considerations, is too poorly attested for acceptance as the text.

Some modern commentators[4] take μονογενής as a noun and punctuate so as to have three distinct designations of him who makes God known (μονογενής, θεός, ὁ ὢν εἰς τὸν κόλπον τοῦ πατρὸς ...).

[It is doubtful that the author would have written μονογενὴς θεός, which may be a primitive, transcriptional error in the Alexandrian tradition (ΥΣ/ΘΣ). At least a D decision would be preferable. A.W.]

1.19 [πρὸς αὐτόν] {C}

It is difficult to decide whether the phrase πρὸς αὐτόν was deleted in some witnesses (𝔓[66*, 75] ℵ C[3] L W[supp] f[1] al) as being essentially redundant in view of αὐτόν later in the verse, or whether it was added either here (B C* 33 892[c] 1010 al) or following Λευίτας (𝔓[66c vid] A Θ Ψ f[13] al) in order to clarify the statement. The Committee decided that the least unsatisfactory resolution of the problem was to adopt the reading of B al, but to enclose the phrase within square brackets to indicate considerable doubt that it belongs in the text.

1.21 Τί οὖν; Σὺ Ἠλίας εἶ; {C}

Confronted with a multiplicity of competing variant readings, the Committee made its choice on the basis of age and diversity of supporting evidence.

1.26 ἕστηκεν {B}

The perfect tense, so frequently employed with theological overtones by the Fourth Evangelist, conveys a special force here (some-

---

[4] E. g. E. A. Abbott, *Johannine Grammar* (London, 1906), p. 42; J. H. Bernard, *A Critical and Exegetical Commentary on the Gospel According to St. John*, I (New York, 1929), p. 31; John Marsh, *The Gospel of St. John* (Penguin Books, 1969), p. 112; and (in effect) Raymond E. Brown, *The Gospel According to John*, I (New York, 1966), p. 17.

thing like, "there is One who has taken his stand in your midst"), a force that was unappreciated by several Greek witnesses (B L *f*[1] Origen Cyril) as well as by a variety of Latin, Syriac, and Coptic witnesses (it[a, b, c, e, ff2, l, q] syr[c, s, p, h, pal] cop[sa, bo]), all of which preferred the more syntactically appropriate present tense. Other readings (the imperfect ἐστήκει and the pluperfect εἱστήκει), besides being inappropriate in the context, are insufficiently supported. (On the forms of στήκω see Blass-Debrunner-Funk, § 73.)

1.28   ἐν Βηθανίᾳ ἐγένετο   {C}

The earliest and most widely attested reading is Βηθανίᾳ. Origen, who in his travels was unable to locate a Bethany by the Jordan, adopted the reading Βηθαβαρᾷ, which he apparently found in a few copies current in his day (he declares that Βηθανίᾳ is the reading of "nearly all the manuscripts"), and to which he was attracted because of what he regarded as an edifying etymology: "The etymology of the name [Bethabara] corresponds with the baptism of him who made ready for the Lord a people prepared for him; for it yields the meaning 'House of preparation,'[5] while Bethany means 'House of obedience.' Where else was it fitting that he should baptize, who was sent as a messenger before the face of Christ, to prepare his way before him, but at the 'House of preparation'?"[6] John Chrysostom, perhaps following Origen, also declares that instead of Bethany the "more accurate of the copies" read Bethabara; for, he explains, "Bethany is neither beyond the Jordan nor in the desert, but is somewhere near Jerusalem." A majority of the Committee favored Βηθανίᾳ on the basis of (*a*) age and distribution of evidence, as well as (*b*) the consideration that, if Βηθαβαρᾷ were original, there is no adequate reason why it should have been altered to Βηθανίᾳ.

---

[5] Origen is misinformed; actually the meaning of Bethabara appears to be "House [or Place] of passing over."

[6] *Commentary on John*, bk. vi, § 24 (40). In the manuscripts of Origen's Commentary the spelling of Bethabara varies, reading Βηθαρᾷ, Βαθαρᾷ, or Βηθαραβᾷ. The last mentioned form, found also in א[b] syr[hmg], is an orthographical variant (by metathesis) of Βηθαβαρᾷ.

1.34 ὁ υἱός {B}

Instead of "the Son of God" several witnesses, chiefly Western (codex Bezae is defective here), read "the chosen one of God" ($\mathfrak{P}^{5vid}$ $\aleph^*$ it$^{b, e, ff2^*}$ syr$^{c, s}$ Ambrose) and a few read "the chosen Son of God" (it$^{a, ff2^c}$ syr^{palmss} cop^{sa}). On the basis of age and diversity of witnesses a majority of the Committee preferred the reading ὁ υἱός, which is also in harmony with the theological terminology of the Fourth Evangelist.

1.41 πρῶτον {B}

The reading πρῶτος, attested by $\aleph^*$ and the later Greek tradition, means that Andrew was the first follower of Jesus who made a convert. The reading πρῶτον, which means that the first thing that Andrew did after having been called was to find his brother, was preferred by a majority of the Committee because of its early and diversified support ($\mathfrak{P}^{66, 75}$ $\aleph^c$ B Θ f^1 f^{13} cop arm geo *al*). The reading πρωΐ ("in the morning"), implied by the word *mane* in two or three Old Latin manuscripts, avoids the ambiguities of πρῶτος/πρῶτον and carries on the narrative from ver. 39.

1.42 Ἰωάννου {B}

A majority of the Committee regarded Ἰωνᾶ (read by A B^3 Δ f^1 f^{13} and most of the later Greek witnesses) as a scribal assimilation to Bar-Jona of Mt 16.17. The reading Ἰωάν(ν)α reflects further scribal confusion with the name of a woman mentioned only by Luke (cf. Lk 8.3; 24.10). See also the comment on Jn 21.15, 16, 17.

2.3 ὑστερήσαντος οἴνου

Several witnesses ($\aleph^*$ it$^{a, b, ff2, j, r}$ syr^{hmg} eth) paraphrase by reading οἶνον οὐκ εἶχον, ὅτι συνετελέσθη ὁ οἶνος τοῦ γάμου· εἶτα ("They had no wine, because the wine of the wedding feast had been used up; then …"). Two Old Latin witnesses (it$^{e, l}$) describe the situation as follows: *et factum est per multam turbam vocitorum vinum* *consummari* ("It happened that, because of the great crowd of those who had been invited, the wine was finished"). The shorter reading, adopted for the text, is attested by $\mathfrak{P}^{66,\,75}$ $\aleph^a$ and all known uncial and minuscule manuscripts, as well as all versional witnesses not cited above.

2.10   μεθυσθῶσιν

The Textus Receptus (following $\aleph^c$ A X Γ Δ Θ Λ Π and many other witnesses) makes a smoother reading by adding τότε. The shorter reading adopted for the text is decisively supported by $\mathfrak{P}^{66,\,75}$ $\aleph^*$ B L 083 0141 57 248 573 579 1010 1279 l^{185} it$^{a,\,e,\,ff2,\,l,\,q}$ syr^{pal} cop$^{sa,\,bo}$ eth.

2.12   καὶ ἡ μήτηρ αὐτοῦ καὶ οἱ ἀδελφοὶ [αὐτοῦ] καὶ οἱ μαθηταὶ αὐτοῦ {C}

The manuscripts present many differences as to the sequence of words as well as the omission of one or more words. The αὐτοῦ following ἀδελφοί is lacking in $\mathfrak{P}^{66*,\,75}$ B Ψ 0162; the αὐτοῦ following μαθηταί is absent from L 0141; the phrase καὶ οἱ μαθηταὶ αὐτοῦ precedes καὶ ἡ μήτηρ in W^{supp}; and the phrase καὶ οἱ μαθηταὶ αὐτοῦ is lacking in $\aleph$ *al.* The reading that, in the judgment of the Committee, best accounts for the rise of the other readings is supported by $\mathfrak{P}^{66c}$ A Δ Θ 0233 f^1 f^{13} *al*, but in view of the weight of the witnesses that lack the first αὐτοῦ, it seemed appropriate to enclose it within square brackets.

2.15   φραγέλλιον {B}

Several witnesses, including the two oldest ($\mathfrak{P}^{66,\,75}$ L W^{supp} X 0162 f^1 33 565 *al*), prefix ὡς. If this word had been present in the original text, there is no good reason that would account for its having been omitted from the other witnesses. On the other hand, it is probable that copyists introduced the word in order to soften somewhat the bald statement that Jesus made a whip of cords; "he made a kind of whip of cords."

2.24 αὐτόν (1) {C}

In place of the first αὐτόν, many witnesses clarify the sense by writing ἑαυτόν (𝔓⁶⁶ ℵ² Aᶜ Wˢᵘᵖᵖ Θ Ψ *al*). Although the word was omitted (probably accidentally) by a few copyists, the Committee judged that there was sufficiently weighty support (ℵ* A* B L 700 *al*) to warrant including it.

3.5 τοῦ θεοῦ

A few Greek manuscripts (ℵ* 245 291 472 1009 *l*²⁶) and a wide range of early patristic writers replace τοῦ θεοῦ with τῶν οὐρανῶν. Although it may be argued that the latter reading is original and that τοῦ θεοῦ was introduced in order to make the passage harmonize with ver. 3, the Committee was impressed by (*a*) the age and diversity of the witnesses that support τοῦ θεοῦ, and (*b*) the probability that copyists introduced τῶν οὐρανῶν in imitation of the frequently recurring expression in Matthew (εἰσέρχεσθαι [εἰσελθεῖν] εἰς τὴν βασιλείαν τῶν οὐρανῶν occurs in Mt 5.20; 7.21; 18.3; 19.23), whereas εἰσελθεῖν εἰς τὴν βασιλείαν τοῦ θεοῦ occurs only once elsewhere (Mt 19.24), while the combination of ἰδεῖν with τὴν βασιλείαν τῶν οὐρανῶν occurs nowhere (and therefore it is not surprising that copyists refrained from introducing τῶν οὐρανῶν into ver. 3).

3.13 ἀνθρώπου {B}

On the one hand, a minority of the Committee preferred the reading ἀνθρώπου ὁ ὢν ἐν τῷ οὐρανῷ, arguing that (1) if the short reading, supported almost exclusively by Egyptian witnesses, were original, there is no discernible motive that would have prompted copyists to add the words ὁ ὢν ἐν τῷ οὐρανῷ, resulting in a most difficult saying (the statement in 1.18, not being parallel, would scarcely have prompted the addition); and (2) the diversity of readings implies that the expression ὁ υἱὸς τοῦ ἀνθρώπου ὁ ὢν ἐν τῷ οὐρανῷ, having been found objectionable or superfluous in the context, was modified either by omitting the participial clause, or by altering it so as to avoid suggesting that the Son of Man was at that moment in heaven.

On the other hand, the majority of the Committee, impressed by the quality of the external attestation supporting the shorter reading, regarded the words ὁ ὢν ἐν τῷ οὐρανῷ as an interpretative gloss, reflecting later Christological development.

3.15 ἐν αὐτῷ {B}

Exegetical as well as textual problems are involved in deciding among the variant readings. Except for this passage, the fourth evangelist always uses εἰς after πιστεύειν (34 times), never ἐν. On the other hand, if ἐν αὐτῷ is original here, the meaning may well be, "that every one who believes shall in him [i. e. resting upon him as the cause] have eternal life." In support of such an interpretation is John's manner of placing an adverbial phrase with ἐν before its verb when the phrase is emphatic or metaphorical (cf. 5.39; 16.33; and 1 Jn *passim*). On balance, therefore, the reading of 𝔓⁷⁵ B *al*, being ambiguous, seems to account best for the rise of the other readings.

3.25 μετὰ Ἰουδαίου {B}

Both Ἰουδαίου and Ἰουδαίων are ancient readings, and external support is rather evenly divided. On the whole, however, it is more likely that the singular (which is unique in John) would have been changed to the more customary plural than vice versa.

3.31-32 ἐρχόμενος [ἐπάνω πάντων ἐστίν·] ὃ ἑώρακεν καὶ ἤκουσεν τοῦτο μαρτυρεῖ {C}

Several variations are involved here. The word καί is omitted by overwhelming authority, and may be set aside at once. On the other hand, the omission of τοῦτο in several witnesses is sufficiently explained as arising from a certain unnecessary pleonasm. The chief problem – the presence or absence of ἐπάνω πάντων ἐστίν – is less easy to solve. Good reasons may be adduced to account for scribal deletion of the words (as redundant after the opening part of ver. 31) or for their mechanical addition after the second instance of ἐρχόμενος by an inattentive scribe. In view of the balance of both external evidence and transcriptional probabilities, the Committee decided to retain the words but to enclose them within square brackets.

3.34 τὸ πνεῦμα {B}

By some oversight, the scribe of B had originally omitted the words τὸ πνεῦμα, but they were subsequently added in the margin by the same hand. In order to make certain that the reader would understand that ὁ θεός earlier in the verse functions also as the subject of δίδωσιν, several witnesses repeat the words before δίδωσιν (A C² D Δ Ψ 086 f¹³ al). The shorter text is strongly supported by 𝔓⁶⁶, ⁷⁵ ℵ B² C* L Wˢᵘᵖᵖ 083 f¹ 33 565 1241.

4.1 Ἰησοῦς {C}

As between Ἰησοῦς and κύριος the Committee preferred the former. Had κύριος been present in the original text, it is unlikely that a scribe would have displaced it with Ἰησοῦς, which occurs twice in the following clauses. On the other hand, in accord with the increasing use of κύριος in reference to Jesus, and in order to relieve the clumsy style, more than one copyist may have smoothed the passage by changing the first instance of Ἰησοῦς to κύριος.

It has been conjectured that originally the verb ἔγνω was without an expressed subject, and that subsequently some copyists inserted Ἰησοῦς and others κύριος.

4.3 πάλιν {A}

The omission of πάλιν from A B* Γ Λ Π Ψ 28 249 579 700 1194 1424 syrʰ al, if not accidental, may have been occasioned by a desire to clarify the evangelist's meaning – for (a) Jesus does not actually arrive in Galilee until two days later (ver. 43), after an interlude in Samaria; and (b) an overly punctilious reader could take πάλιν to mean that Jesus returned *a second time* to Galilee after having left Judea. *Πάλιν* is strongly attested by 𝔓⁶⁶, ⁷⁵ ℵ B² C D L M W Θ 053 083 0141 *f*¹ *f*¹³ 33 565 itᵃ, ᵇ, ᶜ, ᵉ, ᶠᶠ², ¹ vg syrᶜ, ˢ, ᵖᵃˡ copˢᵃ, ᵇᵒ arm eth *al.*

4.5 Συχάρ {A}

Despite the problems of identifying Sychar, the Committee was unwilling to accept Συχέμ (= Shechem) on the basis of only syrᶜ, ˢ and several patristic witnesses. The reading Σιχάρ in 69 is a late Greek orthographic variant of the prevailing Συχάρ.

4.9 οὐ γὰρ συγχρῶνται Ἰουδαῖοι Σαμαρίταις {A}

This explanatory comment is omitted in several witnesses (ℵ* D itᵃ, ᵇ, ᵈ, ᵉ, ʲ copᶠᵃʸ). Although some have thought (Blass-Debrunner-Funk, § 193, 5) that the words are an early marginal gloss that eventually got into the text of most witnesses, such comments are typical of the evangelist. The omission, if not accidental, may reflect scribal opinion that the statement is not literally exact and therefore should be deleted.

4.11 αὐτῷ [ἡ γυνή] {C}

It is difficult to decide whether ἡ γυνή is a natural addition introduced by copyists in order to clarify the subject of λέγει (as ἐκείνη was added in ℵ*), or whether the absence of the words in two Alexandrian witnesses (𝔓⁷⁵ B), joined by two versional witnesses (syrˢ copᵃᶜʰ²), is the result of a pruning of the text of unnecessary words. In order to reflect the balance of possibilities, the words were retained in the text but enclosed within square brackets.

4.35-36 θερισμόν. ἤδη ὁ {B}

The word ἤδη may be taken either as concluding ver. 35 or as beginning ver. 36. In order to prevent it from being taken with what follows, the scribes of A C³ Θ *f*¹ *f*¹³ *al* inserted καί at the beginning of ver. 36. Since it is more in accord with John's style for ἤδη to begin a sentence, the Committee punctuated accordingly.

4.51 παῖς αὐτοῦ {B}

There are two sets of variation: παῖς ‖ υἱός and αὐτοῦ ‖ σου. In the former case it must be observed that, though Matthew and Luke use παῖς freely, this word appears nowhere else in John, who prefers υἱός. Apparently the reading υἱός is due to scribal assimilation (which began at least as early as 𝔓⁶⁶ᶜ) to the usage of the context (verses 46, 47, 50, and 53). The reading σου arose when ὅτι was taken by some copyists to be ὅτι *recitativum,* introducing the actual words of the servants (compare also Jesus' words to the father, ὁ υἱός σου ζῇ, ver. 50).

5.1 ἑορτή {A}

Strong external evidence favors the anarthrous ἑορτή (𝔓⁶⁶, ⁷⁵ A B D Θ *f*¹³ 28 syrᶜ, ᵖ); likewise, the natural tendency of scribes would have been to identify an otherwise indeterminate feast by inserting ἡ (with a reference probably to Passover), a tendency that accounts also for such supplements in isolated manuscripts as ἀζύμων before Ἰουδαίων (in Λ) and ἡ σκηνοπηγία after Ἰουδαίων (in 131).

5.2 Βηθζαθά {C}

Of the several variant readings, Βηθσαϊδά has strong attestation but is suspect as an assimilation to the town of Bethsaida on the Sea of Galilee, mentioned in 1.44. Βηθεσδά, though widely supported, is also suspect as a scribal alteration originally introduced because of its edifying etymology (בֵּית חִסְדָּא, "House of [Divine] Mercy"). In the opinion of a majority of the Committee the least unsatisfactory reading appears to be Βηθζαθά (א 33 Eusebius), of which Βηζαθά (L itᵉ) and perhaps Βελζεθά (D it⁽ᵃ⁾, ᵈ, ʳ¹) may be variant spellings. The Copper Scroll discovered at Qumran contains a reference to a pool at

Betheshdathayim,[1] which the minority of the Committee interpreted as corroborating the reading Βηθεσδά.

5.3   ξηρῶν {A}

Because the man whom Jesus heals appears to have been a paralytic (a word that occurs nowhere in John), after ξηρῶν the Western text (D it[a, b, d, j, l, r1] geo[2]) inserts παραλυτικῶν, which, however, was not taken up in any known later text. A variety of witnesses add, perhaps in order to explain the reference in ver. 7 to the troubling of the water, ἐκδεχομένων τὴν τοῦ ὕδατος κίνησιν. The reading, however, is lacking in the oldest and best witnesses (𝔓[66, 75] ℵ A* B C* L al) and contains two non-Johannine words (ἐκδέχεσθαι and κίνησις).

5.4   omit verse {A}

Ver. 4 is a gloss, whose secondary character is clear from (1) its absence from the earliest and best witnesses (𝔓[66, 75] ℵ B C* D W[supp] 33 it[d, l, q] the true text of the Latin Vulgate syr[c] cop[sa, bomss, ach2] geo Nonnus), (2) the presence of asterisks or obeli to mark the words as spurious in more than twenty Greek witnesses (including S Λ Π 047 1079 2174), (3) the presence of non-Johannine words or expressions (κατὰ καιρόν, ἐμβαίνω [of going into the water], ἐκδέχομαι, κατέχομαι, κίνησις, ταραχή, δήποτε, and νόσημα – the last four words only here in the New Testament), and (4) the rather wide diversity of variant forms in which the verse was transmitted.

5.17   δὲ [Ἰησοῦς] {C}

It is difficult to decide whether Ἰησοῦς was added by scribes in order to provide a subject for ἀπεκρίνατο, or whether the absence of

---

[1] The word, the termination of which signifies the Hebrew dual number, appears to be connected with the Aramaic אֶשֶׁד, "to pour out" (perhaps therefore "Place of poured-out [water]"); cf. J. T. Milik in: M. Baillet, J. T. Milik, and R. de Vaux, Les 'Petites Grottes' de Qumrân (= Discoveries in the Judaean Desert of Jordan, III), Textes (Oxford, 1962), p. 271; and J. Jeremias, The Rediscovery of Bethesda (Louisville, 1966), pp. 12 and 35.

the name from $\mathfrak{P}^{75}$ ℵ B W *al* is an Alexandrian deletion prompted by stylistic considerations. As a compromise a majority of the Committee decided to retain the word enclosed within square brackets. The readings with κύριος are clearly secondary.

5.32 οἶδα {A}

The Western reading οἶδατε (ℵ* D *l*[547] it[a, d, e, q] syr[c] arm geo) reflects the desire of copyists to heighten the argument by forcing the Jews to admit that they know the evidence of Jesus' μαρτυρία to be true (the textual alteration, however, is contradicted by the implication of ver. 37b). Other copyists, prompted perhaps by the recollection of instances of οἶδαμεν in John (3.2; 4.42; 7.27; 9.20, 24, 29, 31; 16.30; 21.24), changed οἶδα to οἶδαμεν (56 58 61).

5.36 μείζω

Instead of μείζω (accusative case), read by the majority of witnesses (ℵ H K L S U V Γ Δ Θ Π and most minuscules; D reads the alternative accusative form μείζονα), the variant reading μείζων (properly the nominative case) is found in $\mathfrak{P}^{66}$ A B E G M N W Λ Ψ *f*[13] 33 397 472 579 713 1071 2430 *al*. The latter reading, however, gives an antithesis ("I who am greater than John have the testimony") that is out of accord with the context. (It is possible, however, that μείζων is a solecistic form of the accusative [see Moulton, *Prolegomena*, p. 49]; the meaning would be the same as that given by μείζω.)

5.44 θεοῦ {B}

Although early and important witnesses ($\mathfrak{P}^{66, 75}$ B W *al*) omit θεοῦ, it seems to be required in the context. The absence of the word can be accounted for through transcriptional oversight; the letters ΘῩ (the customary contraction for θεοῦ) were accidentally omitted from ΤΟΥΜΟΝΟΥΘῩΟΥ.

6.1   τῆς Γαλιλαίας {A}

The clumsiness of the two successive genitives, both identifying the same sea, prompted some copyists to omit τῆς Γαλιλαίας (0210 1242* 1344 2174 *l*[184]), and others to add after Γαλιλαίας either καί (V goth) or εἰς τὰ μέρη (D Θ 892 1009 1230 1253 it[b, d, e, r1] geo). The meaning of the last, which is the smoothest reading, is "across the sea of Galilee to the regions of Tiberias." If this reading were original, it would be difficult to account for the rise of the others.

6.14   ὃ ἐποίησεν σημεῖον {B}

Although the combination of 𝔓[75] B it[a] in support of ἃ ... σημεῖα is impressive, the plural seemed to the Committee to have arisen from scribal assimilation to 2.23 and 6.2. The addition of ὁ Ἰησοῦς was made by copyists in the interest of clarity.

6.15   ἀνεχώρησεν {A}

While it is possible that ἀνεχώρησεν (a word frequently used by Matthew but which occurs nowhere else in John) may have been substituted by copyists for φεύγει (because flight would seem to be unbecoming for Jesus), a majority of the Committee was impressed by the ancient and widespread testimony supporting ἀνεχώρησεν. It regarded φεύγει as a typical Western reading introduced in several witnesses to enliven the narrative. (Syr[c] conflates both readings, "he left them and fled again....")

6.22   ἕν {A}

In order to clarify the evangelist's statement about the boat, copyists added, in one form or another, the explanation that it was the one "into which his [Jesus'] disciples had entered." The variety of wording of the addition condemns it as secondary, just as the age and variety of witnesses which support the shorter reading confirm that as original.

6.23   *ἄλλα ἦλθεν πλοιά[ρια] ἐκ Τιβεριάδος* {C}

Amid the multiplicity of variants, the text of 𝔓⁷⁵, supported by several other widely scattered representative witnesses, was regarded by a majority of the Committee as the reading that best explains the origin of the others. As for the variation involving *πλοῖα* and *πλοιάρια*, in order to represent the balance of evidence and transcriptional probabilities it was decided to print *πλοιά[ρια]*.

6.23   *εὐχαριστήσαντος τοῦ κυρίου* {B}

On the one hand, the rarity of *κύριος* in referring to Jesus in Johannine narrative and the absence of the clause from certain Western witnesses (D 091 it^(a, d, e) syr^(c, s) arm geo¹ Diatessaron^(l, v)) may suggest that the words are a gloss that crept into the other texts. On the other hand, however, in view of the widespread currency of the words in most text-types, a majority of the Committee was reluctant to omit them.

6.27   *ὑμῖν δώσει* {A}

Several witnesses (ℵ D it^(d, e, ff2, j) syr^(c, pal) Chrysostom) read the present tense, which appears to be the result of assimilation to *δίδωσιν ὑμῖν* in ver. 32. The reading *ὑμῖν δώσει*, which is strongly supported by 𝔓⁷⁵ A B W Θ *f*¹ 28 33 565 700 *al*, is clearly to be preferred.

6.36   *[με]* {C}

A few witnesses (ℵ A it^(a, b, e, q) syr^(c, s)) lack *με*. It is possible that this is the original reading and that *με* has crept into the other witnesses from the context. In this case Jesus' statement, "I said to you that you saw and yet do not believe," clearly refers to the signs that the people had witnessed (ver. 26). On the other hand, a majority of the Committee, impressed by the age and diversity of the external attestation supporting *με*, preferred to retain the word in the text, but to enclose it within square brackets.

6.47 πιστεύων {A}

The addition of εἰς ἐμέ as the object of the verb "believe" was both natural and inevitable; the surprising thing is that relatively many copyists resisted the temptation. If the words had been present in the original text, no good reason can be suggested to account for their omission. The reading of the Old Syriac has been assimilated to the text at 14.1.

6.52 [αὐτοῦ] {C}

Since external evidence for and against the presence of αὐτοῦ is so evenly balanced, and since considerations of internal probabilities are not decisive, the Committee decided to retain the word enclosed within square brackets.

6.56 αὐτῷ

After αὐτῷ codex Bezae adds what appears to be a homiletic expansion, καθὼς ἐν ἐμοὶ ὁ πατὴρ κἀγὼ ἐν τῷ πατρί. ἀμὴν ἀμὴν λέγω ὑμῖν, ἐὰν μὴ λάβητε τὸ σῶμα τοῦ υἱοῦ τοῦ ἀνθρώπου ὡς τὸν ἄρτον τῆς ζωῆς, οὐκ ἔχετε ζωὴν ἐν αὐτῷ ("As the Father is in me, I also am in the Father. Truly, truly, I say to you, if you do not receive the body of the Son of Man as the bread of life, you have no life in him"; the sentence "if you … in him" is also read by it[a, ff2]). For the thought, compare 10.38 and 6.53.

6.58 οἱ πατέρες {A}

Since the evidence for οἱ πατέρες is predominantly Egyptian, one might argue that the absence of ὑμῶν is the result of Alexandrian pruning. On the whole, however, it is more probable that, owing to the statement οἱ πατέρες ὑμῶν ἔφαγον ἐν τῇ ἐρήμῳ τὸ μάννα καὶ ἀπέθανον in ver. 49, a variety of copyists introduced ὑμῶν (or, by itacism, ἡμῶν) into the present passage. In any case, the reading τὸ μάννα in later witnesses is clearly secondary.

6.64 τίνες εἰσὶν οἱ μὴ πιστεύοντες καί {B}

The omission of these words from several witnesses (𝔓⁶⁶* 1344* itᵉ syrᶜˋ ˢ) is no doubt the result of oversight in transcription, occasioned perhaps by homoeoarcton (τίνες … τίς). The omission of μή by ℵ Xᶜᵒᵐᵐ *al* is less easy to account for, but it may be the result of a desire to indicate that Jesus knew his own, rather than those who were not his own. The parallelism, however, with the first part of the verse seems to require the presence of the negative.

6.69 ὁ ἅγιος τοῦ θεοῦ {A}

The reading adopted for the text, decisively supported by 𝔓⁷⁵ ℵ B C* D L W *al*, was expanded in various ways by copyists, perhaps in imitation of expressions in 1.49; 11.27; and Mt 16.16.

6.71 Ἰσκαριώτου

Several witnesses (ℵ* Θ *f*¹³ syrʰᵐᵍ ᵍʳ) interpret "Iscariot" as ἀπὸ Καρυώτου, that is, אִישׁ קְרִיּוֹת (*ish Qᵉriyyot(h)*) "man of Kerioth" [a town in southern Judea]. On the basis of preponderant external evidence (𝔓⁶⁶, ⁷⁵ B C L W Ψ 33 *al*) the genitive case Ἰσκαριώτου, agreeing with Σίμωνος, is to be preferred to the accusative case Ἰσκαριώτην, agreeing with Ἰούδαν. (The omission of "Simon" from syrˢ and one ms. of the Vulgate is undoubtedly accidental.) For the spelling Σκαριώθ (D itᵃˑ ᵇˑ ᵈˑ ⁽ff²⁾ˑ ʳ¹) and its variants, see the comment on Mt 10.4.

7.1 ἤθελεν {A}

Although it can be argued that, in view of John's usage elsewhere of ἔχειν ἐξουσίαν, meaning "to be able" (10.18, twice; compare 19.10), the reading of W itᵃˑ ᵇˑ ff²ˑ ¹ˑ ʳ¹ syrᶜ Chrysostom (εἶχεν ἐξουσίαν) should be regarded as original, particularly because it also appears to be the more difficult reading. Since, however, the idiom is not peculiar to John but occurs elsewhere as well, the Committee judged that the overwhelming weight of external evidence supporting ἤθελεν more than counterbalances any considerations bearing on the more difficult versus the less difficult reading.

7.8 οὐκ {C}

The reading οὔπω was introduced at an early date (it is attested by 𝔓⁶⁶, ⁷⁵) in order to alleviate the inconsistency between ver. 8 and ver. 10.

7.9 αὐτός {B}

The reading αὐτός, supported by 𝔓⁶⁶ ℵ D* W f¹ 565 al, is to be preferred as congruent with Johannine style. Copyists, however, apparently regarded it as superfluous and altered it to αὐτοῖς (𝔓⁷⁵ B Dᵇ Θ al), or replaced it with ὁ Ἰησοῦς as being more specific (itᶜ), or omitted it altogether (1365 l²⁶ itᵉ syrᶜ, ᵖ geo¹ al).

7.10 ἀλλὰ [ὡς] {C}

On the one hand, external evidence strongly supports the reading with ὡς (𝔓⁶⁶, ⁷⁵ B L W Θ Ψ f¹ f¹³ 28 33 565 700 al). On the other hand, transcriptional probability seems to favor the originality of the reading without ὡς (ℵ D itᵃ, ᵇ, ᵈ, ᵉ, ʳˡ syrᶜ, ˢ copˢᵃ, ᵇᵒᵐˢ, ᵃᶜʰ², ᶠᵃʸ geo Cyril), since a copyist may have inserted the word in order to soften the force of the expression ἐν κρυπτῷ. In order to represent the balance, a majority of the Committee preferred to retain the word in the text but to enclose it within square brackets to indicate doubt that it has a right to stand there.

7.36

At the close of ver. 36 manuscript 225 (copied A.D. 1192) inserts the pericope of the adulteress, usually found at Jn 7.53–8.11.

7.37 πρός με {B}

A majority of the Committee judged that the absence of πρός με from several witnesses (𝔓⁶⁶* ℵ* D itᵇ, ᵈ, ᵉ al) was probably due to scribal oversight.

7.39 οἱ πιστεύσαντες {B}

A majority of the Committee judged that the tendency among copyists would have been to replace the aorist participle (read by 𝔓⁶⁶, ⁷⁵ᵛⁱᵈ B L T W *l*¹⁸ syrˢ geo¹ *al*) with the present participle (read by ℵ D K X Δ Θ Π Ψ *f*¹ *f*¹³ 28 33 565 700 *al*).

7.39 πνεῦμα {A}

The reading that best explains the origin of the others is πνεῦμα, supported by 𝔓⁶⁶ᶜ, ⁷⁵ ℵ K T Θ Π Ψ 1079 *al*. The tendency to add ἅγιον was both natural and widespread among Christian scribes, whereas if the word had been present in the original, its deletion would be inexplicable. Furthermore, lest an uninformed reader imagine that John meant that the Spirit was not in existence prior to Jesus' glorification, copyists introduced a variety of modifications: (1) "the (Holy) Spirit was not yet *given* (δεδομένον)," read by B 1230 itᵃ, ᵇ, ᶜ, ᵉ, ff², ˡ, q, ʳ¹ vg syrᶜ, ˢ, ᵖ, ᵖᵃˡ geo² *al*; (2) "the Holy Spirit was not yet *upon them*," read by D* itᵈ goth; and (3) "not yet *came* the Holy Spirit," eth.

7.40 τῶν λόγων τούτων

Despite the simple, straightforward nature of the account, a curious multiplicity of variant readings developed during the transmission of the text. They include the following:

(1) τῶν λόγων τούτων 𝔓⁶⁶ᶜ, ⁷⁵ ℵᶜ B L T U itᵃ, ᵇ, ᵉ, q syrʰᵐᵍ, ᵖᵃˡ copˢᵃ, ᵇᵒ goth arm

(2) τῶν λόγων αὐτοῦ K W Π syrᶜ, ᵖ, ʰᵗˣᵗ

(3) αὐτοῦ τῶν λόγων τούτων 𝔓⁶⁶* ℵ* D Θ

(4) τῶν λόγων E H M Γ Δ*

(5) τὸν λόγον S Δ² Λ

(6) τὸν λόγον τοῦτον X many minuscules copˢᵃ eth

(7) τούτων τῶν λόγων G

(8) αὐτοῦ τὸν λόγον 124

(9) *omit* 106 *l*⁴⁴ syrˢ

Although John prefers to use the singular number of λόγος (the plural occurs elsewhere only in 10.19; 14.24; and 19.13), an analysis of the external evidence suggests that the singular number (variants 5, 6, and 8) is a secondary development from the plural. Likewise, the omission (9) must be accounted accidental. Reading (3) has the appearance of being a conflation. Of the other readings a majority of the Committee preferred (1) on the basis of age and diversity of external attestation.

7.46 ἐλάλησεν οὕτως ἄνθρωπος {B}

The crisp brevity of the reading supported by 𝔓⁶⁶ᶜ, ⁷⁵ B L T W copᵇᵒ al was expanded for the sake of greater explicitness in various ways, none of which, if original, would account for the rise of the others.

7.52 ἐκ τῆς Γαλιλαίας προφήτης {B}

The external evidence for the two readings is rather evenly divided. On the whole, however, the Committee was inclined to prefer the reading supported by 𝔓⁷⁵ᵛⁱᵈ B, thinking that a desire on the part of copyists to avoid hiatus may have given rise to the other reading.

7.53–8.11 Pericope of the Adulteress

The evidence for the non-Johannine origin of the pericope of the adulteress is overwhelming. It is absent from such early and diverse manuscripts as 𝔓⁶⁶, ⁷⁵ ℵ B L N T W X Y Δ Θ Ψ 0141 0211 22 33 124 157 209 788 828 1230 1241 1242 1253 2193 al. Codices A and C are defective in this part of John, but it is highly probable that neither contained the pericope, for careful measurement discloses that there would not have been space enough on the missing leaves to include the section along with the rest of the text. In the East the passage is absent from the oldest form of the Syriac version (syrᶜ, ˢ and the best manuscripts of syrᵖ), as well as from the Sahidic and the sub-

Achmimic versions and the older Bohairic manuscripts. Some Armenian manuscripts[1] and the Old Georgian version[2] omit it. In the West the passage is absent from the Gothic version and from several Old Latin manuscripts (it[a, l*, q]). No Greek Church Father prior to Euthymius Zigabenus (twelfth century) comments on the passage, and Euthymius declares that the accurate copies of the Gospel do not contain it.

When one adds to this impressive and diversified list of external evidence the consideration that the style and vocabulary of the pericope differ noticeably from the rest of the Fourth Gospel (see any critical commentary), and that it interrupts the sequence of 7.52 and 8.12 ff., the case against its being of Johannine authorship appears to be conclusive.[3]

At the same time the account has all the earmarks of historical veracity. It is obviously a piece of oral tradition which circulated in certain parts of the Western church and which was subsequently incorporated into various manuscripts at various places. Most copyists apparently thought that it would interrupt John's narrative least if it were inserted after 7.52 (D E (F) G H K M U Γ Π 28 700 892 *al*). Others placed it after 7.36 (ms. 225) or after 7.44 (several Georgian mss.)[4] or after 21.25 (1 565 1076 1570 1582 arm[mss]) or after Lk 21.38

---

[1] According to a note in Zohrab's edition of the Armenian version, "Only five of the thirty manuscripts we used preserve here the addition [i. e. the pericope of the adulteress] found in Latin manuscripts. The remainder usually agree with our exemplar in placing it as a separate section at the end of the Gospel, as we have done. But in six of the older manuscripts the passage is completely omitted in both places" (translated by Erroll F. Rhodes, who comments as follows in a note to the present writer: "When the pericope is found in manuscripts after 7.52, it is frequently accompanied with an asterisk or other symbol").

[2] The pericope is lacking in the Adysh ms. (A.D. 897), the Opiza ms. (A.D. 913), and the Tbet' ms. (A.D. 995).

[3] Occasionally an attempt is made to support the Johannine authorship of the pericope by appealing to linguistic and literary considerations (e. g. J. P. Heil in *Biblica*, LXXII [1992], pp. 182–191); for a convincing rebuttal of such arguments, see D. B. Wallace in *New Testament Studies*, XXXIX (1993), pp. 290–296. For patristic evidence of other forms and interpretations of the pericope, see B. D. Ehrman, *New Testament Studies*, XXXIV (1988), pp. 24–44.

[4] So Eberhard Nestle, who, however, identifies no specific manuscripts (*Einführung*

(f^{13}). Significantly enough, in many of the witnesses that contain the passage it is marked with asterisks or obeli, indicating that, though the scribes included the account, they were aware that it lacked satisfactory credentials.

Sometimes it is stated that the pericope was deliberately expunged from the Fourth Gospel because Jesus' words at the close were liable to be understood in a sense too indulgent to adultery. But, apart from the absence of any instance elsewhere of scribal excision of an extensive passage because of moral prudence, this theory fails "to explain why the three preliminary verses (vii 53; viii 1–2), so important as apparently descriptive of the time and place at which all the discourses of c. viii were spoken, should have been omitted with the rest" (Hort, "Notes on Select Readings," pp. 86 f.).

Although the Committee was unanimous that the pericope was originally no part of the Fourth Gospel, in deference to the evident antiquity of the passage a majority decided to print it, enclosed within double square brackets, at its traditional place following Jn 7.52.

Inasmuch as the passage is absent from the earlier and better manuscripts that normally serve to identify types of text, it is not always easy to make a decision among alternative readings. In any case it will be understood that the level of certainty ({A}) is within the framework of the initial decision relating to the passage as a whole.

8.6 τοῦτο δὲ ... αὐτοῦ {A}

A few manuscripts omit the first nine words of this verse, preferring to introduce the statement either after ver. 4 (D 1071) or after ver. 11 (M).

---

in das Griechische Neue Testament, 3te Aufl. [Göttingen, 1909], p. 157). According to information kindly provided by Dr. J. N. Birdsall, the pericope follows 7.44 in Sinai ms. georg. 16.

In the *editio princeps* of the Georgian Bible (Moscow, 1743), as well as the editions of the New Testament of 1816, 1818, 1878 (Gospels), and 1879, the pericope stands in its traditional place after 7.52.

8.7 *αὐτόν … αὐτοῖς* {A}

A few witnesses omit *αὐτόν* as superfluous, while others replace *αὐτοῖς* with the prepositional phrase *πρὸς αὐτούς*. Neither reading commended itself to the Committee.

8.8 *γῆν*

In order to satisfy pious curiosity concerning what it was that Jesus wrote upon the ground, after *γῆν* several witnesses (U Π 73 331 364 700 782 1592 arm^mss) add the words *ἑνὸς ἑκάστου αὐτῶν τὰς ἁμαρτίας* ("the sins of every one of them").

8.9 *οἱ δὲ ἀκούσαντες ἐξήρχοντο εἷς καθ' εἷς* {A}

The basic text of the pericope continued to be amplified by the addition of explanatory glosses. The Textus Receptus adds the statement that the woman's accusers were themselves "reproved by their conscience" *(ὑπὸ τῆς συνειδήσεως ἐλεγχόμενοι).*

8.9 *πρεσβυτέρων* {A}

The reading *πρεσβυτέρων* was enhanced by adding a clause (in one form or another) indicating that all of the woman's accusers went away.

8.10 *Ἰησοῦς* {A}

The text was elaborated by adding (in one form or another) a clause referring to Jesus' looking at the woman.

8.10 *ποῦ εἰσιν* {A}

The Textus Receptus, following E F G K 1079 *al*, adds *ἐκεῖνοι οἱ κατήγοροί σου* ("those accusers of yours").

8.16 *πατήρ* {A}

Although a minority of the Committee argued that *πατήρ*, which is absent from ℵ* D it^d syr^c, s, has crept into all other witnesses by assimilation to ver. 18, the majority of the Committee was impressed by the age, range, and diversity of evidence that attests the word, and judged that its omission from four or five manuscripts was due to transcriptional oversight.

8.25 ὅ τι {B}

Since the older Greek manuscripts lack punctuation and are written without division between words, it is possible to interpret Τὴν ἀρχὴν ... ὑμῖν in several ways:

1. As a question, with ὅτι = why? ("Why do I speak to you at all?").
2. As an exclamation, with ὅ τι in the sense of the Hebrew מָה ("That I speak to you at all!").
3. As an affirmation, with ὅ τι and supplying ἐγώ εἰμι ("[I am] from the beginning what I am telling you" or "Primarily [I am] what I am telling you" or "[I am] what I have told you from the beginning").

Several Latin witnesses (and the Gothic), misunderstanding the Greek, translate *Principium, qui et loquor vobis* ("[I am] the Beginning, even I who speak to you"). The Ethiopic omits ὅτι ("[I am] the Beginning, and I told you so"). The Bodmer Papyrus II ($\mathfrak{P}^{66}$) reads, according to a marginal correction that may be by the original scribe, Εἶπεν αὐτοῖς ὁ Ἰησοῦς, Εἶπον ὑμῖν τὴν ἀρχὴν ὅ τι καὶ λαλῶ ὑμῖν ("Jesus said to them, I told you at the beginning what I am also telling you [now]").[1]

8.34 τῆς ἁμαρτίας {A}

A majority of the Committee explained the absence of τῆς ἁμαρτίας from several witnesses of the Western text (D it[b, d] syr[s] cop[bomss] Clement *al*) as a stylistic improvement introduced by copyists either (*a*) because τὴν ἁμαρτίαν occurs just a few words

---

[1] For full discussions of the difficulties of the passage, see R. W. Funk, *Harvard Theological Review*, LI (1958), pp. 95–100, and E. R. Smothers, S.J., *ibid.,* pp. 111–122, who independently prefer the reading of $\mathfrak{P}^{66c}$.

earlier or (*b*) in order to make a closer connection with the following general expression ὁ δὲ δοῦλος.

8.38   παρὰ τῷ πατρί   {B}

The addition of μου after πατρί and/or the addition of ταῦτα as correlative to ἅ appear to be natural explications that copyists would have been inclined to make in the interest of greater clarity; whereas, if either or both had been present originally, it is difficult to explain their omission in the oldest witnesses. (See also the comment on the following variant reading.)

8.38   ἠκούσατε παρὰ τοῦ πατρὸς ποιεῖτε   {B}

Although ἑωράκατε is early and widespread ($\mathfrak{P}^{66}$ ℵ* D Δ Ψ the Old Latin vg syr[s, p, h] cop[sa, bo][mss, ach2] *al*), a majority of the Committee judged that it was introduced by copyists in order to balance ἑώρακα in the preceding clause; on the other hand, if ἑωράκατε were original, there is no reason why scribes should have substituted ἠκούσατε. A majority of the Committee regarded ὑμῶν after τοῦ πατρός (or τῷ πατρί, the dative having been introduced for the sake of uniformity with the preceding clause) and ταῦτα as scribal refinements, the former having been inserted in an attempt to clarify what was taken to be a contrast between God and the devil. (This contrast, however, seems to be introduced at ver. 41.) Without the possessive pronouns, both instances of the word "father" in ver. 38 seem to refer to God, and ποιεῖτε is probably imperative mood.

8.39   ἐποιεῖτε   {B}

It appears that the original text of this verse involved a mixed conditional sentence, with εἰ … ἐστε in the protasis, and ἐποιεῖτε in the apodosis ("If you are really Abraham's children, you would be doing the works of Abraham"). The variant readings arose in an effort to make a more grammatically "correct" condition; thus, instead of ἐστε ($\mathfrak{P}^{66, 75}$ ℵ B D L T Ψ 070 1321 *l*[60] it[ff2] vg syr[s]), the later text reads ἦτε (C N W X Γ Δ Θ Λ Π *f*[1] *f*[13] it[a, b, c, e, l, q] cop[sa, bo] *al*), which, with ἐποιεῖτε, makes a condition contrary to fact. Other witnesses add ἄν, even though in koine Greek "the addition of ἄν to the apodosis is no longer obligatory" (Blass-Debrunner-Funk, *Grammar*, § 360, 1).

8.44   οὐκ ἕστηκεν {C}

The form ἕστηκεν (imperfect of στήκω), supported by 𝔓⁶⁶ ℵ B* C D L W X Δ Θ Ψ f¹³ 33 892 *al*, follows more naturally after ἦν than does the perfect tense ἕστηκεν (𝔓⁷⁵ B³ K Π f¹ 28 565 700 *al*).

8.54   θεὸς ἡμῶν {B}

The reading ὑμῶν (ℵ B* D X Ψ 700 *al*) makes the words following ὅτι indirect discourse, whereas ἡμῶν (𝔓⁶⁶, ⁷⁵ A B² C K L W Δ Θ Π f¹ f¹³ 28 33 565 892 *al*) involves direct discourse. The Committee, noting that both readings have good manuscript support, judged that the change was more likely to go from direct to indirect discourse than vice versa.

8.57   πεντήκοντα ἔτη

In an attempt to harmonize the statement more closely with Lk 3.23, a few witnesses (Λ 239 262 1355 1555 Chrysostom Ps-Athanasius) read τεσσεράκοντα ("You are not yet *forty* years old").

8.57   ἑώρακας {B}

A few witnesses (𝔓⁷⁵ ℵ* 0124 syrˢ copˢᵃ, ᵇᵒᵐˢ, ᵃᶜʰ²) read ἑώρακέν σε ("… has Abraham seen you?"). This is doubtless a scribal assimilation of the Jews' question to Jesus' previous statement ("Abraham … [saw] my day," ver. 56). The reading chosen for the text, besides having much stronger manuscript attestation (𝔓⁶⁶ ℵᶜ A Bᶜ (B* W Θ 28 ἑώρακες) C D K L X Δ Π Ψ f¹ f¹³ 33 565 700 892 many others), is more fitting on the part of the Jews, who, assuming the superiority of Abraham (ver. 53), would naturally represent Jesus as seeing Abraham rather than Abraham as seeing Jesus.

8.59 ἱεροῦ {A}

The true text almost certainly closes with ἱεροῦ, which is attested by 𝔓[66, 75] ℵ* B D W Θ* it[a, b, c, d, e, ff2, l] vg syr[s] cop[sa, bomss, ach2] arm geo[1] *al*. In order to give the impression that Jesus escaped by miraculous power, copyists expanded the text by borrowing διελθὼν διὰ μέσου αὐτῶν from Lk 4.30, and then continuing with καὶ παρῆγεν οὕτως in preparation for the statement in 9.1. If any of these longer texts were original, there is no reason why the best representatives of the earliest text-types should have omitted it.

9.4 ἡμᾶς δεῖ ... πέμψαντός με {C}

Although it is difficult to choose among the readings, a majority of the Committee preferred ἡμᾶς δεῖ, (*a*) because of its somewhat superior external support, and (*b*) because it is slightly more probable that copyists would have altered ἡμᾶς to ἐμέ than vice versa. The reading πέμψαντος ἡμᾶς, which is a non-Johannine expression, appears to have been introduced into several witnesses (𝔓[66, 75] ℵ* L W cop[bo] *al*) as correlative with ἡμᾶς δεῖ at the beginning of the sentence.

9.21 αὐτὸν ἐρωτήσατε

In the interest of making a smoother sequence of clauses (cf. the sequence in ver. 23), the Textus Receptus, following A Γ Δ Λ most minuscules it[l, q] goth syr[p, h] *al*, transposes the words αὐτὸν ἐρωτήσατε to follow ἡλικίαν ἔχει. The omission of the clause in a few witnesses (ℵ* it[b] cop[sa] Chrysostom) is probably accidental (𝔓[75] replaces the clause with αὐτός).

9.35 ἀνθρώπου {A}

The external support for ἀνθρώπου (𝔓[66, 75] ℵ B D W syr[s] cop[sa, boms, ach2, fay] *al*) is so weighty, and the improbability of θεοῦ being altered to ἀνθρώπου is so great, that the Committee regarded the reading adopted for the text as virtually certain.

9.38-39 ὁ δὲ ἔφη ... καὶ εἶπεν ὁ Ἰησοῦς {B}

Several witnesses lack the words ὁ δὲ ἔφη, Πιστεύω κύριε·
καὶ προσεκύνησεν αὐτῷ. καὶ εἶπεν ὁ Ἰησοῦς (𝔓⁷⁵ ℵ* W itᵇ· ⁽¹⁾
copᵃᶜʰ; Diatessaronᵛ lacks verses 38 and 39 entirely¹). Since ἔφη is
rare in John (only at 1.23 and in some witnesses at 9.36) and since
προσκυνέω occurs nowhere else in John concerning Jesus, Brown
suggests that the words may be "an addition stemming from the
association of John ix with the baptismal liturgy and catechesis."²
Apart from the question whether such liturgical influence would have
been likely as early as 𝔓⁷⁵, in view of the overwhelming preponderance of external attestation in favor of the longer text it appears that
the omission, if not accidental, is to be regarded as editorial, made in
the interest of unifying Jesus' teaching in verses 37 and 39.

10.7 ἡ θύρα

The reading ὁ ποιμήν (𝔓⁷⁵ copˢᵃ· ᵃᶜʰ· ᵐᶠ) is an early alleviation of the
text, introduced by copyists who found the expression "the door of
the sheep" too difficult.

10.8 ἦλθον [πρὸ ἐμοῦ] {C}

It is difficult to decide whether copyists added πρὸ ἐμοῦ, before or
after ἦλθον, in order to make more sense from a highly compressed
statement, or whether they omitted the words in order to lessen the
possibility of taking the passage as a blanket condemnation of all Old
Testament worthies. Although the external evidence for the shorter
text is impressive (𝔓⁴⁵ᵛⁱᵈ· ⁷⁵ ℵ* E F G M S U Γ Δ 28 892 and most
minuscules, itᵃ· ᵇ· ᶜ· ᵉ· ff², l, q, rl vg syrˢ· ᵖ· ʰ· ᵖᵃˡ copˢᵃ· ᵇᵒᵐˢ· ᵃᶜʰ² goth al), and
although the divided testimony regarding the position of πρὸ ἐμοῦ
would normally suggest the secondary character of the words, a
majority of the Committee, observing that several witnesses (D itᵇ· ᵈ

---

¹ The editor, Alberto Vaccari, suggests that the two verses have dropped out
accidentally because verses 37 and 39 begin in the same way (*Dixit ei Iesus*).
² Raymond E. Brown, *The Gospel According to John (i–xii)* (New York, 1966),
p. 375.

vg^{ms}) omit πάντες in order to lessen the scope and drastic nature of the statement, judged that the least unsatisfactory decision was to retain the words πρὸ ἐμοῦ after ἦλθον but to enclose them within square brackets.

10.11 τίθησιν {B}

Instead of the expression "to lay down one's life," which is characteristically Johannine (10.15, 17; 13.37, 38; 15.13; 1 Jn 3.16 *bis*), several witnesses ($\mathfrak{P}^{45}$ א* D *al*) substitute the expression "to give one's life," which occurs in the Synoptic Gospels (Mt 20.28; Mk 10.45).

10.15 τίθημι {B}

See the comment on ver. 11.

10.16 γενήσονται {C}

Although both readings are well attested, the Committee judged that the plural γενήσονται has slightly stronger support ($\mathfrak{P}^{45}$ א^c B D L W X Θ Ψ f^1 33 565 *al*) than the singular γενήσεται ($\mathfrak{P}^{66}$ א* A K Δ Π f^{13} 28 700 *al*). Furthermore, the singular number appears to be a stylistic correction.

10.16 μία ποίμνη

All known witnesses except the Latin Vulgate read "one flock." Jerome's erroneous rendering *unum ovile* ("one fold") was followed by Wycliff and the translators of Cromwell's Great Bible, the Geneva Bible, the Bishops' Bible, the Rheims-Douay Bible, and the Authorized or King James Bible.

10.18 αἴρει {B}

Although the aorist ἦρεν ("No one *has taken* [my life] from me") has early and good support ($\mathfrak{P}^{45}$ א* B), and although it may seem to be preferred as the more difficult reading, a majority of the Committee judged that its external attestation was too limited in extent, representing, as it does, only a single textual type (the Egyptian).

10.19 πάλιν {B}

Although the external evidence for ($\mathfrak{P}^{66}$ A D Δ Θ Ψ *al*) and against ($\mathfrak{P}^{75}$ ℵ B L W *al*) the presence of οὖν in the text is rather evenly balanced, the Committee considered it more likely that the word would have been added than omitted in transcription.

10.22 τότε {B}

Of the four variant readings, δὲ τότε (1321 cop[samss, bo, ach2]) can be dismissed as a conflation, and the absence of any particle (f^1 565 1010 1344 it[a, b] syr[s] geo[1] *al*) is due either to an accident in transmission or to deliberate omission at the beginning of a lection. Both τότε and δέ are well attested. In view of the preceding ἐγένετο the origin of either reading *(εγενετοτοτε or εγενετοδε)* is susceptible of explanation on transcriptional grounds (dittography or haplography), followed by confusion (not infrequent in some Greek manuscripts) of δέ and τε. After considerable debate a majority of the Committee preferred τότε as "too appropriate not to have been included originally."

10.26 ἐμῶν {B}

The two readings, which are almost equally well attested, can be evaluated in different ways. On the one hand, a minority of the Committee explained the absence of the clause καθὼς εἶπον ὑμῖν to be the result of deliberate deletion by copyists who could find in the previous account no saying of Jesus that the Jews were not of his sheep. On the other hand, the majority of the Committee regarded the clause as an obvious scribal accretion to the text.

10.29 ὃ δέδωκέν μοι πάντων μεῖζόν ἐστιν {D}

In sorting out this nest of variant readings that present all possible combinations of the masculine or neuter relative pronoun and the masculine or neuter comparative adjective, only those readings need be seriously considered which involve the sequence ὁ πατήρ μου ὅ … (for the sequence ὁ πατήρ μου ὅς, if original, would almost certainly not have been altered). The reading of ℵ L W Ψ is impossible Greek, and cannot be construed. This leaves the reading of B*, which is supported by the Old Latin, Vulgate, Bohairic, Gothic, Ambrose, and Augustine (the difference of sequence of μεῖζον πάντων in the versions may be accounted for as translational variation). It thus appears that the reading ὁ πατήρ μου ὅ δέδωκέν μοι πάντων μεῖζόν ἐστιν, because of the unexpected sequence of neuter relative pronoun after ὁ πατήρ μου ("my Father," by hyperbaton, functions as subject of δέδωκεν within the relative clause), best explains the origin of the other readings.

10.38 καὶ γινώσκητε {B}

Copyists seem to have regarded the reading καὶ γινώσκητε, which has early and diversified support (𝔓[45, 66, 75] B L (W X γινώσκετε) Θ f[1] 33 565 al), to be pleonastic after γνῶτε, and therefore either replaced the verb with πιστεύσητε (as in (ℵ πιστεύητε) A K Δ Π Ψ f[13] 28 700 al) or omitted it entirely (as in D it[a, b, c, d, e, ff2, l] syr[s] al).

10.39 ἐζήτουν [οὖν] {C}

The absence of οὖν, a favorite connective in the Fourth Gospel, may be accounted for through haplography (ἐζήτουν), but its replacement with δέ or καί in other witnesses was deemed by the Committee as sufficient reason to enclose the word within square brackets.

11.17 τέσσαρας ἤδη ἡμέρας

There are four variant readings:
(1) τέσσαρας ἤδη ἡμέρας 𝔓[75] B C* Θ f[13] al
(2) τέσσαρας ἡμέρας ἤδη ℵ A[c] C[3] L W X Γ Δ Λ Π f[1] Byz

(3) ἤδη τέσσαρας ἡμέρας 𝔓⁶⁶ itᵃ, ˡ, ᵖ goth

(4) τέσσαρας ἡμέρας A* D 237 itᵉ syrˢ, ᵖ copˢᵃ, ᵇᵒ, ᵃᶜʰ arm eth geo

Among the several readings, that chosen for the text is the best supported and also accounts best for the rise of the others. Copyists were either dissatisfied with ἤδη separating τέσσαρας ἡμέρας and so moved it before or after the phrase, or, in a few cases, they omitted the word by an accident in transcription, either when "four" was written as a word (ΤΕϹϹΑΡΑϹΗΔΗΗΜΕΡΑϹ) or, more likely, when it was represented as a numeral (ΔΗΔΗΗΜΕΡΑϹ).

11.21   κύριε {A}

The absence of κύριε (see ver. 32), though supported by two early witnesses of different text types (B and syrˢ), is probably the result of transcriptional oversight.

11.25   καὶ ἡ ζωή {A}

The omission of καὶ ἡ ζωή from several witnesses (𝔓⁴⁵ itˡ syrˢ, ᵖᵃˡᵐˢ Diatessaronˢʸʳ Cyprian Paulinus-Nola) is puzzling. Was it added in the great mass of witnesses in anticipation of the thought expressed by the following ζήσεται and ὁ ζῶν, or was it omitted, perhaps by accident in transcription or because ver. 24 makes mention of the resurrection alone? On the basis of considerations of the age, weight, and diversification of witnesses that include the words, a majority of the Committee preferred to retain them in the text.

11.31   δόξαντες {B}

The manuscript support for δόξαντες is early (the nonsensical reading δοξάζοντες of 𝔓⁷⁵ 33 is tantamount to testimony supporting δόξαντες) and widely diversified (ℵ B C* D L W X f¹ f¹³ 700 syrˢ, ᵖ, ʰᵐᵍ copᵇᵒ arm eth geo). The reading λέγοντες may have arisen when it was asked how the evangelist could have known the thoughts of the Jews (as also in 11.13, where ms. X substitutes ἔλεγον for ἔδοξαν).

11.32 πρός

The reading πρὸς τοὺς πόδας (in the description of Mary's falling *at* Jesus' feet) is supported by early and diverse attestation ($\mathfrak{P}^{75}$ ℵ B C* D L W X Ψ *f*[1] 33 *al*); other witnesses (including $\mathfrak{P}^{66}$ A C³ Γ Δ Θ Λ Π *f*[13] *al*) read εἰς τοὺς πόδας. Although the latter expression is admittedly strange, and therefore likely to be altered, a majority of the Committee was impressed by the superior external evidence supporting πρὸς τοὺς πόδας.

11.33 ἐνεβριμήσατο τῷ πνεύματι καὶ ἐτάραξεν ἑαυτόν

Instead of the reading adopted as the text, several witnesses ($\mathfrak{P}^{45}$ ($\mathfrak{P}^{66?}$) D Θ *f*[1] 22 131 660 1582 2193 it^p cop^{sa, ach} arm) read ἐταράχθη τῷ πνεύματι ὡς ἐμβριμούμενος. Since the latter is the easier reading (for it softens the statement by inserting ὡς), a majority of the Committee regarded it as a secondary improvement, introduced from a sense of reverence for the person of Jesus.

11.50 ὑμῖν {B}

The second person pronoun, which is strongly supported ($\mathfrak{P}^{45, 66}$ B D L X *al*), is in accord with the tone of contempt represented by the closing words of ver. 49. The omission of the pronoun from ℵ and a few other witnesses may be accidental or under the influence of 18.14.

11.51 τοῦ ἐνιαυτοῦ ἐκείνου

Through carelessness the scribes of $\mathfrak{P}^{66}$ and D omit ἐκείνου, doubtless because of confusion arising from the ending of the previous word. The whole expression "of that year" is omitted by $\mathfrak{P}^{45}$ it^e syr^s, perhaps as redundant after ver. 49.

12.1 Λάζαρος {A}

Although the absence of ὁ τεθνηκώς from ℵ B L W X it^{a, c, e, rl} syr^{p, pal} cop^{sa, boms} eth *al* can be explained as a deliberate deletion because it seemed entirely superfluous in view of the following clause, a majority of the Committee, impressed by the external attestation supporting the shorter reading, judged the words to be a scribal gloss that was added at an early date (it is read by 𝔓⁶⁶).

12.4 Ἰούδας ὁ Ἰσκαριώτης εἷς [ἐκ] τῶν μαθητῶν αὐτοῦ

The identification of Judas as Σίμωνος (A K X Δ Θ Π Ψ 065 *f*¹³ 28 *Byz*) or as Σίμων (1195 1242* 1344 2148 *al*) is a scribal accretion derived from 6.71. These same witnesses also smooth the sequence by placing the name after the indefinite εἷς ἐκ τῶν μαθητῶν αὐτοῦ and before ὁ μέλλων αὐτὸν παραδιδόναι. It was thought best to retain the words εἷς ἐκ, an expression that occurs in eleven other passages in the Fourth Gospel, but in view of the absence of ἐκ in such early and noteworthy witnesses as 𝔓⁶⁶, ⁷⁵ᵛⁱᵈ B L W 33, to enclose it within square brackets. (For the reading of D, see the comments on 6.71 and Mt 10.4.)

12.8 *include verse* {A}

The omission of μεθ' ἑαυτῶν ἐμὲ δὲ οὐ πάντοτε ἔχετε by 𝔓⁷⁵ and Λ* is clearly the result of parablepsis, the eye of the scribe passing from ἔχετε to ἔχετε. The omission of verses 7 and 8 from 0250 seems also to be due to a transcriptional accident, the scribe's eye passsing from ΕΙΠΕΝΟΥΝ to ΕΓΝΩΟΥΝ. It is much more difficult to account for the absence of ver. 8 from D itᵈ syrˢ. On the one hand, it can be argued that the words were added at an early date by a copyist who recalled the similar statement in Mt 26.11 and Mk 14.7. On the other hand, the overwhelming manuscript support for the verse seemed to a majority of the Committee to justify retaining it in the text.

12.9 Ἔγνω οὖν [ὁ] ὄχλος πολὺς ἐκ τῶν Ἰουδαίων {C}

It is natural to regard ὄχλος πολύς (𝔓⁶⁶*, ⁷⁵ A B³ K X Δ Θ Π Ψ *f*¹ 33 *Byz*) and ὁ ὄχλος ὁ πολύς (𝔓⁶⁶ᶜ W 0250 1010) as scribal ameliorations of the difficult reading ἔγνω οὖν ὁ ὄχλος πολύς (ℵ B* L 28 892 *al*). But the expression ὁ ὄχλος πολύς serving as the subject of a verb is such unusual Greek (with πολύς in the predicate position) that serious doubts arise whether the evangelist could have written it thus. A majority of the Committee therefore thought it appropriate to enclose ὁ within square brackets.

12.17 ὅτε {B}

The reading ὅτε is preferable to ὅτι because it is supported by generally superior external testimony, and because ὅτι appears to be an attempt to clarify the account, which otherwise could be taken to refer to two crowds (cf. ver. 18).

12.28 σου τὸ ὄνομα {A}

Instead of the reading "glorify thy name," found in all the early and in most of the later witnesses, several of the later witnesses (L X *f*¹ *f*¹³ 33 1071 1241 *al*), influenced by the recollection of the opening of Jesus' high-priestly prayer (17.1), read "glorify thy Son." In codex Bezae the assimilation takes a different form; while retaining τὸ ὄνομα, the scribe of D continues with words that recall 17.5, which in that manuscript reads ... τῇ δόξῃ ᾗ εἶχον παρὰ σοὶ πρὸ τοῦ τὸν κόσμον γενέσθαι.

12.32 πάντας ἑλκύσω {B}

Since the reading πάντα, supported by 𝔓⁶⁶ ℵ* D it vg syr^s, p, pal cop^sa, bo, ach2 goth eth geo¹ *al*, is ambiguous ("everyone," "all things," "all"), it is possible that copyists, desiring to remove the ambiguity, added a sigma. A majority of the Committee, however, favored the reading πάντας because of the weight of its external attestation and because it appears to be more congruent with Johannine theology. The reading πάντα, which suggests ideas of a cosmic redemption, may have arisen under the influence of Col 1.16-17 and/or Gnostic speculation.

12.40   ἐπώρωσεν {C}

The reading ἐπήρωσεν ($\mathfrak{P}^{66, 75}$ ℵ K W Π *al*) appeared to a majority of the Committee to have arisen in an attempt to supply a somewhat more suitable verb with τὴν καρδίαν than ἐπώρωσεν or πεπώρωκεν. The form πεπώρωκεν (B³ Δ *f*¹ 565 700 *Byz al*) has doubtless been assimilated to the tense of the preceding verb (τετύφλωκεν).

12.41   ὅτι {B}

A majority of the Committee preferred ὅτι to ὅτε, chiefly because of the age and weight of the supporting evidence ($\mathfrak{P}^{66, 75}$ ℵ A B L X Θ Ψ *f*¹ 33 *al*), but also because ὅτι appears, on the surface, to be somewhat less appropriate in the context than either ὅτε or ἐπεί (W), and so would be likely to provoke scribal alteration.

12.43   ἤπερ

The comparative particle ἤπερ, which occurs only here in the New Testament, is attested by $\mathfrak{P}^{75}$ A B D Γ Δ Π *al*. It was altered to the much more usual ὑπέρ by $\mathfrak{P}^{66c}$ ℵ L W X *f*¹ 33 69 565 *al*. In koine and Byzantine Greek the two words were pronounced alike.

13.2   γινομένου {B}

This verse contains two serious textual problems. The first involves but a single letter: δείπνου γενομένου is generally taken to mean "supper being ended" (AV), whereas δείπνου γινομένου means "during supper" (NRSV). The former reading is by far the more difficult, for it stands in opposition to the following context, which indicates that the supper was still in progress (verses 4 and 26). On the basis of what was felt to be superior manuscript evidence (ℵ* B L W X Ψ *al*), a majority of the Committee preferred the present tense. On the other hand, the minority, while preferring the aorist, interpreted it as an ingressive aorist, "supper having been served."

13.2 Ἰούδας Σίμωνος Ἰσκαριώτου {C}

There are several variations: the nominative or genitive case of "Judas," the position of the name in the sentence, and the case of "Iscariot." The genitive case Ἰούδα, with the transposition of the name so as to follow καρδίαν (A D K Δ Θ Π *f*¹ 28 33 700 892 *Byz*), is obviously the easier reading, which, if original, would not have been altered to a more difficult construction (Ἰούδας following ἵνα παραδοῖ αὐτόν, 𝔓⁶⁶ ℵ B L W X Ψ 0124 1241 *al*). Since, according to the best witnesses, John elsewhere (6.71 and 13.26) construes Iscariot with Simon, the father of Judas, a majority of the Committee thought it wise to adopt Ἰσκαριώτου with L Ψ 0124 1241 *al* (the reading Ἰούδα Σίμωνος Ἰσκαριώτου, found in most witnesses, may, of course, also be translated "[the heart] of Judas, the son of Simon Iscariot"). On the reading ... ἀπὸ Καρυώτου ... (D it⁽ᵈ⁾, ᵉ), see the comment on 6.71.

13.10 οὐκ ἔχει χρείαν εἰ μὴ τοὺς πόδας νίψασθαι {B}

The rearrangement of οὐκ ἔχει χρείαν to οὐ χρείαν ἔχει (C³ D E* K L Γ Δ Θ *f*¹³ 892 *al*) seems to have been made in the interest of euphony. Instead of εἰ μή the Textus Receptus (following C³ E* Δ *f*¹ 28 700 *al*) substitutes ἤ, which is to be construed as though the evangelist had written something like οὐκ ἄλλου τινὸς χρείαν ἔχει. The insertion of μόνον in two of the readings shows the influence of the preceding verse. More difficult to assess is the reading οὐκ ἔχει χρείαν νίψασθαι (ℵ it^c vg Tertullian Origen), for whose originality more or less plausible arguments can be advanced. Because, however, the words εἰ μὴ τοὺς πόδας may have been omitted accidentally (or even deliberately because of the difficulty of reconciling them with the following declaration, ἀλλ' ἔστιν καθαρὸς ὅλος), a majority of the Committee considered it safer to retain them on the basis of the preponderant weight of external attestation.

13.18 μου {C}

Although μετ' ἐμοῦ (𝔓⁶⁶ ℵ A D K W Δ Θ Π Ψ *f*¹ *f*¹³ 28 33 700 it vg syr^s, p, h, pal goth arm geo *al*) is much more widely attested than μου

(B C L 892 1071 1230 cop^{sa} eth *al*), which is also the reading of the
Septuagint, a majority of the Committee preferred the latter reading
because μετ᾽ ἐμοῦ may be an assimilation to Mk 14.18.

13.26   βάψω τὸ ψωμίον καὶ δώσω αὐτῷ   {C}

It is more likely that scribal alteration went from the simple
(δώσω) to the compound verb (ἐπιδώσω), which John uses nowhere
else. Furthermore, the Semitic, paratactic style of two finite verbs
connected by καί is typically Johannine, whereas the omission of the
conjunction and the hypotactic construction involving a participle
(βάψας) has the appearance of being a stylistic modification introduced by copyists in the interest of elegance. Likewise, the redundant
αὐτῷ after δώσω, so characteristic of a primitive, Semitic style,
would almost certainly be deleted by copyists. See also the comment
on the following variant reading.

13.26   βάψας οὖν τὸ ψωμίον [λαμβάνει καὶ] δίδωσιν   {C}

It is difficult to decide whether the words λαμβάνει καί were
added by copyists to recall Jesus' deliberate action at the Last Supper
in *taking* bread (Mt 26.26; Mk 14.22; Lk 22.19; 1 Cor 11.23), or
whether the words were omitted as irrelevant and unnecessary. In
order to reflect the balance of both external attestation and transcriptional probabilities, a majority of the Committee decided to retain the
words enclosed within square brackets.

13.26   Ἰσκαριώτου

Both the weight of manuscript evidence and transcriptional probability, along with what seems to be Johannine usage elsewhere (6.71;
13.2), appeared to the Committee to favor the genitive Ἰσκαριώτου.
On the reading of codex Bezae, see the comment on 6.71.

13.32   [εἰ ὁ θεὸς ἐδοξάσθη ἐν αὐτῷ]   {C}

Normally the age and range of the witnesses that support the
shorter text (𝔓⁶⁶ ℵ* B C* D L W X Π *f*¹ *al*) would seem to create a

presumption that the clause εἰ ὁ θεὸς ἐδοξάσθη ἐν αὐτῷ is a secondary intrusion into such witnesses as ℵ^c A C² K Δ Θ Ψ f^13 28 33 565 700 892, followed by the Textus Receptus. On the other hand, however, the absence of the words can be accounted for either as the result of (a) transcriptional oversight because of homoeoteleuton (ἐν αὐτῷ … ἐν αὐτῷ) or (b) deliberate deletion because of supposed redundancy of thought (yet there is a logical connection rightly expressed between the earlier and subsequent glorification, and the step-parallelism is characteristically Johannine). Faced with this dilemma a majority of the Committee preferred to retain the words in the text but to enclose them within square brackets.

13.32 ἐν αὐτῷ (2) {B}

In view of the parallelism in the successive clauses of verses 31 and 32, a majority of the Committee preferred to adopt the reading of 𝔓^66 ℵ^{*, b} B 2148 syr^{p, h, palmss} cop^{sa, bo, ach2, fay}, and to use the smooth breathing on αὐτῷ. Despite what appears to be Hellenistic usage, a minority of the Committee strongly preferred to use the rough breathing on αὑτῷ.

13.37 Κύριε {A}

Κύριε, which is absent from ℵ* 33 565 vg syr^s cop^{sams, bomss}, may be regarded as an accretion in the other witnesses by assimilation to ver. 36. On the other hand, however, in view of early and widespread manuscript support for the word, a majority of the Committee voted to retain it, explaining its omission as either accidental (κύριε was often contracted to κ̅ε̅) or deliberate (because it seemed redundant so soon after Κύριε in ver. 36).

14.2 ὅτι {B}

In this passage, where ὅτι may mean either "that" or "because," its absence from some witnesses (𝔓^{66*} C^{2vid} Δ Θ 28 700 Byz Lect, followed by the Textus Receptus) is probably to be explained as a simplification introduced by copyists who took it as ὅτι recitativum, which is often omitted as superfluous.

14.4 τὴν ὁδόν {B}

The syntactical harshness of the shorter reading ὅπου ἐγὼ ὑπάγω οἴδατε τὴν ὁδόν (𝔓⁶⁶ᶜ ℵ B C* L W X 33 1071 itᵃ, ʳlᵛⁱᵈ copᵇᵒ eth) seems to invite amelioration. Since Thomas in ver. 5 distinguishes between "where" and "the way," copyists improved ver. 4 by expanding so as to read ὅπου ἐγὼ ὑπάγω οἴδατε καὶ τὴν ὁδὸν οἴδατε.

14.7 ἐγνώκατέ με {C}

The reading adopted by a majority of the Committee here and in the following set of variants involves a promise: "If you have come to know me [as in fact you do], you shall know my Father also." Despite the harmony between this statement and the rest of ver. 7, another interpretation of Jesus' words gained wide currency, this one a reproach: "If you had come to know me [which, alas, you do not], you would have knowledge of my Father also." The latter construction (a condition contrary to fact) seems to have arisen either because copyists recalled Jesus' reproach against unbelieving Jews in 8.19 or because Philip's question (ver. 8) and Jesus' reply (ver. 9) suggested to them that the disciples knew neither Jesus nor the Father.

[The purpose of the Evangelist as well as the laws of textual development have been misunderstood. If a negative and a positive statement about the Apostles stand side by side in the textual tradition, the positive one is usually the later. K.A.]

14.7 γνώσεσθε {C}

See the comment on the preceding set of variants.

14.11 πιστεύετε {B}

A variety of witnesses, including several of the earliest (𝔓⁶⁶, ⁷⁵ ℵ D L W 33 1071* itᶜ, ᵈ, ᵉ, ʳl vg syrᶜ, ᵖ, ᵖᵃl copˢᵃ, ᵇᵒᵐˢ, ᵃᶜʰ²), have resisted the temptation to assimilate the construction to the preceding πιστεύετέ μοι.

14.14　*include verse* {A}

Ver. 14 is omitted by a scattering of witnesses, including several important ancient versions (X *f*¹ 565 1009 1365 *l*⁷⁶, ²⁵³ it^b vg^ms syr^c, s, pal arm geo Nonnus). Furthermore, Λ* omits ver. 14 and the last seven words of ver. 13, the eye of the scribe having passed from ποιήσω to ποιήσω. The omission of ver. 14 can be variously explained: (*a*) it was due to an accident in transcription, the eye of the scribe having passed from ϵⲀⲚ to ϵⲀⲚ; (*b*) similarity in sentiment and even in expression with the first part of ver. 13 prompted parsimonious scribes to delete; (*c*) it was deliberately omitted in order to avoid contradiction with 16.23.

14.14　*με* {B}

Either the unusual collocation, "ask *me* in *my* name," or a desire to avoid contradiction with 16.23 seems to have prompted (*a*) the omission of *με* in a variety of witnesses (A D K L Π Ψ *Byz al*) or (*b*) its replacement with τὸν πατέρα (249 397). The word *με* is adequately supported (𝔓⁶⁶ ℵ B W Δ Θ *f*¹³ 28 33 700 *al*) and seems to be appropriate in view of its correlation with ἐγώ later in the verse.

14.15　*τηρήσετε* {C}

A majority of the Committee preferred the future tense *τηρήσετε*, read by B L Ψ 1010 1071 1195* 2148 *al* (and perhaps supported indirectly by witnesses that read the aorist subjunctive *τηρήσητε*, 𝔓⁶⁶ ℵ 060 33 *al*), instead of the imperative *τηρήσατε*, which, though rather well supported (A D K W X Δ Θ Π *f*¹ *f*¹³ 28 565 700 892 *Byz*), accords less well with ἐρωτήσω in the following verse.

14.17　*μένει ... ἔσται* {C}

A majority of the Committee interpreted the sense of the passage as requiring the future ἔσται, which is adequately supported by 𝔓⁶⁶ᶜ, ⁷⁵ᵛⁱᵈ ℵ A Θ Ψ *f*¹³ 28 33ᵛⁱᵈ 700 syr^s, h *al*.

14.22   Ἰούδας, οὐχ ὁ Ἰσκαριώτης {A}

The singular and sub-singular readings in several versional witnesses are interesting from the standpoint of later hagiographical tradition. On the reading of codex Bezae, see the comments on 6.71 and Mt 10.4.

14.26   [ἐγώ]

The emphatic pronoun ἐγώ, read by B L 060 0141 (33 ἐγὼ εἶπον ὑμῖν, cf. ver. 28) 127 1819, is omitted (perhaps as unnecessary) by 𝔓[75vid] ℵ A D Γ Δ Θ *f*[1] *f*[13] *Byz.* In the absence of any compelling internal considerations, and in order to reflect the somewhat unusual division of external attestation, the Committee thought it necessary to retain the word in the text, but to enclose it within square brackets.

It is possible to punctuate by taking ἐγώ with the following sentence, but this obscures the prominence otherwise given to εἰρήνην.

15.6   αὐτά

The plural αὐτά, attested by A B Γ Θ Λ *al*, appears to have been altered by copyists to the singular αὐτό (ℵ D L X Δ Π 0141 *f*[1] *f*[13] 33 565 1071 *al*) in order to agree grammatically with τὸ κλῆμα.

15.8   γένησθε {C}

The Committee found it exceedingly difficult to decide between γένησθε, which depends upon ἵνα and is coordinate with φέρητε, and γενήσεσθε, which probably[1] must be construed as an independent clause or sentence. The former was finally chosen, chiefly on the basis of the age and diversity of the external support (𝔓[66vid] B D L X Θ Π 0250 *f*[1] 565 1079 *al*).

---

[1] Yet on rare occasions the future indicative occurs with ἵνα; see Blass-Debrunner-Funk, § 369 (2).

16.4　*ὥρα αὐτῶν μνημονεύητε αὐτῶν* {B}

The double *αὐτῶν* is to be preferred both because of the strength of the external evidence ($\mathfrak{P}^{66vid}$ A B Θ Π* 33) and because *αὐτῶν* after *ὥρα* was more likely to be removed as superfluous than added by copyists.

16.13　*ὁδηγήσει ὑμᾶς ἐν τῇ ἀληθείᾳ πάσῃ* {B}

The construction of *εἰς* and the accusative seems to have been introduced by copyists who regarded it as more idiomatic after *ὁδηγήσει* than the construction of *ἐν* and the dative (ℵ D L W Θ *f*[1] 33 565 1071 *al*).

16.13　*ὅσα ἀκούσει*

The reading *ὅσα ἀκούσει,* supported by B D E* H W Y Ψ 1 213 397 579 1071 1689 *al,* is to be preferred as best accounting for the origin of the other readings: *ὅσα ἀκούει* (ℵ L 33 1819 *al*) is a dogmatic improvement, introduced to suggest the eternal relationship of the Holy Spirit with the Father, and *ὅσα ἂν ἀκούσῃ* (A G K M S U Γ Δ Π *al*) is a grammatical improvement.

16.16　*ὄψεσθέ με* {A}

Wishing to prepare for the disciples' question in ver. 17 about Jesus' going to the Father (and overlooking Jesus' statement in ver. 10), after *ὄψεσθέ με* copyists added, with minor variations, *ὅτι ὑπάγω πρὸς τὸν πατέρα.*

16.18　*[ὃ λέγει]* {C}

The repetitious character of the text in this verse has facilitated the emergence of variant readings, the evaluation of which is correspondingly difficult. In order to represent the balance of the weight of witnesses that support the presence of *ὃ λέγει* (ℵ[2] A B D[2] L Θ Ψ *al*) or its absence ($\mathfrak{P}^{5, 66}$ ℵ* D* W *f*[13] *al*), and in view of the possibility that the phrase was deleted either as being not absolutely necessary for the sense or was added in order to clarify the sense, the Committee decided to retain the words but to enclose them within square brackets.

16.22 ἔχετε {B}

In the opinion of a majority of the Committee the future ἕξετε (𝔓⁶⁶ ℵᶜ A D W* Θ Ψ 33 *al*) appears to have been introduced by copyists to bring the statement in accord with λυπηθήσεσθε in ver. 20. The present ἔχετε is strongly supported by 𝔓²² ℵ* B C K Wᶜ Δ Π *f*¹ *f*¹³ 28 565 700 892 *al*.

16.22 αἴρει {B}

Although the future ἀρεῖ is rather well supported (𝔓⁵ B D* *al*), a majority of the Committee was inclined to think that copyists would have been more likely to change the present tense to the future than vice versa. The external attestation for αἴρει is both ancient and widely diversified.

16.23 ἄν τι {B}

The thought of the clause is expressed with virtually identical meaning in four slightly different readings. On the basis of the weight of the combination of 𝔓⁵ᵛⁱᵈ B C and D* Ψ, the Committee regarded ἄν τι as most nearly representing the original text.

16.23 ἐν τῷ ὀνόματί μου δώσει ὑμῖν {C}

A majority of the Committee preferred the reading that places ἐν τῷ ὀνόματί μου between the verbs αἰτήσητε and δώσει, because (*a*) the external support for this reading is more diversified, whereas the witnesses that support the order δώσει ὑμῖν ἐν τῷ ὀνόματί μου are chiefly Egyptian, and (*b*) the context has to do with prayer, which the evangelist elsewhere links with the name of Jesus (14.13, 14; 16.15, 24, 26).

16.25 ἔρχεται

The abruptness of the shorter reading, supported by early and good witnesses (𝔓⁶⁶ᵛⁱᵈ ℵ B C* D* L W X Y 1 13 33 69 213 1582 itᵃ, ᵇ, ᵈ, ᵉ vg syrᵖᵃˡ copˢᵃ, ᵇᵒ arm), was alleviated by copyists who inserted ἀλλ᾽ or ἀλλά before ἔρχεται.

16.27 [τοῦ] θεοῦ {C}

The reading τοῦ πατρός, though strongly supported by B C* D L X *al*, is probably secondary, having arisen by assimilation to ἐξῆλθον παρὰ τοῦ πατρός of the following verse. The balance of evidence for and against the definite article is so close that a majority of the Committee thought it necessary to enclose the word within square brackets.

16.28 ἐξῆλθον παρὰ τοῦ πατρός {C}

Most members of the Committee regarded the omission in D W itᵇ, ᵈ, ᶠᶠ² syrˢ copᵃᶜʰ² as accidental, and, on the basis of slightly stronger external evidence (𝔓⁵, ²² ℵ A C² K Δ Θ Π *f*¹ *f*¹³ 28 565 700 892 *Byz Lect*), preferred the reading with παρά. The reading with ἐκ (B C* L X Ψ 33 *al*) seems to have arisen through assimilation to the compound verbs in the context.

17.1 ὁ υἱός {B}

It is difficult to decide whether σου was omitted because copyists thought it superfluous, or whether it was added in order to enhance the solemnity of the style. On the basis of the weight of 𝔓⁶⁰ᵛⁱᵈ ℵ B C* W 0109 itᵈ, ᵉ, ᶠᶠ² *al*, the shorter reading was preferred.

17.7 ἔγνωκαν

Although there is impressive support for the first person singular (ἔγνων, ℵ itᵃ, ᵇ, ᶜ, ᵉ, ᶠᶠ², ᑫ syrˢ, ᵖ, ʰᵐᵍ, ᵖᵃˡ copˢᵃ, ᵃᶜʰ goth pers; ἔγνωκα, W 7

118 138* 579 1188 2145* *l*³², ³⁶, ⁴⁴, ⁶⁰), a majority of the Committee regarded it either as a mistaken correction of a copyist influenced by the first person in ver. 6, or (in the case of ἔγνωκα) as an accidental error in transcription (loss of horizontal line over α, representing final ν). The reading ἔγνωκαν (A B C D L Y Θ *al*) accords with the Johannine use of the perfect tense; the aorist ἔγνωσαν (C U X Ψ *f*¹³ 33 *al*) appears to be a scribal assimilation to ver. 8.

17.8 καὶ ἔγνωσαν

It is curious that several witnesses (ℵ* A D W a few minuscules it^{a, e, q} goth) lack the words καὶ ἔγνωσαν. Lagrange suggests *(ad loc.)* that the phrase may have been deleted because it seemed to contradict 6.69.

17.11 ᾧ δέδωκάς μοι {B}

The reading that best accounts for the origin of the others has also the strongest attestation: the difficulty of ᾧ (which is read by 𝔓^{60vid, 66vid} ℵ A B C K L W Δ Θ Π Ψ 054 *f*¹ *f*¹³ 28 565 700 *Byz Lect*) prompted some copyists to replace the dative (which is attracted to the case of the antecedent) with the accusative ὅ (D* X 2148 *al*) or with the plural οὕς (D^b 892^{vid} 1009 vg goth eth geo² *al*). The latter correction could also have been prompted by the recollection of ver. 6 or the statement in 18.9. The omission of one or more clauses from several ancient witnesses (𝔓^{66*} it^{a, b, c, e, ff2, r1} syr^s cop^{ach2}) may be due to the difficulty of the original reading, or it may be accidental.

17.12 ᾧ δέδωκάς μοι, καί {B}

See the comment on ver. 11.

17.14 καθὼς ἐγώ … κόσμου {A}

Homoeoteleuton accounts for the accidental omission of the clause in several textual traditions.

17.21 ὦσιν (2) {B}

The better attested reading is ὦσιν ($\mathfrak{P}^{66vid}$ B C* D W it[a, b, c, d, e] syr[s] cop[sa, bomss, ach2] arm geo *al*). The pedantic addition of ἕν before ὦσιν (א A C³ K L X Δ Θ Π Ψ *f*¹ *f*¹³ 28 33 565 700 892 *Byz Lect*), which comes from ἕν ὦσιν earlier in the verse, clouds the thought more than illumines it.

17.23 ἠγάπησας (1) {A}

The Western reading, ἠγάπησα (D 0141 it syr), arose either through scribal inattentiveness or as a deliberate accommodation to 15.9.

17.24 ὅ δέδωκάς μοι {B}

The difficult ὅ, read by good representatives of several text-types ($\mathfrak{P}^{60}$ א B D W it[d] syr[s, pal] cop[bo] goth geo¹), was replaced in most witnesses by the easier οὕς, which prepares for the following κἀκεῖνοι.

18.1 τοῦ Κεδρών

There are three principal readings:

(a) τῶν κέδρων ("of the cedars") א[c] B C L N X Y Γ Δ Θ Ψ *f*¹ *f*¹³ *al*,

(b) τοῦ κέδρου ("of the cedar") א* D W it[a, b, r1] cop[sa, bomss, ach],

(c) τοῦ Κεδρών ("of Kidron") A S Δ 123 it[c, e, q] vg syr[s, p, pal] goth.

Despite weakness of external evidence a majority of the Committee considered that reading (c) accounts best for the origin of the other two readings (that is, what appears to be a lack of concord between article and noun was "corrected" by copyists who took the indeclinable proper noun Κεδρών (= קִדְרוֹן) to be the common word κέδρος). Indeed, the converse change, from (a) or (b) to (c), is scarcely conceivable, the tendency being to assimilate terminations.

18.5   Ἐγώ εἰμι. {C}

In considering the variant readings of this verse it must be recalled that normally scribes contracted the name Ἰησοῦς to ͞ι͞ς. On the one hand, it is possible that, if ὁ Ἰησοῦς stood originally after αὐτοῖς, the words may have been accidentally omitted through an oversight in transcription (ᴀͰΤΟΙϹΟΙϹ); or, if Ἰησοῦς stood originally before εἰστήκει (which in many manuscripts is written ἱστήκει), it may also have been accidentally omitted in transcription (͞ι͞ϹΙϹΤΗΚƐΙ). On the other hand, if ἐγώ εἰμι were the original reading, it is probable that copyists would have identified the speaker by inserting the proper name. The variation of position of (ὁ) Ἰησοῦς before or after ἐγώ εἰμι is further indication of the secondary character of the longer readings.

18.13-27   *order of verses* {A}

Because the usual sequence of these verses involves difficulties (in ver. 13 Jesus is brought before Annas first and what follows is apparently before him, whereas the Synoptists say nothing of the part played by Annas; ver. 24, in its present position, leaves the reader wondering what happened at the trial before Caiaphas), several witnesses seek to ease the sense by rearranging the order. Thus 225 (copied A.D. 1192) interpolates ver. 24 into the middle of ver. 13 (after πρῶτον), and 1195 (copied A.D. 1123) – joined by the marginal reading of the Harclean Syriac, by codex A of the Palestinian Syriac Lectionary, and by Cyril of Alexandria – interpolates ver. 24 after ver. 13. In spite of the interpolation, however, these witnesses have ver. 24 also in its proper position. A more elaborate rearrangement of the text is given by the Sinaitic Syriac (probably following Tatian's Diatessaron), namely verses 13, 24, 14-15, 19-23, 16-18, 25-27. (Luther, quite independently, proposed a similar order.)

18.27

See the comment on ver. 13.

18.30 κακὸν ποιῶν {B}

In the opinion of a majority of the Committee, the periphrastic construction ἦν ... κακὸν ποιῶν (ℵ^c B L W it^e syr^{h, pal} *al*; κακοποιῶν C* Ψ 33 *al*) was modified by copyists who introduced, perhaps from 1 Pe 2.12; 4.15, the substantive κακοποιός (A C³ D^{supp} K X Δ Θ Π 054 *f*¹ *f*¹³ 28 565 700 892 *Byz Lect*).

19.14 ἕκτη

Instead of "about the sixth hour" several witnesses (ℵ^c D^{supp} L X^{txt} Δ Ψ 053 72 88 123*^{mg} 151 Eusebius Nonnus) read "about the third hour" *(ὥρα ... ὡς τρίτη),* an obvious attempt to harmonize the chronology with that of Mk 15.25 (see the comment there on the converse corruption). Although one may conjecture that the disagreement originally arose (as Ammonius,[1] followed by Eusebius[2] and Jerome,[3] suggested) when copyists confused the Greek numerals Γ (= 3) and F (= 6),[4] the manuscript evidence is overwhelmingly in support of ἕκτη (𝔓⁶⁶ ℵ* B E H I K M S U W Y Γ Θ Λ Π *f*¹ *f*¹³ all minuscules (except those cited above) Old Latin vg syr^{p, h, pal} cop^{sa, bo} arm eth geo pers *al*).

19.16 Παρέλαβον ... Ἰησοῦν {B}

Both the ambiguity of "they" (those previously mentioned are the chief priests, whereas in ver. 18 "they" must refer to Roman soldiers) and the brevity of expression called for supplementation. Some scribes added καὶ ἤγαγον after Ἰησοῦν (D^{supp} Δ Θ *al*), others added

---

[1] Migne, *Patrologia Graeca,* LXXXV, col. 1512B.

[2] Migne, *Patrologia Graeca,* XXII, col. 1009B.

[3] Migne, *Patrologia Latina,* XXVII, col. 1108C.

[4] For a full discussion see Sebastián Bartina, S.J., "Ignotum *episèmon* gabex," *Verbum Domini,* XXXVI (1958), pp. 16–37, who reproduces a portion of Papyrus Berolinensis 8279 of A.D. 42 (edited by Wilhelm Schubart in *Papyri Graecae Berolinenses* [Bonn, 1911], p. XV, nr. 16a) showing first century specimens of the Greek numerals for 3 and 6. *Gabex (γαβέξ)* is the name given by Ammonius to the sign denoting six (see above, footnote 1).

ἀπήγαγον (‭א‬ A N W *f*¹ *al*), which is the reading at Mt 27.31 and Lk 23.36, while others enlarged the account still further, continuing with εἰς τὸ πραιτώριον (700 *al*), or with καὶ ἐπέθηκαν αὐτῷ τὸν σταυρόν (*f*¹³). The reading that apparently gave rise to the other readings is supported by B L Ψ 0141 33 it cop[bo].

19.20 Ἑβραϊστί, Ῥωμαϊστί, Ἑλληνιστί

The sequence "Hebrew, Latin, Greek" (i. e. the national language, the official language, the common language) is strongly supported by ‭א‬[a] B L N X 33 74 89 90 234 248 317 483 484 713 945 1321 1346 it[e, ff²] syr[pal] cop[sa, bo] arm eth. The sequence "Hebrew, Greek, Latin," which is read by A D[supp] I Y Γ Θ Λ Π most minuscules most of the Old Latin vg syr[p, h], appears to be a secondary development, with the languages arranged in accord with a geographical order going from East to West. The scribes of W and 1194 became confused and produced Ἑβραϊστί, Ῥωμαϊστί, Ἑβραϊστί. See also the comment on Lk 23.38, where the several forms of the Johannine reading have intruded into the Lukan text.

19.24 [ἡ λέγουσα] {C}

It is difficult to decide whether ἡ λέγουσα is an explanatory clause added to the text in most witnesses in order to let the reader know that what follows is a citation from Scripture (no similar addition, however, is found in similar cases at 13.18 and 19.36), or whether the clause was inadvertently omitted by two early Greek witnesses (‭א‬ B) and a variety of versions. Taking into account both of these possibilities, the Committee decided to include the clause but to enclose it within square brackets.

19.29 ὑσσώπῳ {A}

One eleventh-century manuscript (476*) reads ὑσσῷ ("a javelin"; compare *perticae* (it[b, ff², n, v] "a pole or long staff"), a reading which, though more appropriate in the context, seems to have arisen accidentally through haplography (ΥϹϹΩΠΕΡΙΘΕΝΤΕϹ being written for ΥϹϹΩΠΩΠΕΡΙΘΕΝΤΕϹ).[5] Influenced by Mt 27.34 several witnesses (Θ 892 1195 2174 *al*) read μετὰ χολῆς καὶ ὑσσώπου "with gall and hyssop." One Old Latin witness (it[c]) omits "hyssop" and reads merely *cum felle permixtum* "mixed with gall."

19.35 πιστεύ[σ]ητε

See the comment (with footnote 1) on 20.31.

19.39 μίγμα {B}

Although ἕλιγμα (ℵ* B W cop[boms]), being the more difficult reading (the word normally means "a fold, a wrapping," and not "a roll, a package," which would be required here), might seem to be preferable as explaining the rise of the other readings, a majority of the Committee was impressed by the earlier and more diversified testimony supporting μίγμα (𝔓[66vid] ℵ[c] A D[supp] K L X Δ Θ Π 054 *f*[1] *f*[13] 28 33 565 700 *Byz Lect*). Whether σμίγμα (Ψ 892 2174 *l*[47]) and σμῆγμα (1242* *l*[181] syr[pal]) developed from ἕλιγμα or from μίγμα is uncertain.

20.19 μαθηταί {A}

Before διά the Textus Receptus, following ℵ[2] Θ L Δ Ψ 33 *al*, adds the very natural supplement, συνηγμένοι, perhaps in recollection of Mt 18.20.

---

[5] Among modern translations that adopt "javelin" (or something similar) are those of Moffatt, Goodspeed, Phillips, C. K. Williams, Schonfield, and the NEB. G. D. Kilpatrick points out, however, that ὑσσός (Latin *pilum*) was not used by Roman auxiliary troops, but only by legionary troops, and that the latter were first sent to Judea A.D. 66 (*The Bible Translator,* IX [1958], pp. 133 f.); cf. R. G. Bratcher's remarks, "It may be granted that a 'javelin' and not a stalk of 'hyssop' would be the means of conveying the sponge to the lips of Jesus; this does not mean, however, that the author of the Gospel necessarily wrote ὑσσῷ; on the contrary the evidence is that he wrote … ὑσσώπῳ" (*Babel: Revue internationale de la traduction,* VII [1961], p. 61). For a wide-ranging discussion of the uses of hyssop see F. G. Beethan and P. A. Beethan, "A Note on John 19.29," *Journal of Theological Studies,* N.S. XLIV (1993), pp. 163–169.

20.21   *[ὁ Ἰησοῦς] πάλιν* {C}

It is difficult to decide whether ὁ Ἰησοῦς (written as a *nomen sacrum,* oιc) was accidentally added after ᴀᵧτoιc by dittography or omitted by haplography. On the basis of what was taken as the preponderant weight of the external evidence, a majority of the Committee considered the longer reading to be original.

20.23   *ἀφέωνται* {B}

Although the perfect tense ἀφέωνται could be regarded as a secondary assimilation to κεκράτηνται at the end of the sentence, a majority of the Committee interpreted the present tense ἀφίενται and the future ἀφεθήσεται as scribal simplifications which weaken the sense. To the external evidence supporting ἀφέωνται (‭א‬ᶜ A D (L) X 050 *f*¹ *f*¹³ 33ᵛⁱᵈ 565 *al*) should perhaps be added B*, which reads ἀφείονται (*ιο* being written for ω).

20.30   *μαθητῶν [αὐτοῦ]* {C}

In order to represent the close balance of external attestation for (𝔓⁶⁶ ‭א‬ C D L W X Θ Ψ *f*¹ *f*¹³ 33 565 700 892 *al*) and against (A B K Δ Π 0250 *al*) the inclusion of αὐτοῦ, the Committee retained the word enclosed within square brackets.

20.31   *πιστεύ[σ]ητε* {C}

Both πιστεύητε and πιστεύσητε have notable early support. The aorist tense, strictly interpreted, suggests that the Fourth Gospel was addressed to non-Christians so that they might come to believe that Jesus is the Messiah; the present tense suggests that the aim of the writer was to strengthen the faith of those who already believe ("that you may continue to believe").[1] In view of the difficulty of choosing between the readings by assessing the supposed purpose of the evan-

---

[1] In 19.35 πιστεύητε is read by ‭א‬* B Ψ Origen; apparently all other witnesses read πιστεύσητε.

gelist (assuming that he used the tenses of the subjunctive strictly), the Committee considered it preferable to represent both readings by enclosing σ within square brackets.

21.4   εἰς

Copyists have substituted the more "correct" ἐπί (ℵ A D L M U X Θ Ψ 33 700 1071 1188 1375 *al*) for the more difficult εἰς (B C E G H K P S W Γ Δ Λ Π *f¹ al*); the latter preposition with ἔστη in accounts of appearances of the risen Christ occurs elsewhere in the Fourth Gospel (20.19 and 26).

21.15, 16, 17   Ἰωάννου {B}

In place of Ἰωάννου, the Textus Receptus, following A C² Δ Θ Ψ *f¹ f¹³ al*, reads Ἰωνᾶ, an assimilation to Mt 16.17. See also the comment on Jn 1.42.

21.22, 23

The Latin Vulgate manuscripts of these verses present an interesting variant reading that played a considerable part in later mediaeval discussions of the preeminence of the Greek text over the Latin Vulgate when they differ, and in the question of possible dominical sanction of celibacy. The official Clementine edition of the Latin Vulgate reads *Sic eum volo manere donec veniam* ("I wish him [Peter] to remain thus until I come"). In the fifteenth century Cardinal Bessarion wrote a pamphlet[2] pointing out, among other errors in the Vulgate, that by a copyist's oversight the text reads *sic* instead of *si* (= ἐάν). According to modern critical editions of the Vulgate (those of Wordsworth and White[3] and of Robert Weber), Jerome's text

---

[2] Reprinted in Migne, *Patrologia Graeca,* vol. CLXI, cols. 623–640 (cf. an opposing position, set forth by George of Trebizond, *ib.,* cols. 867–882). For a brief account of the altercation, see L. D. Reynolds and N. G. Wilson, *Scribes and Scholars: a Guide to the Transmission of Greek and Latin Literature* (Oxford, 1968), pp. 127 f.

[3] See their note *in loc.*

originally contained both words, *si sic,* just as codex Bezae in ver. 22
(not however ver. 23) adds οὕτως after μένειν.[4]

21.23   ἔρχομαι, *[τί πρὸς σέ·]* {C}

Several witnesses, including ℵ* C² *f*¹ 565 it^(a, e) syr^s arm, lack the
words τί πρὸς σέ.[5] Although Tischendorf (8th ed.) and von Soden
regarded the shorter text as original (the evangelist often varies the
wording in a repeated phrase), it is also possible that copyists omitted
the clause in order to draw attention to what was taken as the primary
element in Jesus' reply (codex Bezae accomplishes the same effect
by omitting τί). In view of the close balance of probabilities, a majority of the Committee preferred to retain the clause, but to enclose it
within square brackets to indicate doubt that it belongs in the text.

21.25   βιβλία.

Many later manuscripts, followed by the Textus Receptus, conclude the Gospel with ἀμήν. See also the comment on Mt 28.20.

After ver. 25 several Greek minuscules (1 565 1076 1570 1582)
and many Armenian manuscripts[6] add the pericope of the adulteress
(7.53–8.11).

---

[4] According to J. R. Harris, the variant reading of codex Bezae in Jn 21.22 was
appealed to in private discussions of the question of celibacy during the earlier years of
the Council of Trent (*A Study of Codex Bezae* [Cambridge, 1891], pp. 36–39).

[5] The text of the same phrase in ver. 22 is firm.

[6] See footnote 1 on p. 188.

THE ACTS OF THE APOSTLES

Introduction

The text of the book of the Acts of the Apostles circulated in the early church in two quite distinct forms, commonly called the Alexandrian and the Western. The former, which has been traditionally regarded as the authentic text of Acts, is represented by $\mathfrak{P}^{45}$ $\mathfrak{P}^{74}$ ℵ A B C Ψ 33 81 104 326 and 1175. The other form is represented chiefly by D and the fragmentary papyri $\mathfrak{P}^{29}$, $\mathfrak{P}^{38}$, and $\mathfrak{P}^{48}$, by the readings marked with an asterisk or standing in the margin of the Harclean Syriac version (syr^h with *, syr^hmg), by the African Old Latin ms. h (a fifth or sixth century fragmentary palimpsest that preserves about 203 of the 1007 verses of Acts), and by the citations of Acts made by Cyprian and Augustine. These, which are the primary witnesses to the Western text in Acts, are sometimes joined by others that present mixed texts with a relatively high proportion of Western elements. Among such are the Armenian version of the commentary on Acts by Ephraem Syrus, the Old Georgian version of Acts, several mixed Old Latin and Vulgate manuscripts, and a few Greek minuscule manuscripts that were included by von Soden in his *I*-group. More recent discoveries of witnesses with decided Western affiliations include a Palestinian Syriac fragment (syr^msK) from the Kastellion Monastery at Khirbet Mird, dating from the sixth century,[1] and a Coptic manuscript (cop^G67) written in the Middle Egyptian dialect and dated by its editor in the late fourth or early fifth century.[2]

---

[1] The fragment, which preserves the text of Acts 10.28-29, 32-41, was edited by Charles Perrot in an article, "Un fragment christo-palestinien découvert à Khirbet Mird," *Revue Biblique*, LXX (1963), pp. 506–555.

[2] The manuscript, which contains the text of Acts 1.1–15.3 and is now in the Glazier Collection in the Pierpont Morgan Library in New York, was described and edited in a preliminary fashion by the late Fr. T. C. Petersen in an article, "An Early Coptic Manuscript of Acts: An Unrevised Version of the Ancient so-called Western Text," *Catholic Biblical Quarterly*, XXVI (1964), pp. 225–241. For a critique of Petersen's evaluation of the Coptic manuscript, see Ernst Haenchen and Peter Weigandt, "The

The two forms of text differ in character as well as length. The Western text is nearly one-tenth longer than the Alexandrian text,[3] and is generally more picturesque and circumstantial, whereas the shorter text is generally more colorless and in places more obscure (see also pp. 5*–6* above).

The relationship between the two forms of Acts has been the subject of much discussion;[4] the chief theories that have been proposed are the following.

(1) Both forms of text proceed from the author, who produced two editions of his work. The first to make this suggestion appears to have been Jean Leclerc, who, however, later rejected his own hypothesis.[5] In more modern times Bishop J. B. Lightfoot[6] took a rather favorable view of this theory, and it was subsequently adopted and developed

---

Original Text of Acts?" *New Testament Studies,* xiv (1967–68), pp. 469–481, who date the manuscript in the fifth or sixth century. A definitive edition, with a German translation on facing pages, was published by Hans-Martin Schenke, *Apostelgeschichte 1,1–15,3 im mittelägyptischen Dialekt des Koptischen (Codex Glazier) (Texte und Untersuchungen,* 137; Berlin, 1991).

[3] More precisely, it appears that in the text edited by Westcott and Hort (which is a typically Alexandrian type of text) the book of Acts has 18,401 words, whereas in the text established by A. C. Clark (which is a typically Western type of text) Acts has 19,983 words; that is, the latter text is about $8^1/_2\%$ longer (the figures are those of F. G. Kenyon, *The Western Text in the Gospels and Acts* [= *Proceedings of the British Academy,* vol. xxiv; London, 1939], p. 26).

[4] For a summary of the principal stages of this discussion, see A. F. J. Klijn, *A Survey of the Researches into the Western Text of the Gospels and Acts* (Utrecht, 1949); this was supplemented by Klijn to cover the research of 1949–1959 in an article in *Novum Testamentum,* iii (1959), pp. 1–27, 161–172; the latter material has been incorporated in a volume that covers the research of the period 1949 to 1969 and is entitled *A Survey of the Researches into the Western Text of the Gospels and Acts, Part Two* (Leiden, 1969). See also Eldon Jay Epp, *The Theological Tendency of Codex Bezae Cantabrigiensis in Acts* (Cambridge, 1966), pp. 1–21, and W. A. Strange, *The Problem of the Text of Acts* (Cambridge, 1992), pp. 2–34.

[5] *Sentiments de quelques théologiens de Hollande,* 1685, *Ep.* xvii (p. 451), dated Nov. 2, 1684 [quoted by A. C. Clark (see footnote 23 below), p.xxi]. For an instructive monograph on second editions in antiquity, see Hilarius Emonds, *Zweite Auflage im Altertum. Kulturgeschichtliche Studien zur Überlieferung der antiken Literatur* (Leipzig, 1941).

[6] *On a Fresh Revision of the English New Testament* (London, 1871), p. 29; 3rd ed. (1891), p. 32.

with much learning by the German professor of classics, Friedrich Blass.[7] According to Blass, Luke, having made a rough draft of his history of the primitive church, perhaps on the back of some previous manuscript, desired to present a handsome copy of his work to his distinguished friend Theophilus. Not being rich enough to employ a professional scribe to make the copy, Luke had to make it himself; naturally, instead of slavishly following his first draft, he exercised the freedom that an author can lawfully take with a work of his own, in altering phraseology and deleting superfluities. From both forms of Acts, according to Blass, copies were made; the text current in most manuscripts represents the polished, second edition prepared for Theophilus, while copies were also made from the original (longer) draft, which Blass supposed was treasured and preserved in the Roman church.

Nothing in this theory is inherently unreasonable, and it attracted the support of a number of other scholars, including Theodor Zahn,[8] Eberhard Nestle,[9] J. M. Wilson,[10] and M.-É. Boismard.[11] Other

---

[7] See his *Acta apostolorum, sive Lucae ad Theophilum liber alter,* editio philologica (Göttingen, 1895), and the more abbreviated edition, *Acta apostolorum ... secundum formam quae videtur Romanam* (Leipzig, 1896).

[8] *Introduction to the New Testament,* Eng. trans. from the third German ed., III (Edinburgh, 1909), pp. 8 ff.; and *Die Urausgabe der Apostelgeschichte des Lucas,* being vol. IX of his *Forschungen zur Geschichte des neutestamentlichen Kanons und der altkirchlichen Literatur* (Leipzig, 1916).

[9] *Philologica sacra* (Berlin, 1896).

[10] *The Acts of the Apostles, translated from the Codex Bezae, with an Introduction on its Lucan Origin and Importance* (London, 1923).

[11] "The Text of Acts: A Problem of Literary Criticism?" in *New Testament Textual Criticism; Its Significance for Exegesis,* ed. by E. J. Epp and G. D. Fee (Oxford, 1981), pp. 147–157. A very much more extensive discussion, supported by wide-ranging information from early versions, was published in two volumes by Boismard assisted by A. Lamouille under the title, *Le Texte Occidental de Actes des Apôtres; Reconstruction et réhabilitation* (Paris, 1984). Here they refine Blass's view as follows: "Luke wrote a first edition of Acts, of which we find an echo in the 'Western' text; a certain number of years later he thoroughly revised his earlier work, not only from the point of view of style (as Blass emphasized), but also from the point of view of content. These two editions were subsequently fused into a single edition so as to produce the present text of Acts, or more exactly, the Alexandrian text (in a form that is purer than that which we now have)," vol. i, p. 9.

scholars, however, found it difficult to understand the motives of the author in choosing to omit certain details found in the presumed earlier account; the gain in space is small and the loss in information and descriptiveness is sometimes great. Is it plausible that the author would have omitted a clause from the decrees of the Jerusalem council (15.20, 29), or have altered the language of the letter of Claudius Lysias (23.26-30) or Festus's speech to Agrippa concerning Paul's culpability (25.24-25)? Furthermore, sometimes the shorter form contradicts the longer form. For example, having described (in the first person plural) a break in the journey from Caesarea to Jerusalem at the house of Mnason (so the Western text of 21.16), the author would not be likely to alter it so as to suggest that Mnason lived in Jerusalem (as is implied in the shorter text).

It has also been pointed out that in many cases the text that Blass regarded as the earlier, unrevised form of Acts exhibits the clear characteristics of later additions. Thus, for example, in a devastating review of Blass's edition, another classical scholar, T. E. Page,[12] assembled numerous examples where the Western text heightens

---

For a critique of Boismard and Lamouille's analysis evidence on which to judge Lukan style, see F. Neirynck and F. van Segbroeck, "Le Texte des Actes des Apôtres et les caractéristiques stylistiques lucaniennes," *Ephemerides theologicae Lovanienses,* LXI (1985), pp. 304–339.

[12] See *Classical Review,* XI (1897), pp. 317–320. The Western variants (identified by β) are listed by Page in four groups, which he describes as follows: "The characteristic of variants in group *A* is to exaggerate the emphasis, in *B* to bring in religious formula, in *B* and *C* to substitute for the simpler and natural names of Jesus a later and more theological title, and in *D* to emphasize words and actions as inspired…. The whole of them bear traces of being subsequent corrections of the text by a second-rate hand; that they were Luke's original version is incredible."

Group *A:* 5.32 τῶν ῥημάτων τούτων; β. adds πάντων. / 6.10 ἀντιστῆναι τῷ πνεύματι ᾧ ἐλάλει; β. adds διὰ τὸ ἐλέγχεσθαι ὑπ' αὐτοῦ μετὰ πάσης παρρησίας. / 9.5 ὁ δὲ (εἶπεν); β. gives ὁ δὲ τρέμων τε καὶ θαμβῶν ἐπὶ τῷ γεγονότι αὐτῷ εἶπεν. / 9.20 ἐκήρυσσεν; β. adds μετὰ πάσης παρρησίας. / 10.33 παραγενόμενος; β. ἐν τάχει παραγενόμενος. / 10.41 συνεπίομεν αὐτῷ μετὰ τὸ ἀναστῆναι; β. συνεπίομεν αὐτῷ καὶ συνεστράφημεν μετ' αὐτοῦ ἡμέρας τεσσεράκοντα μ. τ. α. / 12.23 σκωληκόβρωτος ἐξέψυξεν; β. adds ἔτι ζῶν before ἐξ. / 14.9 ἤκουεν τοῦ Π.; β. ἡδέως ἤκουεν. / 14.10 καὶ ἥλατο; β. καὶ εὐθέως παραχρῆμα ἥλατο. / 19.8 ἐπαρρησιάζετο; β. adds ἐν δυνάμει μεγάλῃ. / 20.1 παρακαλέσας; β. πολλὰ παρακαλέσας.

or exaggerates the emphasis of the passage, where it introduces religious formulae and substitutes for the simpler and natural names of Jesus fuller and more elaborate theological titles, and where it emphasizes words and actions as inspired by the Spirit.

For these and other reasons many scholars today are reluctant to adopt Blass's theory of two editions of Acts.

(2) Contrary to the theory proposed by Blass, who thought that the

---

Group *B:* 6.8 ἐποίει … σημεῖα μεγάλα ἐν τῷ λαῷ; β. adds διὰ τοῦ ὀνόματος κυρίου ('Ιησοῦ χριστοῦ). / 9.17 ἐπιθεὶς ἐπ' αὐτὸν τὴν χεῖρα; β. ἐπέθηκεν αὐτῷ τὴν χεῖρα ἐν τῷ ὀνόματι Ἰησοῦ χριστοῦ. / 9.40 Ταβιθὰ ἀνάστηθι· ἡ δὲ ἤνοιξεν … ; β. Ταβιθὰ ἀνάστηθι ἐν τῷ ὀνόματι Ἰησοῦ χριστοῦ· ἡ δὲ παραχρῆμα ἤνοιξεν. / 14.10 ἀνάστηθι; β. σοὶ λέγω, ἐν τῷ ὀνόματι τοῦ κυρίου Ἰησοῦ χριστοῦ ἀνάστηθι. / 16.4 παρεδίδοσαν αὐτοῖς φυλάσσειν τὰ δόγματα; β. has ἐκήρυσσον αὐτοῖς μετὰ πάσης παρρησίας τὸν κύριον Ἰησοῦν χριστόν, ἅμα παραδίδοντες … / 18.4 διελέγετο; β. adds ἐντιθεὶς τὸ ὄνομα τοῦ κυρίου Ἰησοῦ. / 18.8 ἐπίστευον καὶ ἐβαπτίζοντο; β. has ἐβαπτίζοντο πιστεύοντες τῷ θεῷ διὰ τοῦ ὀνόματος τοῦ κυρίου Ἰησοῦ χριστοῦ. / 8.37 is inserted from β. εἶπε δὲ αὐτῷ ὁ Φίλιππος· εἰ πιστεύεις ἐξ ὅλης τῆς καρδίας σοι· ἀποκριθεὶς δὲ εἶπε· πιστεύω τὸν υἱὸν τοῦ θεοῦ εἶναι τὸν Ἰησοῦν.

Group *C:* 7.55 Ἰησοῦν; β. Ἰησοῦν τὸν κύριον. / 13.33 Ἰησοῦν; β. τὸν κύριον Ἰησοῦν χριστόν. / 20.21 εἰς τὸν κύριον ἡμῶν Ἰησοῦν; β. διὰ τοῦ κυρίου ἡμῶν Ἰησοῦ χριστοῦ.

Group *D:* 15.7 Πέτρος εἶπεν; β. Πέτρος ἐν πνεύματι ἁγίῳ εἶπεν. / 15.29 εὖ πράξετε; β. εὖ πράξετε, φερόμενοι ἐν τῷ ἁγίῳ πνεύματι. / 15.32 προφῆται ὄντες; β. προφῆται ὄντες πλήρεις πνεύματος ἁγίου. / 19.1 ἐγένετο … Παῦλον διελθόντα; β. θέλοντος δὲ τοῦ Παύλου κατὰ τὴν ἰδίαν βουλὴν πορεύεσθαι εἰς Ἱερ. εἶπεν αὐτῷ τὸ πνεῦμα. / 20.3 ἐγένετο γνώμης ὑποστρέφειν; β. εἶπεν δὲ τὸ πνεῦμα αὐτῷ ὑποστρέφειν.

Since the *Classical Review* may not be readily available to the readers of the present volume, perhaps it will be useful to quote also the concluding paragraph of Professor Page's review: "On the whole the value of the β variants seems very small. The question of their origin may occupy the attention of scholars with ample leisure and does not seem to admit of any solution, but they add practically nothing to our real knowledge of the Acts, while they frequently mar and spoil what they seek to improve. The final verses of our present text are a model of powerful composition, while the rhythmic beauty of their closing cadence – μετὰ πάσης παρρησίας ἀκωλύτως – might strike even an unpractised ear, but, when there is a desire to drag in theological formulae, nothing is sacred, and the β text tacks on to it the words λέγων ὅτι οὗτός ἐστιν ὁ χριστὸς ὁ υἱὸς τοῦ θεοῦ, δι' οὗ μέλλει πᾶς ὁ κόσμος κρίνεσθαι. 'Non inepte,' says Dr. Blass, 'hoc in fine libri ponitur.' Most people will not agree with him, and, even on his own theory, the opinion of Luke must have been different for, after writing the words he deliberately struck them out" (p. 320).

shorter form of Acts was produced when Luke pruned the earlier, longer text of his book, other scholars have considered it much more probable that the Western text of Acts was produced by the expansion of an earlier form of the text. Several theories have been proposed that attribute the process of expansion essentially to Luke himself. One of these was put forward by the Irish polymath, George Salmon, who suggested that "Luke may have continued to reside at Rome after the expiration of Paul's two years [of Roman imprisonment], and may there have given readings of his work; and explanatory statements which he then made were preserved in the West."[13] Although it is possible to point to examples of authors in antiquity who gave public readings of their literary works, it is difficult to imagine the historical circumstances that would account for the preservation in written form of the oral comments made by Luke.

(3) A much more elaborately argued case was made by Édouard Delebecque[14] on the basis of his extensive analyses of stylistic features of the longer text of Acts. Delebecque agrees with Blass that this form of text displays the same characteristics as those found in Luke's undisputed writings; he differs, however, in holding that the longer text is evidently secondary and a development of the shorter text. The relation of the two is explained by a series of hypotheses as follows. The earlier, shorter text was written while Paul was a prisoner in Rome. Subsequently, following his release from imprisonment, the apostle undertook further travels to Spain and also once again in the Aegean region, where he was eventually imprisoned again (at Ephesus). At this time, Paul dictated 2 Timothy to Luke. After Paul's death in Ephesus, Luke revised and enlarged Acts, probably shortly after A.D. 67.

---

[13] *Some Thoughts on the Textual Criticism of the New Testament* (London, 1897), p. 140. Salmon supported his argument with the following comments: "It need hardly be mentioned that public recitation was a form of publication which prevailed in the days when Juvenal counted it as one of the plagues of Rome that even the month of August put no stop to the recitation of their works by poets. We may give no credence to the account that Herodotus read his history at the Olympian games; but at the time when Lucian told the story that must have seemed a natural mode of publication" (*ibid.*).

[14] *Les Deux Actes des Apôtres* (Paris, 1986).

(4) In his Oxford D. Phil. thesis, W. A. Strange[15] developed yet another theory to account for the two forms of the text of Acts. This theory begins by supposing that Luke left the manuscript of Acts unfinished at his death. This rough draft contained here and there annotations in the form of marginal and interlinear notes. After the middle of the second century, this annotated, author's copy of Acts came into the hands of two editors who, working independently, produced the two textual traditions that we have today. The Western fullness of expression in Acts is the result of the editor's wish to preserve the annotated and interlinear material that one might expect in an author's working copy. On the other hand, the non-Western editor did not include the annotated material in his version. He did, however, attempt occasionally to clear up passages that were obscure or that might give potential support for mid-second-century Gnostic sects.

(5) Still other scholars have explained the distinctive form of the Western text as having arisen from interpolation. It is maintained that in the early ages of the church the text of the New Testament was not looked upon as sacred, and therefore scribes felt at liberty to modify the form as well as to incorporate from oral tradition all kinds of additional details. Thus the Western text, according to this explanation, represents a wild and uncontrolled growth of the text during the first and second centuries.

This view has been widely held by scholars of various backgrounds, such as Westcott and Hort,[16] W. H. P. Hatch,[17] and F. G. Kenyon.[18]

Still others have held that one of the rival texts is derived from the other, not merely by a haphazard accumulation of glosses added over the years by numerous scribes, but by a deliberate revision made early in the second century by someone who was not satisfied with

---

[15] *The Problem of the Text of Acts* (Cambridge University Press, 1992).

[16] *The New Testament in the Original Greek*, [vol. II,] *Introduction [and] Appendix* (London, 1881; 2nd ed. 1896), pp. 120–126.

[17] *The "Western" Text of the Gospels* (Evanston, 1937).

[18] *The Western Text in the Gospels and Acts*, in *Proceedings of the British Academy*, XXIV (1939), pp. 287–315.

the existing form of the book. The problem is to determine which form was primary and which was secondary. The following two theories give diametrically opposing answers to the problem.

(6) The view that in general the Alexandrian text preserves more accurately the work of the original author and that the Western text reflects the work of a reviser was set forth with great learning by James Hardy Ropes in his edition of the text of Acts,[19] and has been championed more recently by R. P. C. Hanson, who, however, instead of referring to a Western reviser, prefers to speak of a Western interpolator.[20]

An interesting hypothesis that Ropes threw out for further discussion is the suggestion that "the preparation of the 'Western' text, which took place early in the second century, perhaps at Antioch, was incidental to the work of forming a collection of Christian writings for general Church use which ultimately, somewhat enlarged, became the New Testament; in a word, the 'Western' text was the text of the

---

[19] *The Text of Acts,* being vol. III of *The Beginnings of Christianity,* edited by F. J. Foakes Jackson and Kirsopp Lake (London, 1926). Ropes describes the character of the Western text of Acts as follows: "The purpose of the 'Western' reviser, as shown by his work, was literary improvement and elaboration in accordance with his own taste, which was somewhat different from that of the author. He aimed at bettering the connexion, removing superficial inconsistency, filling slight gaps, and giving a more complete and continuous narrative. Where it was possible he liked to introduce points from parallel or similar passages, or to complete an Old Testament quotation. Especially congenial to his style were heightened emphasis and more abundant use of religious commonplaces. This effort after smoothness, fulness, and emphasis in his expansion has usually resulted in a weaker style, sometimes showing a sort of naïve superabundance in expressly stating what every reader could have understood without the reviser's diluting supplement. Occasionally it relieves a genuine difficulty and is a real improvement… In his language he uses a vocabulary notably the same as that of the original author, but with a certain number of new words – about fifty. One trick of his style is the frequent introduction of τότε as a particle of transition …" (pp. ccxxxi f.).

[20] "The Provenance of the Interpolator in the 'Western' Text of Acts," *New Testament Studies,* XII (1965–66), pp. 211–230. Hanson seeks to show that "it is likely that an interpolator was at work on the text of Acts some time between A.D. 120 and 150 approximately, in the city of Rome. He was a Christian of some wealth and education with no strong connexions with Judaism. His additions to and alterations of the text somehow became incorporated in the MS tradition which we call the 'Western' text and which originated somewhere about the middle of the second century" (p. 223).

primitive 'canon' (if the term may be pardoned in referring to so early a date), and was expressly created for that purpose."[21]

(7) The opposite point of view, namely that the Western text of Acts is primary and the Alexandrian is a deliberate modification of it, was championed by Albert C. Clark, Corpus Professor of Latin in the University of Oxford. In his earlier publications Clark explained the shortened form as being the result of a scribe's accidentally missing here and there one or more lines of his exemplar.[22] Since, however, accidental omissions would not account for the regular correspondence of the omissions with breaks in the sense, nor does the theory explain the numerous differences in wording where no omission is involved, in a subsequent publication Clark practically abandoned the theory of accidental omission and revived the theory of a deliberate editorial shortening of the Western text. The Alexandrian abbreviator, he thinks, excised passages throughout the book for a variety of reasons; in some cases we can deduce that he eliminated what he considered to be otiose, but in other cases the excisions, Clark admits, show a singular want of taste.[23]

Still other theories of a linguistic sort have been proposed over the years to account for the unusual phenomena of codex Bezae.

(8) J. Rendel Harris revived the theory of Mill, Wettstein, Middleton, and other eighteenth century scholars that "the whole of the Greek text of Codex Bezae from the beginning of Matthew to the end

---

[21] *Ibid.*, p. ix; compare pp. ccxlv and ccxc f.

[22] *The Primitive Text of the Gospels and Acts* (Oxford, 1914). Clark had previously applied the theory of accidental omission of lines to the transmission of the manuscripts of Cicero's letters.

In the preceding century Clark's view of the Western text was anticipated by F. A. Bornemann, who regarded codex Bezae as preserving the original text of Acts and explained the shorter, common text as having arisen from the negligence or ignorance of copyists, who passed over many passages due to homoeoteleuton (*Acta Apostolorum ab Sancto Luca conscripta ad Codicis Cantabrigiensis fidem recensuit* [Grossenhain and London, 1848]). Clark, however, pointed out later (p. xxiv of his work cited in the following footnote) that several of Bornemann's examples are somewhat forced, and that in the majority of omitted passages homoeoteleuton does not exist.

[23] *The Acts of the Apostles, a Critical Edition with Introduction and Notes on Selected Passages* (Oxford, 1933; reprinted, 1970), pp. xlv ff.

of Acts is a re-adjustment of an earlier text to the Latin version."[24] The theory finds little or no support among present-day scholars.

(9) The view that codex Bezae embodies an appreciable amount of Semitic coloring has been examined and adopted in various forms by several scholars. Frederic Henry Chase sought to prove that the Bezan text of Acts is the result of assimilation of a Greek text to a Syriac text that antedated the Peshitta version.[25] In the case of the Gospels, Julius Wellhausen frequently argued for the primitive nature of the readings in codex D.[26] This point of view was discussed further by A. J. Wensinck in a study entitled, "The Semitisms of Codex Bezae and their Relation to the Non-Western Text of the Gospel of Saint Luke,"[27] and particularly by Matthew Black in his volume *An Aramaic Approach to the Gospels and Acts,*[28] in which he gathers, classifies, and carefully evaluates a large amount of relevant material. According to Black, "The Bezan text in all the Synoptic Gospels, if less so in some respects in Mark, is more frequently stained with Aramaic constructions and idiom than the B ℵ text."[29] A somewhat similar conclusion concerning the Western text of Acts was also reached by Max Wilcox in his monograph (originally a doctoral dissertation written under the guidance of Black) entitled *The Semitisms of Acts.*[30]

Another hypothesis that seeks to account for Semitisms in codex Bezae was proposed by a specialist in the Semitic languages, C. C. Torrey. After having published several monographs on details of Aramaic coloring in the Gospels and the first half of the book of Acts, Torrey advanced the theory that the Gospels and Acts were translated from Greek into an Aramaic "Targum" towards the end of the first

---

[24] *Codex Bezae, A Study of the So-Called Western Text of the New Testament* (= *Texts and Studies,* vol. II, no. 1; Cambridge, 1891), p. 41; compare Harris's *Four Lectures on the Western Text of the New Testament* (London, 1894), pp. 68–90.

[25] *The Old Syriac Element in the Text of Codex Bezae* (London, 1893).

[26] *Einleitung in die drei ersten Evangelien* (Berlin, 1905; 2nd ed., 1911). Wellhausen, however, regarded the Bezan text of Acts to be the later and inferior text.

[27] *Bulletin of the Bezan Club,* XII (1937), pp. 11–48.

[28] (Oxford, 1946; 2nd ed., 1954; 3rd ed., 1967).

[29] *Ibid.,* (1st and 2nd edition), p. 212; (3rd edition), p. 277.

[30] (Oxford, 1965); see especially p. 185.

century, and that this "Targum," being mistaken for the original Semitic text of these books, was very soon afterwards retranslated into Greek with constant reference to the existing Greek text. This retranslation, Torrey held, was the basis of the Western text in the Gospels and Acts.[31]

Although F. F. Bruce described Torrey's hypothesis as "very plausible ... [for] it seems to satisfy many of the *linguistic* phenomena better than any other,"[32] most other scholars have rejected it as too complicated to be probable. Moreover, though such an hypothesis may account for certain linguistic phenomena, it offers no help in explaining how the Bezan text of Acts became nearly one-tenth longer than the Alexandrian text.

Dissatisfied with the methodology of those who adduce sporadic examples of Semitisms without controlling their results by a systematic examination of opposing linguistic phenomena, the present writer suggested to a student of his that he make a comprehensive study of all the distinctive features of the Greek of codex Bezae. James D. Yoder, having assembled a *Concordance to the Distinctive Greek Text of Codex Bezae*,[33] collected and analyzed not only instances of Semitisms in Bezae, but also instances where that manuscript lacks Semitisms that are preserved in other Greek witnesses. Yoder's conclusions are: "(1) When one takes into account not only the instances of Semitic phenomena in codex Bezae, but also the Bezan variants which abandon Semitisms found in other MSS, the net increase of Semitisms [in Bezae compared with other Greek witnesses] is sometimes inconsequential, while in other respects this MS actually reveals fewer Semitisms than [the number] found in the B ℵ text; and (2) ofttimes the data are concentrated in limited areas of the text, thus detracting from the supposed homogeneity of the Bezan text."[34]

---

[31] "The Origin of the 'Western' Text," in *Documents of the Primitive Church* (New York, 1941), pp. 112–148.

[32] *The Acts of the Apostles, the Greek Text with Introduction and Commentary* (London, 1951), p. 45.

[33] The concordance is published in the series, *New Testament Tools and Studies*, vol. II (Leiden and Grand Rapids, 1961).

[34] James D. Yoder, "Semitisms in Codex Bezae," *Journal of Biblical Literature*,

After surveying the chief theories that have been offered to explain the origin of the Western text, one is impressed by the wide diversity of hypotheses and the lack of any generally accepted explanation. A failing common to many of the theories is the attempt to account for the Western text by concentrating upon only one aspect of the problem. The complex phenomena, however, that characterize the Western text in relation to the Alexandrian text include, as Haenchen points out in a brief but incisive discussion,[35] at least three kinds or levels of variant readings. There are, first, not only for Acts but for the Gospels and the Pauline corpus as well, a great number of minor variants that seek to clarify and explain the text and make it smooth. Occasionally pious phrases are introduced. This form of text, widely current in the early church and used by Marcion, Tatian, Irenaeus, and others, cannot be regarded as a "recension," for it is not and never was a unity.

Secondly, there are variants of another kind, peculiar to the Western text of Acts. These include many additions, long and short, of a substantive nature that reveal the hand of a reviser. Working upon a copy of the "Western" text in the first sense, the reviser, who was obviously a meticulous and well-informed scholar, eliminated seams and gaps and added historical, biographical, and geographical details. Apparently the reviser did his work at an early date, before the text of Acts had come to be generally regarded as a sacred text that must be preserved inviolate.

Thirdly, there are still other variants which are not to be associated with the Western text as such, nor with its reviser, but which belong to a particular manuscript, namely codex Bezae. This witness, copied, according to Haenchen, about A.D. 500,[36] exhibits a variety of scribal

---

LXXVII (1959), p. 317; cf. also *idem,* "The Language of the Greek Variants of Codex Bezae," *Novum Testamentum,* III (1959), 241–248. Both articles rest upon Yoder's unpublished doctoral dissertation, "The Language of the Greek Variants of Codex Bezae Cantabrigiensis" (1958), on deposit in the library of Princeton Theological Seminary.

[35] Ernst Haenchen, *The Acts of the Apostles; A Commentary* (Philadelphia, 1971), pp. 50–60.

[36] *Idem,* p. 53.

Scholars have proposed a wide range of dates for codex Bezae; e. g. fourth century

idiosyncrasies, some of which, though suggesting Aramaisms, are nothing more than errors of a scribe, or possibly two successive scribes. It follows, in the words of Haenchen's conclusion, that "in none of the three cases does the 'Western' text of Acts preserve for us the 'original' text of that book; this is the lesson that we are gradually beginning to learn."[37]

In a more recent discussion of the origin of the Western text of Acts, Barbara Aland[38] traces the several stages in the development of this form (or of such forms) of text. In the second century copyists introduced interpolations, omissions, and alterations in the text of Acts that tended in the direction of the Western type of text. In the first half of the third (?) century a redactor revised a manuscript that contained a form of text that belonged to the first stage, and this resulted in a text embodying the well-known "Western" characteristics. At the third stage the redactor's exemplar was copied by various persons who dealt with the text in a rather free manner.

By way of summing up at least some of the analyses of the Western text, one may conclude that it would be more appropriate to

---

(H. J. Frede, *Altlateinische Paulus-Handschriften* [Freiburg, 1964] p. 18, note 4); beginning of the fifth century (John Chapman, *Zeitschrift für die neutestamentliche Wissenschaft,* VI [1905], pp. 345 f.); a little before the middle of the fifth century (Guglielmo Cavallo, *Ricerche sulla maiuscola biblica* [Florence, 1967], p. 75); the fifth century (E. A. Lowe, *Codices Latini antiquiores,* II (Oxford, 1936), item 140; J. H. Ropes, *The Text of Acts,* p. lvii; A. C. Clark, *The Acts of the Apostles,* p. xv; Kirsopp Lake, *The Text of the New Testament,* 6th ed. [London, 1933], p. 16; F. C. Burkitt, *Journal of Theological Studies,* III [1901–02], pp. 501–513; and W. H. P. Hatch, *Principal Uncial Manuscripts of the New Testament* [Chicago, 1939], pl. XXII); probably the fifth century (F. C. Kenyon, *The Text of the Greek Bible* [London, 1937], p. 89); late fifth century (Eldon J. Epp, *The Theological Tendency of Codex Bezae Cantabrigiensis in Acts* [Cambridge, 1966], p. 7); the sixth century (Kurt Aland, *Kurzgefasste Liste der griechischen Handschriften des Neuen Testaments,* I [Berlin, 1963], p. 37; Ernst von Dobschütz, *Eberhard Nestle's Einführung in das griechische Neue Testament,* 4te Aufl. [Göttingen, 1923], p. 89; C. R. Gregory, *Textkritik des Neuen Testamentes,* I [Leipzig, 1900], p. 43; and Heinrich Joseph Vogels, *Codicum Novi Testamenti specimina* [Bonn, 1929], p. 7); and seventh century (or later) (K. Sneyders de Vogel, *Bulletin of the Bezan Club,* III [1926], pp. 10–13).

[37] *Idem,* p. 56

[38] "Entstehung, Charakter und Herkunft des sog. westlichen Textes untersucht an der Apostelgeschichte," *Ephemerides theologicae Lovanienses,* LXII (1985), pp. 5–65.

speak of Western *texts,* rather than of *a* Western text. At the same time, one can recognize a, so-to-speak, Western tendency that is shared by many such witnesses. In this sense, as Strange declares, "it is legitimate to refer to *the* Western text, as long as it is understood that what is meant is a broad stream of textual tradition, and a way of handling the text, rather than a coherent recension of the text, created at a specific time."[39] Understood in this way, Codex Bezae frequently offers the most original form of the Western text. At the same time, of course, D has a manuscript history of its own,[40] and does not invariably preserve the earliest form of the Western text. To ascertain that stage one must also take into account the evidence of other witnesses, both versional and patristic. For such study we now have available the extensive collection of textual information presented in vol. ii, *Apparat critique,* of Boismard and Lamouille's *Le Texte Occidental de Actes des Apôtres.*[41]

Inasmuch as no hypothesis thus far proposed to explain the relation of the Western and the Alexandrian texts of Acts has gained anything like general assent, in its work of editing that book the United Bible Societies' Committee proceeded in an eclectic fashion, judging that neither the Alexandrian nor the Western group of witnesses always preserves the original text, but that in order to attain the earliest text one must compare the two divergent traditions point by point and in each case select the reading that commends itself in the light of transcriptional and intrinsic probabilities.

In reviewing the work of the Committee on the book of Acts as a whole, one observes that more often than not the shorter, Alexandrian text was preferred. At the same time the Committee recognized that some of the information incorporated in certain Western expansions may well be factually accurate, though not deriving from the original author of Acts.[42] In the following comments the present writer has at-

---

[39] *Op. cit.,* p. 37.

[40] For a magisterial study of the palaeography of codex Bezae, see D. C. Parker, *Codex Bezae; An Early Christian Manuscript and Its Text* (Cambridge University Press, 1992).

[41] See p. 224, n. 11. above.

[42] Who it was that was responsible for the additional information concerning the apostolic age or where it came from is entirely unknown. According to F. G. Kenyon,

tempted to set before the reader a more or less full report (with an English translation) of the several additions and other modifications that are attested by Western witnesses, whether Greek, Latin, Syriac, or Coptic. Since many of these have no corresponding apparatus in the text-volume, care was taken to supply an adequate conspectus of the evidence that supports the divergent reading(s).

1.1   ὁ Ἰησοῦς

Against all other witnesses B and D omit ὁ before Ἰησοῦς, a reading adopted by Tregelles, Westcott-Hort, and A. C. Clark. These scholars were probably impressed by the nature of the external evidence as well as by the circumstance that this is the first instance of Ἰησοῦς in the book of Acts, and therefore, according to Attic Greek standards, would not call for the use of the article.

On the other hand, Luke may well have wished, by the presence of the article, to bring to the reader's mind the content of the Gospel narrative in his first volume.[1] The absence of the article in two manuscripts may be accounted for by assuming either that by inadvertence in transcription ὁ was, so to speak, swallowed up by the preceding o-sound of ἤρξατο,[2] or that the scribes of B and D, observing that this is the first occurrence of Ἰησοῦς in Acts, decided to omit ὁ.

1.2   ἡμέρας ... ἀνελήμφθη {A}

The text of the opening sentence of Acts circulated in several different forms in the early church. The ordinary text, witnessed by all

---

"What one would like to suppose (but for which there is no external evidence) is that one of St. Paul's companions transcribed Luke's book (perhaps after the author's death), and inserted details of which he had personal knowledge, and made other alterations in accordance with his own taste in a matter on which he was entitled to regard himself as having authority equal to that of Luke" (*The Text of the Greek Bible* [London, 1937], pp. 235 f.).

[1] So B. Weiss, "Der Gebrauch des Artikels bei den Eigennamen," *Theologische Studien und Kritiken,* LXVIII (1913), p. 355, and Blass-Debrunner-Funk, § 260 (1).

[2] So B. Weiss, *Der Codex D,* p. 107; compare H. von Soden, *Die Schriften des Neuen Testaments,* I, ii (Berlin, 1907), p. 1408.

extant ancient Greek manuscripts with the exception of codex Bezae, can be rendered as follows:

In the first book, O Theophilus, I have dealt with all that Jesus began to do and to teach, until the day when he was taken up, after he had given commandment through the Holy Spirit to the apostles whom he had chosen (… ἄχρι ἧς ἡμέρας ἐντειλάμενος τοῖς ἀποστόλοις διὰ πνεύματος ἁγίου οὓς ἐξελέξατο ἀνελήμφθη).

The text of codex Bezae, on the other hand, differs in two respects: (1) ἀνελήμφθη is moved forward so that it follows ἄχρι ἧς ἡμέρας, and (2) after ἐξελέξατο it adds a further clause so as to read as follows: … ἄχρι ἧς ἡμέρας ἀνελήμφθη ἐντειλάμενος τοῖς ἀποστόλοις διὰ πνεύματος ἁγίου οὓς ἐξελέξατο καὶ ἐκέλευσε κηρύσσειν τὸ εὐαγγέλιον. A text like that of codex Bezae is attested by Thomas of Harkel for the Greek manuscript that he collated at the Monastery of the Antonians, except that in this manuscript διὰ πνεύματος ἁγίου probably followed ἐξελέξατο. The Sahidic version also agrees with D in moving ἀνελήμφθη earlier in the sentence, but after ἁγίου it seems to have rendered a Greek text that read κηρύσσειν τὸ εὐαγγέλιον οὓς ἐξελέξατο.

Before proceeding further an attempt must be made to understand how this form of the Western text should be construed. Is καὶ ἐκέλευσε to be coordinated with ἀνελήμφθη? In this case the sequence is very awkward, particularly in view of the statement that the ascension terminates the Third Gospel. On the other hand, to coordinate the finite verb ἐκέλευσε with the participle ἐντειλάμενος, while satisfactory from the standpoint of sense, is grammatically intolerable. The only remaining possibility is to take the added clause as parallel with ἐξελέξατο and to render "whom he had chosen and commanded to proclaim the gospel." It must be acknowledged, however, that this destroys the balance of the sentence, which has already expressed the idea of Jesus' giving commandment to the apostles (ἐντειλάμενος).

Another form of the Western text, which does not involve the difficulties exhibited by the Bezan text, is preserved in several Old Latin witnesses, particularly in codex Gigas and in the quotations of

Augustine and Vigilius. On the basis of what is assumed to be the common text lying behind these Latin witnesses, which differ slightly from one another, Blass, followed by Clark and, in most respects, by Ropes, reconstructed the following Greek text: ἐν ᾗ ἡμέρᾳ τοὺς ἀποστόλους ἐξελέξατο διὰ πνεύματος ἁγίου καὶ ἐκέλευσεν κηρύσσειν τὸ εὐαγγέλιον. This text (and what goes before) may be rendered as follows:

> (In the first book, O Theophilus, I have dealt with all that Jesus began to do and teach,) on the day when he chose the apostles through the Holy Spirit and commanded them to proclaim the gospel.

This form of text differs in two particulars from the text of all other witnesses: (1) no mention is made of the ascension, and (2) the "day" that is specified is the occasion during Jesus' public ministry when he chose the apostles. According to the opinion of Ropes and Clark, whose text-critical views usually differ from each other, this form of the Western text must be regarded as original and the Alexandrian as corrupt, while the text preserved in D syr[hmg] cop[sa] is a conflation of the two.

The following considerations, however, seem to the present writer to lead to the conclusion that the Old Latin form of Western text, though stylistically smoother than the Bezan form, is equally difficult to accept as original.

First, it is incredible that Luke should have said that Jesus' public ministry began when he chose his apostles; the third Gospel records many details of what Jesus began to do and to teach prior to Lk 6.13 ff. (= choosing the Twelve).

Second, as Lake points out in a note in which he expresses dissent to Ropes's reconstruction of the text, "in a preface to the second book the important point to be noticed is that which was reached at the end of the first, so that ἄχρι is essential to the sense."[3]

---

[3] Kirsopp Lake, *The Beginnings of Christianity,* Part I, *The Acts of the Apostles,* vol. v (London, 1933), p. 2 (hereafter referred to merely as *The Beginnings of Christianity*).

For further discussion of the diminution in the Western text of observable aspects of

Although Lake regarded the greater part of the Alexandrian text of ver. 2 as original, he agreed with Ropes in rejecting ἀνελήμφθη, and accepted Ropes's view that the omission of ἀνελήμφθη in the Old Latin is to be connected with the omission (in ℵ* D Old Latin) of καὶ ἀνεφέρετο εἰς τὸν οὐρανόν in Lk 24.51.

It can be agreed that the two omissions belong together, and that (as Lake pointed out) "it is surely illogical to do as Westcott and Hort did, namely, select a text of the gospel which does not mention the ascension, and a text of Acts which says that the gospel did mention it."[4] Lake's attempt, however, to reconstruct the Greek text of verses 1-4 without ἀνελήμφθη[5] can hardly be pronounced successful. The main verb in the clause that begins with ἄχρι must be παρήγγειλε of ver. 4, and this, as Lake candidly admits, "makes a very bad sentence."[6] There are, as Creed pointed out, at least three objections to Luke's having written such a prefatory sentence: (1) the exceptionally long parenthesis, extending from οἷς at the beginning of ver. 3 to συναλιζόμενος αὐτοῖς in ver. 4, though grammatically possible, is stylistically intolerable; (2) ἐντειλάμενος ... παρήγγειλεν is badly redundant; (3) whereas on the usual punctuation συναλιζόμενος runs happily with παρήγγειλεν, it makes a weak third to ὀπτανόμενος αὐτοῖς and λέγων τὰ περὶ τῆς βασιλείας τοῦ θεοῦ.[7]

If it be assumed that the original text was that which is testified by all known Greek manuscripts except D, simple explanations lie near at hand to account for the several forms of the Western text. Codex Bezae moved ἀνελήμφθη earlier in the sentence in order to make its

---

the ascension, see E. J. Epp, "The Ascension in the Textual Tradition of Luke-Acts," in *New Testament Textual Criticism, Its Significance for Exegesis,* ed. by E. J. Epp and G. D. Fee (Oxford, 1981), pp. 131–145.

[4] K. Lake, "The Practical Value of Textual Variation, Illustrated from the Book of Acts," *Biblical World,* N.S. XIX (1902), p. 363; compare also F. Graefe, "Der Schluss des Lukasevangeliums und der Anfang der Apostelgeschichte," *Theologische Studien und Kritiken,* LXI (1888), pp. 522–541; and *ibid.,* LXXI (1898), pp. 136–137.

[5] For the Greek text see *The Beginnings of Christianity,* vol. V, p. 2, and for an English translation see *ibid.,* vol. IV, pp. 2–4.

[6] *The Beginnings of Christianity,* vol. V, p. 2.

[7] J. M. Creed, "The Text and Interpretation of Acts i 1–2," *Journal of Theological Studies,* XXXV (1934), p. 180.

construction with ἄχρι clearly apparent, and added καὶ ἐκέλευσε κηρύσσειν τὸ εὐαγγέλιον in order to make explicit what is implied in ἐντειλάμενος. The Old Latin translator(s), who were often exceedingly free in their rendering, were perfectly capable of modifying the text on which they were working so as to omit the reference to the ascension.

If, however, for the sake of the argument it be assumed that a Greek text once existed which lacked reference to the ascension, its origin can be explained on the basis of either doctrinal or stylistic reasons. Plooij argued that the alteration in ver. 2 is only part of a deliberate attempt made by the Western reviser (whose work is seen also in 1.9 and 11 as well as in Lk 24.51) to excise as much as possible of what might imply the bodily ascension of Jesus into heaven.[8] Without referring to doctrinal considerations Creed made a strong case that the real difficulty is stylistic and is inherent in the narrative itself. He writes:

> "Here as so often in the Lucan writings, a smooth surface covers real incongruity. The author of Acts begins with part of a Preface, composed in the accepted manner, which resumes the contents of the preceding volume. This leads us to expect that he will take up the thread where he has dropped it. But instead of this, what he does is to give us a new version of the last scene between Jesus and the disciples.... This overlapping of Gospel and Acts inevitably dislocates a preface which presupposes continuity of narrative. Luke covers up the seam by introducing a relative clause after ἀνελήμφθη which enables him to return to the last appearance. Ropes' defense of the Old Latin text on the grounds that it avoids a premature reference to the ἀνάλημψις before the narrative of the last appearance is based upon a true perception of the difficulty, but he does not recognize that the difficulty is inherent in Gospel and Acts, apart from the particular word ἀνελήμφθη.... Since the slenderly supported omission of ἀνελήμφθη creates a number of

---

[8] D. Plooij, *The Ascension in the 'Western' Textual Tradition* (= *Mededeelingen der koninklijke Akademie von Wetenschappen,* Afdeeling letterkunde, Deel 67, Serie A, no. 2; Amsterdam, 1929), p. 15 [= p. 53].

other difficulties to which no satisfactory answer is forth-
coming, the word should be retained with all the Greek MSS."[9]

1.4 συναλιζόμενος

The textual problems involving συναλιζόμενος and its variants
are less perplexing than the lexical considerations concerning the
meaning of the word. All known uncial manuscripts, with the
possible exception of D, and the overwhelming majority of the
minuscule manuscripts read συναλιζόμενος. The first hand of
codex Bezae reads συναλισκόμενος μετ' αὐτῶν, which has been
corrected by a subsequent hand to συναλισγόμενος μετ' αὐτῶν.
Since, however, the meaning of συναλίσκεσθαι is intolerable in the
context (the verb means *to be taken captive together*), and since -σκ-
(as well as -σγ-) is not far phonetically from -ζ-, Ropes is justified in
correcting the spelling to συναλιζόμενος in his transcription of the
manuscript. About thirty-five minuscule manuscripts, including 614
(which is a relatively important witness to the Western text) and
several manuscripts of family 1 (e. g. 1, 69), as well as many patristic
witnesses, read συναυλιζόμενος, a verb that means literally *to
spend the night with,* and then also generally *to be with, to stay with.*

The Committee agreed that the manuscript evidence requires the
adoption of the reading συναλιζόμενος. This verb, spelled with a
long α, is common in classical and Hellenistic Greek and means
collect or *assemble*. The same verb, spelled with a short α, means *eat
with* (literally, *eat salt with another*).This meaning is extremely rare
in Greek literature; it does not appear before the end of the second
century after Christ, and no example has turned up in the papyri.[10]
Many of the early versions took the word in this sense; it is found in
the Old Latin, the Vulgate, the Coptic (both Sahidic and Bohairic),
the Peshitta and the Harclean Syriac, the Armenian, and the Ethiopic.

Since the use of συναλίζεσθαι in its regular sense *to assemble,
gather* is awkward when only one person is mentioned, and partic-

---

[9] *Op. cit.,* p. 181.

[10] The statement is based on information kindly supplied by Prof. Herbert C. Youtie
of the University of Michigan, who, at the request of the present writer, consulted his
comprehensive *index verborum* of the Greek papyri.

ularly awkward in its use in ver. 4 where the present tense is joined with the aorist παρήγγειλεν αὐτοῖς, and since, as was mentioned above, συναλίζεσθαι in the sense *to eat with* is unknown in the first Christian century, it has been proposed to regard συναλιζόμενος as an orthographic variant for συναυλιζόμενος. This theory, which Cadbury supported with many examples of similar exchange of -α- and -αυ-,[11] was adopted by the RSV and the NRSV ("while staying with them").

The conjectural emendation proposed by I. A. Heikel[12] to read συναλιζομένοις, suggested previously by T. Hemsterhusius (whom Heikel does not mention), is only superficially attractive, for if Luke had originally written the dative plural he would not have been likely to follow it two words later with αὐτοῖς. (The passage in Lk 8.4 that Heikel adduces as a parallel is not pertinent, for it has nothing corresponding to αὐτοῖς.)

1.4   ἠκούσατέ μου

The phrase φησὶν διὰ τοῦ στόματός μου of D it^p vg eth Hilary Augustine, which replaces the simple μου of all the other witnesses, is, as Ropes points out, probably "an expansion, ameliorating the transition to direct discourse and avoiding the awkward μου."[13] (For a similar example of the vivid and homely style of the Western paraphrast, see the final comment on Mt 6.8.)

1.5   ἐν πνεύματι βαπτισθήσεσθε ἁγίῳ

The great majority of witnesses read Ἰωάννης μὲν ἐβάπτισεν ὕδατι, ὑμεῖς δὲ βαπτισθήσεσθε ἐν πνεύματι ἁγίῳ. Several

[11] H. J. Cadbury, "Lexical Notes on Luke-Acts; III, Luke's Interest in Lodging," *Journal of Biblical Literature,* XLV (1926), pp. 310–317. For a discussion of various possible Semitic words lying behind the Greek, see Max Wilcox, *The Semitisms of Acts* (Oxford, 1965), pp. 106 ff.

[12] "Konjekturen zu einigen Stellen des neutestamentlichen Textes," *Theologische Studien und Kritiken,* CVI (1934–35), p. 314.

[13] James Hardy Ropes, *The Text of Acts,* being vol. III of *The Beginnings of Christianity,* ed. by K. Lake and F. J. Foakes Jackson (London, 1926), p. 2.

important witnesses have a different order of words, involving chiasmus: thus ℵ* B 81 915 Didymus read … *ἐν πνεύματι βαπτισθήσεσθε ἁγίῳ,* and D Hilary Augustine read *ἐν πνεύματι ἁγίῳ βαπτισθήσεσθε.* The chiastic order of words does not seem to be merely an Alexandrian refinement, for it is not confined to the Alexandrian text.

The less elegant order in the great bulk of witnesses can be explained as a harmonization with the sequence of words in the parallel reported in the Synoptic Gospels, all of which place *ἐν πνεύματι ἁγίῳ* after the word *baptize* (Mt 3.11; Mk 1.8; Lk 3.16).

The envelope construction of the Alexandrian text (placing the verb between the noun and the adjective) may be an editorial refinement, or it may reproduce an emphasis intended by the author. A majority of the Committee preferred the Alexandrian text, considering the weight of ℵ* B 81 915 Didymus to be superior to that of D (the evidence of Latin Fathers does not count for much on a point concerned with the presence or absence of the envelope construction in Greek).

1.5 *ἡμέρας*

At the end of the verse several Western witnesses (D cop[sa, G67] Ephraem Augustine Cassiodorus) add *ἕως τῆς πεντηκοστῆς,* thus explaining more precisely the date of the coming of the Holy Spirit.

1.7 *Οὐχ ὑμῶν ἐστιν γνῶναι*

Lake and Cadbury render the verse, "And he [Jesus] said to them, 'No one can know times or seasons which the Father fixed by his own authority,'" and comment on *No one can know:* "This is the Western reading; the Neutral and later text is 'it is not yours to know.' The Western reading is preferable because the paraphrast is unlikely to have ascribed ignorance to Jesus."[14] The expression "the Western

---

[14] *The Beginnings of Christianity,* vol. IV, p. 8.

reading" is used here in a rather deceptive manner. No New Testament manuscript in any language contains this reading; only Cyprian (*Test.* iii, 89) and Augustine (*Ep.* 197) quote the form, "Nemo potest cognoscere tempus." Moreover, in a reply to Augustine, Hesychius, Bishop of Salona in Dalmatia (*Ep.* 198, 2), corrects Augustine's quotation, pointing out that "in the most ancient books of the churches it is not written, 'No one can,' but it is written, 'It is not yours to know times and seasons, which the Father put in his own power.'"[15]

In support of the reading involving the second person plural, Hesychius appropriately draws Augustine's attention to the continuation of the passage in Acts, which reads, "But you will be witnesses. ..." In his subsequent reply to Hesychius (*Ep.* 199, 1 ff.), the Bishop of Hippo tacitly accepts the correction and henceforth quotes the passage, "It is not for you to know. ..."

In view of such slender evidence it is better, with Haenchen, to regard the text quoted by Cyprian and Augustine as simply a reproduction of Mk 13.32, and not as testimony for the existence of a similar reading in Acts.

1.8 [ἐν] πάσῃ

The preposition ἐν is read before πάσῃ by 𝔓[74vid] ℵ B C² E Ψ most minuscules *Lect* vg syr[p, h] arm, whereas it is absent from A C* D 81 181 206 322 323 328 429* 945 1611 1704 *al.* Because the repetition of the same preposition before successive coordinate phrases is more typical of Semitic style than Greek, it can be argued that the word is probably original and was deleted subsequently by Greek scribes who felt the repetition to be unidiomatic. On the other hand, it is also possible that copyists, noticing that Jerusalem is a city whereas Judea and Samaria are countries, inserted the second ἐν in order to balance the two entities. Unable to determine which consideration is more probable, and in view of more or less equally weighty external evidence, a majority of the Committee voted to include ἐν in the text, but to enclose it within square brackets.

---

[15] *Corpus Scriptorum Ecclesiasticorum Latinorum,* vol. LVII, p. 236, lines 6–11.

1.11 [ἐμ]βλέποντες

The external evidence is rather evenly divided between βλέποντες
(ℵ* B E^{gr} 33 81 180 218 440 522 614 630 642 945 1245 1642 1704
1739 1831 1875 1884 1891 2298 2495 *al*) and ἐμβλέποντες (𝔓⁵⁶ ℵ^c
A C (D ἐνβλέποντες) Ψ and most minuscules). It is difficult to
decide whether copyists heightened the account by introducing the
compound form (which seems to imply a degree of intensity not suggested by the simple form), or whether the initial syllable was
accidentally dropped in copying. In order to represent the even balance of textual evidence and of transcriptional probabilities, a majority of the Committee preferred to print the compound form, but to
enclose the initial syllable within square brackets to indicate that it
may be a scribal accretion.

1.11 εἰς τὸν οὐρανόν (2) {A}

The third of the four occurrences of the phrase εἰς τὸν οὐρανόν in
verses 10 and 11 is omitted by D 33^c 242 326* and several Old Latin
witnesses, including it^{gig} Augustine Vigilius. Ropes judges that it is
correctly omitted, but Haenchen thinks that Luke wished to lay
emphasis upon the idea by a fourfold repetition. A majority of the
Committee preferred to retain the phrase, considering it more likely
that the words were accidentally omitted than deliberately inserted in
a context that was already liberally supplied with instances of the
same phrase.

1.13

The omission in Codex Bezae of καί both before the first
occurrence of Ἰάκωβος and before Σίμων is to be accounted for
(as Ropes points out) by the arrangement of the apostles' names in
two columns in that manuscript; as it happens both names appear
in the first column, where none of the names is preceded by
καί.

The later manuscripts (E and most minuscules), followed by the
Textus Receptus, alter the sequence to the more accustomed order of

"James and John." Furthermore, in E the name of Andrew is moved forward to follow that of Peter (his brother).

1.14   τῇ προσευχῇ

The addition of καὶ τῇ δεήσει after τῇ προσευχῇ in the later witnesses (C³ and most minuscules), followed by the Textus Receptus ("in prayer and supplication," AV), is due to the influence of Php 4.6.

1.14   γυναιξίν

Instead of the colorless σὺν γυναιξίν codex Bezae reads σὺν ταῖς γυναιξὶν καὶ τέκνοις ("with their wives and children"); compare 21.5, where the Tyrian Christians accompany Paul to his ship σὺν γυναιξὶν καὶ τέκνοις,[16] and the Dura fragment of Tatian's Diatessaron, which apparently[17] refers to the wives of those who accompanied Jesus from Galilee.

1.14   τοῖς ἀδελφοῖς

The Textus Receptus, following B C³ E 33 81 326 and most minuscules, reads σύν before τοῖς ἀδελφοῖς, whereas the preposition is absent from ℵ A C* D 88 104 134 241 464ᶜ 468 547 876 915 1175 1311 1758 1765 1838 al. Since σύν seems to separate Jesus from his ἀδελφοί, and is therefore suspect as a scribal addition made

---

[16] George Salmon finds here "an illustration of the tendency of scribes to refuse to allow two words to part company which usually go together (such as eating and drinking, fasting and praying, wives and children), and when one occurs to add the other, with or without authority" (*Hermathena*, IX [1896], p. 235; compare Metzger, *The Text of the New Testament*, p. 198).

[17] Unfortunately the text is fragmentary, but Kraeling is no doubt correct in restoring it to read αἱ γ γναῖκες [τῶν συ]νακολουθησάντων αὐ[τ]ῷ ἀπὸ τῆς [Γαλιλαί]ας (Lk 23.49); see Carl H. Kraeling, *A Greek Fragment of Tatian's Diatessaron from Dura* (London, 1935); it was re-edited by C. Bradford Welles, *et al.*, *The Parchments and Papyri* (*The Excavations at Dura-Europos,* Final Report V, Part I; New Haven, 1959), p. 74 (the latter makes slight modifications in Kraeling's transcription, namely … [τῶν συ]νακολουθησάντων αὐ[τ]ῷ ν ἀπὸ τῆς [Γαλιλαί]ας, where ν [= *vacat*] signifies a blank space great enough for one letter).

in the interest of supporting the perpetual virginity of Mary, a majority of the Committee preferred the shorter text.

1.15 ἀδελφῶν

The Western text (D it$^{e, gig, p}$ Cyprian Augustine) has substituted μαθητῶν for ἀδελφῶν of א A B C *al.* The reason is obvious: to prevent the reader from confusing these "brethren" with the brothers of Jesus (ver. 14). (The word μαθητής is used nowhere else in the first five chapters of Acts.) For the same reason the scribe of the Bodmer Papyrus of Acts seems to have substituted ἀποστόλων (𝔓^{74vid}).

1.18 πρηνὴς γενόμενος

The enigmatic πρηνὴς γενόμενος (literally "having become prone"; AV, ASV, and RSV "falling headlong," NEB "fell forward on the ground") is interpreted variously in the early versions.

(1) The Latin versions attempt to harmonize the account in Acts with the statement in Matthew that Judas "went out and hanged himself" (Mt 27.5). The Old Latin version current in North Africa, according to a quotation by Augustine in his *contra Felicem,* i.4, seems to have read *collum sibi alligavit et deiectus in faciem diruptus est medius, et effusa sunt omnia viscera eius* ("*he bound himself around the neck* and, having fallen on his face, burst asunder in the midst, and all his bowels gushed out"). On the basis of this sole patristic witness Blass introduced καὶ κατέδησεν αὐτοῦ τὸν τράχηλον into his edition of the Roman form of the Acts, and Clark inserted the line καὶ τὸν τράχηλον κατέδησεν αὐτοῦ into his stichometric edition of Acts. Jerome, who may have known this rendering, reads in the Vulgate *suspensus crepuit medius et diffusa sunt omnia viscera eius* ("*being hanged,* he burst asunder in the midst, and all his bowels gushed out").

(2) A different tradition is represented in the Armenian version and the Old Gregorian version; these describe Judas's end thus: "*Being swollen up* he burst asunder and all his bowels gushed out." What the Greek may have been from which this rendering was made is problematical. Papias, who according to tradition was a disciple of the

apostle John, described Judas's death with the word πρησθείς (from Epic πρήθειν, *to swell out by blowing*).[18]

According to a conjecture of Eberhard Nestle, who compares Nu 5.21-27, the word that stood originally in Ac 1.18 was either πρησθείς or πεπρησμένος.[19]

It has also been argued[20] that πρηνής, besides its common meaning "prone," had a medical meaning "swollen"; but the evidence for this specialized significance is disputed.

1.19 τῇ ἰδίᾳ διαλέκτῳ αὐτῶν

A majority of the Committee preferred to adopt the reading ἰδίᾳ, which is supported by almost all witnesses and is in accord with Luke's expression in 2.6 and 8. The absence of ἰδίᾳ from 𝔓⁷⁴ᵛⁱᵈ ℵ B* D was explained as due to haplography (ΤΗΙΔΙΑΔΙΑΛΕΚΤѠ).

1.19 Ἀκελδαμάχ

The great majority of Greek manuscripts read Ἀκελδαμά, which represents חֲקֵל דְּמָא (Aramaic for "field of blood"). The earlier Greek uncials, however, spell the word with a final consonant, -χ (ℵ A B D), or -κ (E); the Old Latin, Vulgate, Sahidic, and Bohairic also read a final consonant.

---

[18] Papias's work, *Exegeses of the Lord's Oracles,* is extant only in fragments; the text of this fragment is quoted in two forms by Apollinarius of Laodicea (see K. Lake in *The Beginnings of Christianity,* vol. v, pp. 23 f.). According to Bihlmeyer's reconstruction of the text, Papias's commentary read as follows: "Judas's earthly career was a striking example of impiety. His body bloated to such an extent that, even where a wagon passes with ease, he was not able to pass; no, not even his bloated head by itself could do so. His eyelids, for example, swelled to such dimensions, they say, that neither could he himself see the light at all, nor could his eyes be detected by a physician's optical instrument: to such depths had they sunk below the outer surface" (translated by James A. Kleist in *Ancient Christian Writers,* vol. vi [Westminster, Md., 1948], p. 119; the passage continues with other revolting details).

[19] *Expository Times,* xxiii (1911–12), pp. 331 f.

[20] See F. H. Chase, "On πρηνὴς γενόμενος in Acts i 18," *Journal of Theological Studies,* xiii (1911–12), pp. 278–285, and 415; J. R. Harris, "St. Luke's Version of the Death of Judas," *American Journal of Theology,* xviii (1914), pp. 127–131; and Alexander Souter, *A Pocket Lexicon to the Greek New Testament* (Oxford, 1916), *s.v.*

The usual explanation is that the consonant represents nothing in the Aramaic pronunciation, but is an orthographical device to transliterate the final א, just as Σειραχ represents Sira (סירא) in the name of the author of Ecclesiasticus. Dalman compares Ἰωσήχ of Lk 3.26, which represents יוסי, and says that the final χ marks the word as indeclinable.[21]

1.21   Ἰησοῦς

After Ἰησοῦς several Western witnesses (D syr^h cop^G67 eth Augustine) add Χριστός. On this kind of secondary accretion, see the examples listed in Groups B and C in footnote 12 on pp. 225 f. above.

1.23   ἔστησαν {A}

Instead of a democratic proposal made by the community of 120 (see ver. 15), the Western reading ἔστησεν (D it^gig Augustine) emphasizes the role of Peter in nominating two persons. Here and elsewhere in the Western text, one recognizes clearly the later point of view, according to which Peter rules the church with the authority of the monarchical episcopate.[22]

1.25   τόπον (1) {B}

Under the influence of τὸν κλῆρον τῆς διακονίας ταύτης (ver. 17), the Textus Receptus, following א C³ E and the overwhelming bulk of the minuscules, replaces τόπον (1) with κλῆρον; the former reading, however, is strongly supported by 𝔓⁷⁴ A B C* D Ψ it^d, gig vg syr^hmg cop^sa, bo Augustine.

---

[21] Gustav Dalman, *Grammatik des jüdisch-palästinischen Aramäisch,* 2te Aufl. (Leipzig, 1905), p. 202, note 3. Compare Moulton-Howard, *Grammar,* II, pp. 108 f.

[22] Cf. Carlo M. Martini, S.J., "La figura di Pietro secondo le varianti del codice D negli Atti degli Apostoli," *San Pietro* (= *Atti della XIX Settimana Biblica*; Brecia, [1967]), pp. 279–289.

1.26 αὐτοῖς {B}

Instead of αὐτοῖς, which is well attested by ℵ A B C 33 81 1739 vg cop^{sa. bo} *al,* the Textus Receptus, following D* E Ψ most minuscules, reads αὐτῶν. In the opinion of a majority of the Committee, the ambiguity of αὐτοῖς (is it intended as indirect object, "they gave lots *to* them," or as ethical dative, "they cast lots *for* them"?) prompted copyists to replace it with the easier αὐτῶν.

1.26 συγκατεψηφίσθη μετὰ τῶν ἔνδεκα ἀποστόλων

The scribe of codex Bezae replaced the rare verb συγκατα-ψηφίζεσθαι with the more common συμψηφίζειν. Then, taking μετά in the sense of "among," he substituted "the *twelve* (ιβ) apostles" for "the eleven apostles." Not satisfied with this, other pedantically-minded scribes produced the conflate reading, "he was counted among the eleven apostles as the twelfth" (so the Armenian catena, the Georgian version, and Augustine).

2.1-2 Καὶ ἐν τῷ συμπληροῦσθαι τὴν ἡμέραν τῆς πεντη-κοστῆς ἦσαν πάντες ὁμοῦ ἐπὶ τὸ αὐτό. (2) καὶ ἐγένετο

The Bezan text, preferred by Ropes, reads καὶ ἐγένετο ἐν ταῖς ἡμέραις ἐκείναις τοῦ συνπληροῦσθαι τὴν ἡμέραν τῆς πεντη-κοστῆς ὄντων αὐτῶν πάντων ἐπὶ τὸ αὐτό, καὶ εἰδοὺ ἐγένετο, which means, he says, "And it came to pass in those days of the arrival of the day of pentecost that while they were all together behold there came," etc.[1] He explains the unusual Greek as the result of translation from Aramaic (compare Torrey's suggestion that the original read וּבְמִשְׁלַם שָׁבוּעַיָּא "and when the Weeks were fulfilled").[2]

---

[1] *The Text of Acts,* p. 10

[2] C. C. Torrey, *The Composition and Date of Acts* (= *Harvard Theological Studies,* ɪ; Cambridge, 1916), p. 28. For a full discussion of the exegetical problems of the passage, see J. H. Ropes, *Harvard Theological Review,* xvɪ (1923), pp. 168–175.

2.5   κατοικοῦντες Ἰουδαῖοι, ἄνδρες εὐλαβεῖς {B}

Behind the familiar words, "Now there were dwelling in Jerusalem Jews, devout men from every nation under heaven," lie several interesting and provocative textual problems. Why should Luke
think it necessary to mention that Jews were dwelling in Jerusalem?
Likewise, why should it be said that they were devout men; would
not this be taken for granted from the fact that they were Jews? Most
amazing of all is the statement that these Jews were persons from
every nation under heaven. Out of all *lands* under heaven could be
understood – but since Jews were already an ἔθνος, to say that
these were from another ἔθνος is tantamount to a contradiction of
terms.

Now it is certainly significant that the word Ἰουδαῖοι, which
creates so many exegetical problems in the verse, is absent from ℵ,
and is variously placed in two other uncial manuscripts: C reads
ἄνδρες Ἰουδαῖοι and E reads Ἰουδαῖοι κατοικοῦντες, whereas in
the rest of the Greek witnesses Ἰουδαῖοι follows κατοικοῦντες and
precedes ἄνδρες. Does not this mean, as Blass, followed by Ropes,
suggested, that the word is an early, perhaps pre-Western, variant that
found lodgment at various places in the sentence?[3]

On the other hand, one must ask what would have motivated
several different scribes to insert a word that raises so many questions in the reader's mind?[4] It is easier to understand that, being
present in the original text and witnessed by the overwhelming mass
of manuscripts, Ἰουδαῖοι was either dropped as seemingly contradictory to ἀπὸ παντὸς ἔθνους, or moved to a position considered
less objectionable from a stylistic point of view.

---

[3] See F. Blass, "Zur Textkritik von Apostelgeschichte 2,5," *Neue kirchliche Zeitschrift,* III (1892), pp. 826–830, and Ropes, *The Text of Acts,* pp. 12–13.

[4] A. C. Clark suggests that "the confusion was caused by a very ancient note
Ἰουδαῖοι placed in the margin, to show that the ἄνδρες εὐλαβεῖς in *v.* 5 were Jews by
religion, though by race or residence they were Parthians, Medes, &c" (*The Acts of the
Apostles,* pp. 338 f.). But this explanation assumes that all three forms of text were
direct descendants from the one manuscript that had the marginal note, and that three
scribes independently thought it necessary to incorporate the note into the text at different places – which is a rather improbable assumption.

2.6   ἤκουον

The variations are between the imperfect and the aorist tense and the singular and the plural number. A majority of the Committee regarded ἤκουεν (C 81 467 547 1311 1739 vg syr^ph cop^sa geo) as a correction of ἤκουον (A D E I^vid most minuscules Chrysostom) under the influence of the following εἷς ἕκαστος. The readings ἤκουσεν (ℵ B 181 241 307 327 614 917 1874) and ἤκουσαν (181 460) seem to have arisen from harmonization with adjacent verbs in the aorist tense.

2.6   τῇ ἰδίᾳ διαλέκτῳ λαλούντων αὐτῶν

Ropes suggests that the sequence of the Western reading, λαλούντας ταῖς γλώσσαις αὐτῶν (D syr^p, hmg Augustine), "is perhaps intended to make it clear that the speaking, not the hearing only, took place in these languages."[5]

2.7   ἐξίσταντο δέ

The insertion of πάντες (or ἅπαντες) after ἐξίσταντο δέ (ℵ* A C E S most minuscules, including 33 81 181, followed by the Textus Receptus) was probably made under the influence of ver. 12. It is lacking not only in B but in the Western text as well (D it^gig Augustine), and is the kind of heightening of the narrative that would occur independently to more than one scribe.

2.7   λέγοντες

The addition of πρὸς ἀλλήλους before (Ψ it^gig) or after λέγοντες (C^3 D E most minuscules) is a typical scribal addition of circumstantial detail. Had it been present originally there is no discernible reason why it should have been deleted. On the other hand, in view of the narrative style (similar to that in Lk 2.15) there would have been great temptation for scribes to insert the phrase.

---

[5] *The Text of Acts*, p. 13.

A majority of the Committee preferred the shorter text, which is strongly supported by $\mathfrak{P}^{74}$ ℵ A B C* 81 it[57] vg cop[sa, bo] *al.*

2.7 οὐχ

Although the iota of *οὐχί* (attested only by B) may have fallen out before *ἰδού,* resulting in the reading *οὐχ* (ℵ D E 81 98 794 915 1175 1827), it may have been added in order to produce a more emphatic expression. The reading *οὐκ* (A C most minuscules), which entered the Textus Receptus, is the orthographically correct form. A majority of the Committee was of the opinion that *οὐχ* best explains the rise of both other readings.

2.9 Ἰουδαίαν

Although solidly supported by external evidence (by all Greek witnesses, and almost all versional and patristic witnesses, except those mentioned below), the word *Ἰουδαίαν* has frequently been suspected because (1) it stands in an unusual sequence in the list (between Mesopotamia and Cappadocia); (2) it is properly an adjective and therefore when used as a substantive (as here) it ought to be preceded by the definite article;[6] (3) it is absent from the astrological geography of Paulus Alexandrinus,[7] with which Luke's list is otherwise in partial agreement; and (4) it involves the curious anomaly that the inhabitants of Judea should be amazed to hear the apostles speak in their own language (ver. 6).[8]

---

[6] According to Blass-Debrunner-Funk, "anarthrous *Ἰουδαίαν* is certainly corrupt," § 261 (4).

[7] On Paulus Alexandrinus and his geographical list, see Stefan Weinstock, "The Geographical Catalogue in Acts ii.9–11," *Journal of Roman Studies,* XXXVIII (1948), pp. 43–46, and the article by the present writer in the Festschrift in honor of F. F. Bruce (*Apostolic History and the Gospel,* edited by W. Ward Gasque and Ralph P. Martin [Exeter and Grand Rapids, 1970], pp. 123–133), reprinted in Metzger, *New Testament Studies* (Leiden, 1980), pp. 46–56.

[8] It is not sufficient to turn the force of this argument to say, as Denk does, that the dialect of Galileans differed from the dialect used in Judea (Jos. Denk, *Zeitschrift für katholische Theologie,* XXXIV [1910], p. 606).

For these reasons some ancient and many modern writers have proposed the names of other countries. Thus, Tertullian and Augustine (once) substitute *Armeniam,* Jerome substitutes (*habitantes in*) *Syria,* and Chrysostom Ἰνδίαν. Modern scholars have proposed a wide variety of conjectures, including Idumaea (Caspar, Spitta, Lagercranz), Ionia (Cheyne), Bithynia (Hemsterhuis, Valckenaer), Cilicia (Mangey), Lydia (Bentley, Bryant), India ([following Chrysostom] Erasmus, Schmid), Gordyaea (Greve, Burkitt), Yaudi (Gunkel), Adiabene (Eberhard Nestle), and Aramaea (Hatch).[9] Others, including Eusebius, Harnack, and C. S. C. Williams, omit the word altogether, considering it a scribal gloss.

Despite internal difficulties, the Committee was impressed by the overwhelming preponderance of external evidence supporting Ἰουδαίαν, and therefore retained it in the text.

2.12 διηπόρουν

The middle voice of διαπορεῖν (א A B 076) is so appropriate here that, if it were original, it is difficult to account for its being altered to the active voice in the great mass of witnesses (C D E I and apparently all minuscules). On the other hand, if Luke wrote διηπόρουν it is easy to see why Egyptian witnesses adopted an Alexandrian refinement.

2.12 ἄλλον

The addition in D syr[hmg] Augustine of ἐπὶ τῷ γεγονότι ("concerning what had taken place") after ἄλλον is a typical expansion so characteristic of the Western text.

2.14 σταθεὶς δὲ ὁ Πέτρος σὺν τοῖς ἔνδεκα

Instead of σταθεὶς δὲ ὁ Πέτρος σὺν τοῖς ἔνδεκα codex Bezae reads τότε σταθεὶς δὲ ὁ Πέτρος σὺν τοῖς δέκα ἀποστόλοις,

---

[9] For discussions of the last two proposals mentioned above, see Eberhard Nestle, *Zeitschrift für die neutestamentliche Wissenschaft,* IX (1908), pp. 253–254, and W. H.

suggesting that the source from which this account came either disregarded or was ignorant of the election of Matthias.

Codex Bezae enhances the prominence of Peter by inserting
πρῶτος after ἐπῆρεν (see also the comment on 1.23).

2.16 προφήτου Ἰωήλ {B}

A majority of the Committee judged that the name Ἰωήλ had
fallen out accidentally from the Western text (D it[d, h, 57] Irenaeus
Rebaptism Ephraem Hilary Gregory of Elvira Augustine).

2.17-21

The quotation from Jl 2.28-32 (= LXX 3.1-5) is preserved in two
forms, represented by codex Vaticanus and by codex Bezae. The former agrees almost exactly with the text of the Septuagint, whereas the
latter embodies a series of changes from the Septuagint, most of
which make the quotation more suitable for the occasion. This adaptation may be the work of the original author, and the agreement of
the B-text with the Septuagint may have been produced by an editor.
On the other hand, however, it is equally possible that the author
copied exactly, or nearly so, from his Septuagint, and that the
modifications were introduced by the Western reviser. In favor of the
latter view is the fact that in other formal quotations the author of
Acts displays a remarkable degree of faithfulness to the text of the
Septuagint. Moreover, several of the Western modifications appear to
reflect an emphasis on Gentile interests,[10] sometimes approaching
what has been called the anti-Jewish bias of the Western reviser. The
problem is a complex one, however, and the possibility must be left
open that occasionally the text of B represents a secondary development.

P. Hatch, *ibid.,* pp. 255–256 (the latter lists most of the conjectures that are mentioned
above).

[10] See Elden J. Epp, *The Theological Tendency of Codex Bezae Cantabrigiensis in
Acts* (Cambridge, 1966).

2.17 ἐν ταῖς ἐσχάταις ἡμέραις

It was probably the author himself who substituted ἐν ταῖς ἐσχάταις ἡμέραις (ℵ A D E I P S 462 vg syr Irenaeus Hilary Macarius Chrysostom Augustine *al*) for μετὰ ταῦτα of the Septuagint (Jl 2.28 [= LXX 3.1]), which is inappropriate for the context of the narrative in Acts. The presence of the words μετὰ ταῦτα in B 076 cop^sa Cyril of Jerusalem, therefore, should be regarded as the work of an Alexandrian corrector who brought the quotation in Acts into strict conformity with the prevailing text of the Septuagint.[11]

2.17 λέγει ὁ θεός

Instead of λέγει ὁ θεός, which is read by most of the manuscripts, the Western text reads λέγει κύριος (D E 242 467 1845 Old Latin Vulgate Irenaeus). The Septuagint lacks the clause. Kilpatrick thinks that "in general the tendency may have been to change κυριοσ to θεοσ as κυριοσ is ambiguous and may mean God or Christ, but θεοσ like Ιησουσ or Χριστοσ is not."[12]

There is, however, no evidence that such a tendency as Kilpatrick suggests operated in the case of codex Bezae. A glance at Yoder's *Concordance to the Distinctive Greek Text of Codex Bezae* reveals that ten times D reads κύριος for θεός in other manuscripts, and eleven times D reads θεός for κύριος in other manuscripts.

In the present passage the textual decision must be made on the basis of external evidence, and when the geographical distribution of

---

[11] For a discussion of the textual merits of each reading, see E. Haenchen, "Schriftzitate und Textüberlieferung in der Apostelgeschichte," *Zeitschrift für Theologie und Kirche*, LI (1954), p. 162 (and his *The Acts of the Apostles, A Commentary* (Oxford, 1971), *in loc.*), who argues for the originality of μετὰ ταῦτα on the ground that it agrees better with Luke's theology; and F. Mussner, "'In den letzten Tagen' (Apg. 2, 17a)," *Biblische Zeitschrift*, N.F. v (1961), pp. 263–265, who disputes Haenchen's interpretation on both textual and theological grounds.

[12] G. D. Kilpatrick, "An Eclectic Study of the Text of Acts," *Biblical and Patristic Studies in Memory of Robert Pierce Casey*, edited by J. Neville Birdsall and Robert W. Thomson (Freiburg, 1963), pp. 65–66.

witnesses is taken into account, it seems to be obvious that λέγει ὁ θεός should be preferred to λέγει κύριος.

2.17

The substitution of αὐτῶν (in D it^gig Rebaptism Hilary) for the first two instances of ὑμῶν, as well as the omission of the next two instances of ὑμῶν (in the former case by D Rebaptism; in the latter by D E it^p Rebaptism), may have been motivated by the Western reviser's wish to make the prophetic oracle apply to Gentiles and not exclusively to the Jews to whom Peter was speaking:

> "I will pour out my Spirit upon all flesh,[13] and their sons and their daughters shall prophesy, and the young men shall see visions, and the old men shall dream dreams."

That such was in fact his intention seems to be evident by what follows in ver. 39, where the Western text alters the second person pronouns to the first person, thus implying that the promises belong to the spiritual Israel, the new people of God, and not to the Israel κατὰ σάρκα, to which Peter is speaking.

2.18 ἐν ταῖς ἡμέραις ἐκείναις {A}

On the basis of the testimony of the overwhelming mass of witnesses, a majority of the Committee preferred to retain ἐν ταῖς ἡμέραις ἐκείναις, explaining the absence of the words in D it^d, gig, r Rebaptism Priscillian as due either to an accident in transmission or to a feeling that they were otiose after ἐν ταῖς ἐσχάταις ἡμέραις in ver. 17.

2.18 καὶ προφητεύσουσιν {A}

The omission of καὶ προφητεύσουσιν in the Western text (D it^p, r Tertullian Rebaptism Priscillian) brings the passage into

---

[13] Codex Bezae alters πᾶσαν σάρκα to πάσας σάρκας, perhaps in order to emphasize still further the universality of the gift of the Spirit (yet the change may be merely stylistic; cf. Lk 24.39 where D alters σάρκα to σάρκας).

harmony with the Septuagint (and Hebrew) text. Ropes prefers the shorter text and explains the addition as a Western non-interpolation, made before the formation of the text of B.

Ropes's pronouncement that, "if [the words] were originally present, the only reason for omitting them in D would have been the desire to conform to the LXX, but, as has been shown, this motive is the opposite of that which, under any hypothesis, governed the formation of the D-text,"[14] fails to take into account the possibility of accidental omission.

A majority of the Committee preferred the non-parallel reading, which is supported by the preponderant attestation.

2.19 αἷμα καὶ πῦρ καὶ ἀτμίδα καπνοῦ {A}

The omission of the words αἷμα καὶ πῦρ καὶ ἀτμίδα καπνοῦ from the Western text (D it^gig, p, r Priscillian) may have resulted from parablepsis when the eye of the scribe passed from the preceding word κάτω to the final word καπνοῦ. A majority of the Committee preferred the longer text, supported as it is by 𝔓^74vid ℵ A B C *al.*

2.20 καὶ ἐπιφανῆ

A majority of the Committee regarded the absence of καὶ ἐπιφανῆ in ℵ D it^gig, r Priscillian as the result of scribal oversight, occasioned either by the presence of two groups of similar letters, μεγαλην and επιφανη, or by the homoeoarcton involved in what follows, καιεπιφανη καιεσται. The text adopted is supported by the preponderant weight of external evidence (𝔓^74 A B C E P, apparently all other Greek witnesses, vg *al*).

2.23 ἔκδοτον

The addition of λαβόντες after ἔκδοτον in ℵ^c C³ D E P 614 *al,* followed by the Textus Receptus, is a typical scribal expansion, introduced in order to fill out the construction.

---

[14] *The Text of Acts*, p. 17.

2.24 θανάτου {A}

The Western substitution of ᾅδου (D it[d, e, gig] vg syr[p] cop[bo] Polycarp Irenaeus[lat] Ephraem Augustine) for θανάτου appears to be an assimilation to the use of ᾅδην in verses 27 and 31.

2.26 ἡ καρδία μου

The sequence of μου ἡ καρδία, attested by ℵ* B Clement, is a more artificial order that may have been introduced by Alexandrian scribes in order to provide a chiastic contrast with the following ἡ γλῶσσά μου. Therefore, despite the agreement of ἡ καρδία μου with the Septuagint (Ps 16.9 [= LXX 15.9]), a majority of the Committee preferred the latter order, supported as it is by all other witnesses (𝔓[74] ℵ[c] A C D E P al).

2.30 ὀσφύος

The substitution of καρδίας in D* for ὀσφύος has been explained in terms of an Aramaic source[15] or as a false retranslation from the Latin text it[d] (praecordis, which means both "belly" and "heart").[16] The reading κοιλίας (1311 it[gig, p] vg[2 mss] syr[p] Irenaeus[lat]) is a scribal assimilation to the text of the Septuagint (Ps 132.11 [= LXX 131.11]).

2.30 καθίσαι {B}

The Hebraic use of the phrase ἐκ καρποῦ as a noun, the object of καθίσαι, is extremely harsh in Greek and has given rise to various explanatory expansions (derived perhaps from 2 Sm 7.12). Thus, before καθίσαι D[gr*] inserts κατὰ σάρκα ἀναστῆσαι τὸν Χριστὸν καί, and the Textus Receptus, folllowing P 049 056 0142 most minuscules Lect it[d] syr[h] cop[G67] al, reads τὸ κατὰ σάρκα ἀναστήσειν τὸν Χριστόν.

---

[15] So C. C. Torrey, *Documents of the Primitive Church* (New York, 1941), p. 145.
[16] So E. Haenchen, *Zeitschrift für Theologie und Kirche*, LI (1954), pp. 164 f.

2.31

Through an accidental oversight on the part of the scribe, codex Bezae (D* itᵈ) lacks προϊδὼν ἐλάλησεν περὶ τῆς.

2.31 ᾅδην

The construction εἰς ᾅδου (standing for εἰς ᾅδου οἶκον [or δόμον]) is usual in classical Greek (where Hades is the god of the nether world). In the Septuagint text of Ps 16.10 (= LXX 15.10) ᾅδου is read by A and ᾅδην by ℵ B and the papyrus designated U by Swete. The Committee saw no reason to depart from ᾅδην (ℵ B 81 1739 al), which occurs also in ver. 27 (ℵ A B C D 81 al).

2.33

The insertion of ὑμῖν after ἐξέχεεν in codex Bezae and the insertion of τὸ δῶρον before ὑμεῖς in E itᵖ syr copˢᵃ Irenaeusˡᵃᵗ are obviously scribal embellishments.

2.37

The replacement of ἀκούσαντες δέ with τότε πάντες οἱ συνελθόντες καὶ ἀκούσαντες in D syrʰᵐᵍ and the insertion in D of τινες ἐξ αὐτῶν before εἶπον (because the entire crowd could not speak to Peter and the apostles) and of ὑποδείξατε ἡμῖν ("Show us") after ἀδελφοί in D E Old Latin syrʰᵐᵍ copᴳ⁶⁷ are typical Western expansions.[17]

2.37 λοιπούς {A}

The omission of λοιπούς from D 241 itᵍⁱᵍ, ⁵⁷ copᵇᵒ²ᵐˢˢ Hippolytusᵃʳᵐ Augustine seems to have been accidental, occasioned perhaps because of homoeoteleuton (ΚΑΙΤΟΥϹΛΟΙΠΟΥϹΑΠΟϹΤΟΛΟΥϹ).

---

[17] For an interesting attempt to show that Luke himself was responsible for the colloquial ὑποδείξατε ἡμῖν, see C. A. Phillips, *Bulletin of the Bezan Club,* VIII (1930), pp. 21–24.

2.38 *Μετανοήσατε, [φησίν,]*

The witnesses offer a wide variety of readings: (*a*) *Πέτρος δὲ πρὸς αὐτούς· Μετανοήσατε,* B 218 606 630 1835 *al*; (*b*) *Πέτρος δὲ αὐτούς· Μετανοήσατε, φησίν,* 𝔓[74vid] ℵ A C 81 630 1642* 1704 1739 1891 vg *al;* (*c*) *Πέτρος δὲ πρὸς αὐτούς φησιν· Μετανοήσατε,* D it[d, p] Irenaeus; (*d*) *Πέτρος δὲ ἔφη πρὸς αὐτούς· Μετανοήσατε,* E P Ψ *Byz* it[gig] vg[mss]; (*e*) *Πέτρος δὲ πρὸς αὐτοὺς ἔφη. Μετανοήσατε,* 2147; (*f*) *εἶπε δὲ Πέτρος πρὸς αὐτούς· Μετανοήσατε,* 42 51 57 223 582 1405 *al*; (*g*) as (*f*) followed by *φησίν,* 206; (*h*) *Πέτρος δὲ ἔφη πρὸς αὐτούς· Μετανοήσατε, φησίν,* 36 180 453 1642[c]; and (*i*) *Πέτρος δὲ πρὸς αὐτούς· Μετανοήσατε ἔφη,* 945 *al*. A majority of the Committee was impressed by the diversity of early testimony supporting reading (*b*), but preferred to enclose *φησίν* within square brackets because of the weight of codex B, which lacks the word.

[Only reading (*a*) adequately accounts for the rise of the other readings, for the absence of an explicit verb of saying prompted copyists to add, at various places, *φησίν* or *ἔφη* or *εἶπεν*; there is no good reason why any of these verbs, if original, should have been omitted or altered to a different verb. It ought to be noted also that elsewhere Luke occasionally dispenses with a verb of saying (25.22a; 26.28). B.M.M.]

2.38 *ἐπί*

A majority of the Committee preferred *ἐπί* (ℵ A E almost all minuscules), which is the more unusual preposition in such a context, and explained *ἐν* (B C D 429 522 1739 2298 *al*) as a scribal accommodation to the more accustomed expression (cf. 10.48 where *ἐν* occurs with no variant reading).

2.38 *ὑμῶν* (2)

The omission of *ὑμῶν* after *εἰς ἄφεσιν τῶν ἁμαρτιῶν* by D it[gig] syr[p, h] Irenaeus Augustine *al* is, as Ropes points out, "conformation to the solemn formula of the Gospels, not an original shorter reading," for there is a "complete absence of tendency to expand in Matt. xxvi.28, Mk. i.4, Lk. iii.3."[18]

2.39

For the second person pronouns in the Western text, see the final comment on ver. 17 above.

2.41

The substitution in D of πιστεύσαντες for ἀποδεξάμενοι was doubtless motivated by theological concern that faith in, and not merely reception of, the word preached by Peter is prerequisite to receiving baptism. The addition of ἀσμένως before ἀποδεξάμενοι ("they that *gladly* received his word") in E P 614 cop[G67] Augustine *al*, followed by the Textus Receptus, is an obvious accretion, deriving either from 21.17 or from a feeling that such a description would be eminently appropriate for Peter's hearers.

2.42   τῶν ἀποστόλων

After τῶν ἀποστόλων codex Bezae adds ἐν Ἰερουσαλήμ. The Latin text of codex Bezae reads, with vg syr[p] cop[sa, bo], "in the fellowship of the breaking of bread."

2.43   διὰ τῶν ἀποστόλων ἐγίνετο   {C}

It is exceedingly difficult to ascertain the original text of this passage. It can be argued, as Ropes does, that the words ἐν Ἰερουσαλήμ, φόβος τε ἦν μέγας ἐπὶ πάντας καί were omitted because they seem to repeat ver. 43a. On the other hand, Haenchen supposes that the words are an expansion smoothing the way for ver. 44. A majority of the Committee preferred to follow B (D) 614 1739 it[d, gig, p*, r] syr[h] cop[sa] *al*.

---

[18] *The Text of Acts*, p. 22.

2.44 πιστεύοντες

In the book of Acts the absolute use of the participle of πιστεύειν occurs as a designation of Christians.[19] The present participle πιστεύοντες (A C D E P most minuscules) indicates the continuance of the state of believing, whereas the aorist πιστεύσαντες (ℵ B 0142 28 42 88 104 431 *al*) specifies merely that the adoption of the faith had taken place sometime in the past, near or remote. The aorist occurs also in 4.32, where the text is firm. In the present passage a majority of the Committee understood the context to refer not to converts but to believers, and therefore preferred the present tense.

2.44 ἦσαν ἐπὶ τὸ αὐτὸ καί {A}

The reading ἐπὶ τὸ αὐτό (B 234 it^p Origen Speculum Salvian) gives the impression of being a stylistic improvement, paring away every superfluity of expression. (For the expression ἐπὶ τὸ αὐτό, which occurs three times in the Western text of verses 44-47, and twice in the B text, see the comment on ver. 47.)

2.45-47

The Bezan text of these verses differs in numerous details from that of the other witnesses; sometimes a reason for the alteration is apparent, but in other cases it is not clear what motivated the Western reviser.

In ver. 45 the reading "and as many as had possessions or goods sold them" (καὶ ὅσοι κτήματα εἶχον ἢ ὑπάρξεις ἐπίπρασκον, D (syr^p)) may have been introduced in order to avoid giving the impression that all Christians were property-owners.

Codex Bezae has moved καθ' ἡμέραν from ver. 46, where it described the attendance in the temple, to ver. 45 and attached it to the verb διεμέριζον, thus suggesting a daily distribution of the profits from the sale of property (compare ἐν τῇ διακονίᾳ τῇ καθημερινῇ

---

[19] See H. J. Cadbury in *The Beginnings of Christianity*, vol. v, p. 382.

in 6.1). The same manuscript heightens the account of the early community of believers by inserting πάντες before προσκαρτεροῦντες in ver. 46, and by declaring in the following verse that the believers had favor with all the "world" (not merely with the Jewish "people").[20] On the other hand, it is not clear (*a*) why the scribe of codex Bezae rejected ὁμοθυμαδόν from one clause and inserted ἐπὶ τὸ αὐτό in the following clause (which then constitutes the second in a series of three instances of the same phrase within three verses); (*b*) why he moved κατ᾿ οἶκον from the phrase "breaking bread in their homes" to the previous clause, producing the curious description, "All were regular in attendance at the temple and in their homes [were] together" (πάντες τε προσεκαρτέρουν ἐν τῷ ἱερῷ καὶ κατ᾿ οἴκους ἄν ἐπὶ τὸ αὐτό, where the word ἄν is an obvious corruption); or (*c*) why the phrase ἐν τῇ ἐκκλησίᾳ was introduced in ver. 47.[21] (Since the last reading passed into the Textus Receptus, it happens that in the AV the earliest mention of the word "church" in the book of Acts is at this verse; in the other witnesses the word first appears at 5.11.)

2.47–3.1   ἐπὶ τὸ αὐτό. Πέτρος δέ {B}

The difficulty arises chiefly from the obscurity of the phrase ἐπὶ τὸ αὐτό. Torrey explains it as a mistranslation of a Judean Aramaic word meaning "greatly," and translates the reconstructed Greek text, "And the Lord added greatly day by day to the saved."[22] Although de Zwaan characterized this a "splendid observation,"[23] it was rejected

---

[20] It is possible, however, that this last variant does not represent a deliberate heightening. Several scholars have conjectured that the reading of codex Bezae is due to a confusion between עָלְמָא "the world" and עַמָּא "the people." C. C. Torrey, who was disposed to look favorably on this conjecture, pointed out also that "in popular Aramaic speech עָלַם is sometimes used in a looser way, exactly like the French *tout le monde*" (*Documents of the Primitive Church*, p. 145).

[21] Moulton and Howard suggest that ἐν τῇ ἐκκλησίᾳ may have crept into the text from being originally a marginal gloss written by a scribe who recognized that this was the meaning of ἐπὶ τὸ αὐτό (*Grammar*, II, p. 473).

[22] C. C. Torrey, *The Composition and Date of Acts*, pp. 10–14.

[23] *The Beginnings of Christianity*, vol. II, p. 55.

on linguistic and exegetical grounds by F. C. Burkitt,[24] M. Black,[25] and H. F. D. Sparks.[26]

The phrase ἐπὶ τὸ αὐτό, which is common enough in classical Greek and in the Septuagint, acquired a quasi-technical meaning in the early church. This meaning, which is required in 1.15; 2.1, 47; 1 Cor 11.20; 14.23, signifies the union of the Christian body, and perhaps could be rendered "in church fellowship."[27] Not perceiving this special usage of the word in ver. 47, scribes attempted to rearrange the text, either by moving the phrase to the following sentence (3.1) or by glossing it with an equivalent phrase, ἐν τῇ ἐκκλησίᾳ.

The Committee preferred to adopt the reading of 𝔓[74] ℵ A B C G 81 1175 it[gig] vg cop[sa, bo] arm eth *al.*

3.1 Πέτρος δέ

Haenchen observes (*in loc.*) that the scribe of codex Bezae regarded the absence of a connection as a deficiency and therefore introduced ἐν δὲ ταῖς ἡμέραις ταύταις at the beginning of chap. 3 (the same phrase also appears in it[p] and cop[G67]). But there is also another (or a further) explanation of the origin of the words. Bengel, in the apparatus of his 1734 edition of the Greek Testament, suggests that the phrase may have been borrowed from Greek lectionaries, which normally introduce a lection with ἐν ταῖς ἡμέραις ἐκείναις. Eberhard Nestle, who characterizes Bengel's observation as "not unsound," qualifies it, however, by pointing out that the phrase could not have been borrowed from a separate Greek lectionary (for lectionary manuscripts are more recent than the age of codex Bezae), but may have been written in the margin of the codex from which D was copied.[1]

---

[24] *Journal of Theological Studies,* xx (1919), pp. 321 ff.

[25] *An Aramaic Approach to the Gospels and Acts,* pp. 9 f.

[26] "The Semitisms of Acts," *Journal of Theological Studies,* N. S. I (1950), pp. 17–18.

[27] For a collection of passages illustrating the meaning of the phrase in Thucydides, the Septuagint, and the Apostolic Fathers, see A. A. Vazakas, *Journal of Biblical Literature,* xxxvii (1918), pp. 106–108.

[1] *Expository Times,* xiv (1902–03), p. 190.

3.1 ἱερόν

Not satisfied with the account that "Peter and John were going up to the temple at the hour of prayer, the ninth hour,"[2] codex Bezae adds (after ἱερόν) yet another circumstantial detail: it was "toward evening" (τὸ δειλινόν, *ad vesperum*). The word δειλινός appears nine times in the Septuagint but nowhere else in the New Testament.

3.2 τις

Ropes argues (*in loc.*) that the addition of ἰδού (before τις) in D it[p] vg[ms] syr[p] "may be original, since it is more Semitic." On the other hand, however, in this instance as well as in the two others in Acts where codex Bezae introduces ἰδού (2.2; 13.47) the explanation may well be that it was a Jewish Christian who prepared the Western text of Acts.

3.3 λαβεῖν

The presence of λαβεῖν ($\mathfrak{P}^{74}$ ℵ A B C E G 33 81 614 1739 *al*) seems to overload the expression (... ἠρώτα ἐλεημοσύνην λαβεῖν) and so was omitted by Western and Byzantine witnesses (D P most minuscules). For other examples of the infinitive after ἐρωτᾶν, see Blass-Debrunner-Funk, § 392, 1 (*c*).

3.3-5

The usual text reads, "Seeing (ὃς ἰδών) Peter and John about to go into the temple, he [the lame man] asked... And Peter directed his gaze (ἀτενίσας) at him, with John, and said, 'Look at us' (βλέψον). And he fixed his attention (ὁ δὲ ἐπεῖχεν) upon them..." Codex Bezae rewrites the passage, using the verb ἀτενίζειν of the lame man: οὗτος ἀτενίσας τοῖς ὀφθαλμοῖς αὐτοῦ καὶ ἰδών... ἐμβλέψας δὲ ὁ Πέτρος εἰς αὐτὸν σὺν Ἰωάνῃ καὶ εἶπεν· Ἀτένεισον εἰς ἡμᾶς. ὁ δὲ ἀτενείσας αὐτοῖς...

---

[2] The "ninth hour" of the day was 3:00 p.m.

These changes are especially curious in view of the fact that in stories of miracles it is usual to employ ἀτενίζειν of the person who effects the cure. Lake and Cadbury comment on this passage: "If it were not for general considerations it would by tempting here to accept the Western text as original and regard the B-text as an accommodation to the typical vocabulary of a miraculous story."[3]

3.6 [ἔγειρε καὶ] περιπάτει {C}

It is difficult to decide whether the words ἔγειρε καί are a gloss, introduced by copyists who were influenced by such well-known passages as Mt 9.5; Mk 2.9; Lk 5.23; Jn 5.8, or were omitted in several witnesses as superfluous, since it is Peter himself who raises up the lame man (ver. 7). A majority of the Committee considered it more probable that the words were present originally; in deference, however, to the strong combination of witnesses that support the shorter reading (א B D cop^sa), it was decided to enclose them within square brackets.

3.8 περιεπάτει

In periphrastic fashion the Bezan text adds after περιεπάτει the participle χαιρόμενος (which Ropes, on the basis of the testimony of it^h, thinks may be for χαίρων καὶ ἀγαλλιώμενος) and omits περιπατῶν καὶ ἁλλόμενος καί. Lake and Cadbury, however, are inclined to regard the omission as original, "for the Neutral text with its 'walking and jumping' seems intended to magnify the miracle."[4]

3.11

The two forms of text of this verse involve a particularly difficult set of problems, some textual, some archaeological. Instead of the usual text, codex Bezae reads ἐκπορευομένου δὲ τοῦ Πέτρου καὶ

---

[3] *The Beginnings of Christianity*, vol. IV, p. 33.
[4] *Ibid.*, p. 34.

Ἰωάνου συνεξεπορεύετο κρατῶν αὐτούς, οἱ δὲ θαμβηθέντες ἔστησαν ἐν τῇ στοᾷ, ἡ καλουμένη Σολομῶνος, ἔκθαμβοι, which may be rendered as follows (the material in square brackets is not in D but is added here from the Alexandrian text in order to make sense of the phraseology of D): "And as Peter and John went out, he went out with them, holding on to them; and [all the people ran together to them and] stood wondering in the portico that is called Solomon's, astounded."

The differences between the Alexandrian and Western texts involve the location of Solomon's portico. According to the Alexandrian text (*a*) Peter and John healed the lame man at the Beautiful gate; (*b*) they went into the temple (ver. 8); and (*c*) they became the center of a crowd that ran together to them in Solomon's portico. From this account the reader would conclude that Solomon's portico was inside the ἱερόν. On the other hand, according to the Western text the apostles (*a*) heal the lame man at the Beautiful gate, (*b*) they go into the temple, and then (*c*) the apostles and the healed man go out to Solomon's portico. This envisages the location of Solomon's portico outside the ἱερόν (see however the Western text and the comment at 5.12).

Commentators try in various ways to resolve the difficulty. Dibelius regards the Western text as an editorial attempt to cover up the seam left by Luke between his own work and the preceding narrative that he incorporated from an older source.[5] According to F. F. Bruce, this is another instance where the Western text makes explicit what is implicit in the Alexandrian text, as if the readers could not be trusted to draw the correct inference for themselves.[6] On the other hand, after a painstaking analysis of the topographical evidence of the temple area, Kirsopp Lake concludes that the Western text must be accepted as the original.[7]

---

[5] M. Dibelius, "The Text of Acts," in his *Studies in the Acts of the Apostles* (New York, 1956), p. 85.

[6] *The Book of Acts,* p. 106.

[7] *The Beginnings of Christianity,* vol. v, p. 484. On somewhat different grounds Jean Duplacy comes to the same conclusion; see his contribution to *Mémorial Gustave Bardy,* entitled, "A propos d'une variante 'occidental' des *Actes des Apôtres* (III, 11)," *Revue des études augustiniennes,* II (1956), pp. 231–242.

It may be conceded that Luke was less well acquainted with the topography of the temple than was the person who was responsible for the tradition embodied in codex Bezae. At the same time, however, even the most ardent proponent of the Western text would scarcely be prepared to accept the wording of the text of D, as it stands, as the work of so careful an author as Luke. For, in addition to the need for identifying the "they" in ver. 11 in some such way as is done in the Alexandrian text (enclosed in square brackets in the translation given above), the atrocious grammar of ἐν τῇ στοᾷ, ἡ καλουμένη Σολομῶνος, reminds one of the solecisms perpetrated by the author of the Apocalypse.

The least unsatisfactory text, therefore, seems to be that preserved in ℵ A B C 81 *al*. The reading κρατοῦντος δὲ τοῦ ἰαθέντος χωλοῦ (P S most minuscules, followed by the Textus Receptus), which identifies the colorless αὐτοῦ of the earlier witnesses, is obviously a secondary development, probably connected with the beginning of an ecclesiastical lection at this point.

3.12   εὐσεβείᾳ

The word εὐσεβείᾳ, which is, as Lake and Cadbury declare, "certainly the right reading,"[8] was taken as ἐξουσίᾳ in some early versions (it[h, p], some manuscripts of the Vulgate, the Peshitta, and the Armenian). Irenaeus omits ἢ εὐσεβείᾳ. The word ἐξουσίᾳ seemed to scribes to be a more natural complement after δυνάμει in describing a miracle (cf. Lk 4.36; 9.1).

3.14   ἠρνήσασθε {A}

In order to avoid the repetition of ἠρνήσασθε in two successive clauses (cf. ver. 13), codex Bezae substitutes ἐβαρύνατε. This word, which appears in ℵ* at 28.27 and in D H *al* at Lk 21.34, but nowhere else in Luke-Acts, is so manifestly inappropriate in the context (it means "weighed down, burdened, oppressed") that many scholars have suspected something other than an ordinary corruption. Among

---

[8] *The Beginnings of Christianity,* vol. IV, p. 35.

proposals that postulate a Syriac or Hebrew original, Chase,[9] followed by Nestle[10] and Blass,[11] suggested that the error arose in Syriac
where ⲁⲟⲃⲓⲟⲃⲕ was corrupted into (or misread as) ⲁⲃⲓⲃⲅⲃⲕ,
the former meaning ἠρνήσασθε, and the latter ἐβαρύνατε. Harris,[12]
on the other hand, was inclined to describe the variant reading as a
Latinizing error, related to Irenaeus's quotation of 2.14 *aggravastis et
petistis virum homicidam.* Ropes, without mentioning Harris, also
took ἐβαρύνατε as "a retranslation of the Latin *gravastis* [in it[d]]. But
why the Latin translation took this turn is not explained."[13] Yet
another conjecture was offered by Torrey; rejecting Nestle's suggestion that the confusion arose in Hebrew when כפרתם, "you
denied," was copied as כבדתם, "you weighed down, oppressed," he
proposed that "the Aramaic editor rendered ἠρνήσασθε by כַּדֶּבְתּוּן,
'you denied, declared false'…. It was wrongly copied as כַּבֶּדְתּוּ,
which could only be translated (regarded as a Hebraism) by the
Greek ἐβαρύνατε."[14]

3.16

The text of the first part of ver. 16 is exceedingly awkward; literally it runs, "And by faith in his name has his name made this man
strong, whom you behold and know." The proposal of Burkitt[15] to
place a colon before τοῦτον, thus taking the preceding words with
ver. 15, only partly relieves the difficulty, for it is still awkward, as
Bruce points out, "to have the genitive οὗ and the dative τῇ πίστει
together dependent on μάρτυρές ἐσμεν."[16]

---

[9] F. H. Chase, *The Old Syriac Element in the Text of Codex Bezae,* p. 38.

[10] Eberhard Nestle, *Theologische Studien und Kritiken,* LXIX (1896), pp. 102 ff.; and
Philologica Sacra (Berlin, 1896), pp. 40 f.

[11] F. Blass, *Philology of the Gospels* (London, 1898), pp. 194 f.

[12] *Codex Bezae* (Cambridge, 1891), pp. 162 f.

[13] *The Text of Acts,* p. 28.

[14] *Documents of the Primitive Church,* p. 145. It is, however, as F. F. Bruce points
out, "by no means certain that *kabbēdtūn* could mean ἐβαρύνατε. One might think
rather of the Aphel ʾ*akhbēdtūn*" (*The Acts of the Apostles* (1951), p. 109).

[15] *Journal of Theological Studies,* xx (1919), pp. 324 f.

[16] *The Acts of the Apostles,* (1951), p. 110.

Torrey argued that the original Aramaic, in an unpointed text, was ambiguous, and that what was "originally intended was not הְקֵף שְׁמֵהּ, ἐστερέωσε τὸ ὄνομα αὐτοῦ, but הְקֵף שְׁמֵהּ, ὑγιῆ ἐποίησεν (or κατέστησεν) αὐτόν."[17] The meaning, therefore, is "and by faith in his name he [either Ἰησοῦς or ὁ θεός] has made whole this man whom you see and know." The difficulty with this suggestion, however, as with so many explanations that postulate a misunderstanding of an Aramaic original, is how one can explain psychologically that such a misunderstanding could ever have arisen.

These proposals do not relieve the redundancy that remains when one continues with the second part of ver. 16: "and the faith which is through him [Jesus] has given him [the cripple] this perfect health in the presence of you all." Following a suggestion made by his father, C. F. D. Moule refers to several passages in Acts that seem to preserve alternative drafts of the same sentence. He writes: "If it is conceivable that the writer of the Acts really did leave his work unrevised, and that each of these passages represents several different attempts to say the same thing, which were eventually copied collectively, instead of the alternatives being struck out, it would offer a more plausible explanation of these passages (I suggest) than either the hypothesis of intolerably bad mistranslation, or that of an unaccountable conflation of simpler texts; and it might throw an extremely interesting light on the writer's style and sensitiveness to alternative possibilities in idiom."[18]

In the present passage Moule, using Westcott and Hort's text, suggests that the three drafts of the sentence that were combined were:

(a) τῇ πίστει τοῦ ὀνόματος αὐτοῦ [οὗτος ἐσώθη – or equivalent, this alternative being defective].

(b) τοῦτον ... ἐστερέωσεν τὸ ὄνομα αὐτοῦ.

(c) ἡ πίστις ἡ δι᾽ αὐτοῦ [or τοῦ ὀνόματος αὐτοῦ] ἔδωκεν αὐτῷ τὴν ὁλοκληρίαν ταύτην....

Interesting though this suggestion is, it leaves the modern editor in a quandry: shall one assume that the last of the three rival drafts best

---

[17] *The Composition and Date of Acts,* p. 16. For objections against Torrey's proposal, see Max Wilcox, *The Semitisms of Acts* (Oxford, 1965), pp. 144 ff.

[18] *Expository Times,* LXV (1954), p. 220.

represents the intention of the author, or – since apparently the author could not make up his mind – must one not reproduce the several clauses, redundant though they are? In the latter case, much can be said in favor of punctuating (with Lachmann, followed by Blass) by placing a colon after ἐστερέωσεν (omitting, of course, the comma after τὸ ὄνομα αὐτοῦ).

3.16 ὅν θεωρεῖτε καὶ οἴδατε

The Greek (but not the Latin) text of codex Bezae omits ὅν before θεωρεῖτε and adds ὅτι after οἴδατε, so as to read, "And by faith in his name you behold this (man) and know that his name has made him strong...."

3.17

The Western text (D E itʰ· ᵖ copᴳ⁶⁷) introduces several changes: it (a) expands ἀδελφοί into the more usual expression ἄνδρες ἀδελφοί, (b) accommodates the verb to the plural (ἐπιστάμεθα for οἶδα) in harmony with the preceding ἡμεῖς (ver. 15), and (c) adds πονηρόν after ἐπράξατε in order to express the idea that, though the Jews' part in bringing about Jesus' death was done in ignorance, it was nevertheless a crime. By inserting μέν in ver. 17 a sharper contrast is afforded between the act of the Jews over against the purpose of God, expressed in ver. 18. The heightened emphasis in the D-text is apparent: "*We* know that *you,* on the one hand, did a *wicked thing* in ignorance ..., but, on the other hand, God ... fulfilled [his purpose]."[19]

3.19 εἰς

Despite Ropes's declaration that "the only ground of decision [between προς (ℵ B) and εἰς (all other witnesses)] is the relative

---

[19] For anti-Judaistic tendencies in codex D, see P. H. Menoud in the *Bulletin* of the Studiorum Novi Testamenti Societas, II (1951), p. 24, and Eldon Jay Epp, *The Theological Tendency of Codex Bezae Cantabrigiensis in Acts* (Cambridge, 1966), pp. 41 ff.

value ascribed to the opposing groups [of witnesses],"[20] a majority of the Committee was impressed by the fact that, except for Lk 18.1, the construction of πρὸς τό with infinitive is not found elsewhere in Luke-Acts.

3.20   τὸν ... Χριστὸν Ἰησοῦν

On the basis of the combination of Alexandrian and Western witnesses (ℵ B D E syr[h] cop[sa]), the Committee preferred the sequence Χριστὸν Ἰησοῦν. The alternative sequence, Ἰησοῦν Χριστόν (𝔓[74] A C Ψ most minuscules vg syr[p] cop[bo] eth, followed by the Textus Receptus), seems to have arisen as an adaptation to the somewhat more usual appellation (in the New Testament Ἰησοῦς Χριστός occurs 152 times, and Χριστὸς Ἰησοῦς 107 times). In any case, the copyists who introduced the sequence Ἰησοῦν Χριστόν failed to perceive that here τὸν ... Χριστόν means "the Messiah."

3.21   ἀπ᾽ αἰῶνος αὐτοῦ προφητῶν {B}

Variation in wording seems to have been occasioned by the possibility of taking τῶν ἁγίων as a noun followed by an appositive. The omission of ἀπ᾽ αἰῶνος in the Western text may be either accidental or the result of asking whether prophets actually existed from the beginning. A majority of the Committee preferred, as the least unsatisfactory reading, that attested by 𝔓[74vid] ℵ* A B* C 81 1739 it[e].

3.22   εἶπεν {B}

The Committee regarded the several additions before or after εἶπεν as natural expansions to the text, made by scribes who may have recollected the phrase ὁ θεὸς τῶν πατέρων in ver. 13.

---

[20] *The Text of Acts*, p. 30.

3.22 ὁ θεὸς ὑμῶν {C}

The quotation is from Dt 18.15 f. (where the Septuagint reads ὁ θεός σου) and Lv 23.29. It appears that the Alexandrian text, with its usual tendency toward parsimoniousness, has eliminated the pronoun after θεός. In view of the interchange of ἡμῶν and ὑμῶν through itacism it is difficult to decide between the two chief readings; a majority of the Committee, however, judged that external evidence seems to support ὑμῶν.

3.25 ὑμῶν {C}

A majority of the Committee considered it probable that the second person pronoun ὑμῶν has been conformed to the general usage of Acts in referring to "our fathers."

3.26 ὑμῶν

The more difficult reading is the plural pronoun, which B omits, probably for stylistic reasons. The singular αὐτοῦ (5 88 241 257 322 323 915) is a scribal conformation to the preceding ἕκαστον. Both external evidence and internal considerations strongly favor ὑμῶν.

4.1-4

In these verses codex Bezae makes a number of modifications for reasons that are not always clear. The addition of τὰ ῥήματα ταῦτα in ver. 1 was probably made in the interest of fullness of expression in accord with the Semitic love for cognate accusatives. The absence of καὶ ὁ στρατηγὸς τοῦ ἱεροῦ must be due to scribal idiosyncrasy, for other Western witnesses have the words. In ver. 2 the modification of καταγγέλλειν ἐν τῷ Ἰησοῦ τὴν ἀνάστασιν τὴν ἐκ νεκρῶν into ἀναγγέλλειν τὸν Ἰησοῦν ἐν τῇ ἀναστάσει ἐκ νεκρῶν is curious, to say the least. In ver. 3, after altering ἐπέβαλον into ἐπιβαλόντες the scribe of D, as Haenchen remarks, overlooked the need of omitting καί before ἔθεντο (a subsequent corrector has deleted the superfluous word). In ver. 4 the addition of "also" in the sentence "and the number also of the men came to be about five thousand" (καὶ ἀριθμός τε ἐγενήθη ἀνδρῶν ὡς χιλιάδες ε) was probably intended to heighten the point of the statement, though it does so at the expense of good literary style.

4.1 ἱερεῖς {B}

The word ἱερεύς occurs 31 times in the New Testament; the word ἀρχιερεύς occurs 122 times. It is more likely that scribes would have substituted the more frequently used word for the other than vice versa, especially since in this instance the modification was also in the interest of heightening the seriousness of the persecution.[1]

4.4 [ὡς]

It is difficult to decide whether the passage originally stated that the number of the believers was five thousand ($\mathfrak{P}^{74}$ ℵ A 81 vg cop$^{sa, bo}$ eth) and copyists added ὡς (B D 0165 1611) or ὡσεί (E P most minuscules), on the pattern of 2.41; or whether the qualifying word (which seems to be a favorite of Luke when referring to numbers) was dropped by scribes for whom the number 5000 had become a firmly fixed tradition.

To reflect the dubiety in the interpretation of the evidence the Committee preferred to retain ὡς, which is supported by B and D, but to enclose the word within square brackets.

4.5

According to Chase the addition in codex Bezae of ἡμέραν after τὴν αὔριον seems to reflect Semitic usage: "the Syriac Vulgate has ܪܝܘ ܐ ܪܗ ܠ ܐ, where the word 'day' is necessary."[2]

---

[1] The reason given in the Appendix of the NEB Greek text for preferring ἀρχιερεῖς (namely, that "action by *superior* officials seems to be indicated") is exactly why copyists would have been likely to alter ἱερεῖς to ἀρχιερεῖς!

[2] F. H. Chase, *The Old Syriac Element in the Text of Codex Bezae* (London, 1893), p. 43.

According to Harris the Greek side of Bezae was assimilated to the Bezan Latin, *crastinum diem*[3] (but compare σήμερον ἡμέρα in Ac 20.26; Ro 11.8; 2 Cor 3.14).

4.6 Ἰωάννης {A}

Both John and Alexander are unknown. Codex Bezae, in substituting Jonathan for John, agrees with information given by Josephus, who says that Jonathan, son of Annas, was appointed high priest in A.D. 36 in succession to Caiaphas (*Antiquities* XVIII.iv.3).

Either the reading of Bezae is a correction of Luke, in accord with what may be historical fact, or scribes substituted the familiar name Ἰωάννης for the less familiar Ἰωνάθας. A majority of the Committee was impressed by the former possibility, when considered in the light of the preponderance of external evidence.

4.8 πρεσβύτεροι {B}

The addition of the words τοῦ Ἰσραήλ was probably made in the interest of symmetry and balance with the preceding τοῦ λαοῦ. The shorter text is supported by a diversified group of witnesses (𝔓[74] ℵ A B 0165 629 1175 it[ar, c, ph] vg cop[sa, bo] eth Cyril Fulgentius).

4.10 ὑγιής {A}

After ὑγιής several Western witnesses, including E it[h] syr[hmg] Cyprian Bede, add καὶ ἐν ἄλλῳ οὐδενί. The words are obviously an intrusion from ver. 12. (See also the comment on ver. 12.)

4.12 καὶ οὐκ ἔστιν ἐν ἄλλῳ οὐδενὶ ἡ σωτηρία {A}

The opening clause καὶ … σωτηρία is lacking in certain Old Latin witnesses (it[h] Irenaeus Rebaptism Cyprian Priscillian Augustine). Several witnesses (D it[p]) omit ἡ σωτηρία, probably because the word seemed pleonastic before ἐν ᾧ δεῖ σωθῆναι ἡμᾶς.

---

[3] J. Rendel Harris, *Codex Bezae*, p. 91

Kilpatrick (following A. C. Clark) argues that the words καὶ ἐν ἄλλῳ οὐδενί were original in ver. 10, but that after they had been accidentally omitted from that verse they were later inserted erroneously into ver. 12, with the addition of οὐκ ἔστιν in order to make the insertion construe; but it construed with so little sense that ἡ σωτηρία was subsequently added, producing the current printed text.[4] Although each of these steps is possible, the combination of all of them appeared to the Committee to be highly improbable.

4.13-16

The Western text, preserved most fully in it[h] and cop[G67], rewrites the account, emphasizing the perplexity of the Sanhedrin:

> "Now when they all heard the firmness of Peter and John, convinced that they were uneducated and common men, they were amazed; (14) but seeing the lame man standing with them, cured, they could make no opposition in deed or word (cop[G67] omits: in deed or word). But some of them recognized that they had been with Jesus. (Then they talked with each other [cop[G67]])."

Codex Bezae stands between the full-blown Western form of text and the text of most of the old uncials. The scribe of D omits καὶ ἰδιῶται (ver. 13), perhaps because the double expression ἀγράμματοί εἰσιν καὶ ἰδιῶται seemed to depreciate the apostles too much. In order to heighten the Sanhedrin's inability to cope with the situation, D inserts ποιῆσαι ἤ after εἶχον, "they had nothing *to do or* say in opposition" (ver. 14). For the more neutral, "When they [the Sanhedrin] commanded them to go aside (ἀπελθεῖν) out of the council," Bezae substitutes a more picturesque word, "... commanded that they *should be led* (ἀπαχθῆναι) out of the council" (ver. 15). Instead of saying simply that "it is clear" (φανερόν) that a notable sign had been performed through the apostles, D enhances

---

[4] G. D. Kilpatrick, "An Eclectic Study of the Text of Acts," in *Biblical and Patristic Studies in Memory of Robert Pierce Casey,* edited by J. Neville Birdsall and Robert W. Thomson (Freiburg, 1963), pp. 68 f.

the account by using the comparative φανερότερον (instead of φανερώτερον) in the elative sense, "it is all too clear" (ver. 16).

4.18 καὶ καλέσαντες αὐτούς

Several Western witnesses (D it^{gig, h} syr^{hmg} cop^{G67} Lucifer) expand the text by replacing καὶ καλέσαντες αὐτούς with the circumstantial clause συγκατατιθεμένων δὲ αὐτῶν πάντων (om. πάντων D it^h syr^{hmg}) τῇ γνώμῃ (om. τῇ γνώμῃ it^{gig} Lucifer) φωνήσαντες αὐτούς ("And when they all had agreed to the decision, having called them …").

4.18 τὸ καθόλου

The Alexandrian omission (only ℵ* B) of τό in the expression παρήγγειλαν τὸ καθόλου μὴ φθέγγεσθαι was perhaps a precautionary measure, lest the reader suppose that the article was to be taken with the infinitive (compare Blass-Debrunner-Funk, § 399, 3).

4.19 ὁ δὲ Πέτρος καὶ Ἰωάννης ἀποκριθέντες εἶπον

The reading of D it^{gig} syr^p Lucifer, ἀποκριθεὶς δὲ Πέτρος καὶ Ἰωάνης εἶπον, which Kilpatrick[5] prefers to the ordinary text, is rather to be regarded as an alteration made in the interest of enhancing the position of Peter as chief speaker.[6]

4.22 γεγόνει

Manuscripts B and D unite in attesting γεγόνει, whereas all other witnesses read ἐγεγόνει. According to Moulton-Howard, in the New Testament the augment of the pluperfect is usually dropped (*Grammar,* p. 190). They go on to comment that "in Attic writers the temporal augment is omitted, but not the syllabic, MSS and edd. not-

---

[5] *Ibid.,* p. 69.

[6] Cf. Joseph Crehan, S.J., "Peter According to the D-Text of Acts," *Theological Studies,* XVIII (1957), pp. 596–603.

withstanding (see *e. g.* Ti[schendorf] on Ac 4²² …)." In the light of the evidence that they produce to substantiate their dictum, it appears that ἐγεγόνει is the result of the Atticistic revival in the early Christian centuries.[7]

4.24 ἀκούσαντες

After ἀκούσαντες D and copᴳ⁶⁷ add καὶ ἐπιγνόντες τὴν τοῦ θεοῦ ἐνέργειαν ("And when they heard it, *and recognized the working of God …*"), a clause which Harris was at first inclined to explain as a Montanist gloss,[8] but which he subsequently described as "either a part of the primitive Greek text of the Acts or an extremely early Greek expansion, with a strong balance of probability in favour of the former."[9] The use of ἐνέργεια here, as Blass had earlier observed, is in accord with the account of the interposition of divine providence in 3 Macc 4.21, with which Harris compares a similar usage in 3 Macc 5.12, 28 and 2 Macc 3.29. Against Harris's strong preference for regarding the clause as original is the fact Luke nowhere else uses ἐνέργεια (in the New Testament the word appears only in Paul).

4.24 σύ {B}

The shortest form of text appears to be the oldest; the additions were doubtless made in the interest of heightening the apostles' reverence in prayer. If one of the longer expressions were original, no scribe would have abbreviated it.

4.25 ὁ τοῦ πατρὸς ἡμῶν διὰ πνεύματος ἁγίου στόματος Δαυὶδ παιδός σου εἰπών {C}

The text of this verse is in a very confused state. The reading of the old uncials is anomalous both grammatically (how is the phrase τοῦ

---

[7] For further information on the pluperfect see Blass-Debrunner -Funk, § 66 (1), and P. Chantraine, *Histoire du parfait grec* (Paris, 1927).

[8] J. Rendel Harris, *Codex Bezae,* p. 152.

[9] "Two Important Glosses in the Codex Bezae," *Expositor,* Sixth Series, ɪɪ (1900), p. 399.

πατρὸς ἡμῶν to be construed?) and theologically (where else does God speak through the Holy Spirit?). Many attempts have been made to account for the confusion in the manuscripts. On his theory of a written Aramaic source Torrey reconstructed the text as follows: היא די אבונא לפום רוחא די קודשא דויד עדבך אמר which means, "That which our father, thy servant David, said by (or, by the command of) the Holy Spirit." According to Torrey, this clear statement became chaotic when "the י of היא was lengthened into ו (perhaps the most common of all accidents in Hebrew-Aramaic manuscripts, and here made especially easy by the preceding context) [and] the whole passage was ruined. הוא די אבונא was of necessity ὁ τοῦ πατρὸς ἡμῶν, and every other part of our Greek text followed inevitably; there is no other way in which a faithful translator would have been likely to render it."[10]

Objections to this superficially attractive proposal can be made on psychological and grammatical grounds. According to Lake and Cadbury, "It is hard to believe that a writer of Luke's general ability would have produced what Torrey rightly calls 'an incoherent jumble of words,' and … אמר היא (for 'said it') is regarded as harsh by some authorities on Aramaic idiom."[11]

According to an interesting theory first proposed by H. W. Moule,

"the words as we have them contain traces of three or more alternative ways of writing the sentence, any one of which could introduce the quotation ἵνα τί κ.τ.λ. Thus:

1. ὁ διὰ πνεύματος ἁγίου εἰπών
2. ὁ διὰ στόματος Δαυεὶδ [τοῦ] παιδός σου εἰπών
3. ὁ διὰ στόματος τοῦ πατρὸς ἡμῶν Δαυεὶδ εἰπών.

[Luke] knew his own marks for deletion or addition, but one of the earliest copyists misunderstood them, combined words which were really alternative, and thereby sowed the seed of confusion for all time. Some such theory as this is perhaps both simpler and less unlikely than those generally put forward."[12]

---

[10] C. C. Torrey, *The Composition and Date of Acts,* pp. 17 f.

[11] *The Beginnings of Christianity,* vol. IV, pp. 46 f.

[12] *Expository Times,* LI (1939–40), p. 396.

However the variant readings arose, it is widely agreed that (*a*) the more complicated readings could scarcely have arisen through additions to the simpler text of 049 056 0142 and most minuscules, followed by the Textus Receptus (for no adequate reason can be assigned why it should have been glossed so ineptly), and (*b*) the earliest attainable text appears to be that attested by $\mathfrak{P}^{74}$ ℵ A B E 33 *al*. What the author wrote originally and what kind of textual corruption was responsible for the multiplication of variant readings are questions that have been answered variously. Lachmann[13] traced all the trouble to the addition of the word πνεύματος (though surely ἁγίου is involved too, for to leave it in the text, as Lachmann does, results in the utterly unlikely expression διὰ ἁγίου στόματος Δαυείδ). Westcott and Hort, who marked the passage with an obelus indicating the presence of a primitive error, made two different suggestions concerning the origin of the error.[14] According to Westcott, "a confusion of lines ending successively with ΔΙΑ ΑΑΑ ΔΙΑ may have brought πνεύματος ἁγίου too high up, and caused the loss of one διά." According to Hort, "if τοῦ πατρός is taken as a corruption of τοῖς πατράσιν, the order of words in [the W-H] text presents no difficulty, David (or the mouth of David) being represented as the mouth of the Holy Spirit."

Recognizing that the reading of $\mathfrak{P}^{74}$ ℵ A B E *al* is unsatisfactory, the Committee nevertheless considered it to be closer to what the author wrote originally than any of the other extant forms of text.

4.27   ἐν τῇ πόλει ταύτῃ ... λαοῖς

Because it is not represented in the passage from Ps 2, which the author just quoted, the phrase ἐν τῇ πόλει ταύτῃ is omitted by P S 1 69 462 *al* and the Textus Receptus.

Not noticing that λαοῖς Ἰσραήλ is plural because of parallelism with Ps 2.1 f., some witnesses (including E 3 326 Hilary Augustine Theophylact) read λαὸς Ἰσραήλ. The Peshitta has "synagogue (or, assembly [ܟܢܘܫܬܐ]) of Israel."

---

[13] See pp. vii f. of the Preface to vol. II of his second edition (Berlin, 1850).
[14] "Notes on Select Readings," p. 92.

4.28 βουλή [σου]

The word βουλή without σου is read by A* B E*vid 945 1704 1739 itgig vgmss *al*, whereas βουλή σου is read by ℵ A² D Ec vid P Ψ *Byz al.* In order to represent the balance of external evidence it was decided to include σου in the text but to enclose it within square brackets.

4.30 τὴν χεῖρά [σου] ἐκτείνειν σε

Instead of τὴν χεῖρά σου, read by 𝔓⁴⁵ (ἐκτείνειν before τὴν χεῖρά σου) ℵ Dgr E P Ψ and most minuscules, a few witnesses have merely χεῖρα (𝔓⁷⁴ A (but σε ἐκτείνειν) B 1175 itd. gig Lucifer). It is difficult to determine whether the pronoun, which suits the character of the diction of prayer, was deleted by Atticizing copyists as superfluous with parts of the body, or was added from verses 27 and 29. In order to represent the balance of evidence and of probabilities, the Committee retained the word but enclosed it within square brackets.

4.31

At the end of the verse codex Bezae and some other witnesses (including E, certain Greek manuscripts known to Bede, vg³ mss copG67 Irenaeus Ephraem Augustine) add, a little naïvely but conformably to the spirit of the recital, παντὶ τῷ θέλοντι πιστεύειν ("to every one who wished to believe"). According to Rendel Harris,

> "Its origin is evidently an attempt to assimilate the fulfilment of the prayer to the prayer itself which is in v. 29
>
> μετὰ πάσης παρρησίας λαλεῖν τὸν λόγον σου
> cum fiducia omni loqui verbum tuum.
>
> Hence we expect naturally the addition of πάσης, and a number of MSS. show it. (For example, the Gigas reads *loquebantur verbum dei cum omni fiducia.*) This is the cause of the *omni* at the beginning of the gloss; but this *omni* separated from *fiducia*

by the line division has been read as a dative, and turned back into Greek as παντί with the result that it has itself become the subject of expansion, in order to limit the extravagance of the statement and to round off the sentence."[15]

Although one may have reservations about the validity of the several steps in Harris's ingenious theory, the words nevertheless are obviously an accretion to the text.

4.32 μία

After μία several Western witnesses (D E Cyprian Zeno Ambrose) add καὶ οὐκ ἦν διάκρισις (χωρισμός E) ἐν αὐτοῖς οὐδεμία (τις E) ("and there was no quarrel among them at all" ["and there was not any division among them," E]). According to A. C. Clark, the shorter text was formed by the accidental omission of a stichos, facilitated by the presence of μία at the end of successive stichoi.[16] On the other hand, since such an explanation fails to account for the reading of E, it is more likely that the Western reading is an expansion of the original text, made in the interest of emphasizing the unity of the primitive church.

4.33 τῆς ἀναστάσεως τοῦ κυρίου Ἰησοῦ {C}

Of the four major variant readings, that supported by 𝔓[8] (fourth century) P Ψ 049 056 0142 it[gig] syr[h] cop[sa] eth *al* best accounts for the origin of the others. In B the order of the last two phrases is reversed, perhaps in order to connect τοῦ κυρίου Ἰησοῦ with οἱ ἀπόστολοι (so Ropes); it should be noted, moreover, that Luke never joins "the apostles" as a fixed title with a genitive (Haenchen). The other two variant readings are characterized by the natural addition of Χριστοῦ. Although agreeing that the sequence of Ἰησοῦ Χριστοῦ

---

[15] *Four Lectures on the Western Text of the New Testament* (London, 1894), pp. 89 f.

[16] *The Acts of the Apostles*, p. xxiv.

τοῦ κυρίου (in ℵ A *al*) is unusual, the Committee disagreed with Tischendorf's view (*in loc.*) that this reading could account for the rise of the other variant readings (what scribe would have eliminated Χριστοῦ?).

4.36 Ἰωσήφ

The Textus Receptus, following P Ψ 1 33 69 326 440 522 623 920 1611 1827 *al,* reads Ἰωσῆς, a spelling that reflects the tendency to replace a non-Greek ending *(-φ)* with one more congenial to Byzantine scribes.

4.37 πρὸς τοὺς πόδας

The Textus Receptus, following 𝔓[57, 74] A B D P Ψ and most minuscules, reads παρὰ τοὺς πόδας, whereas E 36 94 180 307 327 453 1884 *al* read πρὸς τοὺς πόδας. Since παρὰ τοὺς πόδας is the more urbane expression, and since there is no fluctuation of witnesses in 4.35 and 5.2, where παρὰ τοὺς πόδας appears, it is altogether probable that in 4.37 the original reading was πρὸς τοὺς πόδας, which scribes altered so as to bring it into harmony with the adjacent passages 4.35 and 5.2. It should also be observed that the same tendency to alter the less elegant expression appears in 5.10, where πρός (ℵ A B D) is replaced in various witnesses by παρά or ἐπί or ὑπό.

5.3 ὁ Πέτρος, Ἀνανία

Instead of ὁ Πέτρος, Ἀνανία codex Bezae reads Πέτρος πρὸς Ἀνανίαν. Did πρός come from partial dittography of Πέτρος, or is the commonly received reading the result of accidental omission of the preposition and of the final ν (perhaps written as a horizontal line over the final α) of Ἀνανίαν?

In view of the tendency of the Western text to expand readings, it is probable that the scribe of D filled out the expression either accidentally or deliberately (compare the insertion by E 321 syr[p. h with*] cop[sa, bo] eth *al* of πρὸς αὐτόν before or after Πέτρος).

5.3 *ἐπλήρωσεν* {B}

Since the expression *ἐπλήρωσεν ὁ Σατανᾶς τὴν καρδίαν σου* seems somehow to involve an inappropriate use of the verb "to fill," it has been argued that the original text read either *ἐπήρωσεν*[1] or *ἐπείρασεν*.[2]

It is more probable, however, that the reading *ἐπήρωσεν* ("disabled, maimed") arose through accidental omission of λ from *ἐπλήρωσεν*. In codex Sinaiticus (fol. 102, col. *a,* of the New Testament) the lines are arranged as follows (spaces are left between the words here):

> ΑΝΑΝΙΑ ΔΙΑΤΙ ΕΠΗ
> ΡωϹΕΝ Ο ϹΑΤΑΝΑϹ
> ΤΗΝ ΚΑΡΔΙΑΝ ϹΟΥ
> ↓ΕΥϹΑϹΘΑΙ ϹΕ ΤΟ
> Π͞ΝΑ ΤΟ ΑΓΙΟΝ ΚΑΙ

From *ἐπήρωσεν* it was an easy step, by itacism and correction *ad sensum,* to the production of the verb that above all others seems to be admirably suited, *ἐπείρασεν* ("tempted").

But what seems to have been generally overlooked, as Girard has pointed out,[3] is that the expression "to *fill* the heart" is a Hebraism that means "to dare (to do something)." Thus, in Ec 8.11: מָלֵא לֵב בְּנֵי־הָאָדָם בָּהֶם לַעֲשׂוֹת רָע the Septuagint translates literally: *ἐπληροφορήθη καρδία υἱῶν τοῦ ἀνθρώπου ἐν αὐτοῖς τοῦ ποιῆσαι τὸ πονηρόν.* In place of *ἐπληροφορήθη καρδία…,* Aquila employs *ἐτόλμησαν,* and the Vulgate translates … *absque timore ullo filii hominum perpetrant mala.* Again, in Est 7.5 the Hebrew reads מִי הוּא … אֲשֶׁר־מְלָאוֹ לִבּוֹ לַעֲשׂוֹת כֵּן which the Septuagint renders *Τίς οὗτος, ὅστις ἐτόλμησε ποιῆσαι τὸ πρᾶγμα*

---

[1] So, e. g., Adhémar d'Alès, "Actes, V. 3," *Recherches de science religieuse,* XXIV (1934), pp. 199–200.

[2] So, e. g., Paul Joüon, "Actes, 5, 3," *ibid.,* pp. 474 f.

[3] L. Saint-Paul Girard, "Actes des apôtres 5, 3: *ἐπλήρωσεν* ou *ἐπήρωσεν?*" in *Mélanges Maspéro,* vol. II, being *Mémoires de l'institut français d'archéologie orientale du Caire,* vol. LXVII (1934–37), pp. 309–312.

τοῦτο; and the Vulgate, *Quis est iste ... ut haec audeat facere?*[4] The combination, therefore, of superior external attestation and the possibility of explaining the idiom in terms of Semitizing Greek led the Committee to prefer the reading ἐπλήρωσεν.

5.4-5 τὸ πρᾶγμα τοῦτο ... πεσών

In order to make the account in ver. 4 more vivid, codex Bezae reads ποιῆσαι πονηρὸν τοῦτο, and to heighten the dramatic effect in ver. 5 it inserts before πεσών the adverb παραχρῆμα (from ver. 10).

5.8-10

Codex Bezae alters ver. 8 by replacing ἀπεκρίθη with εἶπεν and by rephrasing Peter's inquiry, ἐπερωτήσω σε εἰ ἄρα τὸ χωρίον τοσούτου ἀπέδοσθε ("I will ask you if indeed you sold the land for so much"). In view of the use of the interrogative prefix ἐρωτήσω ὑμᾶς in Lk 20.3, C. A. Phillips argued that the reading of codex Bezae in ver. 8 preserves a genuine Lukan trait.[5] Cop^G67 reads, "Peter said to her, I asked you about the sale. Did you sell the garden for this money?"

In ver. 9 the expression τὸ πνεῦμα κυρίου, which, apart from Old Testament quotations, is very rare in the New Testament, is replaced in 𝔓^74 1522 1838 geo by the more usual expression τὸ πνεῦμα τὸ ἅγιον.

In ver. 10 the Greek text of codex Bezae adds συνστείλαντες ("having wrapped her up"), derived from ver. 6.

5.12 ἅπαντες

After ἅπαντες several witnesses add ἐν τῷ ἱερῷ (D 42 cop^sa,G67 eth *al*). This is clearly an interpolation (which even Blass refused to

---

[4] These examples are cited by Girard, *ibid.,* p. 311.

[5] *Bulletin of the Bezan Club,* VIII (1930), pp. 23 f.

admit into his Roman text of Acts), for according to the Western text
of 3.11 Solomon's portico was outside τὸ ἱερόν.

5.13

The ordinarily received text is difficult to interpret because κολλᾶσθαι (meaning "to join") seems to be inappropriate in the context
(contrast ver. 14), and because the identity of τῶν λοιπῶν is not disclosed. Among the attempts to clarify the verse, several conjectures
may be mentioned. Pallis emended κολλᾶσθαι αὐτοῖς to κωλῦσαι
αὐτούς, and adopted A. Hilgenfeld's emendation of λοιπῶν to
Λευειτῶν, producing thereby the sentence, "And of the Levites none
dared to prevent them [from holding meetings in the Temple pre-
cincts]."[6]

Torrey conjectured that the original Aramaic was שִׂיבוּתָא, "the
elders," which was misread as שִׁירִיתָא, "the rest," the meaning being,
"of the elders no one dared join himself to them; nevertheless the
common people magnified them,… multitudes both of men and
women."[7]

Without resorting to an Aramaic original, Dibelius conjectured
that τῶν δὲ λοιπῶν came from τῶν ἀρχόντων. He writes, "The
number of letters is the same, and the changes, at least from A to Δ
and from X to Λ, are easily understood. 'Of the leaders no one dared
join them, but the people made much of them, and more believers
than ever were won for the Lord.' Thus the sentence becomes intelligible."[8] Against this proposal, however, is the disappearance of the
connecting particle.

5.15

At the end of the verse codex Bezae adds ἀπηλλάσσοντο γὰρ
ἀπὸ πάσης ἀσθενείας ὡς εἶχεν ἔκαστος αὐτῶν ("for they were

[6] Alex. Pallis, *Notes on St Luke and the Acts* (London, 1928), pp. 54–55.

[7] C. C. Torrey, *Documents of the Primitive Church*, p. 96; compare *idem, Expository
Times*, XLVI (1934–35), pp. 428 f.

[8] M. Dibelius, *Studies in the Acts of the Apostles* (New York, 1956), p. 91.

being set free from every sickness, such as each of them had"). A similar statement *(καὶ ῥυσθῶσιν ἀπὸ πάσης ἀσθενείας ἧς εἶχον)* is read by E it[gig. p] vg[mss] cop[G67] Lucifer.

5.16   Ἰερουσαλήμ   {B}

Not observing that *πέριξ* governs Ἰερουσαλήμ,[9] most copyists understood *τῶν πέριξ πόλεων* as "the surrounding cities" and therefore added *εἰς* or *ἐν* before Ἰερουσαλήμ.

5.17   ἀναστὰς δέ   {A}

Instead of *ἀναστάς* it[p] has "Annas," which Dibelius,[10] following Blass,[11] was inclined to accept as original. But *ἀνίστημι,* which is a favorite Lukan word (out of 107 occurrences in the New Testament, 26 appear in the third Gospel and 45 in Acts), in this passage reflects the usage of Septuagint Greek, where it is often little more than a copula.[12] Furthermore, as Lake and Cadbury point out, "no reviser or scribe is likely to have objected to the ascription of the high priesthood to Annas, but *ἀναστάς* may easily have been read accidentally as Ἄννας, especially after the phrase in iv.6."[13]

5.18   δημοσίᾳ

Codex Bezae adds, with typical circumstantial detail, *καὶ ἐπορεύθη εἰς ἕκαστος εἰς τὰ ἴδια* ("and each one went to his own home"). A similar sentence appears in the *pericope de adultera,* [Jn] 7.53, *ἐπορεύθησαν* (D *ἐπορεύθη*) *ἕκαστος εἰς τὸν οἶκον αὐτοῦ.* The phrase *εἰς τὰ ἴδια* is characteristic of John, but it is also found in Ac 21.6.

---

[9] On the separation of a preposition from the word it governs, see Schöne in *Hermes,* LX (1925), pp. 167 f., and Blass-Debrunner-Funk, § 474, 8.

[10] M. Dibelius, *Studies in the Acts of the Apostles* (New York, 1956), p. 91.

[11] F. Blass, *Theologische Studien und Kritiken,* LXIX (1896), p. 459.

[12] Cf. C. C. Torrey, *The Composition and Date of Acts,* p. 32.

[13] *The Beginnings of Christianity,* vol. IV, p. 56.

5.21-22

The Western text of these verses is variously preserved in D E and other witnesses. Instead of the opening words ἀκούσαντες δέ, E reads ἐξελθόντες δὲ ἐκ τῆς φυλακῆς, which is received by Blass into his Roman form of the text. Codex Bezae paints more vividly the circumstances of the trial by adding a phrase that is analogous to the reading of D in ver. 18: "the high priest came and those who were with him, *having risen early, and (ἐγερθέντες τὸ πρωΐ καί)* called together the council." In ver. 22 the Western text (D it^p vg syr^hmg) adds the detail, "But when the officers came *and opened the prison (καὶ ἀνοίξαντες τὴν φυλακήν),* they did not find them *inside (ἔσω* D)."

5.28   *[Οὐ] παραγγελία* {C}

A majority of the Committee interpreted the absence of οὐ from several witnesses as due to their copyists' desire to transform thereby the high priest's question into a rebuke. In view, however, of the weight of the external evidence supporting the shorter reading, it was decided to print οὐ within square brackets.[14]

[From the standpoint of transcriptional probability, it appears that οὐ is a scribal addition, occasioned by the influence of the verb ἐπηρώτησεν in ver. 27 (compare 4.17). For this reason, as well as the strong combination of 𝔓^74 ℵ* A B it^d, gig vg cop^sams, bo geo Lucifer *al,* the word should be omitted from the text. B.M.M.]

5.29   *ἀποκριθεὶς δὲ Πέτρος καὶ οἱ ἀπόστολοι εἶπαν* {A}

Codex Bezae enhances the role of Peter by omitting "and the apostles answered and," and by altering εἶπαν to εἶπεν. The Old Latin text (it^h) continues by adding: *cui obaudire oportet, deo an hominibus? ille aut[em ait, deo]. et dixit Petrus ad eum* ("'Whom is it right to obey, God or man?' and he said, 'God.' And Peter said to him" [then ver. 30 follows]). A similar addition occurs also in cop^G67.

---

[14] Ropes *(The Text of Acts, ad loc.)* follows von Soden in including οὐ.

The declarative form of the B-text is witnessed as early as the second and third century in Polycrates's letter to Pope Victor (quoted in Eusebius, *Eccl. hist.*, v.xxiv.7), Origen (*contra Celsum*, VIII.26), and Hippolytus (*c. Noët.*, 6 fin.).

5.31

The Western reading, "God exalted him *for his glory*" (τῇ δόξῃ αὐτοῦ), supported by D it$^{gig. p}$ cop^{sa} Irenaeus Augustine, seems to be an ancient transcriptional error (ΔΟΞΗ for ΔΕΞΙΑ). Nestle[15] draws attention to the same confusion in the manuscripts of the Septuagint at 2 Chr 30.8 and Is 62.8.

The presence of ἐν αὐτῷ (D* it$^{d, h, p}$ cop^{sa} eth^{ro} Augustine) after ἄφεσιν ἁμαρτιῶν appears to be a typical Western expansion. (See also the next variant.)

5.32 ἐσμεν μάρτυρες {B}

A majority of the Committee regarded the reading ἐσμεν μάρτυρες (𝔓^{74} ℵ (A) D^{gr*} 915 vg syr^h cop$^{sa, bo}$ *al*) to be original. The insertion of αὐτοῦ (D^b E P (Ψ) *Byz*) doubtless reflects recollection of the words of Jesus reported in 1.8, καὶ ἔσεσθέ μου μάρτυρες. The words ἐν αὐτῷ (which in B replace ἐσμεν) appear to be the result of scribal inadvertence; perhaps they are somehow connected with the Western variant at the close of ver. 31 (see the preceding variant).

5.32 ὅ

The omission of ὅ by B and a few other witnesses was probably accidental. The masculine gender ὅν (D* E) appears to be a theological correction *ad sensum*. There may be, as Ropes suggests, some deeper but hidden factor which led to the omission of both ἐσμεν and ὅ in the B-text of this verse.

---

[15] Eberhard Nestle, *Expositor,* Fifth Series, II (1895), pp. 238 f.

5.33 ἐβούλοντο {B}

A majority of the Committee interpreted the context as favoring ἐβούλοντο (which occurs 13 times elsewhere in Acts), for the members of the Sanhedrin, being enraged, were scarcely in a mood quietly to take counsel. The reading ἐβουλεύοντο (a word that occurs elsewhere in Acts only in 27.39) seems to have arisen accidentally through a scribal blunder.

5.34 τοὺς ἀνθρώπους

Copyists no doubt deemed the expression τοὺς ἀνθρώπους (א A B vg cop^bo arm) too undignified for Luke's narrative (it reappears in Gamaliel's speech in verses 35 and 38) and substituted τοὺς ἀποστόλους (so the Textus Receptus, following D E H P most minuscules syr^p, h cop^sa eth).

5.35 αὐτούς

Codex Bezae and cop^sa replace the ambiguous αὐτούς, which a careless reader might take to refer to the apostles, with τοὺς ἄρχοντας καὶ τοὺς συνέδρους ("the rulers and the members of the council"; the last word D misspells συνεδρίους, but intends to use the word σύνεδρος, which is found nowhere else in the New Testament).

5.36 ἑαυτόν

The addition of μέγαν before or after ἑαυτόν in A^2 D E 614 it^gig, h syr^p cop^G67 Origen Jerome Cyril is an interesting example of a Western reading that gained wide currency; it probably came into the text here from 8.9.

5.36 προσεκλίθη

Instead of προσεκλίθη (א A B C^2 al), which occurs only here in the New Testament, (C*) D* E H P al read προσεκλήθη (by itacism). In 33 *al* Old Latin vg (and the Textus Receptus) the reading προσεκολλήθη is an interpretation of or substitution for προσεκλίθη.

5.36 ἀνηρέθη

Instead of using ἀνηρέθη to describe the death of Theudas, the Greek text of codex Bezae (but not it^d or it^h) employs the curious expression διελύθη αὐτὸς δι᾽ αὐτοῦ ("he was destroyed by himself").[16] (The same verb is used more idiomatically in verses 38 and 39.) Bezae's account of Theudas's suicide is contrary to that of Josephus, who expressly says that Theudas, having been captured alive, was beheaded (*Antiquities*, XX.v.1) – or is the disagreement between the two accounts an added argument supporting the theory that Josephus and Acts refer to two different persons with the same name?

5.37 λαόν {A}

This verse provides a clear example of a growing text. Dissatisfied with the unadorned account that Judas the Galilean "drew away some of the people after him" (ἀπέστησεν λαὸν ὀπίσω αὐτοῦ), various scribes undertook to heighten the account by the addition of πολύν or ἱκανόν before or after λαόν. It is significant that the Latin text of codex Bezae agrees with the earlier and shorter reading.

5.38-39

The Western text has, as Lake and Cadbury admit, "a vigorous and attractive paraphrase," which Rendel Harris was tempted to regard as possibly original.[17] In the following translation the chief expansions are italicized: "So in the present case, *brethren,* I tell you, keep away

---

[16] The alternative suggestion, made by Ropes, that ὅς διελύθη was taken to refer to ἀριθμός, with καὶ πάντες in apposition, is highly improbable in view of the resulting tautology.

[17] *Expositor,* Sixth Series, II (1900), pp. 399–400.

from these men and let them go, *without defiling your hands; for if this plan or this undertaking is of human origin, it will fail; (39) but if it is of God, you will not be able to overthrow them – neither you nor kings nor tyrants. Therefore keep away from these men,* lest you be found opposing God!" (For each expansion, see the following comments.)

5.38   νῦν

After νῦν D it^h cop^G67 add ἀδελφοί (compare a similar addition in the Western text of 20.18).

5.38   αὐτούς

Harris suspected the Western addition μὴ μιάναντες (μολύνοντες E) τὰς χεῖρας (+ ὑμῶν E it^h) of D E it^h cop^G67 to be of Montanist origin.[18]

5.39   αὐτούς {A}

The expansion in D, οὔτε ὑμεῖς οὔτε βασιλεῖς οὔτε τύραννοι· ἀπέχεσθε οὖν ἀπὸ τῶν ἀνθρώπων τούτων (similarly 614 1108 1611 2138 syr^h with * cop^G67), doubtless shows the influence of a passage in the Wisdom of Solomon where the writer is dealing with the same problem as in Acts, namely the question whether it is safe to oppose God. The passage (Wis 12.13 f.) is as follows: οὔτε γὰρ θεός ἐστιν πλὴν σοῦ ... οὔτε βασιλεὺς ἢ τύραννος ἀντοφθαλμῆσαι δυνήσεταί σοι περὶ ὧν ἐκόλασας ("For neither is there any God besides thee, ... nor can any king or tyrant confront thee about those whom thou hast punished"). In E the word τύραννοι (which is not a New Testament word) is replaced by ἄρχοντες, but at the expense of the sense, for now Gamaliel seems to refer to the Sanhedrin twice ("neither *you* ... nor *rulers*").

The addition of ἀπέχεσθε οὖν ἀπὸ τῶν ἀνθρώπων τούτων is, as

---

[18] J. R. Harris, *Codex Bezae* (Cambridge, 1891), p. 198.

Weiss characterizes it, "an empty repetition of ver. 38; but it serves at the same time as an appropriate connection for the following μήποτε καί...."[19]

5.41   ὑπὲρ τοῦ ὀνόματος

After ὑπὲρ τοῦ ὀνόματος scribes could not resist the temptation to add such words as Ἰησοῦ (33 it^{gig, h} vg), τοῦ κυρίου Ἰησοῦ (E 383 614 syr^h), τοῦ Χριστοῦ (69 328 al), and αὐτοῦ (88 242 255 431 460 808 917 1518 eth Origen).

6.1   αὐτῶν

At the end of the verse codex Bezae adds the phrase ἐν τῇ δια-κονίᾳ τῶν Ἑβραίων ("in the ministration of the Hebrews"), which is quite superfluous in view of the preceding context. Old Latin h reads *a ministris Hebraecorum,* representing ὑπὸ τῶν διακόντων τῶν Ἑβραίων ("by the ministers of the Hebrews").

6.3

Codex Bezae and codex Vaticanus have each altered the opening words of the verse in accord with the predilections of its scribe. The former (supported by it^h and cop^{G67}) prefaces the suggestion made by the apostles with an introductory interrogative phrase, τί οὖν ἐστιν, ἀδελφοί; which lends a colloquial touch to the narrative (compare also the Western readings mentioned at 2.37 and 5.8). The phrase seems to have come to the present passage from 21.22.

The unique reading ἐπισκεψώμεθα in codex Vaticanus, as Ropes remarks, is probably "due to the desire not to exclude the apostles from a share in the selection of the Seven. It is clearly inconsistent with vs. 6 in the usual text. Perhaps the 'Western' οὗτοι ἐστάθησαν in the latter verse has arisen from the same motive."[1]

---

[19] Bernhard Weiss, *Der Codex D* (Leipzig, 1897), p. 66.

[1] J. H. Ropes, *The Text of Acts,* p. 56.

THE ACTS OF THE APOSTLES 295

6.3 δέ {B}

The reading οὖν is so appropriate in the context that, if it were original, there would have been no reason why the other readings should have arisen. The Committee agreed with Tischendorf *(ad loc.)* that the presence of δέ in both the preceding and following sentences prompted scribes to alter δέ in this verse (א B cop^sa) to either δή (A) or οὖν (C E P Ψ 33 614 1739 *Byz,* followed by the Textus Receptus), or to omit it entirely (𝔓^74 cop^sams arm eth geo *al*). The conflation δὲ οὖν is read by 1175.

6.3 πνεύματος

It was natural for scribes to add ἁγίου after πνεύματος (A C* H P S vg cop^sa eth), and the word passed into the Textus Receptus. The shorter text is supported by 𝔓^8, 74 א B D 431 614 2412 syr^h Chrysostom.

6.5 πλήθους

The Western text (D it^h cop^G67) adds τῶν μαθητῶν lest παντὸς τοῦ πλήθους be taken to refer to the non-Christian multitude.

6.5 πλήρης

The undeclinable form πλήρης, read by א A C D E H P and many minuscules, was corrected in B and several minuscules to πλήρη, a reading that passed into the Textus Receptus.

6.5 Τίμωνα

Instead of Τίμωνα Old Latin h reads *Simonem.* Since the name Τίμων is unique in the Bible, it is altogether probable that a scribe (or translator) misread the Greek name as Simon, a name more familiar to readers of the New Testament.[2]

---

[2] See K. Pieper, "Zu Apg. 6, 5," *Biblische Zeitschrift,* IX (1911), p. 184.

6.7 θεοῦ {B}

Acts contains examples of both ὁ λόγος τοῦ θεοῦ (4.31; 6.2; 11.1; 13.5, 7; 17.13; 18.11) and ὁ λόγος τοῦ κυρίου (8.25; 13.49; 15.35, 36; 19.10, 20; 20.35 [plural λόγοι]); the reading is in doubt at 12.24; 13.44; 16.32; 19.20.

In the present verse the Committee preferred ὁ λόγος τοῦ θεοῦ, which, in view of ver. 2, seems to be the more appropriate reading, and which is supported by superior external evidence (including 𝔓⁷⁴ ℵ A B C 33 1739 itᵍⁱᵍ syrᵖ copˢᵃ, ᵇᵒ).

6.7 τῶν ἱερέων

The more unusual reading τῶν ἱερέων (𝔓⁷⁴ A B C D *al*) is to be preferred to the more commonplace τῶν Ἰουδαίων (ℵ* 142 424 453 2401 *al* syrᵖ) and to the obviously corrupt ἐν τῷ ἱερῷ that underlies itʰ *(in templo)*.

6.8 χάριτος

The earlier text describes Stephen as a man "full of *grace*" (χάριτος, with 𝔓⁷⁴ ℵ A B D vg syrᵖ copˢᵃ, ᵇᵒ arm). The later text was assimilated to ver. 5, "full of *faith*" (πίστεως, with H P S most minuscules, followed by the Textus Receptus). Both readings are conflated in E (χάριτος καὶ πίστεως).[3]

6.8 λαῷ

The Western text adds διὰ τοῦ ὀνόματος (τοῦ) κυρίου Ἰησοῦ Χριστοῦ (D 5 33 431 453 876 2412 copˢᵃ Augustine), an interpolation probably derived from 4.30.

6.9 Λιβερτίνων

Since the other synagogues mentioned in this verse are named from countries, and since there were freedmen in every country,

---

[3] For a discussion of the variant readings, see Metzger, *The Text of the New Testament*, pp. 221–223.

many scholars from Beza onwards have suggested that instead of Λιβερτίνων we should read Λιβιστίνων or Λιβυστίνων ("Libyans").[4] Schulthess proposed Λιβύων τῶν κατὰ Κυρήνην (compare 2.10). One of the Arabic versions reads "Corinthians."

In Ropes's opinion, the explanation "Libyans," which is quoted from Chrysostom in the Armenian catena and is found in the Armenian vulgate text, may be an interpretation, not a variant reading.[5]

On the other hand, it is possible, as Lake and Cadbury suggest (in loc.), that the Greek text refers to only one synagogue; thus, the NEB renders the verse: "But some members of the synagogue called the Synagogue of Freedmen, comprising Cyrenians and Alexandrians and people from Cilicia and Asia, came forward and argued with Stephen." With this interpretation emendation is not necessary, and even on the usual view that several synagogues are intended, there is no compelling reason to depart from the text of the Greek witnesses.

6.9 καὶ Ἀσίας

The omission of καὶ Ἀσίας from A D* *l*[60] seems to have been accidental, occasioned by parablepsis (compare the similar ending of Κιλικίας, which immediately precedes).

6.10-11

A Western expansion, in slightly different forms, appears in D E vg[vmss] syr[hmg] cop[G67] and the Bohemian (Old Czech) version. The Bezan form, which according to Harris displays traces of Montanist interest in the Paraclete,[6] is as follows: οἵτινες οὐκ ἴσχυον ἀντιστῆναι τῇ σοφίᾳ τῇ οὔσῃ ἐν αὐτῷ καὶ τῷ πνεύματι τῷ ἁγίῳ ᾧ ἐλάλει, διὰ τὸ ἐλέγχεσθαι αὐτοὺς ἐπ' αὐτοῦ μετὰ πάσης παρρησίας. μὴ δυνάμενοι οὐ<ν> ἀντοφθαλμεῖν τῇ

---

[4] The history of this emendation is given by J. Rendel Harris, *Expositor*, Sixth Series, VI (1902), pp. 379–385.

[5] *The Text of Acts*, p. 58; see also Conybeare, *American Journal of Philology*, XVII (1896), p. 152.

[6] J. Rendel Harris, *Codex Bezae*, p. 150.

ἀληθείᾳ ("who could not withstand the wisdom *that was in him* and the *holy* Spirit with which he spoke, *because they were confuted by him with all boldness. Being unable therefore to confront the truth,* …).

The word ἀντοφθαλμεῖν is used in Wsd 12.14, a passage that may have influenced the Western reviser of Ac 5.39.

6.13   λαλῶν ῥήματα

Instead of λαλῶν ῥήματα the Textus Receptus reads ῥήματα βλάσφημα λαλῶν with E H P *al* arm; βλάσφημα is an interpolation from ver. 11.

6.13   [τούτου]

The phrase κατὰ τοῦ τόπου τοῦ ἁγίου (𝔓⁷⁴ ℵ A D E H P Ψ 066 0175 it^gig vg arm eth) refers, of course, to the temple. The addition of τούτου after ἁγίου (B C 33 69 1739 syr^p, h cop^sa, bo) allows (if indeed it does not require) the phrase to refer to the place of assembly of the Sanhedrin, which may have been situated on the Temple Mount on the western side of the enclosing wall.

The omission may have occurred accidentally (many words in the context end in -ου), or the word may have been deleted because the scene, according to ver. 12, took place in the assembly room of the Sanhedrin, for which a reference suited to the temple was inappropriate. On the other hand, the word may have crept into the text from the next verse, where the text is firm.

In view of the balance of these possibilities the Committee decided to retain the word but to enclose it within square brackets.

6.15   ἀγγέλου

After ὡσεὶ πρόσωπον ἀγγέλου the Greek text of codex Bezae (supported by it^h cop^G67) adds the phrase ἑστῶτος ἐν μέσῳ αὐτῶν ("all who sat in the council saw that his face was like the face of an angel *standing in their midst*"). Since, however, the Latin text of

Bezae reads *stans in medio eorum,* Harris argues[7] that the nominative form of the participle shows that the gloss originally belonged to the first verse of the following chapter, describing the position of the high priest "standing in their midst" (compare Mk 14.60). But this explanation overlooks the fact that what is needed to describe the action of the high priest is not merely that he was standing, but that (as the Markan passage shows) he stood up in their midst and spoke;[8] the gloss therefore belongs (as the Greek text of Bezae indicates) with what precedes.[9]

7.1

After εἶπεν δὲ ὁ ἀρχιερεύς the Western text (D E it[gig, h] vg[mss] cop[G67]) adds the very natural supplement τῷ Στεφάνῳ.

7.3-51

In addition to several direct quotations from the Septuagint, Stephen's speech consists of a series of allusions to and summaries of Israelitish history. In these phrases drawn from the Old Testament about thirty variants between B and D occur in which one agrees with the Septuagint against the other. In most of the cases it is codex Bezae that has been conformed to the text of the Septuagint; according to Ropes's judgment,[1] in only one instance (ἤδει in ver. 18)

---

[7] J. Rendel Harris, *Four Lectures on the Western Text* (London, 1894), pp. 70–75.

[8] So Peter Corssen, *Göttingische gelehrte Anzeigen,* CLVIII (1896), pp. 434 f.

[9] Harris remained enamoured of his proposal and a third of a century later offered as an added testimony for the Western reading a stray reference in the Life of St. Kentigern in Capgrave's *Nova Legenda Angliae* (ed. Horstmann, II, 121), where it is said that the face of St. Kentigern, while he was at prayer, sometimes appeared to bystanders as it had been the face of an angel standing in their midst ("Intuebantur enim faciem eius tanquam vultum angeli *stantis inter illos*"). Since, however, nothing is mentioned in the context that would connect the description of St. Kentigern with the account of Stephen in the book of Acts, the force of Harris's newly found "authority" for the Bezan text is minimal. Cf. Harris's article, "A New Witness for a Famous Western Reading," *Expository Times,* XXXIX (1927–28), pp. 380–381; see also Harris, *ibid.,* pp. 456–458.

[1] *The Text of Acts,* pp. 60–61.

is there reason to suspect that the B-text has been conformed to the Septuagint.

7.3-4

Several Old Latin witnesses (including it[gig. p]) remove the clause μετὰ τὸ ἀποθανεῖν τὸν πατέρα αὐτοῦ from its place in ver. 4 and insert it just before ver. 3. Probably the motive for this alteration was to bring the text into closer accord with the interpretation that the ordinary reader of Gn 11.27 ff. would be likely to derive from the progress of the narrative.[2]

7.4

The Western text presents several minor expansions, including the addition of Ἀβραάμ after τότε (D syr[h]); κἀκεῖ ἦν instead of κἀκεῖθεν and the corresponding insertion of καί before μετῴκισεν (D*); and the addition after κατοικεῖτε of καὶ οἱ πατέρες ὑμῶν (D ἡμῶν) E syr[h with *] Augustine. D further adds οἱ πρὸ ἡμῶν (syr[h with *] ὑμῶν). Since the last addition goes ill with κατοικεῖτε (for κατῴκησαν is needed), there is a possibility that the Western text is original and was subsequently deleted. On the other hand, however, since the entire context deals with the fathers, the opportunity for making such an addition was near to hand; it is also the kind of superfluity that is characteristic of the Western text.

7.12 σιτία

The Textus Receptus reads σῖτα ("wheat, grain") with H P and many minuscules, whereas $\mathfrak{P}^{74}$ ℵ A B C D E *al* read σιτία ("food [made from grain]"). Σιτίον is found only here in the New Testament, and only once in the Septuagint (Pr 30.22); scribes would

---

[2] In actuality, however, a strict analysis of the account in Genesis proves that Abraham departed from Haran many years before his father's death at the age of 205 years (Gn 11.32). According to Gn 11.26 Terah was 70 years old when Abraham was born, and according to Gn 12.4 Abraham was 75 years old when he left Terah, who therefore had sixty more years of life (205–[70+75] = 60).

therefore be tempted to assimilate it to the more frequently used σῖτον, which occurs 14 times in the New Testament, and 79 times in the Septuagint.

7.13 ἀνεγνωρίσθη

It is probable that scribes changed the verb ἀνεγνωρίσθη (𝔓⁷⁴ ℵ C D E H P most minuscules) to the simple form ἐγνωρίσθη (A B itᵖ vg) because the compound form seems to imply that Joseph had also made himself known to his brothers on their first visit to Egypt. (According to Brooke and McLean, in the Septuagint of Gn 45.1 three manuscripts read ἀνεγνωρίζετο for ἐγνωρίζετο.)

7.13 [τοῦ] Ἰωσήφ

The Textus Receptus, following D H P and many minuscules, reads τοῦ Ἰωσήφ, whereas the article is absent from B C 88 90 915 al, and instead of τοῦ Ἰωσήφ ℵ A E 181 1895 vg arm al read αὐτοῦ.

The Committee was divided in its evaluation of the evidence. Some members regarded αὐτοῦ as original and thought that copyists replaced it with Ἰωσήφ or τοῦ Ἰωσήφ for the sake of perspicuity. Others held that since Joseph had already been mentioned in the previous clause, scribes were led by stylistic considerations to substitute αὐτοῦ for the proper name. It was finally decided that the least unsatisfactory solution was to print τοῦ enclosed within square brackets.

7.16 ἐν Συχέμ {C}

The author has combined the accounts of two transactions: (a) Abraham bought a burial plot from Ephron the Hittite in Machpelah east of Hebron (Gn 23.3-20), where Abraham, Sarah, Isaac, Rebekah, Leah, and Jacob were buried (Gn 49.31; 50.13), and (b) Joseph was buried in a plot that Jacob bought from the sons of Hamor, the father of Schechem (Gn 33.19; Jos 24.32). Except for the two passages just mentioned, in the Old Testament Shechem is always the name of a place, not of a person. The variant readings in

Ac 7.16 reflect the two traditions concerning the name Shechem, except that the Western and Antiochian texts reverse the relationship, making Shechem the father instead of the son of Hamor. In seeking an explanation to account for the curious reading τοῦ ($\mathfrak{P}^{74}$ D^{gr} *al*), it should be observed that the Harclean Syriac reads "who was from Shechem"; could it be that παρά or ἀπό has fallen out of the archetype of the Western group of witnesses?

All things considered, the Committee judged ἐν to be the least unsatisfactory reading, supported, as it is, by ℵ* B C 88 1739 cop$^{sa, bo, fay}$ arm geo *al*.

7.17 ὡμολόγησεν {B}

The verb ὀμνύειν (ὀμνύναι) is used frequently throughout the Septuagint to render שָׁבַע. On the other hand, ὁμολογεῖν and ἐπαγγέλειν are used infrequently in the Septuagint (ὁμολογεῖν occurs a total of 14 times and ἐπαγγέλειν occurs 11 times; neither verb appears in the Pentateuch or the historical books). It is probable, therefore, that in the present passage scribes substituted ὤμοσεν for one of the other two verbs. Furthermore, since the verb ὁμολογεῖν acquired a technical meaning in the early church ("to make one's confession"),[3] there was added reason for copyists to alter it here. The verb ἐπηγγείλατο may have arisen as an echo of the previous τῆς ἐπαγγελίας.

7.18 [ἐπ' Αἴγυπτον] {C}

On the one hand, if the shorter reading be regarded as original, it is easy to see how Ex 1.8 in the Septuagint (ἀνέστη δὲ βασιλεὺς ἕτερος ἐπ' Αἴγυπτον, ὃς οὐκ ᾔδει τὸν Ἰωσήφ) would have influenced scribes to insert the phrase, ἐπ' Αἴγυπτον. On the other hand, since the preceding verse in Acts speaks of the people of Israel being ἐν Αἰγύπτῳ, it may be that the phrase was deleted as superfluous. Confronted with such a balance of probabilities, a majority of the

---

[3] On the semantics of ὁμολογεῖν, see Vernon H. Neufeld, *The Earliest Christian Confessions* (Leiden and Grand Rapids, 1963), pp. 13–20.

Committee decided to retain the words in the text but to enclose them within square brackets.

7.18 ᾔδει

For "another king who had not known Joseph" the Western text (D E it$^{gig, p}$ Chrysostom) reads "another king who did not *remember* (ἐμνήσθη) Joseph." Lake and Cadbury suggest that the B-text (ᾔδει) may be an accommodation to the Septuagint.[4] On the other hand, the Western text so often goes its own way that it would be extremely unwise to accept its text of Old Testament quotations as original whenever they differ from the Septuagint text.

7.19 [ἡμῶν] {C}

On the one hand, external evidence tends to favor the reading without ἡμῶν. On the other hand, the presence of ἡμῶν four words earlier with τὸ γένος may well have prompted copyists to delete the second instance of the pronoun as superfluous. In order to represent both considerations, a majority of the Committee decided to include the word in the text, but to enclose it within square brackets in order to indicate a measure of doubt that it belongs there.

7.21 αὐτοῦ

The Western text includes the added detail that Pharaoh's daughter found the infant Moses after he had been cast out "into the river," εἰς (παρὰ D) τὸν ποταμόν (D E syr$^{h \text{ with } *}$ cop^{G67}).

7.24

The Western text adds details from the Septuagint of Ex 2.11-12, "And seeing one *of his race* (ἐκ τοῦ γένους αὐτοῦ, D E syr$^{p, h \text{ with } *}$ cop^{G67} eth [D omits αὐτοῦ]) being wronged, he defended the op-

---

[4] *The Beginnings of Christianity,* vol. IV, p. 74.

pressed man and avenged him by striking the Egyptian, *and he hid him in the sand*" (καὶ ἔκρυψεν αὐτὸν ἐν τῇ ἄμμῳ, D cop^fay eth).

7.26

Codex Bezae (but not other members of the Western text) makes three additions to the verse: it prefixes τότε at the beginning (omitting τε); adds καὶ εἶδεν αὐτοὺς ἀδικοῦντας ("and he saw them doing injustice") after μαχομένοις; and reads τί ποιεῖτε, ἄνδρες ἀδελφοί; instead of ἄνδρες, ἀδελφοί ἐστε.

7.29   ἔφυγεν δὲ Μωϋσῆς

Hilgenfeld, followed by A. C. Clark, accepted the reading of codex Bezae as original, οὕτως καὶ ἐφυγάδευσεν Μωϋσῆς (E reads ἐφυγάδευσεν δὲ Μωϋσῆν, which means that the verb is transitive, with ὁ ἀδικῶν of ver. 27 understood as the subject). The word φυγαδεύειν appears nowhere else in the New Testament; in the Septuagint it occurs both transitively and intransitively, but generally the latter. Although it is just possible that the more commonly used verb φύγειν may be a corruption of the less usual φυγαδεύειν, on the whole the Western reading has little to recommend it in the face of the overwhelming weight of evidence against it (all other witnesses support ἔφυγεν δὲ Μωϋσῆς).

7.30   ἄγγελος

The Western and the Antiochian texts (D H P S 614 syr^{p. h} arm eth Augustine) insert κυρίου, a natural adition, especially in the light of Ex 3.2. The AV follows the expanded text with "an angel of the Lord."

7.31-34

The manuscript cop^{G67} is unique in making extensive additions to Stephen's account from the Old Testament and from tradition: "… as he [Moses] drew near to look (there came the voice of the Lord saying), *the Lord spoke to him in a voice saying, Moses, Moses! But he said, Who art thou, Lord? But he said to him, Do not draw near to this place. Take thy shoes off thy feet, for the place on which thou standest is a holy place. He said to him,* I am the God ... and of Jacob. But Moses (trembled and did not dare to look) *turned away his face, for he feared to look straightforwardly at God.* Then (the Lord) *God* said *this* to (him) *Moses,* (Loose the sandals from thy feet, for the place where thou art standing is holy ground). *Seeing* I have seen the oppression of my people in Egypt. I have heard their groaning *about their slave-labor, for I know their heartache.* I have come down to deliver them *from the hand of the Egyptians.* (And now) come, I (will) send thee to Egypt *that thou mayest bring them out of that land and take them into another land, which is good and plentiful, a land abundant with milk and honey, the place of the Canaanites and Hittites and Amorites and Pheresites and Hevites and Gergesites and Jebusites. And the cry of the children of Israel has come up to me, some of the sufferings with which the Egyptians have afflicted them. Now come, and I send thee to Pharaoh, the king of Egypt, and thou wilt bring my people, the children of Israel, out of the land of Egypt."*[5]

7.33 εἶπεν δὲ αὐτῷ ὁ κύριος

Instead of the commonplace introductory clause, "And the Lord said to him," codex Bezae substitutes the more colorful expression, καὶ ἐγένετο φωνὴ πρὸς αὐτόν ... (*"And there came a voice to him, 'Loose the shoes...'"*).

7.34 αὐτῶν

Since the singular number αὐτοῦ (B D 321 1838 syr[p]) is the more correct form grammatically (it refers to τοῦ λαοῦ), it is probable that

---

[5] Theodore C. Petersen's translation (see *Catholic Biblical Quarterly*, XXVI [1964], pp. 234 f.). Words which are absent from the Coptic manuscript, but which are present in the Vulgate text, are enclosed by Petersen within parentheses. For the Coptic text with a German translation (with Western readings similarly italicized), see Hans-Martin Schenke's edition in *Texte und Untersuchungen*, vol. 137 (1991).

αὐτῶν ($\mathfrak{P}^{74}$ ℵ A C E H P nearly all minuscules and versions) is the original reading that was altered by punctilious scribes.

7.35 δικαστήν

In this verse reference is made to the earlier citation (ver. 27) of the quotation from Ex 2.14. It was almost inevitable, therefore, that scribes would fill out the shorter reading here ($\mathfrak{P}^{45,\ 74}$ A B H P most minuscules vg syr^htxt) with the phrase "over us." The variant readings ἐφ' ἡμῶν (ℵ C D *al*) and ἐφ' ἡμᾶς (E 0142 33 61 *al*) occur also in the manuscripts of Ex 2.14.

7.35 [καί] (2)

The absence of καί after θεός in $\mathfrak{P}^{45,\ 74}$ ℵ* A C and many other witnesses, as well as the more deliberate emphasis that its presence gives to the text ("both ruler and deliverer"), led some members of the Committee to regard the word as a scribal addition. On the other hand, the strong external support in its favor (including B D) made other members of the Committee reluctant to omit the word entirely. As a compromise it was decided to retain the word enclosed within square brackets.

7.36 γῆ Αἰγύπτῳ

The reading γῆ Αἰγύπτου ($\mathfrak{P}^{74}$ D^gr 1611 1739 vg syr^p, h *al*) is obviously a correction of γῆ Αἰγύπτῳ (ℵ A E N P 81 many minuscules). The witnesses of both readings, however, unite in their support of γῆ against τῆ, which is read by B C 38 69 94 255 307 it^d cop^sa. The Septuagint text at Ex 7.3, to which the present passage seems to allude, reads γῆ. Although normally the Committee preferred readings that depart from the Septuagint, in this case the palaeographical possibility that scribes misread ΓΗΑΙΓΥΠΤΩ for the more usual (and therefore more to be expected) ΤΗΑΙΓΥΠΤΩ was regarded as the probable explanation for the emergence of scattered witnesses attesting τῆ. A few secondary witnesses (4 122* 181 241 460 1898 2180) omit both γῆ and τῆ, reading simply Αἰγύπτῳ.

7.37 ὁ θεός

The original text, ὁ θεός (𝔓⁷⁴ ℵ A B D 81 vg cop^sa, bo eth), has undergone various expansions. Since the Septuagint reads κύριος before ὁ θεός (Dt 18.15), it was natural for scribes to insert the word here (C E H P *al*). Later the expression was expanded still more (through assimilation to 3.22) by the addition of ἡμῶν (E H and most minuscules) or ὑμῶν (P some minuscules, followed by the Textus Receptus).

At the end of the verse the addition of the words αὐτοῦ ἀκού-σεσθε ("You shall hear him" [referring to the Messiah]), is a scribal assimilation to Dt 18.15 and/or Ac 3.22, which is read by C D E most minuscules vg syr^p, h cop^bo arm eth, followed by the Textus Receptus.

7.38 ἡμῖν {B}

As usual the manuscripts differ in their testimony to the first and second person plural pronouns, which, being pronounced alike, were constantly confused by scribes. It appears from the context that what is needed is ἡμῖν (A C D *al*), for Stephen does not wish to dis-associate himself from those who received God's revelation in the past, but only from those who misinterpreted and disobeyed that revelation. The erroneous ὑμῖν is read by 𝔓⁷⁴ ℵ B 36 76 257 307 467 489 913 1838 2138 cop^sa, bo geo. (See also the comment on ver. 39.)

7.39 ἡμῶν

Instead of "*our* fathers" several witnesses (including 36 81 242 2401 cop^G67 geo Irenaeus) read "*your* fathers." (See also the comment on ver. 38.)

7.42

Instead of "book of the prophets" cop^G67 reads "Amos the prophet." (See also the comment on ver. 48.)

7.43 ἐπέκεινα Βαβυλῶνος

The reading of codex Bezae ἐπὶ [τὰ μέ]ρη Βαβυλῶνος ("into the parts of Babylon"), instead of ἐπέκεινα Βαβυλῶνος ("beyond Babylon"; compare the Septuagint of Am 5.27, ἐπέκεινα Δαμασκοῦ), is received as original by Blass and Hilgenfeld, and its originality is judged "not impossible" by Knowling.[6] It is difficult to imagine, however, that a corrector would have replaced the Septuagint ἐπέκεινα (which is *hapax legomenon* in the New Testament) by ἐπὶ τὰ μέρη without also altering Βαβυλῶνος to the Septuagint Δαμασκοῦ. With Ropes and Haenchen the Committee regarded the Western reading as a scribal improvement, bringing the statement into better agreement with historical fact.

7.46 οἴκῳ {B}

Of the two readings, οἴκῳ is to be preferred on the basis of both external evidence (it is supported by a combination of Alexandrian and Western witnesses: 𝔓[74] ℵ* B D cop[sapt] *al*) and transcriptional probability, for there is no good reason why scribes should have altered θεῷ to οἴκῳ, whereas the apparent difficulty of the expression "a habitation for the house of Jacob" as well as the temptation to assimilate it to the Septuagint text of Ps 132.5 [= LXX 131.5] (ἕως οὗ εὕρω τόπον τῷ κυρίῳ, σκήνωμα τῷ θεῷ Ἰακώβ) would have influenced many to emend the text.

Some scholars who regard the reading οἴκῳ as intrinsically too difficult in the context ("[David] found favor in the sight of God and asked leave to find a habitation for the house of Jacob. (47) But it was Solomon who built a house for him"), and yet who acknowledge that θεῷ is secondary to οἴκῳ, believe that a primitive error has corrupted all extant witnesses. Lachmann conjectured that the original reading was εὑρεῖν σκήνωμα τῷ οἴκῳ τοῦ θεοῦ Ἰακώβ,[7] and Hort suggested that κυρίῳ had fallen out of the text (ΤΩΚΩ being mistaken for ΤΩΟΙΚΩ).[8] Against Hort's suggestion, however, is

---

[6] *The Expositor's Greek Testament*, vol. II, p. 195.

[7] *Novum Testamentum graece et latine*, vol. II (Berlin, 1850), p. viii.

[8] "Notes on Select Readings," p. 92.

the absence in both Old and New Testament of the expression "Lord of Jacob," whereas "God of Jacob" and "house of Jacob" are both well known.

Without indicating a preference, Knowling observes that "in LXX, Ps. cxxxi.3, we have σκήνωμα οἴκου, and a similar expression *may* have been the orig. reading here; again, in Ps. xxiv.6, Heb., we have 'Jacob' = 'the God of Jacob' (LXX 23.6), and it has been suggested that some such abbreviation or mode of speech lies at the bottom of the difficulty here."[9] Ropes also was dissatisfied with οἴκῳ and concludes his discussion of the variant readings with the supposition that "if we have here a translation from an Aramaic source, it is easy to suppose that the Aramaic equivalent of the Hebrew phrase was first rendered by τῳ κυριῳ ιακωβ, and then this unusual expression corrupted to the familiar-sounding but inappropriate phrase τῳ οικῳ ιακωβ."[10]

Not all scholars, however, are agreed that the reading οἴκῳ is so lacking in sense as to require conjectural emendation. Lake and Cadbury, for example, remark that "after all, the Temple, like the Tabernacle, was a house or tent 'of meeting,' and it was to be used by the house of Jacob as well as by the Almighty."[11] Furthermore, as Klijn points out, Stephen's "idea of a house within the house of Israel as a substitute for the temple and thus as the real temple of God," an idea not known heretofore in Jewish literature, has now been paralleled in the *Manual of Discipline* from Qumran – a fact that seems to support the originality of the reading οἴκῳ.[12]

7.48 προφήτης

After "prophet" cop[G67] adds "Isaiah" (see also the comment on ver. 42).

---

[9] *The Expositor's Greek Testament,* vol. II, p. 198.

[10] *The Text of Acts,* p. 72.

[11] *The Beginnings of Christianity,* vol. IV, p. 81. The same idea is set forth at length by José M.ª Bover in his "Notas de crítica textual neotestamentaria," *Emérita, boletín de lingüística y filología clásica,* XVIII (1950), pp. 381–385; Eng. summary, pp. 581 f. Compare also F. C. Synge in *Theology,* LV (1952), pp. 25–26.

[12] A. F. J. Klijn, "Stephen's Speech – Acts vii. 2–53," *New Testament Studies,* IV (1957), pp. 25–31, especially 29–31.

7.50 ταῦτα πάντα

Since the Septuagint text of Is 66.2 reads πάντα ταῦτα, it is probable that the sequence ταῦτα πάντα of ℵ B H 33 81 *al* is original and that in 𝔓⁷⁴ A C D E P Ψ *al* scribes assimilated the order to the Septuagint reading.

7.55 Ἰησοῦν

After Ἰησοῦν the Western text (D it^(gig, h, p) cop^(sa^pt, G67)) characteristically adds τὸν κύριον (see also the examples in Groups *B* and *C* in footnote 12, p. 226 above).

7.56 τὸν υἱὸν τοῦ ἀνθρώπου

Instead of τοῦ ἀνθρώπου a few witnesses (𝔓⁷⁴ 614 cop^(bo2 mss) geo) read τοῦ θεοῦ, which Kilpatrick thinks may possibly be original.[13] (See also the comment on the same variant readings at Jn 9.35.)

7.56 ἐκ δεξιῶν ἑστῶτα

The sequence ἐκ δεξιῶν ἑστῶτα in 𝔓⁷⁴ ℵ^c B D H P *al* was altered to ἑστῶτα ἐκ δεξιῶν in 𝔓⁴⁵ ℵ* A C E 69 *al*, probably by assimilation to ver. 55.

8.1

Once again Western witnesses expand the text with additions that underline the obvious. If "a great persecution arose against the church in Jerusalem," one would expect, without being told, that it would also involve "affliction" (after διωγμὸς μέγας D adds καὶ θλῖψις; it^h and cop^sa introduce θλῖψις καί before διωγμὸς μέγας); and if "they all were scattered abroad throughout the region of Judea and Samaria, except the apostles," we do not need the information that the

---

[13] G. D. Kilpatrick, *Theologische Zeitschrift,* XXI (1965), p. 209.

latter "remained in Jerusalem" (οἳ ἔμειναν ἐν Ἰερουσαλήμ, D* (1175) it^gig, h cop^sa, G67 Augustine). Compare ver. 6.

8.4 τὸν λόγον

After τὸν λόγον several Western witnesses (E it^p2 syr^p Augustine) add τοῦ θεοῦ; other Western witnesses (it^pl vg^mss) add *circa ciuitates et castella iudee,* which A. C. Clark introduces into his edition of Acts in the form κατὰ τὰς πόλεις καὶ κώμας τῆς Ἰουδαίας.

8.5 [τήν] {C}

It is difficult to decide the textual problem involving the presence or absence of the article. Since in the New Testament Samaria denotes the district, not the city of that name, the phrase εἰς τὴν πόλιν τῆς Σαμαρείας means "to the [main] city of Samaria." But which city did Luke intend by this circumlocution; was it Sebaste, the name given by Herod the Great to the city previously called Samaria, or was it Neapolis (Nablus), the ancient Shechem, the religious head-quarters of the Samaritans?[1] And why did he choose to refer to it without mentioning its name? It is not probable that he thought that Samaria had only one city.

On the other hand, the reading without the article ("to a city of Samaria") makes excellent sense in the context, and is the natural antecedent for the reference in ver. 8, where the author states that "there was much joy in that city."[2]

The Committee was of the opinion that the external evidence supporting the article (𝔓^74 ℵ A B 69 181 460* 1175 1898) was so strong that the word ought not be omitted from the text altogether. Yet because internal considerations favor the absence of the article, it was considered best to enclose it within square brackets.

---

[1] For a discussion favoring the latter possibility, see Julius Boehmer, "Samaria Stadt oder Landschaft?" *Zeitschrift für die neutestamentliche Wissenschaft,* IX (1908), pp. 216–218.

[2] It is because of this verse that C. C. Torrey rightly hesitated to solve the problem by assuming that the phrase ἡ πόλις τῆς Σαμαρίας is a mistranslation of מדינת שמרין "the *province* of Samaria"; see his *Composition and Date of Acts,* p. 18, n. 2.

8.6 προσεῖχον δὲ οἱ ὄχλοι

Here the jejune superfluity of the expansions of the Western text was too much even for Blass,[3] who refused to adopt the addition of D, ὡς δὲ ἤκουον πᾶν (it[d] πάντες), οἱ ὄχλοι προσεῖχον … ("And *when they heard everything*, the multitudes gave heed …"), with which is related the still more turgid reading of syr[p] ("And when the men who were there had heard his preaching, they gave heed to him and acquiesced to all that he said …").[4]

8.7

The grammar of the reading that is attested by the earlier and better witnesses (πολλοὶ γὰρ τῶν ἐχόντων πνεύματα ἀκάθαρτα βοῶντα φωνῇ μεγάλῃ ἐξήρχοντο, 𝔓[74] ℵ A B C *al*) is strained, for the author begins with πολλοί as the subject and πνεύματα ἀκάθαρτα as object of τῶν ἐχόντων, and then proceeds as though πνεύματα were the subject of the main verb ἐξήρχοντο ("For many of those who had unclean spirits, crying with a loud voice they came out"). In order to improve the syntax scribes altered the *nominativus pendens* into πολλοῖς (so codex Bezae)[5] or πολλῶν (so H P *al* cop[bo] arm Chrysostom); the latter reading passed into the Textus Receptus.

Modern scholars, dissatisfied with the anacoluthon and recognizing that πολλῶν is a secondary development, have proposed several conjectural emendations. For example, Lachmann suggested that πολλά should be read instead of πολλοί.[6] Blass, followed by

---

[3] B. Weiss (*Der Codex D,* p. 68) expresses surprise at this rejection by Blass, for the reading "is not more superfluous than innumerable additions in D" (compare the comments on 8.1 above).

[4] On the probable origin of this expanded reading, see F. H. Chase, *The Old Syriac Element in the Text of Codex Bezae* (London, 1893), pp. 75–77.

[5] Before πολλοῖς there is an erasure in D; Wetstein read ἀπὸ πολλοῖς *a prima manu*; Scrivener was inclined to read π[αρ]ά; and Blass thought that the scribe wrote π[αμ] (*Theologische Studien und Kritiken*, LXXXI [1898], p. 540).

[6] Preface in his *Novum Testamentum graece et latine,* 2nd ed., vol. II (Berlin, 1850), p. viii.

Hilgenfeld, thought that ἅ had fallen out after ἀκάθαρτα; with the relative pronoun restored, πολλοί is to be construed (along with the following πολλοί) as the subject of ἐθεραπεύθησαν.

On the other hand, however, Torrey argued that the Greek, rough though it is, ought not to be emended, since it represents the conjectural Aramaic original, in which the suspended construction is not unusual.[7]

Irrespective of one's view concerning the hypothetical Aramaic original, it is perhaps best to retain the anacoluthon and to conclude, with Lake and Cadbury, that we have here "one of those tricks of mental 'telescoping' to which all writers are liable," and that, as such, "it is one of several indications in the text that it was never finally revised."[8]

8.9 μέγαν

Struck by the syntax of the expression λέγων εἶναί τινα ἑαυτὸν μέγαν, several scholars have proposed emendations. Valckenaer, van de Sande Bakhuyzen, and Blass[9] regard μέγαν as an interpolation. Bowyer, Mangey, van Manen, and (tentatively) Lake and Cadbury prefer to read μάγον. In view, however, of ver. 10, which may illustrate what Lake and Cadbury thought was Luke's tendency to repeat a word soon after he has used it, it seems best to retain μέγαν.[10]

8.10 καλουμένη {A}

The awkward καλουμένη is omitted by the later Byzantine text; it is replaced by λεγομένη in several minuscules. Klostermann thought that Μεγάλη was a transliteration of the Samaritan מגלא or מגלי,

---

[7] *The Composition and Date of Acts,* pp. 33 f.

[8] *The Beginnings of Christianity,* vol. IV, p. 90; cf. also Cadbury's discussion, "Four Features of Lucan Style," in *Studies in Luke-Acts,* ed. by Leander E. Keck and J. Louis Martyn (New York, 1966), pp. 87–102.

[9] Besides Blass's edition of Acts (*in loc.*), see Blass-Debrunner-Funk, § 301, 1.

[10] *The Beginnings of Christianity,* vol. IV, p. 91.

meaning "he who reveals, the revealer,"[11] in which case καλουμένη apologizes for the foreign term (compare 1.12; 3.2, 11; 6.9).

8.18 πνεῦμα {B}

A majority of the Committee was of the opinion that the shorter reading, although supported by only ℵ B cop[sa] Apostolic Constitutions, was to be preferred to the reading of the overwhelming mass of witnesses, for after τὸ πνεῦμα the addition of τὸ ἅγιον was as natural for Christian scribes to make as its deletion would be inexplicable.

8.19 λέγων

In order to strengthen Simon's request the Western text (D it[gig, p]) inserts παρακαλῶν καί before λέγων (compare ver. 24 where παρακαλῶ occurs in D it[gig] syr[hmg]); the combination of verbs is not infrequent, e. g. Mt 8.5, 31; 18.29; Mk 5.12, 23; Ac 2.40; 16.9, 15.

8.24 ἐπ' ἐμὲ ὧν εἰρήκατε {A}

The Bezan text differs from that of other witnesses in several striking particulars: "And Simon answered and said *to them*, '*I beseech you,* pray for me *to God,* that none *of these evils* of which you have spoken *to me* may come upon me' – *who did not stop weeping copiously.*" The last clause is attached so awkwardly to the close of the sentence that Blass conjectured καί for the ὅς of D, which reads ... ὅπως μηδὲν ἐπέλθῃ μοι τούτων τῶν κακῶν ὧν εἰρήκατέ μοι, ὃς πολλὰ κλαίων οὐ διελίμπανεν. The addition gives the suggestion that Simon's tears are of remorse and perhaps of repentance; in the Clementine tradition Simon's tears are tears of rage and disappointment (*Clem. Hom.* xx.21; *Recog.* x.63).

Curiously the verb διαλιμπάνειν appears again in codex Bezae at 17.13 and nowhere else in the New Testament.

---

[11] A. Klostermann, *Probleme im Aposteltexte* (1883), pp. 15–20.

8.33 ταπεινώσει [αὐτοῦ]

The pronoun αὐτοῦ, present in most witnesses, is absent from 𝔓[74] ℵ A B 103 629 1642* 1739ᶜ vg *al*. Although such testimony in support of the shorter text generally carries conviction of originality, in this case, since the Septuagint text of Is 53.8 lacks αὐτοῦ, copyists would have been tempted to conform the New Testament quotation to the Old Testament text. In order to represent the conflict between external evidence and transcriptional probability, it was thought best to include αὐτοῦ in the text, but to enclose it within square brackets.

8.35

CopG67 reads, "Then Philip *took his* beginning from the scripture, *and now he was in the spirit*; he began *to explain to him* from the scripture, (and) preached *the Lord* Jesus *Christ* to him."

8.37 *omit verse* {A}

Ver. 37 is a Western addition, not found in 𝔓[45, 74] ℵ A B C 33 81 614 vg syrᵖ, ʰ copˢᵃ, ᵇᵒ eth, but is read, with many minor variations, by E, many minuscules, itᵍⁱᵍ, ʰ vgᵐˢˢ syrʰ ʷⁱᵗʰ * copG67 arm. There is no reason why scribes should have omitted the material, if it had originally stood in the text. It should be noted too that τὸν Ἰησοῦν Χριστόν is not a Lukan expression.

The formula πιστεύω … Χριστόν was doubtless used by the early church in baptismal ceremonies, and may have been written in the margin of a copy of Acts. Its insertion into the text seems to have been due to the feeling that Philip would not have baptized the Ethiopian without securing a confession of faith, which needed to be expressed in the narrative. Although the earliest known New Testament manuscript that contains the words dates from the sixth century (ms. E), the tradition of the Ethiopian's confession of faith in Christ was current as early as the latter part of the second century, for Irenaeus quotes part of it (*Against Heresies,* III.xii.8).

Although the passage does not appear in the late medieval manuscript on which Erasmus chiefly depended for his edition (ms. 2), it stands in the margin of another (ms. 4), from which he inserted it into his text because he "judged that it had been omitted by the carelessness of scribes *(arbitror omissum librariorum incuria)*."

8.39   πνεῦμα {A}

Instead of πνεῦμα κυρίου several witnesses, including A (correction by the first hand) 36ᵃ 94 103 307 322 323 385 467 1739 1765 2298 itᵖ vgᵐˢˢ syrʰ ᵂⁱᵗʰ * arm Ephraem Jerome Augustine (D is defective here), read πνεῦμα ἅγιον ἐπέπεσεν ἐπὶ τὸν εὐνοῦχον, ἄγγελος δέ ("the *Holy* Spirit *fell on the eunuch, and an angel* of the Lord caught up Philip"). Some scholars, holding the longer reading to be original, have explained its absence in the other witnesses as due either to accidental omission or to deliberate excision because of its variance with the account in verses 15–18, where it is implied that the Holy Spirit was bestowed only through the laying on of the hands of the apostles.

On the other hand, most scholars have been impressed by the weight of attestation supporting the shorter text as well as by the probability that the words were added in order (*a*) to make explicit that the baptism of the Ethiopian was followed by the gift of the Holy Spirit, and (*b*) to conform the account of Philip's departure to that of his commission (by an angel of the Lord, ver. 26).

9.2   τῆς ὁδοῦ ὄντας

There are six variant readings: τῆς ὁδοῦ ὄντας (B C E H L P many minuscules), ὄντας τῆς ὁδοῦ (𝔓⁷⁴ ℵ A 81 88 242 323 467 915 1739 2298), τῆς ὁδοῦ ταύτης ὄντας (181 1838 *al*), ὄντας τῆς ὁδοῦ ταύτης (104), τῆς ὁδοῦ (33 429* 522 1175 1827 1891 copˢᵃ, ᵇᵒ), τῆς ὁδοῦ ταύτης (itᵉ vg). It is clear that ταύτης was introduced at various positions by scribes who wished thereby to relieve the peculiarity of the term ἡ ὁδός, used here for the first time in reference to Christianity. The choice between the reading of B C *al* and of 𝔓⁷⁴ ℵ A 81 1739 seems to depend upon which order would have appeared more difficult and therefore more likely to be altered to an easier sequence. It is probable that scribes, in order to prevent the reader from taking ὄντας chiefly with what follows ("being both men and women"), moved the participle nearer τινάς.

9.4-5 διώκεις

The clause σκληρόν σοι πρὸς κέντρα λακτίζειν is included after διώκεις (ver. 4) in E 431 vg^mss syr^p, h with * Petilianus Jerome Augustine; and after διώκεις (ver. 5) in it^gig, h, p vg^ms Lucifer Ambrose. Although Clark argued that it would have been "inartistic" of Luke not to include the clause in one or the other verses (Clark prefers ver. 4),[1] it is more probable that the words were introduced by copyists who assimilated the passage to the account of Paul's conversion given in 26.14, where the clause follows διώκεις (the text is firm). In support of this judgment is the lack of any reason that would satisfactorily account for the omission of the clause from verses 4 or 5, had it stood there originally. Likewise, it is always suspicious when a variant reading, which agrees with a parallel passage, has no fixed location but vacillates between two points of attachment in Western witnesses.

---

[1] Clark expresses himself as follows: "I find it difficult to believe that the writer of Acts would reserve this picturesque detail for the third occasion on which the story is told. Could he have been, to say the least, so inartistic? We should have expected the three accounts to agree, or, failing this, that, if a striking detail was dropped, it would be in xxii.7 or xxvi.14" (*The Acts of the Apostles,* p. 345). Luke evidently thought otherwise, for the second account of Paul's conversion is longer than the first, and the third account is longer than the second; for a convenient arrangement of the Greek text of the three accounts in parallel columns, see Erwin Preuschen's commentary in the series *Handbuch zum Neuen Testament* (Tübingen, 1912).

Haenchen makes a threefold answer to Clark's *a priori* argument: (*a*) Luke felt no obligation to repeat a description schematically; (*b*) the hellenistic proverb σκληρόν κ. τ. λ. is appropriately introduced only before the hellenistic audience in chap. 26; and (*c*) a good author holds something in reserve so that he can make a special point when he repeats an account. Therefore, it is not the B-text, but the D-text that is "inartistic" here! (E. Haenchen, "Zur Text der Apostelgeschichte," *Zeitschrift für Theologie und Kirche,* LIII [1956], pp. 27 f.)

9.5-6 διώκεις· ἀλλά

After διώκεις (and omitting ἀλλά of ver. 6) the Textus Receptus adds σκληρόν σοι πρὸς κέντρα λακτίζειν. (6) τρέμων τε καὶ θαμβῶν εἶπε, Κύριε, τί με θέλεις ποιῆσαι; καὶ ὁ κύριος πρὸς αὐτόν, which is rendered in the AV as follows: "it is hard for thee to kick against the pricks. (6) And he trembling and astonished said, Lord, what wilt thou have me to do? And the Lord said unto him." So far as is known, no Greek witness reads these words at this place; they have been taken from 26.14 and 22.10, and are found here in codices of the Vulgate, with which it[h, p] syr[h with *] cop[G67] substantially agree (all except the Vulgate add after θαμβῶν the words ἐπὶ τῷ γεγονότι αὐτῷ, taken from 3.10). The spurious passage came into the Textus Receptus when Erasmus translated it from the Latin Vulgate into Greek and inserted it in his first edition of the Greek New Testament (Basel, 1516). See p. 8* above.

9.8 ἠγέρθη ... γῆς

Instead of the statement ἠγέρθη δὲ Σαῦλος ἀπὸ τῆς γῆς, several Western witnesses heighten the pathos of the account by reading ἔφη δὲ πρὸς αὐτούς, Ἐγείρατέ με ἀπὸ τῆς γῆς (it[h, p] vg[mss]), followed by καὶ ἐγειράντων αὐτόν (it[h] Ephraem).

9.8 οὐδέν

Instead of οὐδέν (𝔓[74] ℵ A* B it[e] vg syr[p, h] cop[sa, G67]) οὐδένα is read by A[2] C E[gr] H L P 614 and many others (in codex Sinaiticus the letter α seems to have been begun above the line, but was left unfinished). The latter reading entered the Textus Receptus and lies behind the AV, "he saw no man."

9.12

Because the verse is absent from the Old Latin h, Blass omitted it from his Roman edition of Acts and Hilgenfeld bracketed it. There is, however, as Knowling remarks,[2] no apparent reason why it should have been inserted if not genuine, as it is not influenced by any parallel passage. After a lengthy discussion of problems, some real, some imaginary, which have been found in the verse, Corssen[3] contents himself with the deletion of ἐν ὁράματι and Ἀνανίαν ὀνόματι. Clark, without manuscript support, prefers to place ver. 12 immediately after ver. 9. Although he professes to find "admirable sense" in this sequence,[4] the rearrangement leaves the introduction of ver. 10 (Clark's ver. 11) extremely inept, for now Ananias is introduced as though he were unknown (ἦν δέ τις μαθητὴς ἐν Δαμασκῷ ὀνόματι Ἀνανίας) despite his having been mentioned by name in the immediately preceding sentence.

It seems best to regard the absence of the verse from it[h] as due to an accident in transcription, occasioned perhaps by the presence of the name Ananias early in both ver. 12 and ver. 13.

9.12   ἄνδρα [ἐν ὁράματι] {C}

The fact that the words ἐν ὁράματι stand in several positions in the manuscripts may suggest that the phrase is an explanatory gloss introduced to complete the sense of εἶδεν. On the other hand, since ἐν ὁράματι had just been used (in ver. 10), the second instance (though referring to a different vision) may have been omitted as apparently redundant. Moreover, inattentive scribes would be likely to confuse ὁράματι with the following ὀνόματι, which also varies in position (the Textus Receptus, following H L P and many other manuscripts, reads ὀνόματι Ἀνανίαν, and ὀνόματι is omitted by cop[sa] eth[ro] Chrysostom). It should be noted, as Haenchen observes, that the sequence of words in B C is unusual (but not unknown to Luke; cf. the preferred reading in 14.8), and therefore may have been amended in the later manuscripts.

In view of the balance of possibilities a majority of the Committee

[2] R. J. Knowling, *The Expositor's Greek Testament,* vol. II, p. 235.

[3] Peter Corssen, *Der Cyprianische Text der Acta apostolorum* (Berlin, 1892), pp. 21–23.

[4] A. C. Clark, *The Acts of the Apostles,* pp. liii and 345.

decided to retain the words in the text enclosed within square brackets.

9.17 Ἰησοῦς

Although the word Ἰησοῦς, which is absent from H L P Ψ 5 218 255 257 326 383 431 467 623 927 1311 1838 2143 cop^sa eth^ro, may have come into the text from ver. 5 (as John Mill thought), a majority of the Committee was impressed by the weight of early and diverse external support for its inclusion (𝔓^45, 74 ℵ A B C E most minuscules vg).

9.18 ἀνέβλεψέν τε

In order to heighten the account concerning the restoration of Paul's eyesight, παραχρῆμα is added by C² E L many minuscules syr^p cop^sa arm^mss eth Chrysostom. The gloss came into the Textus Receptus, whence the AV renders "and he received sight forthwith" (the translators avoided using "immediately" because they had employed this word earlier in the sentence for εὐθέως).

9.19 ἡμέρας τινάς

The reading of 𝔓^45 ἡμέρας ἱκανάς (compare it^h *dies plurimos*) is a scribal modification, introduced perhaps under the influence of the similar phrase in ver. 23.

9.20 Ἰησοῦν

The reading Ἰησοῦν (𝔓^45, 74 ℵ A B C E 61 vg syr^p, h cop^sa, bo *al*) was displaced (probably for doctrinal reasons) by the reading Χριστόν (H L P arm^mss *al*), which was taken into the Textus Receptus and so into the AV. But, as Alford pointed out long ago, "the following τὸ ὄνομα τοῦτο (ver. 21) is decisive for the reading Ἰησοῦν, and οὗτός ἐστιν ὁ χριστός (ver. 22) still more so" (*The Greek Testament, ad loc.*).

9.22 ἐνεδυναμοῦτο

Copyists added the words ἐν τῷ λόγῳ (C (om. ἐν) E 467 it[h. p] cop[G67]) to make it clear that the statement, "Saul increased all the more in strength," refers to his power in preaching and not merely to his recovery of physical strength (compare ver. 19).

9.22 Χριστός

After Χριστός the Western text, preserved in it[gig. h, p], adds ἐν ᾧ (or εἰς ὅν) εὐδόκησεν ὁ θεός. According to Lake and Cadbury, "[this] may be the original reading, for it is not at all the type of addition which was customary at any late date, and it may have been omitted for theological reasons."[5] On the other hand, however, in view of the absence of the reading from all Greek manuscripts of Acts, it is safer to regard the clause as a scribal gloss derived from either Mt 3.17 or Lk 3.22 (compare 2 Pe 1.17).

9.24 ἡμέρας τε καὶ νυκτὸς ὅπως αὐτὸν ἀνέλωσιν

Several witnesses (A 181 242 323 1898), having been conformed to Paul's account of the incident (2 Cor 11.32), read ὅπως πιάσωσιν αὐτὸν ἡμέρας καὶ νυκτός.

9.25 οἱ μαθηταὶ αὐτοῦ

The oldest reading extant in the manuscripts appears to be οἱ μαθηταὶ αὐτοῦ (𝔓[74] ℵ A B C 81* vg al). This was altered (perhaps because in verses 19 and 26 μαθηταί is used absolutely) to οἱ μαθηταὶ αὐτόν (69 81[c]), or to αὐτὸν οἱ μαθηταί (E H L P syr[p. h] cop[sa, bo] arm al, followed by the Textus Receptus), or to οἱ μαθηταί (S 36 429 al).

Since it is scarcely conceivable that Jewish converts to Christianity at Damascus would be called "Paul's disciples," various attempts have been made to alleviate the difficulty that the best attested

[5] *The Beginnings of Christianity,* vol. IV, p. 105.

reading involves. Occasionally the genitive αὐτοῦ is construed as the object of λαβόντες ("taking hold of him"),[6] but the sequence of words as well as the unnatural sense stand against this expedient. To assume, as Rengstorf does, that these disciples had been Paul's "companions on the way to Damascus, who through his own leadership and by his witness had themselves come to the faith,"[7] is totally gratuitous. The most satisfactory solution appears to be the conjecture that the oldest extant text arose through scribal inadvertence, when an original αὐτόν was taken as αὐτοῦ.[8]

9.26 ἐπείραζεν

The reading ἐπειρᾶτο, which is from the usual verb in classical Greek meaning "to try [to do something]," was introduced into the later text (E H L P many minuscules, followed by the Textus Receptus) in place of ἐπείραζεν (𝔓74 ℵ A B C 61 81 *al*). The substitution was made because the latter verb, which is much more common in the New Testament, ordinarily has a different sense ("to make trial of, tempt") from its meaning here.

9.29 Ἑλληνιστάς {A}

The weight of the manuscript evidence is decisively in support of Ἑλληνιστάς, usually rendered "Hellenists" (i.e., Greek-speaking Jews). See also the comment on 11.20.

9.31 ἡ ... ἐκκλησία ... εἶχεν ... οἰκοδομουμένη καὶ πορευο-
μένη ... ἐπληθύνετο {A}

The range and age of the witnesses that read the singular number are superior to those that read the plural. The singular can hardly be a scribal modification in the interest of expressing the idea of the unity

---

[6] So, e. g., Henry Alford, *The Greek Testament, ad loc.*

[7] K. H. Rengstorf in Kittel's *Theologische Wörterbuch zum Neuen Testament*, vol. IV, p. 464 [English trans., p. 459]. The variant reading in 14.20 D E κυκλωσάντων δὲ τῶν μαθητῶν αὐτοῦ provides no real explanation for the present verse.

[8] Compare E. Haenchen, *The Acts of the Apostles, ad loc.*

of the church, for in that case we should have expected similar modifications in 15.41 and 16.5, where there is no doubt that the plural number ἐκκλησίαι is the original text. More probably the singular number here has been altered to the plural in order to conform to the two later passages.

9.34 ἰᾶται

The verb form that is spelled ιαται may be accented either as present tense (ἰᾶται) or perfect tense (ἴαται). The scribe of codex Vaticanus undoubtedly took the form to be the perfect tense, for he wrote it ειαται, as he did also at Mk 5.29 where there is no question that the perfect tense is intended.[9]

9.34 Ἰησοῦς Χριστός

Although the expression Ἰησοῦς ὁ Χριστός ("Jesus the Christ"), read by A B³ E H L P and most minuscules, seems to have a certain primitiveness, a majority of the Committee was impressed by the weight of the witnesses that omit the article (𝔓⁷⁴ ℵ B* C Ψ 048 33 1175 al). The prefixing of ὁ κύριος (in A 36 94 181 307 441 vg copˢᵃ arm eth) is obviously a secondary development.

9.35 Σαρῶνα

The testimony of most early witnesses converges upon the spelling Σαρῶνα (𝔓⁵³, ⁷⁴ (-ρρ- A) B C E). The scribes of 𝔓⁴⁵ and of numerous minuscules (followed by the Textus Receptus), not observing that the word was already accusative from Σαρων, added -ν, making it accusative from Σαρωνᾶς. The spelling with prefixed alpha (Ἀσσάρωνα in H L (Ἀσα- P) 33 al) may be, as Zahn suggested,[10] in imitation of the Hebrew article, although the Aramaic article was already indicated by the final -α.

---

[9] See H. J. Cadbury, "A Possible Perfect in Acts ix.34," *Journal of Theological Studies*, XLIX (1948), pp. 57–58.

[10] Theodor Zahn, *Die Apostelgeschichte des Lucas* (Leipzig und Erlangen, 1919), p. 336, n. 27.

9.38 δύο ἄνδρας

The sending of two messengers (δύο ἄνδρας, read by 𝔓[45, 74] ℵ A B C E and most minuscules) is in accord with Near Eastern customs.[11] The omission of the words in some witnesses (H L P Ψ 104 326 383 440 536 920 *al*) may be due to influence from 10.19 (see the comment there).

9.38

At the close of the verse cop[G67] adds "for the city was not far away. And when the men had gone there, they begged him to come with them without delay."

9.40

After ἀνάστηθι several Western witnesses (it[gig. p] vg[mss] syr[h with *] cop[sa, G67] arm Cyprian Ambrose) add in slightly varying forms the words ἐν τῷ ὀνόματι τοῦ κυρίου ἡμῶν Ἰησοῦ Χριστοῦ ("in the name of our Lord Jesus Christ"); compare 4.10, "in the name of Jesus Christ of Nazareth." Another Western modification is the addition of παραχρῆμα ("immediately") before ἤνοιξεν (E it[gig. p] cop[sa, G67] Speculum).

9.42 τῆς

The word τῆς is absent from 𝔓[53] B C* but present in apparently all other Greek witnesses. Should the acknowledged excellence of codex Vaticanus and the early age of 𝔓[53] (third century) be regarded as decisive in adopting the shorter text, or should the reading of the overwhelming mass of manuscripts be preferred? Since Luke always uses the definite article after καθ' ὅλης (Lk 4.14; 23.5; Ac 9.31; 10.37), and in view of a certain tendency on the part of the scribe of

---

[11] See J. Jeremias, "Paarweise Sendung im Neuen Testament," *New Testament Essays: Studies in Memory of Thomas Walter Manson* ... edited by A. J. B. Higgins (Manchester, 1959), pp. 136–143.

Vaticanus occasionally to omit the article, the Committee regarded its absence from the three witnesses as accidental.

9.43 ἡμέρας ἱκανὰς μεῖναι

There are three variant readings: ἡμέρας ἱκανὰς μεῖναι (𝔓⁵³ ℵ* B 3 209* 216 1175 1739 geo), αὐτὸν ἡμέρας ἱκανὰς μεῖναι (𝔓⁷⁴ ℵᶜ A E 18 81 181 242 323 328 429 441 920 2298 *al*), and ἡμέρας ἱκανὰς μεῖναι αὐτόν (C L P most minuscules, followed by the Textus Receptus). A majority of the Committee preferred ἡμέρας ἱκανὰς μεῖναι as the most difficult reading (it is also the earliest attested reading – 𝔓⁵³ is third century, ℵ and B are fourth). In order to clarify the construction, scribes supplied αὐτόν either before or after ἡμέρας ἱκανὰς μεῖναι.

10.3 περί

The Textus Receptus, following L P Ψ and most minuscules, omits περί. The word, which apparently was dropped by copyists who deemed it superfluous, is decisively supported by 𝔓⁷⁴ ℵ A B C E 36ᵃ 642 808 *al*.

10.5 τινά {B}

The presence of τινά after Σίμωνα is altogether appropriate in the mouth of Cornelius, to whom Peter was unknown. On the other hand, however, the expression "a certain Simon who is called Peter" may have seemed to copyists to lack proper respect for the chief of the apostles, and so the belittling τινά was dropped.

10.6

At the close of the verse several minuscules (321 322 436 453 466 467) add from 11.14 the words ὃς λαλήσει ῥήματα πρός σε, ἐν οἷς σωθήσῃ σὺ καὶ πᾶς ὁ οἶκός σου. A similar phrase, οὗτος λαλήσει σοι τί σε δεῖ ποιεῖν, which is found in 69ᵐᵍ 1611 and in several Latin manuscripts (it is included in the Clementine Vulgate, but not in Wordsworth and White's edition), somehow got into the Textus Receptus (perhaps Erasmus translated it into Greek, on the model of 9.6), and so the AV renders, "he shall tell thee what thou oughtest to do."

10.9 ἕκτην

Instead of "sixth" hour ℵ^c 225 *al* read "ninth" *(ἐνάτην)*, making Peter's prayer coincide with Cornelius's prayer (ver. 30).

10.10 ἐγένετο (2)

Instead of the second instance of ἐγένετο, the later text (E L P many minuscules, followed by the Textus Receptus) substitutes ἐπέπεσεν, which not only avoids the repetition of ἐγένετο but provides a more appropriate word with ἔκστασις.

10.11 καὶ καταβαῖνον σκεῦός τι ὡς ὀθόνην μεγάλην τέσσαρσιν ἀρχαῖς καθιέμενον {C}

Apparently the Western text lacked καταβαῖνον (it is omitted by it^d syr^{p,h} cop^{sa} Didascalia [in Apostolic Constitutions]) and described the vessel as "tied *(δεδεμένον)* at (the) four corners." In the text of the old uncials, which read καταβαῖνον, the vessel is said to be "lowered *(καθιέμενον)* by (the) four corners." A majority of the Committee judged that witnesses that have all three participles are conflate, and preferred the reading supported by 𝔓^{74} ℵ A B (C^2) it^e vg geo.

10.12 τετράποδα καὶ ἑρπετὰ τῆς γῆς {B}

Copyists recollecting the similar but fuller account in 11.6 produced a variety of expanded readings; thus, the usual expression (καὶ) τὰ θηρία was introduced before or after τὰ ἑρπετά, or after τῆς γῆς. The reading that best explains the origin of the others is also well attested ($\mathfrak{P}^{74}$ ℵ A B 81 326 630 it^{gig} vg syr^p *al*).

10.16 εὐθὺς ἀνελήμφθη {B}

The readings with πάλιν before or after ἀνελήμφθη reflect scribal assimilation to the parallel account in 11.10. Of the other readings, a majority of the Committee preferred εὐθὺς ἀνελήμφθη, which is well supported by $\mathfrak{P}^{74}$ ℵ A B C E^{gr} 81 88 1877 vg syr^{hmg} *al*.

[Since the adverb εὐθύς occurs nowhere else in Acts (though εὐθέως occurs nine times), and in view of the unexplained absence of any adverb in $\mathfrak{P}^{45}$ 307 453 610 1175 and a variety of versional and patristic witnesses, it is preferable to enclose εὐθύς within square brackets. B.M.M. and A.W.]

10.17 ἰδού

The Textus Receptus, following C D E L P and most minuscules, reads καὶ ἰδού. A majority of the Committee, impressed by the weight of $\mathfrak{P}^{45, 74}$ ℵ A B 81 181 242 255 429 *al*, preferred the reading ἰδού without καί

[The probability that modification would have gone from the more difficult (Hebraic) reading, involving an apparently superfluous καί, to the easier reading makes it preferable to adopt the reading with καί – or at least to read καί enclosed within square brackets. B.M.M.]

10.19 [αὐτῷ]

The omission of αὐτῷ (in B) appears to be accidental, yet because of the variation in position of the pronoun in the other readings, it was thought best to represent the possibility that the shorter text was original and to enclose αὐτῷ within square brackets. Of the two readings, εἶπεν τὸ πνεῦμα αὐτῷ ($\mathfrak{P}^{74}$ ℵ A C 69 81 431 1898 *al*) and εἶπεν αὐτῷ τὸ πνεῦμα ($\mathfrak{P}^{45}$ D E L P most minuscules, followed by the Textus Receptus), a majority of the Committee preferred the one attested by the oldest known witness ($\mathfrak{P}^{45}$).

10.19 τρεῖς {B}

The evidence for and against each of the four principal readings is curiously kaleidescopic, and a case can be made for each of them.

(1) The reading of B, being the most difficult (because of the discrepancy with ver. 7 and 11.11), is preferred by Ropes, who suggests that the two servants alone (ver. 7) may be thought of as responsible messengers, the soldier merely serving as a guard. Scribes, not observing the reason lying behind the use of δύο, corrected what they supposed was an error either by deleting the word or by substituting τρεῖς (in accord with 11.11).

(2) The reading τρεῖς is strongly supported by diversified external evidence. Assuming this reading to be original, one can explain the origin of δύο as the work of a discriminating scribe and the absence of the word as an accidental omission after ἄνδρες (–ΔΡΕϹΤΡΕΙϹ).

(3) If, as is usual in similar cases, the shortest reading is regarded as original (compare ἄνδρας, ver. 5), recollection of ver. 7 or 11.11 would have induced scribes to include a numeral with ἄνδρες.

On balance, it seemed to the Committee that the least unsatisfactory solution was to adopt the reading supported by the broadest spectrum of external evidence.

10.19 ζητοῦντες

Instead of ζητοῦσιν, supported by the overwhelming number of witnesses, a majority of the Committee preferred ζητοῦντες, read by $\mathfrak{P}^{74}$ ℵ B and 81 (the latter has the orthographic variant -νταις, which in Byzantine Greek was pronounced like -ντες). If the finite verb were original, it is difficult to understand what would have induced scribes to substitute the participle. On the other hand, when the sentence-building power of ἰδού was forgotten, the emergence of the reading ζητοῦσιν would have been almost inevitable.

10.21-23

The Western text differs in several minor details. In ver. 21 instead of καταβὰς δέ D E syr^p read τότε καταβάς, and before τίς D syr^h add the solemn but superfluous τί θέλετε ἤ (by itacism D reads θέλεται). In ver. 22 D syr^p cop^sa add πρὸς αὐτόν after εἶπαν, and after Κορνήλιος D^gr syr^p add τις. In ver. 23 instead of εἰσκαλεσάμενος οὖν (the verb is *hapax legomenon* in the New Testament), D it^p syr^p read τότε εἰσαγαγὼν ὁ Πέτρος.

10.24 εἰσῆλθεν {C}

Although εἰσῆλθον may have been altered to the singular number in order to agree with ἐξῆλθεν in the previous verse, a majority of the Committee judged that transcriptional probability favors εἰσῆλθεν, since it is preceded and followed by plurals (συνῆλθον and αὐτούς) to which copyists would have been tempted to assimilate it.

10.25

The expansion in the Western text of this verse appears to have arisen from reflecting upon the difficulty involved in the ordinary text, that Cornelius could not have known exactly when to go out to meet Peter and to summon his kinsmen and close friends to his home. The text of D, supported by it^gig syr^hmg cop^G67 and in part by it^p and other Latin witnesses, reads: προσεγγίζοντος δὲ τοῦ Πέτρου εἰς τὴν Καισάριαν προδραμὼν εἷς τῶν δούλων διεσάφησεν παραγεγονέναι αὐτόν. ὁ δὲ Κορνήλιος ἐκπηδήσας καὶ ... ("And as Peter was drawing near to Caesarea, one of the servants[1] ran ahead and announced that he had arrived. And Cornelius jumped up and ...").[2]

---

[1] The servant, as it seems, is one of the two whom Cornelius had sent to fetch Peter (verses 7 and 23), and not one posted by Cornelius to watch for the apostle's coming (as E. J. Epp suggests, *The Theological Tendency of Codex Bezae Cantabrigiensis in Acts*, p. 161), nor one of Peter's own servants (as R. P. C. Hanson assumes, *New Testament Studies*, XII [1965–66], p. 221).

[2] For a discussion of the difficulties in both the Alexandrian and the Western forms of text, see Peter Corssen in *Göttingische gelehrte Anzeigen*, CLVIII (1896), pp. 437 f.

10.26-29

Instead of ἀνάστηθι in ver. 26 D reads τί ποιεῖς; (compare 7.26 τί ποιεῖτε; D, and 14.15); both expressions are conflated in it^p syr^hmg, and it^p2 adds *deum adora* (compare τῷ θεῷ προσκύνησον, Re 19.10; 22.9). In the same vein D* E it^gig, p vg^mss add ὡς καὶ σύ after εἰμι. In ver. 27 D omits συνομιλῶν αὐτῷ, perhaps because it was regarded as superfluous. With the addition in ver. 28 of βέλτιον before ἐφίστασθε in D ("you yourselves know *very well*"), compare the similar heightening in D at 4.16. The insertion of ἀνδρί before ἀλλοφύλῳ in D^gr syr^p cop^sa may be due to the presence of the same word earlier in the sentence. In ver. 29 after μεταπεμφθείς D E it^p fill out the expression with the obvious ὑφ᾽ ὑμῶν.

10.30   τὴν ἐνάτην {B}

The Textus Receptus, supported by a diversified and respectable array of witnesses, appears to be clear and straightforward: Ἀπὸ τετάρτης ἡμέρας μέχρι ταύτης τῆς ὥρας ἤμην νηστεύων, καὶ τὴν ἐνάτην ὥραν προσευχόμενος ἐν τῷ οἴκῳ μου, which ought to mean, "From the fourth day until this hour I was fasting, and while keeping the ninth hour of prayer in my house" (the reading in D ἀπὸ τῆς τρίτης ἡμέρας may have arisen when the scribe counted the three instances of ἐπαύριον in verses 9, 23, and 24). The superficial impression, however, that Cornelius had been fasting for the immediately preceding four days is clearly erroneous, for the terminus of the fasting was the sudden appearance of a man in bright clothing who told him to send to Joppa, etc. Instead, therefore, of counting forward four days (or three, according to D), we must take ἀπὸ τετάρτης ἡμέρας to mean "four days ago."[3]

Great difficulty arises with μέχρι ταύτης τῆς ὥρας, which ought to be "until this (very) hour" (the variant reading in D μέχρι τῆς ἄρτι ὥρας has substantially the same sense), but which, since the preceding ἀπό cannot signify "from," must mean either "at this (very) hour" or "about this (very) hour."

---

[3] For this use of ἀπό, see Bauer-Arndt-Gingrich-Danker, *s.v.* (II.2.a).

Since, however, it is highly questionable whether μέχρι can bear either of these meanings, several scholars have proposed conjectural emendations in order to remove the word from the text. Lake and Cadbury, for example, think it possible that either "the author or a scribe was misled by the suggestion of ἀπό to write its usual correlative μέχρι."[4] Blass and Schmiedel rewrite the passage, getting rid of both ἀπό and μέχρι. The former conjectures τετάρτην ἡμέραν ταύτην ἤμην,[5] and the latter proposes πρὸ τετάρτης ἡμέρας ἀπὸ ταύτης τῆς ὥρας ἤμην.[6]

Since, however, it is just possible that the Greek may be explained as colloquial koine or as Semitized Greek,[7] the Committee decided to retain both the ἀπό and the μέχρι phrases.

Although the words νηστεύων καί may have been deleted in some copies because nothing is said in the previous account of Cornelius's fasting, it is more probable that they were added to the text by those who thought that fasting should precede baptism (compare 9.9 and Didache 7.4 κελεύσεις δὲ νηστεῦσαι τὸν βαπτιζόμενον πρὸ μιᾶς ἢ δύο).

10.32 θάλασσαν {B}

The concluding clause, ὅς παραγενόμενος λαλήσει σοι (translated in the AV "Who, when he cometh, shall speak unto thee"), appears to be an innocuous expansion in the Western text (D E it[d, e, gig, 63, 67] syr[msK]) that was later incorporated into the Byzantine text (H L P many minuscules). Although it can be argued that the clause was pruned from the Alexandrian text as an unnecessary and, indeed, an awkward appendage (strictly ὅς refers to Σίμων

---

[4] *The Beginnings of Christianity*, vol. IV, p. 118. Haenchen adopts the view that a scribe was the culprit who erroneously introduced μέχρι (*The Acts of the Apostles, ad loc.*).

[5] *Theologische Studien und Kritiken*, LXIX (1896), pp. 463 f., and *Acta apostolorum ... secundum formam quae videtur Romanam* (Leipzig, 1896), *ad loc.*

[6] P. W. Schmiedel, "Ein Paar Konjekturen zum Text des Neuen Testamentes," *Festgabe Adolf Kaegi von Schülern und Freunden ...* (Frauenfeld, 1919), pp. 179–181.

[7] For the latter explanation, see C. C. Torrey, *The Composition and Date of Acts*, pp. 34 f., who supposes the Greek to represent מִן יוֹמָא רְבִיעָיָא עַד שַׁעְתָא דָא.

βυρσεύς), a majority of the Committee regarded it as a circumstantial expansion, to be compared with the partial parallel in 11.14.

10.33

The Western text modifies the verse in several respects: "So I sent to you at once, *asking you to come to us* (*παρακαλῶν ἐλθεῖν σε* [D* omits *σε*] *πρὸς ἡμᾶς,* D itᵖ vgᵐˢ syrʰ· ᵐˢᴷ copᴳ⁶⁷), and you have been kind enough to come *quickly* (*ἐν τάχει* D). Now *behold* (*ἰδού* D syrʰ instead of *οὖν,* and *πάρεσμεν* omitted), we all are before *you* (*σου* instead of *τοῦ θεοῦ,* see following comment), *wishing* to hear *from you* (*βουλόμενοι παρὰ σοῦ* D*) the things that you have been commanded *from God* (*ἀπὸ τοῦ θεοῦ* instead of *ὑπὸ τοῦ κυρίου* [see following comment])."

Of these alterations, Ropes *(in loc.)* thinks that the Semitism involved in *ἰδού,* with the omission of the following *πάρεσμεν,* may be preferable to the usual reading with *οὖν.* On the other hand, the presence of *οὖν* twice in the previous verse may have led to its being dropped here.

10.33   *ἐνώπιον τοῦ θεοῦ*

Although Ropes and Haenchen hold *ἐνώπιόν σου* (D* itᵖ vg syrᵖ· ᵐˢᴷᵛⁱᵈ copˢᵃ) to be preferable to the more religious phrase *ἐνώπιον τοῦ θεοῦ,* a majority of the Committee preferred the latter reading, which is supported by 𝔓⁷⁴ ℵ A B C D² E H L P and almost all minuscules, and which is a Septuagintal phrase very much in the style of Luke.

10.33   *ὑπό*

There are four variant readings: *ἀπό* (𝔓⁷⁴ A C D), *παρά* (E), *ὑπέρ* (1175), and *ὑπό* (ℵ* B H L P and apparently all other witnesses). The reasons for variety in the preposition are not clear, though possibly the variant readings *κυρίου* and *θεοῦ* may have had some influence. On the basis of the weight of the external evidence the Committee preferred *ὑπό.*

10.33 τοῦ κυρίου {C}

Although θεοῦ may have been altered to κυρίου in order to avoid repetition with the preceding θεοῦ, the Committee was not impressed by the weight of the evidence supporting θεοῦ. Considerations of intrinsic fitness are inconclusive, for, although it may be argued that θεός would be more appropriate than κύριος in the mouth of a Gentile proselyte, it is possible that a copyist as well as the author may have been moved by such a consideration.

10.36-38

In several respects the Greek of the Alexandrian text is harsh: (1) both sentences lack connecting particles; (2) ἀρξάμενος cannot be syntactically construed; and (3) the abrupt apposition of Ἰησοῦν τὸν ἀπὸ Ναζαρέθ to ῥῆμα is far from idiomatic. Besides several scribal efforts at amelioration, modern attempts to account for the unusual Greek include (1) the theory that an Aramaic original was translated literalistically into poor Greek (see the following comments); and (2) the suggestion that the text, being unrevised, is a conflation of two different drafts of essentially the same sentence, namely (a) ὑμεῖς οἴδατε τὸν λόγον ὃν ἀπέστειλεν ... (οὗτός ἐστιν πάντων κύριος) and (b) ὑμεῖς οἴδατε τὸ γενόμενον ῥῆμα ... Ἰησοῦν.[8]

Despairing of construing the text as it stands, Preuschen conjectured that originally the text may have run as follows, ὑμεῖς οἴδατε τὸν λόγον, ὃν ἀπέστειλεν τοῖς υἱοῖς Ἰσραὴλ εὐαγγελιζόμενος εἰρήνην διὰ Ἰησοῦ Χριστοῦ τοῦ ἀπὸ Ναζαρέθ, ὡς ἔχρισεν αὐτὸν κ.τ.λ.[9]

10.36 [ὅν] {C}

Either the addition or the omission of ὅν can be defended on palaeographical grounds (dittography or haplography with the preceding -ov). Of the two readings the one with the relative pronoun is the more difficult. According to Torrey, the un-Greek suspended

---

[8] C. F. D. Moule, *Expository Times,* LXV (1953–54), pp. 220 f.

[9] Erwin Preuschen in *Handbuch zum Neuen Testament, ad loc.*

construction of τὸν λόγον ὅν reflects exactly a perfectly idiomatic sentence in Aramaic.[10]

Considering the alternative possibilities, none of which is free from difficulties, a majority of the Committee judged that the least unsatisfactory solution was to retain ὅν in the text, enclosed within square brackets.

10.37 ἀρξάμενος {B}

The use of the pendent nominative, ἀρξάμενος (𝔓[74] ℵ A B C D E H 1739 *al*), which is to be taken in a quasi-adverbial sense, can be paralleled not only in Greek inscriptions and papyri[11] but also in Xenophon and Plutarch[12]; one is therefore not compelled to resort, as Torrey does, to an Aramaic idiom in which מִשָׁרֵא מִן amounts to not much more than "from."[13] In any case, however, the *nominativus pendens* is sufficiently unusual so that scribes would have attempted to improve the grammar either by altering it to the accusative (𝔓[45] L P 69 81 most minuscules, followed by the Textus Receptus), or by retaining the nominative and adding γάρ (𝔓[74] A D it[e, p] syr[msK] Irenaeus[lat]) – which is described by Blass-Debrunner as a futile attempt to ameliorate the construction.[14]

10.40 [ἐν] τῇ τρίτῃ ἡμέρᾳ {C}

The reading μετὰ τὴν τρίτην ἡμέραν (D* it[d, l, t]) may be either an attempt to harmonize the expression with that of Mt 27.63, etc.,

---

[10] C. C. Torrey, *The Composition and Date of Acts,* pp. 27 and 35 f. He suggests that the postulated Aramaic original might also be translated, "As for the word which the Lord of All sent to the children of Israel, proclaiming good tidings of peace through Jesus Christ, you know what took place...."

[11] See J. H. Moulton, *Prolegomena,* 3rd ed., p. 240, and Moulton and Milligan, *Vocabulary, s.v.*

[12] See J. W. Hunkin, "Pleonastic ἄρχομαι in the New Testament," *Journal of Theological Studies,* xxv (1924), pp. 391 ff.

[13] C. C. Torrey, *The Composition and Date of Acts,* pp. 25 ff. Cf. Max Wilcox, *The Semitisms of Acts* (Oxford, 1965), p. 150, who finds no reason to regard the expression as an Aramaism.

[14] Blass-Debrunner-Funk, § 137, 3.

or, as Harris argues, may be an idiosyncrasy of codex Bezae (as also in Mt 16.21; 17.23) that reflects the Latin *post tertium diem,* meaning "the third day after."[15]

In support of the reading ἐν τῇ τρίτῃ ἡμέρᾳ (ℵ* C *al*) Tischendorf observes that ἐν after ἤγειρεν could have easily fallen out, and that scribes would have a tendency to substitute the much more customary expression τῇ τρίτῃ ἡμέρᾳ. On the other hand, however, a majority of the Committee, judging that it was also possible that ἐν had been accidentally introduced through dittography, considered it preferable to enclose the word within square brackets, indicating thereby a certain doubt that it belongs in the text.

10.41

Toward the end of the verse several Western witnesses (with minor variations) make two additions to the usual text: "who ate and drank with him *and accompanied (him),* after he rose from the dead, *for forty days*" (after αὐτῷ D² it^{gig. p} syr^h add καὶ συνανεστράφημεν [D reads συνεστράφημεν], and ἡμέρας [δι᾽ ἡμέρων E] τεσσερά-κοντα is added before μετά by it^p vg^{ms} syr^h and after νεκρῶν by D E it^{gig} vg^{mss} cop^{sa}). It may be observed that in Acts codex Bezae is fond of συστρέφειν, which it introduces also in 11.28; 16.39; 17.5.

10.42 οὗτος

Instead of οὗτος (B C D^{gr} E^{gr} 33 94 103 104 307 323 489 614 623 913 1739 1765 1827 1838 1891 syr^{p. h} cop^{sa. bo} *al*) the Textus Receptus, following 𝔓^{74} ℵ A H P 69 81 it^e vg eth *al*, reads αὐτός. A majority of the Committee was impressed not only by the weight of the witnesses that support οὗτος, but also by the consideration that since οὗτος might be taken to have a depreciatory implication, it was more likely to be altered to αὐτός than vice versa.

---

[15] J. R. Harris, *Codex Bezae,* pp. 91 f.

10.46 γλώσσαις

Several Western witnesses qualify "tongues" with one or another adjective; thus it[d] (D[gr] has an erasure at this point) reads *praevaricatis linguis,* which may presuppose an original Greek reading ποικίλαις (Hilgenfeld), or καιναῖς (Blass), or ἑτέραις (Ropes and A. C. Clark); a manuscript of the Vulgate reads *linguis variis*; cop[sa, bopt] read "other tongues"; and the anonymous treatise on Rebaptism reads *linguis suis.*

10.48 αὐτούς

Since προστάσσειν is usually construed with the dative of the person commanded and the accusative of the thing commanded, it is probable that αὐτοῖς ($\mathfrak{P}^{74}$ ℵ A 33 *al*) is a learned correction introduced by those who did not perceive that αὐτούς serves as the subject of the following infinitive.

10.48 ἐν τῷ ὀνόματι Ἰησοῦ Χριστοῦ βαπτισθῆναι {B}

Although it may be argued that the primitive reading was τοῦ κυρίου, which was expanded or supplanted by Ἰησοῦ Χριστοῦ in order to denote more precisely the specific character of the baptism, the Committee was impressed by the weight and diversity of the witnesses that read Ἰησοῦ Χριστοῦ. In any case, the reading τοῦ κυρίου Ἰησοῦ Χριστοῦ is clearly a conflation. The position of βαπτισθῆναι was moved forward in order to make it plain that ἐν τῷ ὀνόματι goes with it and not with προσέταξεν αὐτούς.

11.1 Ἤκουσαν ... Ἰουδαίαν

Instead of the customary text codex Bezae, substantially supported by syr[p], reads Ἀκουστὸν δὲ ἐγένετο τοῖς ἀποστόλοις καὶ τοῖς ἀδελφοῖς τοῖς (οἱ D*) ἐν τῇ Ἰουδαίᾳ. Although Ropes preferred the Western reading because it is more Semitic than the B-text, a majority of the Committee was unwilling to abandon the weight of the testimony of the rest of the witnesses, particularly since in this case D contains the word ἀκουστόν, which appears nowhere else in the

New Testament. It may also be pointed out that at the end of the verse several Western witnesses add the comment, "and they glorified God" (it^gig, pc^ vg^mss^ syr^h with *^).

11.2   ὅτε δὲ ... περιτομῆς {A}

The text of several Western witnesses (D it^d, p^ vg^mss^ syr^h with *^ cop^G67^) differs widely from that preserved in other witnesses. Codex Bezae reads ὁ μὲν οὖν Πέτρος διὰ ἱκανοῦ χρόνου ἠθέλησε πορευθῆναι εἰς Ἱεροσόλυμα· καὶ προσφωνήσας τοὺς ἀδελφοὺς καὶ ἐπιστηρίξας αὐτούς, πολὺν λόγον ποιούμενος, διὰ τῶν χωρῶν διδάσκων αὐτούς· ὃς καὶ κατήντησεν αὐτοῖς καὶ ἀπήγγειλεν αὐτοῖς τὴν χάριν τοῦ θεοῦ. οἱ δὲ ἐκ περιτομῆς ἀδελφοὶ διεκρίνοντο πρὸς αὐτόν ("Peter, therefore, for a considerable time wished to journey to Jerusalem; and having called to him the brethren and having strengthened them [he departed], speaking much throughout the country [and] teaching them; he [lit. who] also went to meet them[1] and reported to them the grace of God. But the brethren of the circumcision disputed with him, saying ...").

According to Clark the omission of the passage from the other Greek witnesses is to be accounted for by homoeoteleuton, when "the eye of a copyist passed from τοῦ θεοῦ at the end of ver. 1 to τοῦ θεοῦ later on."[2] This explanation, however, accounts for only part of the difference between the Western text and that of the old uncials, for after τὴν χάριν τοῦ θεοῦ codex Bezae goes on with οἱ δὲ ἐκ περιτομῆς ἀδελφοὶ διεκρίνοντο, whereas the other witnesses read ὅτε δὲ ἀνέβη Πέτρος εἰς Ἱερουσαλήμ, διεκρίνοντο πρὸς αὐτὸν οἱ ἐκ περιτομῆς. Since the information given in the Alexandrian text (that Peter went up to Jerusalem) is (as Clark admits) "indispensable to the sense," it is obvious that parablepsis on the part of a scribe is not sufficient to explain the differences between the two forms of text.

---

[1] I. e. the Jerusalem representatives. It should be observed that nowhere in the Alexandrian text of Luke-Acts is κατανταν construed with the dative case; indeed, the construction, as Ropes says, "is hardly tolerable."

[2] A. C. Clark, *The Acts of the Apostles*, p. 347.

The motives for the expansion in the Western text appear to be connected with the tendency in that text to avoid putting Peter in a bad light.[3] In order to prevent the reader of the Alexandrian text from gaining the impression that the conversion of Cornelius compelled Peter to break off his missionary work and go to Jerusalem in order to justify himself, the Western reviser introduces a passage (in the style[4] of 8.25 and 15.3) that describes how Peter continued his missionary work for a considerable length of time, and how, finally, on his own initiative, he went up to Jerusalem, where, so far from being called to give an account of himself, he voluntarily sought out the brethren at Jerusalem "and reported to them the grace of God."[5]

11.3 εἰσῆλθες ... συνέφαγες

Instead of εἰσῆλθες ... συνέφαγες, $\mathfrak{P}^{45}$ B L 33 81 614 1175 1611 1827 syr[p. h txt] *al* read εἰσῆλθεν ... συνέφαγεν. Since in later Greek usage ὅτι may stand for τί ("Why ...?"),[6] a majority of the Committee held that failure to recognize this idiom led copyists to produce the reading involving the third person, in which ὅτι is taken as recitative introducing direct discourse (either as a statement, "saying, You went in ..." or as a question, "saying, Did you go in ...?").[7] The text is supported by $\mathfrak{P}^{74}$ (lacuna at εἰσῆλθες) ℵ A D E H P most minuscules vg syr[hmg] cop[sa. bo] eth.

---

[3] See Joseph Crehan, "Peter according to the D-Text of Acts," *Theological Studies,* XVIII (1957), pp. 596–603, and E. J. Epp, *The Theological Tendency of Codex Bezae Cantabrigiensis in Acts,* pp. 105–107.

[4] Except for the construction of κατανταν (see footnote 1 above).

[5] Crehan finds a desire in the Western text to enhance the position of Peter by "pairing off" episodes in the history of Peter with those in the history of Paul; "for at 15:41 and 16:1 there is just such a passage as this about Paul, and the word *katantaō* is used again of his turning aside from Cilicia to visit Derbe and Lystra" (*op. cit.,* p. 598).

[6] See E. A. Sophocles, *Greek Lexicon of the Roman and Byzantine Periods, s.v.* ὅστις, § 4; J. H. Moulton, *Prolegomena,* pp. 93 f.; H. J. Cadbury, *Journal of Biblical Literature,* XLVIII (1929), pp. 423 ff.; Blass-Debrunner-Funk, § 300, 2; and Nigel Turner, *Syntax,* pp. 49 f.

[7] So Lake and Cadbury in *The Beginnings of Christianity,* vol. IV, p. 124.

11.5 ἄχρι

Codex Bezae and 241 read ἕως; 𝔓⁷⁴ ℵ A B* 104 1319 read ἄχρι; all other witnesses read ἄχρις. While the reading ἕως may be ignored, the two others deserve comment.

In Attic Greek ἄχρι was used predominantly, and it is found extensively in the Septuagint and the New Testament. In later Greek the form with the final sigma came into ever wider usage, though it was condemned by Phrynichus and other grammarians.

Whether Luke followed Attic preference and later scribes corrupted it, or whether he followed the growing tolerance for ἄχρις and later purist scribes, reacting against the prevailing usage, corrected the spelling according to archaic standards, is a difficult question to answer. A majority of the Committee decided that it was wisest to err (if indeed it is to err) in company with 𝔓⁷⁴ ℵ A B* *al.*

11.11 ἦμεν {C}

The more difficult reading is ἦμεν, which because of its apparent irrelevancy was assimilated to ἤμην of ver. 5.

11.12 μηδὲν διακρίναντα {C}

Although it may be, as Lake and Cadbury admit, that the Western text preserves the original reading and that the words were interpolated from the parallel account in 10.20 (μηδὲν διακρινόμενος), a majority of the Committee was not persuaded, chiefly because the earliest form(s) of the reading utilize the active (not the middle) voice of the verb. The reading of H L P *al* was interpreted as due to the influence of 10.20, not for the insertion but for the assimilation of the voice of the participle.

11.17 ὁ θεός {A}

The omission of ὁ θεός by D vg^ms Rebaptism Augustine (but not syr^h, as is sometimes stated) is probably due, as Ropes observes, "to the 'Western' reviser's view that the Holy Spirit was the gift of Christ."[8]

11.17 θεόν {A}

In order to explain the meaning of the expression κωλῦσαι τὸν θεόν codex Bezae, with support, in whole or in part,[9] from other Western witnesses (467 it^p vg^{ms} syr$^{h \text{ with } *}$ cop^{G67}) adds τοῦ μὴ δοῦναι αὐτοῖς πνεῦμα ἅγιον πιστεύσασιν ἐν αὐτῷ ("that he should not give them the Holy Spirit after they had believed on him").

11.20 Ἑλληνιστάς {C}

The textual problems of this verse are compounded by the diversity of views concerning the meaning of Ἑλληνιστής. This noun, which appears to be a new formation from ἑλληνίζειν, "to speak Greek" or "to practice Greek ways," is found nowhere in previous classical Greek literature or in hellenistic-Jewish literature; in the New Testament it occurs only here and in 6.1 and 9.29. According to the prevailing opinion, current since the time of Chrysostom,[10] the Ἑλληνισταί of 6.1 were Greek-speaking Jews (or Jewish-Christians) in contrast to those speaking a Semitic language (so Thayer, Souter, Bauer-Arndt-Gingrich-Danker). Since, however, in the present passage the author seems to draw a contrast between Ἑλληνιστάς (or the variant reading Ἕλληνας) and Ἰουδαίοις of ver. 19, it has been urged that the word must possess some more distinctive meaning than merely "Greek-speaking Jews." Thus, Warfield[11] and Cadbury[12] argue that it means Gentiles (and so is synonymous with

---

[8] *The Text of Acts,* p. 105.

[9] The great diversity of testimony among the Western witnesses indicates, as Zahn correctly points out, the secondary character of the addition *(Die Apostelgeschichte des Lucas,* p. 365, Anm. 90).

[10] Migne, *Patrologia Graeca,* LX, col. 113.

[11] B. B. Warfield, "The Readings Ἕλληνας and Ἑλληνιστάς, Acts xi.20," *Journal of Biblical Literature,* [III], 1883, pp. 113–127.

[12] H. J. Cadbury, "The Hellenists," *The Beginnings of Christianity,* vol. v, pp. 59–74.

Ἕλληνας); the former translates it "Graecizers" and the latter "Hellenists." Other alternatives include the proposal to take Ἑλληνιστάς as connoting proselytes,[13] or to interpret it as referring to a radical, reforming, "gentilistic" sect within Judaism, to which Stephen may have belonged before he became a Christian.[14] None of these views, however, is entirely free from more or less serious difficulties,[15] and perhaps the least unsatisfactory assumption to make is that the meaning of the word, though quite definite in the early church, was lost to Christian usage. When the word reappears in patristic literature (other than that influenced by Chrysostom's exegesis of 6.1), it means "a defender of paganism" (E. A. Sophocles's *Lexicon*), or simply, "a pagan" (Lampe's *Patristic Greek Lexicon*).

In assessing the evidence for the variant readings in the present passage, no weight can be attached to the fact that the early versions all read "Greeks" (so the Latin, Syriac,[16] Coptic, Armenian, Old Georgian, and Ethiopic), for, as Hort justly observes, they "would naturally be at a loss to provide a distinctive rendering for so rare and so peculiar a word as Ἑλληνιστής."[17] The first hand of codex Sinaiticus, which already in ver. 19 gives the meaningless Ἰουδαῖοι without subsequent correction, writes in ver. 20 the equally meaningless πρὸς τοὺς εὐαγγελιστάς, which, however, has been corrected by a later hand to Ἕλληνας.[18] Likewise the testimony of

---

[13] So E. C. Blackman (reviving the view of Salmasius of the seventeenth century), *Expository Times,* XLVIII (1936–37), pp. 524 ff.

[14] So Oscar Cullmann, "The Significance of the Qumran Texts for Research into the Beginnings of Christianity," *Journal of Biblical Literature,* LXXIV (1955), pp. 220 ff., and Marcel Simon (partly following G. P. Wetter and W. Bauer), *St. Stephen and the Hellenists* (New York, 1958). The latter nevertheless admits that "the term Hellenists, as used by Luke, includes all Greek-speaking Jews," and that "to the author of Acts, the word apparently has no other meaning" (p. 15).

[15] See C. F. D. Moule's critique, "Once More, Who Were the Hellenists?" *Expository Times,* LXX (1959), pp. 100–102. Moule adopts the traditional definition of the word, but refines it slightly; thus, "Jews who spoke *only* Greek" in contrast to Ἑβραῖοι, "Jews who, while able to speak Greek, knew a Semitic language *also*."

[16] In 9.29 the Syriac Peshitta renders Ἑλληνιστάς "Jews who understood Greek," which may show a connection between Chrysostom and the Peshitta.

[17] "Notes on Select Readings," p. 93.

[18] It is often assumed that the reading of ℵ* presupposes Ἑλληνιστάς, on account

codex Alexandrinus is weakened, if not discredited, when one observes that in 9.29 the scribe substituted Ἕλληνας for Ἑλληνιστάς, which is acknowledged to be the true reading.

Transcriptional probability is all in favor of Ἑλληνιστάς, for the temptation to editor or scribe was to substitute an easy and familiar word (Ἕλληνας) for one which was by no means familiar. There is no counter temptation to set against this, so that the argument drawn from it is a strong one.

Perhaps the chief objection of modern scholars to adopting Ἑλληνιστάς here is the belief that it always means "Greek-speaking Jews," and therefore is inappropriate to stand in contrast with the preceding Ἰουδαῖοι. But since Ἑλληνιστής is derived from ἑλληνίζειν, it means strictly "one who uses Greek [language or customs]"; whether the person be a Jew or a Roman or any other non-Greek must be gathered from the context. In 6.1 the contrast is no doubt between Greek-speaking Jewish Christians and Semitic-speaking Jewish Christians. What the word connotes in 9.29 is not altogether clear; in any case they are not believers as in 6.1. In the present passage, where the preponderant weight of the external evidence combines with the strong transcriptional probability in support of Ἑλληνιστάς, the word is to be understood in the broad sense of "Greek-speaking persons," meaning thereby the mixed population of Antioch in contrast to the Ἰουδαῖοι of ver. 19.

11.22 οὔσης

The word οὔσης is read by 𝔓⁷⁴ ℵ B E 33 81 614 1611 1852 2138 al, and is absent from A D H L P most minuscules and the Textus Receptus. Since the present participle ὤν is used elsewhere in Acts with the special meaning "the *local* ..." (13.1; 28.17), the Committee considered it more probable that copyists would have deleted than added the word here.

---

of its similar termination. But since it seems certain that εὐαγγελιστάς was suggested by, and results from, the proximity of εὐαγγελιζόμενοι, which follows immediately, it is with considerable hesitation that one can take the weight of ℵ* to be in favor of Ἑλληνιστάς.

11.22 *[διελθεῖν]* {C}

On the one hand, the weight of external evidence ($\mathfrak{P}^{74}$ ℵ A B 81 629 1642 1739 1891 *al*) favors the shorter reading without *διελθεῖν*. On the other hand, the expression *διελθεῖν ἕως* (D E H L P S Ψ most minuscules it^(gig, p) vg^(mss) syr^h) is in accord with the style of Luke (cf. 9.38; 11.19; Lk 2.15), and the absence of *διελθεῖν* in the other witnesses may be the result of deliberate excision to simplify the construction. For these reasons the word is retained in the text, but enclosed within square brackets to indicate doubt that it belongs there.

11.23 *[τήν]*

The definite article *τήν* after *χάριν,* which is read by $\mathfrak{P}^{74}$ D E H L P and almost all minuscules, is absent from ℵ A B 927. On the one hand, since the usual construction is *ἡ χάρις τοῦ θεοῦ,* the article after *χάριν* appears to have a special force, suggesting that Barnabas rejoiced because he recognized that the grace was obviously that of God *(τὴν τοῦ θεοῦ).* Scribes, not observing this nuance, may have dropped the article as unnecessary. On the other hand, it can be argued that *τήν* is a pedantic insertion made by Alexandrian scribes. In view of the balance of probabilities a majority of the Committee thought it best to retain the word but to enclose it within square brackets.

11.23 *τῷ κυρίῳ* {B}

The use of *ἐν* before *τῷ κυρίῳ* reminds one of Pauline usage; since this characteristic expression is found nowhere else in Acts, its presence in B Ψ 181 *al* was judged to be due to scribes rather than the author.

11.25-26

Codex Bezae, supported in part by other Western witnesses, reads *ἀκούσας δὲ ὅτι Σαῦλός ἐστιν εἰς Θαρσὸν ἐξῆλθεν ἀναζητῶν αὐτόν, καὶ ὡς συντυχὼν παρεκάλεσεν ἐλθεῖν εἰς Ἀντιόχειαν.*

οἵτινες παραγενόμενοι ἐνιαυτὸν ὅλον συνεχύθησαν ὄχλον ἱκανόν, καὶ τότε πρῶτον ἐχρημάτισαν ἐν Ἀντιοχείᾳ οἱ μαθηταὶ Χρειστιανοί ("And *having heard that Saul was at Tarsus, he went out to seek him; and when he had met him, he entreated him to come* to Antioch. *When they had come,* for a whole year a large company of people *were stirred up,* and *then* for the first time the disciples in Antioch were called Christians").

Ropes was inclined to think that the verb συνεχύθησαν, so unexpected in the context, was original, and that συναχθῆναι was substituted in all other texts. The variation of verbs, however, is more probably part of a corruption that involved also the accidental omission of the words τῇ ἐκκλησίᾳ καὶ ἐδίδασκον between the verb and ὄχλον ἱκανόν ("*When they had come,* for a whole year [people] *were stirred up* in the church, and they were teaching a large company of people").

It is difficult to see why the Western text should have been shortened if it were original; on the other hand, the Alexandrian text may have been rewritten to show more clearly why Barnabas went to Tarsus, and to indicate that Saul was not "brought" to Antioch, but was "entreated" to come.

11.26 καὶ ἐνιαυτὸν ὅλον

The presence of καί before ἐνιαυτὸν ὅλον, "even for a whole year" ($\mathfrak{P}^{74}$ ℵ A B 33 614 syr[h]), is unusual, and it is not strange that the later text has omitted it (E H L P 383 *al,* as well as the Textus Receptus). Since the expression καί followed by ἐνιαυτόν or by a year is not New Testament usage, Blass thinks that the καί may have come from some other reading, and compares καί in ver. 1.[19]

11.28 ἀναστὰς δὲ ... ἐσήμανεν {A}

An important Western reading, preserved in D (it[p]) (cop[G67]) Augustine, supplies the first "we"-passage[20] in any text of Acts: ἦν δὲ

---

[19] F. Blass, *Acta apostolorum* ... editio philologica, p. 136.

[20] Harnack, however, argued that the original form of the Western addition was ...

πολλὴ ἀγαλλίασις· συνεστραμμένων δὲ ἡμῶν ἔφη εἷς ἐξ αὐτῶν
ὀνόματι "Αγαβος σημαίνων ... ("And there was much rejoicing;
and when we were gathered together one of them named Agabus
spoke, signifying ..."). On the verb συστρέφειν, see the final comment on 10.41.

12.1

After ἐκκλησίας the Western text adds the information that it was
the church in Judea which Herod was persecuting (ἐν τῇ Ἰουδαίᾳ, D
614 it[p] syr[h with *] cop[G67]). In this way the following account is brought
into closer connection with the preceding resolve to send relief from
Antioch to the brethren in Judea (11.29 f.).

12.2

The proposal of Eisler[1] and others to emend the text of this verse
by inserting the words Ἰωάννην καί after ἀνεῖλεν has been made in
the interest of bolstering the exceedingly weak evidence for the early
death of the apostle John. Still less defensible is the view of Pallis[2]
that the entire verse is spurious.

12.3

In order to define more specifically what it was that Herod did
that pleased the Jews, the Western text adds after τοῖς Ἰουδαίοις
the words ἡ ἐπιχείρησις αὐτοῦ ἐπὶ τοὺς (+ ἁγίους καί it[p])
πιστούς (D (it[p]) syr[hmg]), which, in the context, may be rendered, "and
when he saw that *his attack upon the (saints and) faithful* pleased the

---

συνεστραμμένων δὲ αὐτῶν ..., and that the αὐτῶν was later "corrected" to ἡμῶν in
order to avoid confusion with the following αὐτῶν (see his "Über den ursprünglichen
Text Act. Apost. 11, 27.28," *Sitzungsberichte der königlich preussischen Akademie der
Wissenschaften zu Berlin,* 1899, pp. 316–327, reprinted in his *Studien zur Geschichte
des Neuen Testaments und der alten Kirche*; vol. I, *Zur neutestamentlichen Textkritik*
[Berlin and Leipzig, 1931], pp. 33–47).

[1] Robert Eisler, *The Enigma of the Fourth Gospel* (London, 1938), pp. 73–77.
[2] Alex. Pallis, *Notes on St Luke and the Acts* (London, 1928), p. 63.

Jews ..." Although Luke uses the verb ἐπιχειρεῖν (Lk 1.1; Ac 9.29; 19.13), the noun ἐπιχείρησις appears nowhere else in the New Testament.

12.5

Several Western witnesses (but not codex Bezae) expand the statement, "So Peter was kept in prison," by adding the words "by a cohort of the king" (*a cohorte regis*, it^{p1} vg^{ms} syr$^{h with *}$ cop^{G67}). What relation this cohort had to the sixteen soldiers of ver. 4 is not clear.

12.5 ἐκτενῶς

Instead of ἐκτενῶς ($\mathfrak{P}^{74}$ ℵ A^{*vid} B 33 181 216 440 453 1898 it^e vg Lucifer), the Textus Receptus, following A^2 E H L P and most minuscules, reads ἐκτενής. It is more likely that the adverb (which was condemned by Phrynichus as poor Greek)[3] would be altered to the adjective than vice versa. Codex Bezae rewrites the sentence avoiding both adjective and adverb (notice also the heightening of the account by the addition of πολλή as well as the redundant περὶ αὐτοῦ): πολλὴ δὲ προσευχὴ ἦν ἐν ἐκτενείᾳ περὶ αὐτοῦ ἀπὸ τῆς ἐκκλησίας πρὸς τὸν θεὸν περὶ αὐτοῦ ("but *much* prayer *in earnestness* was [made] *for him* by the church to God for him"). For the expression ἐν ἐκτενείᾳ compare 26.7 and Judith 4.9.

12.6 προαγαγεῖν

There are four variant readings: προαγαγεῖν ($\mathfrak{P}^{74}$ A 8 36^a 51 81 307 337 460 467 915 1874 *al*), προσαγαγεῖν (B 33 254), προσάγειν (ℵ Ψ 5 323 436 440 450 2180), and προάγειν (D E H L P most minuscules). In each pair of variant readings, the aorist tense is to be preferred to the present. As between the two verbs, a majority of the Committee regarded the compound with πρό to be more appropriate in the context.

---

[3] W. G. Rutherford, *The New Phrynichus* (London, 1881), pp. 365 f.

12.7

The Western text differs in several respects from the generally received text: an angel of the Lord appeared "to Peter" (ἐπέστη [lit. "stood by"] + τῷ Πέτρῳ, D itᵖ syrʰ ᵂⁱᵗʰ * copˢᵃ); light "shone *forth from him* [the angel]" (ἐπέλαμψεν, D, + ἀπ' αὐτοῦ, itᵍⁱᵍ· ᵖ syrʰᵐᵍ); instead of ἐν τῷ οἰκήματι, itᵈ· ᵍⁱᵍ· ⁽ᵖ⁾ Lucifer read "in that place" (*in illo loco*); and instead of the angel's "striking" (πατάξας) Peter on the side in order to waken him, D itᵍⁱᵍ Lucifer speak of his "nudging" (νύξας) the sleeping apostle.[4]

12.8-9

Between verses 8 and 9 copᴳ⁶⁷ adds the sentence, "But he [the angel] seized him [Peter] and drew him along and took him out, and Peter followed."

12.10 ἐξελθόντες {A}

The circumstantial detail in codex Bezae, namely that Peter and the angel when coming out of prison "walked down the seven steps" (κατέβησαν τοὺς ζ βαθμοὺς καί), has seemed to many scholars to possess a verisimilitude that reflects local knowledge of Jerusalem. It should not be overlooked, however, as Lake and Cadbury remind us, that "we have no knowledge as to (i) where the prison was …, and (ii) whether there really were seven steps."[5]

A trace of the same reading is preserved in itᵖ and copᴳ⁶⁷, "they descended (the) steps" (without "seven"). The reading of the Latin side of codex Bezae is slightly expanded, "when they went out *they descended (the) seven steps and went on one step,* and immediately

---

[4] According to C. S. C. Williams (*Alterations in the Synoptic Gospels and Acts,* 1951, p. 81) both participles may be derived from the same Syriac word (ܡܚܐ); F. H. Chase, however, argues for the influence of Jn 19.34 on the mind of the scribe of the Western text (*The Old Syriac Element in the Text of Codex Bezae,* 1893, p. 88).

[5] *The Beginnings of Christianity,* vol. IV, p. 136.

the angel left him" (… *descenderunt septem grados et processerunt gradum unum* …).

Other references elsewhere to specified numbers of steps include the mention of seven steps and eight steps in Ezekiel's vision of the temple (Eze 40.22, 26, 31), and the mention of fourteen steps, five steps, and fifteen steps in Josephus's description of the temple complex (*Jewish Wars,* v.v.2–3). Later in the book of Acts (21.35, 40) the author refers to the steps that led from the barracks of Antonia into the temple area, but, as Knowling says, "there is no connection between them and the definite seven steps here, which are evidently presupposed (note the article) to be well known to the reader."[6]

12.12 συνιδών

Dissatisfied with συνιδών Hammond[7] conjectured that the text originally read σπεύδων ("making haste"), and Pallis[8] emended it to read συντείνων ("hurrying").

12.13 προσῆλθεν

Instead of προσῆλθεν a few witnesses (‭א‬ B² 3 itᵖ vg) read προῆλθεν, "she came forward" (i. e. from the house itself, to answer the knock at the gate).

---

[6] R. J. Knowling, *The Expositor's Greek Testament,* vol. ii, p. 275.

[7] Because of its quaint diffidence Hammond's comment may be quoted in its entirety: "The word συνιδών is so near in likeness (tho' far enough off in the nature and signification of it) to σπεύδων, that it is very possible one of these may here by the transcriber be put for the other. And indeed the signification of the latter σπεύδων, *making haste,* seems that which is fitter for the turn in this place, where being left alone in the street by the Angel, he was in reason to make haste to some place of safety and privacy, and such was that which he here chose. If this conjecture (which I mention only as such, having no authority for it) be not too remote, then may it also probably belong to another place, *c.* 14.6 συνιδόντες κατέφυγον, perhaps for σπεύδοντες, *they made haste and fled,* as out of a great danger" (Henry Hammond, *A Paraphrase and Annotations upon … the New Testament,* 7th ed. [London, 1702], p. 334).

[8] Alex. Pallis, *Notes on St Luke and the Acts* (London, 1928), p. 64.

12.15 ὁ ἄγγελος

By prefixing τυχόν ("*Perhaps* it is his angel") the Western text (D syr^p) enhances the naïveté of the account, softening the definiteness of the explanation offered to solve the enigma. Except as a Bezan variant reading in Lk 20.13, τυχόν occurs elsewhere in the New Testament only in 1 Cor 16.6.

12.17 σιγᾶν

In order to prevent the reader of the generally received text from supposing that Peter made his explanation while still standing at the door of the gateway, the Western text adds the graphic touch that, "having motioned to them with his hand that they should be silent, he *came in and* described to them how the Lord had brought him out of the prison" (instead of σιγᾶν D it^p vg^ms syr^p, h with * read ἵνα σιγάσω-σιν εἰσῆλθεν καί).

12.20-22

The account in the Western text of the last days and death of Herod Agrippa I differs in several respects from that in the commonly received text. By using γάρ instead of δέ (ver. 20) the scribe of D indicates more clearly the reason why it was that, according to ver. 19, Herod had gone down "from Judea to Caesarea"– it was to hold an audience with representatives from two neighboring cities, Tyre and Sidon.

The non-Western text declares that the people of Tyre and Sidon "came to him in a body" (ὁμοθυμαδὸν δὲ παρῆσαν πρὸς αὐτόν). Taken literally this is clearly an exaggeration; the Western reviser, however, skillfully rewrote it, while still retaining ὁμοθυμαδόν, to suggest that some from both of the cities came in a body to the king (οἱ δὲ ὁμοθυμαδὸν ἐξ ἀμφοτέρων τῶν πόλεων παρῆσαν πρὸς τὸν βασιλέα, D (614 syr^h with *)).

Between verses 21 and 22 the Western text inserts καταλλαγέν-τος δὲ αὐτοῦ τοῖς Τυρίοις (D it^p (syr^h with *) cop^G67; it^p2 vg^mss continue with *et Sidoniis*), that is, "And on the occasion of his reconciliation with the Tyrians (and the Sidonians)."

12.23 γενόμενος σκωληκόβρωτος {A}

After τῷ θεῷ codex Bezae, supported in part by cop^G67 and by Ephraem,[9] continues καὶ καταβὰς ἀπὸ τοῦ βήματος, γενόμενος σκωληκόβρωτος ἔτι ζῶν καὶ οὕτως ἐξέψυξεν ("and *he came down from the platform,* [and] *while he was still living* he was eaten by worms and *thus* died"). The additional material (italicized in the translation) informs the reader that, though an angel of the Lord smote him immediately after his address, he did not expire at once, but was able to descend from his throne.[10] The addition of ἔτι ζῶν, as Bruce observes, "emphasizes the unpleasantness of his disease."[11]

12.24 θεοῦ

Instead of θεοῦ codex Vaticanus and the Latin Vulgate unite to read κυρίου, having been influenced by the expression ἄγγελος κυρίου of ver. 23.

12.25 Σαῦλος

After Σαῦλος several Western witnesses (614 it^p syr^h with * cop^G67) add ὃς ἐπεκλήθη Παῦλος ("who was called Paul"). This appears to be a scribal anticipation of 13.9 (Σαῦλος ὁ καὶ Παῦλος), introduced here because of the presence later in the verse of a similar identification of John Mark (Ἰωάννην τὸν ἐπικληθέντα Μᾶρκον).

Furthermore, instead of Σαῦλος manuscripts 2 57 326 436 441 *al* read Παῦλος (102 reads Σαῦλος Παῦλος).

12.25 εἰς Ἰερουσαλήμ {C}

Many attempts have been made to account for the origin of the reading εἰς in this verse. The natural impression one gets when

---

[9] See F. C. Conybeare in *Zeitschrift für die neutestamentliche Wissenschaft,* XX (1921), pp. 41–42, and J. H. Ropes, *The Text of Acts,* p. 416.

[10] According to Josephus, Herod's death occurred five days after being stricken with a pain in his abdomen (*Antiquities,* XIX.viii.2).

[11] F. F. Bruce, *The Acts of the Apostles,* 3rd ed. (1990), p. 289.

reading the section 11.27 to 13.1 is that 11.30 refers to the arrival of Paul and Barnabas at Jerusalem and that 12.25 ought to tell of their departure *from* Jerusalem. On the one hand, all the canons of textual criticism favor the more difficult reading εἰς, supported as it is by the earliest and best witnesses. Furthermore, the *lectio facilior* is not only divided against itself (ἀπό and ἐξ), but it is also discredited by the fact that it is not the common usage of Acts to specify the place *whence* return is made (1.12 is the only such instance of the twelve occurrences of the verb ὑποστρέφειν in Acts).

On the other hand, as Westcott and Hort declare, "εἰς Ἱερουσαλήμ, which is the best attested and was not likely to be introduced, cannot possibly be right if it is taken with ὑπέστρεψαν."[12] Their conclusion is that the passage contains a primitive error that has infected all extant witnesses, and they propose that the sequence of words be emended to read ὑπέστρεψαν τὴν εἰς Ἱερουσαλὴμ πληρώσαντες διακονίαν ("having fulfilled their mission at Jerusalem they returned").

Much more extreme is the remedy proposed by Simcox, who decided that the whole verse is an interpolation that should be omitted.[13] Others have suggested that the variations arose from a confusion of marginal glosses. Thus, Alford, who adopted ἐξ Ἱερουσαλήμ as the text, conjectured that εἰς Ἀντιόχειαν may have been an explanatory gloss that was later substituted for ἐξ Ἱερουσαλήμ; then Ἀντιόχειαν may have again been corrected to Ἱερουσαλήμ, leaving the εἰς standing.[14] Less complicated is the suggestion of Bartlet,[15] which is adopted by Bruce,[16] that originally the passage had

---

[12] "Notes on Select Readings," p. 94.

[13] G. A. Simcox, "A Point in Pauline Chronology," *Journal of Theological Studies,* II (1900–01), pp. 586–590.

[14] Henry Alford, *The Greek Testament,* new ed. (London, 1881), vol. II, p. 137 (Alford prefers the rough breathing on Ἱερουσαλήμ).

[15] J. Vernon Bartlet, "The Acts" in *The Century Bible* (London, 1901), *ad loc.* Bartlet subsequently changed his mind and argued for the originality of ἀπὸ Ἱερουσαλήμ; see his "Note on Acts xii 25," *Journal of Theological Studies,* IV (1902–03), pp. 438–440.

[16] F. F. Bruce, *The Acts of the Apostles, ad loc.;* Bruce admits that this solution "cuts the knot instead of untying it."

no prepositional phrase and that all the variant readings represent additions to the simple verb "returned."

Other scholars, preferring what appears to be the best attested reading *(εἰς)*, attempt to alleviate the contextual difficulties by making various lexical or grammatical suggestions. Thus, instead of taking the aorist participle πληρώσαντες in its normal sense "when they had fulfilled," several writers regard it as an instance of the rare usage of the "futuristic" aorist[17] expressing purpose. Attractive though this proposal may be, it involves taking also the following aorist participle *(συμπαραλαβόντες)* as an aorist of subsequent action – a category whose existence is denied by most grammarians.[18] Less violent to Greek syntax and lexical usage is the proposal that a comma be placed after ὑπέστρεψαν and εἰς be taken as the hellenistic equivalent of ἐν, so that the meaning would be "Barnabas and Saul returned,[19] after they had fulfilled at Jerusalem their mission, bringing with them John whose other name was Mark."[20]

After long and repeated deliberation the Committee decided that the least unsatisfactory[21] decision was to adopt εἰς.

---

[17] See, e. g., C. D. Chambers, "On a Use of the Aorist Participle in Some Hellenistic Writers," *Journal of Theological Studies,* XXIV (1922), pp. 183–187, and W. F. Howard, "On the Futuristic Use of the Aorist Participle in Hellenistic," *ibid.,* pp. 403–406.

[18] See, e. g., J. H. Moulton, *Prolegomena,* pp. 132 ff.; A. T. Robertson, *A Grammar of the Greek New Testament in the Light of Historical Research,* 5th ed. (New York, 1931), pp. 861 ff.

[19] I. e. returned to Antioch; see 13.1, and compare Ephraem on 12.25 (in Ropes's *The Text of Acts,* p. 416).

[20] So, e. g., H. H. Wendt, *Die Apostelgeschichte,* 5te Aufl. (Göttingen, 1913), pp. 199 f.; E. Haenchen, *The Acts of the Apostles* (Philadelphia, 1971), p. 380; Blass-Debrunner-Funk, § 205. For a full discussion of the textual and literary problems, see J. Dupont, "La Mission de Paul 'à Jérusalem' (Actes xii 25)," *Novum Testamentum,* I (1956), pp. 275–303.

[21] The Committee confesses that more than once K. Lake's frank admission of despair reflected its own mood: "Which is the true text? No ones knows.... For my part, I am in the same frame of mind as was the scribe of Codex B, who began to write ἀπό and ended by writing εἰς" ("The Practical Value of Textual Criticism, Illustrated from the Book of Acts," *Biblical World,* N. S. XIX [1902], p. 366). For a much more confident discussion, concluding that εἰς is indeed the correct reading, see Pierson Parker, *Journal of Biblical Literature,* LXXXIII (1964), pp. 168–170.

13.1 ἦσαν δέ

The later text (E H L P 33 *al* syr[h] arm and Textus Receptus) interpolates τινες after ἦσαν δέ in order to imply that the six persons about to be mentioned were not the only prophets and teachers in the church at Antioch. Codex Bezae[gr] and the Vulgate achieve the same end by replacing ὅ τε with ἐν τοῖς ("among whom [were]").

13.1 τετραάρχου

Since the tendency in hellenistic Greek was to permit hiatus for the sake of etymological clarity,[1] the Committee adopted the spelling τετραάρχης (instead of τετράρχης) at each occurrence of the word, in accord with the following witnesses: Mt 14.1 ℵ C Z Δ cop[samss, bo]; Lk 3.1 (three times) ℵ* C cop[sa, bo]; 3.19 ℵ* C cop[sa, bo]; 9.7 ℵ[a] (ℵ* omits ὁ τετρ.) C Ξ* cop[sams, bo]; Ac 13.1 ℵ* cop[sa, bo].

13.3 προσευξάμενοι

The addition of πάντες after προσευξάμενοι in codex Bezae is a typical Western expansion. The omission of ἀπέλυσαν by the same manuscript must be accounted a scribal blunder, for its absence ruins the syntax. (Blass and Clark retain the word in their editions.) After ἀπέλυσαν E vg cop[sa, bo] syr[p, h with obelus] add αὐτούς.

13.5

Instead of τὸν λόγον τοῦ θεοῦ codex Bezae[gr] it[gig] syr[p] read τὸν λόγον τοῦ κυρίου. The latter reading reflects the Christianization of the traditional expression.[2]

---

[1] Cf. Moulton-Howard, p. 63; Blass-Debrunner-Funk, § 124.

[2] The two expressions occur 32 times in the manuscripts of Acts. In nine of these passages the manuscript tradition shows no appreciable variation. Three of the nine instances read "word of the Lord" (13.49; 15.36; 19.10); six of the instances read "word of God" (4.31; 6.2; 11.1; 13.7; 17.13; 18.11). The firm attestation for "the word of God" is thus more frequent; it is also the only form of the expression that appears in

Instead of ὑπηρέτην, D 614 it^p syr^hmg cop^sa read ὑπηρετοῦντα αὐτοῖς and E vg read εἰς διακονίαν. According to Weiss,[3] these alterations were made in order to avoid describing Mark as a (menial) ὑπηρέτης. On the other hand, however, in Lk 1.2 the word seems to have an honorable connotation, for ὑπηρέται τοῦ λόγου are mentioned along with eyewitnesses of Jesus' ministry.[4]

13.6 διελθόντες

According to Haenchen, the Western reading, "And when they had gone *around* the whole island as far as Paphos …" (καὶ περιελθόντων (+ δέ D, omit it^d) αὐτῶν, D it^gig vg Lucifer), replaced the commonly received text (διελθόντες) in order to explain why no other places on Cyprus are mentioned: the missionaries sailed southwards from Salamis around the island as far as Paphos.[5]

13.6 Βαριησοῦ

Various witnesses give the name "Bar-Jesus" in various forms: Βαριησοῦ (𝔓^74 ℵ 181 242 257 460 it^gig, pvid vg syr^htxt cop^bo), Βαριησοῦς (B C E 33 many minuscules cop^sa), Βαριησοῦν (A D^2 H L P 81 104 326 614 1108 1611 2127 syr^hgr *al*), Βαριησουαν (D*, -uam it^d), Βαριησουμ (Ψ), Βαρσουμα (syr^p Ephraem), *bariesuban* (Lucifer), *varisuas* (*Opus imperfectum in Matt.* xxiv.3). With some hesitation the Committee agreed with Tischendorf and Ropes that the form Βαριησοῦ best accounts for the other variant readings; the nominative is an attempt to improve the grammar, and the accusative appears to be in apposition with ψευδοπροφήτην. The reading of D presupposes a more exact transliteration of the Semitic Bar Jeshua'

---

the Third Gospel (Lk 5.1; 8.11, 21; 11.28). For these statistics and a discussion of the passages where the evidence is divided, see Jacques Dupont, "Notes sur les Actes des Apôtres," *Revue Biblique,* LXVI (1955), pp. 47–49.

[3] *Der Codex D,* p. 73.

[4] For the wide variety of the usages of ὑπηρέτης in the Greek papyri, see Moulton-Milligan, *Vocabulary,* and B. T. Holmes, "Luke's Description of John Mark," *Journal of Biblical Literature,* LIV (1935), pp. 63–72.

[5] E. Haenchen, *The Acts of the Apostles,* p. 397.

(בַּר יֵשׁוּעַ),[6] which passed into *bariesuban* of Lucifer and *varisuas*
[i. e. *barisuas*] of the anonymous *Opus imperfectum in Matt.*

13.8 Ἐλύμας

Instead of Ἐλύμας codex Bezae reads (with a lacuna of one letter)
Ἐτ.]ιμας. That it should be spelled Ἐτοιμᾶς is shown by the Latin
side of the manuscript, which reads *Etoemas,* as does also Lucifer;
the manuscripts of Ambrosiaster vary between *ethimas, etymas,
tymas, thimas,* and *atrmas.* Manuscripts of Pacianus read *hetymam* or
hetym mam. Likewise in support of the reading of Bezae is the addition in some Old Latin witnesses at the end of ver. 6, where E reads
ὁ μεθερμηνεύεται Ἐλύμας, but where it[gig] vg[mss] Lucifer read *para-
tus* [i. e. Ἕτοιμος].

It is possible, as Harris suggested,[7] that the Western tradition of
Ἐτοιμᾶς (or Ἕτοιμος) goes back to a source similar to the one used
by Josephus when he mentions the part played by a Jewish magician
who lived in Cyprus about this time and who helped the procurator
Felix to win Drusilla (Ac 24.24), the wife of king Aziz of Emesa
(*Antiquities,* xx.vii.2). Although most of the manuscripts of Josephus
call the magician Simon, one eleventh-century manuscript, supported
by the Epitome of the *Antiquities,* give him the name Atomos
(Ἄτομος).[8]

While some scholars (including Zahn, Clemen, Wellhausen,
Ropes, A. C. Clark, and C. S. C. Williams) have been impressed by
the parallel in Josephus, Burkitt hesitated to accept the identification
and proposed the conjectural emendation of ὁ λοιμός, a word that
occurs in 24.5 and that was used by Demosthenes for a φαρμακός
("sorcerer"). The passage, as Burkitt would read it, runs: ἀνθίστατο

---

[6] On the name "Barjesus" see P. W. Schmiedel in *Encyclopaedia Biblica,* cols.
478–480 and 4556, and G. R. Driver's note in A. C. Clark, *The Acts of the Apostles,*
pp. 353 f.

[7] J. Rendel Harris, "A Curious Bezan Reading Vindicated." *Expositor,* Fifth Series,
v (1902), pp. 189–195.

[8] Niese, the editor of Josephus's works, preferred the more unusual name, since the
other probably arose from conflation with the familiar cycle of stories regarding Simon
Magus.

δὲ αὐτοῖς ὁ λοιμός, ὁ μάγος, οὕτως γὰρ μεθερμηνεύεται τὸ ὄνομα αὐτοῦ, "Now they were withstood by the pestilent fellow, the sorcerer I mean, for 'pestilent fellow' is the interpretation of the name."[9]

Despite Harris's ingenious argument, which broadens the testimony supporting the Western reading(s), the Committee did not feel itself justified in disregarding the weight of the manuscript evidence attesting Ἐλύμας.[10]

13.8 πίστεως

At the close of the verse codex Bezae, with the support of E syr[hmg] cop[G67], adds the reason why Elymas sought to turn away the proconsul from the faith: ἐπ<ε>ιδὴ ἥδιστα ἤκουεν αὐτῶν ("because he [the proconsul] was listening with the greatest pleasure to them").

13.11 παραχρῆμά τε

External evidence is divided between παραχρῆμά τε, read by 𝔓[45] ℵ C 81 623 1175 vg syr[p] cop[bo] eth, and παραχρῆμα δέ, read by 𝔓[74] A B E H L P most minuscules syr[h] cop[sa] arm, while codex Bezae goes its own way with καὶ εὐθέως. The frequent use of τε in Acts and Luke's fondness for παραχρῆμα (all but two of its 18 occurrences in the New Testament are in Luke-Acts) led the Committee to prefer the reading of 𝔓[45] ℵ C 81 al.

13.12

Curiously, though codex Bezae is especially fond of τότε,[11] here it substitutes δέ for τότε.

---

[9] F. C. Burkitt, "The Interpretation of Bar-Jesus," Journal of Theological Studies, IV (1902–03), pp. 127–129.

[10] For further discussion that derives Ἐλύμας from the Aramaic haloma (= magician), see L. Yaure, "Elymas – Nehelamite – Pethor." Journal of Biblical Literature, LXXIX (1960), pp. 297–314.

[11] See the list drawn up by Lake and Cadbury, who observe that "it [τότε] is found more than twice as often in the Western text of Acts as in the Neutral," The Beginnings of Christianity, vol. IV, p. 123.

In order to heighten and clarify the narrative D E it^gig syr^p Lucifer Ephraem and Vigilius add ἐθαύμασεν καί before ἐπίστευσεν, and D adds τῷ θεῷ after it. ("The proconsul, when he saw what had occurred, *marvelled and* believed *in God,* being astonished ...")

13.18 ἐτροποφόρησεν {C}

The evidence is singularly evenly balanced between ἐτροπο-φόρησεν ("he bore with [them]") and ἐτροφοφόρησεν ("he cared for [them]").[12] The author is doubtless alluding to Dt 1.31, where the Septuagint text, in rendering נָשָׂא, presents the same two variant readings: ἐτροφοφόρησεν (so B and 28 other mss.; ἐτροποφορ. ten mss.) σε κύριος ὁ θεός σου, ὡς εἴ τις τροφοφορήσει (B^c *al*; τροποφορ. B* N 75 Origen^3/6) ἄνθρωπος τὸν υἱὸν αὐτοῦ. In Acts a majority of the Committee regarded ἐτροποφόρησεν to be slightly better attested (by Alexandrian and several Western witnesses). On the other hand, one has the feeling that in the context it is more likely that reference should be made to God's interposition and efforts in behalf of the Israelites rather than his forbearance in the face of their ingratitude; the problem is whether the greater appropriateness was sensed by the author or by copyists. On balance it seemed best to adopt the reading that differs from the prevailing Septuagint text, on the ground that scribes would have been more likely to accommodate the two than to make them diverge.

13.19 καὶ καθελών

The initial καί is absent from B 81 cop^sa; it is present in 𝔓^74 ℵ A C D E H L P and almost all minuscules. Despite Ropes's argument for taking (as Westcott and Hort did) the preceding ὡς as "when," the Committee regarded it as less cumbersome syntax and more in the

---

[12] Lake and Cadbury raise the question whether there is evidence that the word τροφοφορεῖν really existed in Greek, and refer to Blass's statement, "Non video quomodo formari potuerit τροφοφ., at est formatum τροποφ. (Cic. ad Att. 13, 29, 2) = φέρειν τὸν τρόπον τινός, patienter ferre aliquem. Etiam 2 Macc. 7.27 minime de τροφῇ agitur," *Acta apostolorum* ... editio philologica, p. 149.

style of Luke when numerals are involved to understand ὡς as "about," and therefore was disposed to explain the absence of καί as haplography due to the following καθελών.

13.19 τὴν γῆν αὐτῶν {B}

Although αὐτοῖς may have been omitted because it seemed to be too clumsy with the following αὐτῶν, a majority of the Committee preferred the shorter reading (supported, as it is, by early witnesses representing the Alexandrian and the Western types of text), and explained the insertion of αὐτοῖς either as an assimilation to Dt 3.28 or as an expansion made in the interest of clarification ("he gave *them* their land as an inheritance"). D* *al* read "he gave the land of the foreigners."

13.20 ὡς ἔτεσιν ... μετὰ ταῦτα {C}

The problems of verses 19 and 20 are both textual and exegetical. The Textus Receptus (following Dᵇ E P Ψ and most minuscules) speaks of the period of the judges following the division of Canaan: "and after that he gave unto them judges about the space of four hundred and fifty years, until Samuel the prophet" (AV). On the other hand the Alexandrian text transfers the temporal clause to the end of ver. 19, and thus makes the four hundred fifty years cover a period prior to the institution of the judges: "... when he had destroyed seven nations in the land of Canaan, he gave them their land as an inheritance, for about four hundred and fifty years. (20) And after that he gave them judges until Samuel the prophet" (RSV).

The chronological reckoning involved in the reading of the Textus Receptus agrees almost exactly with that of Josephus (443 years, according to *Antiquities,* VIII.iii.1), and both differ widely from 1 Kgs 6.1, where it is said that Solomon (who lived long after the judges) began his temple in the four hundred and eightieth (so the Hebrew text; but the Septuagint text reads four hundred and fortieth) year after the Exodus. The reckoning that lies behind the Alexandrian text evidently covers the four hundred years of the stay in Egypt (ver. 17) plus the forty years in the wilderness (ver. 18), plus about ten years for the distribution of the land (Jos 14).[13]

On the surface, however, the Alexandrian text appears to limit the four hundred fifty years to the time that passed between the division of the land by Joshua and the institution of the judges.[14] It was probably in order to prevent the reader from drawing such an erroneous conclusion that scribes transposed the temporal clause to the following sentence, producing the reading of the Textus Receptus.

It may be added that when modern translators of the Alexandrian text break up the one Greek sentence of verses 17, 18, and 19 into several different sentences, it is almost inevitable that the reader will take the temporal clause of ver. 19 as referring only to the final sentence.[15]

13.23 ἤγαγεν {B}

Not only does ἤγαγεν have strong and varied support, but in view of the presence of ἤγειρεν in ver. 22, it is easy to understand how copyists would have altered the less usual verb to the more characteristic expression.

13.23 σωτῆρα Ἰησοῦν

Instead of reading "God has brought to Israel a Saviour, Jesus," 𝔓[74] H L and about fifty minuscules read "God has brought to Israel salvation." The error arose, as Tischendorf observes, through a palaeographical oversight, when c̅p̅α̅ ι̅ν̅ (= σωτῆρα Ἰησοῦν) was read as c̅p̅ι̅α̅ν̅ (= σωτηρίαν), or cⲱⲧⲏⲣⲁⲓⲛ as cⲱⲧⲏⲣⲓⲁⲛ.

---

[13] So, e. g., Lake and Cadbury, Haenchen, et al.

[14] That the author of the Alexandrian text cannot have intended such a meaning is shown by (1) the verb κατεκληρονόμησεν, which refers to a definite point of time and not to a period of more than four centuries; and (2) the usage of the dative case (in distinction from the accusatives of time in verses 18 and 21) to embrace the whole period from the date implied in ver. 17 to the division of the promised land.

[15] The New American Standard Bible (La Habra, Calif., 1963) attempts to prevent the reader from drawing such an inference by punctuating ver. 19 with a dash ("... distributed their land as an inheritance – all of which took about four hundred and fifty years").

13.25 Τί ἐμέ {B}

The reading τί ἐμέ is supported by 𝔓[74] ℵ A B (81 τί μαι [= με]) 915 cop[sa] eth, whereas the reading τίνα με is supported by 𝔓[45vid] C D E H L P Ψ most minuscules vg syr[p, h] cop[bo] arm. Here the Alexandrian text corresponds to Aramaic usage,[16] and the Western and the Byzantine Greek texts reflect linguistic improvement.

It is possible to take τί as equivalent to a relative pronoun[17] and so to replace the question mark after εἶναι with a comma (resulting in the meaning, "I am not what you think I am"; so Haenchen and REB).

13.26 ἡμῖν {B}

The interchange of ὑ for ἡ (both were pronounced ēē), and vice versa, was a common blunder among Greek scribes (for example, earlier in the verse A D 81 read ἐν ἡμῖν instead of the obviously correct ἐν ὑμῖν). In the present case the context as well as a combination of Alexandrian and Western witnesses strongly support the first person pronoun.

13.27 τοῦτον ἀγνοήσαντες καὶ τὰς φωνὰς ... κρίναντες {A}

The text of verses 27–29 circulated in a variety of forms, the shortest being that of the Alexandrian witnesses. Several forms of the Western text (or, several Western types of text) supply various additions in order to provide a more complete, though summary, account of Jesus' trial and death. Here and there the text of codex Bezae is ungrammatical and obviously corrupt. By using evidence from the Harclean Syriac and the Old Latin witnesses Blass, Hilgenfeld, Zahn, Ropes, and Clark reconstructed what each regarded as the original Western text. Ropes's reconstruction,[18] which may be selected as representative of a median text, is as follows: (27) οἱ γὰρ κατοικοῦντες ἐν Ἱερουσαλὴμ καὶ οἱ ἄρχοντες αὐτῆς, μὴ

---

[16] C. C. Torrey, *The Composition and Date of Acts*, pp. 37 f.

[17] See Blass-Debrunner-Funk, § 298, 4, and C. F. D. Moule, *An Idiom Book of New Testament Greek* (Cambridge, 1953), p. 124.

[18] J. H. Ropes, "Detached Note on xiii.27–29," *The Text of Acts*, pp. 261–263.

συνιέντες τὰς γραφὰς τῶν προφητῶν τὰς κατὰ πᾶν σάββατον ἀναγεινωσκομένας ἐπλήρωσαν, (28) καὶ μηδεμίαν αἰτίαν θανάτου εὑρόντες ἐν αὐτῷ, κρείναντες αὐτόν, παρέδωκαν Πειλάτῳ εἰς ἀναίρεσιν· (29) ὡς δὲ ἐτέλουν πάντα τὰ περὶ αὐτοῦ γεγραμμένα, ᾐτοῦντο τὸν Πειλᾶτον μετὰ τὸ σταυρωθῆναι αὐτὸν ἀπὸ τοῦ ξύλου καθαιρεθῆναι, καὶ ἐπιτυχόντες καθεῖλον καὶ ἔθηκαν εἰς μνημεῖον ("For those who live in Jerusalem and her rulers, not understanding[19] the scriptures of the prophets, which are read publically every sabbath, have fulfilled them, (28) and though they found no cause of death in him, after having judged him they delivered him to Pilate for destruction. (29) And when they were completing all the things that had been written concerning him, they requested Pilate after his crucifixion that he might be taken down from the tree, and having gained their request they took him down and laid him in a tomb."

13.31 [νῦν]

The evidence for and against the inclusion of νῦν is curiously ambiguous. On the one hand, its varying position (after εἰσί in ℵ, before it in A C 81), its expanded form (ἄχρι νῦν in D), and its omission altogether by B and the ecclesiastical text, suggest that it was added in various places. On the other hand, however, the fact that in similar passages (2.32; 3.15; 5.32; 10.39) it is not read (even as a variant reading), suggests that it was not added here by scribes but comes from the author. Its absence in some witnesses may be accounted for either because it was regarded as unnecessary, or because the apostles not only now first, but for a long time past, were witnesses.

In order to represent the balance of possibilities, the Committee decided to print νῦν before εἰσίν but to enclose it within square brackets.

---

[19] On the difference between the Alexandrian and the Western representation of the Jews' culpability, see E. J. Epp, "The 'Ignorance Motif' in Acts and Anti-Judaic Tendencies in Codex Bezae," *Harvard Theological Review*, LV (1962), pp. 57–59, and *idem, The Theological Tendency of Codex Bezae Cantabrigiensis in Acts* (Cambridge, 1966), pp. 41–51.

13.33 [αὐτῶν] ἡμῖν {C}

Although ἡμῶν is by far the best attested reading, it gives a most improbable sense (since the promise was made to the fathers, we expect to read that it was fulfilled, not "to *our* children" but "to *their* children").[20] On the other hand, both αὐτῶν and αὐτῶν ἡμῖν are so eminently appropriate that if either had been the original reading, one cannot understand how the readings ἡμῶν and ἡμῖν could have arisen.

Several conjectural emendations have been proposed, including ἐφ' ἡμῶν ("in our time") by Lachmann[21] and ἐκπεπλήρωκεν ἡμῖν καὶ τοῖς τέκνοις ἡμῶν by Chase,[22] who compares 2.39. While the scribe of ms. 142 (eleventh century) has preserved what many regard as the correct reading, he has done so only, so to speak, accidentally or by a happy conjecture. At the same time it is possible to argue that the reading αὐτῶν ἡμῖν in the great majority of witnesses is a conflate reading and therefore presents a strong presumption for the early existence of the reading ἡμῖν.

The Committee, though agreeing with Hort's judgment that "it can hardly be doubted that ἡμῶν is a primitive corruption of ἡμῖν,"[23] felt compelled by the predominance of external evidence to print αὐτῶν ἡμῖν, but, in view of the transcriptional considerations mentioned above, to enclose αὐτῶν within square brackets. Besides the customary rendering of αὐτῶν ἡμῖν, it has been proposed to take ἡμῖν with what follows and to translate, "This promise God has fulfilled for the children, having for us raised up Jesus" (so W. F. Burnside, *The Acts of the Apostles* [Cambridge, 1916], p. 163).

---

[20] G. D. Kilpatrick, who adopts ἡμῶν, suggests that here the author himself made a slip of the pen and wrote nonsense ("An Eclectic Study of the Text of Acts," *Biblical and Patristic Studies in Memory of Robert Pierce Casey,* edited by J. Neville Birdsall and Robert W. Thomson [Freiburg, 1963], p. 74).

[21] Preface to his 2nd edition, vol. II, p. ix.

[22] F. H. Chase, *The Credibility of the Book of the Acts of the Apostles* (London, 1902), p. 187, n. 1.

[23] "Notes on Select Readings," p. 95. With Hort agree, e. g., Souter (*Expositor,* Eighth Series, x [1915], p. 438), Ropes (*The Text of Acts,* p. 124), Haenchen (*Commentary, ad loc.*), and Evald Lövestam (*Son and Saviour* [Lund, 1961], pp. 7–8).

13.33   Ἰησοῦν

Several Western witnesses expand Ἰησοῦν by reading τὸν κύριον Ἰησοῦν Χριστόν (D cop^sa Ambrose) or τὸν κύριον ἡμῶν Ἰησοῦν (614 syr^h Hilary). It is obvious that if either of these had been the original reading, copyists would not have deliberately shortened the text so as to produce Ἰησοῦν, which is read by the overwhelming mass of witnesses.

13.33   τῷ ψαλμῷ γέγραπται τῷ δευτέρῳ   {B}

It is not known when numerals were first assigned to the Psalms. There is some patristic and rabbinical evidence that in the early Christian period what is now reckoned as the second Psalm was regarded as the continuation of the first Psalm. In his comments on the second Psalm Origen states that he had two Hebrew manuscripts, in one of which the second Psalm was joined to the first. In illustration of such an ordering of the Psalms he refers to the present passage in Acts, where the statement, "Thou art my Son, today I have begotten thee," is identified as a quotation from the first Psalm, whereas in the Greek manuscripts (here Origen means the Septuagint) this Psalm is indicated (μηνύει) as the second. At the same time, one should not overlook the fact, he adds, that no Hebrew manuscript of the Psalms actually contains a number, such as "first" or "second" or "third."

Both the Jerusalem and the Babylonian Talmuds contain examples of rabbinical exegesis that count the first and second Psalms as one Psalm.[24] In quoting the two Psalms Justin Martyr passes from the first to the second without indicating any break (*Apol.* I.40), and Eusebius, Apollinaris, and Euthymius Zigabenus (all of whom, however, are probably dependent upon Origen) refer to this Hebrew practice.

---

[24] See Jerusalem Talmud, *Taanith,* fol. 65, 3, quoted by John Lightfoot, *Horae hebraicae et talmudicae,* ed. by Robert Gandell, vol. IV (Oxford, 1859), pp. 119 f., and Babylonian Talmud, *Berakoth,* fol. 9b, translated by Maurice Simon, in the Soncino edition (London, 1948), pp. 50 f. In both cases the purpose of making such an enumeration is to enable the opening verse of Psalm 20 to stand immediately after the eighteenth Psalm, in the interest of drawing a parallel with the Eighteen Benedictions.

On the Latin side Hilary discusses at length in his treatise on the Psalms whether the apostle Paul made an error when, in Acts, he designated the quotation as coming from the first Psalm. Likewise in some manuscripts Tertullian (*adv. Marcionem*, IV.22) and Cyprian (*Testimonia*, I.13; III.112) adduce passages from the second Psalm under the rubric of *in primo psalmo*.[25]

In evaluating the Greek manuscript evidence of Ac 13.33 it is apparent that the reading "second Psalm" was very widely disseminated – all uncials except D read δευτέρῳ.

On the other hand, the patristic evidence for πρώτῳ is, if not overwhelming (as Clark characterizes it), at least very impressive.[26]

The textual critic must weigh probabilities: was it more likely that Luke was acquainted with the tradition that counted the first two Psalms as one, and later editors or transcribers altered his πρώτῳ to δευτέρῳ to conform to what became the usual enumeration, or was πρώτῳ substituted by someone who was acquainted with the rabbinical practice of combining them?

Or is the reading of 𝔓⁴⁵, τοῖς ψαλμοῖς, to be preferred, not only because it is the oldest, but for transcriptional reasons as well?[27] The variety of positions at which the numeral (whether πρώτῳ or δευτέρῳ) is introduced makes both numerals suspect. The rabbinical

---

[25] In his edition of Tertullian in the *Corpus Scriptorum Ecclesiasticorum Latinorum* Kroymann abandons the oldest manuscript evidence and prints *in secundo psalmo*. The manuscript testimony of Cyprian in the two passages mentioned is divided, some reading *in primo psalmo;* in five other instances all manuscripts of *Testimonia* cite passages from the second Psalm as *in psalmo secundo*. For other patristic references see Paul de Lagarde, "Novae Psalterii Graeci editionis specimen," *Abhandlungen der königlichen Gesellschaft der Wissenschaften zu Göttingen,* XXXIII (1886), pp. 16–18; for a discussion, see Zahn, *Die Urausgabe der Apostelgeschichte des Lucas* (Leipzig, 1916), pp. 83 and 234 f.

[26] A. C. Clark, *The Acts of the Apostles,* p. 356. Ropes, who devotes an extended note to the problem (*The Text of Acts,* pp. 263–265), also adopts πρώτῳ as original in Acts.

[27] Tischendorf and Souter cite (but with a question mark) the tenth or eleventh century semi-uncial manuscript 0142 in support of the omission of the numeral; upon inspection by Dom G. Morin, however, it has been ascertained that this manuscript reads ὡς καὶ ἐν τῷ β̄ ψαλμῷ γέγραπται (see E. R. Smothers in *Recherches de science religieuse,* XXIV [1934], pp. 467 f.).

evidence for counting the two Psalms as one is linked, as was mentioned above, with the currency of the Eighteen Benedictions; but it is generally agreed that in the first century this liturgical set of prayers contained fewer than eighteen (perhaps twelve) benedictions, and so such an incentive to join the two Psalms could not have operated at that early date.

Yet, if the shorter reading is regarded as original, one has the difficulty of explaining why, in this passage alone in the New Testament, almost all scribes thought it necessary to identify the quotation by using a numeral with ψαλμῷ. Does not this tradition suggest that the author had used one or the other numeral?[28]

In view of the balance in transcriptional probabilities a majority of the Committee, impressed by the weight of four of the great uncials, supported as they are by $\mathfrak{P}^{74}$ 33 81 *al,* preferred the reading τῷ ψαλμῷ γέγραπται τῷ δευτέρῳ.

13.33 σε

The Western text (D vg[ms] syr[hmg] cop[G67]) continues the quotation by adding Ps 2.8, αἴτησαι παρ' ἐμοῦ καὶ δώσω σοι ἔθνη τὴν κληρονομίαν σου, καὶ τὴν κατάσχεσίν σου τὰ πέρατα τῆς γῆς ("Ask of me and I will give you Gentiles for your inheritance, and for your possession the ends of the earth").

13.34 ὅτι (1)

Instead of ὅτι (1), which resumes the quotation begun at the beginning of ver. 33 *(ὅτι),* D 614 2412 it[gig] vg[ms] Hilary continue with a somewhat easier and more loosely articulated construction introduced by ὅτε.

---

[28] According to Zahn, in his first edition of Acts Luke followed the old Jewish synagogal usage in the public reading of Psalms 1 and 2 as one, whereas later either Luke himself altered the numeral (to accommodate the reference to the scriptural usage current in Greek congregations) or various scribes made the alteration (see *Die Apostelgeschichte des Lucas* [Leipzig and Erlangen, 1921], p. 443). It may be asked, however, what evidence exists to prove that in the first century the Psalms were included in the lectionary of scripture readings for synagogue services?

Cop^G67 expands ver. 34 with the following material: "He has raised him up from the dead *in such a way as* never again to return to decay, *that all the people may know* (it) *and repent. For thus it stands written in the prophet Isaiah,* 'I will make *with you an everlasting covenant,* the sure mercies of David.'"

13.38 διὰ τούτου

The reading διὰ τούτου ("through this man," ℵ A B³ C D L P many minuscules) is more appropriate in the context (compare ἐν τούτῳ, ver. 39) than διὰ τοῦτο ("for this reason," 𝔓⁷⁴ B* 61 326 436 1175 1838 *al*). The latter reading may have arisen accidentally when Υ fell out by haplography. The reading διὰ αὐτοῦ (E 218 425 611 642 808 *al*) softens what could be taken as a slightly disrespectful tone in τούτου ("this fellow"). The reading διὰ τοῦτον (919) is an orthographic variant.

13.38-39

In order to smooth the construction by amplifying the sense the Western text makes several insertions: "Through this man forgiveness of sins is proclaimed to you, and *repentance* (μετάνοια, D vg^ms (syr^h with * and cop^G67 before καταγγέλεται)) from all those things from which you could not be freed by the law of Moses; by him *therefore* (οὖν, D 614 syr^hmg) every one that believes is freed *before God*" (παρὰ θεῷ D (syr^hmg ὑπὸ θεοῦ)).

13.40 ἐπέλθῃ {B}

The addition of ἐφ' ὑμᾶς seems to be a natural supplement that scribes felt to be necessary in the context. Had it been present originally, there is no good reason that would account for its being dropped.

13.40 ἐν τοῖς προφήταις

Cop^G67 makes the reference more explicit, "what is said in Habakkuk the prophet."

13.41 ἔργον (2)

The second instance of ἔργον ($\mathfrak{P}^{74}$ ℵ A B C 33 81 1765 1827 vg cop^{sa, bo}) was omitted (D E L P 104 216 326 429 915 1881 it^{gig, p} syr^{p, h} *al*) either because it was felt to be redundant, or in order to assimilate the text to the Septuagint text of Hab 1.5.

13.41 ὑμῖν

At the close of Paul's speech D adds καὶ ἐσίγησαν, and 614 syr^{h with *} cop^{G67} add καὶ ἐσίγησεν. The former reading describes the deep impression that the apostle's words made on his hearers; the latter reading indicates merely that he had finished his address.

13.42 αὐτῶν {A}

The ambiguity of the earliest text ("as they [i. e. the apostles] went out, they [i. e. the people] besought them ...") was relieved by expansions serving to identify the several groups. Thus, in the Textus Receptus (following P 049 056 and most minuscules) the subject of ἐξιόντων is τῶν Ἰουδαίων, and this is balanced by τὰ ἔθνη as the subject of παρεκάλουν (see the comment on the following set of variants).

13.42 παρεκάλουν εἰς τὸ μεταξὺ σάββατον {B}

The Textus Receptus (see the comment on the preceding set of variants) add τὰ ἔθνη, probably because it was considered necessary that the request to speak again should be ascribed to the Gentiles, in view of the hostility of the Jews (ver. 45).

Instead of μεταξύ, which more properly means "between" and only in common parlance "next," codex Bezae preferred the unambiguous ἑξῆς.

Codex Laudianus (E), which has very short lines (sometimes but a single word), accidentally omits παρεκάλουν; codex Vaticanus likewise omits it, but inserts another verb (which can also mean "they were asking") after σάββατον.

The fact that there is a certain amount of repetition between verses 42 and 43, as well as the ambiguity referred to in the comments on the previous set of variants, accounts for the multiplication of variant readings. Hort was inclined to think that the exegetical difficulties pointed to the existence of a primitive error that had infected all witnesses, and suggested that "perhaps Ἀξιούντων should replace Ἐξιόντων, and παρεκάλουν and the stop at the end of the verse be omitted."[29] The resulting text, however, which involves two genitives absolute before the main verb, can hardly be regarded as superior to the reading attested by the majority of the old uncials. Even less plausible is the proposal to take παρεκάλουν as "a corruption of παρ᾽ Ἀμβακούμ (or perhaps παρ᾽ Ἀβακούμ – a possible form) – i. e. 'from Habakkuk': originally a sidenote to the effect that the quotation in v. 41, with which Paul's speech ends, was made from that prophet."[30] Apart from the fact that παρά was not the preposition normally used to denote the origin of a quotation, the resulting syntax of the sentence without παρεκάλουν is impossibly chaotic.

13.43   Βαρναβᾷ {A}

After Βαρναβᾷ 614 al syr[h with *] insert ἀξιοῦντες βαπτισθῆναι ("asking that they be baptized"), an addition which, as Haenchen says, was made in order to give content to the exhortation that they "continue in the grace of God."

13.43   Θεοῦ. {A}

At the close of ver. 43 codex Laudianus (E) cop[G67] and the Greek text known to Bede add ἐγένετο δὲ κατὰ πᾶσαν πόλιν φημισθῆναι τὸν λόγον ("And it came to pass that the word was spread throughout all the city"). The verb φημίζειν occurs elsewhere in the

---

[29] "Notes on Select Readings," p. 95. The emended text could be translated, "When they asked that they speak these words to them on the next sabbath, and after the synagogue [meeting] was dismissed, many Jews and devout converts to Judaism followed Paul...."

[30] So E. E. Kellett, "Note on Acts xiii.42," *Expository Times,* xxxiv (1922–23), pp. 188–189.

New Testament only at Mt 28.15 as a variant reading of *δια-φημίζειν*. The addition was probably made in order to explain how it was that on the following sabbath almost the whole city gathered together.

Codex Bezae, supported in part by syr[hmg] cop[G67], makes even more extensive additions: "And it came to pass that the word of God went throughout the whole city *(ἐγένετο δὲ καθ' ὅλης τῆς πόλεως δι-ελθεῖν τὸν λόγον τοῦ θεοῦ)*. And the next sabbath almost the whole *(ὅλη* for *πᾶσα)* city gathered together to hear Paul. And when he made a long discourse about the Lord *(ἀκοῦσαι Παύλου. πολύν τε λόγον ποιησαμένου*[31] *περὶ τοῦ κυρίου)* and the Jews saw the multitudes, they were filled with jealousy, and contradicted the words *(τοῖς λόγοις)* spoken by Paul, contradicting and *(ἀντιλέγοντες καί)* blaspheming."

13.44   *τὸν λόγον τοῦ κυρίου* {C}

Luke, as well as other New Testament writers, uses the expression *ὁ λόγος τοῦ θεοῦ* more frequently than *ὁ λόγος τοῦ κυρίου*.[32] In view of the rather evenly balanced external attestation, a majority of the Committee judged it more probable that the more frequently used phrase was substituted for the less frequently used one, than vice versa.

13.45   *βλασφημοῦντες* {B}

A majority of the Committee preferred the shorter text, regarding the longer reading as a Western expansion. The reading *ἐναντιού-μενοι καί* appears to be an attempt to avoid the tautology that *ἀντιλέγοντες* makes with *ἀντέλεγον*.

13.48   *τὸν λόγον τοῦ κυρίου* {C}

The accusative is the object of *ἐδόξαζον*. Now, the expression *δοξάζειν τὸν θεόν* occurs frequently, but *δοξάζειν τὸν λόγον τοῦ*

---

[31] Compare the Western addition at 11.2, *πολὺν λόγον ποιούμενος*.
[32] For statistics, see above, pp. 353 f., footnote 2.

θεοῦ (or κυρίου) is not found elsewhere. Probably for this reason codex Bezae substitutes ἐδέξαντο ("received"). Other scribes and translators omitted τὸν λόγον and made τὸν θεόν the object of the verb, and several (including those responsible for 614 876 1799 2412 and syrʰ) reworded the text to produce ἐδόξαζον τὸν θεὸν καὶ ἐπίστευσαν τῷ λόγῳ τοῦ κυρίου ("glorified God and believed the word of the Lord").

As was the case in ver. 44, so here also the Committee judged that it was more likely that τὸν λόγον τοῦ κυρίου would be supplanted by the more frequent τὸν λόγον τοῦ θεοῦ, than vice versa, especially since ὁ λόγος τοῦ κυρίου occurs in ver. 49.

13.50 διωγμόν

Codex Bezae, partly supported by E, adds θλῖψιν μεγάλην καί before διωγμόν ("… stirred up *great affliction and* persecution against Paul and Barnabas"); for a similar Western expansion, see 8.1.

14.2-7

The Western text of these verses adds a number of details that serve, among other things, to smooth away what, in the ordinary text, is a seeming lack of coherence between verses 2 and 3 (where mention is made of the opposition of the Jews: therefore the apostles remained for a long time). According to codex Bezae (with support in part from syrʰᵐᵍ and copᴳ⁶⁷) the passage runs as follows (italics mark the chief additions and changes): "But *the chiefs of the synagogue of the Jews and the rulers of the synagogue* [syrʰᵐᵍ omits "of the synagogue," thus identifying 'the rulers' as those of the previously mentioned Iconians] *stirred up for themselves*[1] *persecution against the righteous* (οἱ δὲ ἀρχισυνάγωγοι τῶν Ἰουδαίων καὶ οἱ ἄρχοντες

---

[1] It is not quite certain how αὐτοῖς is to be taken. Normally one would regard it as the object of ἐπί in the verb, "stirred up persecution against them," but the following κατὰ τῶν δικαίων seems to render it superfluous. It may represent, as Torrey suggests, the Aramaic ethical dative (*Documents of the Primitive Church*, pp. 125, 138, 147), and it is taken thus in the translation above. See also the comment on ver. 27.

τῆς συναγωγῆς ἐπήγαγον αὐτοῖς διωγμὸν κατὰ τῶν δικαίων), and poisoned the minds of the Gentiles against the brethren. *But the Lord soon gave peace (ὁ δὲ κύριος ἔδωκεν ταχὺ εἰρήνην)*. (3) So they remained for a long time, speaking boldly for the Lord, who bore witness to the word of his grace, granting signs and wonders to be done by their hands. (4) But the people of the city were divided; some sided with the Jews, and some with the apostles, *cleaving to them on account of the word of God (κολλώμενοι διὰ τὸν λόγον τοῦ θεοῦ)*. (5) When an attempt was made [*again,* so syr[hmg] cop[G67]] by both Gentiles and Jews, with their rulers, to molest them [*a second time,* so syr[hmg] cop[G67]] and to stone them [it[d] and syr[hmg] state that they did stone them], (6) they learned of it and [syr[hmg] cop[G67] om. "learned of it and"] fled to Lystra and Derbe, cities of Lycaonia, and to the *whole* (ὅλην is added after περίχωρον) surrounding country; (7) and there they preached the gospel, *and the whole multitude was moved by* [*drew near to,* cop[G67]] *the teaching. And Paul and Barnabas stayed on in Lystra (καὶ ἐκεινήθη ὅλον τὸ πλῆθος ἐπὶ τῇ διδαχῇ. ὁ δὲ Παῦλος καὶ Βαρναβᾶς διέτριβον ἐν Λύστροις).*"

The greater smoothness of the Western text is probably a mark of its secondary character,[2] for all the additions seem to be comments calculated to remedy difficulties in the ordinary text.[3]

Wendt[4] and Moffatt[5] secure a smoother text by transposing ver. 3 to what they assume to be its original position between verses 1 and 2. Haenchen takes the aorist verbs in ver. 2 as ingressive (Blass-Debrunner-Funk, § 318) and regards the Western text as an unnecessary expansion of what is already expressed in the usual text.[6]

14.3 *[ἐπὶ] τῷ λόγῳ*

On the one hand, the overwhelming weight of external evidence reads τῷ λόγῳ (𝔓[74] ℵ[c] B C D E L P Ψ and apparently all minuscules),

---

[2] So F. F. Bruce, *The Acts of the Apostles,* (1951), p. 277.

[3] So Cadbury and Lake, *The Beginnings of Christianity,* vol. IV, p. 161.

[4] *Die Apostelgeschichte,* 1913, p. 218, Anm. 2.

[5] *The New Testament, a New Translation, in loc.*

[6] *The Acts of the Apostles, ad loc.*

whereas only a few witnesses read ἐπὶ τῷ λόγῳ (אׁ* A syrᵖ copᵇᵒ). On the other hand, ἐπί is such an unusual construction after μαρτυρεῖν that, according to the opinion of Ropes (*ad loc.*), it is probably genuine, perhaps being derived from an Aramaic original (עַל). Desiring to take into account both these considerations, a majority of the Committee decided to include ἐπί in the text, but to enclose it within square brackets.

14.6   συνιδόντες κατέφυγον

For συνιδόντες κατέφυγον, Hammond conjectured σπεύδοντες, "they made haste and fled" (see footnote 7 on p. 348).

14.6   Λυκαονίας

After Λυκαονίας the palimpsest itʰ adds (as deciphered by E. S. Buchanan)[7] *sicut ī͞hs dixerat eis LX [XII]* ("just as Jesus had said to the Seventy-two"). The reference is to the words of Jesus in Lk 10.10-12.

14.8   ἀδύνατος ἐν Λύστροις

The omission of the phrase ἐν Λύστροις in D E copˢᵃ is to be accounted for either because it was felt to be unnecessary owing to its presence in the immediately previous sentence (in D), or because it dropped out due to palaeographical similarity with the adjacent ἀδύνατος, when written in uncials.

Despite the rather slender external support for the reading ἀνὴρ ἀδύνατος ἐν Λύστροις τοῖς ποσίν (only אׁ* B 1175), a majority of the Committee preferred it to the reading ἀνὴρ ἐν Λύστροις

---

[7] It should be mentioned that some of Buchanan's palaeographical work has come under severe criticism; see H. A. Sanders, "Buchanans Publikationen altlateinischer Texte, eine Warnung," *Zeitschrift für die neutestamentliche Wissenschaft*, XXI (1922), pp. 291–299, and compare the annotation on item no. 936 in B. M. Metzger's *Annotated Bibliography of the Textual Criticism of the New Testament, 1914–1939* (Copenhagen, 1955). As Ropes points out (*ad loc.*) "no other authority seems to give any hint of this gloss."

ἀδύνατος τοῖς ποσίν (𝔓⁷⁴ ℵᶜ A C H L P most minuscules) because the former has the appearance of being primitive and seems to cry out for rearrangement, whereas if the latter reading, which is the smoother of the two, were original, it is difficult to account for the emergence of the other.

14.8-9

Several Western witnesses introduce a variety of expansions. At the close of ver. 8 itʰ adds (according to Berger) the phrase *[habens ti]morem dei* ("having the fear of God") [Buchanan could not read *dei* in the manuscript, which is a palimpsest]. According to Blass, the intention of the addition is to describe the cripple as a Jewish proselyte. In accord with this interpretation of the phrase is the addition to ver. 9 in the same witness, "he heard the apostle *gladly*" (*libenter* = ἡδέως). Codex Bezae moves the phrase to ver. 9, and after λαλοῦντος reads ὑπάρχων ἐν φόβῳ, where its meaning is more difficult to interpret; Zahn thinks it means "being in despair," but Ramsay still takes it to mean that he was a "Godfearer."[8] The reading of itᵍⁱᵍ makes the man's faith the result of Paul's preaching, *hic cum audisset Paulum loquentem, credidit* ("When he had heard Paul speaking, *he believed*"). After "speaking" copᴳ⁶⁷ expands with circumstantial detail: "*He had been wishing to hear Paul speak. When Paul saw him he looked in his face; he knew in the spirit* that he had *true* faith to be cured."

14.10

The Western text is assimilated to the account of Peter's healing the lame man at the Beautiful gate of the temple (3.6). After φωνῇ C D (E) 223 614 876 (2412) itʰ syrʰᵐᵍ copˢᵃ, ᵇᵒᵖᵗ, ᴳ⁶⁷ Irenaeus add σοι λέγω ἐν τῷ ὀνόματι τοῦ κυρίου Ἰησοῦ Χριστοῦ, and after ὀρθός D itʰ syrʰᵐᵍ copᴳ⁶⁷ add καὶ περιπάτει (compare Lk 5.23).

At the close of the verse several Western witnesses emphasize that the cure was instantaneous (compare 3.7): after καί D adds εὐθέως

---

[8] W. M. Ramsay, *St. Paul the Traveller and the Roman Citizen* (London, 1905), p. 116.

παραχρῆμα, E adds παραχρῆμα, and syr[hmg] reads "at once that same hour."

14.13

The reading of codex Bezae, οἱ δὲ ἱερεῖς τοῦ ὄντος Διὸς πρὸ πόλεως ... ἤθελον ἐπιθύειν ("But the priests of the local Zeus-before-the-city," i. e. the Zeus whose temple was in front of the city) is, according to Lake and Cadbury, "either original or represents a correction based on exact knowledge of the probable situation."[9] Despite Blass's protestations to the contrary,[10] a college of priests was usually connected with great temples.

Ropes, on the other hand, thinks that "the unhellenic phrase of the B-text τοῦ Διὸς τοῦ ὄντος πρὸ τῆς πόλεως may well reflect a Semitic original."[11]

14.14 οἱ ἀπόστολοι

Weiss thinks that the omission of οἱ ἀπόστολοι (D it[gig, h] syr[p]) may have been deliberate because offense was taken at the extension of the title to Barnabas, who, moreover, is here mentioned before Paul.[12]

14.19 ἐπῆλθαν δὲ ... καὶ πείσαντες τοὺς ὄχλους

In the Western text the abruptness of the transition to a new scene is softened by the insertion of a circumstantial clause, which is followed by an expansion that may represent, as Lake and Cadbury suggest, "a perverted tradition as to the Judaistic controversy in

---

[9] *The Beginnings of Christianity*, vol. IV, p. 165.

[10] F. Blass, *Acta apostolorum* ... editio philologica, p. 158.

[11] *The Text of Acts*, p. 132.

[12] *Der Codex D in der Apostelgeschichte*, p. 78. Kilpatrick, however, prefers the reading of Bezae, which has the participle in the singular number (ἀκούσας δὲ Βαρναβᾶς καὶ Παῦλος); see G. D. Kilpatrick in *Biblical and Patristic Studies in Memory of Robert Pierce Casey*, edited by J. Neville Birdsall and Robert W. Thomson, pp. 69 f.

Galatia."[13] The expanded form of text, preserved in D (in part) it[h] syr[hmg] and other Western witnesses (including the more recently discovered cop[G67]) was reconstructed by A. C. Clark as follows: διατριβόντων δὲ αὐτῶν καὶ διδασκόντων ἐπῆλθόν τινες Ἰουδαῖοι ἀπὸ Ἰκονίου καὶ Ἀντιοχείας καὶ διαλεγομένων αὐτῶν παρρησίᾳ ἔπεισαν τοὺς ὄχλους ἀποστῆναι ἀπ' αὐτῶν λέγοντες ὅτι οὐδὲν ἀληθὲς λέγουσιν, ἀλλὰ πάντα ψεύδονται. καὶ ἐπισείσαντες τοὺς ὄχλους ... ("But while they were staying there and teaching, certain Jews came from Iconium and Antioch, and openly disputed [it[h] adds: the word of God]; these persuaded the multitudes to withdraw from them, saying that they were not telling the truth at all, but were liars at every point. And having incited the multitudes ...").

It is noteworthy that cop[G67] omits "and Antioch," either by accident or perhaps because it was thought unlikely that Jews would come from so distant a city (Pisidian Antioch was one hundred miles away from Lystra) in order to oppose the work of the apostles.

14.20

The ordinary text is expanded in several Western witnesses: "Then the disciples [*brethren,* cop[G67]] gathered around him, *and the crowd left* [it[h] cop[G67]]. And when evening had come [when the day grew late *and darkness had come on,* Ephraem], he *rose up* [*with difficulty,* it[p2]] *and went into the city*" [it[h] cop[sa, G67]].

14.25 λόγον {B}

The tendency to add either τοῦ κυρίου (ℵ A C 614 vg syr[p, h with *] arm *al*) or τοῦ θεοῦ ($\mathfrak{P}^{74}$ E it[gig]) after λαλήσαντες τὸν λόγον must have been very strong, whereas no one would have omitted either of the qualifying genitives if it had been present originally. The shorter text is strongly supported by B D H L P most minuscules cop[sa, bo] eth *al.*

---

[13] *The Beginnings of Christianity,* vol. IV, p. 167.

14.25 Ἀττάλειαν

After Ἀττάλειαν, which was a harbor city, the Western text makes the statement that the apostles conducted a preaching mission there before sailing for Antioch; D (383) 614 syr^h with * cop^G67 add εὐαγγελιζόμενοι αὐτούς (αὐτοῖς 383).

14.27 ἐποίησεν

After ὅσα ὁ θεὸς ἐποίησεν codex Bezae continues with a pleonastic combination of pronouns, αὐτοῖς μετὰ τῶν ψυχῶν αὐτῶν. It is generally recognized that the reading μετὰ τῶν ψυχῶν αὐτῶν reflects Semitic influence and is linguistically equivalent to μετὰ αὐτῶν in the usual text. The preceding αὐτοῖς is less easy to account for, but it probably represents the Aramaic proleptic pronoun, which is superfluous in Greek.

Torrey thinks that the second-century editor wished to emphasize the twofold work of God ("for them" and "for the Gentiles"), and therefore wrote עבד עמהון נפשהון, "had done for them themselves," which was then turned back more literally into the Greek of D.[14]

15.2 ἔταξαν ... ἐξ αὐτῶν {A}

The Western text has introduced several extensive alterations into the text of verses 1-5. "And some men *of those who had believed from the party of the Pharisees* (Ἰουδαίας] + τῶν πεπιστευκότων ἀπὸ τῆς αἱρέσεως τῶν Φαρισαίων, Ψ 614 1799 2412 syr^hmg) came down from Judea and were teaching the brethren, 'Unless you are circumcised *and walk* according to the custom of Moses (καὶ τῷ ἔθει Μωϋσέως περιπατῆτε, D syr^hmg cop^sa), you cannot be saved.' (2) And when Paul and Barnabas had no small dissension and debate with them – *for Paul spoke maintaining firmly that they* [i. e. the converts] *should stay as they were when converted; but those who had*

---

[14] C. C. Torrey, *Documents of the Primitive Church,* p. 146. The suggestion, however, involves Torrey's improbable theory of multiple translations (see above, pp. 231 f.).

come from Jerusalem ordered them, Paul and Barnabas and certain others, to go up to Jerusalem (ἔταξαν … ἐξ αὐτῶν] ἔλεγεν γὰρ ὁ Παῦλος μένειν οὕτως καθὼς ἐπίστευσαν διϊσχυριζόμενος, οἱ δὲ ἐληλυθότες ἀπὸ Ἱερουσαλὴμ παρήγγειλαν αὐτοῖς τῷ Παύλῳ καὶ Βαρναβᾷ καί τισιν ἄλλοις ἀναβαίνειν, D (it^gig syr^hmg cop^G67)) to the apostles and elders *that they might be judged before them* (Ἱερουσαλήμ] + ὅπως κριθῶσιν ἐπ᾽ αὐτοῖς, D 1799 syr^h with * (αὐτῶν, 614 2412)) about this question. (3) So, being sent on the way … [verse 3 as in ordinary text]. (4) When they came to Jerusalem, they were welcomed *heartily* (παρεδέχθησαν] + μεγάλως, C D (μέγως) 614 1799 2412 syr^h with * cop^sa) by the church and the apostles and the elders, having declared all that God had done with them. (5) But *those who had ordered them to go up to the elders* (ἐξανέστησαν δέ τινες τῶν] οἱ δὲ παραγγείλαντες αὐτοῖς ἀναβαίνειν πρὸς τοὺς πρεσβυτέρους ἐξανέστησαν (+ κατὰ τῶν ἀποστόλων, syr^hmg) λέγοντες τινες, D (syr^hmg) and omit subsequent λέγοντες), namely certain believers who belonged to the party of the Pharisees, rose up *(against the apostles),* and said, 'It is necessary to circumcise them, and to charge them to keep the law of Moses.'"

The Western form of text is obviously written from a different point of view from the B-text. In the latter certain unidentified persons "arranged" (ἔταξαν) for Paul and Barnabas, with others, to go from Antioch to Jerusalem; in the D-text, on the other hand, the envoys from Jerusalem "ordered" (παρήγγειλαν) Paul and others to go up to Jerusalem in order to give an account of themselves to the apostles and elders (ὅπως κριθῶσιν ἐπ᾽ αὐτοῖς). One cannot say, however, that the Western paraphrast was anti-Pauline, for not only does he describe the Jerusalem church's welcome to the apostles as *hearty* (ver. 4), but he displays no trace whatever of the animus against Paul that is so apparent in the circles represented by the later Clementine *Homilies,* where Paul appears as ἐχθρὸς ἄνθρωπος. The most that can be said is that the B-text reflects the point of view of Paul, whereas the D-text is more sympathetic to the local tradition of the church at Jerusalem. It should be noted that in ver. 1 the Western text makes the demands still more sweeping by adding "*and walk* according to the custom of Moses." Likewise, the designation in ver. 1 of the brethren arriving from Judea as former Pharisees is drawn from ver. 5, where perhaps it was intended that the clause should be omitted.

In ver. 2 αὐτοῖς (after παρήγγειλαν), which Ropes says "is not easily explained," appears to be a clear example of the Semitic proleptic pronoun.

15.4 ἀπό

The more Semitic ἀπό of agent (B C 36ᵃ 94 307 326 431 1175), a construction that appears elsewhere in Acts (e. g. 2.22; 15.33; 20.9), was replaced (perhaps under the influence of ver. 3) by the more classical ὑπό (𝔓⁷⁴ ℵ A D E H L P most minuscules).

15.6 πρεσβύτεροι {A}

After πρεσβύτεροι 614 1799 2412 syrʰ add the words σὺν τῷ πλήθει ("with the congregation"). The gloss was probably suggested by verses 12 and 22, where reference is made to "the assembly" and "the whole church."

15.7 ἀναστὰς Πέτρος {A}

In order to enhance the solemnity of the occasion and the authority of the apostle Peter's speech,[1] several Western witnesses add, before or after Πέτρος, "in the (Holy) Spirit" (ἐν πνεύματι, D; + ἁγίῳ 614 1799 2412 syrʰᵐᵍ); see also the comment on 15.12. The scribe of 𝔓⁴⁵ has amplified the text by repeating information from 15.2.

15.9 οὐθέν

During the Christian era the less usual form was οὐθέν.[2] Copyists would therefore be inclined to change it to οὐδέν.

---

[1] Cf. C. M. Martini, S.J., "Le figura di Pietro secondo le varianti del codice D negli Atti degli Apostoli," *San Pietro* (= *Atti della XIX Settimana Biblica*; Brescia [1967]), pp. 279–289.

[2] See Henry St John Thackeray, *A Grammar of the Old Testament in Greek* (Cambridge, 1909), pp. 58–62; Moulton-Howard, *Grammar*, pp. 111 f.; Moulton-Milligan, *Vocabulary, s.v.* οὐθείς.

15.12 Ἐσίγησεν δέ {A}

Perhaps in order to enhance the prestige of Peter (see the comment on 15.7), several Western witnesses (D syr^(h with *) Ephraem) add at the beginning of the verse the words συνκατατεθεμένων δὲ τῶν πρεσβυτέρων τοῖς ὑπὸ τοῦ Πέτρου εἰρημένοις ("And when the elders assented to what had been spoken by Peter").

15.16 κατεσκαμμένα

Instead of κατεσκαμμένα (A C D E L P (σκα- H) (ἀνεσκ- E) most minuscules), several witnesses (ℵ (-ρεμ- B) 33 61 104 326 915) read κατεστραμμένα. The Septuagint text of Am 9.11 f., which is quoted here, also presents a variant reading involving the same word; A^c Q* read κατεστραμμένα and B Q^a read κατεσκαμμένα. The verb κατασκάπτειν occurs elsewhere in the New Testament only at Ro 11.3. A majority of the Committee preferred the rarer verb, supported as it is by representatives of the Alexandrian and the Western texts.

15.17-18 ταῦτα γνωστὰ ἀπ' αἰῶνος {B}

Since the quotation from Am 9.12 ends with ταῦτα, the concluding words are James's comment. The reading γνωστὰ ἀπ' αἰῶνος, however, is so elliptical an expression that copyists made various attempts to recast the phrase, rounding it out as an independent sentence.

15.20, 29; 21.25

The text of the Apostolic Decree, as it is called, is given at 15.29; it is referred to proleptically in 15.20 and retrospectively in 21.25. The three verses contain many problems concerning text and exegesis: (1) Are Gentiles commanded to abstain from four things (food offered to idols, blood, strangled meat, and unchastity) or from three (omitting either strangled meat or unchastity); and (2) are the three or four prohibitions entirely ceremonial, or entirely ethical, or a combination of both kinds?

(a) The Alexandrian text, as well as most other witnesses, has four items of prohibition.

(b) The Western text omits "what is strangled" and adds a negative form of the Golden Rule in 15.20 and 29.

(c) Several witnesses omit "unchastity" from 15.20 (so 𝔓⁴⁵ [which unfortunately is not extant for 15.29 or 21.25] and eth) and from 15.29 (so Origen, *contra Celsum,* VIII.29, as well as vgᵐˢ Vigilius and Gaudentius).

The occasion for issuing the Apostolic Decree, it should be observed, was to settle the question whether Gentile converts to Christianity should be required to submit to the rite of circumcision and fulfill other Mosaic statutes. The Council decided that such observance was not required for salvation; at the same time, however, in order to avoid giving unnecessary offense to Jewish Christians (and to Jews contemplating becoming Christians), the Council asked Gentile converts to make certain concessions for prudential reasons, abstaining from those acts that would offend Jewish scruples and hinder social intercourse, including joint participation in the Lord's Supper.

As concerns transcriptional probabilities, $τῆς πορνείας$ may have been omitted because this item seemed, superficially, to be out of place in what otherwise appeared to be a food law. Although such a consideration may well account for its absence, it is possible that what was intended by the Jerusalem Council was to warn the Gentile believers to avoid either marriage within the prohibited Levitical degrees (Lv 18.6-18), which the rabbis described as "forbidden for $πορνεία$," or mixed marriages with pagans (Nu 25.1; also compare 2 Cor 6.14), or participation in pagan worship, which had long been described by Old Testament prophets as spiritual adultery and which, in fact, offered opportunity in many temples for religious prostitution.

Another way to make sure that the list deals entirely with ritual prohibitions is to remove $πορνείας$ by emending the text. Bentley,[3] for example, conjectured that the Apostolic Decree was an injunction to abstain "from pollutions of idols and *swine's* flesh $(χοιρείας)$ and things strangled and from blood." A similar conjecture, intended to

---

[3] So A. A. Ellis in *Bentleii Critica Sacra* (1862), p. 25, quoted by J. Rendel Harris, *Side-Lights on New Testament Research* (London, 1908), p. 188.

produce the same dietetic interpretation, is to read πορκείας[4] instead of πορνείας. But there is no known example of such a word in Greek, and if an example were found it would be an abstract noun (from πόρκος) meaning "piggishness."[5]

Concerning (b), it is obvious that the threefold prohibition (lacking τοῦ πνικτοῦ) refers to moral injunctions to refrain from idolatry, unchastity, and blood-shedding (or murder), to which is added the negative Golden Rule. But this reading can scarcely be original, for it implies that a special warning had to be given to Gentile converts against such sins as murder, and that this was expressed in the form of asking them to "abstain" from it – which is slightly absurd!

It therefore appears to be more likely that an original ritual prohibition against eating foods offered to idols, things strangled and blood, and against πορνεία (however this latter is to be interpreted) was altered into a moral law by dropping the reference to πνικτοῦ and by adding the negative Golden Rule, than to suppose that an original moral law was transformed into a food law.

The alternative to accepting the fourfold decree is to argue, as P. H. Menoud has done,[6] that the original text involved a twofold prohibition, namely to abstain from pollutions of idols and from blood, and that to this basic decree respecting *kosher* foods, 𝔓[45] *al* added "and from what is strangled," thus extending the food-law concerning blood to all flesh improperly slaughtered. In the Western tradition the twofold decree was understood to be a moral injunction relating to idolatry and murder, and these witnesses added the prohibition against another major sin, unchastity. Subsequently the injunction concerning the negative Golden Rule was appended to the Western text, which thus extends the moral application far beyond the three

---

[4] Who first proposed the emendation is not known; it found champions in such diverse persons as William E. Gladstone and Joseph Halévy – indeed, the latter unguardedly gives the impression that it is actually found in manuscripts of Acts (*Revue Sémitique,* x [1902], pp. 238 f.).

[5] J. U. Powell's verdict in his article, "On the suggestion πόρκεια in the Acts of the Apostles, xv, 20, 29," is that (quoting the words of F. W. Farrar), "There is not the faintest atom of probability in it" (*Classical Review,* XXXIII [1919], p. 152).

[6] "The Western Text and the Theology of Acts," *Bulletin* of the Studiorum Novi Testamenti Societas, II (1951), pp. 22–28.

basic prohibitions. Finally, the text of the great mass of witnesses represents a conflation of several Western expansions of the basic twofold decree.

Attractive though this theory is on the surface, the textual evidence is not really susceptible of such an interpretation. First, there is no manuscript evidence for the hypothetical twofold decree. Menoud does indeed shrink from pressing his conjecture concerning the two-fold decree, and is prepared, with Lagrange, to adopt the reading of $\mathfrak{P}^{45}$ as the original text.[7] But such an alternative proposal leaves the text critic with exactly the same problems that confronted him before, namely, how to explain the deletion as well as the addition of certain items in the decree.

Secondly, the fact that in 15.20 πνικτοῦ precedes καὶ τοῦ αἵματος is hardly compatible with the theory that it was added in order to clarify and extend the meaning of αἵματος.

In conclusion, therefore, it appears that the least unsatisfactory solution of the complicated textual and exegetical problems of the Apostolic Decree is to regard the fourfold decree as original (foods offered to idols, strangled meat, eating blood, and unchastity – whether ritual or moral), and to explain the two forms of the threefold decree in some such way as those suggested above.[8]

An extensive literature exists on the text and exegesis of the Apostolic Decree. For what can be said in support of the Western text see, e. g., A. Hilgenfeld, "Das Apostel-Concil nach seinem ursprüng-lichen Wortlaut," *Zeitschrift für wissenschaftliche Theologie*, XLII (1899), pp. 138–149; Gotthold Resch, *Das Aposteldecret nach seiner*

---

[7] "If our conjecture about the original text appears to be too hazardous, this text of $\mathfrak{P}^{45}$ can be regarded as the original," *op. cit.,* p. 24, with a reference to M.-J. Lagrange, in *Revue Biblique,* XLIII (1934), p. 168, and *La Critique textuelle* (Paris, 1935), p. 414.

[8] An ingenious attempt to solve the problem by proposing that *both* the Alexandrian and the Western readings are, in a certain sense, original was made by Karl Six, S.J., who asks, "Could not James, who according to tradition was more legalistic than the rest, have included the prohibition of πνικτόν in his proposal, while in the composi-tion of the letter it was omitted, either in the interest of conciseness or because it seemed to be comprehended in the prohibition of blood?" (*Das Aposteldekret (Act 15, 28.29). Seine Entstehung und Geltung in den ersten vier Jahrhunderten* [Innsbruck, 1912], p. 18). The difficulty with this theoretical solution is that it is unsupported by the evidence of the manuscripts in 15.20 and 29.

ausserkanonischen Textgestalt (Texte und Untersuchungen, N.F. XIII,
3; Leipzig, 1905); A. von Harnack, *Beiträge zur Einleitung in das
Neue Testament,* III (1908), pp. 188–198, and IV (1911), *The Acts of
the Apostles* (London, 1909), pp. 248–263; K. Lake, *The Earlier
Epistles of St. Paul, their Motive and Origin* (London, 1911), pp.
48–60; *idem, The Beginnings of Christianity,* vol. V, pp. 205–209;
J. H. Ropes, *The Text of Acts,* pp. 265–269; A. C. Clark, *The Acts of
the Apostles,* pp. 360–361; Thorleif Boman, "Das textkritische
Problem des sogenannten Aposteldekrets," *Novum Testamentum,* VII
(1964), pp. 26–36.

Those who have argued in support of the fourfold decree[9] include
Theodor Zahn, *Introduction to the New Testament,* III (Edinburgh,
1909), pp. 18–22; *idem, Die Apostelgeschichte des Lucas* (Leipzig
and Erlangen, 1921), pp. 523 ff.; William Sanday, "The Apostolic
Decree (Acts XV. 20–29)," *Theologische Studien Theodor Zahn …
dargebracht* (Leipzig, 1908), pp. 317–338; *idem,* "The Text of the
Apostolic Decree (Acts XV.29)," *Expositor,* Eighth Series, VI (1913),
pp. 289–305; E. Jacquier, *Les Actes des Apôtres* (Paris, 1926), pp.
455–458; Hans Lietzmann, "Der Sinn des Aposteldekretes und seine
Textwandlung," in *Amicitiae corolla, a Volume of Essays Presented
to James Rendel Harris,* ed. by H. G. Wood (London, 1933), pp.
203–211; W. G. Kümmel, "Die älteste Form des Aposteldekrets,"
Spiritus et veritas [Festschrift Carlo Kundziņš] (Eutin, 1953), pp.
83–98; E. Haenchen, *Die Apostelgeschichte, ad loc.*; Marcel Simon,
"The Apostolic Decree and its Setting in the Ancient Church,"
Bulletin of the John Rylands Library, LII (1969–70), pp. 437–460;
C. M. Martini, "Il Decreto del Concilio di Gerusalemme," *Atti della
XXII Settimana Biblica* (Brescia, 1973), pp. 345–355; C. K. Barrett,
Australian Biblical Review, XXXV (1987), pp. 50–59.

15.20   καὶ τῆς πορνείας {A}

See the preceeding comments.

---

[9] According to Jacques Dupont, "Present day scholarship is practically unanimous
in considering the 'Eastern' text of the decree as the only authentic text (in four items)
and in interpreting its prescriptions in a sense not ethical but ritual," *Les problèmes du
Livre des Actes d'après les travaux récents* (Louvain, 1950), p. 70.

15.20 καὶ τοῦ πνικτοῦ {C}

See the preceding comments.

15.20 αἵματος {A}

See the preceding comments.[10]

It is of historical interest that according to Aelius Lampridius, the biographer of Severus Alexander (A.D. 222–235), the Emperor "would often exclaim what he had heard from someone, either a Jew or a Christian, and always remembered, and he also had it announced by a herald whenever he was disciplining anyone, 'What you do not wish to be done to you, do not do to another.' And so highly did he value this sentiment that he had it inscribed on the Palace and on public buildings."[11]

15.22 Βαρσαββᾶν

In estimating the standard of accuracy displayed by the scribe of codex Bezae one must take into account the transforming of Βαρσαββᾶν into Βαραββᾶν here and into Βαρνάβαν in 1.23.

15.23 ἀδελφοί {B}

The addition of καὶ οἱ before ἀδελφοί appears to be an emendation made in order to avoid what in Greek is a somewhat harsh

---

[10] On the negative Golden Rule, see G. B. King, "The 'Negative' Golden Rule," *Journal of Religion,* VIII (1928), pp. 268–279, and XV (1935), pp. 59–62; L. J. Philippides, *Die "Goldene Regel" religionsgeschichtlich untersucht* (Leipzig, 1929), and *Religionswissenschaftliche Forschungsberichte über die Goldene Regel* (Athens, 1933); A. Dihle, *Die Goldene Regel, eine Einführung in die Geschichte der antiken und frühchristlichen Vulgärethik* (Göttingen, 1962); and Johannes Straub, *Heidnische Geschichtsapologetik in der christlichen Spätantike,* chap. iv "Die Goldene Regel" (Bonn, 1963), pp. 106–124.

[11] *Scriptores Historiae Augustae,* Severus Alexander, LI,7–8: Clamabatque saepius, quod a quibusdam sive Iudaeis sive Christianis audierat et tenebat, idque per praeconem, cum aliquem emendaret, dici iubebat: quod tibi non vis, alteri ne feceris. quam sententiam usque adeo dilexit, ut et in Palatio et in publicis operibus perscribi iuberet.

apposition of ἀδελφοί with both οἱ ἀπόστολοι and οἱ πρεσβύτεροι.[12] The omission of the word by a few witnesses may be accidental due to similar endings.

15.24 [ἐξελθόντες] {C}

Despite the possibility that ἐξελθόντες was added, either under
the influence of Ga 2.12 or "to guard against the appearances that
τινὲς ἐξ ἡμῶν belonged to the senders of the letter" (Knowling, *ad
loc.*), a majority of the Committee was impressed by the weight of
external evidence in support of its inclusion in the text. To represent
the equivocal evidence, however, it was thought best to enclose the
word within square brackets.

15.24 ὑμῶν {A}

The expansion, which, though absent from D, is probably part
of the original Western text, appears to be an addition derived from
verses 1 and 5 and inserted here in order to specify in what particulars
the Judaizers had sought to trouble the Antiochian Christians. The
interpolation passed into the Textus Receptus.

Other witnesses add still further details; Chrysostom, for example,
read λέγοντες περιτέμνειν αὐτοὺς τὰ τέκνα καὶ τηρεῖν τὸν
νόμον, and after νόμον the Old Georgian adds "of Moses."

15.25 ἐκλεξαμένοις {C}

It is difficult to decide whether ἐκλεξαμένους was corrected to
the dative for grammatical reasons, or whether ἐκλεξαμένοις was
altered to the accusative to accord with the prevailing text of ver. 22.
On the basis of what was considered superior manuscript evidence a
majority of the Committee preferred the reading ἐκλεξαμένοις, a

---

[12] In Aramaic, however, such apposition is entirely idiomatic; see C. C. Torrey, *The
Composition and Date of Acts*, p. 39. The translation "and the elder brethren" in the
Revised Version of 1881, taking πρεσβύτεροι as an adjective, is inadmissible (see H.
Hyman, *Classical Review*, III [1889], pp. 73 f.), and was not followed by the American
Standard Version of 1901.

reading that one member of the Committee preferred for ver. 22 also (where the dative is read by 𝔓⁷⁴ 33 206 242 614 630 642* 945 1704 1739 1891).

15.26

At the close of the verse the Western text (D E 614 1799 2412 syr^hmg) adds εἰς πάντα πειρασμόν ("they risked their lives for the sake of our Lord Jesus Christ *in every trial*"). The addition was probably prompted, as Lake and Cadbury remark *(ad loc.),* by the fact that παραδοῦναι τὴν ψυχήν is not usually applied to a man who is still alive. The gloss may be a reminiscence of 20.19 (so B. Weiss)[13] or of Sirach 2.1 ἑτοίμασον τὴν ψυχήν σου εἰς πειρασμόν (so J. Rendel Harris).[14]

15.28 τούτων τῶν ἐπάναγκες

The difficulty of the Greek τούτων τῶν ἐπάναγκες (ℵ^c B C H 69 81 429 436 611 614 1799 2412 *al*) prompted the alteration to the easier sequence of τῶν ἐπάναγκες τούτων (E L P most minuscules, followed by the Textus Receptus). The reading τῶν ἐπάναγκες (A 76 94 307 431) probably arose through the accidental omission of τούτων. Whether τούτων ἐπάναγκες (ℵ* D 33) arose from haplography or whether τῶν came into the other readings by dittography is uncertain, but the former is perhaps slightly more probable.

15.29 καὶ πνικτῶν {B}

The plural number was assimilated to the singular in ver. 20. Concerning the omission, see the comments on ver. 20.

15.29 καὶ πορνείας {A}

See the comments on ver. 20.

---

[13] *Der Codex D* (Leipzig, 1897), p. 82.
[14] *Four Lectures on the Western Text of the New Testament* (London, 1894), pp. 85 f.

15.29   πράξετε {A}

The future tense is to be preferred on grounds of both external evidence and transcriptional probability. The addition in the Western text, "being borne along by the Holy Spirit" (for the sense compare Php 3.15), reminds one of similar interpolated references to the Holy Spirit.[15] Whether it arose among Montanists, who would naturally desire some reference to the Paraclete, or whether it is a misplaced gloss that was intended to explain ἀπολυθέντες (ver. 30),[16] or whether it is merely a pious expansion to give a specifically Christian turn to an otherwise secular close of the apostolic letter, which was inspired by the Holy Spirit (ver. 28), it is difficult to decide.

15.30   ἀπολυθέντες

After ἀπολυθέντες D^{gr*} it^d add ἐν ἡμέραις ὀλίγαις, which Blass, followed by Belser, takes to reflect the joyous speed with which they carry the letter to Antioch, in contrast to the more leisurely journey from Antioch to Jerusalem (ver. 3). On the other hand, however, Weiss interprets it not of the time consumed in the journey, but of the time of their departure, i. e. shortly after the close of the council they returned to put an end to the troubles at Antioch (compare ver. 24).[17]

15.32   ὄντες

After ὄντες codex Bezae, with its characteristic interest in the Holy Spirit,[18] adds πλήρεις πνεύματος ἁγίου ("who were themselves prophets *filled with the Holy Spirit*").

---

[15] See, for example, the list in Group *D* in the footnote on p. 226 above.

[16] Thus J. Rendel Harris (*Four Lectures on the Western Text,* p. 77), who translates, "So they were led by the Holy Spirit and came down to Antioch."

[17] *Der Codex D* (Leipzig, 1897), p. 82.

[18] See the Western text of 15.7, 29; 19.1; 20.3, and cf. E. J. Epp, *The Theological Tendency of Codex Bezae Cantabrigiensis in Acts* (Cambridge, 1966), pp. 68–70, 116–118, and other pages cited in the index, *s.v.* "Holy Spirit."

15.33   πρὸς τοὺς ἀποστείλαντας αὐτούς

Instead of πρὸς τοὺς ἀποστείλαντας αὐτούς (𝔓⁷⁴ ℵ A B C D vg cop^{sa, bo} *al*) the Textus Receptus, following H L P S many minuscules syr^{p, h} cop^{bo} arm eth^{ro} Bede^{acc. to Greek mss}, reads πρὸς τοὺς ἀποστόλους. The latter appears to be a deliberate alteration introduced by copyists in order to bring the apostolate into greater prominence.

15.34   *omit verse* {A}

The later Greek text, followed by the Textus Receptus, reads, "But it seemed good to Silas to remain there" (several manuscripts, including C, read αὐτούς for αὐτοῦ, i. e. "But it seemed good to Silas that they should remain"). Codex Bezae presents a still more expanded reading, "But it seemed good to Silas that they remain, and Judas journeyed alone."

The insertion, whether in the longer or the shorter version, was no doubt made by copyists to account for the presence of Silas at Antioch in ver. 40.

15.38

Codex Bezae has expanded the sentence with additional clauses, which, however, considerably weaken the force of the B-text (which closes with τοῦτον in a most emphatic position): Παῦλος δὲ οὐκ ἐβούλετο, λέγων τὸν ἀποστ<ατ>ήσαντα ἀπ᾽ αὐτῶν ἀπὸ Παμφυλίας καὶ μὴ συνελθόντα εἰς τὸ ἔργον εἰς ὃ ἐπέμφθησαν τοῦτον μὴ εἶναι σὺν αὐτοῖς ("But Paul *was not willing, saying that* one who had withdrawn from them in Pamphylia, and had not gone with them to the work *for which they had been sent, should not be with them*").

15.40   κυρίου {B}

Instead of κυρίου, which is strongly attested by both Alexandrian and Western evidence (𝔓⁷⁴ ℵ A B D 33 61 81 326 441 vg cop^{sa}), other witnesses, some of them ancient (𝔓⁴⁵ C H L P most minuscules syr^{p, h} cop^bo arm *al*), read θεοῦ. The latter reading appears to be a scribal assimilation to 14.26.

15.41 τὰς ἐκκλησίας {A}

At the close of the verse codex Bezae adds the supplementary clause παραδιδοὺς τὰς ἐντολὰς τῶν πρεσβυτέρων ("delivering [to them] the commands of the elders"). This is expanded still further in syr^hmg, with support from several Latin Vulgate manuscripts, "… commands of the *apostles and* elders." Both additions, which contribute nothing new, make quite explicit what anyone could deduce from the previous narrative and what is expressly stated in 16.4.

16.1

The Western text (D it^gig vg^mss syr^hmg Cassiodorus), continuing its expansion of the last verse of the preceding chapter, reads διελθὼν δὲ τὰ ἔθνη ταῦτα κατήντησεν εἰς Δέρβην καὶ Λύστραν ("And having passed through these nations he came to Derbe and Lystra"). The effect of the addition is to show that Lystra and Derbe were not included in Syria and Cilicia mentioned in the previous verse.

16.3 ὅτι Ἕλλην ὁ πατὴρ αὐτοῦ

The Textus Receptus, following 𝔓^45vid D E H L P most minuscules syr^p, h arm Chrysostom *al*, reads τὸν πατέρα αὐτοῦ ὅτι Ἕλλην, whereas 𝔓^74 ℵ A B C Ψ 33 61 69 81 307 441 467 1739 1891 1898 cop^sa, bo *al* read ὅτι Ἕλλην ὁ πατὴρ αὐτοῦ. A majority of the Committee was of the opinion that the reading that found its way into the Textus Receptus is an intentional transposition into the usual mode of expression by attraction (Blass-Debrunner-Funk, § 408). If the reading of 𝔓^74 ℵ A B 33 81 1739 *al* were a resolution of the attraction, Ἕλλην would not have been placed first.

16.4

The Western text (D syr^hmg Ephraem) expands the first part of the verse, reading διερχόμενοι δὲ τὰς πόλεις ἐκήρυσσον [καὶ παρεδίδοσαν αὐτοῖς, so D, spoiling the syntax] μετὰ πάσης παρρησίας τὸν κύριον Ἰησοῦν Χριστὸν ἅμα παραδιδόντες καὶ τὰς ἐντολὰς ἀποστόλων καί ... ("And while going through the cities *they preached [and delivered to them], with all boldness, the Lord Jesus Christ,* delivering *at the same time also* the commandments of the apostles and ..."). It may well be that, as Weiss suggests,[1] the addition was made in order to provide an explanation for the growth of the church, described in ver. 5.

16.6 τὴν Φρυγίαν καὶ Γαλατικὴν χώραν

The Textus Receptus, following E H L P and most minuscules, reads τὴν Φρυγίαν καὶ τὴν Γαλατικὴν χώραν. Although Kirsopp Lake, in discussing the textual evidence of this passage, overstated the case ("A reading found in the later MSS., but in neither the Neutral nor the Western text, has no claim to be considered"),[2] the Committee gave careful consideration to the later text, only to decide that there was no reason to abandon the combined testimony of $\mathfrak{P}^{74}$ ℵ A B C D *al*, despite the fact that, as Bruce points out, "there is no direct evidence elsewhere for the adjectival use of Φρυγία."[3]

16.6 τὸν λόγον

The addition by the Western text of τοῦ θεοῦ (D it^gig syr^p cop^bo eth Ephraem Speculum) after τὸν λόγον is obviously a secondary modification.

16.7 Ἰησοῦ {A}

The expression τὸ πνεῦμα Ἰησοῦ ($\mathfrak{P}^{74}$ ℵ A B C² D E 33 69 81* 326 467 vg syr^p, h cop^bo arm^mss), which appears nowhere else in the New Testament, is so unusual that various attempts were made to modify it, such as replacing Ἰησοῦ with κυρίου (C* it^gig *al*) or with

---

[1] B. Weiss, *Der Codex D*, p. 84.

[2] *The Beginnings of Christianity*, vol. v, p. 228.

[3] F. F. Bruce, *The Acts of the Apostles* (1951), p. 310.

τὸ ἅγιον (arm^mss Epiphanius), or omitting the modifier altogether (H L P 81^c and most minuscules cop^sa arm^mss Ephraem Chrysostom *al*, followed by the Textus Receptus). One Armenian manuscript known to Zohrab reads, "the Spirit of Christ," which he adopted as text in his two editions (the text of the American Bible Society's edition of the Armenian New Testament reads "the Spirit of Jesus").

16.8 παρελθόντες

The Western reading, "passing through Mysia" (διελθόντες, D it^gig vg syr^h, instead of παρελθόντες), is distinctly the easier reading, for the ordinary sense of παρελθεῖν, "to pass alongside," does not fit the context, which requires something like "passing by" in the sense of neglecting. It seems unlikely, as Knowling observes, "that διελθ., a common word, should have been changed to παρελθ. – the converse is far more probable."[4]

16.9 ὅραμα

In view of the external attestation (all witnesses except D^gr it^e syr^p Irenaeus) as well as intrinsic probability (elsewhere in Acts Luke says "saw a vision"), a majority of the Committee had no hesitancy in preferring ὅραμα. Codex Bezae (supported in part by other Western witnesses) alters the structure of the verse: καὶ ἐν ὁράματι διὰ νυκτὸς ὤφθη τῷ Παύλῳ ὡσεὶ ἀνὴρ Μακεδών τις ἑστὼς κατὰ πρόσωπον αὐτοῦ παρακαλῶν καὶ λέγων ... ("And *in* a vision in the night there appeared to Paul, *as it were* a man of Macedonia, standing *before his face*, beseeching and saying ..."). See also the following comments.

16.9 ἀνήρ

Against all other witnesses D syr^p cop^sa and Ephraem read ὡσεὶ ἀνήρ. Although ὡσεί appears to be something of a favorite with

---

[4] R. J. Knowling, *The Expositor's Greek Testament, ad loc.*

Luke (15 of its 21 occurrences in the New Testament are in Luke-Acts), a majority of the Committee considered it more likely that the qualifying word would have been added than deleted in the present passage.

16.9 ἀνήρ Μακεδών τις ἦν

A majority of the Committee judged that the combination of $\mathfrak{P}^{74}$ ℵ A B C D² 33 69 81 1739 *al* could not be set aside in favor of the witnesses supporting any of the other variant readings, namely (1) ἀνὴρ Μακεδών τις D* E 209* 1311; (2) ἀνήρ τις Μακεδὼν ἦν 630 (om. τις 431 1891) syrʰ arm; and (3) ἀνήρ τις ἦν Μακεδών H L P and most minuscules.

16.9 ἑστώς

Although the expression κατὰ πρόσωπον αὐτοῦ occurs in the New Testament only in Luke-Acts (Lk 2.31; Ac 3.13; 25.16), a majority of the Committee agreed with Corssen[5] in judging that it had been added here by the Western reviser (D 257 383 614 syrʰ ᵂⁱᵗʰ * copˢᵃ) in the interest of clarity of description.

16.10

Codex Bezae, supported in part by copˢᵃ, recasts the verse to read, διεγερθεὶς οὖν διηγήσατο τὸ ὅραμα ἡμῖν, καὶ ἐνοήσαμεν ὅτι προσκέκληται ἡμᾶς ὁ κύριος εὐαγγελίσασθαι τοὺς ἐν τῇ Μακεδονίᾳ ("*When therefore he had risen up, he related to us the vision,* and we perceived that *the Lord* had called us to preach the gospel to *those who were in Macedonia*"). The purpose of the banal addition is clear enough: the reviser wanted to make sure that the reader will understand how it was that Paul's companions knew what he had seen in the vision – Paul told them!

---

[5] *Göttingische gelehrte Anzeigen*, 1896, pp. 436 f.

16.10   θεός {B}

Since internal considerations offer no decisive help in choosing between the variant readings, the Committee preferred to rely upon the strong combination of 𝔓⁷⁴ ℵ A B C 33 81 *al*.

16.11   ἀναχθέντες δέ {B}

It is easy to understand how, at the beginning of a new section, δέ (𝔓⁷⁴ ℵ A (D) E 33 51 69 81 181 326 441 467 1898 vg syr^hmg cop^bo Chrysostom) was replaced by οὖν (B C H L most minuscules syr^htxt cop^sa arm Irenaeus^lat). The Western text (D 257 383 614 2147 syr^hmg), in the light of its revision of ver. 10 (see above), leaves nothing to the reader's imagination and reads τῇ δὲ ἐπαύριον ἀναχθέντες (D* ἀχθ-), thus showing the alacrity with which Paul and his companions responded to the Macedonian call.

16.11   Νέαν Πόλιν

The Textus Receptus, following C D* E H L P *al*, reads Νεά-πολιν, whereas 𝔓⁷⁴ ℵ A B D² 467 1175 1739 1838 *al* read Νέαν Πόλιν. A majority of the Committee preferred to adopt the classical usage, witnessed also in inscriptions, and to spell the name in two words.

16.12   πρώτη[ς] μερίδος τῆς {D}

The oldest form of text in the extant Greek witnesses appears to be πρώτη τῆς μερίδος Μακεδονίας πόλις, "a first city of the district of Macedonia." Hort denied that μερίς could ever denote a geographical division, and for this, and other reasons, regarded the passage as primitively corrupt. Subsequent to Hort, however, examples of such a geographical usage have turned up in papyri, in an inscription, and in late writers.[6] But what is the meaning of πρώτη? (1) Against the translation "chief" city (AV) is the fact that not Philip-

---

[6] See Moulton and Milligan, *Vocabulary, s.v.,* and p. xvi.

pi but Thessalonica was acknowledged to be the chief city of Macedonia and Amphipolis the chief city of the district in which Philippi was situated. (2) Some have suggested that the author means that Philippi was the first Macedonian city to which Paul and his companions came in that district. But as a matter of fact the apostle first set foot in Neapolis, which apparently belonged to the same district as Philippi. Furthermore, apart from questions of geography one may well wonder why, on this interpretation of the meaning of πρώτη, Luke should have wished to call attention to something so inconsequential to his narrative. (3) In view of the use of πρώτη as a title of honor (found on coins of Pergamum and Smyrna as well as in inscriptions referring to Thessalonica), Lake and Cadbury translate the passage, "Philippi, which is a first city of the district of Macedonia, a colony." In their comments, however, they point out that as a definite title the word has been found so far only in the cases of cities that were members of a κοινόν (league or union) in their particular province, and were not Roman colonies at the time. Since Philippi does not qualify in either respect, they conclude that it is more probable that "the meaning of πρώτη in this passage is simply 'a leading city'" (the rendering subsequently adopted by the RSV).

The difficulties involved in the reading πρώτη led to attempts at correction in other branches of the tradition. Among these, however, πρώτη μερίς is impossible because a city cannot be called a μερίς. The omission of τῆς μερίδος results in calling Philippi πρώτη τῆς Μακεδονίας πόλις, which merely increases the problem, as does also the curious replacement of πρώτη by κεφαλή, which is generally explained as a Latinism (rendering *caput*) or which may suggest influence from Syriac, where ܪܫܝ means both "head" and "foremost."[7]

Dissatisfied for various reasons with all these readings in Greek witnesses, a majority of the Committee preferred to adopt the conjecture proposed by a number of scholars from Le Clerc to Blass and

---

[7] See G. Zuntz, "Textual Criticism of Some Passages of the Acts of the Apostles," *Classica et Mediaevalia*, III (1940), pp. 36 f. A. C. Clark argues that κεφαλή can have the meaning "extremity," "apex," or "frontiertown"; see *The Acts of the Apostles* (Oxford, 1933), pp. 363 ff.

Turner,[8] namely to read πρώτης for πρώτη τῆς, with the resultant meaning, "a city of the first district of Macedonia." Those who adopt this conjecture usually explain the origin of the commonly received text (πρώτη τῆς μερίδος) as due either (a) to the accidental reduplication of the letters τη, or (b) to a misunderstanding of the correction if by mistake a copyist had written πρώτη and then -της were written over it to correct it. (The reading πρώτης μερίδος is paralleled by *primae partis* found in three late Vulgate manuscripts, but it is doubtful whether this versional reading represents an original Greek witness or whether it originated within the Latin tradition.) At the same time, in order to take into account the overwhelming manuscript evidence supporting πρώτη, the majority decided to enclose the final sigma of πρώτης within square brackets.

[Despite what have been regarded as insuperable difficulties involved in the commonly received text (πρώτη τῆς μερίδος), it appears ill-advised to abandon the testimony of 𝔓[74] ℵ A C 81 *al*, especially since the phrase can be taken to mean merely that Philippi was "a leading city of the district of Macedonia"; cf. Bauer's *Griechisch-Deutsches Wörterbuch,* 6te Aufl. (1988), *s.v.* μερίς. K.A. and B.M.M.]

16.13   ἐνομίζομεν προσευχήν {C}

In view of the wide range of variables in lexicography, syntax, palaeography, and textual attestation, the difficulties presented by this verse are well-nigh baffling.

Was ἐνομίζετο, supported by the later Byzantine text, original and subsequently altered, as Ropes argued, in order to avoid the less usual sense of the verb (ἐνομίζετο = "according to custom"; ἐνομίζομεν = "we thought"; ἐδόκει = "it seemed")? How shall the following προσευχή[ν] be spelled and construed? The nominative as subject of an impersonal verb, though not impossible, is certainly not as common as the accusative, especially with εἶναι following. Furthermore,

---

[8] See C. H. Turner, "Philippi," in Hastings's *Dictionary of the Bible,* vol. III, p. 838, col. a.

in the uncial book-hand it is perfectly possible to take προσευχή as dative case, "to be at prayer." Finally, the textual critic is confronted with the bewildering diversity of variant readings of the early uncial manuscripts, as well as by the perplexing circumstance that what is good external support for προσευχή is relatively poor as regards the previous word.

Changing μ to ν Blass *(ad loc.)* conjectured that the original read οὗ ἐνόμιζον ἐν προσευχῇ εἶναι, "where they were accustomed to be at prayer" (cf. Blass-Debrunner-Funk, § 397, 2).

Faced with these difficulties the Committee decided that the least unsatisfactory solution was to print ἐνομίζομεν προσευχὴν εἶναι, even though A² and Ψ appear to be the only uncials that give precisely this reading. It was felt, however, that the manifestly erroneous reading ἐνόμιζεν of 𝔓⁷⁴ ℵ probably testifies to an earlier ἐνομίζομεν, and that προσευχή in 𝔓⁷⁴ A B may have resulted from accidental omission of the horizontal stroke over the η, signifying a final ν.

16.15 ὁ οἶκος

The Western text characteristically expands the narrative by adding πᾶς before ὁ οἶκος (D; compare *cum omnibus suis,* it^gig).

16.16 πύθωνα

The more difficult reading appears to be πύθωνα (𝔓⁷⁴ ℵ A B C* D* 81 326 1837 vg arm), which has been replaced in some manuscripts (𝔓⁴⁵ C³ D² E H L P most minuscules it^gig syr^hmg(gr)) by πύθωνος.

16.17 ὑμῖν {B}

The second person plural pronoun, which is more appropriate to the context, is supported by weighty evidence.

16.26 παραχρῆμα

In the opinion of a majority of the Committee the omission of παραχρῆμα from B it^gig Lucifer must be accidental. The word appears to be a favorite with Luke, occurring in fifteen other passages in Luke-Acts, and in the rest of the New Testament only twice.

16.27 ὁ δεσμοφύλαξ

After ὁ δεσμοφύλαξ several manuscripts, including 614 1799 and 2147, identify the jailer as ὁ πιστὸς Στεφανᾶς ("faithful Stephanas").

16.28 μεγάλῃ φωνῇ [ὁ] Παῦλος

The manuscripts present a wide variety of readings: (*a*) μεγάλῃ φωνῇ Παῦλος, 𝔓⁷⁴ Ψ itᵈ; (*b*) same as (*a*) but ὁ Παῦλος, A 1875 1898; (*c*) φωνῇ μεγάλῃ Παῦλος, ℵ C* 33; (*d*) same as (*c*) but ὁ Παῦλος, C³ Dᵍʳ E P most minuscules; (*e*) Παῦλος μεγάλῃ φωνῇ, B; (*f*) same as (*e*) but ὁ Παῦλος, 181 431 927; (*g*) ὁ Παῦλος φωνῇ μεγάλῃ, 36 180 629 itᵍⁱᵍ. The overwhelming weight of external evidence reads φωνῇ near ἐφώνησεν δέ. It appears that several copyists, disliking this Semitic type of construction, moved φωνῇ farther away from the verb. In view of the division of testimony for and against the presence of ὁ, it seemed best to include the word on the basis of the combined testimony of 𝔓⁷⁴ A Ψ 1875 1898 *al,* but to enclose it within square brackets.

16.29 προσέπεσεν

After προσέπεσεν the Western text (D* itᵈˑ ᵍⁱᵍ vgᶜˡ syrʰ ʷⁱᵗʰ ᵒᵇᵉˡᵘˢ copˢᵃˑ ᵇᵒ Lucifer Cassiodorus) introduces the natural supplement πρὸς τοὺς πόδας.

16.30 ἔξω

The Western text adds the detail that the jailer "secured the rest" of the prisoners before he addressed Paul and Silas (after ἔξω D syrʰ ʷⁱᵗʰ * read τοὺς λοιποὺς ἀσφαλισάμενος). Despite Sir William Ramsay's inclination to accept the addition as genuine, "suggestive of the orderly, well-disciplined character of the jailor,"[9] the great probability is that after an earthquake the average Near Eastern jailer was hardly likely to exhibit such a degree of discipline as either Ramsay or the Western glossator attributes to him!

16.32 τοῦ κυρίου {B}

Although Weiss argues that the reference in ver. 31 to the Lord Jesus influenced scribes to alter "the word of God" to "the word of the Lord,"[10] in view of the preponderant weight of external testimony the Committee preferred κυρίου. What Ropes describes as a special force residing in θεοῦ, which calls attention to the divine truth of the answer of ver. 31, so far from supporting the genuineness of θεοῦ, suggests rather the work of scribal refinement.

16.32 σύν

The Textus Receptus, following E H L P most minuscules, replaces σύν (𝔓⁷⁴ A B C D 33 36ᵃ 61 81 181 242 431 441 927 1837 1873 *al*) with καὶ, thus attaining greater simplicity, and paralleling σὺ καὶ ὁ οἶκος of the previous verse.

16.35 ἀπέστειλαν οἱ στρατηγοί {A}

In order to explain the sudden change of attitude on the part of the magistrates, who now entreat the apostles to leave, D syr^hmg Cassiodorus and Ephraem read, (35) ἡμέρας δὲ γενομένης συνῆλθον οἱ στρατηγοὶ ἐπὶ τὸ αὐτὸ εἰς τὴν ἀγορὰν καὶ ἀναμνησθέντες τὸν σεισμὸν τὸν γεγονότα ἐφοβήθησαν, καὶ ἀπέστειλαν τοὺς ῥαβδούχους λέγοντας ... ("But when it was day the magistrates *assembled together in the market place, and recollecting the earthquake that had taken place, they were afraid; and* sent the police, saying ...").

---

[9] *St. Paul the Traveller and the Roman Citizen*, p. 222.
[10] B. Weiss, *Die Apostelgeschichte, textkritische Untersuchungen und Textherstellung*, pp. 5–6.

16.35 ἐκείνους {A}

Here D 614 1799 2412 syrʰ add the rather superfluous clause οὓς ἐχθὲς παρέλαβες ("whom you took into custody yesterday").

16.36 ἐν εἰρήνῃ {A}

Although Ropes thought that ἐν εἰρήνῃ "is inappropriate in the mouth of a Greek jailer," a majority of the Committee did not regard such a consideration to be germane to the question whether Luke may not have thus described the words of farewell uttered by the newly converted jailer. The omission of the phrase from two manuscripts (D itᵍⁱᵍ) appears to be accidental.

16.36-38

Leaving nothing to the imagination of the reader, in ver. 36 codex Bezae reads καὶ εἰσελθὼν ὁ δεσμοφύλαξ ἀπήγγειλεν, while syrᵖ, still more circumstantial, reads καὶ ἀκούσας ὁ δεσμοφύλαξ εἰσελθὼν ἀπήγγειλεν. Similarly in ver. 38 codex Bezae is extremely pleonastic in reading ἀπήγγειλαν δὲ αὐτοῖσοι [sic] στρατηγοῖς οἱ ῥαβδοῦχοι τὰ ῥήματα ταῦτα τὰ ῥηθέντα πρὸς τοὺς στρατηγούς ... ("And the police reported to the magistrates *themselves* these words *which were spoken for the magistrates* ...").

In order to emphasize the innocence of Paul and Silas, and the desire of the magistrates to avoid an unpleasant case, in ver. 37 the Western reviser (D syrᵖ) substitutes ἀναιτίους ("innocent") for the unusual word ἀκατακρίτους ("uncondemned"), found only here and in 22.25.

16.39 ἐλθόντες ... τῆς πόλεως {A}

Verses 39 and 40 in codex Bezae, supported in part by 614 syrʰ ʷⁱᵗʰ * and Ephraem, read as follows: καὶ παραγενόμενοι μετὰ φίλων πολλῶν εἰς τὴν φυλακὴν παρεκάλεσαν αὐτοὺς ἐξελθεῖν εἰπόντες, Ἠγνοήσαμεν τὰ καθ' ὑμᾶς ὅτι ἐστὲ [D = ἔσται] ἄνδρες δίκαιοι. καὶ ἐξαγαγόντες παρεκάλεσαν αὐτοὺς λέγον-

τες, Ἐκ τῆς πόλεως ταύτης ἐξέλθατε μήποτε πάλιν συν-
στραφῶσιν ἡμῖν ἐπικράζοντες καθ᾽ ὑμῶν. (40) ἐξελθόντες δὲ
ἐκ τῆς φυλακῆς ἦλθον πρὸς τὴν Λυδίαν, καὶ ἰδόντες τοὺς
ἀδελφοὺς διηγήσαντο ὅσα ἐποίησεν κύριος αὐτοῖς παρα-
καλέσαντες αὐτούς, καὶ ἐξῆλθαν ("And *having arrived with
many friends at the prison,* they besought them to go forth, *saying,
'We did not know the truth about you, that you are righteous men.'*
And when they had brought them out they besought them saying,
'Depart from this city, *lest they again assemble against us, crying out
against you.'* (40) So they went out from the prison, and visited
Lydia; and when they had seen the brethren, *they reported the things
which the Lord had done for them,* and having exhorted them they
departed"). On the verb συστρέφειν, see the final comment on
10.41.

16.39 καὶ ἐξαγαγόντες ἠρώτων

The Committee was not impressed by Ropes's complicated argument that the absence of the words καὶ ἐξαγαγόντες ἠρώτων is a
Western non-interpolation,[11] but preferred to explain their omission in
several witnesses (257 383 614 2147 syr^h with *) as occasioned by their
redundancy with the preceding παρεκάλεσαν.

The redundancy may also suggest, as P. W. Schmiedel pointed out
long ago (*Encyclopædia Biblica,* vol. I, col. 52), the fusion of two
texts, in one of which παρεκάλεσαν stood with indirect speech,
and in the other with direct speech. See also the comment on 4.25,
especially H. W. Moule's suggestion.

17.1

Unlike the generally accepted text, διοδεύσαντες δὲ τὴν Ἀμφίπολιν καὶ τὴν Ἀπολλωνίαν ἦλθον εἰς Θεσσαλονίκην ("Now
when they had passed through Amphipolis and Apollonia, they came
to Thessalonica"), the reading of codex Bezae implies that Paul and
Silas stopped off at Apollonia, διοδεύσαντες δὲ τὴν Ἀμφίπολιν

---

[11] J. H. Ropes, *The Text of Acts,* p. 160.

καὶ κατῆλθον εἰς Ἀπολλωνίδα κἀκεῖθεν εἰς Θεσσαλονίκην
("Now when they had passed through Amphipolis they *went down* to
Apollonia, *and thence* to Thessalonica").

17.3 ὁ Χριστὸς [ὁ] Ἰησοῦς {C}

The wide variety of readings seems to have arisen from the unusual reading preserved only in codex Vaticanus. Since, however, the
Committee was reluctant to accord a decisive role to one manuscript,
it preferred to indicate the slender basis of the reading by enclosing
within square brackets the definite article before Ἰησοῦς.

For the change to direct discourse from indirect compare 1.4 f.;
23.22; Lk 5.14.

17.4 ἐπείσθησαν

On the strength of the confused text of codex Bezae, ἐπίσθησαν
καὶ προσεκληρώθησαν τῷ Παύλῳ καὶ τῷ Σιλαίᾳ τῇ διδαχῇ
πολλοὶ τῶν σεβομένων ..., A. C. Clark, following the suggestion
of Blass, reconstructs the text as follows: ἐπείσθησαν τῇ διδαχῇ,
καὶ προσεκληρώθησαν τῷ Παύλῳ καὶ τῷ Σιλᾷ πολλοὶ τῶν
σεβομένων ... ("... were persuaded *by the teaching,* and *many* of the
devout joined Paul and Silas ...").

17.4 Ἑλλήνων {B}

The unusual collocation of σεβομένων Ἑλλήνων, not found elsewhere, prompted several copyists (𝔓⁷⁴ A D 33 *al*) to insert καί, so as
to indicate two classes instead of one.

17.4 γυναικῶν τε {A}

It is possible to translate γυναικῶν τε τῶν πρώτων "and wives of
the leading men," an interpretation that the Western text enforced by
reading καὶ γυναῖκες τῶν πρώτων. A majority of the Committee
preferred the reading supported by 𝔓⁷⁴ ℵ A B E P Ψ 33 81 614 1739
al, not only because of superior external attestation, but also because

it was thought much more likely that copyists would replace the less usual connective by the more common καί (or δέ, as in *l*[1021]).

17.5 ζηλώσαντες δὲ οἱ Ἰουδαῖοι καὶ προσλαβόμενοι

Part of the distinctive reading of codex Bezae, οἱ δὲ ἀπειθοῦντες Ἰουδαῖοι συνστρέψαντές τινας ἄνδρας τῶν ἀγοραίων πονηροὺς ἐθορυβοῦσαν τὴν πόλιν ("But the Jews *who disbelieved assembled* some wicked fellows of the rabble and set the city in an uproar"), is preserved in the later Byzantine text, προσλαβόμενοι δὲ οἱ Ἰουδαῖοι οἱ ἀπειθοῦντες *(al οἱ ἀπειθ. Ἰουδ.)* (H L P most minuscules), and in the Textus Receptus, ζηλώσαντες δὲ οἱ ἀπειθοῦντες Ἰουδαῖοι καὶ προσλαβόμενοι (a reading that lacks any significant support in the manuscripts). On the verb συστρέφειν, see the final comment on 10.41.

17.9 καὶ λαβόντες

On the strength of syr[hmg], with indirect support from Ephraem, A. C. Clark prints οἱ μὲν οὖν πολιτάρχαι λαβόντες. The reading, however, appears to be an obvious amelioration introduced in order to smooth the sequence between verses 8 and 9.

17.11 οὕτως

At the close of the verse the Western text, represented by 383 614 1799 2412 it[gig] vg[mss] syr[h with *] Ephraem Priscillian, expands by adding καθὼς Παῦλος ἀπαγγέλλει ("examining the scriptures daily to see if these things were so *as Paul was proclaiming*").

17.12

After beginning the verse with a rather banal observation, τινὲς μὲν οὖν αὐτῶν ἐπίστευσαν, τίνες δὲ ἠπίστησαν ("Some of them, therefore, believed, but some did not believe," cf. 28.24), codex Bezae smooths the grammar of the generally received text and reads καὶ τῶν Ἑλλήνων καὶ τῶν εὐσχημόνων ἄνδρες καὶ γυναῖκες ἱκανοὶ ἐπίστευσαν ("and many of the Greeks and men and women of high standing believed"). Besides being better Greek the readjusted order has the effect of lessening any importance given to women (cf. comments on ver. 34 and on 18.26). According to Menoud, "the antifeminist tendency of the writer of D seems to be more or less general in the last decades of the first century. In any case it is not one of the major trends in the thought of the Western recension."[1]

17.13 καὶ ταράσσοντες τοὺς ὄχλους {B}

Many witnesses, including 𝔓⁴⁵ E P 049 056 0120 0142 *al*, followed by the Textus Receptus, lack the words καὶ ταράσσοντες. The shorter text appears to be the result of transcriptional oversight, occasioned by homoeoteleuton with the preceding σαλεύοντες. The vernacular διαλιμπάνειν occurs in D only here and at 8.24.

17.14-15

Codex Bezae, with occasional support from other Western witnesses, recasts these two verses as follows: τὸν μὲν οὖν Παῦλον οἱ ἀδελφοὶ ἐξαπέστειλαν ἀπελθεῖν ἐπὶ τὴν θάλασσαν· ὑπέμεινεν δὲ ὁ Σιλᾶς καὶ ὁ Τιμόθεος ἐκεῖ. οἱ δὲ καταστάνοντες τὸν Παῦλον ἤγαγον ἕως Ἀθηνῶν, παρῆλθεν δὲ τὴν Θεσσαλίαν, ἐκωλύθη γὰρ εἰς αὐτοὺς κηρύξαι τὸν λόγον, λαβόντες δὲ ἐντολὴν παρὰ Παύλου πρὸς τὸν Σιλᾶν καὶ Τιμόθεον ὅπως ἐν τάχει ἔλθωσιν πρὸς αὐτὸν ἐξῄεσαν ("The brethren therefore sent Paul off to go to the sea, but Silas and Timothy remained there. (15) And those who conducted Paul brought him as far as Athens, and he passed by Thessaly, for he was prevented from proclaiming the word to them; and having received a command from Paul for Silas

---

[1] P. H. Menoud, "The Western Text and the Theology of Acts," in the *Bulletin* of the Studiorum Novi Testamenti Societas, II (1951), pp. 30 f.; compare Ropes, *The Text of Acts,* p. ccxxxiv, who finds in Ac 17.12 and chap. 18 several indications of what may fairly be called an "anti-feminist" tendency. See also Metzger, *The Text of the New Testament,* 3rd ed., pp. 295 f.

and Timothy to come to him quickly, they departed"). The purpose of the addition in ver. 15 is to explain why nothing happened on Paul's journey through Thessaly.

17.14 ἕως

The Western text (D it^{d, gig} *al*) reads ἐπὶ τὴν θάλασσαν. The introduction of ὡς in the Byzantine text suggests an attempt to foil the Jews by a ruse ("then immediately the brethren sent away Paul to go as it were to the sea," AV). Inasmuch as ἕως with a following preposition occurs elsewhere in Luke-Acts (cf. Lk 24.50; Ac 21.5; 26.11), the Committee preferred to follow the combination of 𝔓^{74} ℵ A B 33 81 1739 vg *al*.

17.18 ὅτι … εὐηγγελίζετο

It is curious that D it^{gig} omit the explanatory clause. Although some scholars have regarded the reading as a Western non-interpolation, it is more likely that the words were omitted because "the writer scrupled to appear to class Ἰησοῦς among the δαιμόνια" (so Knowling; i. e. the clause implies that Paul's hearers understood Ἀνάστασις as a female deity parallel with Jesus).

17.19 ἐπιλαβόμενοί τε αὐτοῦ

The Western text embroiders the sentence by prefixing μετὰ δὲ ἡμέρας τινὰς ἐπιλαβόμενοι αὐτοῦ (D syr^h) and by adding πυνθανόμενοι καί after Πάγον (D; "And *after some days* they took hold of him and brought him to the Areopagus, *inquiring and* saying …").

17.26 ἐξ ἑνός {B}

The Western text, with the support of a wide range of early versions and patristic witnesses, adds αἵματος after ἑνός. This reading passed into the Textus Receptus and lies behind the AV. In support of the longer text is the palaeographical consideration that αἵματος may have been accidentally omitted because it ends in the same letters as the preceding ἑνός. It is also possible, though perhaps not probable, that someone deliberately deleted the word, since it appears to contradict the statement in Genesis that God made man from dust – not blood (Gn 2.7). Likewise, there is some force in the consideration that αἵματος is not a very natural gloss on ἑνός – for that one would have expected ἀνθρώπου or something similar.

On the other hand, a majority of the Committee was impressed by the external evidence supporting the shorter text, and judged that αἵματος was a typical expansion so characteristic of the Western reviser.

17.27 ζητεῖν τὸν θεόν {A}

The reading κύριον undoubtedly arose from the careless substitution by a scribe of K̄N̄ for Θ̄N̄, an exchange that occurs frequently. In any case, the argument of Kilpatrick, who assumes that κύριον was original and that scribes felt it to be ambiguous,[2] is difficult to reconcile with the circumstance that the following verb "to feel after" agrees better with κύριον than with either θεόν or θεῖον.

Although it is doubtless true, as Nestle pointed out, that scribes would be more likely to alter θεόν to θεῖον,[3] the fact that θεῖον occurs in ver. 29 may account for its intrusion here. Furthermore, since θεός is the subject of the sentence (cf. ver. 24), there was an added incentive for scribes to alter θεόν to either θεῖον or κύριον.

It should be noted that the present text of codex Bezae, μάλιστα ζητεῖν τὸ θεῖόν ἐστιν, cannot be construed with the rest of the sentence and must be emended either by altering τό to ὅ (as Clark does in accord with the testimony of it^gig and Irenaeus) or by deleting ἐστιν (as Ropes and Streeter[4] prefer). In either case the presence of

---

[2] "An Eclectic Study of the Text of Acts," *Biblical and Patristic Studies in Memory of Robert Pierce Casey,* ed. by J. Neville Birdsall and R. W. Thomson, p. 75.

[3] Eberhard Nestle, *Philologia sacra* (Berlin, 1896), p. 42; cf. also Nestle, *Introduction to the Textual Criticism of the Greek New Testament* (London, 1901), pp. 295 f.

[4] *Journal of Theological Studies,* XXXIV (1933), p. 238.

μάλιστα gives the impression that the reading is a secondary qualification.

17.28 ὡς καί τινες τῶν καθ' ὑμᾶς ποιητῶν {A}

Codex Bezae adds to the quotation the phrase τὸ καθ' ἡμέραν ("in him we live and move and have our being *day by day*").

According to Rendel Harris this reading arose from a misread and misplaced marginal annotation. He suggests that a corrector who wished to alter τῶν καθ' ὑμᾶς in the next line to "some of our own poets" "indificated this in the margin in a sort of short-hand, which was misunderstood as τὸ καθ' ἡμέραν and inserted as an expansion into the previous line."[5] Williams, however, agrees with W. L. Knox that "a more likely explanation is that it was a 'favourite phrase of D.'"[6]

Although Clark thinks that "it would be difficult to find a more typical example of a gloss than the addition of ποιητῶν,"[7] it is also possible, as Lake and Cadbury remark, that the Western editor may have had some moral objection to quoting poets. At any rate, the Peshitta Syriac, the Armenian, and the Ethiopic versions read "sages" or "wise men" instead of "poets."

Scribal confusion between ὑμᾶς and ἡμᾶς, which were pronounced alike, was common. It is scarcely likely that Paul would have represented himself as one of the Greeks.

17.30 τῆς ἀγνοίας

The addition in codex Bezae and the Vulgate of ταύτης after τῆς ἀγνοίας, thought by Epp[8] to involve a deliberate contrast to the ignorance referred to in 3.17, is more probably an innocent heightening

---

[5] *Bulletin of the Bezan Club*, VIII (1930), p. 6.

[6] C. S. C. Williams, *Alterations to the Text of the Synoptic Gospels and Acts*, p. 69, n. 1.

[7] *The Acts of the Apostles*, p. 367. Blass and Ropes also omit ποιητῶν.

[8] E. J. Epp, *The Theological Tendency of Codex Bezae Cantabrigiensis in Acts* (Cambridge, 1966), pp. 48–50.

with no subtle allusion to a different attitude of God toward Jewish (as distinguished from Gentile) ignorance.

17.31 ἐν ἀνδρί {A}

After ἀνδρί several Western witnesses (D vg^ms and Irenaeus) add the identifying Ἰησοῦ.

17.34

The omission in codex Bezae of the words καὶ γυνὴ ὀνόματι Δάμαρις has been taken by some (e. g. Wm. M. Ramsay) to be another indication of the anti-feminist attitude of the scribe (see the comment on ver. 12 above).[9] It is, however, more likely, as A. C. Clark suggests,[10] that a line in an ancestor of codex Bezae had been accidentally omitted, so that what remains in D is ἐν οἷς καὶ Διο-νύσιός τις Ἀρεοπαγείτης εὐσχήμων καὶ ἕτεροι σὺν αὐτοῖς ("among whom also was a *certain* Dionysius, *an* Areopagite of *high standing,* and others with them"). In either case, however, the con-cluding phrase σὺν αὐτοῖς suggests that Luke originally specified more than one person (Dionysius) as among Paul's converts.

It is curious that codex Bezae reads εὐσχήμων to indicate the high standing of Dionysius, though being an Areopagite would naturally imply his honorable estate without adding the adjective.[11] Its pres-ence, according to an ingenious explanation proposed by J. Armitage Robinson,[12] is to be accounted for as follows. According to Robinson it is significant that in Acts the word εὐσχήμων is used only of women (13.50; 17.12). Under the influence of its usage earlier in Acts some gallant scribe added the word after Δάμαρις.[13] Later, after the

---

[9] *The Church in the Roman Empire,* pp. 161 f.

[10] *The Acts of the Apostles,* p. 367.

[11] Notice that Lk 23.50 does not retain εὐσχήμων of Mk 15.43.

[12] Reported by W. M. Ramsay, *The Church in the Roman Empire,* p. 161.

[13] Ramsay observes that "it was impossible in Athenian society for a woman of respectable position and family to have any opportunity of hearing Paul; and the name Damaris (probably a vulgarism for *damalis,* heifer) suggests a foreign woman, perhaps

church had taken her stand against the pagan or heretical claims advanced in behalf of her ambitious women, a more orthodox if less chivalrous transcriber deleted the name of Damaris altogether, but left the adjective standing, a witness at once against his own deed and the deed of the scribe who had gone before him.

18.1 ἐκ {B}

The insertion of the subject was apparently made in the interest of clarifying the passage when it was read as the opening sentence of an ecclesiastical lesson. Certainly if the words ὁ Παῦλος were present originally, no one would have deleted them.

18.2-4

The original form of the Western text, which in verses 2 and 3 codex Bezae presents in a form somewhat accommodated to the Alexandrian text, appears to have been the following (reconstructed by Ropes, chiefly on the basis of it[h] and syr[hmg]): καὶ εὗρεν Ἀκύλαν, Ποντικὸν τῷ γένει, Ἰουδαῖον, προσφάτως ἐληλυθότα ἀπὸ τῆς Ἰταλίας σὺν Πρισκίλλῃ γυναικὶ αὐτοῦ, καὶ προσῆλθεν αὐτοῖς· οὗτοι δὲ ἐξῆλθον ἀπὸ τῆς Ῥώμης διὰ τὸ τεταχέναι Κλαύδιον Καίσαρα χωρίζεσθαι πάντας Ἰουδαίους ἀπὸ τῆς Ῥώμης· οἳ καὶ κατῴκησαν εἰς τὴν Ἀχαίαν. ὁ δὲ Παῦλος ἐγνωρίσθη τῷ Ἀκύλᾳ (3) διὰ τὸ ὁμόφυλον καὶ ὁμότεχνον εἶναι, καὶ ἔμεινεν πρὸς αὐτοὺς καὶ ἠργάζετο· ἦσαν γὰρ σκηνοποιοὶ τῇ τέχνῃ. (4) εἰσπορευόμενος δὲ εἰς τὴν συναγωγὴν κατὰ πᾶν σάββατον διελέγετο, καὶ ἐντιθεὶς τὸ ὄνομα τοῦ κυρίου Ἰησοῦ, καὶ ἔπειθεν δὲ οὐ μόνον Ἰουδαίους ἀλλὰ καὶ Ἕλληνας ("And he found Aquila, [a man] of Pontus by race, a Jew, who had lately come from Italy *with* Priscilla, his wife, and he went to them. Now these had come out from Rome because Claudius *Caesar* had commanded all Jews to leave Rome; *and they settled in Greece*. And Paul *became known* to Aquila (3) because he was of *the same tribe and* the

---

one of the class of educated *Hetairai,* who might very well be in his audience," *St. Paul the Traveller and the Roman Citizen,* p. 252.

same trade, and he stayed with them and worked; for they were tent-makers by trade. (4) And *entering into* the synagogue each sabbath day, he held a discussion, *introducing the name of the Lord Jesus,* and persuaded *not only* Jews *but also* Greeks").

Lake and Cadbury remark on verses 2 and 3 that "the awkwardness of the Greek in the B-text may be at least partly responsible for the interesting and smoother version of the Western text."[1] (On ἠργάζετο in ver. 3, see the comment on that verse.) In ver. 4 the Western addition implies that in his expounding of the Old Testament scriptures Paul would "insert the name of the Lord Jesus" where, according to Christian theology, it was appropriate. Compare also the addition in D syr[hmg] it[h] at the beginning of ver. 6. At the end of ver. 3 codex Bezae and it[gig] lack the statement, "for they were tentmakers by trade"; the absence is due no doubt to accidental omission of a line of text.

18.3   ἠργάζετο / εἰργάζετο {B}

The plural ἠργάζοντο in several Alexandrian witnesses is probably an accommodation to the plural forms immediately preceding and following.

18.5   λόγῳ {B}

The expression that Paul συνείχετο τῷ λόγῳ ("was wholly absorbed with preaching," so Bauer-Arndt-Gingrich-Danker) seems to have been misunderstood, so that πνεύματι was either deliberately substituted for λόγῳ or, being added as an explanation in the margin, eventually usurped the place of λόγῳ, with the resultant meaning "was urged on by the Spirit" or "was pressed in the spirit" (so the AV).

18.6

At the beginning of the verse the Western text (D syr[hmg] it[h]) inserts πολλοῦ δὲ λόγου γινομένου καὶ γραφῶν διερμηνευομένων

---

[1] *The Beginnings of Christianity,* vol. IV, p. 221.

("And after there had been much discussion, and interpretations of the scriptures had been given ..."). Compare also the comments on verses 2 and 3.

18.7 ἐκεῖθεν

The Western reviser emended ἐκεῖθεν to ἀπὸ τοῦ Ἀκύλα (D it^h), and other witnesses conflated the two readings; thus ἐκεῖθεν ἀπὸ τοῦ Ἀκύλα, 614 (1799) 2412. But it is unlikely that opposition of the Jews in the synagogue would have caused Paul to change his residence from the home of Aquila, with whom Paul continued to have good relations. The Western revision reflects, as Bruce[2] points out, "a misunderstanding of Luke's meaning; Paul did not remove his private lodgings from Aquila's house to that of Justus, but made Justus's house his preaching headquarters instead of the synagogue," which was next door.

18.7 Τιτίου Ἰούστου {C}

There is a considerable amount of divergency among the witnesses. Ropes argued that the reading with a single name Ἰούστου is probably original, and by dittography ονομαΤΙΙΟΥστου gave rise to Τιτίου. But, as Goodspeed pointed out, the hypothesis is seriously weakened by the absence of the word ὀνόματι from codex Alexandrinus, the chief ancient support for the omission of Titus.[3] Furthermore, the opposite error, that of haplography, is perhaps even more likely to have occurred, and from ΤΙΤΙΤΙ and (Ι)ΟΥΙΟΥ in ὀνόματι Τιτίου Ἰούστου came the shortened form in most of the uncial manuscripts.[4] In any case Τίτου seems to be a secondary correction, as the more familiar name.

---

[2] F. F. Bruce, *Commentary on the Book of the Acts; the English Text* ... (London, 1954), p. 370, n. 17.

[3] *Journal of Biblical Literature*, LXIX (1950), p. 383.

[4] A. van Veldhuizen, "Hand. 18:7. Titius Iustus of Iustus?" *Theologische Studiën*, XX (1902), pp. 422–423.

18.8 καὶ ἐβαπτίζοντο {A}

The verb ἐβαπτίζοντο was supplemented by scribes with the addition of "through the name of the Lord Jesus Christ" (614 syr^(h with *)) or "believing God through the name of our Lord Jesus Christ" (D); the latter ignored the redundancy that was created with the previous ἐπίστευον.

18.12 Ἰουδαῖοι

After Ἰουδαῖοι the Western text (D it^h and partly syr^(h with *)) continues with the more colorful account συνλαλήσαντες μεθ᾽ ἑαυτῶν ἐπὶ τὸν Παῦλον, καὶ ἐπιθέντες τὰς χεῖρας ἤγαγον αὐτὸν πρὸς τὸν ἀνθύπατον (D has ἐπὶ τὸ βῆμα), καταβοῶντες καὶ λέγοντες … ("*having talked together among themselves* against Paul, *and having laid hands upon him* they brought him *to the governor, crying out and* saying …").

18.17 πάντες {B}

In order to identify the "all" who seized and beat Sosthenes, the ruler of the synagogue, the Western and later ecclesiastical texts (and hence the AV) add the identifying words, "the Greeks," i. e. the Gentile community. Several minuscule manuscripts read "all the Jews," which is much more unlikely to represent the real situation.

At the close of the verse the Latin text of codex Bezae reads *tunc Gallio fingebat eum non videre* ("Then Gallio pretended not to see him"). The line in the Greek text of codex Bezae after βήματος is erased and nothing is now legible, but it is fair to assume that it corresponded to the Latin; Clark reconstructs τότε ὁ Γαλλίων προσεποιεῖτο μὴ ἰδεῖν.[5]

---

[5] According to a suggestion made by C. A. Phillips, behind the two forms of text one may postulate the Syriac verb ܐܘܫܝ, which, according to Brockelmann's *Lexicon Syriacum*, means primarily *avertit (occulos, faciem)* but also *non curavit, neglexit* (*Bulletin of the Bezan Club*, v [1928], p. 44; cf. D. Plooij, *ibid.*, IX [1931], p. 16).

18.18

One form of the Western text, preserved in it[h], reads *Aquila, qui votum cum fecisset [Cenchris], caput tondit*, from which Blass produced Ἀκύλας, ὅς εὐχὴν ἔχων ἐν Κεγχρειαῖς τὴν κεφαλὴν ἐκείρατο ("Aquila, who, having made a vow at Cenchreae, had cut his hair"). Several manuscripts of the Latin Vulgate read the plural, "Priscilla and Aquila, who had cut their hair at Cenchreae, for they had a vow."

18.19   κατήντησαν {B}

The Textus Receptus, following 𝔓[74] P Ψ most minuscules *al*, alters κατήντησαν to the singular in conformity with the other verbs in the context.

18.21   εἰπών {A}

The addition made by the Western reviser, which has passed into the later ecclesiastical text (and therefore is represented in the AV: "I must by all means keep this feast that cometh in Jerusalem"), is loosely paralleled by the similar statement in 20.16, and by the Western text of 19.1 (see the comment on the latter passage). The interpolation (for thus it must be accounted, there being no reason why, if original, it should have been deleted in a wide variety of manuscripts and versions) may well give, as Bruce observes, "the true reason for Paul's hasty departure, the feast probably being passover."[6]

18.24   Ἀπολλῶς ὀνόματι

The name Ἀπολλῶς is an abbreviated form of Ἀπολλώνιος (read here by D). It may be that the variant reading Ἀπελλῆς[7] (ℵ* 307 431 453 536 610 cop[bo] arm geo (eth) Didymus Ammonius) is an Egyptian

---

[6] F. F. Bruce, *The Acts of the Apostles* (1951), p. 349.

[7] Cf. Blass-Debrunner-Funk, § 29, 4.

preference.[8] On the other hand, despite its meager attestation here and in 19.1, Kilpatrick suggests that Ἀπελλῆς is the original reading in Acts and that scribes assimilated it in most witnesses to the name of the Ἀπολλῶς of 1 Corinthians.[9] (See also the comment on 19.1.)

18.25 οὗτος ἦν κατηχημένος τὴν ὁδὸν τοῦ κυρίου

The Western addition (D it[gig]) of ἐν τῇ πατρίδι after κατηχημένος ("who had been instructed *in his own country* in the word of the Lord") implies that Christianity had reached Alexandria by about A.D. 50. Whether the statement of the Western reviser depends upon personal knowledge or is based on inference, the implication of the statement no doubt accords with historical fact.

The reading τὸν λόγον (D 35 36[a] 94 142 242 307 309 323 429 431) instead of τὴν ὁδόν is, as Ropes declares, "clearly an attempt to make a hard word easier" *(ad loc.)*; the same type of change appears also in ver. 26.

18.25 τοῦ Ἰησοῦ {A}

The Committee preferred the reading Ἰησοῦ, not only because of the stronger and more diversified external witnesses in its support, but also because it appears that the readings with κυρίου arose from assimilation with the previous instance of κυρίου in the same sentence.

18.26 Πρίσκιλλα καὶ Ἀκύλας

Apparently the Western reviser (D it[gig] syr cop[sa] arm *al*) desired to reduce the prominence of Priscilla, for he either mentions Aquila first (as here) or inserts the name of Aquila without including Priscilla (as in verses 3, 18, and 21). The unusual order, the wife before the hus-

---

[8] So Theodor Zahn, *Introduction to the New Testament,* I (Edinburgh, 1909), p. 270, note 10; cf. Henry Offermann, "Apollos, Apelles, Apollonios," *Lutheran Church Review,* XXXVIII (1919), pp. 145–150.

[9] *Journal of Biblical Literature,* LXXXIX (1970), p. 77.

band, must be accepted as original, for there was always a tendency among scribes to change the unusual to the usual. In the case of Priscilla and Aquila, however, it was customary in the early church to refer to her before her husband (cf. Ro 16.3; 2 Tm 4.19).[10] On an anti-feminist tendency, see the comment on 17.12 above.

18.26 τὴν ὁδὸν [τοῦ θεοῦ] {C}

While appreciating the force of the consideration urged by Alford, Ropes, and others, namely that τὴν ὁδόν in the Western text is original and the other readings are attempts to render it more intelligible, a majority of the Committee was reluctant to accord primary weight to the testimony of D here inasmuch as in ver. 25 it is clearly secondary, having substituted λόγον for ὁδόν. On the other hand, in view of the usage in 9.2; 19.9, 23; 22.4; 24.14, 22, it was agreed to represent the possibility that the Western text may be original and to enclose τοῦ θεοῦ (ℵ* A B) within square brackets.

18.27

The Western reviser (D, supported in large part by syr^hmg) expanded and paraphrased this verse as follows: ἐν δὲ τῇ Ἐφέσῳ ἐπιδημοῦντές τινες Κορίνθιοι καὶ ἀκούσαντες αὐτοῦ παρακάλουν διελθεῖν σὺν αὐτοῖς εἰς τὴν πατρίδα αὐτῶν. συνκατανεύσαντος[11] δὲ αὐτοῦ οἱ Ἐφέσιοι ἔγραψαν τοῖς ἐν Κορίνθῳ μαθηταῖς ὅπως ἀποδέξωνται τὸν ἄνδρα· ὃς ἐπιδημήσας εἰς τὴν Ἀχαίαν πολὺ συνεβάλλετο ἐν ταῖς ἐκκλησίαις ("And some Corinthians who were on a visit to Ephesus and had heard him invited him to cross over with them to their native place. When he agreed, the Ephesians wrote to the disciples to receive the man; and when he took up residence in Achaia he was of great help in the churches").

---

[10] See Adolf Harnack, "Über die beiden Recensionen der Geschichte der Prisca und des Aquila in Act. Apost. 18, 1-27," *Sitzungsberichte der königlich preussischen Akademie der Wissenschaften zu Berlin*, 1900, pp. 2–13.

[11] The verb συγκατανεύειν occurs nowhere else in the New Testament.

The unusual orientation and outlook, as well as certain internal difficulties of the passage, have been pointed out more than once.[12] For example, nowhere else in Acts do we read of members of one church acting in another church, nor do we ever hear of an invitation to an apostle or evangelist to come to a church (16.9 is not a parallel). But there is a more serious difficulty. If Apollos's visit is made at his own initiative, an introductory letter recommending him to the Corinthians is appropriate; if, on the other hand, he goes at the invitation of members of the Corinthian church, why is it necessary that the Ephesians supply such a letter?

18.28 *δημοσίᾳ ἐπιδεικνύς*

The Western text (𝔓[38] D 383 614 it[d]) expands the account so as to read *δημοσίᾳ διαλεγόμενος καὶ* (𝔓[38] om. *καί*) *ἐπιδεικνύς* ("discoursing publicly and showing").

19.1 *Ἐγένετο … εἰς Ἔφεσον* {A}

Omitting the clause *Ἐγένετο δὲ ἐν τῷ τὸν Ἀπολλῶ εἶναι ἐν Κορίνθῳ,* the Western text (𝔓[38] D syr[hmg], with partial support from it[gig] and Ephraem) substitutes the following: *Θέλοντος δὲ τοῦ Παύλου κατὰ τὴν ἰδίαν βουλὴν πορεύεσθαι εἰς Ἱεροσόλυμα εἶπεν αὐτῷ τὸ πνεῦμα ὑποστρέφειν εἰς τὴν Ἀσίαν, διελθὼν δὲ τὰ ἀνωτέρικα μέρη ἔρχεται εἰς Ἔφεσον* ("And *although Paul wished, according to his own plan, to go to Jerusalem, the Spirit told him to return to Asia.* And having passed through the upper country he *comes* to Ephesus …").

It is difficult to understand why so much is said about a purpose that was not accomplished. Weiss is correct in observing that "the whole antithesis between *ἰδία βουλή* and an order of the Spirit is neither in the character of Paul nor of Luke, who brings expressly into prominence how Paul allows all his decisions to be made by the will

---

[12] See, e. g., F. W. Grosheide, *Bulletin of the Bezan Club,* VIII (1930), pp. 18–20, and G. Zuntz, *Classica et mediaevalia,* III (1940), pp. 26–33.

of God made known to him through the Spirit."[1] (See also the comment on 18.21.)

19.1 Ἀπολλῶ

Instead of Ἀπολλῶ, 𝔓[74] A[c] 181 read Ἀπολλών, and ℵ* 307 431* 453 536 610 cop[bo] read Ἀπελλῆν. (See also the comment on 18.24.)

19.5 Ἰησοῦ

The Western text (𝔓[38] D 383 614 syr[h with *]) expands the brief statement, "they were baptized in the name of the Lord Jesus," by continuing Χριστοῦ (not 𝔓[38]) εἰς ἄφεσιν ἁμαρτιῶν. The addition, though intended to be edifying, is inept, because these persons had previously received John's baptism for the remission of sins.

19.6

Instead of ἦλθε codex Bezae and Jerome read the more colorful εὐθέως ἐπέπεσεν ("the Holy Spirit *immediately fell* upon them").

After γλώσσαις the Western text (represented by syr[hmg] and, in part, by it[p] vg[mss] and Ephraem) adds "*other* tongues, *and they* themselves *knew them, which they also interpreted for themselves; and certain* also prophesied." Although Clark professes to believe that "it is more natural to suppose that the words … were struck out as inconsistent with ch. 2, than that they were introduced as an interpolation from 1 Cor. xiv,"[2] it is much more probable that the Western form of text arose by scribal embroidering of the Alexandrian text than that the text in all known Greek manuscripts has been curtailed because of what might possibly be regarded as an inconsistency with the account of Pentecost in Acts 2.

---

[1] *Der Codex D*, p. 94, Anm. 1.
[2] A. C. Clark, *The Acts of the Apostles*, p. 370.

19.8 *ἐπαρρησιάζετο*

The Western text (D syr^h) reads *ἐν δυνάμει μεγάλῃ ἐπαρ-ρησιάζετο* ("spoke boldly *with great power*").

19.9 *Τυράννου* {B}

The interesting addition in the Western text ("[Paul] argued daily in the hall of Tyrannus *from the fifth hour to the tenth*" [i. e. from 11:00 a.m. to 4:00 p.m.]) may represent an accurate piece of information, preserved in oral tradition before being incorporated into the text of certain manuscripts. Were it present in the original text, there is no good reason why it should have been deleted. (Instead of "to the tenth" two Latin manuscripts of the Vulgate read "to the ninth" (G), "to the ninth and tenth" (D).)

19.14, 16

The Western text (codex Bezae and, in part, 𝔓^38 it^gig syr^hmg Ephraem) rewrites ver. 14 as follows: *ἐν οἷς καὶ υἱοὶ* [+ *ἑπτά* syr^hmg] *Σκευᾶ τινος ἱερέως ἠθέλησαν τὸ αὐτὸ ποιῆσαι (ἔθος εἶχαν τοὺς τοιούτους ἐξορκίζειν), καὶ εἰσελθόντες πρὸς τὸν δαιμονι-ζόμενον ἤρξαντο ἐπικαλεῖσθαι τὸ ὄνομα λέγοντες, Παραγ-γέλλομέν σοι ἐν Ἰησοῦ ὃν Παῦλος ἐξελθεῖν κηρύσσει* ("In this connection also [seven] sons of a certain priest named Sceva *wished* to do *the same thing (they were accustomed to exorcize such persons). And they entered into the one who was demon-possessed and began to invoke the Name, saying, 'We command you, by Jesus* whom Paul preaches, *to come out'*").

Some have felt a difficulty that *ἑπτά* in ver. 14 changes in ver. 16 to "two" (*ἀμφότεροι*, though occasionally in substandard Greek *ἀμφότεροι* has the meaning "all"). Codex Gigas emends *ἑπτά* to *duo*; others (D it^57) omit the numeral entirely. In ver. 16 ms. E omits *ἀμφότεροι* and others (including H L P S *al*, followed by the Textus Receptus) replace it with *αὐτῶν*.

Among modern proposals, Moulton reports a conjecture of J. B. Shipley, that *ἑπτά* has arisen from a gloss, in which the name *Σκευᾶ* was taken to be the Hebrew שבע, which can be read as the numeral seven (ἑπτά).[3]

A. C. Clark argued that by mistake a marginal note of interrogation ζ (= ζήτει), meaning "query," being taken as the numeral seven, was erroneously incorporated into the text.[4] Torrey, following Overbeck, conjectured that the error of "seven" for "two" arose because in the first century the Greek β (= 2) and ζ (= 7) were made very much alike.[5] Finally, it may be reported that at the end of the last century the Dutch classical scholar Naber proposed that ἀμφότεροι be emended to ἄφνω "suddenly,"[6] a reading that J. M. S. Baljon adopted in his edition (1898).

The difficulty of reconciling ἑπτά with ἀμφότεροι, however, is not so great as to render the text that includes both an impossible text. On the other hand, however, the difficulty is so troublesome that it is hard to explain how ἑπτά came into the text, and was perpetuated, if it were not original, whereas, in view of ἀμφότεροι, it is easy to see how it might have been omitted by certain witnesses.

19.20   τοῦ κυρίου ὁ λόγος ηὔξανεν καὶ ἴσχυεν {B}

A majority of the Committee preferred the Alexandrian reading (ℵ* A B), on the consideration that it is more likely that the less usual order was altered into the characteristic order, than vice versa. The substitution of θεοῦ for κυρίου appears to be a secondary correction. Codex Bezae presents a conflate reading, οὕτως κατὰ κράτος ἐνίσχυσεν καὶ ἡ πίστις τοῦ θεοῦ ηὔξανε καὶ ἐπλήθυνε ("So mightily it prevailed; and *the faith of God* grew and *multiplied*"). Although it could be argued that ἐνισχύειν is a Lukan word (it appears twice in the New Testament, Lk 22.43 and

---

[3] J. H. Moulton, *Prolegomena,* p. 246; compare Moulton and Milligan, *Vocabulary,* p. 577, col. a. On the other hand, Robert Eisler conjectured that "cκεγⲁ might be a misreading of cκεγⲁⲓ, 'investigate' 'look up!', wedged between ⲅⲓⲟⲓ and ⲁⲅⲟ," *Bulletin of the Bezan Club,* XII (1937), p. 78; compare H. A. Sanders, *ibid.,* XI (1936), p. 14.

[4] *The Acts of the Apostles,* pp. 371–373.

[5] *Anglican Theological Review,* XXVI (1944), pp. 253–255.

[6] *Mnemosyne,* XXIX (1881), p. 289.

Ac 9.19), the expression ἡ πίστις τοῦ θεοῦ occurs nowhere in Luke-Acts.

19.22-26

In these verses various witnesses of the Western text incorporate a variety of picturesque details. After χρόνον in ver. 22 the Greek text of codex Bezae adds ὀλίγον ("stayed in Asia for a *little* while"). In ver. 25 after Ἄνδρες D and syr[h with *] add συντεχνῖται ("fellow-craftsmen"), a word that does not appear elsewhere in the New Testament. In ver. 26 after ὁ Παῦλος οὗτος codex Bezae adds τίς τοτε [which, in the light of it[gig] *hic Paulus nescio quem,* is to be read τίς ποτε], that is, colloquially "this Paul, *a somebody.*"

19.28 Θυμοῦ {A}

Following Θυμοῦ codex Bezae syr[hmg] (614) (1799) 2401[c] 2412 add καὶ δράμοντες εἰς τὸ ἄμφοδον ("*and running into the street* they cried out").[7]

19.33 συνεβίβασαν {B}

The difficulty of understanding συνεβίβασαν in the context doubtless led scribes to change it to κατεβίβασαν or to προεβίβασαν.

19.37 ἡμῶν {B}

The Textus Receptus, following the later manuscripts, replaces ἡμῶν with ὑμῶν, which copyists apparently regarded as suiting better the second person plural ἠγάγετε.

19.39 περαιτέρω {B}

The comparative adverb περαιτέρω (which appears nowhere else in the New Testament) is appropriate in this context, whereas περὶ ἑτέρων is not. Probably the latter arose from itacism.

---

[7] The word ἄμφοδον appears elsewhere in the New Testament only in Mk 11.4.

19.40 [οὐ] {C}

Neither variant reading is without difficulty, and Hort, followed by Ropes, suspected the presence of a primitive error that has infected all texts. Hort conjectured that "probably αἴτιοι ὑπάρχοντες should be read for αἰτίου ὑπάρχοντος, with the construction μηδενὸς αἴτιοι ὑπάρχοντες περὶ οὗ οὐ κ.τ.λ. ('although we are guilty of nothing concerning which' &c.)."[8]

C. F. D. Moule supposes that the author made a rough draft that involved several alternative forms of the sentence, and that he neglected finally to delete the ones with which he was dissatisfied.[9]

The Committee, reluctant to resort to conjectural emendation, regarded οὐ as the least unsatisfactory reading; at the same time, however, in order to reflect the evidence for the absence of οὐ it was thought best to enclose the word within square brackets.

20.3-4

Codex Bezae, supported in part by syr[hmg] and Ephraem, presents the following text of verses 3 and 4: ποιήσας δὲ μῆνας γ καὶ γενηθείς<ης> αὐτῷ ἐπιβουλῆς ὑπὸ τῶν Ἰουδαίων ἠθέλησεν ἀναχθῆναι εἰς Συρίαν, εἶπεν δὲ τὸ πνεῦμα αὐτῷ ὑποστρέφειν διὰ τῆς Μακεδονίας. (4) μέλλοντος οὖν ἐξειέναι αὐτοῦ [+ συν-είποντο αὐτῷ syr[hmg]] μέχρι τῆς Ἀσίας Σώπατρος Πύρρου Βεροιαῖος [ms.: Βερυιαιος], Θεσσαλονικέων δὲ Ἀρίσταρχος καὶ Σεκοῦνδος, καὶ Γάϊος Δουβ[έ]ριος καὶ Τιμόθεος, Ἐφέσιοι δὲ Εὔτυχος καὶ Τρόφιμος ("And when he had spent three months there, and when a plot was made against him by the Jews, he *wished* to sail for Syria, *but the Spirit told him* to return through Macedonia. (4) *Therefore when he was about to leave,* Sopater of Beroea, the son of Pyrrhus, and of the Thessalonians Aristarchus and Secundus, and Gaius of *Douberios,* and Timothy, went with him *as far as Asia*; but the *Ephesians Eutychus* and Trophimus ...").

---

[8] "Notes on Select Readings," p. 97. For other conjectures see W. C. van Manen, *Conjecturaal-Kritiek* ... (Haarlem, 1880), p. 246, and W. H. van de Sande Bakhuyzen, *Over de toepassing van de Conjecturaal-Kritiek* ... (Haarlem, 1880), pp. 225 f.

[9] *Expository Times,* LV (1954), p. 221.

According to the generally received text Paul was intending to go to Syria in order to carry the collection for the poor of Jerusalem; the Western reviser, however, ascribes the reason for the journey to the Jews' plot. Furthermore, in characteristic fashion (cf. 19.1) the Western text introduces the prompting of the Spirit to account for Paul's going by a land route rather than by sea, as the apostle had formerly planned to do.

In ver. 4 Bezae's identification of Paul's companions as *Ephesians* rather than *Asians* (the Harclean Syriac margin conflates the two, *ex Asia Ephesii*) may suggest that the Western reviser belonged to, or was closely connected with Ephesus. The substitution of Εὔτυχος for Τυχικός may be an emendation based on ver. 9.

20.4   συνείπετο δὲ αὐτῷ {B}

It is difficult to understand how, if ἄχρι τῆς Ἀσίας were original, the phrase would have been omitted. Furthermore, as Conzelmann points out,[1] it appears that the author of 1 Timothy envisaged a situation in Paul's activities that is reflected in a text of Acts lacking the addition.

20.4   Πύρρου {B}

Although Ropes conjectured that ΠΥΡΡΟΥ had somehow arisen out of the preceding ΠΑΤΡΟΣ, the Committee, impressed by the external evidence supporting Πύρρου, regarded its omission as the result of an accident in transcription.

20.4   Δερβαῖος {B}

The generally received text of Acts involves a well-known crux: in 20.4 Gaius is called a man of Derbe, whereas in 19.29 he, along with a certain Aristarchus, is identified as a Macedonian. The discrepancy has been resolved (*a*) by emending Μακεδόνας in 19.29 to Μακεδόνα (which is indeed the reading of 307 and a few other manuscripts), thus identifying only Aristarchus as a Macedonian; or (*b*) by assuming that two different persons bearing the name Gaius

---

[1] *Zeitschrift für die neutestamentliche Wissenschaft,* XLV (1954), p. 266.

are meant; or (c) by following the Western reading Δοβήριος at 20.4 (it^{gig}, compare D* Δουβ[έ]ριος and it^d *doverius* [= *doberius*]) and identifying this place with a Macedonian post-town by that name near Mt. Pangaios, on the road from Philippi. Although this identification has been widely approved (e. g. by A. C. Clark, B. S. Streeter, Lagrange, C. S. C. Williams, G. Zuntz [*Gnomon*, XXX (1958), p. 26], F. F. Bruce, and a scant majority of the translators of the New English Bible[2]), a majority of the Committee was hesitant to do so, for (a) Δερβαῖος applied to a man apparently called a Macedonian in the context would have been the harder reading in the second century, when everyone knew that Derbe[3] was in Asia Minor, and (b) Δοβήριος would be a natural and intelligible emendation at that period. Furthermore, as Haenchen[4] points out, the grouping of the names in pairs (after the mention of Sopater) according to their place of residence suggests that this Gaius, who is mentioned in company with Timothy, was from Asia Minor and not from Macedonia.

20.8 λαμπάδες

Zuntz[5] argues for the originality of the Bezan reading ὑπο-λαμπάδες, an exceedingly rare word apparently meaning "(small) windows," or "look-out holes."[6]

---

[2] "By a casting vote Δουβέριος, found in D d gig, was preferred to Δερβαῖος, the reading of the other MSS," R. V. G. Tasker, "Notes on Variant Readings," *The Greek New Testament, Being the Text Translated in The New English Bible, 1961* (Oxford and Cambridge, 1964), p. 433.

[3] Epigraphic proof is now available to show that Derbe was situated at Kerti Hüyük, about 60 miles from Lystra. Whether it was within or outside the Province of Galatia is an open question; see George Ogg, "Derbe," *New Testament Studies*, IX (1963), pp. 367–370.

[4] "The Thessalonian Aristarchus (also mentioned in 19.29 and 27.2) and the otherwise unknown Secundus constitute the first pair; the Lycaonian Gaius from Derbe and Timothy (from [the neighboring] Lystra, 16.1; since he is well known to the reader he is not further identified), form the second pair; and the Asians, Tychicus and Trophimus, the third pair" (Ernst Haenchen, *The Acts of the Apostles, A Commentary*, p. 574).

[5] *Gnomon*, XXX (1958), p. 26.

[6] See Harold Smith in *Expository Times*, XVI (1905), p. 478; Moulton-Howard, *Grammar*, II, p. 328; and Moulton-Milligan, *Vocabulary, s.v.*

20.12

Instead of ἤγαγον δὲ τὸν παῖδα ζῶντα D[gr] reads ἀσπαζομένων αὐτῶν ἤγαγεν τὸν νεανίσκον ζῶντα ("And as they were saying farewell, he [Paul] brought the young man alive"). In the interest of making a smoother sequence of events, A. C. Clark[7] transposes (without support from any manuscript) the clauses ἤγαγεν τὸν νεανίσκον ζῶντα, καὶ παρεκλήθησαν οὐ μετρίως to the close of ver. 10, reading Bezae's ἀσπαζομένων δὲ αὐτῶν as ver. 12.

20.13   ἡμεῖς

The Armenian catena, which rests upon the Old Syriac text, expands the "we" into "I, Luke, and those who with me went on board,"[8] a reading that Rendel Harris[9] argued was the original Western reading of this verse.

20.13-14   Ἄσσον

Instead of Ἄσσον, in ver. 13 𝔓[41] L P 237 614 2401 2412 *al* syr[p. h] cop[sa] and in ver. 14 P 614 1799 2401 2412 *al* syr[p. h] cop[sa] read Θάσσον (or Θάσον). Thasos, which is an island east of Amphipolis, is an impossible reading in the context; how it arose in such diverse witnesses is a puzzle.[10]

20.15   τῇ δέ (2) {B}

The information contained in the longer text is, as Ramsay points out, "in itself highly probable, for the promontory of Trogyllian or Trogylia projects far out between Samos and Miletus, and the little

---

[7] *The Acts of the Apostles* (Oxford, 1933), p. liii.

[8] See F. C. Conybeare in J. H. Ropes, *The Text of Acts,* pp. 442 f.

[9] *The British Friend,* April, 1913, quoted in *Expository Times,* XXIV (1912–13), p. 530.

[10] See Ropes, *ad loc.* and p. CCXXXV, note 1, and Edgar R. Smothers, "A Problem of Text in Saint John Chrysostom," *Recherches de science religieuse,* XXXIX (1951–52), pp. 416–427.

coasting vessel would naturally touch there, perhaps becalmed, or for some other reason."[11] Whether the words were present originally and later accidentally fell out of some texts (or were stricken out deliberately in the interests of the rhythm of the sentence, as Weiss supposed), or whether they were inserted by the Western reviser who thought that the run from Samos to Miletus was too long, it is difficult to decide. Chiefly because of superior external attestation, a majority of the Committee preferred the shorter text.

20.18

In this verse codex Bezae makes a number of characteristic additions. After the opening words, "And when they [the Ephesian elders] came to him," the Western reviser added the superfluous ὁμόσε ὄντων αὐτῶν ("while they were together"). It is easy to understand why ἀδελφοί was inserted after ἐπίστασθε. After Ἀσίαν D reads ὡς τριετίαν ἢ καὶ πλεῖον ποταπῶς μεθ' ὑμῶν ἦν [? ἤμην] παντὸς χρόνου ("for about three years or even more …"); the addition may be derived from ver. 31.

20.21 εἰς τὸν κύριον ἡμῶν Ἰησοῦν {B}

There is no good reason why Χριστόν should have been omitted if it were present originally, whereas scribal expansion of the names of the Lord is a frequent occurrence.

20.24

Instead of the awkward, yet idiomatic, ἀλλ' οὐδενὸς λόγου ποιοῦμαι τὴν ψυχὴν τιμίαν ἐμαυτῷ ($\mathfrak{P}^{74}$ ℵ* B C D² copˢᵃ *al*), the Western text (in D) expands to ἀλλ' οὐδενὸς λόγον ἔχω μοι οὐδὲ ποιοῦμαι τὴν ψυχήν μου τιμίαν ἐμαυτοῦ [perhaps for ἐμαυτῷ] ("But I make no reckoning of anything for myself nor do I account my life as precious [to me]"). The Textus Receptus, following E H L P and most minuscules, combines elements of the Alexandrian and

---

[11] W. M. Ramsay, *The Church in the Roman Empire*, p. 155.

Western texts, reading ἀλλ᾽ οὐδενὸς λόγον ποιοῦμαι οὐδὲ ἔχω τὴν ψυχήν μου τιμίαν ἐμαυτῷ.

After διαμαρτύρασθαι the Western text (D it^gig vg cop^sa Lucifer Ephraem) expands by adding Ἰουδαίοις καὶ Ἕλλησιν from ver. 21.

20.25 τὴν βασιλείαν

After τὴν βασιλείαν D and cop^sa add τοῦ Ἰησοῦ; it^gig and Lucifer add τοῦ κυρίου Ἰησοῦ; and E H L P most minuscules vg syr^p al (followed by the Textus Receptus) add τοῦ θεοῦ. The text is adequately supported by 𝔓^74 ℵ* A B C 33 36^a 307 431 al.

20.28 θεοῦ {C}

The external evidence is singularly balanced between "church *of God*" and "church *of the Lord*" (the reading "church *of the Lord and God*" is obviously conflate, and therefore secondary – as are also the other variant readings). Palaeographically the difference concerns only a single letter: Θ̅Υ̅ and Κ̅Υ̅. In deciding between the two readings one must take into account internal probabilities.

The expression ἐκκλησία κυρίου occurs seven times in the Septuagint but nowhere in the New Testament. On the other hand, ἐκκλησία τοῦ θεοῦ appears with moderate frequency (eleven times) in the Epistles traditionally ascribed to Paul, but nowhere else in the New Testament. (The phrase αἱ ἐκκλησίαι πᾶσαι τοῦ Χριστοῦ occurs once in Ro 16.16.) It is possible, therefore, that a scribe, finding θεοῦ in his exemplar, was influenced by Old Testament passages and altered it to κυρίου. On the other hand, it is also possible that a scribe, influenced by Pauline usage, changed κυρίου of his exemplar to θεοῦ.

In support of the originality of κυρίου is the argument (urged by a number of scholars[12]) that copyists were likely to substitute the more

---

[12] E. g., S. P. Tregelles, *An Account of the Printed Text of the Greek New Testament* (London, 1854), pp. 233 f.; Ezra Abbot, "On the Reading 'Church of *God*,' Acts xx.28," *Bibliotheca Sacra*, xxxiii (1876), pp. 313–352 (reprinted in Abbot's *The Authorship of the Fourth Gospel and other Critical Essays* [Boston, 1888], pp. 315 ff.);

common phrase ἡ ἐκκλησία τοῦ θεοῦ for the more rare phrase ἡ ἐκκλησία τοῦ κυρίου.

On the other hand, it is undeniable that θεοῦ is the more difficult reading. The following clause speaks of the church "which he obtained διὰ τοῦ αἵματος τοῦ ἰδίου." If this is taken in its usual sense ("with his own blood"), a copyist might well raise the question, Does God have blood?, and thus be led to change θεοῦ to κυρίου. If, however, κυρίου were the original reading, there is nothing unusual in the phrase to catch the mind of the scribe and throw it off its balance. This and other considerations led the Committee (as well as a variety of other scholars[13]) to regard θεοῦ as the original reading.

Instead of the usual meaning of διὰ τοῦ αἵματος τοῦ ἰδίου, it is possible that the writer of Acts intended his readers to understand the expression to mean "with the blood of his Own." (It is not necessary to suppose, with Hort, that υἱοῦ may have dropped out after τοῦ ἰδίου, though palaeographically such an omission would have been easy.) This absolute use of ὁ ἴδιος is found in Greek papyri as a term of endearment referring to near relatives.[14] It is possible, therefore, that "his Own" (ὁ ἴδιος) was a title that early Christians gave to Jesus, comparable to "the Beloved" (ὁ ἀγαπητός); compare Ro 8.32, where Paul refers to God "who did not spare τοῦ ἰδίου υἱοῦ" in a context that clearly alludes to Gn 22.16, where the Septuagint has τοῦ ἀγαπητοῦ υἱοῦ.

Without committing itself concerning what some have thought to be a slight probability that τοῦ ἰδίου is used here as the equivalent of

---

F. W. Farrar, "A Few Various Readings in the New Testament," *Expositor,* IX (1879), pp. 378 ff.; J. H. Ropes, *The Text of Acts,* pp. 198 f.; and a majority of the NEB translators, according to R. V. G. Tasker, ed., *The Greek New Testament* (1964), p. 433.

[13] E. g., Henry Alford, *The Greek Testament,* new ed., II (Boston, 1881), pp. 230 f.; R. J. Knowling, *The Expositor's Greek Testament,* II (London, 1900), p. 434; E. Jacquier, *Les Actes des Apôtres* (Paris, 1926), p. 615; K. Lake and H. J. Cadbury, *The Beginnings of Christianity,* IV (1933), p. 261; Charles F. De Vine, "The 'Blood of God' in Acts 20:28," *Catholic Biblical Quarterly,* IX (1947), pp. 381 ff.; F. F. Bruce, *The Acts of the Apostles* (London, 1951), p. 381; C. S. C. Williams, *A Commentary on the Acts of the Apostles* (New York, 1957), p. 234; E. Haenchen, *The Acts of the Apostles, A Commentary,* pp. 582 f.

[14] James Hope Moulton, *Prolegomena,* p. 90; and Moulton and Milligan, *Vocabulary, s.v.*

τοῦ ἰδίου υἱοῦ, the Committee judged that the reading θεοῦ was more likely to have been altered to κυρίου than vice versa.

20.28 αἵματος τοῦ ἰδίου {A}

The reading ἰδίου αἵματος is supported by many of the Byzantine witnesses that read the conflation κυρίου καὶ θεοῦ in the preceding variant. It may well be, as Lake and Cadbury point out, that after the special meaning of ὁ ἴδιος (discussed in the previous comment) had dropped out of Christian usage, τοῦ ἰδίου of this passage was misunderstood as a qualification of αἵματος ("his own blood"). "This misunderstanding led to two changes in the text: τοῦ αἵματος τοῦ ἰδίου was changed to τοῦ ἰδίου αἵματος (influenced by Heb. ix.12?), which is neater but perverts the sense, and θεοῦ was changed to κυρίου by the Western revisers, who doubtless shrank from the implied phrase 'the blood of God.'"[15]

20.32 θεῷ {B}

The predominant weight of the witnesses supports θεῷ.

21.1 Πάταρα {A}

Although it is possible (as both Ropes and Clark argue) that καὶ Μύρα was accidentally dropped through homoeoteleuton (παταρακαιμυρα), a majority of the Committee regarded it as slightly more probable that the text has been assimilated either to 27.5 (so Blass and Weiss) or to the narrative in the *Acts of Paul and Thecla* concerning Paul's residence in Myra.[1]

21.8 ἤλθομεν {A}

Before ἤλθομεν the Textus Receptus, following H L P 049 056 0142 and most minuscules, inserts οἱ περὶ τὸν Παῦλον. The reason

---

[15] *The Beginnings of Christianity,* vol. IV, p. 261.

[1] For an account of Paul at Myra, see M. R. James, *The Apocryphal New Testament* (Oxford, 1924), pp. 281–284, or Wilhelm Schneemelcher, *New Testament Apocrypha,* Engl. trans. by R. McL. Wilson, II (Philadelphia, 1964), pp. 363–367.

for the addition arises from the circumstance that an ecclesiastical lesson begins with ἐξελθόντες. For the same reason the Byzantine and Lectionary texts alter ἤλθομεν to ἦλθον.

21.12-15

In these verses one or another Western witness makes sundry small additions. In ver. 12 after οἱ ἐντόπιοι D and it^gig add τὸν Παῦλον; in ver. 13 D^gr adds πρὸς ἡμᾶς before ὁ Παῦλος; after δεθῆναι D and Tertullian add βούλομαι; and after Ἰησοῦ C D it^gig syr^p al add Χριστοῦ; in ver. 14 after εἰπόντες D adds πρὸς ἀλλήλους; in ver. 15 D reads μετὰ δέ τινας ἡμέρας ἀποταξάμενοι … ("And after *some* days *we bade them farewell* …").

21.13   τότε ἀπεκρίθη ὁ Παῦλος {B}

When the word τότε was taken with the preceding sentence, some copula (δέ or τε) became necessary. In several of the later forms of text τότε is omitted altogether.

21.16-17   ξενισθῶμεν Μνάσωνί … 17 Γενομένων δὲ ἡμῶν {A}

The Western text of these verses expands what may be implied in the use of ἀνεβαίνομεν (ver. 15), namely that the journey from Caesarea to Jerusalem took two days, and that Paul and the Caesarean disciples rested the first night at the home of Mnason in a village en route to Jerusalem: "*And these* [the Caesarean disciples] brought us to those with whom we were to lodge; *and when we arrived at a certain village, we stayed* with Mnason of Cyprus, a disciple of long-standing. (17) *And when we had departed* from there we came …" (οὗτοι δὲ ἦγαγον ἡμᾶς πρὸς οὓς ξενισθῶμεν, καὶ παραγενόμενοι εἴς τινα κώμην ἐγενόμεθα παρὰ Μνάσωνί τινι Κυπρίῳ, μαθητῇ ἀρχαίῳ. (17) κἀκεῖθεν ἐξιόντες ἤλθομεν …, D^vid syr^hmg).

21.21   πάντας

Ropes argues that the word πάντας, which is lacking in A D* (E) 33 vg cop^bo geo, "is so awkwardly placed that it is hard to believe it original." On the other hand, however, the argument that the word is awkwardly placed, if valid, is valid also against its having been introduced by copyists. The shorter text appears to be the result of emendation.

21.22 ἀκούσονται {B}

The expanded form of text (which is to be translated either, "There must be a meeting of the whole church" or, less probably, "A mob will congregate") appears to be a Western addition that gained rather wide circulation, though it is not in the Harclean Syriac.

21.25 ἡμεῖς ἐπεστείλαμεν {C}

The Western text brings out the meaning more explicitly by expanding so as to read, "But concerning the Gentiles who have become believers, *they* [i. e., the Jewish Christians] *have nothing to say to you, for* we have sent a letter with our judgment that they should *observe nothing of the kind, except to* keep themselves from what...."

21.25 κρίναντες φυλάσσεσθαι αὐτούς {B}

Although it can be argued that the words μηδὲν τοιοῦτον τηρεῖν αὐτοὺς εἰ μή (or ἀλλά) were deleted because no such clause is found in the Apostolic Decree (15.28), it is more likely that the reading is a Western paraphrase of the intent of the Decree. It is perhaps significant that the negative Golden Rule, which is present in the Western text of the Decree as cited in 15.20 and 29, is absent here.

21.25 τό τε εἰδωλόθυτον καὶ αἷμα καὶ πνικτὸν καὶ
          πορνείαν {B}

See the comments on 15.20.

21.31

At the end of the verse the margin of the Harclean Syriac adds with asterisk the words, "See therefore that they do not make an uprising," which Hilgenfeld, Blass, and Clark render into Greek, ὅρα οὖν μὴ ποιῶνται ἐπανάστασιν (the word ἐπανάστασις, however, does not occur in the New Testament).

22.3 ζηλωτὴς ὑπάρχων τοῦ θεοῦ

Instead of ζηλωτὴς ὑπάρχων τοῦ θεοῦ, Western witnesses offer a variety of readings. The minuscule 614 and codex Toletanus of the Vulgate omit τοῦ θεοῦ, a reading that Blass regards as original. Instead of τοῦ θεοῦ, the Vulgate reads "(zealous of) the law" (*legis*), and the margin of the Harclean Syriac reads with asterisk "(zealous of) my ancestral traditions" (representing τῶν πατρικῶν μου παραδόσεων, from Ga 1.14).

22.5 ὁ ἀρχιερεύς

After ὁ ἀρχιερεύς several Western witnesses (including 614 and syrʰ ᵂⁱᵗʰ *) add Ἀνανίας (compare 23.2).

22.7

Several Western witnesses expand the verse from parallel passages. After φωνῆς codex Gigas and the margin of the Harclean Syriac add "in the Hebrew language" (compare τῇ Ἑβραΐδι διαλέκτῳ, 26.14). The words τί με διώκεις; are followed in E 255 itᵍⁱᵍ vgᵐˢˢ syrʰᵐᵍ by σκληρόν σοι πρὸς κέντρα λακτίζειν (from 26.14).

22.9 ἐθεάσαντο {B}

Although it is possible that the phrase καὶ ἔμφοβοι ἐγένοντο fell out of the text because of homoeoteleuton, a majority of the Committee was disposed to regard it as a natural expansion in Western and other witnesses.

22.11 ὡς δὲ οὐκ ἐνέβλεπον

Adopting an expansion in several Western witnesses (it^(d, gig) syr^(hmg) cop^(sa) Ephraem) A. C. Clark reads ὡς δὲ ἀνέστην, οὐκ ἐνέβλεπον ("And when *I rose up,* I could not see"). The reading of codex Vaticanus, οὐδὲν ἔβλεπον ("I saw nothing"), which is preferred by Haenchen, may have been introduced from 9.8.

22.12 κατοικούντων Ἰουδαίων {B}

The difficulty of κατοικεῖν used absolutely in the shorter text probably led scribes to add an explanatory gloss, either ἐν Δαμάσκῳ in the later uncials and many minuscules or ἐκεῖ in it^(gig) and syr^(p). The omission of κατοικούντων in a few witnesses was probably accidental, when the eye of the scribe passed from τῶν before κατοικούντων to the last three letters of that word.

22.26 ἑκατοντάρχης

After ἀκούσας δὲ ὁ ἑκατοντάρχης the Western reviser, who left nothing to the imagination of the reader, added ὅτι Ῥωμαῖον ἑαυτὸν λέγει ("that he called himself a Roman"), a reading preserved in D it^(gig) vg^(2 mss).

22.26 Τί {A}

The reading with ὅρα seems to have arisen in order to soften the abruptness of the text.

22.29

From ἀπ' αὐτοῦ onward the text of codex Bezae is lacking. The Latin side ends in the middle of ver. 20.

Once again the Western reviser leaves nothing to the imagination of the reader; at the close of the verse 614 1611 syr^(h with *) cop^(sa) add καὶ παραχρῆμα ἔλυσεν αὐτόν ("and at once he released him"), thereby rendering ἔλυσεν αὐτὸν καί in ver. 30 otiose.[1]

23.9

In order to balance the protasis *(εἰ δὲ …)* at the close of the verse, the Byzantine text (H L P *al,* followed by the Textus Receptus) adds, perhaps from 5.39, μὴ θεομαχῶμεν ("Let us not fight against God").

23.12   συστροφὴν οἱ Ἰουδαῖοι {B}

The addition of τινες was made in order to provide better accord with ver. 13.

23.15

At the beginning of the verse the Western text (it[gig] syr[hmg] cop[sa] Lucifer) expands by reading (according to A. C. Clark's reconstruction) νῦν οὖν ἐρωτῶμεν ὑμᾶς ἵνα τοῦτο ἡμῖν ποιήσητε· συναγαγόντες τὸ συνέδριον ἐμφανίσατε τῷ χιλιάρχῳ ("Now therefore *we ask you that you do this for us: Gather the Sanhedrin together and* give notice to the tribune"). At the close of the verse the Western text (614 2147 it[h] syr[hmg]) adds ἐὰν δέῃ καὶ ἀποθανεῖν ("even though we must die too").

23.23-24

The Western text, reconstructed by A. C. Clark on the basis chiefly of 614 it[gig, h] vg[mss] syr[hmg], reads as follows: … Ἑτοιμάσατε στρατιώτας, ὅπως πορευθῶσιν ἕως Καισαρείας, ἱππεῖς ἑκατὸν καὶ δεξιολάβους διακοσίους· καὶ ἀπὸ τρίτης ὥρας τῆς νυκτὸς κελεύει ἑτοίμους εἶναι πορεύεσθαι· (24) καὶ τοῖς ἑκατοντάρχοις παρήγγειλεν κτήνη παραστῆσαι, ἵνα ἐπιβιβάσαντες τὸν Παῦλον διὰ νυκτὸς διασώσωσιν εἰς Καισάρειαν πρὸς

---

[1] In ver. 30 cop[sa] omits ἔλυσεν αὐτὸν καί.

Φήλικα τὸν ἡγεμόνα· ἐφοβήθη γὰρ μήποτε ἁρπάσαντες αὐτὸν
οἱ Ἰουδαῖοι ἀποκτένωσι, καὶ αὐτὸς μεταξὺ ἔγκλησιν ἔχῃ ὡς
ἀργύριον εἰληφώς ("... 'Get ready soldiers to go to Caesarea, *a*
hundred horsemen and two hundred spearmen,' and *he commanded*
that they be ready to start at the third hour of the night. (24) *And he*
ordered the centurions to provide mounts for Paul to ride, and bring
him *by night* to Felix the governor; *for he was afraid that the Jews*
would seize him [Paul] *and kill him, and afterwards he would incur*
the accusation of having taken money" [i. e. to allow Paul to be
lynched]). The purpose of the concluding clauses is to provide an explanation for the tribune's action.

23.29 *αὐτῶν ... ἔχοντα ἔγκλημα* {A}

After *αὐτῶν* the Western text (614 2147 syr[hmg]) adds *Μωϋσέως*
καὶ Ἰησοῦ τινος ("of Moses and a certain Jesus"), and after
ἔγκλημα the same witnesses (with it[gig]) add *ἐξήγαγον αὐτὸν μόλις*
τῇ βίᾳ ("I got him away with difficulty, by force" [cf. 24.7]).

23.30 *ἔσεσθαι ἐξαυτῆς* {B}

Of the six variant readings the only ones that have serious claim to
be original are *ἔσεσθαι ἐξαυτῆς* and *ἔσεσθαι ἐξ αὐτῶν*. The former was preferred by the Committee because, being the less usual
expression, copyists were more likely to replace it with the latter than
vice versa. The other readings are either conflations or obvious
expansions.

23.30 *σοῦ*. {B}

The Textus Receptus, following ℵ E Ψ 056 0142 and many minuscules, concludes the sentence with an appropriate epistolary close,
ἔρρωσο. Other witnesses, influenced by 15.29, add *ἔρρωσθε*. If
either of these closing formulas had been present originally, it is difficult to account for its absence from 𝔓[74vid] A B 33 it[gig] cop[sa, bo] *al* (in
15.29 no known witness lacks *ἔρρωσθε*).

23.34

The Western text, which transforms the indirect discourse into direct, is reconstructed by A. C. Clark from 383 614 it[gig] syr[hmg] cop[sa], ἀναγνοὺς δὲ τὴν ἐπιστολὴν ἐπηρώτησεν· Ἐκ ποίας ἐπαρχίας εἶ; ἔφη, Κίλιξ· καὶ πυθόμενος ἔφη … ("And when he had read *the letter,* he asked Paul, 'From what province are you?' *He said, 'A Cilician.'* And when he understood this, he said …").

24.6-8 ἐκρατήσαμεν, {B}

In the opinion of some scholars (e. g. Blass, Clark, Lagrange, Lake and Cadbury), the Western reading, which passed into the Textus Receptus, is necessary to the sense of the verses, for the aorist ἐκρατήσαμεν seems to require some sequel. On the other hand, however, the abruptness of ἐκρατήσαμεν may have prompted a desire for addition and completeness, and it is difficult to account for the omission of the disputed words if they were original. One of the effects of the addition is to change the reference of οὗ in ver. 8 from Paul to Lysias, but whether this is to be interpreted as favoring or opposing the addition is disputed.

A majority of the Committee judged that, all things considered, the passage should not be admitted into the text.

24.10 Ἀπεκρίθη … λέγειν

On the basis of a curious Western expansion in the margin of the Harclean Syriac, A. C. Clark reconstructed the following Greek text: ἀπεκρίθη δὲ ὁ Παῦλος νεύσαντος αὐτῷ τοῦ ἡγεμόνος ἀπολογίαν ἔχειν ὑπὲρ ἑαυτοῦ· ὁ δὲ σχῆμα ἔνθεον ἀναλαβὼν ἔφη[1] … ("And when the governor had motioned for him *to make a defense for himself,* Paul answered; and *having assumed a godlike bearing,* he said …").

---

[1] The Syriac reads ܡ ܡܥܡܠ ܀ܒ ܗܡܠ ܟܠܟܡ ܐܡܪ . For a similar gloss in the margin of the Harclean Syriac, cf. 26.1.

24.20 εὗρον ἀδίκημα {B}

The later manuscripts, followed by the Textus Receptus, incorporate a natural addition, which rounds out the phrase and makes it more explicit.

24.24 Ἰουδαία

After Ἰουδαία the margin of the Harclean Syriac preserves an extended gloss, which A. C. Clark renders into the following Greek: ἥτις ἠρώτησεν ἰδεῖν τὸν Παῦλον καὶ ἀκοῦσαι τὸν λόγον. Θέλων οὖν χαρίζεσθαι ("Felix came with his wife Drusilla, who was a Jewess, *who asked to see Paul and hear the word. Wishing therefore to satisfy her,* he summoned Paul"). As Ropes observes (*ad loc.*), "the purpose of the expansion is to justify the mention of Drusilla by ascribing to her a part in the action."

24.24 Χριστὸν Ἰησοῦν {B}

Acknowledging the difficulty of making a firm decision, the Committtee judged that the weight of the external evidence tends to support the longer reading.

24.26 Παύλου

After Παύλου the later manuscripts (H L P *al,* followed by the Textus Receptus), unwilling to leave anything to the reader's imagination, add ὅπως λύσῃ αὐτόν ("that he should release him").

24.27 θέλων ... δεδεμένον {A}

Corresponding to the paraphrase in ver. 24, after Φῆστον the Western text (614 2147 syr^hmg) substitutes for 27b θέλων ... δεδεμένον the statement τὸν δὲ Παῦλον εἴασεν ἐν τηρήσει διὰ Δρούσιλλαν ("but Paul he kept in prison on account of Drusilla").

25.17 *[αὐτῶν] ἐνθάδε*

On the basis of diversity of external evidence a majority of the Committee preferred the reading *αὐτῶν ἐνθάδε* ($\mathfrak{P}^{74}$ ℵ A E H L P Ψ and most minuscules). Nevertheless, in view of the combined weight of the other readings (*ἐνθάδε*, witnessed by B 0142 5 42 51 97 181 209* 234 453, and *ἐνθάδε αὐτῶν*, witnessed by C 36 180 1518 2495), it was considered advisable to enclose *αὐτῶν* within square brackets.

[The reading that best explains the origin of the others is that supported by B, for *αὐτῶν* is clearly an amelioration of a grammatical difficulty, having been added at different places by different copyists. (For other instances in Luke-Acts where the subject of a genitive absolute is understood from the context, see Lk 12.36; Ac 21.31.) B.M.M.]

25.18 *πονηρῶν* {C}

Although *πονηρῶν* (or *πονηρά* or *πονηράν*) has the appearance of being a gloss added at various places to explain *ὧν* or *αἰτίαν*, a majority of the Committee was impressed by the weight of the witnesses that support *πονηρῶν*, and explained its omission in the later witnesses as due to copyists who wished to make a smoother text.

25.21

On the basis of the testimony of it^{gig} A. C. Clark reconstructed the following Greek text: *τότε ὁ Παῦλος ἐπεκαλέσατο Καίσαρα καὶ ἠτήσατο τηρηθῆναι αὐτὸν εἰς τὴν τοῦ Σεβαστοῦ διάγνωσιν, ἐπειδή τε αὐτὸν οὐκ ἐδυνάμην κρῖναι, ἐκέλευσα ...* ("Then Paul appealed *to Caesar and asked* that he be kept in custody for the decision of the emperor, *and since I was not able to judge him,* I commanded ...").

25.23

Near the close of the verse the margin of the Harclean Syriac reads, "who had come down from the province," a reading that

probably represents the Greek τοῖς κατεβεβηκόσιν ἀπὸ τῆς ἐπ-
αρχείας. It is doubtful whether this Western reading is intended to
take the place of τοῖς κατ᾽ ἐξοχὴν τῆς πόλεως (so Ropes), or is to
be subjoined after πόλεως, with καί supplied (so Blass and A. C.
Clark).

25.24-26 ἐνθάδε

After ἐνθάδε the Western text, preserved in the margin of the
Harclean Syriac, and partially supported by a few other witnesses,
adds the following, as reconstructed by A. C. Clark: ὅπως παραδῶ
αὐτὸν εἰς βάσανον ἀναπολόγητον· (25) οὐκ ἠδυνήθην δὲ
παραδοῦναι αὐτόν, διὰ τὰς ἐντολὰς ἃς ἔχομεν παρὰ τοῦ
Σεβαστοῦ. ἐὰν δέ τις αὐτοῦ κατηγορεῖν θέλῃ, ἔλεγον
ἀκολουθεῖν μοι εἰς Καισάρειαν οὗ ἐφυλάσσετο· οἵτινες
ἐλθόντες ἐβόων ἵνα ἀρθῇ ἐκ τῆς ζωῆς. ἀκούσας δὲ ἀμφοτέρων
κατελαβόμην ἐν μηδενὶ αὐτὸν ἔνοχον εἶναι θανάτου· εἰπόντος
δέ μου, Θέλεις κρίνεσθαι μετ᾽ αὐτῶν ἐν Ἱεροσολύμοις; Καίσαρα ἐπεκαλέσατο· (26) περὶ οὗ ... ("that I should hand him over
to them for punishment without any defense. (25) But I could not hand
him over because of the orders that we have from the Emperor. But if
anyone was going to accuse him, I said that he should follow me to
Caesarea, where he [Paul] was being held in custody. And when they
came, they cried out that he should be put to death. But when I heard
both sides of the case, I found that he was in no respect guilty of
death. But when I said, 'Are you willing to be judged before them in
Jerusalem?' he appealed to Caesar. (26) ...").

26.1

The text of the Western reviser, preserved in the margin of the
Harclean Syriac,[1] adds the words, "*confident, and encouraged by the
Holy Spirit,* Paul stretched out his hand ...," a reading that A. C.
Clark reconstructed in Greek, θαρρῶν καὶ ἐν πνεύματι ἁγίῳ
παράκλησιν λαβών.

---

[1] For a similar gloss in the margin of the Harclean Syriac, cf. 24.10.

26.4 *[οἱ] Ἰουδαῖοι*

Instead of *Ἰουδαῖοι* ($\mathfrak{P}^{74}$ B C* E Ψ 3 33 81 209 234 241 242 489 611 618 642 945 1642 1704 1739 1875 1884 1891 2495), *οἱ Ἰουδαῖοι* is read by the Textus Receptus, following ℵ A C² P and most minuscules. A majority of the Committee thought it best to represent the evidence for both readings by including *οἱ* in the text but enclosing it within square brackets.

[Since *πάντες* normally takes the definite article, it is more likely that *οἱ* would have been added than omitted (note the evidence of codex Ephraemi); therefore the shorter reading is to be preferred. B.M.M.]

26.14 *γῆν*

After *εἰς τὴν γῆν* the Western text (614 1611 2147 it^gig syr^hmg) adds *διὰ τὸν φόβον ἐγὼ μόνος* ("when we had all fallen to the ground *on account of fear, only I* heard …").

26.15 *Ἰησοῦς*

After *Ἰησοῦς* the Western text (181 614 it^gig vg^mss syr^p, hmg with *) adds *ὁ Ναζωραῖος* (from 22.8).

26.16 *[με]* {C}

In order to represent the balance between external evidence and transcriptional probability, a majority of the Committee preferred to include *με* in the text, but to enclose it within square brackets.

26.20

Although the text of $\mathfrak{P}^{74}$ ℵ A B vg^mss, which was adopted by the Committee, is hardly tolerable as Greek, at the same time the addition of *εἰς* before *πᾶσαν* in the Byzantine text (E H L P and apparently all minuscules) has every appearance of being a scribal alleviation of the solecism. Blass emended the passage to read εἰς πᾶσάν τε χώραν Ἰουδαίοις καὶ τοῖς ἔθνεσιν ("in every land to both Jews and Gentiles").

26.28 ποιῆσαι {A}

The difficulty of capturing the nuances intended in this verse is notorious. Without entering into the lexical problems (e. g. does ἐν ὀλίγῳ mean "in a short time" or "with little effort"?), from the standpoint of textual criticism the reading that is supported by $\mathfrak{P}^{74vid}$ ℵ B 33 81 syr^hmg cop^bo al seems to account best for the other readings, which appear to be attempts at smoothing the meaning. Thus, instead of πείθεις codex Alexandrinus reads πείθῃ ("you *trust* [or, *think*] that you can make me a Christian"), which is adopted by Lachmann, Alford, A. C. Clark, though the verb seems to have been suggested by πείθομαι of ver. 26. The reading γενέσθαι of the Byzantine text (E P Ψ 049 most minuscules, followed by the Textus Receptus) appears to have come from the following verse. Hort, who suspected some primitive corruption in the text, suggested that possibly πέποιθας should be read for με πείθεις.

27.1-2

A. C. Clark's reconstruction of the Western text (represented in part by 97 421 syr^p and fairly completely by syr^hmg) reads as follows: Οὕτως οὖν ἔκρινεν ὁ ἡγεμὼν ἀναπέμπεσθαι αὐτὸν Καίσαρι. καὶ τῇ ἐπαύριον προσκαλεσάμενος ἑκατοντάρχην τινὰ ὀνόματι Ἰούλιον, σπείρης Σεβαστῆς, παρεδίδου αὐτῷ τὸν Παῦλον σὺν ἑτέροις δεσμώταις. (2) ἀρξάμενοι δὲ τοῦ ἀποπλεῖν εἰς τὴν Ἰταλίαν ἐπέβημεν πλοίῳ ... ("*So then the governor decided to send him to Caesar; and the next day he called* a centurion named Julius of the Augustan Cohort, and delivered to him Paul with the other prisoners. (2) *And beginning to sail for Italy* we embarked in a ship ..."). According to Ropes the origin of the Western paraphrase is to be accounted for as an attempt to relieve the abruptness of the Alexandrian text. At the close of ver. 2 several witnesses (614 1518 syr^h) add "and Secundus" (Θεσσαλονικέων δὲ Ἀρίσταρχος καὶ

Σεκοῦνδος), who in 20.4 is mentioned along with Aristarchus as a fellow Thessalonian and travel companion.

27.5 κατήλθομεν {A}

The Western text (preserved in 614 1518 2138 it[h vid] vg[mss] syr[h with *]) prefixes δι᾽ ἡμερῶν δεκάπεντε ("for fifteen days"). Ropes, followed by Lake and Cadbury, accepts the longer reading as original, explaining the omission of the words from the Alexandrian text as due to an accident, the scribe's eye wandering from ΔΙΑΠΛΕΥCΑΝΤΕC to the following words ΔΙΗΜΕΡΩΝΔΕΚΑΠΕΝΤΕ. On the other hand, however, neither the general character of the witnesses that include the longer reading, nor the variation of location where it appears in the text, inspires confidence in its originality.

27.14 Εὐρακύλων {B}

The earliest reading, attested by Alexandrian and Western witnesses, appears to be Εὐρακύλων, a hybrid compound of Εὖρος, the east wind, and Latin *Aquilo,* the north wind. The word, which does not occur elsewhere, obviously gave trouble to copyists, who introduced a wide variety of emendations.

27.15 ἐπιδόντες

After ἐπιδόντες the Western text (preserved in 82 614 1518 2125 syr[h with *] Cassiodorus Bede) adds τῷ πνέοντι (614 and 1518 have πλέοντι by error) καὶ συστείλαντες τὰ ἱστία ("when the ship was caught and could not face the wind, we gave way to [the wind] *which was blowing, and having furled the sails* we were driven" (syr[h] continues, *"as chance would have it"*)).

27.16 Καῦδα {B}

According to Blass the true form of the word is Καῦδος or Γαῦδος, but it was frequently spelled with λ.[1] Haenchen, following

---

[1] Cf. also J. Rendel Harris, "Clauda or Cauda?" *Expository Times,* XXI (1909–10), pp. 17–19.

Lake and Cadbury, thinks that Κλαῦδα is the Alexandrian and Καῦδα the Latin form of the name. The form without λ was taken over into modern Greek Γαυδονῆσι (the island *[νῆσος]* of Gaudos). The reading of the Textus Receptus Κλαύδην, following H L P and most minuscules, betrays an editorial hand that corrected the grammar to the accusative.

27.19 ἔρριψαν

Once again the Western text (614 it^{gig, s} vg^{ms} syr^{h with *} cop^{sa}) emphasizes the obvious by adding after ἔρριψαν the words εἰς τὴν θάλασσαν.

27.29-30

At the close of ver. 29 several Western witnesses (it^{gig} vg^{mss}) add *ut sciremus an salvi esse possimus* (*possemus* vg^{mss}) ("that we might know whether we could be saved"), a clause that Blass, following Hilgenfeld, reconstructs in Greek, τοῦ εἰδέναι εἰ σωθῆναι δυνάμεθα. At the close of ver. 30 the same authorities add *ut tutius navis staret* ("so that the ship might ride more safely"), a clause that A. C. Clark, following the Greek reconstruction of Hilgenfeld and Blass, introduces into his text, τοῦ ἀσφαλέστερον τὸ πλοῖον ἑστάναι.

27.34 ὑπάρχει

On the strength of it^{gig} Blass and A. C. Clark add after ὑπάρχει the words ἐλπίζω γὰρ ἐν τῷ θεῷ μου ὅτι ("it will give you strength; *for I hope in my God that* not a hair will perish from the head of any of you").

27.35 ἐσθίειν {A}

After ἐσθίειν the Western text (614 1611 2147 cop^{sa} syr^{h with *}) adds ἐπιδιδοὺς καὶ ἡμῖν ("having given also to us"). If one inquires who, in the mind of the Western reviser, is comprehended by ἡμῖν, it is not enough to suggest (as Ramsay does) Luke and Aristarchus, for, according to the Western text of ver. 2, Secundus should also be included. According to Bruce,[2] "in this narrative ἡμεῖς includes the whole ship's company along with the narrator."

27.37 διακόσιαι ἑβδομήκοντα ἕξ {B}

The reading in B and cop[sa] ("about seventy-six") probably arose by taking πλοιωϲοϲ̅ as πλοιωωϲοϲ̅.[3] In any case, ὡς with an exact statement of number is inappropriate (despite Luke's penchant for qualifying numbers by using ὡς or ὡσεί, cf. Lk 3.23; Ac 2.41; 4.4; 5.7, 36; 10.3; 13.18, 20; 19.7, 34).

Other witnesses present a curious vacillation: codex Alexandrinus reads 275; 69 and Ephraem read 270; occasional Coptic (Bohairic) manuscripts read ρ̅ος̅ (= 176) or ω̅ος̅ (= 876); 522 and *l*[680] read 76; and Epiphanius reads ὡς ἑβδομήκοντα.

27.39 ἐξῶσαι {A}

The reading ἐκσῶσαι, "*to bring* the ship *safe* to shore," apparently arose from an error in hearing; the verb ἐξῶσαι is regularly used of "driving [a ship] ashore."

27.41 ὑπὸ τῆς βίας [τῶν κυμάτων] {C}

While it may be true, as Ropes points out, that "the curtness of ὑπὸ τῆς βίας led to various expansions," it is also true that the penchant of Alexandrian scribes for brevity of expression may account for the deletion of τῶν κυμάτων. Faced with these conflicting possibilities, the Committee decided to retain the words τῶν κυμάτων but to enclose them within square brackets in order to indicate doubt that they belong in the text. The singular readings of 629 and of Ψ are the result of scribal idiosyncrasies.

---

[2] F. F. Bruce, *The Acts of the Apostles* (London, 1951), p. 465.

[3] In Greek the letter sigma may stand for the numeral 200, and omicron for 70; the letter digamma (or stigma) is 6. (See also footnote 4 on page 216 above.)

28.1   Μελίτη {A}

The reading Μελιτήνη (B* *al*) probably arose through dittography of some of the letters in Μελίτη ἡ νῆσος in *scriptio continua*. The reading Μυτιλήνη, presupposed by several Latin witnesses, is a translational or transcriptional error, occasioned perhaps by the recollection of 20.14 (where the alternative spelling Μιτυλήνη occurs).

28.13   περιελόντες {C}

Although it is possible that the reading περιελόντες is simply a scribal mistake (ϴ having fallen out before ο), a majority of the Committee preferred to follow ℵ* B Ψ cop[sa, (bo)], taking the word to be a technical nautical term of uncertain meaning (it may be a shorter expression for τὰς ἀγκύρας περιελόντες, as in 27.40, "weighing (anchor)," "casting loose").[1] The difficulty of the term would have given rise to the variant readings, περιελθόντες, προσελθόντες, and προελθόντες.

28.16   ἐπετράπη τῷ Παύλῳ {A}

The Western text expands ἐπετράπη τῷ Παύλῳ into ὁ ἑκατόνταρχος παρέδωκε τοὺς δεσμίους τῷ στρατοπεδάρχῳ, τῷ δὲ Παύλῳ ἐπετράπη ("the centurion delivered the prisoners to the stratopedarch [captain of the guard]; but Paul was allowed ..."). The expansion passed into the Byzantine text and lies behind the AV.

After καθ' ἑαυτόν the Western text (614 1611 2147 it[gig, p] vg[mss] syr[h with *] Ambrosiaster) adds ἔξω τῆς παρεμβολῆς ("outside the barracks").

28.18   οἵτινες

After οἵτινες the Western text (614 2147 syr[h with *]) adds πολλά ("when they had examined me *concerning many things* [or, after a *long* examination]").

---

[1] See also Westcott and Hort, *Introduction*, pp. 226 f.

28.19 τῶν Ἰουδαίων

Once again the Western text (represented by 614 syr[h with *] and other witnesses) expands the text, adding after τῶν Ἰουδαίων the words καὶ ἐπικραζόντων, Αἶρε τὸν ἐχθρὸν ἡμῶν ("and crying out, 'Away with our enemy!'"). At the close of the verse the same authorities, joined by other minuscules and it[gig, p] vg[mss], continue with the clause ἀλλ' ἵνα λυτρώσωμαι τὴν ψυχήν μου ἐκ θανάτου ("but that I might deliver my soul from death").

28.19 κατηγορεῖν {A}

Following the infinitive several Western witnesses expand by adding, "but that I might deliver my soul from death."

28.25 ὑμῶν {B}

External attestation ($\mathfrak{P}^{74}$ ℵ A B Ψ 33 81 1739 it[p, s] cop[sa, bo] geo *al*) as well as internal considerations (the tone and contents of the speech, conveying censure and rejection) led the Committee to prefer the second person pronoun.

28.29 *omit verse* {A}

The Western expansion (represented by 383 614 it[gig, p] vg[mss] syr[h with *]) was adopted by the Byzantine text and lies behind the AV rendering, "And when he had said these words, the Jews departed, and had great reasoning among themselves." The addition was probably made because of the abrupt transition from ver. 28 to ver. 30.

28.31 ἀκωλύτως. {A}

The artistic literary cadence of the concluding phrase of the book of Acts and the powerful note of triumph expressed by ἀκωλύτως are greatly weakened by the pious Western addition after ἀκωλύτως, found with variations[2] in it^p vg^{mss} syr^{htxt} Ephraem (as reconstructed by Clark): ὅτι οὗτός ἐστιν Ἰησοῦς ὁ υἱὸς τοῦ θεοῦ, δι᾽ οὗ μέλλει ὅλος ὁ κόσμος κρίνεσθαι ("[saying] that this is Jesus the Son of God, through whom the whole world is to be judged").

Following ἀκωλύτως, several later witnesses (Ψ 36 453 614 1175 2495 *al* vg^{ww} syr^h *al*) conclude the book with "Amen," indicating a liturgical use of the text.

---

[2] See Donatien De Bruyne, "Le dernier verset des Actes, une variante inconnue," *Revue Bénédictine*, XXIV (1907), pp. 403 f., who draws attention to a quotation in *Liber de divinis scripturis* (ed. Weirich), chap. 2, *Quibus praedicabat Paulus dicens: hic est Iesus Christus filius dei vivi, per quem iudicabitur omnis orbis terrarum* ("To whom Paul was preaching saying, 'This is Jesus Christ the son of the living God, through whom the whole world will be judged' ").

THE LETTER OF PAUL TO THE ROMANS

1.1 Χριστοῦ Ἰησοῦ {B}

In the opening verses of most of the Pauline letters, the manuscripts vary the sequence between Ἰησοῦ Χριστοῦ and Χριστοῦ Ἰησοῦ. In general, the earlier letters read indubiably Ἰησοῦ Χριστοῦ (or Χριστῷ), while those written later (with the exception of Titus) just as indubiably read Χριστοῦ Ἰησοῦ. For Romans (and 1 Corinthians), however, the weight of the witnesses supporting each sequence is more evenly balanced. On the basis of two fourth-century manuscripts ($\mathfrak{P}^{10}$ and B), supported by 81 and several other witnesses, the Committee preferred the sequence Χριστοῦ Ἰησοῦ.

1.7 ἐν Ῥώμῃ {A}

A majority of the Committee interpreted the absence of the words ἐν Ῥώμῃ in several witnesses (G 1739[mg] 1908[mg] it[g] Origen) either as the result of an accident in transcription, or, more probably, as a deliberate excision, made in order to show that the letter is of general, not local, application. Whether the omission of the designation is also connected with the circulation of an alternative (shorter or longer) form of the letter (see the comment on 14.23) is an open question.

1.7 ἀγαπητοῖς θεοῦ

In view of the early and decisive support for the reading ἀγαπητοῖς θεοῦ ($\mathfrak{P}^{10, 26}$ ℵ A B C Ψ 81 1739 vg syr[p, h, pal] cop[sa, bo] arm Origen[gr, lat] al), the variant ἐν ἀγάπῃ θεοῦ (G it[d*, r, 61] al) was judged by a majority of the Committee to be clearly secondary. Its origin may be connected with the omission of ἐν Ῥώμῃ (see the comment on the previous variant), and the final syllable of ἀγαπητοῖς may have been taken to be a superfluous definite article. The omission of ἀγαπητοῖς θεοῦ in several witnesses (D[abs1] 1915) must be regarded as accidental.

1.13 οὐ θέλω {A}

The reading of D* G it^{d, g} Ambrosiaster Pelagius, οὐκ οἴομαι ("I
do not suppose"), was regarded as a scribal modification limited to
Western witnesses; οὐκ οἴσμαι is still more limited (D^d D^{abs1}). The
reading οὐ θέλω, which is supported by the great mass of the
manuscripts (𝔓^{26vid} ℵ A B C D^c K P Ψ 88 614 1739 *Byz* it^{ar, mon} vg
syr^{(p), h} cop^{(sa), bo} arm *al*), is not only in accord with Paul's usage elsewhere (Ro 11.25; 1 Cor 10.1; 12.1; 2 Cor 1.8; 1 Th 4.13) but seems to
be required in the context (where Paul gives information about his
movements).

1.15 τοῖς ἐν Ῥώμῃ {A}

Two witnesses (the bilingual G and the Latin translation of Origen)
omit τοῖς ἐν Ῥώμῃ, either accidentally, or, more probably, deliberately (to make the letter of general application). See the comment on
ἐν Ῥώμῃ at 1.7.

1.16 πρῶτον

The omission of πρῶτον (B G it^g cop^{sa} Tertullian Ephraem) is
perhaps due to Marcion, to whom the privilege of the Jews was unacceptable. All other witnesses include the word.

1.29 πονηρίᾳ πλεονεξίᾳ κακίᾳ {C}

The Textus Receptus, following L Ψ 88 326 330 614 *Byz Lect* syr^h
arm *al,* inserts πορνείᾳ ("fornication") before πονηρίᾳ. Although it
could be argued that πορνείᾳ had fallen out accidentally in transcription, it is more likely that the word is an intrusion into the text, either
accidentally (when ΠΟΝΗΡΙΑ was erroneously read as ΠΟΡΝΕΙΑ) or
deliberately (when copyists, finding the word in some forms of the
text (D* E G P *al*), inserted it by conflation either before or after
πονηρίᾳ). The fact, however, that Paul argues (verses 24-25) that
such vices as listed here issue from the licentious practices of idolatry, makes it unlikely that he would have included πορνείᾳ within
the list itself.

1.31 ἀστόργους {A}

Recalling a similar catalog of vices in 2 Tm 3.2-5, where ἄστοργος is followed by ἀσπόνδος, copyists inserted the latter word in Romans, some before ἀστόργους (33 1913), and others after (ℵ C Ψ *al*).

2.16 Χριστοῦ Ἰησοῦ {C}

In view of considerable doubt as to which sequence is original, the Committee preferred to adopt the reading supported by the oldest extant witnesses (ℵ* vid B; Origen reads ἐν Χριστῷ Ἰησοῦ).

2.17 εἰ δέ

The Textus Receptus, following the later text (Dᶜ L most minuscules syrʰ), reads ἴδε (whence the AV rendering, "Behold"). This reading arose either as an itacism (ει and ι were pronounced alike) or as a deliberate amelioration of an otherwise extremely long and drawn out sentence (with the apodosis in ver. 21). In any case εἰ δέ is strongly supported by the best representatives of the Alexandrian and the Western types of text (ℵ A B D* K itᵈ, ᵍ vg syrᵖ copˢᵃ, ᵇᵒ arm eth).

3.7 δέ {B}

A majority of the Committee, feeling that Paul's argument requires a parallel between verses 5 and 7, preferred the reading εἰ δέ and regarded εἰ γάρ as a rather inept scribal substitution, perhaps of Western origin.

3.12 [οὐκ ἔστιν] (2) {C}

The second instance of οὐκ ἔστιν is absent from several witnesses (B 1739 syrᵖ Origen), which in this respect differ from the Septuagint text of Ps 13.3. Although the non-Septuagintal reading is generally to be preferred when it appears that the other reading has been assimilated to the Septuagint, in this case a majority of the Committee preferred the longer reading, supported as it is by the mass of witnesses, considering it probable that οὐκ ἔστιν was deleted as superfluous. At the same time, because of the weight of the combination of witnesses that omit the words (B 1739 syrᵖ Origen), it was decided to enclose them within square brackets.

3.22 εἰς πάντας {B}

In place of εἰς πάντας (𝔓⁴⁰ ℵ* B C P Ψ 81 1739 *al*) a few witnesses read ἐπὶ πάντας (vg Pelagius John-Damascus). The Textus Receptus, following ℵᶜ D G K 33 *al,* combines the two readings, producing an essentially redundant and tautological expression.

3.25 διὰ [τῆς] πίστεως {C}

On the one hand, the article may have been added by copyists who wished to point back to διὰ πίστεως Ἰησοῦ Χριστοῦ in ver. 22. On the other hand, later in the chapter when Paul uses πίστις absolutely (i. e. without a modifier), διά is followed by the article (cf. verses 30 and 31). In order to represent the balance in both external evidence and internal considerations, a majority of the Committee preferred to include τῆς in the text, but to enclose it within square brackets to indicate doubt that it belongs there. The omission of the clause in A and 2127 must be accidental.

3.26 Ἰησοῦ

The expansion of Ἰησοῦ (ℵ A B C K P 81 1739 *Byz al*) by the addition of Χριστοῦ (629 it⁽ᵈ*⁾, ⁶¹ copᵇᵒ *al*) is a natural scribal accretion. The reading of syrᵖ *(κυρίου ἡμῶν Ἰησοῦ Χριστοῦ)* corresponds to Syriac ecclesiastical idiom. The omission of Ἰησοῦ by F G 336 itᵍ and the reading Ἰησοῦν in Dᵍʳ Ψ 33 614 *Lect al* are the result of copyists' blunders in transcribing *scriptio continua* ΙΥΠΟΥΟΥΝ. (Ἰησοῦ was usually written ιυ, and Ἰησοῦν, ιν.)

3.28 γάρ {B}

On the whole, the external evidence supporting γάρ (ℵ A D* Ψ 81 1739 Old Latin vg syr^pal cop^sa, bo arm *al*) is slightly superior to that supporting οὖν (B C D^c K P 33 614 *Byz* syr^p, h *al*). The context, moreover, favors γάρ, for ver. 28 gives a reason for the argument in ver. 27, not a conclusion from it. The reading οὖν probably arose when copyists took λογιζόμεθα to mean "we infer, we conclude," rather than "we hold, we consider." Since ver. 28 opens a new lesson (for the third Saturday after Pentecost), the Greek lectionaries omit the conjunction altogether.

4.1 εὑρηκέναι Ἀβραὰμ τὸν προπάτορα ἡμῶν {B}

Although it can be argued that the variation of position of εὑρηκέναι (before Ἀβραάμ, ℵ A C D G Ψ 81 629 *al*; after ἡμῶν, K P 33 88 614 *Byz al*) indicates that the word was added at various places and that therefore the short text (B 1739 Origen) is original, the Committee considered that (*a*) there was no reason why copyists should have decided to add εὑρηκέναι at various places if it did not belong in the text originally, and (*b*) εὑρηκέναι after ἐροῦμεν may have fallen out accidentally because of the similarity of the beginning of both verbs. Of the two readings that include the word, the sequence ἡμῶν εὑρηκέναι was judged inferior both in sense and external support.

The word προπάτορα (which occurs nowhere else in the New Testament) was replaced in the later manuscripts (K P 33 104 614 1739 *Byz Lect al*) by πατέρα (which is the customary designation in the New Testament for Abraham; see Lk 16.24, 30; Jn 8.53; Ac 7.2; Ro 4.12).

4.11 λογισθῆναι [καί] {C}

On the one hand, after the final syllable of λογισθῆναι the word καί, being not indispensable to the sense, could easily have been overlooked in transcription. On the other hand, it is possible that καί has been added by copyists in the interest (at least superficially) of sharpening the argument ("... reckoned to them also"). In view of the balance of transcriptional probabilities, a majority of the Committee thought it best to include καί but to enclose it within square brackets. The reading of 451 is obviously a scribal blunder.

4.15 δέ {B}

As far as external evidence is concerned, the reading οὐ δέ appears to be rather decisively supported (ℵ* A B C 81 *al*). On the other hand, if οὐ γάρ were original, one could understand that some scribes, noticing the presence of γάρ at the beginning of verses 13, 14, and 15, might well have decided to replace the fourth instance of γάρ with δέ. In the face of such considerations, the Committee preferred to adopt the reading supported by the earliest evidence.

4.19 κατενόησεν {C}

Curiously enough, each of the two readings, one positive and one negative, gives good sense: (*a*) κατενόησεν (ℵ A B C 81 1739 vg syr[p] cop[sa, bo, fay] arm *al*) means, "His faith did not weaken when he considered ...," and (*b*) οὐ κατενόησεν (D G K P Ψ 33 *Byz Lect* it[d, g] syr[h] *al*) means, "He was so strong in faith that he did not consider. ..." Whereas reading (*b*), like many other readings of Western origin, appears at first to be preferable, after further reflection it reveals itself to be less appropriate in the context: here Paul does not wish to imply that faith means closing one's eyes to reality, but that Abraham was so strong in faith as to be undaunted by every consideration.

4.19 [ἤδη] {C}

The predominant weight of manuscript evidence, in the opinion of a majority of the Committee, favors the retention of ἤδη (ℵ A C D[gr] K P Ψ 33 81 *Byz Lect* syr[h with *] cop[bo] arm *al*). At the same time, however, the presence of ἤδη gives the impression of a certain heightening of the account. Moreover, who would have omitted the word had it stood in the text originally? As a compromise that reflects the conflict between external evidence and internal considerations, the Committee retained ἤδη in the text but enclosed it within square brackets.

4.22 *[καί]* {C}

In order to represent the balance of external evidence for and against the presence of καί, the Committee decided to print it within square brackets.

5.1 *ἔχομεν* {A}

Although the subjunctive ἔχωμεν (א* A B* C D K L 33 81 it[d, g] vg syr[p, pal] cop[bo] arm eth *al*) has far better external support than the indicative ἔχομεν (א[a] B[3] G[gr] P Ψ 0220[vid] 88 326 330 629 1241 1739 *Byz Lect* it[61vid?] syr[h] cop[sa] *al*), a majority of the Committee judged that internal evidence must here take precedence. Since in this passage it appears that Paul is not exhorting but stating facts ("peace" is the possession of those who have been justified), only the indicative is consonant with the apostle's argument. Since the difference in pronunciation between *o* and *ω* in the Hellenistic age was almost non-existent, when Paul dictated ἔχομεν, Tertius, his amanuensis (16.22), may have written down ἔχωμεν. (For another set of variant readings involving the interchange of *o* and *ω,* see 1 Cor 15.49.)

5.2 *[τῇ πίστει]* {C}

It is doubtful whether the words τῇ πίστει belong to the text or not, for the weight of external evidence is almost evenly balanced between their inclusion (א A C K P Ψ 33 1739 *Byz Lect* it[dc, 61] vg syr[p, h, pal]) and their omission (B D G 0220 it[d*, g] cop[sa]). Furthermore, the sense is not materially changed by their presence or their absence, for Paul has previously declared that faith is necessary for justification, and therefore it may be that copyists dropped the words as redundant and superfluous after ἐκ πίστεως of ver. 1. In order to represent the balance of evidence, a majority of the Committee preferred to retain the words in the text but to enclose the phrase within square brackets. (The reading ἐν τῇ πίστει seems to have arisen by dittography after ἐσχήκαμεν.)

5.6 ἔτι γὰρ ... ἔτι {C}

Although it must be acknowledged that the reading εἴ γε ... ἔτι (B cop^sa) possesses a certain inherent fitness which, despite its very slender external support, makes it most attractive, a majority of the Committee could find no adequate reason why, if this reading were original, the others would have arisen. On the other hand, not only is the external evidence for ἔτι γὰρ ... ἔτι quite overwhelming in weight and variety, but also all witnesses that omit one or the other instance of ἔτι may be held to have originated as scribal improvements to avoid the awkward repetition of the word. Thus, the reading adopted as text seems to be the earliest attainable reading preserved in the manuscripts; whether it originated as a primitive error in the exemplar of the first collection of the Pauline Letters, or whether it arose when, as one may assume, Paul repeated ἔτι, perhaps for the sake of emphasis, while dictating to Tertius (16.22), it is impossible to say.

6.4 οὖν {A}

Uncertain of the appropriateness of οὖν in relating ver. 4 to ver. 3, the Peshitta Syriac version and other witnesses omit the connective, while the Old Latin versions, joined by Origen, substitute γάρ.

6.8 δέ {A}

Instead of δέ, which is supported by a very wide variety of witnesses, a few scribes preferred to use γάρ in order to connect the sentence to what goes before.

6.11 ἐν Χριστῷ Ἰησοῦ {A}

The Textus Receptus, following ℵ C K P 33 81 614 1739^c al, adds τῷ κυρίῳ ἡμῶν. The words appear to be a liturgical expansion, derived perhaps from ver. 23. If they were original, no good reason can be found why they should have been deleted from such weighty witnesses as $\mathfrak{P}^{46}$ A B D G Ψ 1739* it[d, g, 61] syr[h] cop[sa] Tertullian Origen Speculum *al*.

6.12 ταῖς ἐπιθυμίαις αὐτοῦ {B}

The reading ταῖς ἐπιθυμίαις αὐτοῦ, strongly supported by Alexandrian witnesses as well as by a few Western witnesses (א A B C* 81 1739 it[dc, r, 61] vg syr[p] cop[sa, bo] *al*), was replaced in several (chiefly Western) witnesses by αὐτῇ ($\mathfrak{P}^{46}$ D G it[d*, g] Speculum *al*), probably under the influence of the repeated mention of ἁμαρτία in the following verses. The Textus Receptus, following C[3] K P Ψ 614 *Byz Lect* syr[h] *al*, blends the two earlier readings, combined with ἐν, in the conflation αὐτῇ ἐν ταῖς ἐπιθυμίαις αὐτοῦ. The omission of the words from 618 must be accidental.

6.16 εἰς θάνατον

The words εἰς θάνατον, strongly supported by א A B C G K P Ψ 33 81 330 614 it[g, 61] syr[h, pal] cop[bo] arm[mss] eth *al*, are absent from a few witnesses, chiefly versional and patristic (D 1739* it[d, r] vg syr[p] cop[sa] arm Origen[lat] Ambrosiaster Ephraem). Since the phrase seems to be necessary as a correlative to the following phrase εἰς δικαιοσύνην, a majority of the Committee was disposed to regard their omission as an unintentional oversight.

7.14 οἴδαμεν {A}

Influenced by Paul's frequent use of "I" in verses 7 to 25, a few copyists and church Fathers divided the word so as to read οἶδα μέν. But to do this overlooks the need at this point in the apostle's argument for a statement that would command the general assent of his readers – such as he has the habit of introducing by using οἴδαμεν.

7.18 οὔ {B}

The abrupt termination of the sentence with οὔ (א A B C 81 1739 cop[sa, bo] goth arm *al*) prompted copyists to add some kind of supplement: (*a*) εὑρίσκω (D G K P Ψ 33 88* 614 *Byz Lect*), or (*b*) γινώσκω (88ᵐᵍ 2127), or (*c*) *is not in me* (eth).

7.20   *[ἐγώ]* {C}

Not only is the external evidence rather evenly balanced, but also from the point of view of transcriptional probability ἐγώ might have been either accidentally omitted through parablepsis or deliberately added for emphasis in conformity with the following ἐγώ. Accordingly, the Committee decided to retain the word but to enclose it within square brackets.

7.22   θεοῦ {A}

The scribe of B, having noticed τῷ νόμῳ τοῦ νοός in ver. 23, inadvertently replaced θεοῦ with νοός in ver. 22.

7.25   χάρις δὲ τῷ θεῷ {B}

The reading that seems best to account for the rise of the others is χάρις δὲ τῷ θεῷ, supported by ℵ¹ C² Ψ 33 81 88 104 436 2127 *al*. Two Western readings, ἡ χάρις τοῦ θεοῦ (D itᵃʳ, ᵇ, ᵈ, ᵐᵒⁿ, ᵒ vg Irenaeus *al*) and ἡ χάρις κυρίου (G itᵍ), pedantically provide a direct answer to the question τίς με ῥύσεται; in ver. 24. The absence of δέ (B copˢᵃ Origen Methodius Epiphanius Jerome¹ᐟ²) seems to represent a natural development in the light of liturgical usage (δέ is present in the same ascription at 6.17; 2 Cor 2.14; 8.16; and in some witnesses at 2 Cor 9.15). The reading εὐχαριστῶ τῷ θεῷ (ℵ* A K P 614 1739 *Byz Lect*) seems to have arisen through transcriptional error involving the doubling of several letters, ΤΟΥΤΟΥ[ΕΥ]ΧΑΡΙϹ[ΤΩ]ΤΩΘΕΩ.

8.1   Ἰησοῦ {A}

At the close of the verse the later manuscripts introduce an interpolation from ver. 4 in two stages: μὴ κατὰ σάρκα περιπατοῦσιν is read by A Dᵇ Ψ 81 629 2127 itᵈᶜ vg syrᵖ goth arm Speculum *al,* and the same clause followed by ἀλλὰ κατὰ πνεῦμα is read by ℵᶜ Dᶜ K P 33 88 104 614 *Byz Lect* it⁶¹ syrʰ *al*. The shorter text, which makes the more general statement without the qualification that is appropriate enough at ver. 4, is strongly supported by early representatives of both the Alexandrian and the Western types of text (א* B C² D* G 1739 it^{d*, g} cop^{sa, bo} arm^{mss} *al*).

8.2 σε {B}

While it is rather certain that the reading ἡμᾶς is a secondary modification, introduced in order to make the apostle's statement apply to all Christians (as in ver. 4), it is much more difficult to choose between με and σε. The latter, as the more difficult reading, is more likely to have been replaced by the former (which harmonizes better with the argument in chap. 7) than vice versa. On the other hand σε may have originated in the accidental repetition of the final syllable of ἠλευθέρωσεν when the terminal -ν, represented by a horizontal line over the ε, was overlooked.

Although it is possible that the original text was without any object pronoun, the verb being used absolutely (i. e. as a kind of gnomic aorist), the Committee was reluctant to rely upon the slender evidence for omission (arm^{mss} Origen), since the absence of a pronoun in these witnesses may reflect nothing more than freedom of translation or quotation. Impressed by the weight of the combination of Alexandrian and Western witnesses, a majority of the Committee preferred σε as the earliest attainable text.

8.11 τοῦ ἐνοικοῦντος αὐτοῦ πνεύματος {B}

Remembering that in the Pauline corpus the weight of B when associated with D G (as here) is quite considerably lessened, a majority of the Committee preferred the genitive case, on the basis of the combination of text-types, including the Alexandrian (א A C 81), Palestinian (syr^{pal} Cyril-Jerusalem), and Western (it^{61?} Hippolytus).

8.21 ὅτι {A}

The oldest and best witnesses read ὅτι (𝔓^{46} A B C 33 81 614 1739 *al*). Apparently διότι arose accidentally by dittography, ΕΛΠΙΔΙΟΤΙ becoming ΕΛΠΙΔΙΔΙΟΤΙ.

8.23 υἱοθεσίαν {A}

Several witnesses, chiefly Western (𝔓⁴⁶vid D G 614 itᵈ, ᵍ *al*), omit υἱοθεσίαν, a word that copyists doubtless found to be both clumsy in the context and dispensable, as well as seeming to contradict ver. 15.

8.24 τίς {B}

A majority of the Committee, impressed by the weight of the combination of 𝔓⁴⁶ B* 1739ᵐᵍ 1908ᵐᵍ copᵇᵒ Origen, preferred the reading τίς and regarded the other readings as expansions of a strikingly terse and typically Pauline type of question. The expansions may have been introduced by copyists because of the lack of punctuation (after βλέπει) and the ambiguity of ΤΙϹ (interrogative or indefinite) in unaccented script.

8.24 ἐλπίζει {B}

Although ὑπομένει (ℵ* A 1739ᵐᵍ copˢᵃ, ᵇᵒ Origen Ephraem) may appear to be the more difficult reading and therefore deserving of adoption, a majority of the Committee was unwilling to base the text upon such limited support, especially in view of the early and very diversified testimony for ἐλπίζει (𝔓⁴⁶ B C D G Ψ 33 81 614 1739* itᵈ, ᵍ, ⁶¹ vg syrᵖ, ʰ arm eth Clement Origenˡᵃᵗ Cyprian *al*). Furthermore, although the verb ὑπομένειν with object ("to await something") is rather common in the Septuagint, no example for this use can be cited from the New Testament except the present variant reading. On balance, therefore, it is probable that the presence of ὑπομονή in the following verse prompted an early copyist to substitute ὑπομένει for ἐλπίζει.

8.26 ὑπερεντυγχάνει {A}

The Textus Receptus, following ℵᶜ C K P Ψ 33 614 *Byz Lect al*, adds ὑπὲρ ἡμῶν, thus making explicit what is implicit in the compound verb ὑπερεντυγχάνει, which is decisively supported by 𝔓²⁷vid ℵ* A B D G 81 1739 itᵈ*, ᵍ arm Origen *al*.

8.28 συνεργεῖ {B}

Although the reading συνεργεῖ ὁ θεός (𝔓⁴⁶ A B 81 copˢᵃ (eth) Origenᵍʳ²ᐟ⁵) is both ancient and noteworthy, a majority of the Committee deemed it too narrowly supported to be admitted into the text, particularly in view of the diversified support for the shorter reading (ℵ C D G K P Ψ 33 614 1739 *Byz Lect* itᵈˑ ᵍˑ ⁶¹ vg syrᵖˑ ʰ copᵇᵒ arm Clement Origenᵍʳ³ᐟ⁵ˑ ˡᵃᵗ Eusebius Lucifer Cyril-Jerusalem Chrysostom Augustine *al*). Since συνεργεῖ may be taken to imply a personal subject, ὁ θεός seems to have been a natural explanatory addition made by an Alexandrian editor.

8.34 Χριστὸς [Ἰησοῦς] {C}

The weight of the evidence for and against the presence of Χριστός is so evenly balanced that the Committee considered it preferable to retain the word but to enclose it within square brackets.

8.35 Χριστοῦ {A}

Since the reading θεοῦ τῆς ἐν Χριστῷ Ἰησοῦ (B Origenˡᵃᵗ²ᐟ⁷) is in all probability a scribal harmonization with ver. 39, the reading θεοῦ (ℵ 326 330 copˢᵃ Origenᵍʳ¹ᐟ³ˑ ˡᵃᵗ⁴ᐟ⁷ *al*) is doubtless also a partial echo of that verse. The reading Χριστοῦ is strongly supported (A C D G K Ψ 33 614 1241 1739 *Byz Lect* Old Latin vg syrᵖˑ ʰ copᵇᵒ goth arm eth Tertullian Origenᵍʳ²ᐟ³ˑ ˡᵃᵗ¹ᐟ⁷ *al*) and binds together verses 34 and 35.

8.38 οὔτε ἐνεστῶτα οὔτε μέλλοντα οὔτε δυνάμεις {A}

The Textus Receptus, following K L Ψ most minuscule manuscripts syrᵖ goth Chrysostom Theodoret Oecumenius Theophylact, places the words οὔτε δυνάμεις before οὔτε ἐνεστῶτα, thus associating them more closely with ἀρχαί (as also in 1 Cor 15.24; Eph 1.21). The reading adopted for the text is decisively supported by early and good witnesses (𝔓²⁷ˑ ⁴⁶ ℵ A B C D G itᵈ vg syrʰ copˢᵃˑ ᵇᵒ arm eth Origen Eusebius Ephraem Cyril John-Damascus Augustine *al*). There is no reason to expect that the apostle would give a systematic classification of angelic-beings; on the other hand, the rearrangement of the items has every appearance of being the work of copyists or editors who wished to improve the sequence.

9.4 αἱ διαθῆκαι {B}

Although the reading ἡ διαθήκη is strongly supported ($\mathfrak{P}^{46}$ B D^gr it^{61vid?} cop^{sa, bomss} eth *al*), the plural αἱ διαθῆκαι (ℵ C K Ψ 33 81 614 1739 *Byz Lect* it^{d, g} vg syr^{p, h, hgr} cop^bo goth arm *al*) was preferred on the grounds that (*a*) copyists would have been likely to assimilate the plural to the pattern of instances of the singular number in the series, and (*b*) plural covenants may have appeared to involve theological difficulties, and therefore the expression was converted to the singular number. Certainly there is no good reason why the singular, if original, should have been altered to the plural.

9.5 σάρκα, ὁ ὢν ἐπὶ πάντων θεὸς εὐλογητὸς εἰς τοὺς αἰῶνας

Since the earliest manuscripts of the New Testament are without systematic punctuation, editors and translators of the text must insert such marks of punctuation as seem to be appropriate to the syntax and meaning. The present passage has been the object of much discussion[1] as to whether or not Paul intended to refer θεός to ὁ Χριστός. The chief interpretations are the following:

---

[1] Among many earlier discussions pro and con, two may be singled out for special mention as representative of the two points of view. In favor of taking the words as an ascription to Christ, see William Sanday and A. C. Headlam, *A Critical and Exegetical Commentary on the Epistle to the Romans,* 2nd ed. (New York, 1896), pp. 233–238; in favor of taking the words separately from the preceding clause, see Ezra Abbot, "On the Construction of Romans ix.5," *Journal of the Society of Biblical Literature and Exegesis,* 1881, pp. 87–154, and *idem,* "Recent Discussions of Romans ix.5," *ibid.,* 1883, pp. 90–112 (both articles are reprinted in Abbot's posthumously published volume entitled, *The Authorship of the Fourth Gospel and Other Critical Essays* [Boston, 1888], pp. 332–410, and 411–438). For a more recent discussion, see the present writer's contribution to *Christ and Spirit in the New Testament; Studies in honour of C. F. D. Moule,* ed. by Barnabas Lindars and Stephen S. Smalley (Cambridge University Press, 1973), pp. 95–112; reprinted in Metzger's *New Testament Studies* (Leiden, 1980), pp. 56–74.

(*a*) Placing a comma after σάρκα and referring the following words to ὁ Χριστός ("… who is God over all, blessed for ever").

(*b*) Placing a point (either a colon or a full stop) after σάρκα and taking the following words as a clause independent of ὁ Χριστός. (Several translations are possible: "God who is over all be blessed for ever!"; or "He who is God over all be blessed for ever!"; or "He who is over all is God blessed for ever.")

(*c*) Placing a comma after σάρκα and a point (a colon or a full stop) after πάντων. (This, which is a modification of (*b*), is to be translated, "… who is over all. God be [or, is] blessed for ever!")

In deciding which punctuation should be used, the Committee was agreed that evidence from the Church Fathers, who were almost unanimous in understanding the passage as referring to ὁ Χριστός, is of relatively minor significance, as is also the opposing fact that four uncial manuscripts (A B C L) and at least twenty-six minuscule manuscripts have a point after σάρκα, either by the first hand or by subsequent correctors.[2] In both cases the tradition, whether patristic or palaeographical, originated at a time subsequent to Paul's writing (i. e. dictating; cf. 16.22) the passage, and is therefore of questionable authority.

On the one hand, some members of the Committee preferred punctuation (*a*) for the following reasons:

(1) The interpretation that refers the passage to Christ suits the structure of the sentence, whereas the interpretation that takes the words as an asyndetic doxology to God the Father is awkward and unnatural. As Westcott observes, "The juxtaposition of ὁ Χριστὸς κατὰ σάρκα and ὁ ὢν κ.τ.λ. seems to make a change of subject improbable."[3]

---

[2] So Abbot, *op. cit.*, 1883, pp. 107 f. [= pp. 431 f.]. The presence of marks of punctuation in early manuscripts of the New Testament is so sporadic and haphazard that one cannot infer with confidence the construction given by the punctuator to the passage. For example, in Ro 9.2-4 codex Alexandrinus has a colon after μεγάλη in ver. 2, one between Χριστοῦ and ὑπέρ and another after σάρκα in ver. 3, and one after Ἰσραηλῖται in ver. 4. Codex Vaticanus has a colon at the end of Ro 9.3, after both occurrences of Ἰσραήλ in ver. 6, after Ἀβραάμ in ver. 7, Ῥεβέκκα in ver. 10, and αὐτοῦ in ver. 22!

[3] B. F. Westcott in "Notes on Select Readings," in Westcott and Hort, *The New Testament in the Original Greek*, [II], *Introduction [and] Appendix*, 2nd ed. (London,

(2) If the clause ὁ ὢν κ.τ.λ. is an asyndetic doxology to God the Father, the word ὢν is superfluous, for "he who is God over all" is most simply represented by ὁ ἐπὶ πάντων θεός. The presence of the participle suggests that the clause functions as a relative clause (not "he who is ..." but "who is ..."), and thus describes ὁ Χριστός as being "God over all."

(3) Pauline doxologies, as Zahn points out,[4] are never asyndetic but always attach themselves to that which precedes: with ὅς ἐστιν (Ro 1.25); with ὁ ὢν (2 Cor 11.31); with ᾧ (Ga 1.5; 2 Tm 4.18; cf. He 13.21; 1 Pe 4.11); with αὐτῷ (Ro 11.36; Eph 3.21; cf. 1 Pe 5.11; 2 Pe 3.18); with τῷ δὲ θεῷ (Php 4.20; 1 Tm 1.17).

(4) Asyndetic doxologies, not only in the Bible but also in Semitic inscriptions, are differently constructed; the verb or verbal adjective (εὐλογητός, Heb. בָּרוּךְ, Aram. בְּרִיךְ) always precedes the name of God, and never follows it, as here.[5]

(5) In the light of the context, in which Paul speaks of his sorrow over Israel's unbelief, there seems to be no psychological explanation to account for the introduction of a doxology at this point.

On the other hand, in the opinion of others of the Committee, none of these considerations seemed to be decisive, particularly since nowhere else in his genuine epistles[6] does Paul ever designate ὁ Χριστός as θεός.[7] In fact, on the basis of the general tenor of his theology it was considered tantamount to impossible that Paul would have expressed Christ's greatness by calling him God blessed

---

1896), p. 110. Similarly Nigel Turner declares it to be grammatically unnatural that a participle agreeing with Χριστός "should first be divorced from it and then given the force of a wish, receiving a different person as its subject" (*Grammatical Insights into the New Testament* [Edinburgh, 1965], p. 15).

[4] Theodor Zahn, *Der Brief des Paulus an die Römer* (Leipzig, 1910) p. 433, Anm. 78.

[5] The only instance that appears to be an exception is Ps 68.19-20 [= LXX 67.19-20], where the Septuagint reads κύριος ὁ θεὸς εὐλογητός, εὐλογητὸς κύριος ἡμέραν καθ᾽ ἡμέραν. Here, however, the first εὐλογητός has no corresponding word in Hebrew and seems to be a double translation.

[6] Tt 2.13 is generally regarded as deutero-Pauline.

[7] In reply it was argued that if Paul could refer to Χριστὸς Ἰησοῦς as ἴσα θεῷ (Php 2.6), it is not inconceivable that on another occasion he could also refer to ὁ Χριστός as θεός.

for ever. As between the punctuation in (*b*) and (*c*), the former was preferred.

The Committee also considered the possibility that by accident in transcription ὁ ὤν had replaced an original ὤν ὁ (cf. the preceding ver. 4 ὤν ἡ υἱοθεσία …, ver. 5 ὤν οἱ πατέρες), but was unwilling to introduce a conjectural emendation into the text.[8]

9.23 καὶ ἵνα {A}

The absence of καί from several witnesses (B 326 436 1739mg itar, b vg copsa, bomss goth arm) was thought by the Committee to have been the result of an attempt to simplify the construction. The evidence from the versions in this case is of limited significance, since translational freedom, and not a different underlying Greek text, may account for the absence of the conjunction.

9.28 συντέμνων {A}

The Textus Receptus, following ℵc D G K P Ψ 33 88 326 614 1241 *Byz Lect* Old Latin vg syrh goth arm *al,* has filled out the quotation from the Septuagint Is 10.22-23 by inserting ἐν δικαιοσύνῃ, ὅτι λόγον συντετμημένον. Considered in itself, the absence of these words from 𝔓46vid ℵ* A B 1739 1881 syrp copsa, bo eth *al* could be explained as arising when the eye of a copyist accidentally passed from συντέμνων to συντετμημένον. But it is not credible that Paul, who in ver. 27 does not follow the Septuagint closely, should in ver. 28 have copied verbatim a sentence that is so opaque grammatically.

9.32 ἔργων {B}

The Textus Receptus, following ℵc D K P Ψ 33 81 614 *Byz Lect* itd syrp, h, pal goth arm *al,* adds νόμου, imitating Paul's usage in 3.20, 28;

---

[8] For an account of the history of the conjecture, see W. L. Lorimer in *New Testament Studies,* XIII (1966–67), pp. 385 f.

Ga 2.16 (thrice); 3.2, 5, 10. The shorter text is strongly supported by 𝔓⁴⁶ᵛⁱᵈ ℵ* A B G 1739 itᵃʳ, ᵇ, ᶠ, ᵍ, ᵐᵒⁿ, ᵒ vg copˢᵃ, ᵇᵒ *al.*

9.33 καί (2) {A}

Once again the Textus Receptus, following K P Ψ 33 88 326 614 1739 *Byz Lect* itᵈᶜ, ⁶¹ vg syrʰ arm, makes an addition in order to heighten the effectiveness of the quotation; here πᾶς is inserted, imitating Paul's citation of the same quotation in 10.11 (where no manuscript omits πᾶς). The text without πᾶς is strongly supported by ℵ A B D G 81 1881 itᵈ*, ᵍ syrᵖ, ᵖᵃˡ copˢᵃ, ᵇᵒ goth eth *al.*

10.1 αὐτῶν {A}

The shortest reading αὐτῶν is decisively supported by early and representative witnesses of several types of text (𝔓⁴⁶ ℵ* A B D G 1739 1881 1962 itᵈ*, ᵍ syrᵖ, ᵖᵃˡ copˢᵃ, ᵇᵒ goth *al*). The addition of ἐστιν (ℵᶜ K P Ψ 33 81 614 it⁶¹ syrʰ *al*) seems to have been made in the interest of clarifying the grammar, while the addition of τοῦ Ἰσραήλ (K 81 326 614 1241 *Byz Lect al*) may have occurred when this verse was made the beginning of a lesson read in church services (cf. the reference to Israel in 9.31).

10.15 πόδες {A}

Although it is possible that the shorter reading arose because the eye of the scribe passed from τῶν εὐαγγελιζομένων to τῶν εὐαγγελιζομένων, the Committee thought it more probable that the words τῶν εὐαγγελιζομένων εἰρήνην (ℵᶜ D G K P Ψ 33 88 614 1241 *Byz Lect* itᵈ, ᵍ vg syrᵖ, ʰ goth *al*) were inserted in order to make the citation correspond more fully to the Septuagint (Is 52.7; Na 1.15 [=LXX 2.1]).

10.17 Χριστοῦ {A}

Instead of Χριστοῦ, which is strongly supported by early and diverse witnesses (𝔓⁴⁶ᵛⁱᵈ ℵ* B C D* 81 1739 Old Latin vg copˢᵃ, ᵇᵒ, ᶠᵃʸ goth arm *al*), the Textus Receptus, following ℵ^c A D^{b, c} K P Ψ 33 614 1241 *Byz Lect* syr^{p, h} *al*, reads θεοῦ. The expression ῥῆμα Χριστοῦ occurs only here in the New Testament, whereas ῥῆμα θεοῦ is a more familiar expression (Lk 3.2; Jn 3.34; Eph 6.17; He 6.5; 11.3). The omission of Χριστοῦ (or θεοῦ) in an ancestor of several Western witnesses (G it^g Ambrosiaster Hilary Pelagius) is to be attributed to carelessness.

11.1   τὸν λαόν {A}

Instead of τὸν λαόν several witnesses (𝔓⁴⁶ G it^g goth *al*) read τὴν κληρονομίαν, which appears to be a Western assimilation to Ps 94.14 [= LXX 93.14] ὅτι οὐκ ἀπώσεται κύριος τὸν λαὸν αὐτοῦ, καὶ τὴν κληρονομίαν αὐτοῦ οὐκ ἐγκαταλείψει.

11.6   χάρις (2) {A}

After χάρις the Textus Receptus, following ℵ^c (B) L Ψ and later manuscripts, adds εἰ δὲ ἐξ ἔργων οὐκέτι ἐστὶ χάρις ἐπεὶ τὸ ἔργον οὐκέτι ἐστὶν ἔργον ("But if it be of works, then is it no more grace: otherwise work is no more work" AV). There appears to be no reason why, if the words were original, they should have been deleted. The existence of several forms of the addition likewise throws doubt upon the originality of any of them.

11.17   τῆς ῥίζης τῆς πιότητος {B}

The unexpected asyndeton of the reading τῆς ῥίζης, τῆς πιότητος τῆς ἐλαίας, in spite of its rather limited attestation (ℵ* B C Ψ), appears to explain best the origin of the other readings, since the widespread introduction of καί and the omission of τῆς ῥίζης (𝔓⁴⁶ D* G it^{d, g} *al*) are suspicious as ameliorating emendations.

11.21   [μή πως] οὐδέ {C}

On the one hand, the strong combination of ℵ B C 81 1739 in support of the shorter text would normally be preferred. On the other hand, however, (a) μή πως is a typically Pauline expression (it occurs in nine other passages in Paul; only once elsewhere in the New Testament), and (b) copyists may have taken offense at its presence here because of its apparent unrelatedness (Origen substituted the more appropriate πόσῳ μᾶλλον and πόσῳ πλέον – see Tischendorf *in loc.*) and its grammatical inappropriateness with the following future. In order to give due weight to both external evidence and internal considerations, a majority of the Committee considered it necessary to retain μή πως in the text, but to enclose it within square brackets.

11.25 *[παρ']* {C}

Although it can be argued that the simple dative, without a preposition, may be the original reading (supported, as it is, by 𝔓⁴⁶ F G Ψ 1739 *al*) and that the difficulty of construing the sense prompted scribes to insert ἐν or παρ', the Committee decided that it would be safest to adopt παρ', which is strongly supported by ℵ C D *al*, but to enclose it within square brackets in order to indicate considerable doubt whether it belongs in the text.

11.31 *[νῦν]* (2) {C}

Once again external evidence and internal considerations are rather evenly balanced. A preponderance of early and diverse witnesses favors the shorter reading. On the other hand, the difficulty in meaning that the second occurrence of νῦν seems to introduce may have prompted either its deletion or its replacement by the superficially more appropriate ὕστερον. In view of such conflicting considerations it seemed best to retain νῦν in the text but to enclose it within square brackets.

11.32 τοὺς πάντας (1) {A}

Instead of the first occurrence of τοὺς πάντας several witnesses (𝔓⁴⁶ᵛⁱᵈ D* G Old Latin vg Ambrose) substitute τὰ πάντα (or πάντα), a reading that seems to have arisen from scribal recollection of Ga 3.22 *(συνέκλεισεν ἡ γραφὴ τὰ πάντα)*.

12.2 νοός

After νοός the Textus Receptus, following ℵ D^c L P most minuscules it^{d, g} vg syr^{p, h} goth arm eth Speculum *al*, adds ὑμῶν. The shorter text, which is supported by early and good witnesses (𝔓⁴⁶ A B D^{gr*} F G 424^c 1739 Clement Origin Cyprian), is to be preferred because of the preponderance of evidence, as well as the likelihood that ὑμῶν would have suggested itself to scribes as an appropriate parallel to its occurrence in ver. 1.

12.11 κυρίῳ {A}

The reading καιρῷ, supported chiefly by Western witnesses (D* F G 5 it^{d*, g} Origen^{lat} Cyprian Ambrosiaster Jerome *al*), probably arose from a confusion of κ̅ω̅ and κρω (the *nomen sacrum* κυρίῳ was customarily contracted to κ̅ω̅, and the καί compendium was written κ).

12.14 διώκοντας [ὑμᾶς] {C}

It is difficult to decide whether ὑμᾶς was deleted in order to extend the range of the exhortation, or whether copyists, recollecting the parallel sayings in Mt 5.44 and Lk 6.28, added the pronoun. Since both readings are fairly evenly supported in the witnesses, a majority of the Committee preferred to print [ὑμᾶς].

12.17 ἐνώπιον πάντων

Under the influence of Pr 3.4 and 2 Cor 8.21 several witnesses expand by prefixing ἐνώπιον τοῦ θεοῦ καί (A^c) or οὐ μόνον ἐνώπιον τοῦ θεοῦ ἀλλὰ καί (F G it^g vg goth Lucifer Ambrosiaster). On the other hand, perhaps through transcriptional oversight (ΕΝΩΠΙΟΝΠΑΝΤΩΝΑΝΘΡΩΠΩΝ), a few witnesses omit πάντων (181 328 436 876 it^{d, g} Lucifer Speculum) and several substitute τῶν for πάντων (that is, they omit ΠΑΝ, 𝔓⁴⁶ D* F^{gr} G 056 0142 330). The word πάντων, however, is needed to give balance to the earlier μηδενί.

13.1 πᾶσα ψυχὴ ἐξουσίαις ὑπερεχούσαις ὑποτασσέσθω {A}

Adopting a less formal style, perhaps in order to avoid the Hebraic idiom involved in πᾶσα ψυχή, several Western witnesses (𝔓⁴⁶ D* G it^(d*, g, 61) Irenaeus^lat Tertullian Ambrosiaster Speculum) read πάσαις ἐξουσίαις ὑπερεχούσαις ὑποτάσσεσθε.

13.9 οὐ κλέψεις, οὐκ ἐπιθυμήσεις {B}

Under the influence of Ex 20.15-17 and Dt 5.19-21 several witnesses (ℵ P Ψ 048 81 *Byz* it^ar cop^bo arm eth *al*) insert οὐ ψευδομαρτυρήσεις. In the course of transmission other readings arose in various witnesses through omission (perhaps because of homoeoteleuton) or rearrangement of the order of the commandments (the chief manuscripts of the Septuagint vary among themselves and from the Hebrew).

13.11 ὑμᾶς {B}

Although ἡμᾶς has strong support (𝔓^46vid ℵ^c D G Ψ 33 614 1739 *Byz*), a majority of the Committee thought it somewhat more probable that ὑμᾶς was altered to ἡμᾶς in order to conform the person to ἡμῶν in the next clause, than that ἡμᾶς was changed to ὑμᾶς. Several versional and patristic witnesses (syr^h eth Origen^lat Cyril) omit the pronoun altogether, as does also the AV (although the Textus Receptus reads ἡμᾶς).

13.12 ἀποθώμεθα {A}

Instead of ἀποθώμεθα several Western witnesses read ἀποβαλώμεθα (𝔓⁴⁶ D*, ³ F G Old Latin vg). Since the use of ἀποθέσθαι is normal in formulas of renunciation (see E. G. Selwyn, *1 Peter,* pp. 394 ff.), and since the verb ἀποβάλλειν recurs nowhere else in the Pauline Epistles and its middle voice is entirely absent from the New Testament, a majority of the Committee preferred the reading ἀποθώμεθα.

14.4 κύριος {A}

Instead of κύριος, which is strongly supported by 𝔓⁴⁶ ℵ A B C P Ψ cop^(sa, bo) goth arm eth *al,* several uncials and many minuscules read θεός, the copyists having been influenced by θεός in ver. 3.

14.5 *[γάρ]* {C}

On the one hand, the external evidence for the absence of γάρ appears to be slightly superior to that attesting its presence. On the other hand, since the word here expresses merely a continuation rather than a causal relationship, copyists who did not appreciate this Pauline usage of the particle (for examples, see Bauer-Arndt-Gingrich-Danker, *s.v.,* § 4), may have been tempted to delete it. On balance, the Committee thought it best to include the word in the text but enclosed it within square brackets signifying doubt that it belongs there.

14.6 φρονεῖ

The Textus Receptus, following the later witnesses (C³ L P most minuscules syr^(p, h) arm *al*), adds the clause καὶ ὁ μὴ φρονῶν τὴν ἡμέραν κυρίῳ οὐ φρονεῖ. This is a typical Byzantine gloss, prompted by the desire to provide a balanced statement after the model of the clause καὶ ὁ μὴ ἐσθίων later in the verse.

14.9 ἀπέθανεν καὶ ἔζησεν {A}

The oldest and best attested reading appears to be ἀπέθανεν καὶ ἔζησεν (ℵ* A B C 1739 2127 cop^(sa, bo) arm eth *al*). Influenced perhaps by 1 Th 4.14 *(Ἰησοῦς ἀπέθανεν καὶ ἀνέστη)* scribes sought to define more precisely the meaning of ἔζησεν, either by replacing it with ἀνέστη (G 629 it^g vg *al*) or by combining ἀνέστη with the other two verbs, in various sequences.

14.10 θεοῦ {B}

At an early date (Marcion Polycarp Tertullian Origen) the reading θεοῦ, which is supported by the best witnesses (ℵ* A B C* D G 1739 *al*), was supplanted by Χριστοῦ, probably because of influence from 2 Cor 5.10 (ἔμπροσθεν τοῦ βήματος τοῦ Χριστοῦ).

14.12 [τῷ θεῷ] {C}

On the one hand, the combination of such witnesses as ℵ A C D 33 81 614 and most versional testimony makes it difficult to reject the reading τῷ θεῷ. On the other hand, however, it is easy to understand why, if the words were originally absent from the text, copyists would have supplied them in order to clarify the reference of the verb. To represent the balance of external and internal considerations, it was decided to include τῷ θεῷ in the text, but to enclose the words within square brackets.

14.19 διώκωμεν {D}

The question whether in this verse Paul describes the Christian ideal (the indicative διώκομεν continuing the statements made in verses 17 and 18), or whether he now begins his exhortation (the subjunctive διώκωμεν leading to κατάλυε in ver. 20a), is extremely difficult to answer. Despite the slightly superior uncial support for διώκομεν (ℵ A B Gᵍʳ P 048 0209 *al*), and despite the circumstance that elsewhere in Romans the phrase ἄρα οὖν is always followed by the indicative (5.18; 7.3, 25; 8.12; 9.16, 18; cf. 14.12), the Committee felt that, on the whole, the context here calls for the hortatory subjunctive (cf. the imperatives in ver. 13 and ver. 20).

14.21 προσκόπτει {B}

The Textus Receptus incorporates a Western expansion, ἢ σκανδαλίζεται ἢ ἀσθενεῖ, which gained wide circulation (ℵᶜ B D G Ψ 0209ᵛᶦᵈ 33 614 *Byz Lect* vg syrʰ copˢᵃ arm *al*). Other variations in various witnesses suggest that the original text was modified or expanded by copyists who recollected 1 Cor 8.11-13.

14.22 [ἣν] ἔχεις {C}

The relative ἣν is supported by several excellent Alexandrian witnesses (ℵ A B C) and by a few Old Latin manuscripts (itʳ· ᵃʳ). The shorter reading without ἥν is current in the great mass of witnesses, including most of the Old Latin manuscripts and all the other versions. Without ἥν the words σὺ πίστιν ἔχεις can be taken either as a statement or as a question; the latter makes a more lively style, which is appropriate in the context. Was ἥν introduced in order to relieve a certain abruptness, or did the word fall out accidentally in transcription because of itacism after πίστιν (in later Greek ιν and ην were pronounced alike)? In order to represent the balance of possibilities, the Committee decided to retain ἥν with א A B C but to enclose it within square brackets.

14.23 ἐστίν. {A}

A full discussion of the problems of the termination of the Epistle to the Romans involves questions concerning the authenticity and integrity of the last chapter (or of the last two chapters), including the possibility that Paul may have made two copies of the Epistle, one with and one without chap. 16 (chaps. 1–15 being sent to Rome and chaps. 1–16 to Ephesus).[1]

The doxology ("Now to him who is able to strengthen you … be glory for evermore through Jesus Christ!") varies in location; traditionally it has been printed at the close of chap. 16 (as verses 25-27), but in some witnesses it occurs at the close of chap. 14, and in another witness ($\mathfrak{P}^{46}$) at the close of chap. 15. Moreover, several witnesses have it at the close of both chap. 14 and chap. 16, and in others it does not occur at all. (See the comment at 16.25-27.)

It is further to be observed that the benediction ("The grace of our Lord Jesus Christ be with you [all]") is found sometimes after 16.20, sometimes after 16.23, and sometimes in both places. In the last case it is found under three conditions: (1) before the doxology, (2) without it, (3) after it. In its discussion of these problems, the Committee was concerned chiefly with the textual phenomena, and made

---

[1] On the textual history of the Epistle, see Harry Gamble, Jr., *The Textual History of the Letter to the Romans* (Grand Rapids, 1977); Kurt Aland, *Neutestamentliche Entwürfe* (Munich, 1979), pp. 284–301 (who cites manuscript evidence of fifteen different sequences of Romans); and Peter Lampe, *Novum Testamentum,* XXVII (1985), pp. 273–277.

no attempt to formulate a comprehensive literary theory bearing on questions of the authenticity, integrity, and destination(s) of the epistle. (On the positions of the benediction see the comment on 16.20.)

The textual evidence[2] for six locations[3] of the doxology is as follows:

(a)	1.1–16.23 + doxology	$\mathfrak{P}^{61vid}$ ℵ B C D 81 1739 it[d, 61] vg syr[p] cop[sa, bo] eth
(b)	1.1–14.23 + doxology + 15.1–16.23 + doxology	A P 5 33 104 arm
(c)	1.1–14.23 + doxology + 15.1–16.24	L Ψ 0209[vid] 181 326 330 614 1175 *Byz* syr[h] mss[acc. to Origen]lat
(d)	1.1–16.24	F[gr] G (perhaps the archetype of D) 629 mss[acc. to Jerome]
(e)	1.1–15.33 + doxology + 16.1-23	$\mathfrak{P}^{46}$
(f)	1.1–14.23 + 16.24 + doxology	vg[mss] Old Latin[acc. to capitula]

By the way of explanation of the citation of the evidence for the sequence designated (d), it should be said that codex G, a Greek manuscript with a Latin interlinear version, leaves a blank space of six lines between 14.23 and 15.1, i. e. large enough to accommodate the doxology. This suggests that the scribe of G had reason to think that after 14.23 was the place where the doxology should occur, but that it was lacking in the manuscript from which he was copying. Codex F, the Greek text of which seems to have been copied from the same exemplar as G was copied, joins 15.1 immediately to 14.23, and only in its Latin text (written in a column by itself) presents the doxology after 16.24, while the Greek text of F lacks the doxology. Apparently the doxology was lacking also in the exemplar from

---

[2] It should be pointed out that, since $\mathfrak{P}^{61}$ is extremely fragmentary in Romans (preserving only 16.23, 24-27), it could be cited in support of sequence (b) as well as (a).

[3] For two other sequences of the material in Romans (though without the citation of specific manuscript evidence), see K. Aland, *Studien zur Überlieferung des Neuen Testaments und seines Textes* (Berlin, 1967), p. 47.

which codex D was copied, for D is written colometrically (in sense lines) throughout Romans up to 16.24 and the doxology is written stichometrically (in lines straight across the page). This difference in format has been taken to imply that the section was lacking in a recent ancestor of codex D.[4] The capitula that are referred to in the citation of evidence for the sequence designated (*f*) are headings, or brief summaries of sections, that are prefixed to the epistle in many Vulgate manuscripts. The last but one heading (no. 50) begins at the close of 14.14 (see Wordsworth and White, ii, p. 60) and may cover the rest of chap. 14; then the last heading (no. 51) passes at once to the doxology. Since these headings abound in language derived from the Old Latin versions, it appears that the system was drawn up originally for a pre-Vulgate form of the epistle which lacked chaps. 15 and 16, but in which the doxology was appended to the close of chap. 14. This sequence of text is preserved in three Vulgate manuscripts (in Gregory's notation 1648 and 1792, both in Munich, and 2089, in the Monza Chapter Library).[5]

In evaluating the complicated evidence, the Committee was prepared to allow (1) for the probability that Marcion, or his followers, circulated a shortened form of the epistle, lacking chapters 15 and 16, and (2) for the possibility that Paul himself had dispatched a longer and a shorter form of the epistle (one form with, and one without, chapter 16). Furthermore, it was acknowledged that, to some extent, the multiplicity of locations at which the doxology appears in the several witnesses, as well as the occurrence in it of several expressions that have been regarded as non-Pauline, raises suspicions that the doxology may be non-Pauline. At the same time, however, on the basis of good and diversified evidence supporting sequence (*a*), it was decided to include the doxology at its traditional place at the close of the epistle, but enclosed within square brackets to indicate a

---

[4] So Corssen, *Zeitschrift für die neutestamentliche Wissenschaft,* x (1909), pp. 5 f.; but Zahn explains the difference in style of writing (which also occurs occasionally elsewhere in cod. D) as arising from the scribe's attempt to save space (*Introduction to the New Testament,* I, pp. 403 f.).

[5] For a description of these three manuscripts, see R. Schumacher, *Die beiden letzten Kapitel des Römerbriefs* (*Neutestamentliche Abhandlungen* XIV, 4; Münster i. W., 1929), pp. 15 ff.

degree of uncertainty that it belongs there. Some of the other sequences may have arisen from the influence of the Marcionite text
upon the dominant form(s) of the text of the epistle in orthodox
circles. Whether sequence (*e*) is merely one of several idiosyncrasies
of the scribe of $\mathfrak{P}^{46}$, or somehow reflects a stage during which Romans circulated without chapter 16, is difficult to decide. Sequence
(*f*) appears to be peculiar to the transmission of the epistle in Latin.

15.7   *ὑμᾶς* {A}

The reading *ὑμᾶς*, which has superior and more diversified support than the reading *ἡμᾶς*, is in harmony with the other instances of
the second person plural in the context (verses 5-7).

15.15   *ὑμῖν*

The Textus Receptus, following $\mathfrak{P}^{46}$ $\aleph^c$ D F G L P most minuscules
it[d, g] vg syr[p, h, pal] cop[samss] arm, adds *ἀδελφοί* after *ὑμῖν* (in mss. 3 and
209 the word is added after *ἀπὸ μέρους*). Whereas there is no reason
why the word, if original, should have been dropped, its insertion, at
one point or another, would have been prompted by the lectionary use
of the epistle. The shorter text is read by $\aleph^*$ A B C 38 81 218 927
1288 1739 1898 cop[sa, bo] eth Origen Cyprian Chrysostom Augustine.

15.19   *πνεύματος [θεοῦ]* {C}

On the one hand, it can be argued that the presence of *ἁγίου* in
some witnesses and *θεοῦ* in others is suspicious because each can be
explained as a scribal addition to complete what in B and Vigilius
seems to be an unfinished expression. (The reading *πνεύματος θεοῦ
ἁγίου* is an obvious conflation.) On the other hand, despite the generally excellent text preserved by B, a majority of the Committee was
unwilling to adopt a reading based on such slender Greek evidence.
As a compromise, therefore, it was decided to follow the testimony of
the earliest witness ($\mathfrak{P}^{46}$), but in deference to transcriptional considerations to enclose *θεοῦ* within square brackets.

15.24 Σπανίαν {A}

In order to fill out the thought, scribes of later manuscripts added ἐλεύσομαι πρὸς ὑμᾶς. The shorter reading is strongly supported by 𝔓⁴⁶ ℵ* A B C D F G P Ψ 81 *al.*

15.29 Χριστοῦ {A}

The shorter reading εὐλογίας Χριστοῦ, decisively supported by early and good testimony (𝔓⁴⁶ ℵ* A B C D G P 81 1739 Old Latin cop^(sa, bo) arm Clement Origen^(lat)), was expanded in later witnesses (ℵᶜ Ψ 33 88 614 *Byz*) by the insertion of τοῦ εὐαγγελίου τοῦ.

15.31 διακονία {A}

In order to avoid the harshness of διακονία εἰς Ἱερουσαλήμ, several witnesses, chiefly Western (B D* Gᵍʳ Ambrosiaster Ephraem), replace διακονία with δωροφορία ("the bringing of a gift"), a word that occurs nowhere else in the New Testament and is an obvious gloss defining the purpose of Paul's journey. The same Greek witnesses, along with several others (1108 1611 1911 1952), also replace εἰς with the easier ἐν.

15.32 ἐν χαρᾷ ἐλθὼν πρὸς ὑμᾶς διὰ θελήματος θεοῦ συναναπαύσωμαι ὑμῖν {C}

This verse involves a nest of variant readings, the easiest of which to evaluate are those that involve the word or words that qualify θελήματος. Paul nowhere else speaks of θελήματος Ἰησοῦ Χριστοῦ (ℵ*) or θελ. Χριστοῦ Ἰησοῦ (D*) or θελ. κυρίου Ἰησοῦ (B), but always of θελήματος (τοῦ) θεοῦ. The omission of συναναπαύσωμαι ὑμῖν (𝔓⁴⁶ B) is more difficult to account for, but its absence from 𝔓⁴⁶ may have been the result of an accident in transcription when the eye of the copyist passed from ΘΕΛΗΜΑΤΟΣΘΥ to ΟΔΕΘΣ in ver. 33. In a few Western witnesses συναναπαύσωμαι is replaced by ἀναψύξω (D*) or ἀναψύχω (G). The paratactic construction (ἔλθω … καί) appears to be a scribal simplification of the syntax.

15.33 ἀμήν {A}

On the reading of 𝔓⁴⁶, see the comment on 14.23.

[It is difficult to account for the absence of ἀμήν from A G 330 436 451 630 1739 1881 itᵍ al (its omission from 𝔓⁴⁶ is doubtless connected with the presence here of the doxology, concluding with ἀμήν, in that witness). On the other hand, if ἀμήν were not present originally, copyists would have been tempted to add it to such a quasi-liturgical statement as is ver. 33. To represent the conflict between the strong external evidence for its inclusion (א B C D P Ψ 33 81 614 al) and the equally strong transcriptional probability suggesting that it is secondary, the word should be enclosed within square brackets. B.M.M.]

16.3 Πρίσκαν

The Textus Receptus, following 81 209* 255 256 462 489 920 1311 1319 1827 1852 syrᵖˑ ʰ eth al, reads the diminutive form Πρίσκιλλαν. The form Πρίσκαν is decisively supported by 𝔓⁴⁶ (πρεισκαν) A B C D F G L P most minuscules it vg copˢᵃˑ ᵇᵒ arm al. See also the comments on 1 Cor 16.19 and 2 Tm 4.19.

16.7 Ἰουνίαν {A}

On the basis of the weight of manuscript evidence the Committee was unanimous in rejecting Ἰουλίαν (see also the next variant in ver. 15) in favor of Ἰουνιαν, but was divided as to how the latter should be accented. Some members, considering it unlikely that a woman would be among those styled "apostles," understood the name to be masculine Ἰουνιᾶν ("Junias"), thought to be a shortened form of Junianus (see Bauer-Aland, *Wörterbuch,* pp. 770 f.). Others, however, were impressed by the facts that (1) the female Latin name Junia occurs more than 250 times in Greek and Latin inscriptions found in Rome alone, whereas the male name Junias is unattested anywhere, and (2) when Greek manuscripts began to be accented, scribes wrote the feminine Ἰουνίαν ("Junia"). (For recent discussions, see R. R. Schulz in *Expository Times,* ɪɪᴄ (1986–87), pp. 108–

110; J. A. Fitzmyer, *Romans* (Anchor Bible Commentary, 1993), pp. 737 f.; and R. S. Cervin in *New Testament Studies*, XL (1994), pp. 464–470.)

The "A" decision of the Committee must be understood as applicable only as to the spelling of the name Ἰουνιαν, not the accentuation.

16.15   Ἰουλίαν {A}

The scribes of C* F G^gr mistook ιογλιαν for ιογνιαν (compare the contrary error in ver. 7).

16.20   ἡ χάρις τοῦ κυρίου ἡμῶν Ἰησοῦ μεθ᾽ ὑμῶν {A}

The shorter form of the benediction ($\mathfrak{P}^{46}$ ℵ B 1881) appears to be more primitive, for if Χριστοῦ (A C P Ψ 33 81 1739 *Byz* all versions) were present originally there seems to be no reason why a copyist should have deleted it, whereas the general tendency was to expand liturgical formulations. Several Western witnesses (D G it^d*, g Sedulius Scotus) transfer the benediction to follow ver. 23, thus preventing the greetings of verses 21-23 from having the appearance of being an afterthought. Other witnesses (P 33 104 256 263 436 1319 1837 syr^p arm) place ver. 24 following 16.27 (i. e. after the doxology), thus concluding the epistle with a benediction. If, however, it stood in this position originally, there is no good reason why it should have been moved earlier.

16.24   *omit verse* {A}

The earliest and best witnesses omit ver. 24. See the comment on ver. 20.

16.25-27   *The Doxology* {C}

While recognizing the possibility that the doxology may not have been part of the original form of the epistle, on the strength of impressive manuscript evidence ($\mathfrak{P}^{61}$ ℵ B C D 81 1739 it^ar, b, d*, f, o vg syr^p cop^{sa, bo} eth Clement *al*) the Committee decided to include the verses at their traditional place in the epistle, but enclosed within square brackets (for a fuller discussion of the problems involved, see the comment on 14.23).

16.27 αἰῶνας {A}

The shorter text (𝔓⁴⁶ B C Ψ 33 88 104 614 1739 *Byz* syr^h cop^{sa} *al*) was preferred on the ground that the expansion of the doxology by the addition of τῶν αἰώνων (𝔓⁶¹ᵛⁱᵈ ℵ A D P 81 Old Latin vg syr^p cop^{bo} arm eth *al*) was as natural for scribes as it would have been unusual for them to delete the words had they been original.

16.27 *Subscription*

(*a*) The earliest subscription is merely πρὸς Ῥωμαίους ℵ A B* C D* *al*. Other subscriptions include: (*b*) πρὸς Ῥωμαίους ἐγράφη ἀπὸ Κορίνθου B²ᵇ D^b (P); (*c*) πρὸς Ῥωμαίους ἐγράφη διὰ Φοίβης ἀπὸ Κορίνθου 35 (201 om πρ. Ῥωμ.); (*d*) πρὸς Ῥωμαίους ἐγράφη ἀπὸ Κορίνθου διὰ Φοίβης τῆς διακόνου 42 90 216 339 462 466* 642; (*e*) as (*d*) but prefixing τοῦ ἁγίου καὶ πανευφήμου ἀποστόλου Παύλου ἐπιστολή L; (*f*) ἐγράφη ἡ πρὸς Ῥωμαίους ἐπιστολὴ διὰ Τερτίου· ἐπέμφθη δὲ διὰ Φοίβης ἀπὸ Κορινθίων 337; (*g*) as (*d*) but adding τῆς ἐν Κεγχρεαῖς ἐκκλησίας 101 241 460 466^c 469 602 603 605 618 1923 1924 1927 1932, followed by the Textus Receptus.

THE FIRST LETTER OF PAUL
TO THE CORINTHIANS

1.1 Χριστοῦ Ἰησοῦ {B}

The Committee judged the weight of evidence that supports the sequence Χριστοῦ Ἰησοῦ (𝔓⁴⁶ B D F G 33 *al*) to be slightly more impressive than that supporting Ἰησοῦ Χριστῷ (ℵ A L P and the Majority Text). (See also the comment on Ro 1.1.)

1.2 τῇ οὔσῃ ἐν Κορίνθῳ, ἡγιασμένοις ἐν Χριστῷ Ἰησοῦ

On the one hand, a minority of the Committee argued that the reading adopted for the text, which is supported by 𝔓⁶¹ᵛⁱᵈ ℵ A D¹ P Ψ 049 (056 0142 om. Ἰησοῦ) and apparently all minuscules, is secondary, since it is the easier of the two variants. On the other hand, however, the reading ἡγιασμένοις ἐν Χριστῷ Ἰησοῦ τῇ οὔσῃ ἐν Κορίνθῳ, though supported by a notable combination of witnesses (𝔓⁴⁶ B D*, ² F G), appeared to the majority of the Committee to be intrinsically too difficult, as well as quite un-Pauline in comparison with the style of the salutations in other Pauline letters. The reading apparently arose through the accidental omission of one or more phrases and their subsequent reintroduction at a wrong position.

1.4 θεῷ μου {A}

Although it is possible that μου may have crept into the text by assimilation to Ro 1.8 or Php 1.3, the Committee thought it more probable that the word was omitted as inappropriate by several copyists (ℵ* B eth Ephraem). The reading θεῷ μου is strongly supported by a wide variety of Greek and versional witnesses (ℵᵃ A C D G P Ψ 33 614 1739 *Byz Lect* it vg syrᵖ, ʰ copˢᵃ, ᵇᵒ arm). The omission of τῷ θεῷ μου (1984) and the reading θεῷ ἡμῶν (491) are accidental scribal errors.

1.8 *[Χριστοῦ]* {C}

The absence of *Χριστοῦ* from both 𝔓⁴⁶ and B is noteworthy. The presence of *Ἰησοῦ Χριστοῦ* in the preceding and following verses might be thought reason enough for Paul not to use the word here – and for ordinary scribes to insert it! On the other hand, however, the word may have been omitted either accidentally in copying (*Χριστοῦ* was ordinarily written in contracted form, X͞Υ͞) or perhaps deliberately for aesthetic reasons (in order to differentiate the sequence of three instances of *Ἰησοῦ Χριστοῦ*). In view of the strong and varied support for *Χριστοῦ* (ℵ A C D G P Ψ 33 81ᵛⁱᵈ 614 1739 and all versions) the Committee felt obliged to include the word in the text, but decided to enclose it within square brackets to indicate a certain amount of doubt concerning its originality.

1.13 *μεμέρισται* {A}

Since *μεμέρισται ὁ Χριστός* may be read either as a statement or as a question, several witnesses, including 𝔓⁴⁶ 326 1962 *l*⁵⁹⁹ syrᵖ· ᵖᵃˡ copˢᵃ arm, prefix the interrogative *μή,* thus relieving the ambiguity and conforming the clause to the following questions.

1.14 *[τῷ θεῷ]* {C}

It is obvious that the addition of *μου* after *θεῷ* is the result of scribal assimilation to ver. 4. It is more difficult, however, to decide whether *τῷ θεῷ* fell out accidentally in transcription (ΕΥΧΑΡΙϹ-ΤΩΤΩΘΕΩ), or whether copyists supplemented Paul's abbreviated expression with the addition of *τῷ θεῷ,* on the pattern of Ro 1.8; 7.25; 1 Cor 1.4; 14.18; etc. It was considered safer to follow the usage of Paul and to include *τῷ θεῷ* in the text; out of deference, however, to the weight of ℵ* B 1739 *al,* which omit the words, they were enclosed within square brackets.

1.20 *κόσμου*

The Textus Receptus, following later witnesses (ℵᶜ C³ Dᶜ F G L Ψ 6 104 326 623 1739ᶜ *al*), with which some early versions agree (itᵈ· ᵍ· ʳ vg syr^{p, h, pal} cop^{sa, bo} goth arm^{mss}), adds τούτου. Influence from the preceding expression, τοῦ αἰῶνος τούτου, would make the addition of the demonstrative almost a foregone conclusion; the remarkable thing is that so many copyists resisted the urge to assimilate expressions (κόσμου alone is read by 𝔓⁴⁶ ℵ* A B C* D^{gr*} 33 181 206 314 429 917 1610 1758 1827 1836 1898 al).

1.23 ἔθνεσιν

The Textus Receptus, following several later manuscripts (C³ D^c 6 177 206 326 489 919 920 1739 1835 al), replaces ἔθνεσιν with Ἕλλησι. The change was prompted by the desire to make Paul's terminology consistent in verses 22, 23, and 24.

1.28 τὰ μὴ ὄντα {B}

The presence of καί before τὰ μὴ ὄντα (ℵ^c B C³ D^b P Ψ 81 614 Byz al) seems to be an interpolation prompted by the preceding series of objects, each joined to the next by καί (see Blass-Debrunner-Funk, § 490). In adding the word, however, scribes overlooked the force of the expression τὰ μὴ ὄντα, which (as Zahn points out, in loc.) is not another item of the series, but is a comprehensive and climactic characterization of all the preceding items. The shorter reading is strongly supported by 𝔓⁴⁶ ℵ* A C* D* G 0129 33 1739 al.

2.1 μυστήριον {B}

From an exegetical point of view the reading μαρτύριον τοῦ θεοῦ, though well supported (ℵ^c B D G P Ψ 33 81 614 1739 Byz it^{d, g} vg syr^h cop^{sa} arm eth Origen al), is inferior to μυστήριον, which has more limited but early support in 𝔓^{46vid?} ℵ* A C 88 436 it^{r, 61} syr^p cop^{bo} Hippolytus Ambrosiaster Ephraem Ambrose Pelagius Augustine Antiochus. The reading μαρτύριον seems to be a recollection of 1.6, whereas μυστήριον here prepares for its usage in ver. 7.

2.4   πειθοῖ[ς] σοφίας [λόγοις] {C}

Of the eleven different variant readings in this passage, those that read ἀνθρωπίνης before or after σοφίας (ℵ^c A C P Ψ 81 614 1962 2495 *Byz* it° syr^h cop^{bo} *al*) are obviously secondary. If the word were original, there is no good reason why it would have been deleted; on the contrary, it has the appearance of an explanatory gloss inserted by copyists (at different places) in order to identify more exactly the nuance attaching to σοφίας. It is much more difficult to decide what to do with πειθοῖς, an adjective found in no other passage in all of Greek literature. Did the rarity of the word produce confusion in the transmission of the text? Or is it really a *vox nulla,* having arisen from a scribal mistake in copying πειθοῖ σοφίας (πειθοῖ, dative case of the noun πειθώ, meaning "persuasion")? In order to represent the diversity of evidence, a majority of the Committee decided to print πειθοῖ[ς], and, on the strength of 𝔓⁴⁶ G 35* that lack λόγοις, to enclose this latter word within square brackets.

2.10   δέ {B}

The loose use of the connective δέ (ℵ A C D G P Ψ 33 81 614 *Byz al*) is entirely in Paul's manner, whereas γάρ, though strongly supported by 𝔓⁴⁶ B 1739 Clement *al,* has the appearance of being an improvement introduced by copyists.

2.10   πνεύματος

The Textus Receptus, following ℵ^c D F G L almost all minuscules the Old Latin vg syr^{p, h} cop^{sa} arm eth *al,* adds the explanatory αὐτοῦ. The Committee preferred the earlier and shorter reading, supported by 𝔓^{46vid} ℵ* A B C 33^{vid} 1611 cop^{bo} Clement Cyril Basil *al.*

2.12   κόσμου

Influenced by a similar expression in ver. 6 *(τοῦ αἰῶνος τούτου)* copyists added the demonstrative, producing τοῦ κόσμου τούτου (D E F G it^{d, g, r} cop^{samss}). The shorter text is decisively supported by 𝔓⁴⁶ ℵ A B C L P all minuscules^{vid} vg syr^{p, h} *al.*

2.15 *[τὰ] πάντα* {C}

Of the two textual problems involved in this passage, the presence (ℵ[a] B D[b] P Ψ 33 614 1739 *al*) or absence (𝔓[46] A C D* G *al*) of *μέν* is the easier to resolve. Although it is possible that copyists may have omitted the word because it seemed to be inappropriate following *δέ* at the beginning of the sentence, the Committee thought it more probable that the word was added by pedantic copyists in order to provide a correlative for the following *δέ*. It is more difficult to decide what to do with *τά*. Was the word added in order to prevent the reader from taking *πάντα* as masculine singular; or was it omitted, either accidentally (ΤΑΠΑΝΤΑ) or deliberately, so that the statement would be in accord with the precedent in ver. 10? On the strength of 𝔓[46] A C D* *al* the Committee retained the word in the text, but, in view of its absence from many other important witnesses, enclosed the word within square brackets.

2.16 *Χριστοῦ* {B}

The original text appears to be *Χριστοῦ* (strongly supported by 𝔓[46] ℵ A C Ψ 048 *al*), which was assimilated in other witnesses to the preceding *κυρίου*.

3.2 *ἔτι* {A}

The omission of *ἔτι* by 𝔓[45] B 0185 appears to be an Alexandrian improvement of style.[1]

3.3 *ἔρις* {B}

Although the reading *ἔρις καὶ διχοστασίαι* has early and diversified attestation (𝔓[46] D (G) 33 614 *Byz* it[d, g, 61] syr[p, h] Marcion *al*), the absence of *καὶ διχοστασίαι* from such witnesses as 𝔓[11vid] ℵ B C P Ψ 81 1739 *al* led the Committee to suspect the intrusion of a Western

---

[1] See G. Zuntz, *The Text of the Epistles* (London, 1953), p. 40 and addendum on p. 285.

gloss, derived perhaps from the list of vices in Ga 5.20. There being no sufficient reason to account for the omission, if the words were present originally, the shorter reading is to be preferred.

3.5   τί ... τί

Instead of τί ("What?") the Textus Receptus, following $\mathfrak{P}^{46}$ C D F G and most minuscules, reads τίς ("Who?") in both instances. The masculine, however, appears to be a secondary accommodation to suit the personal names; moreover, the implication of the neuter τι in ver. 7 is decisive for τί in ver. 5 (since the answer is "Nothing" the question can scarcely have been "Who?").

3.5   Ἀπολλῶς ... Παῦλος   {A}

The Textus Receptus, following several of the later witnesses (D^b L Ψ 6 88 104 326 915 syr^{p, h} arm eth *al*), reverses the sequence so as to read Παῦλος; τί δέ ἐστιν Ἀπολλῶς;. This transposition was obviously made out of deference to the greater prominence of Paul and because of the sequence in ver. 4. The reading adopted for the text is decisively supported by $\mathfrak{P}^{46vid}$ ℵ A B C D*, c (F G) P 31 33 38 69 181 462 1912 it^{d, g, r} vg cop^{sa, bo}.

3.12   θεμέλιον

On the basis of the testimony of $\mathfrak{P}^{46}$ ℵ* A B C* 6 81 cop^{sa} eth, a majority of the Committee preferred the reading θεμέλιον, regarding the reading θεμέλιον τοῦτον, supported by the rest of the manuscripts, to be a secondary modification introduced in order to clarify the meaning.

3.13   [αὐτό]

The pronoun, which is absent from $\mathfrak{P}^{46vid}$ ℵ D L Ψ 104 177 255 623 1912 it^d vg syr^h cop^{sa, bo} arm eth *al,* is supported by such witnesses as A B C P 33 88 181 326 424 441 915 917 1836 1891 2127 syr^p *al.* Even though the Committee suspected that copyists had omitted the word as pleonastic, yet because external evidence for its inclusion is relatively limited in range, it was decided to enclose the word within square brackets.

3.17 φθερεῖ {B}

Influenced by the preceding word, several witnesses, chiefly Western, read the present tense φθείρει (D^gr G^gr P 81 *l*^809 vg^mss syr^p, h Ephraem) instead of φθερεῖ.

4.17 Χριστῷ ['Ιησοῦ] {C}

Among the several variations presented by the manuscripts, the Western reading of D* F G ("in Lord *[sic]* Jesus") is clearly a scribal corruption (κ̅ω̅ for χ̅ω̅) under the influence of the preceding κυρίῳ. It is more difficult to decide between Χριστῷ 'Ιησοῦ (𝔓^46 ℵ C 33 81 1739 *al*) and simply Χριστῷ (A B Ψ 0150 *al*). In order to represent the balance of evidence, the Committee decided to retain 'Ιησοῦ but to enclose it within square brackets.

5.2 πράξας

The Textus Receptus, following 𝔓^46 B D F G L P Ψ 049 056 0142 and most minuscules, reads ποιήσας, whereas πράξας is read by 𝔓^11vid ℵ A C 33 81 88 104 326 436 462 1912 *al*. The more literary word, πράσσειν, occurs 18 times in Paul's letters; elsewhere in the New Testament, it occurs 20 times (18 times in Luke-Acts, and twice in John). Since the verb ποιεῖν occurs nearly six hundred times in the New Testament, and since the expression ποιεῖν ἔργον was very familiar to transcribers of the New Testament, they were more likely to replace πράξας with ποιήσας than vice versa.

5.4 [ἡμῶν] 'Ιησοῦ (1) {C}

In accord with the solemn character of the address, the Textus Receptus, following 𝔓^46 D^c G P 33 614 *Byz Lect* it^g. 61 vg syr^p, h with * cop[sa, bo] goth arm eth[pp], expands by adding Χριστοῦ after Ἰησοῦ, and 81 transposes to read Ἰησοῦ Χριστοῦ τοῦ κυρίου ἡμῶν. Whether ἡμῶν was added by copyists, or was accidentally omitted by several witnesses (A Ψ 1108 1611 2495 syr[h] eth[ro] Lucifer), is difficult to decide. On the basis of the testimony of B D* 429 918 1175 1739 1836 1984 it[d], the Committee retained the word in the text, but enclosed it within square brackets to indicate a measure of doubt as to its right to stand there.

5.5 κυρίου {B}

The reading that best explains the origin of the other readings is κυρίου, well attested by early and important manuscripts and Fathers. "The name 'Jesus' is twice in the preceding verse: reason enough for Paul not to write it, and for scribes to add it, here."[1]

5.6 ζυμοῖ

Several Western witnesses (D* it[d] vg Marcion Irenaeus[lat] Tertullian Origen[lat] Lucifer Augustine Ambrosiaster) read δολοῖ. The same Western correction occurs in Ga 5.9.

5.10 καί

Instead of καί the Textus Receptus, following 𝔓[46] א[c] D[b, c] L Ψ many minuscules vg syr[p, h] cop[sa, bo] goth arm al, reads ἤ, thus mechanically conforming to the context. The reading καί is strongly supported by both Alexandrian and Western witnesses (א A B C D* F G P 33 88 177 181 326 441 1099 it[d, g] eth).

5.12 οὐχὶ τοὺς ἔσω ὑμεῖς κρίνετε;

Instead of the usual text several early witnesses present interesting variations: (a) 𝔓[46], syr[p], and cop[bo] omit οὐχί and read the verb as an

---

[1] G. Zuntz, *The Text of the Epistles* (London, 1953), p. 184.

imperative, τοὺς ἔσωθεν ὑμεῖς κρίνατε ("Judge ye those who are inside [the church]"); (*b*) the Sahidic apparently took οὐχί with the preceding sentence, reading τί γάρ μοι τοὺς ἔξω κρίνειν καὶ τοὺς ἔσω οὐχί; τοὺς ἔσω ὑμεῖς κρίνετε ("For what have I to do with judging those who are outside and not those who are inside? Judge ye those who are inside").

5.13 κρινεῖ {C}

The earlier manuscripts being without accent marks, κρινει (𝔓[46] א A B* C D[gr *] G[gr]) can be read either as present or future tense. Since the expectation of the parousia was vivid in Paul's day, a majority of the Committee regarded the future tense to be more appropriate in the context.

6.11 Ἰησοῦ Χριστοῦ {C}

The readings with ἡμῶν (B C[vid] P 33 1739 it[ar, r] vg syr[p, h with *] cop[sa, bo] arm eth *al*) appear to have arisen by scribal assimilation to the following ἡμῶν. Even though the Textus Receptus, following A D[c] Ψ 88 614 *Byz Lect* syr[h], has the shortest reading (Ἰησοῦ), a majority of the Committee interpreted the absence of Χριστοῦ to be the result of an accident in transcription and preferred to read Ἰησοῦ Χριστοῦ with 𝔓[11vid, 46] א D* P it[d] Irenaeus[lat] Tertullian, as well as the witnesses (except cop[sa]) that are cited above for ἡμῶν.

[Accidental omission of X̄P̄ is less probable than expansion of an original Ἰησοῦ by pious copyists (compare 5.4). B.M.M.]

6.14 ἐξεγερεῖ {B}

The witnesses are fairly evenly divided as to the tense of the verb: (*a*) the aorist ἐξήγειρεν, 𝔓[46c2] B 424[c] 1739 Origen; (*b*) the present ἐξεγείρει, 𝔓[11, 46 *] A D* P 69 88; and (*c*) the future ἐξεγερεῖ, 𝔓[46c1] א C D[3] K L most minuscules and most versions. The context makes the future necessary as the correlative of καταργήσει in

ver. 13 (compare also the parallel in 2 Cor 4.14). The aorist ἐξήγειρεν (which involves an interpretation that applies it to baptism)
appears to have arisen from mechanical adaptation to the preceding
ἤγειρεν.

It is curious that the original reading of 𝔓⁴⁶ was altered twice.
According to Zuntz, "It is unlikely that the corrector found these
variants, all three, in the manuscript from which 𝔓⁴⁶ was copied.
We seem to be granted a glimpse into a scriptorium where some
authoritative manuscripts were used by the correctors in an
endeavour to bring the productions of the scribes up to a definite
standard."[1]

6.20   δή

Among several variant readings involving δή is (*a*) the interesting
expansion, preserved in Latin witnesses (it^g vg Marcion (Tertullian)
Cyprian Lucifer Ambrosiaster Speculum *al*), *Glorificate et portate
Deum in corpore vestro* ("Glorify *and bear* God in your body").
Apparently this reading arose (in Greek) when ἄρα γε was misread
as ἄρατε (ΑΡΑΓΕ : ΑΡΑΤΕ). Other variant readings include (*b*) οὖν,
syr^p cop^{sa} Pseudo-Athanasius; (*c*) ἄρα γε before δοξάσατε, 1611;
(*d*) δὴ ἄρατε, Chrysostom; (*e*) omission of any particle, ℵ* it^d
syr^{h with *} cop^{bo}. Although the Committee acknowledged that the
clause may have originally lacked a connective and that subsequently
the abrupt anacoluthon was remedied by the addition of one or
another particle, the overwhelming evidence in support of δή (𝔓⁴⁶ ℵ^a
A B C D F G K L P and almost all minuscules) requires that it be
regarded as the earliest definitely ascertainable text (even though Paul
nowhere else uses this particle).

6.20   ὑμῶν {A}

The Textus Receptus, following several of the later uncials and
most of the minuscules (C³ D^c K L P Ψ 1 31 88 915 syr^{p, h}), adds

---

[1] For further discussion see G. Zuntz, *The Text of the Epistles*, pp. 256 f.

after ὑμῶν the words καὶ ἐν τῷ πνεύματι ὑμῶν ἅτινά ἐστι
τοῦ θεοῦ. That these words are a gloss with no claim to be original
is clear (*a*) from the decisive testimony of the earliest and best
witnesses in support of the shorter text ($\mathfrak{P}^{46}$ ℵ A B C* D* F G 33
81 1739* it vg cop[sa, bo, fay] eth Irenaeus[lat] Tertullian Origen Cyprian
al), and (*b*) from the nature of the addition itself (it is not needed
for the argument, which relates to the sanctity of the body, with no
mention of the spirit). The words were inserted apparently with a
desire to soften Paul's abruptness, and to extend the range of his
exhortation.

7.3   ὀφειλήν

Instead of ὀφειλήν, which is overwhelmingly supported by
$\mathfrak{P}^{11, 46vid}$ ℵ A B C D F G P 6 33 181 424[c] 1912 1944 vg cop[sa, bo, fay] arm
eth Tertullian Clement Cyprian Origen Methodius *al*, the Textus
Receptus, following K L most minuscules syr[p, h] *al*, softens the expression (which refers to sexual relations) by substituting the words
ὀφειλομένην εὔνοιαν ("the kindness that is her due").

7.5   τῇ προσευχῇ {A}

The Textus Receptus, following ℵ[c] K L 88 614 *Byz Lect* syr[p, h] goth
al, prefixes τῇ νηστείᾳ καί, and 330 451 John-Damascus add καὶ
νηστείᾳ. Both are interpolations, introduced in the interest of
asceticism. The shorter text is decisively supported by all the early
and best witnesses ($\mathfrak{P}^{11vid, 46}$ ℵ* A B C D G P Ψ 33 81 104 1739 it vg
cop[sa, bo, fay] arm eth *al*).

7.5   ἦτε

In a variety of witnesses, most of them late ($\mathfrak{P}^{46}$ K L P most
minuscules vg syr[p, h] goth arm *al*), the explanatory gloss συν-
έρχησθε (or -εσθε) has replaced the more colorless ἦτε. The latter
is adequately supported by ℵ A B C D F G 33 88 181 255 263
467 618 1838 1912 1944 2127 it[g, r] eth *al*.

7.7   δέ (1) {B}

The reading δέ, which is strongly supported ($\mathfrak{P}^{46}$ ℵ* A C D* G 33^{vid} 81 326 it vg cop^{bo} goth *al*), is preferable to γάρ (ℵ^c B D$^{b, c}$ K P Ψ 88 614 1739 *Byz Lect* syr$^{p, h}$ cop^{sa} arm eth *al*), which appears to be a correction introduced by scribes who did not appreciate the nuance of opposition to the concession mentioned in ver. 6.

7.14   γυναικί

After γυναικί several witnesses, chiefly Western (D F G vg syr^p), add the interpretative gloss τῇ πιστῇ (compare also the addition τῷ πιστῷ in the following comment).

7.14   ἀδελφῷ {A}

Instead of ἀδελφῷ, which is strongly supported by $\mathfrak{P}^{46}$ ℵ* A B C D* G P Ψ 33 1739 it$^{d, g}$ cop$^{sa, bo, fay}$ *al*, the Textus Receptus, following inferior witnesses (ℵ^c D^c K L 81 104 326 614 *Byz Lect* syr^h goth arm eth *al*), reads ἀνδρί, a more appropriate correlative to γυνή, the special force of ἀδελφῷ not having been appreciated. In order to recapture some of the nuance belonging to ἀδελφῷ, in a subsequent modification τῷ πιστῷ was added to ἀνδρί (629 it^{ar} vg syr^p Irenaeus^{lat} Tertullian Ambrosiaster).

7.15   ὑμᾶς {B}

Although ἡμᾶς seems to have slightly stronger external support ($\mathfrak{P}^{46}$ B D G 33 104 614 1739 it vg syr$^{p, h}$ cop$^{sa, fay}$), the Committee preferred ὑμᾶς (ℵ* A C 81 326 2127 cop^{bo}), since the general tendency of scribes is to make modifications in the interest of generalizing the reference of aphorisms (as, in fact, has occurred here in codex Sinaiticus). In later Greek the two words were pronounced alike.

7.28   ἡ παρθένος

Should the definite article be omitted (with B F G 429) or retained (with $\mathfrak{P}^{15, 46}$ ℵ A D K L P and most minuscules)? Although the article may have come into the text by dittography from the preceding -η, the Committee thought it more likely that, because of an apparent lack of appropriateness of the article in the context, it was deleted by several copyists.

7.34 καὶ μεμέρισται. καὶ ἡ γυνὴ ἡ ἄγαμος καὶ ἡ παρθένος {D}

After considering the multiplicity of variant readings and the uncertainties of interpretation, the Committee decided that the least unsatisfactory reading is that supported by early representatives of the Alexandrian and the Western types of text ($\mathfrak{P}^{15}$ B 104 vg cop^sa, bo). The absence of the first καί in some witnesses (D^c F G K L Ψ 614 *Byz*) is to be accounted for either as a palaeographical oversight (after γυναιKI) or (in the case at least of D^c) as a deliberate excision in order to avoid construing ἡ γυνή and ἡ παρθένος with a singular verb (μεριμνᾷ). Its presence is strongly supported by the combination of $\mathfrak{P}^{15, 46}$ ℵ A B D^gr * P 33 81 1739 *al*. The difficulty of distinguishing ἡ γυνὴ ἡ ἄγαμος [the unmarried woman or widow] from ἡ παρθένος may have led copyists to shift the adjective from γυνή to παρθένος (D^gr * and D^c G K Ψ syr^p *al*). The reading of $\mathfrak{P}^{46}$ ℵ A 33 81 *al,* which have ἡ ἄγαμος after both γυνή and παρθένος, has the appearance of a typical scribal conflation.

7.40 θεοῦ {A}

The reading Χριστοῦ in two manuscripts ($\mathfrak{P}^{15}$ 33) arose through faulty transcription.

8.3 τὸν θεόν ... ὑπ' αὐτοῦ {A}

The absence of τὸν θεόν from $\mathfrak{P}^{46}$ Clement was regarded by the Committee to be the result of formal assimilation to ver. 2. The phrase ὑπ' αὐτοῦ is absent from several witnesses, as though ἔγνωσται were active voice. It was to be expected that $\mathfrak{P}^{46}$ Clement should omit the words since their antecedent (τὸν θεόν) is lacking in these witnesses. Their absence also from ℵ* and 33 was regarded by the Committee as accidental, having arisen perhaps from the copyist's expectation that Paul was going to say something like, "If anyone loves God, this man truly knows him." The surprising turn of expression, however, is characteristically Pauline (Ga 4.9; cf. also 1 Cor 13.12).

8.6 αὐτοῦ

At the close of the verse several witnesses (including 0142 234 460 618) expand Paul's reference to one God, the Father, and one Lord, Jesus Christ, by adding καὶ ἓν πνεῦμα ἅγιον, ἐν ᾧ τὰ πάντα καὶ ἡμεῖς ἐν αὐτῷ ("and one Holy Spirit, in whom are all things, and we in him"). The trinitarian form was current as early as the close of the fourth century, for Gregory Nazianzus quotes it (*Orat.* xxxix.12), though omitting the clause beginning with καὶ ἡμεῖς.

8.7 συνηθείᾳ {A}

The reading συνηθείᾳ, strongly supported by ℵ* A B P Ψ 33 81 1739 *al,* was preferred to συνειδήσει (ℵ^c D G 88 614 *Byz Lect*), a reading that apparently arose through assimilation to the following συνείδησις.

8.10 σέ

Several witnesses, including 𝔓⁴⁶ B F G vg Origen^{lat} Augustine Pelagius, lack σέ. Copyists are more likely to have omitted the pronoun, thus generalizing the apostle's statement, than to have inserted it.

8.12 ἀσθενοῦσαν {A}

The absence of ἀσθενοῦσαν from 𝔓⁴⁶ and Clement was regarded as either an accident in transcription or a deliberate modification, introduced to prevent the reader from assuming that wounding a brother's conscience is allowable except when it is "weak."

9.9   κημώσεις

Although the reading φιμώσεις has somewhat stronger external support ($\mathfrak{P}^{46}$ ℵ A B³ C D^{b, c} K L P almost all minuscules), a majority of the Committee preferred κημώσεις (B* D* F G 1739) on transcriptional grounds, for copyists were more likely to alter the less literary word (κημώσεις) to φιμώσεις, which is also the reading of the Septuagint (Dt 25.4), than vice versa.

9.10   ἐπ᾽ ἐλπίδι τοῦ μετέχειν

The reading that best explains the origin of the others is ἐπ᾽ ἐλπίδι τοῦ μετέχειν ($\mathfrak{P}^{46}$ ℵ* (A) B C P 33 69 vg syr^{p, h} cop^{sa, bo, fay} arm *al*). Not observing that ἀλοᾶν must be understood after ἀλοῶν, copyists assumed that μετέχειν was the infinitive after ὀφείλει and therefore adjusted the reading to τῆς ἐλπίδος αὐτοῦ μετέχειν (D* F G 181 917 1836 1896 syr^{hmg}). Later the sense was improved somewhat by combining the readings, thus producing τῆς ἐλπίδος αὐτοῦ μετέχειν ἐπ᾽ ἐλπίδι (ℵ^c D^{b, c} K L Ψ 88 326 623 920 1175 *al*, followed by the Textus Receptus).

9.15   οὐδεὶς κενώσει {B}

According to the view of a majority of the Committee the earliest reading is that supported by $\mathfrak{P}^{46}$ ℵ* B D* 33 1739 it^d syr^p *al*. Not observing that after ἤ Paul breaks off the sentence (a figure of speech called aposiopesis), various copyists attempted in one way or another to ameliorate the construction and to carry on the syntax. The most widespread correction was the replacement of οὐδείς by ἵνα τις (ℵ^c C D^{b, c} K P Ψ 81 88 104 326 330 436 451 614 629 630 1241 1877 1962 1984 1985 2127 2492 2495 *Byz Lect al*). Because of itacism the pronunciation of κενώσει and κενώσῃ was indistinguishable.

Instead of using a dash, it is also possible to punctuate the text with a full stop after ἀποθανεῖν, accenting the next word as ἤ ("Truly no one shall deprive me of my ground for boasting!"). But this use of ἤ, though common in the classics, does not occur elsewhere in Paul.

9.20 μὴ ὢν αὐτὸς ὑπὸ νόμον {A}

The Textus Receptus, following D^grc K Ψ 88 256 326 460 1175 1518 2138 syr^p eth, omits the parenthetical clause μὴ ὢν αὐτὸς ὑπὸ νόμον. The words, which are decisively supported by (𝔓^46) ℵ A B C D* F G P it vg syr^h cop^sa goth arm, probably fell out by accident[1] in transcription, the eye of the copyist passing from ὑπὸ νόμον to ὑπὸ νόμον.

9.22 πάντως τινάς {A}

Instead of πάντως τινάς, strongly supported by a wide spectrum of witnesses, the Western text (D F G lat) reads πάντας, the result of scribal conformation to the preceding clauses.

9.23 πάντα

The reading πάντα is strongly supported by 𝔓^46 ℵ A B C D E F G P 33 69 181 424^c 436 1611 1837 it vg cop^sa, bo arm eth. Later copyists (followed by the Textus Receptus), wishing to define the meaning more precisely, replaced πάντα with τοῦτο (K L Ψ many minuscules syr^p, h goth).

10.2 ἐβαπτίσθησαν {C}

On the basis of what was taken to be superior evidence and Pauline usage, a majority of the Committee preferred the reading ἐβαπτίσθησαν.

[It is more probable that copyists replaced the middle ἐβαπτίσαντο (which corresponds to Jewish practice, according to which the convert baptized himself) with the passive (which is the usual expression in the case of Christian baptism, e. g. 1.13, 15; 12.13; etc.), than vice versa. B.M.M. and A.W.]

---

[1] According to Tischendorf, however, the corrector of the Greek text of D had second thoughts, and, after having fully accented the words, decided to delete them.

10.9 Χριστόν {B}

The reading that best explains the origin of the others is Χριστόν, attested by the oldest Greek manuscript (𝔓⁴⁶) as well as by a wide diversity of early patristic and versional witnesses (Irenaeus in Gaul, Ephraem in Edessa, Clement in Alexandria, Origen in Palestine, as well as by the Old Latin, the Vulgate, Syriac, Sahidic and Bohairic). The difficulty of explaining how the ancient Israelites in the wilderness could have tempted Christ prompted some copyists to substitute either the ambiguous κύριον or the unobjectionable θεόν. Paul's reference to Christ here is analogous to that in ver. 4.

10.11 ταῦτα δέ {B}

Although it is possible that πάντα may have been omitted by copyists who recalled ver. 6, a majority of the Committee thought it more probable that the original ταῦτα (A B 33 630 1739 1881) was expanded by the addition of πάντα, whose varying position in the manuscripts suggests that the word is a gloss, inserted to heighten the narrative.

10.20 ἃ θύουσιν, δαιμονίοις καὶ οὐ θεῷ [θύουσιν] {C}

The words τὰ ἔθνη, though attested by 𝔓⁴⁶ᵛⁱᵈ ℵ A C P Ψ 33 81 1739 *al,* were considered to be an ancient gloss, introduced lest the reader assume that the subject of θύουσιν *(bis)* is Ἰσραὴλ κατὰ σάρκα (ver. 18). The presence of τὰ ἔθνη prompted a subsequent modification in the substitution of ... θύει ... θύει (K 88 326 614 *Byz Lect*), introduced by grammatically-minded scribes to accord with a neuter plural subject. In the interest of greater clarity, the words καὶ οὐ θεῷ were transposed in several witnesses (D F Gᵍʳ) to follow the second θύουσιν.

10.23 πάντα ἔξεστιν ... πάντα ἔξεστιν

In both instances the Textus Receptus reads μοι between πάντα and ἔξεστιν, following ℵᶜ C³ (first time) H K L Ψ most minuscules

THE FIRST LETTER TO THE CORINTHIANS

syr^(p, h) goth (second instance) arm *al*. That the word crept into the text from 6.12 seems to be almost certain, especially in view of the overwhelming testimony supporting the shorter text, namely 𝔓⁴⁶ ℵ* B C (C* first instance) D (F G P first instance; by homoeoteleuton they omit the second πάντα ... οἰκοδομεῖ) it^d vg cop^(sa, bo).

10.28 συνείδησιν {A}

The Textus Receptus, following a few later uncials (H^c K L Ψ) and most minuscules, adds τοῦ γὰρ κυρίου ἡ γῆ καὶ τὸ πλήρωμα αὐτῆς. That this is a gloss derived from ver. 26 is clear from (*a*) the decisive evidence supporting the shorter text (ℵ A B C D F G H* P 33 81 181 1739 it vg syr^p cop^(sa, bo) arm eth *al*), and (*b*) the lack of any good reason to account for deletion of the words, had they been in the text originally.

11.2 ὑμᾶς

It was to be expected that, at the beginning of a new section and following ἐπαινῶ δὲ ὑμᾶς, many witnesses would interpolate ἀδελφοί (D F G K L Ψ 33 88 104 326 623 915 1831 it vg syr^(p, h) goth eth^(pp)). If the word were present originally (as at 10.1 and 12.1, where no witness omits it), its absence from 𝔓⁴⁶ ℵ A B C P 181 206 255 429 441 1758 1836 1898 1912 cop^(sa, bo) arm eth^(ro) *al* would be inexplicable. (Compare also 15.31.)

11.10 ἐξουσίαν {A}

The presumed meaning of the difficult ἐξουσίαν in this passage is given by the explanatory gloss κάλυμμα "a veil," read by several versional and patristic witnesses (cop^(bomss) arm? eth^(ro) Valentinians^(acc. to Irenaeus) Ptolemy^(acc. to Irenaeus) Irenaeus^(gr, lat) Tertullian Jerome Augustine).

11.15 δέδοται [αὐτῇ] {C}

The absence of αὐτῇ in 𝔓⁴⁶ D E F G Ψ and many other witnesses, as well as the variety of its position either before or after δέδοται, might lead one to reject the word (as G. Zuntz argues on the basis of sense; see *The Text of the Epistles*, 1953, p. 127). On the other hand, a majority of the Committee, impressed by the weight of the combination of ℵ A B 33 81 365 2464 *al*, preferred to retain the word, but to enclose it within square brackets to indicate doubt as to its right to be in the text.

11.24   Τοῦτο {A}

The Textus Receptus, following C³ K L P most minuscules syrᵖ·ʰ goth ethᵖᵖ, adds from Mt 26.26 the words λάβετε φάγετε. If these words were present originally in Paul's account, no good reason can be found to explain their absence from 𝔓⁴⁶ ℵ A B C* D F G 33 104 181* 218 424ᶜ 425 618 1906 1912 itᵈ·ᵍ vg copˢᵃ·ᵇᵒ arm Cyprian Basil Cyril Theodoret Chrysostom Euthalius John-Damascus.

11.24   ὑμῶν {A}

The concise expression τὸ ὑπὲρ ὑμῶν, read by 𝔓⁴⁶ ℵ* A B C* 6 33 424ᶜ 1739* arm Origen Cyprian *al*, is characteristic of Paul's style. Attempts to explicate the meaning of the words resulted in the addition of various participles: (*a*) θρυπτόμενον (Dᵍʳ*); (*b*) κλώμενον (ℵᶜ C³ Dᵇ·ᶜ G K P Ψ 81 614 1739ᵐᵍ *Byz Lect* itᵈ·ᵍ syrᵖ·ʰ goth *al*), derived from the preceding ἔκλασεν; (*c*) διδόμενον (vg copˢᵃ·ᵇᵒ eth Euthalius, it⁶¹ *quod tradidi pro vobis*), assimilated to Lk 22.19.

11.29   πίνων ... σῶμα {A}

The meaning of the shorter text, which is preserved in the best witnesses (𝔓⁴⁶ ℵ* A B C* 33 1739 copˢᵃ·ᵇᵒ *al*), was clarified by adding ἀναξίως (from ver. 27) after πίνων and τοῦ κυρίου after σῶμα (ℵᶜ C³ D G K P most minuscules it syrᵖ·ʰ·ᵖᵃˡ goth arm *al*). In each instance there appears to be no good reason to account for the omission if the word(s) had been present originally.

12.9   ἐν τῷ ἐνὶ πνεύματι {A}

Although it could be argued that ἐνί is a variation introduced for stylistic reasons to avoid the monotony of three successive instances of the phrase "the same Spirit," the Committee, impressed by the diversified support for ἐνί (A B 33 81 104 1739 it^ar, d vg Ambrose Speculum Hilary Basil *al*), regarded it more probable that copyists mechanically conformed ἐνί to αὐτῷ (ℵ C³ D^gr G K P 614 *Byz Lect* it^g syr^p, h cop^sa, bo arm *al*). Through an oversight in transcription 𝔓⁴⁶ reads merely ἐν τῷ πνεύματι, and C* and Ψ accidentally omit several words.

13.3   καυχήσωμαι {C}

Did Paul write ἵνα καυχήσωμαι ("that I may glory") or ἵνα καυθήσομαι ("that I should be burned")? To answer this question requires the evaluation of several very evenly balanced considerations.

In support of the reading καυχήσωμαι one can appeal to external evidence that is both early and weighty (𝔓⁴⁶ ℵ A B 6 33 69 1739* cop^sa, bo goth^mg Clement Origen Jerome and Greek mss^acc. to Jerome). Transcriptional considerations likewise favor καυχήσωμαι, for copyists, uncertain of Paul's meaning in linking the idea of glorying or boasting to the preceding clause about the giving up of one's body, may well have sought to improve the sense by substituting the similar sounding word καυθήσομαι. Intrinsic considerations likewise seem to favor καυχήσωμαι, for this verb occurs frequently in the letters traditionally attributed to Paul (a total of 35 times).

On the other hand, in support of καυθήσομαι (-σωμαι) there is an impressive number of witnesses, including C D F G K L Ψ most minuscules it vg syr^p, h goth^txt arm eth^pp, and numerous patristic writers, including Tertullian Aphraates Cyprian Origen Basil Chrysostom Cyril Theodoret Euthalius Maximus-Confessor John-Damascus. It has been argued that in the context καυθήσομαι is as appropriate as καυχήσωμαι is inappropriate, for the reference to burning, whether by martyrdom (as the Three Hebrew Youths in Daniel 3.15 ff.) or by voluntary self-burning, is particularly suitable as the strongest example of sacrifice; whereas, if the motive for giving up life is pride and self-glory, there is no need to declare that such sacrifice is worthless, and therefore Paul's following statement, ἀγάπην δὲ μὴ ἔχω, becomes superfluous.

A majority of the Committee preferred καυχήσωμαι for the following reasons. (a) After the Church entered the epoch of martyrdom, in which death by fire was not rare, it is easier to understand how the variant καυθήσομαι for καυχήσωμαι would creep into the text, than the opposite case. Likewise the passage in Daniel was well known in the Church and might easily have induced a copyist to alter καυχήσωμαι into καυθήσομαι. On the other hand, if the latter reading were original, there is no good reason to account for its being replaced in the oldest copies by the other reading.

(b) The expression παραδῶ τὸ σῶμά μου ἵνα καυθήσομαι, though certainly tolerable in itself, is noticeably cumbersome ("I give up my body, that I may be burnt"); one would have expected, as a more natural expression, ἵνα καυθῇ ("... that it may be burnt"). But in the case of καυχήσωμαι this difficulty disappears.

(c) The reading καυθήσωμαι (= future subjunctive!), while appearing occasionally in Byzantine times, is a grammatical monstrosity that cannot be attributed to Paul (Blass-Debrunner-Funk, § 28; Moulton-Howard, p. 219); occasionally, however, the future indicative after ἵνα occurs (Ga 2.4; Php 2.10-11).

(d) The argument that the presence of the statement, "that I may glory," destroys the sense of the passage loses some of its force when one observes that for Paul "glorying" is not invariably reprehensible; sometimes he regards it as justified (2 Cor 8.24; Php 2.16; 1 Th 2.19; 2 Th 1.4).

13.4 *[ἡ ἀγάπη]* (3) {C}

On the basis of rhythm and sentence structure, the third instance of ἡ ἀγάπη (omitted by B 33 *al*) could be considered to be secondary.[1] On the other hand, a majority of the Committee was impressed

---

[1] So G. Zuntz argues in *The Text of the Epistles* (London, 1953), p. 68. For a correction of Zuntz's citation of the evidence of 𝔓[46], see R.V.G. Tasker in *New Testament Studies*, I (1954-55), p. 191.

by the weight of the witnesses that include the words. In order to represent the balance of these considerations, it was decided to retain the words but to enclose them within square brackets.

13.5 $\dot{\alpha}\sigma\chi\eta\mu\sigma\nu\epsilon\hat{\iota}$ {A}

Instead of $\dot{\alpha}\sigma\chi\eta\mu\sigma\nu\epsilon\hat{\iota}$, the scribe of $\mathfrak{P}^{46}$ unaccountably wrote $\epsilon\dot{\upsilon}\sigma\chi\eta\mu\sigma\nu\epsilon\hat{\iota}$ ("[does not] behave with decorum"!).

13.13 $\pi\acute{\iota}\sigma\tau\iota\varsigma \ldots \tau\alpha\hat{\upsilon}\tau\alpha$

A few early witnesses ($\mathfrak{P}^{46}$ Clement Augustine) transpose so as to read in a much more commonplace sequence: $\tau\grave{\alpha}$ $\tau\rho\acute{\iota}\alpha$ $\tau\alpha\hat{\upsilon}\tau\alpha,$ $\pi\acute{\iota}\sigma\tau\iota\varsigma,$ $\dot{\epsilon}\lambda\pi\acute{\iota}\varsigma,$ $\dot{\alpha}\gamma\acute{\alpha}\pi\eta.$

14.26 $\ddot{\epsilon}\kappa\alpha\sigma\tau\sigma\varsigma$

The Textus Receptus, following $\aleph^{c}$ D F G K L most minuscules it vg syr$^{p,\ h}$ goth arm, adds $\dot{\upsilon}\mu\hat{\omega}\nu$. Although it can be argued that the shorter text ($\mathfrak{P}^{46}$ $\aleph^{*}$ A B P 33 81 206 429 1175 1758 cop$^{sa,\ bo}$) was created by an Alexandrian editor who deleted the pronoun as superfluous, the Committee thought that, on the whole, the tendency of scribes would have been to add the pronoun (as in fact has happened in the case of codex Sinaiticus).

14.34-35 *include verses here* {B}

Several witnesses, chiefly Western, transpose verses 34-35 to follow ver. 40 (D F G 88* it$^{d,\ g}$ Ambrosiaster Sedulius Scotus). Such scribal alterations represent attempts to find a more appropriate location in the context for Paul's directive concerning women.

The evidence of the sixth-century Codex Fuldensis is ambiguous. The Latin text of 1 Cor 14 runs onward throughout the chapter to ver. 40. Following ver. 33 is a scribal siglum that directs the reader to a note standing in the lower margin of the page. This note provides the text of verses 36 through 40. Does the scribe, without actually deleting verses 34-35 from the text, intend the liturgist to omit them when reading the lesson?

14.34 γυναῖκες

The Textus Receptus, following D F G K L many minuscules it[d, g] syr[p, h with obelus] *al*, reads ὑμῶν after γυναῖκες. The Committee regarded this as probably a scribal addition, and preferred the shorter text, which is strongly supported by 𝔓[46vid] ℵ A B C P Ψ 33 43 88 104 256 263 296 436 467 623 915 1319 1739 1837 2127 vg cop[sa, bo, fay] arm eth *al*.

14.38 ἀγνοεῖται {B}

Although the external evidence may at first sight seem to favor ἀγνοείτω (𝔓[46] B K Ψ 81 614 syr[p, h] arm eth *al*), several important representatives of the Alexandrian, the Western, and the Palestinian texts unite to support the indicative (ℵ* A*[vid] D[gr*] 33 1739 it[d] syr[pal] cop[sa, bo, fay] Origen[gr]). The alteration between active and passive forms of the same verb accords with Paul's usage in 8.2-3, whereas the use of the imperative form may have been suggested by Re 22.11. In any case, the imperative gives a less forceful meaning than ἀγνοεῖται. The reading of D[gr*] (ἀγνοεῖτε) is by itacism for ἀγνοεῖται (ε and αι were pronounced alike).

14.40 γινέσθω. {B}

See the comment on verses 34-35.

15.5 δώδεκα

Instead of recognizing that δώδεκα is used here as an official designation, several witnesses, chiefly Western, have introduced the pedantic correction ἕνδεκα (D* F G 330 464* it vg syr[hmg] goth Archelaus Eusebius Ambrosiaster Jerome Pelagius mss[acc. to Augustine] John-Damascus). Compare the similar correction at Ac 1.26.

15.10 *[ἡ] σὺν ἐμοί* {C}

The reading *ἡ εἰς ἐμέ* (𝔓⁴⁶ syrʰᵐᵍ goth Theodoret) is an assimilation to the expression in the first part of the verse. It is more difficult to decide whether *ἡ* was accidentally omitted from several witnesses (א* B D* F G 1739 it vg) or mechanically inserted in other witnesses. In order to represent the balance of probabilities a majority of the Committee decided to retain *ἡ* enclosed within square brackets.

15.14 *ὑμῶν* {B}

Although several important witnesses (including B Dᵍʳ* 33 81 330 1739) read *ἡμῶν*, this may be either itacism for *ὑμῶν* or mechanical assimilation to the previous *ἡμῶν*. In any case, the context seems to require "your faith" as a correlative to "our preaching"; compare also *ἡ πίστις ὑμῶν* in ver. 17, where the reading is firm.

15.31 *[ἀδελφοί,]* {C}

On the one hand, the absence of *ἀδελφοί* from 𝔓⁴⁶ D F G L Ψ 1739 *Byz Lect* itᵈ·ᵍ is surprising, just as the presence of the word in an affectionate asseveration is to be expected. On the other hand, however, because of strong external support for inclusion of the word (א A B 33 81 104 330 1241 itᶠ·ᵃʳ vg syrᵖᵃˡ goth arm), the Committee was reluctant to drop it from the text altogether, and finally decided to enclose it within square brackets. Compare also the comment on 11.2.

15.47 *ἄνθρωπος* (2) {A}

The reading that best accounts for the origin of the others is *ἄνθρωπος*, supported by a strong combination of early and good witnesses representing several text-types (א* B C D* G 33 1739* itᵈ·ᵍ·⁶¹ vg copᵇᵒ *al*). The insertion of *ὁ κύριος* (Marcion preferred *κύριος* as a substitute for *ἄνθρωπος*) is an obvious gloss added to explain the nature of "the man from heaven" (אᶜ A Dᶜ K P Ψ 81 104 614 1739ᵐᵍ *Byz Lect* syrᵖ·ʰ·ᵖᵃˡ goth arm *al*); if this were original there is no reason why it should have been omitted. The singular reading of 𝔓⁴⁶ (ἄνθρωπος πνευματικός) shows the influence of ver. 46, while the omission of ἄνθρωπος (cop^sa Cyril) is merely a transcriptional accident.

15.49 φορέσομεν {B}

Exegetical considerations (i. e., the context is didactic, not hortatory) led the Committee to prefer the future indicative, despite its rather slender external support (B I 38 88 206 218 242 630 915 919 999 1149 1518 1872 1881 syr^p cop^sa eth *al*).

15.51 οὐ κοιμηθησόμεθα, πάντες δὲ ἀλλαγησόμεθα {A}

The reading which best explains the origin of the others is that preserved in B D^c K P Ψ 81 614 *Byz Lect* syr^p, h cop^sa, bo goth eth *al*. Because Paul and his correspondents had died, the statement πάντες οὐ κοιμηθησόμεθα seemed to call for correction. The simplest alteration was to transfer the negative to the following clause (ℵ (A*) C 33 1739 it^g arm eth *al*). That this was an early modification is shown by the artifical conflation of both readings in 𝔓⁴⁶ A^c Origen; οὖν in G^gr may have arisen from a transcriptional blunder, ΟΥ being read as ΟΫ. The most radical alteration, preserved in several Western witnesses (D* it^d, 61 vg Marcion Tertullian *al*), replaces κοιμηθ-ησόμεθα with ἀναστησόμεθα, a reading that apparently arose to counteract (gnostic?) denials of the general resurrection.

15.54 ὅταν δὲ τὸ φθαρτὸν τοῦτο ἐνδύσηται ἀφθαρσίαν καὶ τὸ θνητὸν τοῦτο ἐνδύσηται ἀθανασίαν {B}

The shorter reading, ὅταν δὲ τὸ θνητὸν τοῦτο ἐνδύσηται τὴν ἀθανασίαν, supported, with trifling variations, by several important witnesses (𝔓⁴⁶ ℵ* 088 0121a 0243 1739* it^ar vg cop^sams, bo goth eth Marcion Irenaeus^gr, lat *al*), probably arose accidentally through an oversight in copying, occasioned by homoeoarcton or homoeoteleu-ton. The readings of A 326 cop^sams arm seem to have arisen when the oversight was noticed, but the omitted clause was restored in the wrong sequence. The omission of the entire verse (F G 614* 1877* it^g cop^{boms}) is explained from homoeoteleuton with ver. 53.

15.55 νῖκος; ποῦ σου, θάνατε, τὸ κέντρον; {B}

Two sets of variant readings are involved, both connected with the fact that in Ho 13.14 the Septuagint differs from the Hebrew. The sequence νῖκος ... κέντρον, strongly supported by 𝔓^{46} ℵ* B C 1739*^{vid} vg cop$^{sa, bo}$ al, is to be preferred to the reverse sequence, which arose from scribal assimilation to the text of the Septuagint. The reading ᾅδη (ℵ^c A^c K P Ψ 88 104 614 Byz syr$^{p, h}$ goth arm al) is also an assimilation to the Septuagint; Paul never uses ᾅδης. The reading of 𝔓^{46} B νεῖκος ("strife, dispute") is an itacistic error, having arisen from the similarity of pronunciation of ει and ι.

16.19 Πρίσκα

The Textus Receptus, following A C D F G K L P Ψ most minuscules syr$^{p, h}$ eth, reads Πρίσκιλλα, a diminutive form familiar from the book of Acts (18.2, 18, 26). In the Pauline letters, however, the form Πρίσκα is to be preferred, which in the present passage is supported by 𝔓^{46} (Πρεισκας) ℵ B M P 33 226 vg cop$^{sa, bo}$ goth. See also the comments on Ro 16.3 and 2 Tm 4.19. After Ἀκύλας καὶ Πρίσκα several Western witnesses (D F G goth Pelagius) add the gloss παρ' οἷς (F G^c οὕς) καὶ ξενίζομαι ("with whom also I am lodging").

16.23 Ἰησοῦ

The Textus Receptus, following ℵ^c A C D F G K L M most minuscules, including 6 424^c 920 1739, it$^{d, g, r}$ syr$^{p, h}$ cop$^{sa, bo}$ arm eth, reads Ἰησοῦ Χριστοῦ. The shorter reading Ἰησοῦ, which is supported by ℵ* B 2 33 35 226 356 442 823 1611 1908 2004 vg goth al, is to be preferred. In view of the presence of the longer reading in other Pauline benedictions (Ro 16.24; 2 Cor 13.13; Ga 6.18; Php 4.23; 1 Th 5.28; 2 Th 3.18; Phm 25), as well as the natural proclivity of scribes to expand the sacred name, it is perhaps remarkable that any witnesses should have resisted such pressures.

16.24 Ἰησοῦ. {B}

After Ἰησοῦ (B 0121a 0243 33 630 1739* 1881 it[g, r] syr[p] cop[sa] Ambrosiaster Euthalius) the liturgical ἀμήν is added in most witnesses (ℵ A C D K P Ψ most minuscules and most versions *al*). Other singular or sub-singular variations occur in several of the later witnesses.

16.24 *Subscription*

(*a*) The subscription in ℵ A B C* 33 is πρὸς Κορινθίους α̅. Other subscriptions include: (*b*) πρὸς Κορινθίους α̅ (D[b] adds ἐγράφη ἀπὸ Φιλίππων Μακεδονίας) ἐπληρώθη D; (*c*) ἐτελέσθη πρὸς Κορινθίους α̅ F (πρώτη G), add ἐγράφη ἀπὸ Ἐφέσου B[3]; (*d*) πρὸς Κορινθίους α̅ (L 103 *al* add ἐπιστολή) ἐγράφη ἀπὸ Φιλίππων (add τῆς Μακεδονίας 242 *al*) διὰ Στεφανᾶ καὶ Φορτουνάτου (K *al* Φουρτ-) καὶ Ἀχαϊκοῦ καὶ Τιμοθέου K L many minuscules, followed by the Textus Receptus (with πρώτη for α̅); (*e*) as (*d*) but add ἐγράφη ἀπὸ Ἐφέσου P *al* (462 *al* add τῆς Ἀσίας).

THE SECOND LETTER OF PAUL
TO THE CORINTHIANS

1.1 Χριστοῦ Ἰησοῦ

The Textus Receptus, following A D G K L Ψ most minuscules it^(d, g, r) vg syr^p cop^bo goth arm eth, reads Ἰησοῦ Χριστοῦ. The Committee preferred the sequence Χριστοῦ Ἰησοῦ, supported by 𝔓⁴⁶ ℵ B M P 33 256 1108 1319 1611 2005 vg^mss syr^h cop^sa. Through scribal oversight the words have been omitted from F.

1.6-7 παρακλήσεως καὶ σωτηρίας· εἴτε παρακαλούμεθα, ὑπὲρ τῆς ὑμῶν παρακλήσεως τῆς ἐνεργουμένης ἐν ὑπομονῇ τῶν αὐτῶν παθημάτων ὧν καὶ ἡμεῖς πάσχομεν. (7) καὶ ἡ ἐλπὶς ἡμῶν βεβαία ὑπὲρ ὑμῶν εἰδότες {A}

The reading adopted as text is strongly supported by (𝔓⁴⁶) ℵ A C P Ψ 0243 1739 1881 it^r vg syr^p cop^(sa, bo) eth *al*; it alone gives the needed connection between ver. 6 and ver. 7. The other main variant readings seem to have arisen when, through an oversight due to homoeoteleuton (παρακλήσεως to παρακλήσεως), the words καὶ σωτηρίας εἴτε παρακαλούμεθα, ὑπὲρ τῆς ὑμῶν παρακλήσεως were accidentally omitted (as also happened in 81 104 630) and afterwards were written in the margin. A later copyist, in an ancestor of B (33) 1241, introduced the words at the beginning of ver. 7 after βεβαία ὑπὲρ ὑμῶν and, in order to preserve the sense, transferred καὶ σωτηρίας to the end. Such a text also must lie behind D (G) (K) 0209 (614) 2492 *Byz Lect* it^(d, g, ar) goth *al*, in which, however, for reasons of symmetry, the words καὶ σωτηρίας have been introduced after the first παρακλήσεως. The Textus Receptus, which here is without known manuscript authority, reads παρακλήσεως καὶ σωτηρίας, τῆς ἐνεργουμένης ἐν ὑπομονῇ τῶν αὐτῶν παθημάτων ὧν καὶ ἡμεῖς πάσχομεν· εἴτε παρακαλούμεθα, ὑπὲρ τῆς ὑμῶν παρακλή-

σεως καὶ σωτηρίας· καὶ ἡ ἐλπὶς ἡμῶν βεβαία ὑπὲρ ὑμῶν·
(7) εἰδότες....

1.10 τηλικούτου θανάτου {B}

The text is doubtful. On the one hand, the weight of the external
evidence seems to favor the singular τηλικούτου θανάτου (ℵ A B
C D^gr G^gr K P Ψ 33 614 1739* *Byz Lect* cop^{sa, bo} arm Clement *al*).
On the other hand, the oldest known witness (𝔓^{46}) reads the plural
τηλικούτων θανάτων, an expression which, according to Zuntz
(*The Text of the Epistles,* p. 104), "bears the stamp of genuine Pauline
diction; cf. ib. xi.23 and vi.4 ff.... The singular clearly arose from the
pedantic idea that no one could risk more than one death." A majority
of the Committee was impressed by the preponderance of external
evidence in support of the singular number, and considered that the
plural may have originated from a desire to heighten the intensity of
the account, particularly since Paul himself refers to more than one
deliverance ("has delivered ... and will deliver").

[For the reasons indicated by Zuntz the plural seems preferable. It
is the harder reading, that of the oldest Greek witnesses and of most
Old Latin manuscripts. A.W.]

1.10 καὶ ῥύσεται {B}

In view of the following ῥύσεται the words καὶ ῥύσεται, strongly supported by 𝔓^{46} ℵ B C P 33 it^g vg cop^{sa, bo} arm *al*, seemed to some
scribes to be superfluous and were therefore omitted (A D* Ψ it^{d, 61}
syr^p eth^{pp}); other scribes altered the first ῥύσεται to ῥύεται (D^c G^gr K
614 1739 1881 *Byz Lect* syr^h *al*), thus producing the sequence of past,
present, and future.

1.10 [ὅτι] καὶ ἔτι {C}

A majority of the Committee regarded the rise of variations in the
witnesses as due to the presence of a threefold sequence of particles
(ὅτι καὶ ἔτι), one or another of which was dropped by copyists for

stylistic reasons. Nevertheless, because of the weight of the combination of 𝔓⁴⁶ B Dᵍʳ* 1739 in attesting καὶ ἔτι without ὅτι, it was decided to enclose the latter within square brackets.

If the text is read without ὅτι a full stop should be placed after ἠλπίκαμεν.

1.11 ἡμῶν (2) {B}

The Committee preferred the reading ἡμῶν, which is adequately supported by a variety of witnesses (𝔓⁴⁶ᶜ ℵ A C D* G Ψ 1739 Old Latin vg syrᵖ, ʰ copˢᵃ, ᵇᵒ goth arm *al*). The reading ὑμῶν (𝔓⁴⁶* B Dᶜ K P 614 *al*), which is almost unintelligible in the context, is a scribal blunder, originating from the circumstance that in later Greek η and υ were pronounced alike.

1.12 ἁπλότητι {B}

It is difficult to decide between ἁγιότητι and ἁπλότητι, either of which could be easily confused with the other (ΑΓΙΟΤΗΤΙ and ΑΠΛΟΤΗΤΙ). Although the reading ἁγιότητι has strong and early support (𝔓⁴⁶ ℵ* A B C 33 1739 *al*), a majority of the Committee favored the Western and Byzantine reading ἁπλότητι (ℵᶜ D G 614 *Byz Lect* itᵈ, ᵍ, ᵃʳ vg syrᵖ, ʰ goth) because (*a*) the context seems to require a word meaning "simplicity" rather than "holiness"; (*b*) the word ἁπλότης occurs a number of times in 2 Cor (8.2; 9.11, 13; 11.3); and (*c*) the word ἁγιότης is never used elsewhere by Paul. The readings πραότητι (88 635) and σλπάγχνοις (eth) are secondary variations that presuppose ἁπλότητι.

1.14 τοῦ κυρίου [ἡμῶν] {C}

Although usually the longer readings that involve the sacred names are suspect as scribal expansions, in the present case a majority of the Committee was of the opinion that the expression, "our Lord Jesus," not being a customary liturgical formula, is probably to be attributed to Paul rather than to a copyist. Owing, however, to the balance in weight of the external evidence for and against the presence of ἡμῶν, it was decided to enclose the pronoun within square brackets.

1.15 χάριν {B}

The reading χαράν (ℵ^c B L P 88 614 915 2005 cop^{bo} *al*) appears to be a scribal modification of χάριν (ℵ* A C D G K Ψ 33 1739 *Byz Lect* it vg syr^{p, h} cop^{sa} arm), perhaps under the influence of 2.3.

2.1 γάρ {C}

Although γάρ has rather limited support ($\mathfrak{P}^{46}$ B 31 33 1739 it^r syr^{h, pal} cop^{sams, bo} *al*), a majority of the Committee preferred it to δέ (ℵ A C D^{b, c} (D^{gr*} τε) G K P Ψ 614 most Old Latin vg syr^p *al*), because 2.1 is neither a mere addition nor a contrasting statement to the preceding, but supplies the reason for Paul's delay in visiting the Corinthians (1.23 f.).

2.9 εἰ {A}

The omission of εἰ by $\mathfrak{P}^{46}$ 436 2495 is accidental, occasioned by the juxtaposition of εἰ and εἰς. The reading ᾗ ("whereby"), which is narrowly supported (A B 33), may have arisen as a mere orthographic variant (in later Greek εἰ and ᾗ were pronounced alike). The reading ὡς (460 1836 cop^{sa?}) may have originated through palaeographical confusion (ΥΜѠΕΙΕΙϹ); in any case its external support is negligible, while εἰ is strongly supported by ℵ C D G K L O P Ψ 614 1739 *Byz Lect* it vg syr^{p, h, pal} cop^{bo} goth arm.

2.17 πολλοί {B}

On the basis of ℵ A B C K P Ψ 88 1739 *Byz* it^{d, ar} vg cop^{sa, bo} eth *al* the Committee preferred the reading πολλοί. The reading λοιποί, supported by $\mathfrak{P}^{46}$ D^{gr} G^{gr} 326 614 *Lect* syr^{p, h} arm Marcion *al*, appears to be of Western origin; in any case, however, οἱ λοιποί seems to be too offensive an expression for Paul to have used in the context.

3.2 ἡμῶν (2) {A}

Although ὑμῶν is read by several witnesses (ℵ 33 88 436 1881 eth^{ro}), in view of the overwhelming support for ἡμῶν (𝔓⁴⁶ A B C D G K P Ψ 614 1739 Byz Lect it vg syr^{p, h} cop^{sa, bo} goth arm), as well as Paul's statement in 7.3, the Committee adopted the first person possessive pronoun, which seems to be demanded by the context.

3.3 πλαξίν καρδίαις σαρκίναις {A}

In view of the awkward apposition of καρδίαις to πλαξίν, the genitive singular καρδίας, found in several witnesses (F K 2 489 1912 al it vg syr^p cop^{sa, bo} goth arm – though the testimony of the versions counts but little in this kind of variation), and incorporated in the Textus Receptus, must be regarded as an obvious scribal amelioration.

3.9 τῇ διακονίᾳ {B}

A majority of the Committee, impressed by the weight of the external evidence supporting τῇ διακονίᾳ, was inclined to regard the nominative as due to scribal assimilation to the preceding (and following) διακονία.

3.17 ἐλευθερία

In order to provide a correlative for οὗ the Textus Receptus, following ℵ^c D^{b, c} F G K L P Ψ most minuscules it^{d, g} vg syr^h cop^{sa} goth arm eth, inserts ἐκεῖ before ἐλευθερία. The shorter reading is decisively supported by 𝔓⁴⁶ ℵ* A B C D* 33 424^c 1912 it^r syr^p cop^{bo}; furthermore, the use of ἐκεῖ to balance οὗ is apparently not in Paul's style (cf. Ro 4.15; 5.20).

4.5 Ἰησοῦν (2) {B}

Good representatives of both the Alexandrian and the Western texts (A^{*vid?} B D^{gr} G^{gr}) join in support of the reading Ἰησοῦν. An early variant reading, Ἰησοῦ, also makes good sense, but is slightly less well supported ($\mathfrak{P}^{46}$ ℵ* A^c C 33 1739 it$^{d, g, r}$ vg cop$^{sa, bo}$ Marcion). The other readings, which involve the word "Christ," are obviously secondary.

4.6 [Ἰησοῦ] Χριστοῦ

There are three variants: (a) Ἰησοῦ Χριστοῦ, read by $\mathfrak{P}^{46}$ ℵ C H K L P 049 056 075 0142 0209 most minuscules syr$^{p, h}$ cop^{bo} goth arm al; (b) Χριστοῦ, read by A B 33 1739* cop^{sa} arm^{mss} Marcion Tertullian Origen Ephraem Athanasius Chrysostom al; and (c) Χριστοῦ Ἰησοῦ, read by D F G 6 206 630 1739 1758 1881 1898 it$^{d, g}$ vg al. On the basis of what was regarded as superior external support, a majority of the Committee preferred the reading Ἰησοῦ Χριστοῦ. At the same time, in view of the evidence supporting the shorter reading, it was decided to enclose Ἰησοῦ within square brackets.

[The reading that best explains the origin of the others is Χριστοῦ (cf. the same expression in 2.10), which has significant, though limited, support. Pious scribes could not resist adding Ἰησοῦ before or after Χριστοῦ; if Ἰησοῦ had been present in the text originally, no good reason can account for its absence from such manuscripts as A B 33 1739* as well as important versional and patristic witnesses. B.M.M. and A.W.]

4.14 τὸν κύριον Ἰησοῦν {B}

A majority of the Committee was impressed by the diversity of the witnesses supporting the presence of κύριον (ℵ C D G K L P Ψ 88 614 Byz Lect it$^{d, g}$ syr^h cop^{bo} goth eth al), and explained the shorter reading as an assimilation to Ro 8.11a. The other readings are obvious scribal expansions.

[Due consideration should be given to the weight of the evidence supporting the shortest reading: $\mathfrak{P}^{46}$ B and 33 are strong Alexandrian witnesses; it^r vg and Tertullian are Western; and cop$^{sa, bo ms}$ and arm are proof of still wider dissemination of the reading τὸν Ἰησοῦν. The likelihood that all of these text-types would have undergone scribal assimilation to Ro 8.11 is not nearly so great as the ever-present tendency of pious scribes to expand by adding κύριον – as, in fact, ἡμῶν and Χριστόν also were added later. The word κύριον should therefore not stand in the text. B.M.M.] [Or, if it is admitted into the text, it should be enclosed within square brackets. C.M.M.]

5.3 ἐκδυσάμενοι {C}

It is difficult to decide between ἐνδυσάμενοι and ἐκδυσάμενοι. On the one hand, from the standpoint of external attestation the former reading is to be preferred. On the other hand, internal considerations, in the opinion of a majority of the Committee, decisively favor the latter reading, for with ἐνδυσάμενοι the apostle's statement is banal and even tautologous, whereas with ἐκδυσάμενοι it is characteristically vivid and paradoxical ("inasmuch as we, though unclothed, shall not be found naked"). The reading ἐκλυσάμενοι probably arose through palaeographical confusion when ϵκΔ- was taken as ϵκλ-.

[In view of its superior external support the reading ἐνδυσάμενοι should be adopted, the reading ἐκδυσάμενοι being an early alteration to avoid apparent tautology. B.M.M.]

5.17 καινά {A}

Since the following sentence begins with τὰ δὲ πάντα, one could argue that the original reading was καινὰ τὰ πάντα (D^c K P Ψ 629 Byz^pt Lect syr^h goth eth^pp Marcion al) and that the reading καινά originated when the eye of a scribe accidentally passed over the first τὰ πάντα. Such an explanation, however, does not account for the reading τὰ πάντα καινά, and it also pays insufficient attention to the age and character of the witnesses that support the shorter reading καινά (𝔓^46 ℵ B C D* G 1739 it^d, g, r vg syr^(p), pal cop^sa, bo arm eth^ro Clement Origen). In view of the following τὰ δὲ πάντα, it was perhaps natural that copyists should enhance the meaning of καινά by prefixing or by adding τὰ πάντα.

6.16 ἡμεῖς γὰρ ναὸς θεοῦ ἐσμεν {B}

The reading ἡμεῖς ... ἐσμεν, strongly supported by both Alexandrian and Western witnesses (ℵ* B D* 33 81* it^d cop^{sa, bo} *al*), is to be preferred to ὑμεῖς ... ἐστε (𝔓⁴⁶ C D^c G K Ψ 614 *Byz Lect* it^{g, ar} vg syr^{p, h} goth arm *al*), since the latter reading was very naturally suggested by the recollection of 1 Cor 3.16 as well as by the context (verses 14 and 17), while there was no reason for putting ἡμεῖς ... ἐσμεν in its stead. The plural ναοί (ℵ* 0243 1739 Clement Augustine) is a pedantic correction.

7.8 βλέπω [γάρ] {C}

Because of preponderant attestation, a majority of the Committee preferred the reading βλέπω γάρ and explained the rise of variations as attempts to clear the construction. Thus, copyists rightly sensed that a new portion of the discourse begins with εἰ καὶ μετεμελόμην (whence B inserts δέ after εἰ as an adversative conjunction), and therefore the main clause was taken to begin either at βλέπω, with the consequent omission of γάρ, or at νῦν χαίρω, with the substitution of the participial form βλέπων as a gloss for βλέπω γάρ.

On the other hand the minority of the Committee explained the rise of the variants in another way. Since the reading βλέπω (which is attested by a notable combination of witnesses) involves a typically Pauline anacoluthon, one can understand that copyists would have been inclined to relieve the syntax either by substituting βλέπων or by adding γάρ.

In view of the uncertainty in the evaluation of the evidence, it was thought best to retain γάρ enclosed within square brackets.

8.7 ἡμῶν ἐν ὑμῖν {C}

On the basis of the testimony of several early witnesses (𝔓⁴⁶ B 1739 it^r cop^{sa, bo} Origen^{lat} Ephraem) a majority of the Committee felt a slight preference for the variant ἡμῶν ἐν ὑμῖν, because it is the more difficult reading. At the same time, it must be acknowledged that the reading ὑμῶν ἐν ἡμῖν, which superficially is more appropriate in the context, had very wide circulation in the early church (‭א‬ C D G K P Ψ 81 614 *Byz Lect* it[d, g, 61] vg syr[h] goth eth *al*).

8.9 ὑμᾶς {B}

The second person plural pronoun, which comports with the apostle's argument, is strongly supported by external evidence (𝔓[46] ‭א‬ B D F G L P *al*). Since in later Greek the vowels η and υ came to be pronounced alike, scribes sometimes confused the two, writing ἡμᾶς instead of ὑμᾶς. Furthermore, homiletic or devotional application of the statement to Christian believers in general would have fostered the adoption of the reading ἡμᾶς.

8.19 [αὐτοῦ] {C}

The weight of the witnesses that support the presence of αὐτοῦ is somewhat less than the weight of those that omit the word. On the other hand, its omission produces the easier reading, which is therefore suspect as secondary. The picture is clouded still further by the fact that several witnesses read αὐτήν – yet this may perhaps be taken as indirect support for the earlier presence of αὐτοῦ. On balance, the Committee considered that the least unsatisfactory decision was to retain αὐτοῦ but to enclose it within square brackets.

8.24 ἐνδεικνύμενοι

Since it is now generally recognized by New Testament grammarians that, in accordance with Semitic idiom, occasionally the Greek participle functions as the imperative mood,[1] the Committee preferred ἐνδεικνύμενοι, supported, as it is, by representatives of the Alexandrian and the Western texts (B D* E F G 33 181 1898). If the original reading had been ἐνδείξασθε (‭א‬ C D[b, c] K L P almost all minuscules and many versions – although in such a case the evidence of the versions counts for very little), there is no reason why it should

---

[1] Cf. Blass-Debrunner-Funk, § 468, 2; C. F. D. Moule, *An Idiom-Book of New Testament Greek,* pp. 179 f.; Moulton-Turner, p. 343 (with bibliography).

have been altered to the participial construction; on the other hand, however, it is easy to understand that copyists, unacquainted with the Semitic idiom, would change the participle to the finite verb.

9.4 λέγω {B}

A majority of the Committee preferred to adopt the reading λέγω, supported by 𝔓[46] C* D G it[ar, d, g] cop[samss] goth, and explained λέγωμεν as a scribal assimilation to the preceding καταισχυνθῶμεν ἡμεῖς. Elsewhere in the context Paul uses the first person singular (verses 1, 2, 3, and 5).

9.4 ταύτῃ {B}

The presence of τῆς καυχήσεως in later manuscripts is an explanatory scribal gloss, possibly derived from 11.17.

10.12-13 οὐ συνιᾶσιν. ἡμεῖς δέ {B}

The absence of οὐ συνιᾶσιν. ἡμεῖς δέ in several witnesses of the Western text (D* G it[d, g, ar] Ambrosiaster Vigilius Sedulius Scotus) is doubtless the result of an accident in transcription, when the eye of a copyist passed from οὐ to οὐκ and omitted the intervening words. The reading ἡμεῖς δέ (429 vg Ephraem Pelagius) appears to be an imperfect restoration of the shortened text. The reading οὐ συνίσασιν. ἡμεῖς δέ (ℵ* 88) is an obvious orthographical error, which produces the sense "they compare themselves with themselves without understanding [that they do so]. But we...." In deciding between the alternative spellings of the verb, the Committee preferred to follow the testimony of 𝔓[46] ℵ[a] B H[vid] 33 1739 al.

11.3 ἀπὸ τῆς ἁπλότητος [καὶ τῆς ἁγνότητος] {C}

In this set of variant readings the external evidence and the transcriptional probabilities are susceptible of quite diverse interpretations. On the one hand, assuming that the reading ἀπὸ τῆς ἁπλότητος καὶ τῆς ἁγνότητος (𝔓[46] ℵ* B G 33 451 it[g, r, ar] syr[h with *] cop[sa, bo] goth eth) is original, scribal oversight occasioned by homoeoteleuton

(-ότητος and -ότητος) can easily account for the readings ἀπὸ τῆς ἁπλότητος (‭א‬ᶜ Dᶜ H K P Ψ 614 1739 *Byz Lect* vg syrᵖˑʰ arm) and ἀπὸ τῆς ἁγνότητος (Lucifer Ambrose Augustine Vigilius). It is more difficult to account for the reversed order of words in the reading ἀπὸ τῆς ἁγνότητος καὶ τῆς ἁπλότητος (D* itᵈ Epiphanius), although it may be the result of mere inattention on the part of copyists.

On the other hand, the several readings may also be interpreted as modifications of an original ἀπὸ τῆς ἁπλότητος in the following manner. In order to explain ἁπλότητος in terms of the marriage symbolism of ver. 2 (παρθένον ἁγνήν), in an early copy someone wrote ἁγνότητος in the margin as a gloss, and later copyists introduced the word into the text, either before or after ἁπλότητος. It is more difficult to account for the reading ἀπὸ τῆς ἁγνότητος, although the witnesses (apparently all of them are patristic) may have had special interests that led them to quote only one part of the conflated text.

In view of the age and character of such witnesses as 𝔓⁴⁶ ‭א‬* B 33, the Committee retained the longer reading in the text, but in deference to the testimony of ‭א‬ᶜ Dᶜ H K P Ψ 614 1739 *al* they enclosed καὶ τῆς ἁγνότητος within square brackets.

11.17 κύριον {A}

In place of κύριον (which at this place refers to Jesus), several inattentive scribes substituted θεόν or ἄνθρωπον.

11.21 ἠσθενήκαμεν {B}

The Committee considered the witnesses that support the perfect tense to be of greater weight than those that support the aorist tense. After ἠσθενήσαμεν, a few witnesses (D E *al*) add the gloss ἐν τούτῳ τῷ μέρει ("in this matter").

11.32 πιάσαι με {B}

Although support for the reading πιάσαι με is not extensive, its quality is impressive (B D* itᵈˑᵃʳ vg syrᵖ copˢᵃ arm). If θέλων were original, its omission would be difficult to account for; on the other hand, its insertion at various positions can be explained as the work of copyists in the interest of stylistic amelioration.

12.1 *καυχᾶσθαι δεῖ* {A}

The difficulty of understanding the meaning of the verse led at an early date to various scribal emendations. The original text appears to be preserved in $\mathfrak{P}^{46}$ B D^c G P 33 81 614 1739 it$^{d, g}$ syr$^{p, h}$ goth. (See also the comment on the following set of variant readings.)

12.1 *συμφέρον μέν* {A}

The Committee preferred the reading supported by $\mathfrak{P}^{46}$ $\aleph$ B G^{gr} 33 1739 vg cop$^{sa, bo}$, for the other readings, when considered in the light of the variants earlier in the verse, seem to be the result of attempts to ameliorate the style and syntax.

12.6 *ἀκούει [τι]*

On the one hand, the shorter reading, *ἀκούει,* is supported by a strong combination of witnesses ($\aleph$* B D^c F^{gr} G 33 424^c it^g vg syr^p cop$^{sa, bo}$ arm). On the other hand, however, it is easy to see why *τι* ($\mathfrak{P}^{46}$ $\aleph^c$ D* K L P Ψ 104 326 it^d syr^h goth) should have been dropped by copyists as superfluous and disturbing to the syntax. To indicate this balance of considerations, the Committee decided to retain the word enclosed within square brackets.

12.7 *διό* {C}

Although *διό* is absent from such important witnesses as $\mathfrak{P}^{46}$ D Ψ 88 614 it$^{d, ar}$ vg syr$^{p, h}$ cop^{sa} goth, the Committee preferred to retain the word in the text as the more difficult reading, attested, as it is, by Alexandrian and other witnesses ($\aleph$ A B G 33 81 1739 it^g Euthalius). The excision of the conjunction seems to have occurred when copyists mistakenly began a new sentence with *καὶ τῇ ὑπερβολῇ τῶν ἀποκαλύψεων,* instead of taking these words with the preceding sentence.

12.7 ἵνα μὴ ὑπεραίρωμαι (2) {B}

Several important witnesses (ℵ* A D G 33 629* it^d, g vg eth *al*) omit the second occurence of these words as unnecessary and superfluous; they are well supported, however (𝔓⁴⁶ B Ψ 81 614 1739 syr^p, h cop^sa, bo goth arm), and the repetition has special emphasis in the context.

12.9 δύναμις {A}

The Textus Receptus, following ℵ^c A² D^b, c E K L P most minuscules syr^p, h cop^bo arm, reads ἡ γὰρ δύναμίς μου. The possessive pronoun, which is absent from 𝔓⁴⁶vid ℵ* A* B D* F G 424^c it^d, g vg cop^sa goth eth *al,* was no doubt added by copyists for the sake of perspicuity.

12.15 εἰ {B}

In order to give added emphasis the Textus Receptus, following ℵ^c D^c K L P most minuscules vg syr^p, h goth arm eth, adds καί after εἰ. The reading εἰ is strongly supported by 𝔓⁴⁶ ℵ* A B G^gr 33^vid cop^sa, bo, fay. The omission of εἰ from several Western witnesses (D* it^d, g, r, ar Ambrosiaster) may be due either to an accident in transcription or to deliberate scribal modification.

12.15 ἀγαπῶ[ν], ἧσσον ἀγαπῶμαι; {C}

It is difficult to decide between ἀγαπῶν (𝔓⁴⁶ ℵ^c B D G K P Ψ 81 88 614 1739 *al*) and ἀγαπῶ (ℵ* A 33 104* 330 451 *al*), each of which can be explained on palaeographical grounds as rising from either adding or dropping ν before η (ΑΓΑΠω(Ν)ΗϹϹΟΝ). The more difficult reading is the participial form, which demands that the reader supply mentally the finite verb εἰμί (nowhere else does Paul make this kind of demand on the reader). In order to represent the preponderance of external evidence, a majority of the Committee preferred ἀγαπῶν, but in view of internal considerations it was thought advisable to enclose ν within square brackets.

12.19 πάλαι {A}

The Textus Receptus, following א^c D^{gr} K L P Ψ 104 326 642 1835 it^g syr^{p, h} cop^{bo} goth arm, reads the easier πάλιν. The more difficult reading πάλαι is strongly supported by 𝔓⁴⁶ *(οὐ πάλαι)* א* A B F G^{gr} 33 330 424^c 1319 1845 2127 it^d vg.

12.20 ἔρις

In many witnesses the singular number ἔρις (𝔓⁴⁶ א A 33 1611 1739 2005 syr^p arm) has been changed to ἔρεις (B D F G K L P Ψ most minuscules it vg syr^h cop^{sa, bo} goth) so as to conform to the following plurals.

12.20 ζῆλος

The singular number ζῆλος, which is strongly supported by 𝔓⁴⁶ A B D* F G 33 326 1874 syr^p goth arm, has been changed to ζῆλοι in many witnesses (א D^{b, c} K L P most minuscules it vg syr^h cop^{sa, bo}) so as to conform to the following plurals.

13.2 νῦν

The Textus Receptus, following D^c E K L P Ψ most minuscules syr^{p, h} cop^{sa} goth arm, adds γράφω. Since there is no reason why, if present originally, the word should have been omitted, the shorter text, strongly supported by 𝔓⁴⁶ א A B D* F G 33 424^c 1906* it^{d, g} vg eth^{ro}, is to be preferred.

13.4 ἐν αὐτῷ {A}

Under the influence of the following σὺν αὐτῷ, several witnesses replace ἐν αὐτῷ with σὺν αὐτῷ (א A F G 1311 2495 it^{g, r} syr^p cop^{bo} arab). In other witnesses an inverse assimilation has occurred, the phrase σὺν αὐτῷ being replaced by ἐν αὐτῷ (𝔓^{46vid} D* 33 it^{d, g}). The text adopted *(ἐν αὐτῷ)* is strongly supported by B D K P Ψ 0243 33 614 1739 *Byz Lect* it^{d, 61} vg syr^h cop^{sa, fay} goth.

13.4 εἰς ὑμᾶς {A}

Since it is unclear whether εἰς ὑμᾶς is to be taken with ζήσομεν or with δυνάμεως θεοῦ, the phrase was omitted by a few witnesses (B D² itʳ *al*) as an awkward addendum.

13.13 ὑμῶν.

As would be expected, the Textus Receptus, following ℵᶜ D E K P Ψ most minuscules itᵈ vg syrᵖˑʰ copᵇᵒ goth arm, adds ἀμήν. The text (without ἀμήν) is decisively supported by 𝔓⁴⁶ ℵ* A B F G 33 90 424ᶜ itᵍ vgᵐˢˢ armᵐˢˢ ethʳᵒ.

13.13 *Subscription*

(*a*) The subscription in 𝔓⁴⁶ ℵ* A B* 33 is πρὸς Κορινθίους β̄. Other subscriptions include: (*b*) πρὸς Κορινθίους β̄ ἐγράφη ἀπὸ Φιλίππων Bᶜ P; (*c*) τέλος τῆς πρὸς Κορινθίους β̄ ἐπιστολῆς· ἐγράφη ἀπὸ Φιλίππων 642; (*d*) πρὸς Κορινθίους δευτέρα ἐγράφη ἀπὸ Φιλίππων διὰ Τίτου καὶ Λουκᾶ L *al*; (*e*) πρὸς Κορινθίους β̄ ἐγράφη ἀπὸ Φιλίππων τῆς Μακεδονίας διὰ Τίτου καὶ Λουκᾶ K *al*, followed by the Textus Receptus (with δευτέρα for β̄); (*f*) as (*e*) but concluding … διὰ Τίτου, Βαρναβᾶ, καὶ Λουκᾶ 201 205 209 328 337; (*g*) ἐγράφη ἀπὸ Φιλίππων τῆς Μακεδονίας διὰ Τίτου καὶ Λουκᾶ πρὸς Κορινθίους β̄ ἐπιστολή Euthaliusᵐˢˢ.

THE LETTER OF PAUL TO THE GALATIANS

1.3 πατρὸς ἡμῶν καὶ κυρίου {B}

Although the sequence πατρὸς καὶ κυρίου ἡμῶν has rather strong external support (𝔓⁴⁶, ⁵¹vid B D G H K 88 614 1739 *Byz* itᵈ, ᵍ vg syrᵖ, ʰ, ᵖᵃˡ copˢᵃ, ᵇᵒᵐˢˢ goth arm *al*), a majority of the Committee preferred the sequence πατρὸς ἡμῶν καὶ κυρίου (ℵ A P Ψ 33 81 326 1241 itᵃʳ *al*) because it accords with Paul's usage elsewhere (Ro 1.7; 1 Cor 1.3; 2 Cor 1.2; Eph 1.2; Php 1.2; Phm 3). The apostle's stereotyped formula was altered by copyists who, apparently in the interest of Christian piety, transferred the possessive pronoun so it would be more closely associated with "Lord Jesus Christ."

The other readings, involving the absence of the pronoun altogether (4* 43 206 234 319 424ᶜ 429 547 917 927 941 999 1319 1758 1877 1891 *al*) and its presence after both πατρός and κυρίου (copᵇᵒ eth), must be regarded as secondary developments in the transmission of the text.

1.6 [Χριστοῦ] {C}

The Committee found it difficult to decide whether transcriptional probabilities or external evidence should be allowed the greater weight in choosing among the five variant readings. On the one hand, the absence of any genitive qualifying ἐν χάριτι (𝔓⁴⁶vid G Hvid itᵍ, ᵃʳ Marcion Tertullian Cyprian Ambrosiaster Marius Victorinus Lucifer Ephraem Pelagius) has the appearance of being the original reading, which copyists supplemented by adding Χριστοῦ (𝔓⁵¹vid ℵ A B Ψ 33 81 614 1739 vg syrᵖ, ʰ, ᵖᵃˡ copᵇᵒ goth arm *al*), or Ἰησοῦ Χριστοῦ (D itᵈ syrʰ ʷⁱᵗʰ *), or Χριστοῦ Ἰησοῦ (copˢᵃ Jerome), or θεοῦ (7 327 336 Origenˡᵃᵗ Theodoret). On the other hand however, a majority of the Committee was unwilling to adopt a reading that is supported by only part of the Western tradition; therefore it was decided to print Χριστοῦ on the strength of its strong external support, but to enclose the word within square brackets out of deference to its omission by $\mathfrak{P}^{46vid}$ and certain Western witnesses.

1.8   εὐαγγελίζηται [ὑμῖν] {C}

Since ὑμῖν is absent from several important witnesses (ℵ* G^{gr*} Ψ it^g Tertullian Cyprian Eusebius Ambrosiaster Marius Victorinus Lucifer Cyril), and since it occurs before the verb in some witnesses and after it in others, a strong case can be made for the originality of the shorter text. On the other hand, however, since the presence of the pronoun may seem to limit unnecessarily the range of the statement, copyists may have deleted it in order make Paul's asseveration applicable wherever he or an angel might preach. Because of these conflicting considerations, a majority of the Committee preferred to print the pronoun after the verb (on the strength of preponderant external evidence), but to enclose it within square brackets to indicate a certain doubt about its originality. The reading εὐαγγελίζηται has stronger and more diversified support than either εὐαγγελίζεται or εὐαγγελίσηται.

1.11   γάρ {C}

The weight of manuscript evidence supporting γάρ or supporting δέ is almost evenly balanced. As concerns transcriptional probability, however, the Committee preferred γάρ, and considered that δέ may have arisen from assimilation to 1 Cor 15.1 or 2 Cor 8.1.

1.15   εὐδόκησεν [ὁ θεός] {C}

On the basis of preponderance of external testimony a majority of the Committee preferred the reading with ὁ θεός, yet, in view of the importance of the witnesses that lack the words, it was thought advisable to enclose them within square brackets.

[The reading with ὁ θεός has every appearance of being a scribal gloss making explicit the implied subject of εὐδόκησεν, nor is there any good reason why the words should have been deleted if they had been original (the supposition that they were accidentally omitted is improbable in view of the diversified testimony supporting the shorter text). B.M.M. and A.W.]

1.18 *Κηφᾶν*

The Textus Receptus, following ℵ^c D F G K L P and most minuscules, substitutes the more familiar Greek name *Πέτρον*. The Aramaic name *Κηφᾶν* is supported by 𝔓^{46, 51} ℵ* A B 33 424^c 467 823 920 1739 1912 syr^{p, hmg, pal} cop^{sa, bo} eth. (See also the comments on 2.9, 11, and 14.)

2.1 *πάλιν ἀνέβην* {A}

Of the several variant readings, *πάλιν ἀνέβην* appears to be preferable, being supported by early and diversified witnesses (𝔓⁴⁶ ℵ A B K P Ψ 81 614 1739 vg syr^{(p), h} cop^{sa} arm), whereas *ἀνέβην πάλιν* is supported by predominantly Western witnesses (D G it^{d, g, 61} goth eth Pelagius Jerome) and *πάλιν ἀνῆλθον* has only meager support (C Paschal Chronicle). The absence of *πάλιν* in several versional and patristic witnesses (cop^{bo} Marcion Irenaeus^{lat} Tertullian Ambrosiaster Chrysostom Augustine) is either accidental or the result of scribal uncertainty concerning its precise significance in the context.

2.5 *οἷς οὐδέ* {A}

The omission of *οἷς* in several witnesses (syr^p Marcion Greek mss^{acc. to Ambrosiaster} Ephraem) was probably deliberate, in order to rectify the anacoluthon. Omission of *οὐδέ*, whether with or without omission of *οἷς*, is confined chiefly to Western witnesses (D* it^d Marius Victorinus Latin mss^{acc. to Jerome} Augustine Primasius Latin mss^{acc. to Cassiodorus, Claudius}), and seems to have occurred when certain scribes thought it necessary – in view of the apostle's principle of accommodation (1 Cor 9.20-23) – to find here an analogue to the circumcision of Timothy (Ac 16.3). Since, however, the resulting meaning ("Because of the false brethren ... I yielded for a brief time") seems to be distinctly contrary both to the drift of the apostle's argument and to his temperament, the Committee had little hesitation in adopting the reading οἷς οὐδέ, which is decisively supported by all known Greek manuscripts except D* and by the preponderant weight of versional and patristic witnesses.

2.9 Ἰάκωβος καὶ Κηφᾶς καὶ Ἰωάννης

Several witnesses, chiefly Western, replace the Aramaic name Κηφᾶς with the more familiar Greek name Πέτρος (𝔓[46] D F G it[d, g, r] goth Marcion Origen[lat] Marius Victorinus Ephraem Ambrosiaster Jerome); all but two of the same witnesses (not 𝔓[46] it[r]) give more prominence to Peter by placing his name first in the series, thus also bringing together the familiar pair of names, James and John (this James, however, is not the son of Zebedee and the brother of John, who had been killed by Herod [Acts 12.2], but the brother of Jesus and leader of the Church at Jerusalem [Ga 1.19; Ac 15.13]). (See also the comment on 1.18.)

2.11 Κηφᾶς

Instead of the Aramaic name Κηφᾶς, the Textus Receptus, following D F G K L syr[htxt] goth Marcion Marius Victorinus Chrysostom al, substitutes the more familiar Πέτρος. Κηφᾶς is strongly supported by ℵ A B C H P 33 103 104 181 263 424[c] 436 vg syr[p, hmg] cop[sa, bo] arm eth. (See also the comment on 1.18.)

2.12 τινας {A}

The singular number τινα (𝔓[48vid] it[d, r] Irenaeus), which seems to have originated along with the erroneous reading ἦλθεν (see the following comment), is obviously the result of scribal oversight.

2.12 ἦλθον {A}

Although the reading ἦλθεν is supported by a combination of good and ordinarily reliable witnesses (𝔓[46vid] ℵ B D* 33 330 2492 al), the sense of the passage seems to demand the plural ἦλθον (A C Dᶜ H K P Ψ 81 614 1739 *Byz Lect* itʳˑ ᵃʳ vg syrᵖˑ ʰ copˢᵃˑ ᵇᵒ goth arm *al*). The singular number ἦλθεν is probably due to scribes who either imitated ὅτε δὲ ἦλθεν Κηφᾶς of ver. 11, or were unconsciously influenced by careless assonance with the immediately preceding and following verbs that end in -εν.

2.14 Κηφᾶ

The Textus Receptus, following D F G K L P most minuscules itᵈˑ ᵍ vgᵐˢˢ syrʰ goth *al*, replaces Κηφᾶ (𝔓⁴⁶ ℵ A B C H 10 33 88 255 263 424ᶜ 467 1319 2127 vg syrᵖ copˢᵃˑ ᵇᵒ arm eth) with the more familiar Πέτρῳ. (See also the comment on 1.18.)

2.20 υἱοῦ τοῦ θεοῦ {A}

Although the reading θεοῦ καὶ Χριστοῦ is supported by several important witnesses (𝔓⁴⁶ B D* G itᵈˑ ᵍ Marius Victorinus Pelagius), it can scarcely be regarded as original since Paul nowhere else expressly speaks of God as the object of a Christian's faith. The reading that best explains the origin of the others is the customary Pauline expression τοῦ υἱοῦ τοῦ θεοῦ, which is widely attested by a broad spectrum of Greek, versional, and patristic witnesses. It is probable that in copying, the eye of the scribe passed immediately from the first to the second τοῦ, so that only τοῦ θεοῦ was written (as in ms. 330); since what followed was now incongruous, copyists either added τοῦ υἱοῦ or inserted καὶ Χριστοῦ.

3.1 ἐβάσκανεν

The Textus Receptus, following C Dᶜ K L P Ψ most minuscules vgᵐˢˢ syrʰ goth eth *al*, adds τῇ ἀληθείᾳ μὴ πείθεσθαι from 5.7.

3.1 προεγράφη

The Textus Receptus, following D E F G K L many minuscules itᵈˑ ᵍ syrʰ goth *al*, adds ἐν ὑμῖν, which the AV takes with the following ἐσταυρωμένος ("crucified among you"). The text is decisively supported by ℵ A B C Ψ 33* 104 234 424ᶜ 915 1739 itʳ vg syrᵖ copˢᵃ, ᵇᵒ arm eth *al*.

3.14   ἐπαγγελίαν {A}

Influenced by the occurrence of εὐλογία in the preceding clause, several witnesses, chiefly Western in character (𝔓⁴⁶ D* Fᵍʳ G 88* 489 itᵈ, ᵍ Marcion Ambrosiaster Ephraem Vigilius), replace ἐπαγγελίαν with εὐλογίαν.

3.17   θεοῦ {A}

After θεοῦ the Textus Receptus, following the later uncials and most minuscules (Dᵍʳ Gᵍʳ Iᵛⁱᵈ K 0176 88 614 2127 2495 *Byz Lect* arm *al*), continues with εἰς Χριστόν ("the covenant, that was confirmed before of God in Christ" AV). Apparently the interpretative gloss was added in order to introduce into the argument a reference to Χριστός of the preceding verse. The shorter text is strongly supported by 𝔓⁴⁶ ℵ A B C P Ψ 33 81 1739 Old Latin vg copˢᵃ, ᵇᵒ eth *al*.

3.19   νόμος; τῶν παραβάσεων χάριν προσετέθη {A}

Inattentive copyists have produced several quite idiosyncratic readings: D* reads, "It was established on account of traditions"; F G *al* read, "Why then the law of actions? It was established until …"; 𝔓⁴⁶ reads, "Why then the law of actions?" and omits the other words altogether. The text is strongly supported by ℵ A B C Ψ *al*.

3.21   [τοῦ θεοῦ] {C}

The words τοῦ θεοῦ are absent from several early and important witnesses (𝔓⁴⁶ B itᵈ Ambrosiaster Marius Victorinus). On the one hand, since the shorter reading is terse and entirely in accord with Pauline style, the words τοῦ θεοῦ may be a natural addition made by copyists who recalled such passages as Ro 4.20 or 2 Cor 1.20. On the other hand, however, since the absence of the words in a few witnesses may be due to an accident in transmission, the Committee thought it best to represent the balance of probabilities by retaining the words enclosed within square brackets. The reading of 104 represents the substitution of ⲦⲞⲨⲬⲨ for ⲦⲞⲨⲐⲨ.

3.28 εἷς ἐστε ἐν Χριστῷ {A}

The text is strongly supported by ℵ² B C D Ψ *al.* A number of other readings arose through the inadvertence of scribes. Instead of εἷς, several witnesses read the neuter ἕν, perhaps with some allusion to ἕν σῶμα in 1 Cor 12.12. Two manuscripts read ἔστε Χριστοῦ Ἰησοῦ (𝔓⁴⁶ A; compare ℵ*), "you belong to Christ Jesus," which may be an assimilation to 3.29.

4.6 ἡμῶν {A}

The Textus Receptus, following several of the later uncials (Dᶜ E K L Ψ) and most minuscules, reads ὑμῶν, thus conforming the person of the pronoun to the earlier ἐστε. The first person ἡμῶν is strongly supported by early and diversified witnesses (including 𝔓⁴⁶ ℵ A B C D* G P 104 1241 1739 1881 1962 1984 it vg syrᵖᵃˡ copˢᵃ, ᵇᵒᵐˢˢ arm Marcion Tertullian Origenˡᵃᵗ).

4.7 διὰ θεοῦ {A}

Of the several variant readings, the unusual and unexpected expression, κληρονόμος διὰ θεοῦ, which is well supported by early and diversified witnesses (𝔓⁴⁶ ℵ* A B C*ᵛⁱᵈ 33 itᵍ·ʳ vg copᵇᵒ Clement *al*), seems to account best for the origin of the other readings. In the context one would expect that διά would be followed by the genitive of Χριστοῦ as the Mediator, rather than θεοῦ as the source of the inheritance (nevertheless, on occasion Paul does use διά with θεοῦ, e. g. 1.1 and 1 Cor 1.9). The less frequent expression was altered by copyists in various ways:

(a) θεοῦ ("[an heir] of God"), 1962 arm eth^{ro}

(b) διὰ θεόν ("[an heir] on account of God"), G^{gr} 1881

(c) διὰ Χριστοῦ ("[an heir] through Christ"), 81 630 syr^{pal} cop^{sa} Jerome

(d) διὰ Ἰησοῦ Χριστοῦ ("[an heir] through Jesus Christ"), 1739 *l*⁵⁵

(e) θεοῦ διὰ Χριστοῦ ("[an heir] of God through Christ"), the Textus Receptus, following ℵ^c C² D K P 88 104 614* *Byz Lect* it^{d, 61} goth *al*

(f) θεοῦ διὰ Ἰησοῦ Χριστοῦ ("[an heir] of God through Jesus Christ"), 326 614^c 2127 2495 syr^{p, h} eth^{pp} Theodoret.

(g) διὰ θεοῦ ἐν Χριστῷ Ἰησοῦ ("[an heir] through God in Christ Jesus"), cop^{boms}

(h) μὲν θεοῦ συγκληρονόμος δὲ Χριστοῦ ("[an heir] of God, and fellow heir with Christ"), Ψ 1984 1985 Theodoret Theophylact.

The influence of Ro 8.17 is apparent in variant reading (h).

4.14 τὸν πειρασμὸν ὑμῶν {A}

In order to alleviate the difficulty of the expression τὸν πειρασμὸν ὑμῶν, which is strongly supported by good witnesses of both the Alexandrian (ℵ* A B C^{2vid} 33) and the Western (D* G it^{d, g, r} vg Ambrosiaster *al*) types of text, ὑμῶν was replaced by μοῦ (𝔓⁴⁶ it⁶¹), or by μου τόν (C^{*vid} D^{(b), c} K P Ψ 614 *Byz Lect* syr^h cop^{sa, boms} *al*), or by τόν alone (ℵ^c 81 88 1241 syr^p goth arm eth *al*).

4.25 δὲ Ἁγὰρ Σινᾶ {C}

As between δέ and γάρ, the Committee preferred the former on the strength of superior attestation (𝔓⁴⁶ A B D^{gr} syr^{hmg, pal} cop^{sa, bo}). After γάρ had replaced δέ in some witnesses, the juxtaposition of γὰρ Ἁγάρ led to the accidental omission sometimes of γάρ and sometimes of Ἁγάρ.

4.26 ἡμῶν {A}

The Textus Receptus, following ℵ^c A C² K P 81 614 arm *al,* inserts
πάντων before ἡμῶν (cf. Ro 4.16), an insertion which "gives the
text a broader, pastoral application, but obscures Paul's distinction
between the 'chosen ones' and the 'sons of Hagar'" (Zuntz, p. 223).
The uninterpolated text is strongly supported by 𝔓⁴⁶ ℵ* B C* D G Ψ
33 1739 most Old Latin vg syr^{p, hmg} cop^{sa, bo} goth eth Marcion Irenaeus
al.

4.28 ὑμεῖς ... ἐστέ. {B}

Influenced by the first person pronoun in ver. 26 (cf. also ver. 31),
the Textus Receptus, following ℵ A C D^c K P Ψ 614 *al,* reads ἡμεῖς
... ἐσμέν. The second person ὑμεῖς ... ἐστέ is strongly supported
by early and diverse witnesses (𝔓⁴⁶ B D* G 33 1739 it^{d, g} syr^{pal} cop^{sa}
al).

5.1 τῇ ἐλευθερίᾳ ἡμᾶς Χριστὸς ἠλευθέρωσεν· στήκετε οὖν
{B}

Amid the variety of readings, that adopted for the text seems to
account best for the origin of the others. The apostle's abrupt introduction of exhortations was softened by inserting the relative ᾗ
before or after ἐλευθερίᾳ, or by transferring οὖν to the preceding
clause.

5.9 ζυμοῖ

Several Western witnesses (D* it^d vg goth Marcion Marius Victorinus Ambrosiaster *al*) replace ζυμοῖ with δολοῖ. The same Western
correction occurs in 1 Cor 5.6.

5.20 ἔρις

The Textus Receptus, following C D^{b, c} F G K L N P most minuscules Old Latin vg goth syr^h cop^{bo} *al,* reads the plural ἔρεις. The

earlier representatives of the Alexandrian and the Western types of text (א A B D* 1739 syr^p *al*) support the singular ἔρις. In later Greek both forms were pronounced alike.

5.21 φθόνοι {C}

A wide range of witnesses read φθόνοι φόνοι (A C D G K P Ψ 88 1739 *Byz Lect* most of the Old Latin vg syr^{p, h} cop^{bo} goth arm eth *al*). Although the shorter reading may have originated in accidental omission due to homoeoteleuton, a majority of the Committee, impressed by the age and quality of the witnesses supporting φθόνοι (𝔓^{46} א B 33 81 cop^{sa} Marcion Irenaeus^{lat} Clement Origen^{lat} *al*), was inclined to think that φόνοι was inserted by copyists who recollected Ro 1.29.

5.23 ἐγκράτεια {A}

Several witnesses supplement Paul's list of nine Christian graces: ὑπομονή ("patience") is appended by N^c 442 463, and ἁγνεία ("chastity") by D* F G it^{d, g} goth Cyprian Irenaeus^{lat} Origen^{lat} Ambrosiaster *al*. These are obviously scribal interpolations, for if either had been present originally, no copyist would have ventured to delete it.

5.24 Χριστοῦ ['Ἰησοῦ] {C}

The balance of evidence for and against Ἰησοῦ makes it preferable to retain the word but to enclose it within square brackets in order to indicate considerable doubt that it belongs in the text. Although the presence of the definite article τοῦ with Χριστοῦ Ἰησοῦ is unusual (found elsewhere only in Eph 3.1), few commentators have followed Burton[1] in rendering, "They that belong to the Christ, Jesus, have crucified the flesh."

---

[1] Ernest De Witt Burton, *A Critical and Exegetical Commentary on the Epistle to the Galatians* (New York, 1920), p. 319.

6.2 ἀναπληρώσετε {C}

Although the aorist imperative ἀναπληρώσατε is strongly supported (ℵ A C D^{gr} K P Ψ 614 1739 syr^h arm *al*), the future tense appeared to the Committee to be slightly preferable on the basis of early and diversified external attestation ((𝔓⁴⁶) B G and most ancient versions), as well as transcriptional probability (scribes would be likely to conform the future to the preceding imperatives, *καταρτίζετε* (ver. 1) and *βαστάζετε*¹).

6.10 ἐργαζώμεθα {A}

Although several otherwise strong witnesses read the indicative ἐργαζόμεθα (A B² L P *al*), intrinsic probability as well as significant external attestation favors the hortatory subjunctive in the context. In later Greek ω and ο were scarcely distinguished in pronunciation.

6.15 οὔτε γάρ {A}

Influenced by the similar passage in 5.6, the Textus Receptus, following ℵ A C D F G K L P most minuscules it^{d, g} vg syr^{h with *} cop^{sa, bo} eth^{pp} *al*, reads ἐν γὰρ Χριστῷ Ἰησοῦ οὔτε. The shorter reading has limited but adequate support in 𝔓⁴⁶ B Ψ 33 1175 1611 1739 1908 2005 it^r syr^{htxt, pal} goth arm eth^{ro} *al*.

6.17 Ἰησοῦ

Instead of Ἰησοῦ, which is strongly supported by 𝔓⁴⁶ A B C* 33 1070 1753 most of the Old Latin vg syr^{pal} cop^{sa} *al*, several witnesses (P Ψ 81 255 256 442 463 1175 1319 1908 2127 cop^{bo} arm eth *al*) substitute Χριστοῦ, and others provide various edifying expansions: κυρίου Ἰησοῦ (C³ D^c K L most minuscules, followed by the Textus Receptus; κυρίου Ἰησοῦ Χριστοῦ (ℵ 917 941 it^d *al*); κυρίου ἡμῶν Ἰησοῦ Χριστοῦ (D^{gr*} F^{gr} G 104 1924 syr^p goth); and κυρίου μου Ἰησοῦ Χριστοῦ (Origen^{lat}).

---

¹ Singularly enough, however, ℵ, which reads the future *βαστάσετε* (corrected to -άζετε in ℵ³), has the imperative ἀναπληρώσατε.

6.18   *Subscription*

(*a*) The subscription in ℵ A B* C 33 466 is *πρὸς Γαλάτας*. Other subscriptions include: (*b*) *πρὸς Γαλάτας ἐγράφη* (P -φει) *ἀπὸ Ῥώμης* B^c K P 1908, followed by the Textus Receptus; (*c*) *πρὸς Γαλάτας ἐπληρώθη* D; (*d*) *ἐτελέσθη ἐπιστολὴ πρὸς Γαλάτας* F G; (*e*) *τέλος τῆς πρὸς Γαλάτας· ἐγράφη* (42 add *δέ*) *ἀπὸ Ῥώμης* L 42; (*f*) *ἐγράφη ἀπὸ Ῥώμης ὑπὸ Παύλου καὶ τῶν ἀδελφῶν πρὸς Γαλάτας οἱ* (for *ἡ*) *ἐπιστολὴ αὕτη* Euthalius^mss.

THE LETTER OF PAUL TO THE EPHESIANS

1.1 *[ἐν Ἐφέσῳ]* {C}

The words *ἐν Ἐφέσῳ* are absent from several important witnesses (𝔓⁴⁶ ℵ* B* 424ᶜ 1739) as well as from manuscripts mentioned by Basil and the text used by Origen. Certain internal features of the letter as well as Marcion's designation of the epistle as "To the Laodiceans" and the absence in Tertullian and Ephraem of an explicit quotation of the words *ἐν Ἐφέσῳ* have led many commentators to suggest that the letter was intended as an encyclical, copies being sent to various churches, of which that at Ephesus was chief. Since the letter has been traditionally known as "To the Ephesians," and since all witnesses except those mentioned above include the words *ἐν Ἐφέσῳ*, the Committee decided to retain them, but enclosed within square brackets.

1.6 *ἧς*

The Textus Receptus, following ℵᶜ D G K L Ψ most minuscules itᵈˑ ᵍ vg syrʰ goth, substitutes *ἐν ᾗ* for *ἧς*. The latter reading was preferred by a majority of the Committee on the basis of (*a*) the weight of external support (𝔓⁴⁶ ℵ* A B P 6 33 88 330 424ᶜ 436 1319 1837 1908 2127 Origen Chrysostom Euthalius) and (*b*) the probability that copyists would have been more likely to replace the more difficult construction (*ἧς* stands by attraction for *ἥν*, the cognate accusative) with one that is less difficult, than vice versa.

1.6 *ἠγαπημένῳ* {A}

After *ἠγαπημένῳ* several witnesses, chiefly of a Western textual tradition (D* F G *al*), incorporate an explanatory scribal addition, *υἱῷ αὐτοῦ*.

1.14 ὅ {B}

It is difficult to decide whether copyists altered ὅς to ὅ in order to make it agree with the gender of πνεῦμα, or whether ὅ became ὅς by attraction to the gender of the following ἀρραβών, according to a usual idiom. On the basis of what was taken to be superior external attestation, a majority of the Committee preferred the reading ὅ.

1.15 καὶ τὴν ἀγάπην τὴν εἰς πάντας τοὺς ἁγίους {B}

The shorter reading καὶ τὴν εἰς πάντας τοὺς ἁγίους (𝔓⁴⁶ ℵ* B P 33 1739 *al*) appears to be the result of an accident in transcription, occasioned by homoeoarcton *(τὴν … τὴν)*. If, as some scholars have suggested, the shorter reading is original and the addition is derived from Col 1.4, ἣν ἔχετε would have been inserted instead of the second τήν. The rearrangement of the sequence of the words so as to dispense with the second τήν (81 104 256 *al*) is clearly a secondary modification.

1.18 [ὑμῶν] {C}

Because of the weight of Greek and versional witnesses that support ὑμῶν, the Committee decided that the word should be included in the text, but, in view of its absence from 𝔓⁴⁶ B 33 1739 and other significant witnesses, that it should be enclosed within square brackets.

2.5 τῷ Χριστῷ {B}

The reading ἐν τῷ Χριστῷ (𝔓⁴⁶ B 33 *al*) seems to have arisen from either accidental dittography of the previous -εν, or from deliberate assimilation to ἐν Χριστῷ Ἰησοῦ in ver. 6.

2.5 χάριτι {A}

In order to identify precisely the source of the grace that saves, several witnesses, chiefly Western (D* F G *al*), add οὗ ("whose").

2.17 εἰρήνην (2)

The Textus Receptus, following several later witnesses (K L many minuscules syr[p, h] *al*), omits the second instance of εἰρήνην, probably because it seemed redundant and therefore superfluous. Its presence, however, not only is strongly attested by good witnesses ($\mathfrak{P}^{46}$ ℵ A B D F G P it[d, g] vg cop[sa, bo] goth arm eth *al*), but also adds significantly to the force of the writer's statement.

2.21 πᾶσα οἰκοδομή {B}

Although it is possible that, through itacism, ἡ was accidentally omitted before οἰκοδομή, the anarthrous reading was preferred because of the weight of external evidence (ℵ* B D G K Ψ 33 614 1739* *Byz Lect* Clement *al*) and because copyists would have been tempted to insert ἡ in order to clarify the sense.

3.1 τοῦ Χριστοῦ ['Ιησοῦ] {C}

The balance between the weight of the evidence that supports the presence of 'Ιησοῦ following Χριστοῦ and its absence from several significant witnesses is reflected in the Committee's decision to include the word but to enclose it within square brackets.

3.9 φωτίσαι [πάντας] {C}

Several important witnesses read only φωτίσαι (ℵ* A 424[c] 1739 1881 Origen Ambrosiaster[1/2] Hilary Jerome *al*). It is difficult to decide whether πάντας was omitted, either accidentally or intentionally (as not congruent with τοῖς ἔθνεσιν, ver. 8), or was inserted because the verb φωτίσαι seems to require an expressed accusative (which it usually has elsewhere in the New Testament). Since, however, there are no other variant readings (such as αὐτούς *et sim.*) as would be expected if πάντας were not original, a majority of the Committee preferred to retain the word on the authority of $\mathfrak{P}^{46}$ ℵ[c] B C D G K P Ψ 33 81 614 *Byz Lect* it vg syr[p, h] cop[sa, bo] goth arm *al,* but to enclose it within square brackets, indicating doubt that it has a right to stand in the text.

3.9 οἰκονομία

The Textus Receptus, in company with a scattering of late minuscules, replaces οἰκονομία with the interpretative gloss κοινωνία (hence AV "fellowship"). The true reading is supported by 𝔓⁴⁶, all known uncials, almost all minuscules, all known versions and patristic quotations.

3.9 κτίσαντι

The Textus Receptus, following DᶜKLP many minuscules syrʰ ʷⁱᵗʰ * al, adds διὰ Ἰησοῦ Χριστοῦ. Since there is no reason why, if the words were original, they should have been omitted, the Committee preferred to read simply κτίσαντι, which is decisively supported by 𝔓⁴⁶ ℵ A B C D* F G P 33 1319 1611 2127 and most versions and early patristic quotations.

3.13 ὑμῶν (2) {A}

The second instance of ὑμῶν in ver. 13, supported by early and weighty witnesses, is replaced in later manuscripts with ἡμῶν – which is totally inappropriate in the context. In later Greek the vowels η and υ came to be pronounced alike, and inattentive scribes tended to confuse them.

3.14 πατέρα {B}

After πατέρα, read by 𝔓⁴⁶ ℵ* A B C P 33 81 1739 syrᵖᵃˡ copˢᵃ, ᵇᵒ eth al, a variety of Western and Byzantine witnesses add the words τοῦ κυρίου ἡμῶν Ἰησοῦ Χριστοῦ (ℵᶜ D G K Ψ 88 614 Byz Lect itᵈ, ᵍ, ᵃʳ vg syrᵖ, ʰ goth arm al). The gloss, suggested by 1.3 and similar passages, became part of the Textus Receptus.

3.19 πληρωθῆτε εἰς πᾶν τὸ πλήρωμα τοῦ θεοῦ {A}

Instead of πληρωθῆτε εἰς πᾶν τὸ πλήρωμα τοῦ θεοῦ, which is amply attested by good representatives of both the Alexandrian and the Western types of text (ℵ A C D G it vg syr^p, h, pal cop^bo goth), several witnesses (𝔓⁴⁶ B 462 cop^sa) omit -τε εἰς, reading πληρωθῇ πᾶν τὸ πλήρωμα τοῦ θεοῦ ("[that] all the fullness of God may be filled up"). Several other readings are found in individual manuscripts (81 reads πληροφορηθῆτε, 1881 substitutes Χριστοῦ for θεοῦ, and 33, otherwise following B, adds εἰς ὑμᾶς).

3.20 ὑπέρ {A}

Because of its apparent redundancy several witnesses (𝔓⁴⁶ D E F G it^d, g vg Ambrosiaster) omit ὑπέρ.

4.6 πᾶσιν {A}

The Textus Receptus, following a few minuscules and patristic witnesses (489 Chrysostom Theodoret *al*), adds ὑμῖν; other witnesses (D F G K L Ψ 181 326 917 920 it^d, g vg syr^p, h goth arm *al*) add ἡμῖν. Both readings are explanatory glosses, introduced in order to establish a personal reference of πᾶσιν to the Christians. The reading adopted for the text is strongly supported by 𝔓⁴⁶ ℵ A B C P 082 33 88 104 424^c 436 442 460 462 1912* 1944 cop^sa, bo eth arab *al*.

4.8 ἔδωκεν {B}

On the whole it appears that the reading without καί is to be preferred, not only because it is supported by such diversified witnesses as 𝔓⁴⁶ ℵ* A D* G 33 88 it vg cop^sa, bo Marcion Justin *al,* but also because many a copyist would have been tempted to insert a connective in order to relieve the unidiomatic Greek construction.

4.9 κατέβη {A}

The addition of πρῶτον after κατέβη (ℵ^c B C^c K P Ψ 88 614 *Byz Lect al*) appears to be a natural expansion introduced by copyists to elucidate the meaning. The shorter text is strongly supported by 𝔓⁴⁶ ℵ* A C* D G 1739 *al.*

4.9 *[μέρη]* {C}

Although the presence of *μέρη* in the text is strongly supported by ℵ A B C Ψ *al*, its absence from 𝔓⁴⁶ D* F G *al* leaves one uncertain whether the word was added as an explanatory gloss or deleted as virtually superfluous. The Committee judged that the least unsatisfactory solution was to include the word but to enclose it within square brackets.

4.17 *ἔθνη*

The Textus Receptus adds *λοιπά* before *ἔθνη*, with the correctors of two uncial manuscripts as well as the later uncials and most minuscules (ℵᶜ Dᵇ'ᶜ K L P Ψ arm *al*). The word is obviously an interpretative intrusion; the shorter text is decisively supported by 𝔓⁴⁶ ℵ* A B D* F G 082 33 88 255 256 263 296 424ᶜ 467 1319 itᵈ'ᵍ vg copˢᵃ'ᵇᵒ eth *al*.

4.19 *ἀπηλγηκότες* {A}

Instead of *ἀπηλγηκότες* (from *ἀπαλγέω*, "become callous, without feeling"), a word appropriate to the figure suggested by *πώρωσις* of ver. 18, several Western witnesses read *ἀπηλπικότες* or *ἀφηλπικότες* (from *ἀπελπίζω*, "despair of oneself"). The Committee preferred the reading supported by the earliest manuscripts (𝔓⁴⁶ A B).

4.28 *ταῖς [ἰδίαις] χερσὶν τὸ ἀγαθόν* {C}

The differences of reading are numerous in this brief clause. As concerns the sequence of words, copyists would have been more likely to move *τὸ ἀγαθόν* next to the participle than to separate them; furthermore, the stronger external evidence also supports such a sequence (𝔓⁴⁶'⁴⁹ᵛⁱᵈ ℵ B D G 81 330 451 it vg syrᵖ copˢᵃᵐˢ'ᵇᵒ goth arm eth). It is more difficult to decide whether *ἰδίαις* is an interpolation from 1 Cor 4.12, or whether it was deleted as superfluous, or whether it was accidentally omitted in transcription (ΤΑΙΣΙΔΙΑΙΣΧΕΡΣΙΝ).

On the basis chiefly of external evidence (ℵ* A D G 81 104 it^d, (g), mon syr^p goth arm eth), the Committee preferred the reading ταῖς ἰδίαις χερσίν, the unclassical usage of ἰδίαις being common in colloquial Greek of the time. At the same time, however, in view of the absence of ἰδίαις from such early and notable witnesses as 𝔓^46, 49vid B, it was decided to enclose the word within square brackets. The omission of either τὸ ἀγαθόν (cop^sa Tertullian) or ταῖς (ἰδίαις) χερσίν (P 33 1739 1881 Clement Origen Speculum) may have arisen from the presumed incompatibility of τὸ ἀγαθόν with *manual* labor.

4.29 χρείας {A}

Because χρείας may have seemed ill-suited in the context, several witnesses (chiefly those that present a Western type of text) have substituted πίστεως, which is much easier to construe with οἰκοδομήν.

4.32 ὑμῖν {B}

In the light of the earlier part of the sentence the reading ὑμῖν, which is adequately supported by 𝔓^46 ℵ A G P 81 614 most of the Old Latin cop^sa, bo goth eth *al*, seems to be required by the sense. The origin of the reading ἡμῖν (𝔓^49vid B D^gr K Ψ 33 1739 syr^p, h arm *al*) may have been accidental, through confusion arising from similar pronunciation of υ and η in later Greek. (See also the comments on the next two sets of variant readings.)

5.2 ἡμᾶς {B}

The external evidence supporting the two readings is rather evenly balanced (ἡμᾶς 𝔓^46 ℵ^c D G K Ψ 33 614 1739 it^pt vg syr^p, h goth arm *al*; ὑμᾶς ℵ* A B P 81 it^pt cop^sa, bo eth *al*), with a slight preponderance of weight favoring ἡμᾶς. Since the following set of variant readings seems to require the adoption of the reading ἡμῶν, a majority of the Committee felt that uniformity of the personal pronoun in two successive clauses joined by καί was indispensable, and therefore preferred ἡμᾶς. (See also the comment on 4.32.)

5.2 ὑπὲρ ἡμῶν προσφοράν {A}

In comparison with the external evidence supporting ὑμῶν (B 31 69 442 462 547 it⁸⁶ copˢᵃ, ᵇᵒ eth Speculum *al*), the reading ἡμῶν is much more strongly attested (𝔓⁴⁶, ⁴⁹ ℵ A D F G K L P Ψ 33 81 614 1739 itᵈ, ᵍ, ⁶¹ vg syrᵖ, ʰ goth arm *al*). The reading ὑπὲρ ἡμῶν ἐν φθορᾷ (1241) is the result of a curious transcriptional blunder. (See also the comments on the previous two sets of variant readings.)

5.5 ὅ

Instead of the conventional formula ὅ ἐστιν ("that is to say"), which koine Greek can employ "without reference to the gender of the word explained or to that of the word which explains" (Blass-Debrunner-Funk, § 132 (2), the alteration of ὅ to ὅς (A D K L P most minuscules, followed by the Textus Receptus) appears to be a correction introduced by overly punctilious scribes. The reading ὅ is strongly supported by 𝔓⁴⁶ ℵ B F G Ψ 33 81 256 424ᶜ 915 1175 1319 1739 2005 2127 it vg goth *al*.

5.5 Χριστοῦ καὶ θεοῦ

A curious variety of readings has arisen in the transmission of these words. The reading θεοῦ (𝔓⁴⁶ 1245 2147) originated either through scribal oversight (ΤΟΥΧΥΚΑΙΘΥ) or through the influence of the stereotyped expression *(βασιλεία τοῦ θεοῦ)* in the Gospels. Probably the latter influence is also to be seen in the sequence of the Western reading θεοῦ καὶ Χριστοῦ (Fᵍʳ G itᵍ Ambrosiaster *al*). Other singular or sub-singular readings are Χριστοῦ τοῦ θεοῦ (1739* eth Theodoret), Χριστοῦ (38* 90), and υἱοῦ τοῦ θεοῦ (1836).

5.9 φωτός {A}

Instead of φωτός the Textus Receptus reads πνεύματος, with 𝔓⁴⁶ Dᶜ K Ψ 88 104 614 1739ᵐᵍ *al*. Although it can be argued that φωτός has come in from the influence of the same word in the preceding line, it is much more likely that recollection of Paul's reference in Ga 5.22 to ὁ δὲ καρπὸς τοῦ πνεύματος has led to the introduction of the word here. The reading φωτός is strongly supported by early and diversified witnesses, representing both the Alexandrian and the Western text-types (𝔓[49] ℵ A B D* G P 33 81 1739* it vg syr[p, pal] cop[sa, bo] goth arm eth Origen).

5.14 ἐπιφαύσει σοι ὁ Χριστός {A}

Instead of "Christ will shine upon you," strongly supported by a wide range of witnesses, several Western witnesses substitute either "Christ will touch you" or "You will touch Christ." Apparently the readings arose from the legend that the cross on which Jesus was crucified was erected over the burial place of Adam, who was raised from the dead by the touch of the Savior's blood.[1]

5.15 οὖν ἀκριβῶς πῶς {B}

The Committee preferred the sequence ἀκριβῶς πῶς on the basis of the strength of the external evidence (𝔓[46] ℵ* B 33 81 1739 cop[sa] Origen al) as well as transcriptional probability (πῶς may have been accidentally omitted after -βῶς, and subsequently inserted at the wrong place). The presence of ἀδελφοί in several witnesses (ℵ[c] A 629 it[61] vg cop[bo] Pelagius) is obviously secondary, there being no good reason to account for the deletion of the word if it had been present originally.

5.19 ᾠδαῖς πνευματικαῖς {B}

In the opinion of a majority of the Committee, it is more likely that πνευματικαῖς was accidentally omitted from several witnesses

---

[1] See J. Armitage Robinson, *St. Paul's Epistle to the Ephesians* (London, 1903), p. 119, n.1.

($\mathfrak{P}^{46}$ B it^d Ambrosiaster) because of homoeoteleuton, than added in almost all witnesses by assimilation to Col 3.16, where the text is firm. The addition of *ἐν χάριτι* in A is clearly due to assimilation to Col 3.16.

5.22 *γυναῖκες τοῖς ἰδίοις ἀνδράσιν ὡς* {B}

On the one hand, several early witnesses ($\mathfrak{P}^{46}$ B Clement$^{1/2}$ Origen Greek mss$^{acc.\ to\ Jerome}$ Jerome Theodore) begin the new sentence without a main verb, thus requiring that the force of the preceding *ὑπο-τασσόμενοι* be carried over. On the other hand, the other witnesses read either *ὑποτάσσεσθε* or *ὑποτασσέσθωσαν* after either *γυναῖκες* or *ἀνδράσιν*. A majority of the Committee preferred the shorter reading, which accords with the succinct style of the author's admonitions, and explained the other readings as expansions introduced for the sake of clarity, the main verb being required especially when the words *Αἱ γυναῖκες* stood at the beginning of a scripture lesson.

5.30 *αὐτοῦ* {A}

Although it is possible that the shorter text, which is supported by early and good witnesses (including $\mathfrak{P}^{46}$ ℵ* A B 33 81 1739* cop$^{sa,\ bo}$), may have arisen by accidental omission occasioned by homoeoteleuton *(αὐτοῦ ... αὐτοῦ)*, it is more probable that the longer readings reflect various scribal expansions derived from Gn 2.23 (where, however, the sequence is "bone ... flesh"), anticipatory to the quotation of Gn 2.24 in ver. 31.

6.1 *[ἐν κυρίῳ]* {C}

The words *ἐν κυρίῳ* are absent from several early manuscripts and patristic quotations (B D* G it$^{d,\ g}$ Marcion Clement Tertullian Cyprian Ambrosiaster). It is difficult to decide whether they were added by copyists who recollected 5.22 and/or Col 3.20 ($\mathfrak{P}^{46}$ ℵ A D^c K P Ψ, apparently all minuscules, and the other versional witnesses), or were deleted from several witnesses in order to prevent the reader from supposing that the writer intended to limit or qualify the duty of obedience (rather than merely to characterize the spirit in which obedience is rendered). The longer text was preferred on the basis of (*a*) preponderance of external evidence, and (*b*) the likelihood that if the phrase had been inserted from 5.22 it would have been ὡς τῷ κυρίῳ, or if from Col 3.20 it would have stood after δίκαιον. Nevertheless, in order to reflect the weight of the witnesses that lack ἐν κυρίῳ, a majority of the Committee voted to enclose the words within square brackets.

6.12 ἡμῖν {B}

Whereas the preponderance of external evidence ($\mathfrak{P}^{46}$ B D* G Ψ 81 *al*) appears to support ὑμῖν, the natural tendency of copyists would have been to alter ἡμῖν to ὑμῖν, since the rest of the paragraph involves the second person. A majority of the Committee preferred ἡμῖν as being perhaps the more difficult reading.

6.19 τοῦ εὐαγγελίου {A}

Although it may appear noteworthy that B joins G it[g, mon] *al* in supporting the shorter reading, in the Pauline corpus codex Vaticanus not infrequently displays a strand of Western contamination, and therefore the weight of its testimony, when united with Western witnesses, should not be overevaluated. Moreover, it is significant that besides τοῦ εὐαγγελίου there is no other variation, such as τοῦ Χριστοῦ or τοῦ θεοῦ (for which there are parallels in 3.4; Col 2.2; 4.3), as one might have expected if, in fact, the shorter reading were original and τοῦ εὐαγγελίου were a scribal addition.

6.20 ἐν αὐτῷ {C}

In place of ἐν αὐτῷ (which refers, of course, to τὸ μυστήριον τοῦ εὐαγγελίου of ver. 19), a few important witnesses read αὐτό, thus pointing more directly to the antecedent.

6.24 ἀφθαρσίᾳ. {A}

The Textus Receptus adds the liturgical ἀμήν, with ℵᶜ D K L P most minuscules syrᵖ·ʰ copᵇᵒᵐˢˢ goth armᵐˢˢ ethᵖᵖ. The text is well supported by 𝔓⁴⁶ ℵ* A B F G 33 copˢᵃ·ᵇᵒ·ᶠᵃʸ arm ethʳᵒ.

6.24 *Subscription*

(*a*) The subscription in ℵ A B (D) 33 466 copᶠᵃʸ is πρὸς Ἐφεσίους. Other subscriptions include: (*b*) ἐτελέσθη ἐπιστολὴ πρὸς Ἐφεσίους F G; (*c*) πρὸς Ἐφεσίους ἐγράφη ἀπὸ Ῥώμης Bᶜ P; (*d*) as (*c*) plus διὰ Τυχικοῦ K 31 82 328 436 1908; (*e*) ἐγράφη ἡ ἐπιστολὴ αὕτη ἡ πρὸς Ἐφεσίους ἀπὸ Ῥώμης διὰ Τυχικοῦ L; (*f*) πρὸς Ἐφεσίους ἐγράφη ἀπὸ Ῥώμης διὰ Τυχικοῦ Textus Receptus.

THE LETTER OF PAUL
TO THE PHILIPPIANS

1.1 σὺν ἐπισκόποις

Several witnesses, including B³ Dᶜ K many minuscules itʳ arm Chrysostom Euthalius Cassiodorus Theophylact, read συνεπι-σκόποις ("fellow-bishops"). This reading, which arose no doubt from dogmatic or ecclesiastical interests, is to be rejected[1] because (*a*) the construction would be imperfect, the συν- having no appropriate reference, and (*b*) the letter is obviously intended for the whole community (τοῖς ἁγίοις ... τοῖς οὖσιν ἐν Φιλίπποις (cf. 3.1; 4.1, and especially 15)).

1.11 καὶ ἔπαινον θεοῦ {A}

Although it is not easy to explain how such a wide variety of readings developed, there is little doubt that the original reading is καὶ ἔπαινον θεοῦ, which is supported by good representatives of several types of text, including the Alexandrian and the Western types (א A B Dᶜ I K P Ψ 33 81 614 1739 *Byz Lect* itᵃʳ, ᵈ, ʳ vg syrᵖ, ʰ copˢᵃ, ᵇᵒ, ᶠᵃʸ arm). Instead of θεοῦ, Dᵍʳ* 1962 read Χριστοῦ (Χ͞Υ for Θ͞Υ), from which καὶ ἔπαινον αὐτοῦ (vgᵐˢ) developed as a simplification of the redundancy of the two instances of Χριστοῦ. Very remarkable is the reading καὶ ἔπαινόν μοι (Fᵍʳ G itᵍ), which has no parallel in Paul, and still more astonishing is the early conflate reading in 𝔓⁴⁶, θεοῦ καὶ ἔπαινον ἐμοί.

1.14 λόγον λαλεῖν {B}

It must be acknowledged that, on the basis of weight and variety of external evidence, the reading λόγον τοῦ θεοῦ λαλεῖν seems to be

---

[1] As already Theodore of Mopsuestia recognized (see quotation in Tischendorf's apparatus in his 8th ed.).

preferable (ℵ A B P Ψ 33 81 629 1241 it[ar] vg syr[p, h with *] cop[sa, bo, fay] goth arm eth Clement *al*). Because, however, the position and wording of the genitive modifiers *(τοῦ θεοῦ* and *κυρίου)* vary, a majority of the Committee preferred the reading λόγον λαλεῖν (𝔓[46vid] D[c] K 614 1739 it[r] syr[h] Marcion Chrysostom *al*) as that which best explains the origin of the other readings, which have the appearance of scribal expansions.

2.4 ἕκαστος

On the basis of the weight of external evidence and the fact that everything else in the context is plural, a majority of the Committee preferred ἕκαστος (𝔓[46] ℵ C D K L P most minuscules it[d] syr[p, h] cop[sa, bo] goth *al*), considering ἕκαστοι (A B F G Ψ 33 81 104 462 it[g] vg) to be the result of scribal conformation to the plurals in the context.

2.5 τοῦτο {B}

A majority of the Committee was persuaded that, if γάρ were present originally, no good reason can be found for its deletion,[1] whereas the anacoluthon involved in τοῦτο standing alone seems to cry out for a connective, whether γάρ or οὖν or καί (each of which is found in a variety of witnesses).

2.7 ἀνθρώπων

Instead of ἀνθρώπων several early witnesses read ἀνθρώπου (𝔓[46] syr[p, pal] cop[sa, bo] Marcion Origen Cyprian Hilary Ambrose). Although it is possible that the Adam-Christ typology implicit in the passage accounts for the substitution, it is more likely that the singu-

---

[1] It has sometimes been suggested that the fact that ver. 5 begins a lection would probably facilitate the dropping of γάρ. How far such influence would make itself felt on non-lectionary manuscripts is debatable; in any case, however, ℵ A B C, all of which lack γάρ, probably antedate the presumed date of the origin of the developed lectionary system.

lar number is merely a non-doctrinal conformation to the singular δούλου and the following ἄνθρωπος.

2.9 τὸ ὄνομα {B}

The Textus Receptus, following D F G Ψ and many minuscules, lacks τό, resulting in the meaning that Jesus was given an unspecified name subsequently defined as *that* name which is above every name. While the article before ὄνομα may have been inserted in order to assimilate the expression to a more usual one, it is also possible that the last syllable of ἐχαρίσατο somehow led to the omission of the article. On the whole, the Committee was impressed by the weight of the witnesses that include the word.

2.11 ἐξομολογήσηται {C}

Although the subjunctive may be a scribal assimilation to κάμψῃ, the indicative may be an assimilation to the indicative ὀμεῖται ("shall swear") in Is 45.23. Faced with such a balance of possibilities, the Committee preferred to adopt the reading supported by 𝔓⁴⁶ ℵ B *al*.

2.11 κύριος Ἰησοῦς Χριστός {A}

Several witnesses, chiefly Western, omit Χριστός, perhaps in order to conform the expression to that in ver. 10.

2.12 ὡς {A}

The omission of ὡς from B 33 42 234 618 1241 *al* is probably accidental, although copyists may have deliberately deleted it as superfluous; in any case, the presence of the word is strongly supported by 𝔓⁴⁶ and representatives of both the Alexandrian and the Western types of text (ℵ A C D G K P Ψ 81 614 1739 *Byz Lect*).

2.26 ὑμᾶς {C}

While the external evidence for and against the insertion of ἰδεῖν after ὑμᾶς is very evenly balanced, a majority of the Committee was of the opinion that scribes were more likely to add the infinitive, in accordance with the expression ἐπιποθεῖν ἰδεῖν in Ro 1.11; 1 Th 3.6; 2 Tm 1.4, than to delete it.

2.30   Χριστοῦ {B}

Although it can be argued that the original reading was τὸ ἔργον without any genitive modifier (as in C), and that the variety of readings is due to supplementation made by various copyists, the Committee preferred to regard the omission of the word from one manuscript as due to accidental oversight, and chose to print Χριστοῦ, following the testimony of 𝔓⁴⁶ B G 88 614 1739, supported also (apart from the article τοῦ) by D K 326 630 1984 *Byz Lect* it vg syrᵖ copˢᵃ goth *al.* The reading κυρίου (ℵ A P Ψ 33 81 syrʰ copᵇᵒ arm eth) may have been substituted for Χριστοῦ by copyists who recollected the expression τὸ ἔργον τοῦ κυρίου in 1 Cor 15.58 and 16.10. The reading τοῦ θεοῦ (1985 Chrysostom) seems to have originated from confusion between X̅Y̅ (or K̅Y̅) and Θ̅Y̅.

3.3   θεοῦ {B}

Although some (e. g. the translators of the New English Bible, 1961) have regarded the reading πνεύματι of 𝔓⁴⁶ as original, the Committee preferred the reading πνεύματι θεοῦ, which is amply supported by ℵ* A B C Dᶜ G K 33 81 614 1739 itᵍ syrʰᵐᵍ copˢᵃ, ᵇᵒ *al.* The singular reading of 𝔓⁴⁶ is to be explained as due to accidental oversight, and the reading θεῷ (ℵᶜ D* P Ψ 88 itᵈ, ᵃʳ vg syrᵖ, ʰ goth eth Speculum) appears to be an emendation introduced in order to provide an object for λατρεύοντες (as in Ro 1.9 and 2 Tm 1.3).

3.12   ἔλαβον ἢ ἤδη τετελείωμαι

The Textus Receptus, following several Western witnesses (D* Gᶜ itᵃʳ, ᵈ, (ᵍ) Irenaeusˡᵃᵗ Ambrosiaster) as well as 𝔓⁴⁶, reads ἔλαβον ἢ ἤδη δεδικαίωμαι ἢ ἤδη τετελείωμαι. Although it might be argued that because of homoeoarcton the clause ἢ ἤδη δεδικαίωμαι was accidentally omitted in the other witnesses, the Committee regarded it as more probable that the additional clause was a gloss "of some pious copyist who imagined that the Divine side of sanctification was left too much out of sight" (H. A. A. Kennedy, *Expositor's Greek Testament, ad loc.*). The addition of the clause destroys the balance of the four-part structure of the sentence. The reading adopted for the text is strongly supported by 𝔓[61vid] ℵ A B D[c] K P Ψ 33 81 614 1739 vg syr[p, h] cop[sa, bo] goth arm Clement *al.*

3.12 Χριστοῦ [᾿Ιησοῦ] {C}

Amid a variety of readings that involve the presence, the absence, and the sequence of name and title, on the strength of 𝔓[46, 61] ℵ A Ψ *al*, the Committee decided to adopt the reading Χριστοῦ ᾿Ιησοῦ, but to enclose ᾿Ιησοῦ within square brackets because of its absence from B D* F G 33 *al.*

3.13 οὐ {B}

The reading οὐ, which is amply supported by 𝔓[46] B D[c] G K Ψ 88 1739 most Old Latin vg syr[p, h] cop[sa] arm, appears to have been changed to οὔπω (ℵ A D[gr*] P 33 614 syr[h with *] cop[bo] goth eth Clement) by copyists who considered Paul to be too modest in his protestations.

3.15 φρονῶμεν {A}

In place of the hortatory subjunctive, which is appropriate in the context, the indicative is read by ℵ L and a few other witnesses, probably through scribal inadvertence.

3.16 τῷ αὐτῷ στοιχεῖν {A}

The earliest form of text appears to be that preserved in 𝔓[16, 46] ℵ* A B I[vid] 33 424[c] 1739 cop[sa, bo] eth[ro] *al*. Because of the conciseness of style, copyists added various explanatory words and phrases; e. g. the Textus Receptus reads τῷ αὐτῷ στοιχεῖν κανόνι, τὸ αὐτὸ φρονεῖν with ℵ^c K P Ψ 88 614 syr^{p, h} eth^{pp} *al*, where κανόνι serves to identify the otherwise enigmatic τῷ αὐτῷ, and τὸ αὐτὸ φρονεῖν is a gloss explaining τῷ αὐτῷ στοιχεῖν (compare 2.2 and Ga 6.16); other witnesses insert κανόνι before στοιχεῖν (69 1908), and still others insert τὸ αὐτὸ φρονεῖν before τῷ αὐτῷ, with or without κανόνι (D G 81 330 1241 it vg goth arm Euthalius). The variety and lack of homogeneity of the longer readings make it difficult to suppose that the shorter reading τῷ αὐτῷ στοιχεῖν arose because of homoeoteleuton.

4.3 ναί

The Textus Receptus, in company with 462, erroneously reads καί. All other witnesses, as it seems, read ναί.

4.3 σύζυγε

Some have taken this word as a proper name, Σύζυγε ("Syzygus").

4.3 τῶν λοιπῶν συνεργῶν μου {A}

Because of scribal inadvertence two early witnesses (𝔓^{16vid} ℵ*) read τῶν συνεργῶν μου καὶ τῶν λοιπῶν ("... with Clement and *my fellow workers, and the others* whose names are written ...").

4.7 νοήματα {A}

In order to diversify still further the domains covered by καρδίας and νοήματα, several Western witnesses (F G it^{a, d}) replace the latter with σώματα, while 𝔓^{16vid} adds καὶ τὰ σώματα after νοήματα.

4.8 ἔπαινος {A}

After ἔπαινος, the scribes of several Western witnesses (D* F G it^a), not wishing to leave ἔπαινος without specification, added ἐπιστήμης ("[If there is any] praise of understanding"). The word ἐπιστήμη does not otherwise occur in the New Testament.

4.13   με {A}

In order to identify who it is that strengthens Paul, the Textus Receptus, following several of the later uncials and many minuscules, adds Χριστῷ. If the word had been present in the original text, there would have been no reason to omit it.

4.16   εἰς τὴν χρείαν μοι {C}

The preposition εἰς is lacking in several witnesses, including 𝔓⁴⁶ A Dᵍʳ* 81 330 451 1241 2492 syrʰ goth eth; it seems to have been omitted either accidentally after δίς (ΔΙϹΕΙϹ) or deliberately in order to provide a direct object for the verb ἐπέμψατε. The genitive μου (D P 614 630 *al*) is a scribal replacement for the less usual and far better supported dative μοι. The readings of the Coptic and of itᵍ appear to be overtranslations of the Greek. The reading *in unum mihi* (vgᵐˢ) may be a confused reminiscence of Lk 10.42.

4.19   πληρώσει {B}

Instead of the future indicative ("My God will supply…"), strongly supported by 𝔓⁴⁶ A B D² K L P and many minuscules, the scribes of several Western and other witnesses preferred the aorist optative ("May my God supply…").

4.23   τοῦ πνεύματος

Although some have supposed that the reading τοῦ πνεύματος was introduced by copyists from Ga 6.18 or Phm 25, the Committee was impressed by its distinctly superior attestation (𝔓⁴⁶ ℵ* A B D F G P 6 88 104 241 322 330 424ᶜ 436 442 463 1319 1898 2005 2127 itᵈ, ᵍ, ʳ vg copˢᵃ, ᵇᵒ arm eth), and explained the variant reading πάντων (ℵᶜ K L Ψ most minuscules syrᵖ, ʰ and Textus Receptus) as a scribal substitution of a more familiar termination for a benediction (cf. 1 Cor 16.24; 2 Cor 13.13; 2 Th 3.18; Tt 3.15).

4.23 ὑμῶν. {A}

The ἀμήν (𝔓⁴⁶ ℵ A D K L P almost all minuscules it^(d, r, ar) vg syr^(p, h) cop^(bo) arm eth) appears to have been added by copyists in accord with liturgical practice; if it had been present originally, it would be difficult to account for its omission in B F G 6 1739*^(vid) 1836 1908 it^g syr^(pal) cop^(sa) *al.*

4.23 *Subscription*

(*a*) The subscription in ℵ A B 33 466 is πρὸς Φιλιππησίους. Other subscriptions include: (*b*) πρὸς Φιλιππησίους ἐπληρώθη D; (*c*) ἐτελέσθη πρὸς Φιλιππησίους F G; (*d*) πρὸς Φιλιππησίους ἐγράφη ἀπὸ Ῥώμης δι' Ἐπαφροδίτου K 1908 *al,* followed by the Textus Receptus; (*e*) as (*d*) but prefixing τοῦ ἁγίου ἀποστόλου Παύλου ἐπιστολή L; (*f*) as (*c*) and concluding ἐγράφη ἀπὸ Ῥώμης δι' Τιμοθέου καὶ Ἐπαφροδίτου (cop^(bo)) eth^(pp).

THE LETTER OF PAUL
TO THE COLOSSIANS

1.2 ἡμῶν {A}

After ἡμῶν the Textus Receptus adds καὶ κυρίου Ἰησοῦ Χριστοῦ, with ℵ A C G I 88 614 *Byz Lect al*; the same addition is found also in other witnesses with a second ἡμῶν added to κυρίου, standing before or after Ἰησοῦ Χριστοῦ. The words, which are absent from a variety of witnesses, some of them early (B D K Ψ 33 81 1739 it^ar, d, mon vg syr^p, h cop^sa arm eth^ro), have no doubt been added by copyists who assimilated the text to Pauline usage; certainly no reason for deliberate omission suggests itself.

1.3 θεῷ πατρί {C}

The reading adopted for the text, although it is rather narrowly supported (B C* 1739 Augustine), appears to account best for the origin of the other readings. In order to avoid the very unusual collocation of words, some copyists inserted τῷ (D* G 2005 Chrysostom) and others inserted καί (ℵ A C² D^c I K P Ψ 33 81 614 *Byz Lect*). (See also the comments on ver. 12 and 3.17.)

1.6 ἐστίν

In order to relieve a certain awkwardness of expression, the Textus Receptus reads καὶ ἐστίν, with D^b, c F G K L Ψ most minuscules it^d, g vg syr^p, h *al*. The reading adopted for the text is decisively supported by early and diversified witnesses (𝔓⁴⁶ ℵ A B C D* P 33 88 104 326 330 436 464 489 1837 1944 cop^sa, bo arm eth *al*).

1.7 ὑμῶν {B}

Although on the basis of superior Greek evidence (𝔓⁴⁶ and early Alexandrian and Western authorities) ἡμῶν might seem to be preferable, a majority of the Committee, impressed by the widespread currency of ὑμῶν in versional and patristic witnesses, considered it probable that copyists introduced the first person pronoun under the influence of the preceding ἡμῶν and the following ἡμῖν.

1.12   τῷ πατρί {B}

This verse presents a curious nest of variant readings (see also the following comments). The reading that best explains the origin of the others is τῷ πατρί, supported by a diversified group of witnesses (𝔓⁶¹ A C* D K P Ψ 33 81* 1739* it^{b, d, mon} vg syr^h cop^{sa, bo} goth arm eth). The strangeness of designating God simply as ὁ πατήρ when Christ has not been named in the immediate context doubtless prompted copyists to add either τοῦ Χριστοῦ (330 451 2492) or (τῷ) θεῷ, either in apposition (ℵ it^g syr^p Speculum) or connected with καί (C³ 81^c 88 104 614 1739^{mg} 2495 al). The agreement of 𝔓⁴⁶ and B in prefixing ἅμα is a noteworthy coincidence in error.

1.12   ἱκανώσαντι {B}

Instead of ἱκανώσαντι, which is strongly supported by 𝔓⁴⁶ ℵ A C D^c K L P most minuscules vg syr^{p, h} cop^{bo} al, several witnesses, chiefly Western (D* F G 33 436 1175 it^{d, g} cop^{sa} goth arm eth), substitute καλέσαντι. The latter reading arose either accidentally in transcription (confusion between ΤΩΙΚΑΝΩϹΑΝΤΙ and ΤΩΚΑΛΕϹΑΝΤΙ would be easy), or deliberately as a substitution of a familiar for an unusual expression (ἱκανόω occurs elsewhere in the New Testament only in 2 Cor 3.6). The reading of B is an early conflation of both variants (καλέσαντι καὶ ἱκανώσαντι).

1.12   ὑμᾶς {B}

A majority of the Committee preferred ὑμᾶς (ℵ B 1739 syr^{hmg} cop^{sa} goth arm eth), regarding ἡμᾶς (A C D G K P Ψ 33 614 Byz Lect it vg syr^{p, h} cop^{bo} al) as an assimilation to ver. 13.

1.14 *ἀπολύτρωσιν* {A}

The Textus Receptus, following several secondary witnesses, interpolates from Eph 1.7 the words *διὰ τοῦ αἵματος αὐτοῦ*. If the phrase had been present originally, there would have been no reason for scribes to omit it.

1.20 *αὑτόν*

Some editors (e. g. J. J. Griesbach and J. M. A. Scholz) and grammarians (e. g. C. F. D. Moule[1]) prefer to read *αὑτόν*.

1.20 *[δι' αὐτοῦ]* (2) {C}

According to the view of a majority of the Committee, the phrase *δι' αὐτοῦ*, which is supported by 𝔓⁴⁶ ℵ A C Dᶜ 614 syrᵖ· ʰ copᵇᵒ goth *al,* was omitted from B D* G 81 1739 it vg copˢᵃ arm eth, either accidentally (because of homoeoteleuton) or deliberately (because it is superfluous and obscure). According to the view of the minority, the expression is so disturbing to the sense that it is difficult to attribute it to the author. In order to represent the two points of view it was decided to retain the words in the text, enclosed within square brackets.

1.22 *ἀποκατήλλαξεν* {C}

The conflicting textual phenomena of this verse are difficult to resolve. On the one hand, the reading *ἀποκατήλλαξεν* is well supported (ℵ A C Dᶜ K nearly all minuscules itᵃʳ· ᶠ· ᵐᵒⁿ vg syrᵖ· ʰ copˢᵃ· ᵇᵒ *al*) and provides acceptable sense. On the other hand, however, if this were the original reading, it is exceedingly difficult to explain why

---

[1] "In Col. i.20 *δι' αὐτοῦ* ... *αὑτόν* it is surprising that there appears to be no variant *ἑαυτόν* and that editors [Moule means modern editors] do not print *αὑτόν*, which seems to be required by the sense in order to distinguish *Christ*, referred to in *δι' αὐτοῦ*, from *God*, to whom (probably) the reconciliation is made" (*An Idiom Book of New Testament Greek,* 2nd ed. [Cambridge, 1959], p. 119). In his modern Greek translation of the New Testament P. N. Trempela [Trebela] (2nd ed., Athens, 1955) prints *δι' αὐτοῦ* ... *πρὸς τὸν ἑαυτόν*.

the other readings should have arisen. Faced with this dilemma, and considering a passive verb to be totally unsuitable in the context, a majority of the Committee preferred to follow the preponderance of external testimony and therefore adopted ἀποκατήλλαξεν.

[Despite the harsh anacoluthon that a passive verb creates after ὑμᾶς in ver. 21, only ἀποκατηλλάγητε, which is attested by diversified and early witnesses (B Hilary Ephraem, as well as, in effect, 𝔓⁴⁶ and 33, both of which have scribal misspellings that presuppose -ηλλάγητε), can account for the rise of the other readings as more or less successful attempts to mend the syntax of the sentence. B.M.M.]

2.2 τοῦ θεοῦ, Χριστοῦ {B}

Among what at first sight seems to be a bewildering variety of variant readings, the one adopted for the text is plainly to be preferred (a) because of strong external testimony (𝔓⁴⁶ B Hilary Pelagius Ps-Jerome) and (b) because it alone provides an adequate explanation of the other readings as various scribal attempts to ameliorate the syntactical ambiguity of τοῦ θεοῦ, Χριστοῦ.[1]

2.7 τῇ πίστει {A}

The reading τῇ πίστει, strongly supported by B D* H 33 81 al, best accounts for the rise of the other readings.

2.7 ἐν εὐχαριστίᾳ {B}

Although the reading ἐν αὐτῇ ἐν εὐχαριστίᾳ is rather strongly supported (B D² H K 614 Byz Lect it⁽ᵃʳ⁾, ᵐᵒⁿ, ⁽ᵒ⁾ syrᵖ, ʰ copˢᵃᵐˢ, ᵇᵒ arm al), the Committee regarded it as a copyist's assimilation to 4.2, and explained the reading ἐν αὐτῷ ἐν εὐχαριστίᾳ (ℵᵇ D* itᵈ syrʰᵐᵍ al) as a subsequent modification made under the influence of the preceding phrase ἐν αὐτῷ. The reading ἐν αὐτῇ (P Ψ 048?) no doubt arose through transcriptional oversight by which ἐν εὐχαριστίᾳ was omit-

---

[1] For a fuller discussion see Metzger, *The Text of the New Testament*, pp. 236–38.

ted. The original reading appears to be ἐν εὐχαριστίᾳ, which is adequately supported by ℵ* A C I^vid 33 81 1739 vg cop^sa eth *al.*

2.13 ὑμᾶς (2) {B}

A majority of the Committee preferred ὑμᾶς, which is adequately supported by ℵ* A C K 81 614 1739 syr^p, h cop^sa, bo eth *al,* and explained (*a*) its omission from ℵ^c D G P Ψ *al* on the ground of its seeming to be superfluous, and (*b*) its replacement with ἡμᾶς in 𝔓^46 B 33 88 it^mon, o syr^pal arm *al* as due to a desire to conform the person to the following ἡμῖν.

2.13 ἡμῖν {A}

In later Greek the vowels η and υ came to be pronounced alike. Here the weight of the evidence strongly supports ἡμῖν.

2.18 ἅ {B}

The reading ἅ is strongly supported by 𝔓^46 and good representatives of the Alexandrian and the Western types of the text (ℵ* A B D* I 33 1739 it^d cop^sa, bo Speculum *al*). Apparently the negative (either οὐκ in F G or μή in ℵ^c C D^c K P Ψ 614 it^ar, f, g, mon, o vg syr^p, h goth arm *al*) was added by copyists who either misunderstood the sense of ἐμβατεύων or wished to enhance the polemical nuance that is carried on by the following εἰκῇ φυσιούμενος. The singular reading μή (81) is an accidental scribal error.

2.23 ταπεινοφροσύνῃ [καί] {C}

A minority of the Committee preferred the reading without καί on the basis of strong and early external evidence, and the likelihood that copyists would insert καί on the assumption that ἀφειδίᾳ was the third in a series of datives after ἐν, rather than an instrumental dative qualifying the previous prepositional phrase. On the other hand, the majority of the Committee regarded the omission as accidental and preferred the reading with καί, which is widely supported by ℵ A C

D^gr H K P Ψ 33 81 614 vg syr^p cop^sa arm *al.* As a compromise it was decided to adopt καί but to enclose it within square brackets. The reading ταπεινοφροσύνη τοῦ νοὸς καί (G it^b, mon, o syr^h *al*) is an expansion derived probably from ver. 18.

3.4 ὑμῶν {B}

Although it is possible that ἡμῶν, which is supported by B D^c H K 326 614 1241 syr^p, h cop^sa *al,* was altered by copyists to ὑμῶν in order to agree with the second person pronouns before and after, the Committee was impressed by the considerably stronger manuscript evidence that supports ὑμῶν, including 𝔓^46 and good representatives of both the Alexandrian and the Western text-types (ℵ C D* F G P Ψ 33 81 88 104 1739 it vg cop^bo goth arm eth *al*).

3.6 [ἐπὶ τοὺς υἱοὺς τῆς ἀπειθείας] {C}

It is exceedingly difficult to decide whether the words ἐπὶ … ἀπειθείας were added in most witnesses by copyists who recollected Eph 5.6 (where no manuscript omits the words), or whether they are absent from 𝔓^46 B cop^sa eth^ro and several Fathers (Clement Cyprian Macrobius Ambrosiaster Ephraem Jerome) because of an accident in transmission. In view of (*a*) the very widespread testimony supporting the longer reading (ℵ A C D^vid F G H K L P almost all minuscules it vg syr^p, h cop^bo goth arm eth^pp Clement Chrysostom *al*) and (*b*) the inconcinnity produced by the shorter reading with the following ἐν οἷς, as well as (*c*) the impression that καὶ ὑμεῖς in ver. 7 assumes a previous mention of unbelieving Gentiles, a majority of the Committee decided to retain the words in the text but to enclose them within square brackets in order to indicate a measure of doubt as to their genuineness in Colossians.

3.13 κύριος {C}

On the strength of the weight of 𝔓^46 joined by the best witnesses of both the Alexandrian and the Western texts (A B D* G it^d, g vg Speculum *al*) the Committee preferred κύριος, and explained Χριστός (ℵ^c

C D^c K P Ψ 614 1739 *Byz Lect* it^{b, d, f, g, o} syr^{p, h} cop^{sa, bo} goth eth Clement *al*) as an interpretation by copyists of the more indefinite κύριος, and the other two variant readings (θεός ℵ* and θεὸς ἐν Χριστῷ 33 arm Augustine[1/2]) as due to scribal assimilation (partial or complete) to Eph 4.32.

3.16 Χριστοῦ {A}

Instead of the unusual expression "the word of Christ," which occurs nowhere else in the New Testament, several witnesses substitute the more customary "the word of God" (A C* 33 451 1241 *al*) or "the word of the Lord" (ℵ* I 2127 cop^{bo} Clement). Χριστοῦ is strongly supported by 𝔓[46] ℵ^c B C² D G K P Ψ 81 614 1739 *Byz Lect* it vg syr^{(p), h} cop^{sa, boms} goth arm *al*.

3.16 θεῷ {A}

In place of θεῷ, which is strongly supported by early and diversified testimony (𝔓[46vid] ℵ A B C* D* G Ψ^c 33 81 1739 it^{b, d, f, g} vg syr^{p, h} cop^{sa, bo} arm Clement Speculum *al*), the Textus Receptus, influenced by the parallel in Eph 5.19 (where there is no variation), substitutes κυρίῳ, with C² D^c K Ψ* 614 *Byz Lect* it^{ar} goth *al*.

3.17 θεῷ πατρί {B}

The very unusual collocation τῷ θεῷ πατρί, which is widely supported by 𝔓[46vid] ℵ A B C 81 442 1739 1985 it^{ar, b, mon} syr^p cop^{sa, bo} goth eth Ambrose Speculum, was emended by copyists who inserted καί, thus imitating Eph 5.20 and similar passages. (See also the comments on 1.3 and 12.)

3.21 ἐρεθίζετε {B}

In place of ἐρεθίζετε, supported by 𝔓[46vid] ℵ B Ψ 1739* *al*, a wide spectrum of other witnesses has adopted παροργίζετε from the parallel passage in Eph 6.4 (where the verb is without variant reading).

4.3 Χριστοῦ {A}

Instead of Χριστοῦ, a few witnesses (B* L 1319 *al*), probably under the influence of readings involving a similar expression in many witnesses at 2.2, read θεοῦ.

4.8 γνῶτε τὰ περὶ ἡμῶν {B}

The reading ἵνα γνῶτε τὰ περὶ ἡμῶν ("that you may know how we are"), which is adequately supported by good representatives of the Alexandrian, Western, and Eastern types of text (A B D* G P 33 81 it^(ar, b, d, g, mon) syr^(pal) cop^(sa) arm eth Ephraem *al*), best explains the origin of the other readings. Through inadvertence copyists produced nonsense either by substituting ὑμῶν for ἡμῶν ("that you may know how you are" ℵ* 1241) or by accidentally dropping -τε before τά ("that he may know how we are" 330 451 *l*^(598)). The reading γνῷ τὰ περὶ ὑμῶν (𝔓^(46) ℵ^c C D^c K Ψ 614 1739 *Byz Lect* vg syr^(p, h) cop^(bo) goth *al*) was produced when copyists tried to make sense of ἵνα γνῶτε τὰ περὶ ὑμῶν (*a*) by taking it as ἵνα γνῷ τε τὰ περὶ ὑμῶν and then (*b*) omitting τε as awkward and superfluous. The reading adopted for the text is congruent with the writer's declared purpose of Tychicus's visit (verses 7 and 9).

4.12 Χριστοῦ [Ἰησοῦ] {C}

Ordinarily one might regard this to be a growing text, but the Committee was not impressed by the weight of the witnesses that support Χριστοῦ standing alone. The least unsatisfactory resolution, therefore, seemed to call for Ἰησοῦ to be retained, yet enclosed within square brackets.

4.13 πολὺν πόνον

Instead of πόνον, which is a rare word in the New Testament (it occurs only here and in Re 16.10, 11; 21.4), copyists have introduced various substitutions: πολὺν κόπον D* F G; πολὺν ζῆλον D^(b, c) 33 1906 1908; ζῆλον πολύν K L Ψ most minuscules syr^(p, h), followed by the Textus Receptus; πολὺν πόθον 442 1912; πόθον πολύν 10 104 263; πολὺν ἀγῶνα 6 424ᶜ 1739. The reading adopted for the text is strongly supported by ℵ A B C P 88 296 436 467 1837 1838 Euthalius.

4.15   Νύμφαν καὶ τὴν κατ᾽ οἶκον αὐτῆς {C}

Νυμφαν can be accented Νύμφαν, from the feminine nominative Νύμφα ("Nympha"), or Νυμφᾶν, from the masculine nominative Νυμφᾶς ("Nymphas"). The uncertainty of the gender of the name led to variation in the following possessive pronoun between αὐτῆς and αὐτοῦ. On the basis chiefly of the weight of B 6 424ᶜ 1739 1877 1881 syrʰ· ᵖᵃˡᵐˢ copˢᵃ Origen, the Committee preferred Νύμφαν ... αὐτῆς. The reading with αὐτῶν arose when copyists included ἀδελφούς in the reference.

4.18   ὑμῶν. {A}

The Textus Receptus adds the liturgical ἀμήν, with ℵᶜ D K P Ψ 88 614 1739 Byz Lect itᵃʳ· ᵇ· ᵈ· ᵐᵒⁿ vg syrᵖ· ʰ· ᵖᵃˡᵐˢ copᵇᵒᵐˢˢ goth al. If the word were present originally, however, it is impossible to account for its deletion from such early and varied witnesses as ℵ* A B C G 048 33 81 1881 itᵍ syrᵖᵃˡᵐˢ copˢᵃ· ᵇᵒᵐˢˢ arm ethʳᵒ al.

4.18   *Subscription*

(*a*) In ℵ B* C 33 339 466 1908 the subscription is πρὸς Κολασ-σαεῖς [note the spelling -λα-; Bᶜ D F G L P and most witnesses spell the word with -λο-]. Other subscriptions include: (*b*) πρὸς Κολ. ἐγράφη ἀπὸ Ῥώμης (A om. ἐγρ.) Bᶜ P; (*c*) ἐτελέσθη (F -στη) πρὸς Κολοσσαεῖς F G; (*d*) as (*b*) plus διὰ Τυχικοῦ καὶ Ὀνησίμου K 82 101 122 431 460 1907 1924, followed by the Textus Receptus; (*e*) τοῦ ἁγίου Παύλου ἐπιστολὴ πρὸς Κολοσσαεῖς ἀπὸ Ῥώμης διὰ Τυχικοῦ καὶ Ὀνησίμου L.

THE FIRST LETTER OF PAUL
TO THE THESSALONIANS

1.1 εἰρήνη {A}

Representatives of the Alexandrian and the Western types of text unite in supporting the shorter reading (B G Ψ 1739 it^(ar, b, f, g, o, r) vg syr^(p, palms) cop^(sa, fay)). Other witnesses expand the salutation by adding phrases familiar from the salutations in other Pauline letters. If any one of these expansions had been original, there is no reason why it would have been deleted.

1.5 ἡμῶν {A}

The expression "our gospel," which is solidly based in a diversity of witnesses of every type of textual family, seems to have offended some scribes; ℵ^c C preferred "the gospel of God," and ℵ* preferred "the gospel of our God."

1.7 τύπον

It is more likely that copyists would have altered the singular number τύπον (B D* 6 33 81 104 181 424^c 442 1311 1739 1908 2005 it^(d, r) vg syr^(p, pal) cop^(sa, bo, fay) arm eth arab) to the plural τύπους (ℵ A C F^gr G K L P Ψ most minuscules it^g syr^h *al*) in order to agree with ὑμᾶς than vice versa. The reading τύπος in D^c is a scribal error.

2.7 νήπιοι {B}

From a transcriptional point of view it is difficult to decide whether νήπιοι arose by dittography after the preceding -ν, or whether ἤπιοι arose by haplography. Likewise, considerations of what the author was more likely to have written are equally inconclusive. Thus, though Paul uses νήπιος almost a dozen times elsewhere whereas ἤπιος is found in the Greek Bible only in 2 Tm 2.24, yet the apostle always applies νήπιοι to his converts and nowhere else refers to himself as a νήπιος. Again, though the shift of metaphor from that of babe to that of mother-nurse is admittedly a violent one, it is characteristically Pauline and no more startling than the sudden shift of metaphor in Ga 4.19. In the absence of any strong argument based on internal probabilities, a majority of the Committee preferred to follow what is admittedly the stronger external attestation and to adopt νήπιοι.[1]

[Despite the weight of external evidence, only ἤπιοι seems to suit the context, where the apostle's gentleness makes an appropriate sequence with the arrogance disclaimed in ver. 6. The choice of reading has a bearing on the punctuation; if ἤπιοι is adopted, a full stop should follow ἀπόστολοι, a comma should follow ὑμῶν, and a colon should follow τέκνα. B.M.M. and A.W.]

2.12 καλοῦντος {B}

Apparently under the influence of Ga 1.6 the Textus Receptus adopted the aorist tense καλέσαντος, with א A 104 326 606 1611 1831 1906 1912 2005 and a variety of versions (the weight of whose testimony, however, is diminished by idiomatic considerations). The present tense καλοῦντος, which is appropriate in the context, is strongly supported by B D F G H K L P and most minuscules.

2.15 προφήτας {A}

The Textus Receptus reads ἰδίους προφήτας, following a variety of secondary witnesses (D^c K Ψ most minuscules syr^{p, h} goth al). Whether these somehow derived the reading from Marcion, who inserted the word in order to limit the reference to *Jewish* prophets, or whether they were influenced by ἰδίων in the preceding verse, is immaterial for the present purpose. The shorter reading is decisively supported by the best representatives of several text-types (א A B D* G I P 33 81 1739 it vg cop^{sa, bo, fay} arm eth).

---

[1] For a fuller discussion of the variants, see Metzger, *The Text of the New Testament,* pp. 230–33.

2.16 ὀργή {A}

Several witnesses, chiefly of the Western type of text (D F G *al*), add the clarification that "the wrath" is none other than "the wrath of God." Other witnesses move ὀργή before ἐπ' αὐτούς, preferring to have the subject nearer the verb.

3.2 καὶ συνεργὸν τοῦ θεοῦ ἐν τῷ εὐαγγελίῳ τοῦ Χριστοῦ {B}

Amid the variety of readings, the chief textual questions are whether συνεργόν or διάκονον should be read, and whether τοῦ θεοῦ should be retained or omitted. Although on the basis of external evidence it may appear that the reading καὶ διάκονον τοῦ θεοῦ ... (ℵ A P Ψ 81 629* 1739 itᵃʳ vg syrʰ copˢᵃ, ᵇᵒ, ᶠᵃʸ goth eth) should be adopted, the reading that best accounts for the origin of the others is καὶ συνεργὸν τοῦ θεοῦ ... (D* 33 itᵈ, ⁸⁶* Ambrosiaster Pelagius Ps-Jerome). In order to remove the objectionable character that the bold designation συνεργὸς τοῦ θεοῦ appeared to have, some copyists deleted the words τοῦ θεοῦ (B 1962) or transferred them to qualify τοῦ εὐαγγελίου (arm), while others substituted διάκονον for συνεργόν (for witnesses see preceding sentence). Still later are the conflate readings that embody both διάκονον and συνεργόν (G itᵍ), the latter sometimes qualified by ἡμῶν rather than by τοῦ θεοῦ (Dᶜ K 88 104 614 *Byz Lect* syrᵖ, ʰ ʷⁱᵗʰ * Textus Receptus).[1]

3.13 αὐτοῦ[, ἀμήν]. {C}

Was ἀμήν dropped by copyists who thought it inappropriate in the body of a Pauline epistle (just as ἀμήν was omitted by a scattering of witnesses at the close of Ro 15.33 and 16.24), or was it added as liturgically appropriate in the context, especially when ver. 13 came to be the conclusion of an ecclesiastical lection? Since it is very difficult to reach a confident decision, and since the external attestation is rather evenly balanced, a majority of the Committee decided to include ἀμήν, but to enclose it within square brackets.

---

[1] For a fuller discussion, see Metzger, *The Text of the New Testament*, pp. 240–42.

4.1 καθὼς καὶ περιπατεῖτε {A}

The parenthetical clause καθὼς καὶ περιπατεῖτε is lacking in Dᶜ K L Ψ 177 206 257 623 917 1175 1518 1739 syrᵖ (and the Textus Receptus), having been dropped either accidentally (through confusion with the earlier καθώς clause) or deliberately (as seemingly superfluous). External testimony supporting the clause is strong (ℵ A B D* F G 33 104 181 218 330 1311 1611 1836 1906 1912 2005 2127 itᵈ· ᵍ vg syrʰ copˢᵃ· ᵇᵒ goth arm eth); internal considerations likewise favor the presence of the clause, for ἵνα περισσεύητε presupposes the earlier mention of the Thessalonians having begun the Christian life, but such a beginning is not implied in the preceding text without καθὼς καὶ περιπατεῖτε.

4.9 ἔχετε

Although the construction is harsh (literally, "You have no need to write to you") the reading ἔχετε is not only well supported (ℵ* A Dᶜ K L most minuscules syrᵖ copᵇᵒ eth Origen John-Damascus Theodoret Euthalius) but accounts for the rise of the other readings as scribal alleviations of the irregularity: ἔχομεν (ℵᶜ D* F G Ψ 88 104 142 216 424ᶜ 927 1311 1611 1739 2005 itᵈ· ᵍ vg syrʰ goth); εἴχομεν (B vgᵐˢˢ); and ἔχετε γράφεσθαι (H 81 257 424* 1319 1518 1837 2127).

4.11 [ἰδίαις] {C}

It is difficult to decide whether ἰδίαις is a gloss, added for the sake of symmetry with τὰ ἴδια earlier in the sentence, or whether it accidentally fell out in transcription (ΤΑΙΣΙΔΙΑΙΣ). In view of the balance of these considerations, the Committee decided to retain the word in the text but to enclose it within square brackets.

4.13 κοιμωμένων

The text is somewhat doubtful, external testimony being divided between κοιμωμένων, which is supported by Alexandrian witnesses

(ℵ A B 33 326), and κεκοιμημένων, supported by Western and Byzantine witnesses (D F G K L Ψ 88 104 257 623 915 1245 1518 2005 Hippolytus Cyril-Jerusalem) and adopted by the Textus Receptus. The Committee preferred the former reading, because it is found in the older manuscripts, and because it is more likely to have been altered into κεκοιμημένων than conversely, the latter being the usual expression (cf. Mt 27.52; 1 Cor 15.20).

4.17 οἱ περιλειπόμενοι {A}

By some accidental oversight, several Western witnesses (F G it[ar, b, f, g, o] *al*) omit οἱ περιλειπόμενοι.

5.4 κλέπτης {A}

The reading κλέπτας, supported by three Alexandrian witnesses (A B cop[bo]), appears to have arisen from scribal conformation to the preceding ὑμᾶς, resulting in near nonsense (cf. the similar image in ver. 2).

5.25 [καί] {C}

On the one hand, it can be argued that καί was added by copyists who recalled Col 4.3. On the other hand, however, if the word were present originally it could have fallen out when its reference to ver. 17 was overlooked. In view of the balance of probabilities it was thought best to include καί in the text, but to enclose it within square brackets.

5.27 ἀδελφοῖς {A}

Instead of τοῖς ἀδελφοῖς a variety of witnesses, followed by the Textus Receptus, read τοῖς ἁγίοις ἀδελφοῖς (ℵ[c] A K P Ψ 33 81 614 1739 *Byz Lect* it[61] vg syr[p, h, pal] cop[bo] goth arm eth[pp] *al*). While it is possible to account for the reading τοῖς ἀδελφοῖς on the supposition that ἁγίοις fell out accidentally because of homoeoteleuton, the Committee regarded the shorter reading as original because (*a*) the expression οἱ ἅγιοι ἀδελφοί occurs nowhere else in Paul; (b) the probability of the accidental omission of ἁγίοις is not so great as the probability of its being added from ἁγίῳ in the previous verse; and (c) the weight of the external testimony supporting the shorter reading (ℵ* B D F G 431 436 1311 1835 1907 2004 itd. g. mon copsa ethro Ambrosiaster Ephraem Pelagius Cassiodorus) is slightly superior to that which supports the longer text. The reading τοῖς ἁγίοις (1984 1985 Theophylact) is secondary, having arisen from an oversight in transcription.

5.28 ὑμῶν. {A}

Through the influence of liturgical usage, most witnesses add ἀμήν (ℵ A Dc K L P 614 1739 *Byz Lect* it61. 86 vg syrp. h copbo goth eth). It is absent from good representatives of both the Alexandrian and the Western types of text (B D* F G 33 424c 1881 itd. g syrpal copsa arm Ambrosiaster).

5.28 *Subscription*

(a) The subscription in ℵ B* 33 is πρὸς Θεσσαλονίκεις $\bar{α}$ (33 omits $\bar{α}$). Other subscriptions include: (b) πρὸς Θεσσαλονίκεις $\bar{α}$ ἐπληρώθη D; (c) ἐτελέσθη πρὸς Θεσσαλονίκεις $\bar{α}$ (F) G; (d) πρὸς Θεσσαλονίκεις $\bar{α}$ (or πρώτη) ἐγράφη ἀπὸ Ἀθηνῶν A Bc K 1908 and many other minuscules, followed by the Textus Receptus (reading πρώτη); (e) τοῦ ἁγίου ἀποστόλου Παύλου πρὸς Θεσσαλονίκεις ἐπιστολὴ $\bar{α}$ ἐγράφη ἀπὸ Ἀθηνῶν L; (f) πρὸς Θεσσαλονίκεις $\bar{α}$· ἐγράφη ἀπὸ Κορίνθου ὑπὸ Παύλου καὶ Σιλουανοῦ καὶ Τιμοθέου copbo eth Euthaliusmss.

THE SECOND LETTER OF PAUL
TO THE THESSALONIANS

1.2 πατρὸς [ἡμῶν] καὶ κυρίου {C}

The clause with ἀπό occurs in all the Pauline letters except
1 Thessalonians, and except in Ga 1.3, where the evidence is
divided, ἡμῶν always stands after πατρός. In the present verse it is
difficult to decide whether the pronoun was present originally but was
later omitted by copyists for stylistic reasons (cf. ver. 1 πατρὶ ἡμῶν),
or whether the word, originally absent, was later added by copyists in
imitation of the stereotyped formula. In order to represent the balance
of probabilities, a majority of the Committee decided to include the
word in the text, but to enclose it within square brackets. The sub-
singular readings of syr[p, pal] and cop[sa, bo] are doubtless intra-versional
variants.

2.3 ἀνομίας {B}

Did the apostle write "man of sin," as most witnesses read, or
"man of lawlessness," as ℵ B 81 88[mg] 1739 cop[sa, bo] arm Marcion
Tertullian and others attest? Despite the broader external testimony
supporting ἁμαρτίας (witnesses from each of three text-types: A; D
G it vg; K L P most minuscules), on the whole it appears that the
early Alexandrian witnesses preserve the original reading, ἀνομίας,
a word rarely used by Paul, which was altered by copyists to the
much more frequently used word, ἁμαρτίας. Furthermore, γάρ ...
ἀνομίας in ver. 7 seems to presuppose ἀνομίας here.

2.4 καθίσαι {A}

The interpretative gloss ὡς θεόν is inserted before καθίσαι by a
great number of the later witnesses (D[c] G[c] K L most minuscules, followed by the Textus Receptus), while a few other witnesses (1984
1985 Theophylact) add it after καθίσαι. The shorter text is strongly

supported by early and diversified witnesses (ℵ A B D* Ψ 33 330 1739 it vg syr^h cop^{sa, bo} goth arm eth Marcion *al*).

2.8 *['Ιησοῦς]* {C}

The Textus Receptus, with B D^c K 88 614 1739 1881 *Byz Lect* cop^{boms} *al,* omits *'Ιησοῦς.* On the other hand, the word is present in a wide variety of Greek and versional witnesses (ℵ A D* G P Ψ 33 1241 it vg syr^{p, h} cop^{sa, bo} arm eth *al*). It is difficult to decide whether the word is an addition introduced by pious scribes (vg^{mss} read *'Ιησοῦς Χριστός*), or was omitted either accidentally (ΟΚΣΙΣ) or intentionally (to bring the quotation more nearly into accord with Is 11.4). In order to represent the balance of probabilities the Committee decided to retain the word, but to enclose it within square brackets.

2.13 *ἀπαρχήν* {B}

Although the reading *ἀπ' ἀρχῆς* is strongly supported (ℵ D K L Ψ most minuscules it^{d, g, ar, mon} syr^p cop^{sa} arm eth *al*), the Committee preferred *ἀπαρχήν* (B F G^{gr} P 33 81 1739 vg syr^h cop^{bo} *al*) because (*a*) *ἀπ' ἀρχῆς* occurs nowhere else in the Pauline corpus (*πρὸ τῶν αἰώνων* is used in 1 Cor 2.7 and *ἀπὸ τῶν αἰώνων* in Col 1.26 to express the idea "from eternity"); (*b*) except for Php 4.15, *ἀρχή* in Paul always means "power"; (*c*) *ἀπαρχή* occurs six other places in Paul (though in five of them it is with a qualifying genitive); and (*d*) elsewhere copyists took offense at *ἀπαρχήν* and altered it to *ἀπ' ἀρχῆς* (Re 14.4 ℵ 336 1918, and Ro 16.5 D*) even though the latter expression is inappropriate in these passages. One manuscript (88) emphasizes the middle voice of *εἵλατο* by reading *ἑαυτῷ ἀπ' ἀρχῆς.*

2.16 *[ὁ] θεὸς ὁ πατήρ*

Struck by the unusual expression *ὁ θεὸς ὁ πατὴρ ἡμῶν,* copyists have altered *ὁ πατήρ* (ℵ* (om. ὁ ℵ^c) B D^{gr*} F G 33 431 442 1311

2143 it^g vg^{ms} syr^p cop^{bo} arm eth) to the more familiar Pauline expression καὶ πατήρ (A D^c K L P Ψ 6 81 104 326 917 it^d vg syr^h goth). Since the article before θεός is lacking in B D* K L 33 *al,* a majority of the Committee thought it wise to enclose it within square brackets, thus indicating doubt as to its right to be included in the text.

3.6   παρελάβοσαν {B}

The reading that seems best to explain the origin of the others is παρελάβοσαν (ℵ* A (D* ἐλάβοσαν) 33 88 1827 1845 2005 Basil), whose dialectic termination[1] was corrected later to παρέλαβον (ℵ^c D^c K L P 81 614 1739 *Byz Lect al*). Since the third person is surprising in the context that involves such frequent reference to the second person plural, the introduction of the predominantly Western reading, παρελάβετε (B F^{gr} G 104 327 436 442 1611 2005 2495 syr^h cop$^{sa, (bo)}$ goth arm *al*), is perhaps to be expected. The Textus Receptus παρέλαβε is very weakly attested (5 76 218 234 1962 Basil Ps-Oecumenius) and arose either contextually (appropriate to the subject implied in ἀπὸ παντὸς ἀδελφοῦ) or graphically (from παρελάβε-τε).

3.8   νυκτὸς καὶ ἡμέρας

A majority of the Committee preferred the reading with the genitives (supported by ℵ B F G 33 81 104 255 256 263 442 1611 1845 1908 2005), which is in conformity with Paul's usage in 1 Th 2.9 and 3.10. The reading with the accusatives (supported by A D K L P most minuscules) appears to be a heightening of the apostle's statement, by emphasizing the duration of his labors ("throughout night and day").

---

[1] According to Henry St John Thackeray, "these forms in -οσαν are exceedingly frequent in LXX, being distributed over all the translations (excepting [1–2 Kg, 1–2 Chr]) from the Hexateuch to 2 Esdras" (*A Grammar of the Old Testament in Greek according to the Septuagint,* I [Cambridge, 1909], p. 213); cf. also Moulton-Howard, p. 209.

3.16 τρόπῳ {A}

In several witnesses, chiefly Western (A* D* F G 33 76 it^d, g, 61, 86 vg goth Ambrosiaster Chrysostom), the reading τρόπῳ, which is strongly supported by ℵ A^c B D^c K P Ψ 81 614 1739 *Byz Lect* syr^p, h cop^sa, bo *al,* is replaced by τόπῳ, a more usual expression, in conformity with 1 Cor 1.2; 2 Cor 2.14; 1 Th 1.8; 1 Tm 2.8.

3.18 ὑμῶν. {A}

The liturgical ἀμήν has been introduced by copyists into most witnesses; those that have resisted include ℵ* B 6 33 328 424^c 462 1739 1836 vg^mss cop^sa, bomss arm Ambrosiaster Athanasius Pelagius.

3.18 *Subscription*

(*a*) The subscription in ℵ A B* 33 is πρὸς Θεσσαλονίκεις β̄. Other subscriptions include: (*b*) πρὸς Θεσσαλονίκεις β̄ ἐπληρώθη D; (*c*) ἐτελέσθη (-θαι F) πρὸς Θεσσαλονίκεις F G; (*d*) πρὸς Θεσσαλονίκεις β ἐγράφη ἀπὸ Ἀθηνῶν A B^c K P 31 101 1908 1927 *al,* followed by the Textus Receptus (with δευτέρα for β̄); (*e*) τοῦ ἁγίου ἀποστόλου Παύλου πρὸς Θεσσαλονίκεις δευτέρα· ἐγράφη ἀπὸ Ἀθηνῶν L; (*f*) πρὸς θεσσαλονίκεις δευτέραις (sic) ἐπιστολῆς [add τέλος (?)]· ἐγράφη ἀπὸ Ἀθηνῶν ὑπὸ Παύλου καὶ Σιλουανοῦ καὶ Τιμοθέου cop^bomss Euthalius^mss.

THE FIRST LETTER OF PAUL
TO TIMOTHY

1.1 ἐπιταγήν {A}

Instead of κατ' ἐπιταγήν, Codex Sinaiticus reads κατ' ἐπαγγελίαν, a variant not suitable to the context; it may have arisen inadvertently from the scribe's recollecting 2 Tm 1.1.

1.4 ἐκζητήσεις {B}

Instead of ἐκζητήσεις, a hapax legomenon in the New Testament, several witnesses, chiefly Western (D F G and many minuscules), read the more familiar word ζητήσεις. The meaning of the two words is essentially the same.

1.4 οἰκονομίαν {A}

The Western οἰκοδομήν (D* syr^p, hmg) is the easier reading, but οἰκονομίαν, supported by the overwhelming weight of witnesses, gives a deeper meaning.

1.15 πιστός {A}

Instead of πιστός several Latin witnesses (it^b, mon, ar Ambrosiaster mss^acc. to Jerome Augustine Julian-Eclanum Vigilius), perhaps recollecting a similar reading at 3.1, introduce *humanus* (= ἀνθρώπινος). (See also the comment on 3.1.)

1.17 ἀφθάρτῳ ἀοράτῳ {A}

Instead of ἀφθάρτῳ, several Western witnesses (D*, 2 lat sy^hmg) read ἀθανάτῳ, and others (F G) add ἀθανάτῳ after ἀφθάρτῳ ἀοράτῳ.

1.17 μόνῳ

After μόνῳ the Textus Receptus inserts σοφῷ, with ℵᶜ Dᶜ K L P most minuscules syrʰ goth. The word is no doubt a scribal gloss derived from Ro 16.27; the shorter reading is strongly supported by good representatives of both the Alexandrian and the Western types of text (ℵ* A D* F G H* 33 1739 itᵈ· ᵍ vg syrᵖ copˢᵃ· ᵇᵒ arm eth arab).

2.1 Παρακαλῶ {A}

In place of παρακαλῶ, several Western witnesses (D* (F) (G) itᵇ· ᵈ· ᵍ· ⁽ᵒ⁾ vgᵐˢ) have the imperative παρακάλει, which is obviously a scribal modification intended to give the sentence the form of a specific command to Timothy.

2.7 λέγω {A}

Recollecting Paul's declaration in Ro 9.1, ἀλήθειαν λέγω ἐν Χριστῷ, many witnesses (ℵ* Dᶜ H K 614 1241 *Byz* itᵃʳ goth *al*), followed by the Textus Receptus, have added ἐν Χριστῷ. The emergence of the shorter reading, which is well supported by ℵᶜ A D* G P Ψ 81 629 1739 itᵈ· ᵍ· ʳ vg syrᵖ· ʰ copˢᵃ· ᵇᵒ eth, cannot be adequately explained on the supposition that the longer reading was original. Because of scribal inadvertence several other variant readings occur in various minuscule manuscripts.

3.1 πιστός {A}

The origin of the variant reading ἀνθρώπινος ὁ λόγος ("it is a human saying," i. e. "a common [or popular] saying"), supported by several Western witnesses (D* itᵈ· ⁸⁶ Ambrosiaster mssᵃᶜᶜ· ᵗᵒ ᴶᵉʳᵒᵐᵉ Augustine Speculum Sedulius Scotus), is puzzling. If the evidence were confined to Latin witnesses (as is the case for the similar variant at 1.15), the translation *humanus* could be taken as a very free rendering of πιστός *(hum. = benignus)*, but this leaves unexplained the origin of the reading in D* (the theory that the Greek text of this manuscript was influenced by the Latin translation is disputable).

Perhaps the Greek text arose accidentally when a copyist mistook ΠΙϹΤΟϹ for ANINOC and mistakenly resolved it as ANΘΡΩΠΙΝΟϹ; or (as H. B. Swete proposed[1]) perhaps the translator (or copyist) confused ΠΙϹΤΟϹ, standing at the beginning of a line, with ΠΙΝΟϹ, and considered it to be the final syllables of ἀνθρώπινος; or perhaps a copyist, taking the designation πιστὸς ὁ λόγος to be a formula that introduces a following statement and observing how ill-suited the expression is to introduce ver. 3b, deliberately substituted ἀνθρώπινος for πιστός. In any case, the Committee was impressed by the overwhelming weight and variety of witnesses that support πιστός, and thought it improbable that πιστός was introduced as a substitute for ἀνθρώπινος by copyists who recalled the expression πιστὸς ὁ λόγος at 4.9; 2 Tm 2.11; and Tt 3.8, where the text is firm. In Titus the words cannot be a formula introducing a quotation, but must be taken as a formula of asseveration, relating to what precedes. In the present passage, likewise, πιστός may be taken with 2.15.

3.3 πλήκτην

After πλήκτην the Textus Receptus, as well as many minuscules, inserts μὴ αἰσχροκερδῆ. The words are a gloss derived from Tt 1.7 and are not present in ℵ A D F G K L P 5 33 38 104 181 218 263 323 424ᶜ 436 442 460 462 618 623 635 920 1149 1738 1827 1837 1838 1906* 1944 2004 2125 itᵈ, ᵍ vg syrᵖ, ʰᵗˣᵗ copˢᵃ, ᵇᵒ goth arm eth *al.*

3.16 ὅς {A}

The reading which, on the basis of external evidence and transcriptional probability, best explains the rise of the others is ὅς. It is supported by the earliest and best uncials (ℵ* Aᵛⁱᵈ C* Gᵍʳ) as well as by 33 365 442 2127 syrʰᵐᵍ, ᵖᵃˡ goth ethᵖᵖ Origenˡᵃᵗ Epiphanius Jerome Theodore Eutheriusᵃᶜᶜ· ᵗᵒ ᵀʰᵉᵒᵈᵒʳᵉᵗ Cyril Cyrilᵃᶜᶜ· ᵗᵒ ᴾˢ⁻ᴼᵉᶜᵘᵐᵉⁿⁱᵘˢ Liberatus. Furthermore, since the neuter relative pronoun ὅ must have arisen as a scribal correction of ὅς (to bring the relative into concord with

---

[1] *Journal of Theological Studies,* XVIII (1916–17), p. 1.

μυστήριον), the witnesses that read ὅ (D* it^{d, g, 61, 86} vg Ambrosiaster Marius Victorinus Hilary Pelagius Augustine) also indirectly presuppose ὅς as the earlier reading. The Textus Receptus reads θεός, with ℵ^e (this corrector is of the twelfth century) A² C² D^c K L P Ψ 81 330 614 1739 *Byz Lect* Gregory-Nyssa Didymus Chrysostom Theodoret Euthalius and later Fathers. Thus, no uncial (in the first hand) earlier than the eighth or ninth century (Ψ) supports θεός; all ancient versions presuppose ὅς or ὅ; and no patristic writer prior to the last third of the fourth century testifies to the reading θεός. The reading θεός arose either (*a*) accidentally, through the misreading of oc as ⲑⲥ, or (*b*) deliberately, either to supply a substantive for the following six verbs, or, with less probability, to provide greater dogmatic precision.

4.10 ἀγωνιζόμεθα {C}

It is difficult to decide between ὀνειδιζόμεθα, which is supported by ℵ^c D L P most minuscules it vg cop^{sa, bo} goth arm eth Origen Ambrosiaster *al*, and ἀγωνιζόμεθα, which is read by ℵ* A C F^{gr} G^{gr} K Ψ 33 88 104 326 442 915 1175 1245 1518 1611 1874 *al*. A majority of the Committee preferred the latter, partly because it has slightly better attestation and partly because it seems better suited to the context.

4.12 ἀγάπη

Perhaps under the influence of Col 1.8, after ἀγάπη the Textus Receptus inserts ἐν πνεύματι, with K L P most minuscules John-Damascus Theodoret. The shorter reading is strongly supported by the best representatives of both the Alexandrian and the Western text-types (ℵ A C D F G 33 104 it^{d, g} vg syr^{p, h} cop^{sa, bo} goth arm eth).

5.16 πιστή {B}

Instead of πιστή (ℵ A C F G^{gr} P 33 81 1739 1881 it^{mon} vg cop^{sa, bo} eth^{pp} *al*) the Textus Receptus reads πιστὸς ἢ πιστή with D K L Ψ most minuscules it^{ar, b, d, o} syr^{p, h} *al*. While it is possible that πιστὸς ἢ was omitted accidentally through an oversight in copying, a majority of the Committee, observing that the shorter reading is somewhat better attested than the longer reading, regarded the latter as a natural expansion made by copyists who, in light of ver. 4, felt that a restriction of the principle of this verse to Christian women was unfair. The reading πιστός is confined to versions and may be merely translational in origin.

5.18 τοῦ μισθοῦ {A}

The original hand of codex Sinaiticus reads τῆς τροφῆς, no doubt from having recollected Mt 10.10.

5.19 ἐκτὸς εἰ μὴ ἐπὶ δύο ἢ τριῶν μαρτύρων

These words, found in all extant manuscripts of the passage, were absent from some Latin manuscripts known to Jerome, and perhaps also from the copies used by Cyprian and Ambrosiaster, who quote no farther than παραδέχου.

6.3 προσέρχεται

The reading προσέχεται, which is attested by several witnesses, chiefly Western (ℵ* 1912 it vg arm Cyprian Ambrosiaster Lucifer Pelagius Theodore), appears to be a scribal correction for the more difficult reading προσέρχεται, which is adequately supported by the rest of the witnesses.

6.5 εὐσέβειαν {A}

After εὐσέβειαν the Textus Receptus adds ἀφίστασο ἀπὸ τῶν τοιούτων, with D^c K L P Ψ 061 most minuscules it^ar, b, mon, o syr^p, h goth^ms arm eth^pp Irenaeus Cyprian Ambrosiaster Speculum *al.* Although the reading is ancient, as appears from patristic testimony, it must be rejected as a pious but banal gloss, because (*a*) the best manuscripts of both the Alexandrian and the Western types of text (ℵ A D* F G 048 33 81 88 424^c 1739 1881 it^d, g, r vg cop^sa, bo goth^ms eth^ro

Origen Ambrose) support the shorter reading, and (*b*) if it were present originally, no good reason can be assigned for its omission.

6.7 ὅτι {A}

There is great variation among the witnesses concerning the connection between the two parts of the sentence. Quite secondary are δῆλον ὅτι (ℵᶜ Dᶜ K L P Ψ 104 326 614 *Byz Lect* syrᵖ· ʰ Marcion *al*) and ἀληθὲς ὅτι (D* itᵃʳ· ᵇ· ᵈ· ᵒ goth Cyprian Speculum *al*), each of which is an obvious alleviation introduced in order to clarify the sense. Similarly, the readings καί (copˢᵃ· ᵇᵒ arm eth) and ἀλλ' (Augustine) imply probably nothing more than a free rendering or paraphrase of ὅτι. Thus, the oldest ascertainable reading among the extant witnesses appears to be ὅτι, which is supported, directly or indirectly, by a variety of good witnesses (ℵ* A F G 048 061 33 81 1739 1881 itᵍ· ʳ and the versional evidence supporting καί and ἀλλ'), and which best explains the origin of the other readings. The omission of any connective at all by several patristic writers (Ephraem Orsisius Jerome Augustine Cyril) doubtless reflects merely a rhetorical expedient when quoting a difficult text.

6.9 παγίδα {A}

After παγίδα several Western witnesses (D* F G itᵃʳ· ᵇ· ᵈ· ᶠ· ᵒ) insert τοῦ διαβόλου, derived from 3.7.

6.13 [σοι] {C}

So evenly balanced is the weight of the witnesses that support the presence or the absence of σοι that the Committee thought it best to retain the word but to enclose it within square brackets.

6.17 ἐπὶ θεῷ {A}

After θεῷ the Textus Receptus adds τῷ ζῶντι with D (D* om. τῷ) K L most minuscules itᵈ syrᵖ· ʰ *al*. The shorter reading, which is supported by good representatives of both the Alexandrian and the

Western types of text (ℵ A F G P 33 424ᶜ itᵍ vg copˢᵃ, ᵇᵒ arm eth *al*), was expanded by copyists who recollected the reference to "the living God" in 3.15 or 4.10.

6.19 ὄντως {A}

The Textus Receptus, with Dᶜ K L P 614 1241 *Byz Lect* copᵇᵒᵐˢ Chrysostom *al*, reads αἰωνίου, a manifest correction for the less usual ὄντως, which is supported by the better witnesses of both the Alexandrian and the Western types of text (ℵ A D* F G Ψ 33 81 104 1739 it vg syrᵖ, ʰ copˢᵃ, ᵇᵒ arm eth Ambrosiaster *al*). A few witnesses (69 1175) present the conflated reading αἰωνίου ὄντως (or ὄντως αἰωνίου 296 467).

6.21 ἡ χάρις μεθ' ὑμῶν. {A}

The reading of the Textus Receptus, ἡ χάρις μετὰ σοῦ, which is supported by D² K L Ψ nearly all minuscules itᶠ, ᵒ vg syrᵖ, ʰ copᵇᵒᵐˢ arm eth Theodoret *al*, seems to be a correction introduced as being more appropriate in a letter addressed to an individual than μεθ' ὑμῶν. The latter reading, which occurs also in 2 Tm 4.22 and Tt 3.15 (where a few witnesses have the singular number of the pronoun), is adequately supported by ℵ* A Fᵍʳ G 33 81 1311 itᵍ copᵇᵒᵐˢˢ. Apparently through inadvertence, several versional and patristic witnesses lack the concluding benediction altogether (copˢᵃ Chrysostom Speculum Euthaliusᵐˢˢ). The liturgical ἀμήν, which has been attached to the benediction in most witnesses, is not an original part of the letter, being absent from the earliest representatives of both the Alexandrian and Western types of text (ℵ* A D* Fᵍʳ G 33 81 1311 1881 itᵈ, ᵍ copᵇᵒᵐˢˢ arm).

6.21 *Subscription*

(*a*) The subscription in ℵ A 33 460 *al* is πρὸς Τιμόθεον ᾱ (or πρώτη 460 *al*). Other subscriptions include the following: (*b*) πρὸς Τιμόθεον ᾱ ἐπληρώθη D; (*c*) ἐπληρώθη ἐπιστολὴ πρὸς Τιμόθεον ᾱ F G; (*d*) πρὸς Τιμόθεον ᾱ ἐγράφη ἀπὸ Λαοδικείας A 241

cop^{bomss}; (*e*) πρὸς Τιμόθεον ᾱ ἐγράφη ἀπὸ Νικοπόλεως P 102; (*f*)
πρὸς Τιμόθεον ᾱ (or πρώτη, so also Textus Receptus) ἐγράφη
ἀπὸ Λαοδικείας, ἥτις ἐστὶ (ἐστὶν) μετρόπολις Φρυγίας τῆς
Καπατιανῆς K and many minuscules (1908 *al*, followed by Textus
Receptus, Πακατιανῆς, *al* Παγκα-, Παρακατ-, Καπιανης,
Euthalius^{ms} Πατακατιανης); (*g*) τοῦ ἁγίου ἀποστόλου Παύλου
πρὸς Τιμόθεον ἐπιστολὴ ᾱ ἐγράφη ἀπὸ Λαοδικείας· ἥτις ἐστὶν
μητρόπολης (sic) Φρυγίας τῆς Καπατιανῆς L; (*h*) as (*d*) but ἀπὸ
Μακεδονίας cop^{boms} Euthalius^{mss}; (*i*) as (*d*) but ἀπὸ Ἀθηνῶν διὰ
Τίτου τοῦ μαθητοῦ αὐτοῦ cop^{boms}.

THE SECOND LETTER OF PAUL
TO TIMOTHY

1.11 καὶ διδάσκαλος {B}

Although the overwhelming mass of witnesses (all except ℵ* A I 33 1175 syr^{pal}) read ἐθνῶν, the Committee regarded the word as a gloss introduced by copyists from the parallel passage in 1 Tm 2.7, there being no good reason to account for its omission if it were original here.

2.3 συγκακοπάθησον

The Textus Receptus, following C² Dᶜ K L most minuscules syr^h goth Chrysostom Euthalius Theodoret John-Damascus, reads σὺ οὖν κακοπάθησον. Probably the beginning of ver. 1 gave occasion for the alteration, which was also recommended by the lack of any word to which the prefixed preposition refers. Even the occurrence in some manuscripts (D* E*) of the reading συστρατιώτης for στρατιώτης is an indication that συγκακοπάθησον is original.

2.14 θεοῦ {B}

It is difficult to decide between ἐνώπιον τοῦ θεοῦ and ἐνώπιον τοῦ κυρίου, both of which are supported by weighty evidence. A majority of the Committee preferred the former reading, which is in harmony with 4.1 and 1 Tm 5.4 and 21. The reading Χριστοῦ (206 429 1758) obviously presupposes an earlier κυρίου.

2.18 [τὴν] ἀνάστασιν {C}

In view of the variety of ways in which copyists might have interpreted, or misinterpreted, the significance of the author's reference to ἀνάστασιν, the Committee thought it best, because of nearly overwhelming textual support, to include τήν in the text, but to enclose it within square brackets in order to indicate the possibility that ℵ G 048 33 Cyril may correctly represent the original in omitting the word.

3.8 Ἰάννης καὶ Ἰαμβρῆς

Instead of Ἰάννης C* Euthalius^ms* read Ἰωάννης, and instead of Ἰαμβρῆς certain Western witnesses (F G it^d, g vg goth Cyprian Hippolytus Lucifer Ambrosiaster Augustine Ps-Augustine *al*) read Μαμβρῆς, which in Jewish tradition is a parallel form of the name.[1]

3.11 ἐν Ἰκονίῳ

Before ἐν Ἰκονίῳ the copyist of 181 includes a not very intelligent gloss: ἃ διὰ τὴν Θέκλαν ἔπαθεν ("the things which he [should be *I*] suffered on account of Thecla [in Iconium]").

3.14 τίνων {B}

In order to magnify the apostle Paul's role as Timothy's instructor, the plural was changed to the singular.

3.16 καί

Because the word καί seems to disturb the construction, it is omitted in several versions and Fathers (vg^cl syr^p cop^bo Origen^lat Hilary Ambrosiaster Primasius).

4.1 καὶ τὴν ἐπιφάνειαν {B}

Instead of καί, which involves the more difficult construction, the Textus Receptus substitutes the easier κατά, with ℵ^c D^c K L P Ψ most minuscules syr^p, h cop^sa goth arm eth *al*. The reading adopted

---

[1] See Hugo Odeberg in Kittel's *Theological Dictionary of the New Testament*, III, pp. 192 f.

for the text is amply supported by representatives of both the Alexandrian and the Western types of text (ℵ* A C D* F G 33 424ᶜ 1739 2495 itᵈ·ᵍ·⁶¹ vg copᵇᵒ *al*).

4.8 πᾶσι

Although copyists not infrequently added "all" in order to heighten the account, a majority of the Committee was of the opinion that in the present instance the word is too widely supported in diverse textual traditions to be regarded as a scribal insertion, and interpreted its absence from several witnesses, chiefly Western (D* 424ᶜ 1739* 1881 itᵈ·⁶¹ vg syrᵖ Ambrosiaster Ambrose Augustine Primasius), as the result of an oversight in transcription.

4.10 Γαλατίαν {A}

The reading Γαλατίαν, which is strongly supported by a diversity of Eastern and Western witnesses (A D F G K L P Ψ 33 614 1739 *Byz Lect* itᵃʳ·ᵇ·ᵈ·ᶠ·ᵍ·ᵒ syrᵖ·ʰ copᵇᵒᵐˢˢ goth Irenaeusˡᵃᵗ Ephraem *al*), appears to be the original text, which in some witnesses, chiefly Alexandrian (ℵ C 81 104 326 436 vg copˢᵃ·ᵇᵒᵐˢˢ ethʳᵒ Eusebius Epiphanius), was altered to Γαλλίαν, either accidentally (the second ᴀ being read as ʌ, with the consequent suppression of the ᴛ), or deliberately (by copyists who took it to mean Gaul, which in the early centuries of the Christian era was commonly called Γαλατία).

4.19 Ἀκύλαν

After Ἀκύλαν two minuscules (181 and 460, of the eleventh and thirteenth centuries respectively) insert Λέκτραν τὴν γυναῖκα αὐτοῦ καὶ Σιμαίαν (Σημαίαν 460) καὶ Ζήνωνα τοὺς υἱοὺς αὐτοῦ. Since, according to the apocryphal *Acts of Paul and Thecla* (§ 2), these are the names of the wife and the children of Onesiphorus, the gloss was evidently written first in the margin and later introduced into the text at the wrong place (giving Aquila two wives!).

4.22　κύριος　{B}

Three forms of text are current: (*a*) the shortest is ὁ κύριος μετὰ τοῦ πνεύματός σου, read by ℵ* Fᵍʳ G 33 1739 itᵍ; (*b*) several witnesses expand by including Ἰησοῦς after κύριος (A 102 104 1245); and (*c*) the full formulation κύριος Ἰησοῦς Χριστός occurs in ℵᶜ C D K L P Ψ 6 81 257 326 917 1175 2138 itᵈ vg syrᵖˑʰ (= our Lord …) copˢᵃˑ ᵇᵒ arm John-Damascus Ambrosiaster Chrysostom Euthalius Theodoret *al.*

In the expectation that a letter as late as 2 Timothy would have the fullest formulation, one would be tempted to explain the shorter readings as due to accidental omissions. Such omissions of the sacred name(s), however, are rare,[1] and it is far more probable that the original reading is that preserved by the joint testimony of Alexandrian (ℵ* 33) and Western (Fᵍʳ G itᵍ) witnesses, supported as well by 1739.

4.22　ἡ χάρις μεθ᾽ ὑμῶν. {A}

Of the eight forms of the final sentence of the letter, that attested by ℵ* A C G 33 81 1881 appears to be superior on the score of external evidence and transcriptional probability. The substitution of the first person plural pronoun ἡμῶν (460 1908 1984 copᵇᵒᵐˢ Chrysostom *al*) is perhaps merely an orthographic variant, arising from the circumstance that in late Greek υ and η were pronounced alike. The substitution of σοῦ for the plural pronoun in several versions (syrᵖ copᵇᵒᵐˢ arm) may have been prompted by σου in the preceding sentence, or by the seeming unsuitability of the plural pronoun in a letter addressed to an individual (cf. also the similar variant reading in 1 Tm 6.21). The reading ἔρρωσ᾽ ἐν εἰρήνῃ of several Western witnesses (D* itᵈˑ ⁶¹) combines the usual farewell greeting of Hellenistic letters with the Jewish-Christian expression ἐν εἰρήνῃ. The addition of the liturgical ἀμήν (ℵᶜ Dᶜ K P Ψ itᵃʳˑ ᵈ vg syrᵖˑ ʰ copᵇᵒᵐˢˢ

---

[1] Among the very occasional instances of the accidental omission of *nomina sacra* are the absence of Ἰησοῦς after κύριος in L at Col 3.17, and the reading ὅτι ὁ κύριος in B at 1 Cor 11.23, which has been mechanically conformed to the preceding ἀπὸ τοῦ κυρίου.

eth^{pp} *al*) is natural; its deliberate omission, supposing that it were present originally, is most unlikely in such diversified witnesses as ℵ* A C G 33 81 1881 it^g cop^{bo mss} eth^{ro} Ambrosiaster. In a scattering of witnesses (330 cop^{sa} eth^{pp} Ambrosiaster Pelagius Ps-Jerome) the entire sentence is lacking, probably because it was felt to be superfluous after the preceding sentence.

4.22 *Subscription*

(*a*) The subscription in ℵ C 33 is πρὸς Τιμόθεον. Other subscriptions include the following: (*b*) πρὸς Τιμόθεον δευτέρα 90 *al*; (*c*) πρὸς Τιμόθεον β̄ ἐπληρώθη D; (*d*) ἐτελέσθη πρὸς Τιμόθεον β̄ F G; (*e*) πρὸς Τιμόθεον β̄ ἐγράφη ἀπὸ Λαοδικείας A; (*f*) πρὸς Τιμόθεον β̄ ἐγράφει ἀπὸ Ῥώμης P; (*g*) as (*f*) plus ὅτε ἐκ δευτέρου παρέστη Παῦλος τῷ Καίσαρι Ῥώμης (464 Ῥωμαίων) Νέρωνι 464 Euthalius^{ms}; (*h*) πρὸς Τιμόθεον δευτέρα· τῆς Ἐφεσίων ἐκκλησίας ἐπίσκοπον χειροτονηθένα· ἐγράφη ἀπὸ Ῥώμης ὅτε ἐκ δευτέρου παρέστη Παῦλος τῷ Καίσαρι Ῥώμης Νέρωνι K; (*i*) τοῦ ἁγίου ἀποστόλου Παύλου ἐπιστολὴ β̄ πρὸς Τιμόθεον τῆς Ἐφεσίων ἐκκλησίας πρῶτον ἐπίσκοπον χειροτονηθέντα· ἐγράφη etc. as (*h*) L; (*j*) πρὸς Τιμόθεον δευτέρα, τῆς Ἐφεσίων ἐκκλησίας πρῶτον ἐπίσκοπον χειροτονηθέντα, ἐγράφη ἀπὸ Ῥώμης, ὅτε ἐκ δευτέρου παρέστη Παῦλος τῷ Καίσαρι Νέρωνι Textus Receptus.

THE LETTER OF PAUL TO TITUS

1.4 χάρις καὶ εἰρήνη {A}

The typically Pauline epistolary salutation, χάρις καὶ εἰρήνη, is strongly supported by good representatives of both the Alexandrian and the Western types of text (ℵ C* D G P Ψ it vg). The insertion of ἔλεος (A C² K 81 614 *Byz Lect al* and the Textus Receptus) seems to be an emendation prompted by the analogy of the threefold salutation in 1 Tm 1.2 and 2 Tm 1.2. Other minor fluctuations, such as the insertion of ὑμῖν (33) or σοι (cop^sa), are obviously scribal modifications.

1.9 ἐλέγχειν

After ἐλέγχειν a trilingual manuscript of the thirteenth century (no. 460, Greek with Latin and Arabic versions) adds Μὴ χειροτονεῖν διγάμους μηδὲ διακόνους αὐτοὺς ποιεῖν, μηδὲ γυναῖκας ἔχειν ἐκ διγαμίας· μηδὲ προσερχέσθωσαν ἐν τῷ θυσιαστηρίῳ λειτουργεῖν τὸ θεῖον. τοὺς ἄρχοντας τοὺς ἀδικοκρίτας καὶ ἅρπαγας καὶ ψεύστας καὶ ἀνελεήμονας ἔλεγχε ὡς θεοῦ διάκονος ("Do not appoint those who have married twice or make them deacons, and do not take wives in a second marriage; let them not come to serve the Deity at the altar. As God's servant reprove the rulers who are unjust judges and robbers and liars and unmerciful"). (See also the comment on ver. 11.)

1.10 πολλοὶ [καί] {C}

It is difficult to decide whether καί was added in accordance with the rhetorical usage known as hendiadys, or whether it was omitted by copyists who, not appreciating such usage, deleted it both as unnecessary and as apparently disturbing to the sense. A majority of the Committee preferred to follow the testimony of D G I K Ψ 1739 it^d, g vg Speculum *al,* which read καί, but to enclose the word within square brackets in view of its absence from such weighty authorities as ℵ A C 33 81 it⁶¹ syrᵖˑʰ copˢᵃˑᵇᵒ *al*.

1.11 χάριν

After χάριν the trilingual manuscript 460 (see also the comment on ver. 9) adds τὰ τέκνα οἱ τοὺς ἰδίους γονεῖς ὑβρίζοντες ἢ τύπτονες ἐπιστόμιζε καὶ ἔλεγχε καὶ νουθέτει ὡς πατὴρ τέκνα ("The children who abuse or strike their parents you must check and reprove and admonish as a father his children").

2.5 οἰκουργούς

Instead of the word οἰκουρούς (ℵᶜ Dᶜ H L P most minuscules most Fathers, followed by the Textus Receptus), which occurs frequently in classical Greek, ℵ* A C D* F G I 33 177 330 623 Clement of Rome *al* read οἰκουργούς, which occurs elsewhere only in Soranus, a medical writer of the second century A.D. A majority of the Committee preferred the latter reading because of superior external support, and because it was regarded more probable that an unusual word should have been altered by copyists to a well-known word, than vice versa.

The text may be punctuated with or without a comma after οἰκουργούς.

2.7 ἀφθορίαν

The Committee preferred the reading ἀφθορίαν ("incorruption") because it is supported by good representatives of both the Alexandrian and Western types of text (ℵ* A C D* 33 *al*), and because its rarity explains the origin of the other readings: ἀφθονίαν ("freedom from envy") 𝔓³² Fᵍʳ Gᵍʳ 88 915 copˢᵃ, ἀδιαφθορίαν ("sincerity") ℵᶜ Dᶜ L most minuscules arm (followed by the Textus Receptus), and ἀδιαφορίαν ("indifference") 35ᶜ 205 1905 Theodoretᵐˢ. The last reading is an obvious transcriptional error; all four words are hapax legomena in the New Testament.

3.1 ἀρχαῖς {B}

After ἀρχαῖς the Textus Receptus adds καί, following the later uncials (Dᶜ K P) as well as most of the minuscules, versions, and Fathers. The more difficult asyndetic construction is supported by the best witnesses of both the Alexandrian and the Western types of text (ℵ A C Dᵍʳ* G Ψ 33 1739 itᵍ). It is possible that the conjunction may have fallen out accidentally in transcription (ΑΡΧΑΙϹΚΑΙΕΞΟΥϹΙΑΙϹ). On the other hand, since καί is lacking also between the following two infinitives (according to the decisive weight of witnesses; only Fᵍʳ G itᵍ syrᵖ Basil insert καί), it appears that the author deliberately framed his sentence concisely, and that the presence of καί is the result of the desire of copyists to relieve the asyndeton.

3.9 ἔρεις

On the one hand, from the point of view of transcriptional probability it is more likely that copyists would have altered ἔριν to ἔρεις, in agreement with the plurals before and after it, than vice versa. On the other hand, external evidence appears to favor the plural form: ἔρεις (or its phonetic equivalent, ἔρις) is supported by A C K L P 075 0142 most minuscules itᵈ· ᵍ vg syrᵖ· ʰ copˢᵃ· ᵇᵒ, whereas ἔριν (or its phonetic equivalent ἔρειν) is supported by ℵ* Dᵍʳ* F G Ψ 999 arm eth *al*. A majority of the Committee preferred to be guided in its judgment by the weight of the external evidence (which includes all versions except the Ethiopic), especially since the context seems to call for a reference to a plurality of disagreements.

3.15 μετὰ πάντων ὑμῶν. {A}

The impulse to identify the origin of ἡ χάρις in the benediction prompted copyists to insert τοῦ κυρίου (D) or τοῦ θεοῦ (F G vg). Influence from 2 Tm 4.22 accounts for the substitution of μετὰ τοῦ πνεύματός σου in 33, and for the addition of καὶ μετὰ τοῦ πνεύματός σου in 81. The concluding ἀμήν (ℵᶜ Dᶜ F G H Ψ *al*) is obviously secondary, for the word is absent in a variety of early and diverse witnesses (𝔓⁶¹ᵛⁱᵈ ℵ* A C D* 048 1739 1881 *al*), and the temptation for copyists to add the liturgical conclusion would be great.

3.15 *Subscription*

(*a*) The subscription in ℵ C 33 eth is πρὸς Τίτον. Other subscriptions include the following: (*b*) πρὸς Τίτον ἐπληρώθη D; (*c*) ἐτελέσθη ἐπιστολὴ πρὸς Τίτον F G; (*d*) πρὸς Τίτον ἐγράφη ἀπὸ Νικοπόλεως A P arab; (*e*) πρὸς Τίτον τῆς Κρητῶν ἐκκλησίας πρῶτον ἐπίσκοπον χειροτονηθέντα ἐγράφη ἀπὸ Νικοπόλεως τῆς Μακεδονίας K 101 1908 1927, followed by the Textus Receptus; (*f*) Παύλου ἀποστόλου (L τοῦ ἁγίου ἀποστόλου Παύλου) ἐπιστολὴ πρὸς Τίτον τῆς Κρητῶν (L Κριτῶν) ἐκκλησίας πρῶτον ἐπίσκοπον χειροτονηθέντα· ἐγράφη ἀπὸ Νικοπόλεως τῆς Μακεδονίας H L 462; (*g*) as (*d*) plus τῆς Μακεδονίας Euthalius[ms]; (*h*) To Titus it was finished, it was written in Nicopolis and he sent it by Artemas his disciple, cop[bo]; (*i*) Was finished the epistle to Titus, which was written from Nicopolis and was sent through Zina and Apollo, syr[p]; (*j*) Was finished the epistle to Titus, who was the first bishop of the Church at Crete, which was written from Nicopolis of Macedonia, syr[h].

THE LETTER OF PAUL TO PHILEMON

ver. 2 τῇ ἀδελφῇ {A}

A preponderance of ancient and diversified witnesses (ℵ A D* F G P 048 33 81 1739 1881 *al)* supports ἀδελφῇ. Furthermore, from a transcriptional point of view, it is more likely that ἀγαπητῇ was introduced (in D² Ψ and most minuscules) in conformity with the preceding ἀγαπητῷ (ver. 1) than that ἀδελφῇ was substituted in order to avoid repetition. A few copyists present both words (629 it[ar, b] syr[h]).

ver. 6 ἐν ἡμῖν {B}

Instead of ἐν ἡμῖν the Textus Receptus reads ἐν ὑμῖν, strongly supported by 𝔓[61] ℵ G P 33 1739 *Byz* it[g, 61] vg syr[p, h] cop[sa, bo] arm *al*. The Committee preferred ἐν ἡμῖν, which is perhaps slightly less well supported (A C D K Ψ 81 614 it[d] syr[hmg] *al*), because it is more expressive and because, standing amid other pronouns of the second person singular and plural, ἡμῖν was more likely to be changed by copyists to ὑμῖν than vice versa.

ver. 9 πρεσβύτης

Although the manuscripts support πρεσβύτης ("an old man"), many commentators follow the conjecture of Bentley and others that πρεσβευτής ("an ambassador") should be read (cf. Eph 6.20). J. B. Lightfoot supposed *(Commentary, ad loc.)* that in koine Greek πρεσβύτης may have been written indifferently for πρεσβευτής, for the two forms are interchanged by scribal confusion in the manuscripts of the Septuagint (cf. 2 Chr 32.31; 1 Macc 13.21; 14.21, 22; 2 Macc 11.34; cf. Ignatius, *Smyr.* 11; etc.). On the other hand, other scholars deny that the context permits the meaning "an ambassador" (cf. Theodor Zahn, *Introduction to the New Testament,* vol. i, p. 457, note 6, and the commentaries of M. R. Vincent, Hermann von Soden, M. Dibelius, and M. Meinertz).

ver. 12 ἀνέπεμψά σοι, αὐτόν, τοῦτ᾽ ἔστιν τὰ ἐμὰ σπλάγχνα {B}

The reading of ℵ* A 33, adopted for the text, best explains the origin of the other readings. In order to smooth the syntax, the verb προσλαβοῦ (from ver. 17) was introduced by copyists, either after σπλάγχνα (ℵᶜ C D K P Ψ 81 614 1739 *Byz* it⁶¹ vg syrᵖ· ʰ goth *al*), or after αὐτόν (048 330ᵐᵍ 451 2492 itᵍ syrᵖᵃˡ arm), or before αὐτόν (69 431 462 copˢᵃ· ᵇᵒ). Likewise, the introduction of σύ, either in place of σοι (ℵᶜ Dᶜ Gᵉʳ K P *al*) or in addition to it (C² D* 048 88 *al*), is obviously a further scribal amelioration.

ver. 25 κυρίου {B}

After κυρίου the Textus Receptus adds ἡμῶν, with A C D K Ψ 614 it vg syrᵖ copˢᵃ· ᵇᵒ eth *al*. If the pronoun were present originally, it is difficult to account for its omission in ℵ P 33 81 104 451 1739 1881 2492 syrʰ· ᵖᵃˡ arm, whereas copyists were prone to introduce such natural expansions.

ver. 25 ὑμῶν. {A}

Good representatives of both the Alexandrian and the Western types of text (A D* 048 33 81 1881 itᵈ copˢᵃ· ᵇᵒᵐˢˢ *al*) have resisted the tendency to append the liturgical ἀμήν. The substitution of σου for ὑμῶν (vgᵐˢ) limits the reference to Philemon alone, and agrees with σε in ver. 23.

ver. 25 *Subscription*

(*a*) The subscription in ℵ C 33 ethʳᵒ is πρὸς Φιλήμονα. Other subscriptions include the following: (*b*) πρὸς Φιλήμονα ἐπληρώθη D; (*c*) πρὸς Φιλήμονα ἐγράφει ἀπὸ Ῥώμης P; (*d*) πρὸς Φιλήμονα ἐγράφη ἀπὸ Ῥώμης διὰ Ὀνησίμου οἰκέτου K 1908 (om. οἰκ. 1927) *al*, followed by the Textus Receptus; (*e*) πρὸς Φιλήμονα καὶ Ἀπφίαν δεσπότας τοῦ Ὀνησίμου καὶ πρὸς Ἄρχιππον τὸν διάκονον τῆς ἐν Κολασσαῖς ἐκκλησίας· ἐγράφη ἀπὸ Ῥώμης διὰ

Ὀνησίμου οἰκέτου 101; (*f*) τοῦ ἁγίου ἀποστόλου Παύλου ἐπιστολή plus (*e*), but reading Κολοσσαῖς L; (*g*) πρὸς Φιλήμονα καὶ Ἀπφίαν δεσπότας Ὀνισήμου (sic) καὶ πρὸς Ἄρχιππον διάκονον τῆς ἐκκλησίας ἐγράφη ἀπὸ Ῥώμης διὰ Ὀνησίμου οἰκέτου Euthalius[ms]; (*h*) as (*g*) but after Ῥώμης continue thus: ἐκ προσώπου Παύλου καὶ Τιμοθέου διὰ Ὀνησίμου οἰκέτου· ἀλλὰ δὴ καὶ μάρτυς Χριστοῦ γεγένηται ὁ μακάριος Ὀνήσιμος ἐν τῇ Ῥωμαίων πόλει ἐπὶ Τερτούλλου τοῦ τηνικαῦτα τὴν ἐπαρχικὴν ἐξουσίαν διέποντος τῇ τῶν σκέλων κλάσει τὴν ψῆφον ὑπομείνας τοῦ μαρτυρίου 42 (390); (*i*) ἐτελέσθη ἡ πρὸς Φιλήμονα ἐπιστολή, ἥτις ἐγράφη ἀπὸ Ῥώμης καὶ ἀπεστάλη διὰ Ὀνησίμου syr[p] (cop[bo] arab eth); (*j*) ἐτελέσθη ἡ ἐπιστολὴ πρὸς Φιλήμονα καὶ Ἀπφίαν δεσπότας Ὀνησιφόρου, καὶ πρὸς Ἄρχιππον διάκονον τῆς ἐν Κολασσαῖς ἐκκλησίας, ἥτις ἐγράφη ἀπὸ Ῥώμης διὰ Ὀνησίμου οἰκέτου syr[h]; (*k*) πρὸς Φιλήμονα καὶ Ἀπφίαν δεσπότας Ὀνησίμου, καὶ πρὸς Ἄρχιππον διάκονον τῆς Κολοσσέων ἐκκλησίας, ἐγράφη ἀπὸ Ῥώμης διὰ Ὀνησίμου οἰκέτου arm; (*l*) τέλος τῆς ἐπιστολῆς ἣν ἔγραψεν ἀπὸ Ῥώμης πρὸς Φιλήμονα καὶ Ἀπφίαν δεσπότας Ὀνησίμου καὶ Ἄρχιππον διάκονον τῆς ἐν Κολασσαῖς ἐκκλησίας διὰ Ὀνησίμου οἰκέτου geo.

THE LETTER TO THE HEBREWS

In the manuscripts and versions of the New Testament the position of the Letter to the Hebrews varies widely.[1] It follows (*a*) immediately after Romans in 𝔓[46] 103 455 1961 1964 1977 1994 2104 2576 2685; (*b*) after 2 Corinthians in 1930 1978 1992 2000 2248 cop[sa]; (*c*) after Galatians in an ancestor of codex Vaticanus;[2] (*d*) after Ephesians in 606; (*e*) after 2 Thessalonians in ℵ A B C H I K P 0150 0151 more than eighty minuscules (including 33 81 88 181 436 1739 1877 1881 1962 2127) cop[bo] arm geo[mss] eth[mss]; (*f*) after Titus in 1311 2183 (so too the πίναξ [list] in 1521, but not the text); (*g*) after Philemon in D L Ψ 048 056 075 0142 most minuscules (including 104 326 330 451 614 629 630 1984 1985 2492 2495) it[d] vg syr[p, h] cop[bomss] eth[pp]. There are also the following sequences: (*h*) ... Colossians, Philemon, 1 and 2 Thessalonians, Philippians, *Hebrews,* 1 and 2 Timothy, Titus in 2690 2739, and (*i*) ... 1 and 2 Corinthians,

---

[1] The information given here has been derived chiefly from W. H. P. Hatch, "The Position of Hebrews in the Canon of the New Testament," *Harvard Theological Review,* XXIX (1936), pp. 133–151, with many valuable additions supplied through the kindness of Kurt Aland from the files of the Institute for New Testament Text Research at Münster. For information concerning evidence from early canonical lists and patristic writers, see the article by Hatch.

[2] Although in codex Vaticanus Hebrews follows 2 Thessalonians, the chapter numbers in that manuscript disclose that in an ancestor it occupied a position after Galatians. The chapter numeration of the Pauline Letters begins with Romans and runs continuously through 2 Thessalonians. The Letter to the Galatians concludes with the 58th chapter, whereas the next Epistle, that to the Ephesians, begins with the 70th chapter, and then the numbers continue regularly through Philippians, Colossians, 1 and 2 Thessalonians, ending with the 93rd chapter. Following 2 Thessalonians (as was mentioned above) stands Hebrews, which begins with the 59th chapter, and proceeds with the 60th, 61st, 62nd, 63rd, and 64th chapters, as far as He 9.14, where the manuscript breaks off, the remaining part being lost. Doubtless there were originally eleven chapters in Hebrews (59 to 69). It is clear, therefore, from the sequence of chapter divisions that in an ancestor of codex Vaticanus Hebrews stood after Galatians and before Ephesians, and that the scribe of Vaticanus copied mechanically the chapter numbers even though they no longer were appropriate after Galatians.

Galatians, 1 and 2 Thessalonians, 1 and 2 Timothy, Titus, Philemon, *Hebrews,* James, Romans, Ephesians, Philippians, Colossians, Jude, 1 and 2 Peter, 1 John in 1241 (the manuscript breaks off with 1 John).

Most printed editions of the Greek New Testament have followed the traditional sequence represented by (*g*), with Hebrews at the end of the Pauline canon. Other editions, however, following the witnesses mentioned under (*e*), place it after Paul's Letters to churches and before his Letters to individuals. These include Lachmann (1831), Tregelles (1857–72), Tischendorf (1869–72), Westcott and Hort (1881), B. Weiss (1894–1900), J. M. S. Baljon (1898), and H. von Soden (1913).

1.3 τῆς δυνάμεως αὐτοῦ, καθαρισμόν {B}

Although the reading δι᾽ αὐτοῦ καθαρισμόν ($\mathfrak{P}^{46}$ D^{gr*} 236 263 2005 2127) may appear to be rather strongly supported, the weight of D^{gr*} is considerably weakened when one takes into account the presence of a conflation in that manuscript (τῷ ῥήματι τῆς δυνάμεως αὐτοῦ, δι᾽ αὐτοῦ καθαρισμὸν ...).[1] On the whole the Committee thought it more likely that δι᾽ αὐτοῦ or δι᾽ ἑαυτοῦ (D^c K L M 614 1739 *Byz Lect al*) was added in order to enhance the force of the middle voice of ποιησάμενος, than that the phrase was present originally and then omitted in good representatives of the Alexandrian text (ℵ A B 33 81) as well as in Western witnesses (it^{81} vg).

1.8 σου (2) {B}

Although the reading αὐτοῦ, which has early and good support ($\mathfrak{P}^{46}$ ℵ B), may seem to be preferable because it differs from the reading of the Old Testament passage that is being quoted (Ps 45.7 [= LXX 44.7] σου), to which, on this point of view, presumably the mass of New Testament witnesses have been assimilated, a majority

---

[1] The evidence can be set forth as follows: the phrase τῷ ῥήματι τῆς δυνάμεως is followed by (*a*) αὐτοῦ ℵ A B 33 81 917 1175 1836 it vg arm *al*; (*b*) δι᾽ ἑαυτοῦ (or αὐ-) $\mathfrak{P}^{46}$ 0121 424^c 1739 cop^{sa} *al*; or (*c*) αὐτοῦ δι᾽ ἑαυτοῦ (or αὐ-) D^{gr*} K L most minuscules cop^{bo} *al*.

of the Committee was more impressed (*a*) by the weight and variety of the external evidence supporting σου, and (*b*) by the internal difficulty of construing αὐτοῦ. Thus, if one reads αὐτοῦ the words ὁ θεός must be taken, not as a vocative[2] (an interpretation that is preferred by most exegetes), but as the subject (or predicate nominative),[3] an interpretation that is generally regarded as highly improbable. Even if one assumes that καί, which is absent from the Hebrew and the Septuagint of the Psalm, was inserted by the author with the set purpose of making two separate quotations, with ver. 8a in the second person and 8b in the third person,[4] the strangeness of the shift in persons is only slightly reduced.

1.12 ἐλίξεις {A}

Instead of ἐλίξεις, which is supported by the great preponderance of witnesses, two manuscripts (ℵ* D*) read ἀλλάξεις, (the preponderant reading of Ps 101.27 LXX), subsequently altered by correctors to εἰλίζεις.

1.12 ὡς ἱμάτιον καί {B}

The words ὡς ἱμάτιον, strongly supported by 𝔓⁴⁶ ℵ A B (D*) 1739 (it^d) arm eth, appear to be original with the author of the Letter, who inserted them in his quotation from Ps 102.26 to show that the metaphor of the garment is continued. The absence of the words from most witnesses is the result of conformation to the text of the Septuagint.

2.7 αὐτόν (2) {B}

While external evidence may seem to favor the inclusion of καὶ κατέστησας αὐτὸν ἐπὶ τὰ ἔργα τῶν χειρῶν σου (ℵ A C D* P Ψ

---

[2] "Thy throne, O God, is for ever and ever, and the scepter of righteousness is the scepter of thy kingdom."

[3] "God is thy throne (or, Thy throne is God) for ever and ever, and the scepter of righteousness is the scepter of his [i. e. God's] kingdom."

[4] "'Thy throne, O God, is for ever and ever,' and 'the scepter of righteousness is the scepter of his kingdom.'"

33 (81) 1739 it vg syr[p, h with *] cop[sa, bo, fay] arm eth *al*), the Committee was impressed by the probability that the longer reading may be the result of scribal enlargement of the quotation (Ps 8.7), and therefore preferred the shorter reading, supported by $\mathfrak{P}^{46}$ B D[c] K L *al*.

2.8 [αὐτῷ] (1) {C}

Although the preponderant weight of external evidence might be thought to support αὐτῷ without question, the fact that the earliest Greek witnesses ($\mathfrak{P}^{46}$ B), with support from several early versions, lack the word led the Committee to have some doubt as to whether αὐτῷ belongs in the text, and therefore it was decided to print the word enclosed within square brackets.

2.9 χάριτι θεοῦ {A}

Instead of χάριτι θεοῦ, which is very strongly supported by good representatives of both the Alexandrian and the Western types of text ($\mathfrak{P}^{46}$ ℵ A B C D 33 81 330 614 it vg cop[sa, bo, fay] *al*), a rather large number of Fathers, both Eastern and Western, as well as 0121b 424[c] 1739* vg[ms] syr[pmss], read χωρὶς θεοῦ. The latter reading appears to have arisen either through a scribal lapse, misreading χάριτι as χωρίς, or, more probably, as a marginal gloss (suggested by 1 Cor 15.27) to explain that "everything" in ver. 8 does not include God; this gloss, being erroneously regarded by a later transcriber as a correction of χάριτι θεοῦ, was introduced into the text of ver. 9.

3.2 [ὅλῳ] {C}

Both external evidence and transcriptional probabilities are singularly difficult to evaluate. On the one hand, ὅλῳ is read by a wide variety of text-types, but is suspect as having been conformed to the text of ver. 5 and/or of Nu 12.17 LXX. On the other hand, several early and excellent witnesses ($\mathfrak{P}^{13}$ $\mathfrak{P}^{46vid}$ B, joined by cop[sa, bo, fay] *al*) lack ὅλῳ, but the omission may be a deliberate (Alexandrian?) emendation, introduced in order to render the Old Testament quotation more appropriate to the argument (in ver. 2 "whole" disturbs the parallelism between Moses and Jesus). In the face of such a balance of possibilities, a majority of the Committee thought it best to include ὅλῳ in the text, but to enclose it within square brackets in order to express doubt whether it belongs there.

3.6 οὗ {A}

The reading ὅς, which appears to be predominantly Western in character (𝔓⁴⁶ D* 0121b 88 424ᶜ 1739 itᵃʳ, ᵇ, ᵈ vg Lucifer Ambrose), is probably a scribal modification of οὗ, introduced perhaps for the sake of logical exactitude (Christians are God's house, not Christ's house). The reading οὗ is more than sufficiently supported by early and diversified witnesses (𝔓¹³ᵛⁱᵈ ℵ A B C Dᶜ I K P Ψ 33 81 itᵛ syrᵖ, ʰ, ᵖᵃˡ copˢᵃ, ᵇᵒ arm).

3.6 κατάσχωμεν {B}

After ἐλπίδος the Textus Receptus adds μέχρι τέλους βεβαίαν, with ℵ A C D K P 33 81 629 1739 it vg *al*. It is probable, however, that the phrase is an interpolation from ver. 14, especially since not βεβαίαν but βέβαιον is the gender that one would have expected the author to use, qualifying the nearer substantive τὸ καύχημα.

4.2 συγκεκερασμένους {B}

Among the bewildering variety of readings preserved among the manuscripts (conveniently represented in the apparatus by the use of parentheses), the one that best explains the origin of the others is συγκεκερασμένους. Supported by early and diverse testimony representing both the Alexandrian and the Western types of text (𝔓¹³, ⁴⁶ A B C Dᵍʳ * Ψ (33) 81 1739 *al*), as the more difficult reading it would naturally have been altered to the easier nominative singular (ℵ 57 (102) (itᵈ) syrᵖ copˢᵃ Ephraem Lucifer *al*).

4.3 εἰσερχόμεθα γάρ {A}

Among the connectives γάρ is to be preferred both because of early and good external evidence (𝔓¹³, ⁴⁶ B D K P Ψ 33 614 it vg syrʰ copˢᵃ eth) and because it suits the context. The reading οὖν (ℵ A C

0121b 81 1739 cop^bo), which is considerably less vigorous, was suggested by οὖν in verses 1, 11, 14, and 16, which, however, are not parallel, for here οὖν seems to have a resumptive sense ("well then"). The colorless δέ (syr^p arm) probably represents a mere translational variant. The hortatory subjunctive, εἰσερχώμεθα, which is quite inappropriate with the following οἱ πιστεύσαντες, arose as a secondary development in connection with the misinterpretation that produced οὖν (A C al).

4.3 *[τήν]* {C}

The balance between the weight of evidence for and against the presence of τήν led the Committee to decide to retain the word but to enclose it within square brackets.

5.12 τινά {C}

The Textus Receptus reads the interrogative τίνα (hence AV renders, "ye have need that one teach you again which *[τίνα]* be the first principles of the oracles of God"), with B^c D^c K 88 614 *Byz Lect al*. Since the earliest manuscripts are without accent marks, editors must decide on the basis of context which is the more appropriate form; here the Committee felt that the indefinite pronoun (τινά) gives a sharper antithesis to εἶναι διδάσκαλοι in the preceding clause.

6.2 διδαχῆς {A}

Although the reading διδαχήν, which is in apposition with θεμέλιον of ver. 1, is early (𝔓^46 B it^d), a majority of the Committee regarded it as a stylistic improvement introduced in order to avoid so many genitives. The reading διδαχῆς is strongly supported by good representatives of all the major types of text (ℵ A C D^gr I K P 33 81 614 1739 *Byz Lect al*).

6.3 ποιήσομεν {A}

The future tense ποιήσομεν is to be preferred on the basis of (*a*) the weight of external evidence (𝔓^46 ℵ B I^vid 33 88 614 1739 it^ar, b, d vg syr^{p, h} cop^{sa, bo, fay} *al*) as well as (*b*) its congruence with the follow-ing clause, "if God permits" (which is more appropriate with the future tense than with the exhortation "let us do this"). The reading ποιήσωμεν (A C D^{gr} P Ψ 81 *al*), if it is not merely the result of an orthographic confusion between *ο* and *ω*, probably arose from mechanical conformation with φερώμεθα in ver. 1.

7.21   εἰς τὸν αἰῶνα {A}

On the one hand, the omission of the phrase κατὰ τὴν τάξιν Μελχισέδεκ could be explained if the eye of the scribe wandered from κατά to the κατά that follows Μελχισέδεκ. On the other hand, many scribes would have felt the temptation to add the phrase here (from ver. 17). The Committee judged that the second pos-sibility was much the stronger.[1]

8.8   αὐτούς {B}

The variation between αὐτούς (א* A D* I K P Ψ 33 81 it vg cop^{sa, bo, fay} *al*) and αὐτοῖς (𝔓⁴⁶ א^c B D^c 614 1739 *Byz Lect al*) makes very little difference in sense, though the latter may be construed with either μεμφόμενος or λέγει. Observing the direction in which scribal corrections moved, a majority of the Committee preferred the reading αὐτούς.

8.11   πολίτην {A}

Instead of πολίτην, which is strongly supported by 𝔓⁴⁶ א A B D K L most minuscules it^d syr^{p, h} cop^{sa, bo, fay} arm *al*, the Textus Receptus substitutes the more commonplace πλησίον, with P several minus-cules (including 81) it^{ar, b, comp} vg syr^{hmg} eth *al*.

9.1   [καί] {C}

The evidence, evenly balanced for and against the presence of καί (it is read by א A D *al*; it is lacking in 𝔓^{46vid} B 1739 *al*), is represented

---

[1] See also G. Zuntz, *The Text of the Epistles,* 1953, p. 163.

by the Committee in retaining the word but enclosing it within square
brackets.

9.2   ἄρτων

After ἄρτων several witnesses (B cop^fay eth^ro) add καὶ τὸ
χρυσοῦν θυμιατήριον, and in ver. 4, instead of χρουσοῦν ἔχουσα
θυμιατήριον καί, the same witnesses read only ἔχουσα. The
transposition was obviously made in order to remove the difficulty
concerning the author's statement regarding the location of the
golden altar of incense in the tabernacle.

9.10   βαπτισμοῖς, δικαιώματα {A}

The reading that best explains the origin of the other readings is
βαπτισμοῖς, δικαιώματα, which is supported by early and good
witnesses (including 𝔓^46 ℵ* A I P 33 81 1739 syr^p cop^sa, bo, fay vid
Origen). It is more probable that, in view of the preceding datives,
δικαιώματα was changed into δικαιώμασιν, and joined to them
by means of καί, than that καὶ δικαιώμασιν, if it were original,
was altered, on account of the concluding word ἐπικείμενα, into
δικαιώματα. The singular number δικαίωμα (D* it^d) is a mere
scribal oversight, and the reading βαπτισμοῖς καὶ δικαιώματα (ℵ^c
B 451 2492), which has the appearance of being a conflation, provides no satisfactory sense.

9.11   γενομένων {B}

Although both readings are well supported, on the whole γενομένων appears to have superior attestation on the score of age and
diversity of text type ((𝔓^46) B D* 1739 it^d syr^p, h, pal Origen al). The
presence of the expression τῶν μελλόντων ἀγαθῶν in 10.1, where
the text is firm, seems to have influenced copyists here.

9.14   αἰωνίου {A}

It was no doubt to be expected that, confronted with the rather
unexpected phrase πνεύματος αἰωνίου, copyists would replace the

adjective with ἁγίου, but there was no reason for their replacing ἁγίου with αἰωνίου.

9.14 ἡμῶν {C}

The external evidence for the two readings ἡμῶν (A D* K P 1739* al) and ὑμῶν (ℵ Dᶜ 33 81 1739ᶜ al) is rather evenly balanced. The former was preferred because the author uses the direct address only in the hortatory sections of his Epistle.

9.17 μήποτε {A}

Instead of μήποτε, three Greek manuscripts (ℵ* D* 075* ᵛⁱᵈ) read μὴ τότε, which then requires the reader to understand the sentence as a question ("… since it is not in force as long as the one who made it is alive, is it?"). In all three manuscripts, a later hand has changed τοτε to ποτε.

9.19 μόσχων [καὶ τῶν τράγων] {C}

Although the text without καὶ τῶν τράγων is supported by an impressive combination of witnesses (𝔓⁴⁶ ℵᶜ K L Ψ 181 1241 1739 syrᵖ· ʰ· ᵖᵃˡ Origen), a majority of the Committee thought it probable that the words had been omitted either accidentally (through homoeo-teleuton) or deliberately (to conform the statement to Ex 24.5). Since, however, it is possible that the shorter reading may have been ex-panded by copyists in imitation of ver. 12 διὰ αἵματος τράγων καὶ μόσχων (the sequence of which has influenced the reading of D 365 in the present passage), it was decided to enclose the words within square brackets in order to indicate a certain doubt that they belong there.

10.1 οὐκ αὐτήν {A}

The substitution of καί for οὐκ αὐτήν in the earliest known copy of the Epistle (𝔓⁴⁶) has produced an interesting reading, but one that certainly cannot be original, for the construction of the sentence implies a contrast between *εἰκών* and *σκιά*. The other readings, supported by individual minuscule manuscripts and the Armenian version, are scribal (or translational) idiosyncrasies.

10.1 *δύναται* {B}

Although the reading *δύνανται* (א A C D^{b} P 33 81 *al*) is strongly supported, it appears to have been introduced by copyists who were influenced by *προσφέρουσιν*. After some hesitation, partly because of the presence of other variant readings in the same verse, the Committee preferred *δύναται*, which is supported by 𝔓^{46} D$^{*, c}$ H K Ψ^{vid} 1739 *al.*

10.9 *ποιῆσαι*

After *ποιῆσαι* the Textus Receptus adds *ὁ θεός*, with א^{c} L* 81 104 206 462 489 913 919 1739 2127 vg syr$^{p, h \text{ with } *}$ *al.* This addition, which is clearly a secondary assimilation to ver. 7 and/or to the Septuagint text of Ps 39.9, is absent from 𝔓$^{13, 46}$ א* A C D K P 5 33 383 467 623 794 1319 2004 it^{d} syr^{htxt} cop$^{sa, bo, fay}$ eth.

10.11 *ἱερεύς* {A}

The reading *ἀρχιερεύς* (A C P 88 614 syr$^{p, h \text{ with } *}$ cop$^{sa, fay}$ arm eth) appears to be a correction introduced by copyists who recalled 5.1 or 8.3. In any case, the reading *ἱερεύς* is well supported by early and diverse witnesses (𝔓$^{13, 46}$ א D K Ψ 33 81 1739 it vg syr^{h} cop^{bo} Ephraem Chrysostom *al*).

10.34 *δεσμίοις* {B}

The reading that best explains the origin of the others is *δεσμίοις*, which is supported by good representatives of both the Alexandrian and the Western types of text, as well as by several Eastern witnesses (A D^{gr*} 33 (81) 1739 it$^{ar, b}$ vg syr$^{p, h, pal}$ cop$^{sa, bo}$ arm Ephraem *al*). Through transcriptional oversight the first iota was omitted, resulting in the reading *δεσμοῖς* (𝔓^{46} Ψ 104 Origen). Then, in order to improve the sense, copyists added a personal pronoun, either *αὐτῶν* it^{d, (r), z}), referring to those mentioned in ver. 33b, or *μου* (א D^c K P 88 614 *Byz Lect al*), in imitation of the statements in Php 1.7, 13, 14, 17; Col 4.18. The reading adopted for the text is confirmed by 13.3.

10.34 *ἑαυτούς* {A}

The reading *ἑαυτούς*, which is strongly attested by such Alexandrian and Western witnesses as 𝔓^{13, 46} א A H Ψ 33 81 1739 it vg *al*, was first altered to the dative *ἑαυτοῖς* (D^{gr} K 614 *Byz Lect al*), and this in turn was strengthened by prefixing *ἐν* (1 467 489 1881 *al*). By a curious oversight the pronoun is omitted entirely in P and perhaps in the original of cop^{sa, bo}.

10.38 *δίκαιός μου ἐκ πίστεως* {B}

Influenced by the citation of the same Old Testament quotation in Ro 1.17 and Ga 3.11, where Paul omits the personal pronoun *μου*, 𝔓¹³ and the majority of later witnesses (D^c H^c K P Ψ 81 614 *Byz Lect*), followed by the Textus Receptus, omit the word here. But it undoubtedly belongs in the text, being strongly supported by early and reliable witnesses. The only question, however, is where it belongs, some (𝔓⁴⁶ א A H* 33^{vid} 257 383 1175 1739 1831 1875 it^{ar, comp, r} vg cop^{sa} arm Clement *al*) placing it after *δίκαιος*, and others (D* 1518 1611 it^d syr^{p, h} Eusebius) placing it after *πίστεως*. (The same kind of variation occurs in the manuscripts of the Septuagint of Hab 2.4, where *πίστεώς μου* is read by א B Q W* [W is the Freer papyrus dating from the third century; W^c deletes *μου*], whereas A and the minuscules of the Catena magna read *δίκαιός μου*.) In view of the strong external support, the Committee preferred the reading *δίκαιός μου*.

11.1 *ὑπόστασις, πραγμάτων* {A}

The scribe of 𝔓¹³, a third or fourth century papyrus copy, thoughtlessly wrote *πραγμάτων ἀνάστασις*.[1]

---

[1] According to H. D. F. Sparks, the papyrus reads *ἀποστα[σις]*; see Wordsworth and White, *Novum Testamentum*, Part 2, fasc. vii (Oxford, 1941), p. 743, where a variety of Latin evidence is also cited.

11.11   πίστει καὶ αὐτὴ Σάρρα στεῖρα δύναμιν {C}

The difficulties of this verse are well known (for example, in Greek the expression δύναμιν εἰς καταβολὴν σπέρματος ἔλαβεν is regularly used of the male in begetting, not the female in conceiving) and have led some scholars (including F. Field, Windisch, Zuntz) to suggest that καὶ αὐτὴ Σάρρα στεῖρα is an early gloss that somehow got into the text. Appreciating the lexical difficulty, but unwilling to emend the text, a majority of the Committee understood the words καὶ αὐτὴ Σάρρα στεῖρα to be a Hebraic circumstantial clause,[2] thus allowing Ἀβραάμ (ver. 8) to serve as subject of ἔλαβεν ("by faith, even though Sarah was barren, he [Abraham] received power to beget …").

It is also possible to construe the words ΑΥΤΗ ϹΑΡΡΑ ϹΤΕΙΡΑ as a dative of accompaniment (in uncial script iotas subscript are ordinarily not indicated), so that the sentence runs, "By faith he [Abraham] also, together with barren Sarah, received power to beget…"[3]

A second problem involves στεῖρα, which is absent from several important witnesses (𝔓[13vid] ℵ A D^c 33 614 al). Although admitting that the word might have been added as an interpretative gloss in an ancestor of 𝔓[46] D* P Ψ 81 88 1739 it vg syr[p, h] al, a majority of the Committee regarded it as more likely that the word dropped out through transcriptional oversight (ϹΑΡΡΑϹΤΕΙΡΑ). It was agreed that ἡ (D^b vid 81 88 1739 Euthalius al) and οὖσα (P 104 436 1984 2127 al) are obviously secondary.

11.17   προσενήνοχεν Ἀβραὰμ τὸν Ἰσαὰκ πειραζόμενος

The evidence for the inclusion and for the position of the name Ἀβραάμ fluctuates curiously: (a) most witnesses read προσ-

---

[2] Cf. Matthew Black, "Critical and Exegetical Notes on Three New Testament Texts, Hebrews xi.11, Jude 5, James i.27," in *Apophoreta; Festschrift für Ernst Haenchen* (Berlin, 1964), pp. 41 ff. The discussion of He 11.11 is included also in Black's *Aramaic Approach to the Gospels and Acts,* 3rd ed. (Oxford, 1967), pp. 83–89.

[3] Commentators who prefer to take the words (with or without στεῖρα) as dative include E. Riggenbach, *Der Brief an die Hebraer* (Leipzig, 1913), pp. 356 ff.; O. Michel, *Der Brief an die Hebraer* (Göttingen, 1949), p. 262; and F. F. Bruce, *The Epistle to the Hebrews* (Grand Rapids, 1964), p. 302.

ἐνήνοχεν Ἀβραάμ ...; (b) a few Western witnesses (D it^d) read ... πειραζόμενος Ἀβραάμ; (c) 1912 reads Ἀβραάμ προσενήνο-χεν ...; (d) 1245 1611 arm read ... Ἀβραάμ πειραζόμενος; and (e) the name is omitted by 𝔓⁴⁶ Ψ 330 2005 syr^h Chrysostom.

On the one hand, if the name were not original, the fact that verses 13-16 constitute a parenthesis may have led copyists to insert it in ver. 17, which resumes the narrative concerning Abraham; the variety of positions of the name suggests that it is secondary. On the other hand, if the omission of the name is not accidental, copyists may have felt that the subject of ver. 17 was so obvious that Ἀβραάμ was unnecessary. In any case, the Committee did not see its way clear to disregard the weight of the mass of evidence supporting the reading adopted as text.

11.23 βασιλέως. {A}

After ver. 23, certain witnesses (chiefly Western) add the equiv-alent of a whole verse recounting an additional feat of Moses: Πίστει μέγας γενόμενος Μωϋσῆς ἀνεῖλεν τὸν Αἰγύπτιον κατανοῶν τὴν ταπείνωσιν τῶν ἀδελφῶν αὐτοῦ ("By faith Moses, when he was grown up, destroyed the Egyptian when he observed the humilia-tion of his brothers"). The interpolation, which is read by D* 1827 it^d vg^{mss}, was probably inspired by Ac 7.24 and/or Ex 2.11-12.

11.37 ἐπρίσθησαν {C}

The presence in most manuscripts of the rather general statement ἐπειράσθησαν ("they were tempted") amid the author's enumera-tion of different kinds of violent death has long been regarded by commentators as strange and unexpected. Many have suggested that ἐπειράσθησαν is the corruption of some other word more suitable to the context, or that it entered the text as the result of inadvertent scribal dittography of ἐπρίσθησαν. Among the conjectural emen-dations of ἐπειράσθησαν the following have been proposed (the name of the scholar who, it appears, first proposed it is enclosed within parentheses): ἐπρήσθησαν (Gataker), ἀνεπρήσθησαν (Lücke), ἐπυρώθησαν (Bezae, edd. 3, 4, 5), ἐπυράσθησαν (Junius and Piscator), ἐπυρίσθησαν (Sykes), all of which mean "they were burned"; ἐπάρθησαν (Bezae, edd. 1, 2), "they were pierced" (cf. Luther's "zerstochen"); ἐπηρώθησαν (Faber), "they were mutilated"; ἐπράσθησαν (le Moyne), "they were sold"; ἐσπειράσθησαν or ἐσπειράθησαν (Alberti), "they were strangled" or "they were broken on the wheel"; ἐπηρειάσθησαν (Reiske), "they were ill-treated"; ἐπέρθησαν (Kypke), "they were pierced through"; ἐπεράθησαν (Bryant), "they were stabbed"; ἐπειράθησαν (Wakefield), "they were impaled"; ἐσφαιρίσθησαν (reported by Griesbach), "they were broken on the wheel"; and even ἐταριχεύθησαν (Matthäi), "they were pickled"!

Several singular readings in individual manuscripts are due to carelessness and/or to itacistic confusion: thus D^gr* reads ἐπιράσθησαν, ἐπιράσθησαν *(sic)*, which stands for the aor. pass. ind. of πειράζω, and ms. 1923 reads ἐπρήσθησαν, ἐπειράσθησαν, of which ἐπρήσθησαν is an itacistic spelling of ἐπρίσθησαν ("they were burned").

With some hesitation, but partly on the strength of the uncertain position of ἐπειράσθησαν in the witnesses (sometimes standing before ἐπρίσθησαν, sometimes after it),[4] the Committee decided to adopt the shorter reading preserved in 𝔓^46 1241 1984 *l*^44, 53 syr^p (cop^sa) eth^ro, pp Origen^gr2/7, lat Eusebius Acacius Ephraem Jerome Socrates Ps-Augustine Theophylact, and to print only ἐπρίσθησαν.

12.1 εὐπερίστατον {A}

The reading εὐπερίσπαστον ("easily distracting"), which occurs in 𝔓^46 and 1739 (and perhaps lies behind it^d, z), is either a palaeographical error or a deliberate modification of εὐπερίστατον, which is supported by all the other known witnesses.

12.3 εἰς ἑαυτόν {C}

Although external evidence strongly favors either εἰς ἑαυτούς (ℵ* D^gr* syr^p Ephraem) or εἰς αὐτούς (𝔓^13, 46 ℵ^b Ψ^c 048 33 1739*

---

[4] For a discussion of textual problems in the passage, see G. Zuntz, *The Text of the Epistles,* 1953, pp. 47 f.

Origen *al*), the difficulty of making sense of the plural led a majority of the Committee to prefer the singular number, choosing εἰς ἑαυτόν as the least inadequately supported reading (A P 104 326 1241 John-Damascus). Several versions handle the passage freely, it^d reading *in vobis* and cop^{sa} arm omitting the phrase entirely.

[The plural is the qualitatively best supported and the more difficult (though meaningful) reading, and the one more likely to be altered. A.W.]

12.18 ψηλαφωμένῳ {B}

External evidence strongly supports the reading ψηλαφωμένῳ without ὄρει (𝔓⁴⁶ ℵ A C 048 33 (81) vg syr^p cop^{sa, bo} eth *al*). Moreover, the diversity of position of ὄρει in the witnesses that read the word (it stands before ψηλαφωμένῳ in 69 255 462 syr^h, and after it in D^{gr} K P Ψ 88 614 1739 *Byz Lect*) suggests that it is a scribal gloss derived from ver. 22.

13.15 δι' αὐτοῦ *[οὖν]* {C}

Although most witnesses include οὖν (ℵ^c A C D² K 056 0121b 0142 81 88 614 1739 most minuscules vg syr^h cop^{sa, bo} arm eth *al*), it is absent from several early and important witnesses (𝔓⁴⁶ ℵ* D* P Ψ (it^d) syr^p). It is difficult to decide whether copyists added the word, which seems to be needed at this point, or whether it was accidentally omitted in transcription (ΑΥΤΟΥΟΥΑΝΑ-). In order to reflect the balance of probabilities a majority of the Committee decided to include the word in the text, but to enclose it within square brackets.

13.21 παντὶ ἀγαθῷ {A}

After παντί the Textus Receptus, in company with C D^c K M P almost all minuscules and syr^{p, h} cop^{sa} eth *al,* adds ἔργῳ, an obvious homiletic gloss. If the word had been present originally, no good reason can account for its absence from 𝔓⁴⁶ ℵ D* Ψ it^{ar, b, d} vg cop^{bo} *al*. The singular reading παντὶ ἔργῳ καὶ λόγῳ ἀγαθῷ, in codex A, is from 2 Th 2.17.

13.21 ποιῶν

Although the reading αὐτῷ ποιῶν is strongly attested (ℵ* A C 33* 81 1739ᵐᵍ copˢᵃ), the Committee was disposed to regard the unintelligible pronoun as a dittograph of the preceding αὐτοῦ (as also αὐτό in 𝔓⁴⁶).[1] The reading αὐτὸς ποιῶν (451 2492 itᵈ, ⁶⁵) may be a homiletic expansion. The shorter reading ποιῶν, which was preferred by the Committee, is supported by ℵᶜ Dᵍʳ K P Ψ 88 614 1739* *Byz Lect* it⁶¹ vg syrᵖ, ʰ copˢᵃᵐˢ, ᵇᵒᵐˢ arm *al.*

13.21 ἡμῖν {A}

In view of the preceding ὑμᾶς it is easy to understand why ἡμῖν, which is strongly supported by 𝔓⁴⁶ ℵ A Dᵍʳ K M 33 81 614 1739 syrᵖ copˢᵃ, ᵇᵒ arm *al,* was altered to ὑμῖν (C P Ψ 88 itᵈ, ⁶¹, ⁶⁵ vg syrʰ eth *al*).

13.21 [τῶν αἰώνων] {C}

The phrase εἰς τοὺς αἰῶνας τῶν αἰώνων, which occurs only here in the Epistle to the Hebrews, is attested in all manuscripts in 1 Tm 1.17; 2 Tm 4.18, and in eleven of its twelve occurrences in Revelation. In the doxologies in Ga 1.5; Php 4.20; 1 Pe 4.11; 5.11; and Re 1.6 the words τῶν αἰώνων are omitted by several (mostly later) manuscripts. In He 5.6; 6.20; 7.17, and 21 (all quoting Ps 110.4 [= LXX 109.4]) we find the short form εἰς τὸν αἰῶνα, as also in 2 Cor 9.9 (where F G K 1739 *al* expand by adding τῶν αἰώνων) and 1 Pe 1.25. None of these instances of the short form occurs in a doxology. A quasi-doxology in He 13.8 reads εἰς τοὺς αἰῶνας, with no variations (except the addition of ἀμήν in D* itᵈ).

In view of these data it is difficult to decide whether copyists, influenced by familiarity with the longer form in doxologies elsewhere in the New Testament as well as in current liturgical usage, added τῶν αἰώνων (ℵ A (C*) K P 33 81 614 1739 itᵃʳ, ᵇ, ᶜᵒᵐᵖ, ᶻ vg syrᵖ copˢᵃᵐˢˢ, ᵇᵒ eth *al*), or whether other copyists, either through careless-

---

[1] For a discussion of the dittograph, see G. Zuntz, *The Text of the Epistles,* 1953, p. 62.

ness or in imitation of εἰς τοὺς αἰῶνας in He 13.8, omitted τῶν
αἰώνων (𝔓⁴⁶ C³ Dᵍʳ Ψ 1241 *Lect* syrʰ copˢᵃᵐˢˢ arm *al*). On the whole
the Committee was disposed to prefer the shorter text as original, yet
because of the weight of such witnesses as ℵ A (C*) 33 614 1739 *al,*
it was decided to retain the words τῶν αἰώνων, but to enclose them
within square brackets as an indication that they might well be a
gloss.

13.25 πάντων ὑμῶν. {A}

The later liturgical use of the concluding words ("Grace be with all
of you") must have made it difficult for scribes not to add ἀμήν when
copying the epistle. Several important witnesses, however, including
𝔓⁴⁶ ℵ* Iᵛⁱᵈ 33 vgᵐˢ copˢᵃ arm, have resisted the intrusion. Instead of
ὑμῶν ms. 1241 reads ἡμῶν, and Dᵍʳ* reads τῶν ἁγίων.

13.25 *Subscription*

(*a*) The subscription in ℵ C 33 is πρὸς Ἑβραίους. Other subscriptions include the following: (*b*) πρὸς Ἑβραίους ἐγράφη ἀπὸ
Ῥώμης A; (*c*) πρὸς Ἑβραίους ἐγράφη ἀπὸ Ἰταλίας P 1908;
(*d*) πρὸς Ἑβραίους ἐγράφη ἀπὸ (460 Euthaliusᵐˢ add τῆς)
Ἰταλίας διὰ Τιμοθέου K 102 460 1923 Euthaliusᵐˢ, followed by the
Textus Receptus; (*e*) ἡ πρὸς Ἑβραίους ἐπιστολὴ ἐγράφη ἀπὸ
Ἰταλίας διὰ Τιμοθέου 425 464 *al*; (*f*) Παύλου ἀποστόλου
ἐπιστολὴ πρὸς Ἑβραίους ἐγράφη ἀπὸ Ἰταλίας διὰ Τιμοθέου
404 *al*; (*g*) as (*f*) but instead of ἀπὸ Ἰταλίας it reads ἀπὸ Ἀθηνῶν·
ἄλλοι δέ· ἀπ' Ἰταλίας 1911; (*h*) ἡ πρὸς Ἑβραίους αὕτη
ἐπιστολὴ ἐγράφη ἀπὸ Ἰταλίας διὰ Τιμοθέου τοῦ ἀποστόλου
τοῦ καὶ εἰς αὐτοὺς πεμφθέντος διὰ τοῦ μακαρίου Παύλου ἵν'
αὐτοὺς διορθώσηται 431; (*i*) as (*h*) but after ἐγράφη add
Ἑβραϊστί 104.

THE LETTER OF JAMES

1.3   δοκίμιον {A}

In the context δοκίμιον in its usual meaning ("a means or instrument of testing") gives somewhat less than satisfactory sense; what is needed is an adjective (used as a substantive) meaning "that which is approved, or genuine." This last is supplied by the word δόκιμον, which is read by several witnesses (110 431 1241). It should also be noted that according to evidence from the Greek papyri in koine Greek δοκίμιον was sometimes used as the neuter of an adjective (= δόκιμον). (See also the comment on 1 Pe 1.7.)

1.12   ἐπηγγείλατο {A}

In the style of rabbinical writings, where the word "God" is sometimes to be supplied mentally, the earlier and better witnesses (𝔓²³ ℵ A B Ψ 81 206* 323 it^ff cop^{sa, bo} arm) support the reading ἐπηγγείλατο, without a subject being expressed. Later witnesses, however, fill out what may have seemed to be a lacuna by adding either κύριος (C 1829 *l*⁶⁸⁰) or ὁ κύριος (K L P most minuscules syr^h) or ὁ θεός (33^vid 322 323 463 547 945 1241 1739 2492 vg syr^p eth).

1.17   παραλλαγὴ ἢ τροπῆς ἀποσκίασμα {B}

The obscurity of the passage has led to the emergence of a variety of readings. The reading of ℵ* B (παραλλαγὴ η τροπῆς ἀποσκιάσματος) makes sense only if η is read ἥ ("variation which is of [i. e. consists in, or belongs to] the turning of the shadow") – although even so the expression is excessively turgid. Taking η as ἤ the other witnesses read either the genitive before and after ἤ (παραλλαγῆς ἢ τροπῆς ἀποσκιάσματος 𝔓²³) or the nominative (in a variety of variant readings) before and after ἤ. In the opinion of the Committee the least unsatisfactory reading is παραλλαγὴ ἢ τροπῆς ἀποσκίασμα, supported by ℵ^c A C K P 81 1739 *Byz Lect* vg syr^{p, h} arm *al.* The Sahidic seeks to avoid the difficulties by taking each noun separately: "[there is not any] shadow or change or variation [literally, declining]." At the close of the verse several minuscules (876 1518 1610 1765 2138) add the gloss οὐδὲ μέχρι ὑπονοίας τινὸς ὑποβολὴ ἀποσκιάσματος ("not even the least suspicion of a shadow").

1.19 ἴστε, ἀδελφοί μου ἀγαπητοί· ἔστω δέ {B}

Instead of reading the abrupt ἴστε, the Textus Receptus connects the following ἔστω (dropping δέ) more closely with ver. 18 by substituting ὥστε, in company with a variety of later witnesses (K P² Ψ 614 *Byz* syr^{p, h} *al*). The reading adopted as the text is strongly supported by both Alexandrian and Western witnesses (ℵ^c B C (81) 1739 it^{ff} vg *al*).

1.27 ἄσπιλον ἑαυτὸν τηρεῖν

Instead of the text that is supported by the overwhelming bulk of the witnesses, 𝔓⁷⁴ reads ὑπερασπίζειν αὐτούς ("to protect themselves"). The plural is also read by several minuscules (ἀσπίλους ἑαυτοὺς τηρεῖτε 614 1505 2412 2495).

2.3 ἐκεῖ ἢ κάθου {B}

The reading which, in the opinion of a majority of the Committee, best explains the origin of the others is that supported by A C* Ψ 33 81 614 630 2495 vg syr^h *al*: Σὺ στῆθι ἐκεῖ ἢ κάθου ("'Stand there' or 'Sit [by my footstool]'"). Obviously secondary (though it supports the position of ἐκεῖ after στῆθι) is ἐκεῖ ἢ κάθου ὧδε (𝔓⁷⁴ᵛⁱᵈ ℵ C² K P 049 056 0142 most minuscules syr^p *al*), where ὧδε creates a better parallelism and expresses explicitly what is otherwise implied – namely, that the place ὑπὸ τὸ ὑποπόδιόν μου is thought of as nearer the speaker than the place indicated by the command στῆθι ἐκεῖ. Not recognizing this, B and several other witnesses (including 1739) transposed ἐκεῖ so as to produce a parallelism of two (rather than three) references to places.

2.19 εἷς ἐστιν ὁ θεός {B}

Among the several readings the chief difference turns on the presence or absence of the article: B 614 630 1875 2412 2495 *al* read εἷς θεός ἐστιν ("There is one God"; compare εἷς ἐστιν θεός 945 1241 1739 *al,* and the singular reading of Ψ), whereas the other readings involve ὁ θεός standing either before or after the verb ("God is one"). The reading εἷς ὁ θεός ἐστιν (C 33ᵛⁱᵈ 81 syrʰ *al*) and still more the reading εἷς θεός ἐστιν can be suspected of having been assimilated to the style of the Christian kerygma (1 Cor 8.6; Eph 4.6; 1 Tm 2.5). On the other hand εἷς ἐστιν ὁ θεός (𝔓⁷⁴ ℵ A (945 1241 1739 omit ὁ) 2464 vg syrᵖ copˢᵃ, ᵇᵒ) is in conformity with the prevailing formula of Jewish orthodoxy. Clearly secondary is the reading of the Textus Receptus, ὁ θεὸς εἷς ἐστιν (Kᵐᵍ 049 056 0142 88 436 *Byz Lect al*), in which ὁ θεός is placed first in order to give it a more emphatic position.

2.20 ἀργή {B}

Instead of ἀργή the Textus Receptus reads νεκρά, with ℵ A C² K P Ψ 614 1241 *Byz Lect* syrᵖ, ʰ copᵇᵒ *al*. Since there is considerable suspicion that scribes may have introduced the latter word from either ver. 17 or 26, the Committee preferred ἀργή, which not only is strongly supported by B C* 322 323 945 1739 itᶠᶠ vg copˢᵃ arm, but may also involve a subtle play on words (ἔργων ἀργή [ἀ + ἐργή]). The singular error of 𝔓⁷⁴ (κενή) was suggested by the preceding κενέ.

2.25 ἀγγέλους {A}

So that readers would not mistakenly understand ἀγγέλους as "angels," various witnesses (C L 945 1241 1739 *al*) replaced it with κατασκόπους ("spies," also found in He 11.31) or added τοῦ Ἰσραήλ (61 syrʰ ᵐᵍ).

3.3 εἰ δέ {C}

The itacistic confusion between ει and ι being extremely common, it is possible that a copyist wrote ιδε but meant ει δε, or vice versa (see Moulton-Howard, *Grammar,* pp. 76 f.). The editor must therefore choose the reading that, in his judgment, is most appropriate in the context. Accordingly, a majority of the Committee preferred εἰ δέ as the more difficult reading, and explained the rise of ἴδε partly as the result of itacism and partly in harmonization with ἰδού in verses 4 and 5. The Textus Receptus assimilates to ἰδού, with 36 483 1874 1877.

3.8 ἀκατάστατον {B}

Instead of characterizing the tongue as a "restless (ἀκατάστατον)" evil (ℵ A B K P 1739* *al*), other witnesses of somewhat less weight (C Ψ and most minuscules) describe it as an "uncontrollable (ἀκατάσχετον)" evil. Since the latter involves a more commonplace description, it probably arose through scribal adjustment.

3.9 κύριον {A}

Instead of κύριον, the Textus Receptus reads θεόν, with K L most of the minuscules vg syr^h cop^{sa, bo} *al*. The reading κύριον is to be preferred (*a*) because the combination "Lord and Father" is unusual (it occurs nowhere else in the Bible) and would more likely be changed to "God and Father" than vice versa, and (*b*) because the external evidence supporting κύριον is decidedly superior (ℵ A B C P 33 623 1739 1852 it^{ff} vg^{ms} syr^p cop^{bomss} arm *al*).

3.12 οὔτε ἁλυκόν {B}

Many witnesses, including ℵ C² K L P 049 056 0142 81 104 1739 it^{ff} vg syr^{p, h with *} cop^{bo} *al,* add οὕτως before the negative. Since, however, it was natural for copyists to add such a word to enhance the comparison, and since it is absent from such early and important witnesses as A B C* 88 2492^{txt} syr^h cop^{sa} arm, the Committee preferred the shorter reading. Still less likely to be original is the expansion in the Textus Receptus, which after οὕτως continues οὐδεμία πηγὴ ἁλυκὸν καί, with K (P) 049 056 0142 104 614 917.

4.4 μοιχαλίδες {A}

In scriptural imagery, μοιχαλίς ("adulteress") is used figuratively of Israel as the unfaithful spouse of Jehovah (cf. Ps 73.27; Is 54.5; Jr 3.20; Eze 16 and 23; Ho 9.1; and similarly in the New Testament Mt 12.39; 16.4; Mk 8.38). When copyists, however, understood the word here in its literal sense, they were puzzled why only women were mentioned and therefore considered it right to add a reference to men as well. The shorter reading is strongly testified by both Alexandrian and Western witnesses (ℵ* A B 33 81 1241 1739 it^{ff} vg syr^p cop$^{sa, bo}$ arm eth).

4.5 κατῴκισεν {B}

The two verbal forms, which, because of itacism, were pronounced alike, have slightly different meanings: κατῴκισεν is causative ("the spirit which he [God] has made to dwell in us"), whereas κατῴκησεν is intransitive ("the spirit [or, Spirit] which dwells[1] in us"). On the score of external evidence κατῴκισεν is somewhat better attested ($\mathfrak{P}^{74}$ ℵ A B Ψ 049 104 226 241 462 547 807 1241 1739 1877*) than κατῴκησεν (K L P 056 0142 most minuscules and all versions – most of which, however, could not easily represent the causative idea). On the score of transcriptional probability, since κατοικίζειν occurs nowhere else in the New Testament, copyists were more likely to replace it with the much more common κατοικεῖν, than vice versa.

---

[1] The present tense "dwelleth" of the margin of the ASV, as well as the text of the AV and sixteenth century English versions, is derived by understanding the aorist κατῴκησεν (literally, "he dwelt") in the sense "has taken up [his] dwelling." For another interpretation of the verse see Johann Michl, "Der Spruch Jakobusbrief 4,5," in *Neutestamentliche Aufsätze. Festschrift für Prof. Josef Schmid,* ed. J. Blinzler *et al.* (Regensburg, 1963), pp. 167–174.

4.12 [ὁ] (1) {C}

Because manuscript evidence for and against the inclusion of ὁ before νομοθέτης is rather evenly balanced, with no compelling considerations arising from either palaeography or syntax, the Committee retained the article but enclosed it within square brackets.

4.14 τὸ τῆς αὔριον {B}

Of the several readings, τὰ τῆς αὔριον, though supported by several good witnesses (A P 33 81 1739 *al*), is suspect as a scribal assimilation to Pr 27.1; and, in view of a certain tendency of B to omit the article, the reading τῆς αὔριον cannot be confidently regarded as original. The remaining reading, τὸ τῆς αὔριον, is supported by a wide diversity of witnesses (ℵ K Ψ most minuscules vg syrᵖ arm *al*).

4.14 ποία {B}

Although the reading with γάρ is widespread (𝔓⁷⁴ᵛⁱᵈ ℵᶜ A K L P Ψ 049 056 most minuscules vg syrᵖ copᵇᵒ *al*), the connective appears to have been inserted (perhaps under the influence of the following clause) in order to prevent ambiguity (ποία may introduce an independent question, or may depend upon ἐπίστασθε). The reading ποία is adequately supported by ℵ* B 614 itˢ⁷ syrʰ copᵇᵒᵐˢ arm ethʳᵒ.

4.14 ἀτμὶς γάρ ἐστε ἡ {C}

The connective γάρ, seeming to interrupt the sense after the preceding question, was omitted in A 33 *al*. Although several important witnesses (including B and 1739) lack the article, the Committee considered it more probable that scribes would have accidentally omitted ἡ than added it. Since in later Greek αι and ε were pronounced alike, either ἔσται or ἔστε may have originated through itacistic corruption of the other; the evidence for the two together far outweighs that supporting ἔστιν. As between the second person ἔστε and the third person ἔσται, not only does external evidence on the whole favor the former reading, but it is probable that copyists would tend to prefer the third person in the reply to a question. The omission of ἀτμὶς γάρ ἐστε in ℵ seems to be the result of accidental oversight on the part of the scribe.

5.4   ἀπεστερημένος {A}

The manuscripts present three readings, ἀφυστερημένος (ℵ B*) and two forms of ἀποστερεῖν, the perfect tense, ἀπεστερημένος (A B² P Ψ *al*), and the present tense, ἀποστερήμενος (K L *al*). A majority of the Committee preferred to read ἀπεστερημένος.

[The earliest reading appears to be the rare word ἀφυστερημένος, which copyists emended to a more familiar word. B.M.M.]

5.7   λάβῃ {B}

Since the reading λάβῃ πρόϊμον καὶ ὄψιμον, which is strongly supported by representatives of both the Alexandrian and the Western types of text (𝔓⁷⁴ B 048 1739 vg copˢᵃ), was ambiguous, copyists added what was regarded as an appropriate noun. Thus, in accord with the consistent usage of the Septuagint, ὑετόν is read by A K L P Ψ most minuscules syrᵖˑʰ *al*. Several other witnesses (ℵ 255 398 1175 itff syrʰᵐᵍ (copᵇᵒ) Cassiodorus Antiochus), perhaps not being acquainted with the climate of Palestine and the great importance of the early and the late rain, introduce καρπόν from the previous clause, thus implying that the subject of λάβῃ is "he," i. e. the farmer.

5.14   τοῦ κυρίου {A}

The reading τοῦ κυρίου is supported by the broadest spectrum of witnesses, whereas the omission of τοῦ by A Ψ 81 *al*, and of τοῦ κυρίου by B, probably arose through inadvertence in transcription. The readings Ἰησοῦ Χριστοῦ (6) and τοῦ κυρίου Ἰησοῦ (*l*¹³⁵⁶) are scribal glosses.

5.16   εὔχεσθε

Not counting the present passage, εὔχεσθαι occurs in the New Testament six times; προσεύχεσθαι occurs 85 times. Although *προσεύχεσθαι* appears four other times in this chapter without noteworthy variation among the witnesses, in the present passage the Committee preferred to follow ℵ K P Ψ 056 0142 and most minuscules, which read *εὔχεσθε,* and regarded *προσεύχεσθε,* found in A (B *προσεύχεσθαι*) 048[vid] and a few minuscules, as the result of scribal conformation to the customary Christian usage.

5.20   *γινωσκέτω ὅτι* {B}

The reading *γινώσκετε,* read by B 69 1505 1518 2495 syr[h] eth, appears to be an amelioration, having been introduced either in order to conform to the address (*ἀδελφοί μου,* ver. 19), or in order to avoid the ambiguity of who is to be regarded (the converter or the converted) as the subject of the verb.

5.20   *αὐτοῦ ἐκ θανάτου* {C}

The reading that seems best able to account for the origin of the others is *ψυχὴν αὐτοῦ ἐκ θανάτου,* which is well supported by important witnesses (ℵ A 33 vg). Perplexed by the ambiguity of *ψυχὴν αὐτοῦ* (is it the soul of the converter or of the converted?), scribes either (*a*) transferred *αὐτοῦ* to follow *ἐκ θανάτου* ("from death itself" 𝔓[74] B 614 1108 1611 1852 2138 it[ff]) or (*b*) omitted it entirely (K L Ψ 049 056 0142 most minuscules).

[The reading of 𝔓[74] B *al* seems preferable. Non-recognition of the intensive use of *αὐτός* could explain the omission or transposition. In this position, also, omission might easily be accidental in some witnesses. A.W.]

5.20   *ἁμαρτιῶν.*

After *ἁμαρτιῶν* several of the later witnesses (181 378 614 1518 1765 1898 syr[h]) add *ἀμήν,* and one (330) adds *ὅτι αὐτῷ ἡ δόξα εἰς τοὺς αἰῶνας· ἀμήν.*

THE FIRST LETTER OF PETER

1.7 δοκίμιον {A}

The word δοκίμιον, which in classical Greek meant "a means or instrument of testing," in koine Greek came to be used as an adjective equivalent in meaning to δόκιμον "approved, genuine." Of the two readings here the Committee preferred δοκίμιον, which is supported by all uncials and almost all minuscules. The variant δόκιμον is read by 𝔓[72, 74] 23 56 69 206 429. (See also the comment on Jas 1.3.)

1.8 ἰδόντες {A}

The reading ἰδόντες, which is supported by good witnesses of both the Alexandrian and the Western types of text (𝔓[72] ℵ B C 1739 it[r] vg cop[sa]), is more appropriate in the context than εἰδότες (A K P Ψ 33 81 614 *al*), which seems to have arisen either accidentally (ει and ι being confused through itacism, coupled with the failure of copyists to observe the stroke [representing ν] over the ο), or deliberately (in order to avoid what on the surface seemed to be a pleonasm with μὴ ὁρῶντες).

1.9 [ὑμῶν] {C}

Because in later Greek the vowels η and υ came to be pronounced alike, scribes would sometimes write ὑμῶν when they meant to write ἡμῶν, and vice versa. Since the context of this section in 1 Peter employs the second person plural, the Committee preferred the reading ὑμῶν. Nevertheless, because B and several other witnesses lack the pronoun altogether, the Committee considered it advisable to enclose ὑμῶν within square brackets.

1.12 [ἐν] πνεύματι {C}

On the one hand, the prevailing usage in 1 Peter (as also elsewhere in the New Testament) favors the reading ἐν, attested by ℵ C K P and most other witnesses. On the other hand, in view of the absence of the word from such early and important witnesses as 𝔓⁷² A B Ψ 33 *al* a majority of the Committee thought it necessary to enclose the word within square brackets.

[The reading without ἐν is to be preferred on the basis of (*a*) superior external evidence, (*b*) the tendency of scribes to add ἐν in conformity to the usual expression elsewhere, and (*c*) the absence of any good reason that would account for the omission of the preposition. B.M.M. and A.W.]

1.19-20   Χριστοῦ, προεγνωσμένου

Between verses 19 and 20 several Latin witnesses (vg^mss Bede) insert the equivalent of another verse: *ipse ergo qui et praecognitus est ante constitutionem mundi et novissimo tempore natus et passus est ipse accepit gloriam quam deus verbum semper possedit sine initio manens in patre* ("He himself therefore, who was also known before the foundation of the world and at the last time was born and suffered, received the glory that God the Word always possessed, abiding without beginning in the Father").

1.21   πιστούς

A majority of the Committee preferred the more striking expression πιστούς, preserved in A B 398 vg, and regarded πιστεύοντας (read by the overwhelming mass of witnesses) and πιστεύσαντας (33 *al*) as scribal assimilations to much more commonplace ways of expressing the idea.

1.22   ἀληθείας {A}

After ἀληθείας the Textus Receptus, following the later uncials (K P 049 056 0142) and most minuscules, adds the phrase διὰ πνεύματος. These words, whose absence from such early and good witnesses as 𝔓⁷² ℵ A B C Ψ 33 1739 *al* cannot easily be explained if they were present originally, appear to be a theological expansion introduced by a copyist. In the West several Old Latin manuscripts and the Vulgate replaced ἀληθείας with *caritatis* ("charity"), and one witness (Speculum) expanded with *fidei per spiritum* ("faith through the Spirit").

1.22 ἐκ [καθαρᾶς] καρδίας {C}

On the strength of 𝔓⁷² ℵ* C 81 614, a majority of the Committee preferred the reading ἐκ καθαρᾶς καρδίας, but, in view of the absence of the adjective from A B vg, thought it best to enclose καθαρᾶς within square brackets. The singular reading καρδίας ἀληθινῆς (ℵᶜ) may have arisen through confusion with the following ἀλλήλους.

1.23 μένοντος

After μένοντος the Textus Receptus, in company with K L P most minuscules vg syrᵖ eth, adds εἰς τὸν αἰῶνα. The phrase, which is an intrusion from ver. 25, is absent from a wide variety of representative types of text (𝔓⁷² ℵ A B C 33 322 323 424ᶜ 436 618 1739 1852 2138 vgᵐˢˢ syrʰ copˢᵃ, ᵇᵒ arm Didymus Cyril Jerome).

1.24 αὐτῆς

Instead of αὐτῆς (𝔓⁷² ℵᶜ (-του ℵ*) A B C 206 614 1739 1873 2298 vg syrᵖ, ʰ cop⁽ˢᵃ⁾, ᵇᵒ eth Origen Didymus), the Textus Receptus, following the later uncials (K L P Ψ) and most minuscules, substitutes ἀνθρώπου, thus assimilating the quotation to the Septuagint text of Is 40.6.

2.2 εἰς σωτηρίαν

The Textus Receptus, following L and most minuscules, omits εἰς σωτηρίαν either through an oversight in copying (ειc … ειε) or because the idea of "growing into salvation" was theologically unacceptable.

2.3 εἰ {B}

The reading εἰ, supported by early representatives of the Alexandrian type of text ($\mathfrak{P}^{72}$ ℵ* A B), was improved stylistically in later witnesses by using the more subtle εἴπερ (ℵᶜ C K P Ψ 81 614 1739 vg syrʰ), which among New Testament authors occurs only in Paul.

2.5 εἰς

The Textus Receptus, along with the later uncials (K L P) and most minuscules, omits εἰς, probably because its presence seemed to imply that the Christians were not already priests (compare ver. 9). Its right to be in the text is strongly attested by $\mathfrak{P}^{72}$ ℵ A B C 5 88 307 322 323 424ᶜ 436 441 467 623 915 1739 1852 Origen Eusebius Cyril *al.*

2.19 χάρις {B}

In order to identify more precisely the idea conveyed by χάρις, scribes have added various supplements, παρὰ τῷ θεῷ in C (Ψ 33 omit τῷ) 1739 *al*, θεῷ in 2464, and θεοῦ in 623.

2.19 θεοῦ {B}

The difficulty of interpreting the expression διὰ συνείδησιν θεοῦ, a collocation that occurs only here in the New Testament, prompted copyists to introduce one or another alleviation. In accord with Ac 23.1; 1 Tm 1.5, 19 some witnesses (C 94 206 322 323 424ᶜ 614 915 1175 1518 1739 2298 syrᵖ·ʰ) replace θεοῦ with ἀγαθήν. In other witnesses the two readings are conflated, producing θεοῦ ἀγαθήν (A* Ψ 33) and ἀγαθὴν θεοῦ ($\mathfrak{P}^{72}$ 81). The reading θεοῦ is strongly supported by ℵ A² B K L P most minuscules vg copˢᵃ· ᵇᵒ eth John-Damascus.

2.21 ἔπαθεν {A}

The reading ἔπαθεν, which is strongly supported by $\mathfrak{P}^{72}$ A B Cᵛⁱᵈ 33 81 614 1739 itᵃʳ· ᵗ· ᶻ vg syrʰ copˢᵃ· ᵇᵒ· ᶠᵃʸ ᵛⁱᵈ, was replaced in other witnesses (including א‎ Ψ 209* 2127 syrᵖ arm) by ἀπέθανεν, probably under the influence of the variant reading in 3.18.

2.21 ὑμῶν ὑμῖν {A}

Both external evidence and transcriptional probabilities join in favoring ὑμῶν ὑμῖν as the original reading. Supported by representatives of both the Alexandrian and the Western types of text (𝔓⁷² א‎ A B C 81 itᵃʳ, ʷ, ᶻ vg syrʰ), the reading was altered by copyists either because of carelessness (having confused ὑ and ἡ, which were pronounced alike), or because reference to the work of Christ as an example to the readers alone seemed to be too limited.

2.25 πλανώμενοι {B}

The external evidence for each reading is fairly evenly balanced (-μενοι, א‎ A B 1505 2464 al; -μενα, 𝔓⁷² C Ψ and most minuscules), but in transcription the tendency to change to the neuter form was very natural in view of the word πρόβατα immediately preceding.

3.1 [αἱ] {C}

The weight of external evidence is rather evenly balanced for and against the presence of the article, which perhaps was omitted by scribes in order to indicate more clearly that γυναῖκες is vocative. On the basis of 𝔓⁷² א²‎ C Ψ 33 1739 al, the Committee decided to include the article; in view of its absence, however, from 𝔓⁸¹ א*‎ A B 81 al, the word was enclosed within square brackets.

3.7 συγκληρονόμοις {B}

Of the two chief readings (συγκληρονόμος 2127 can be disregarded as a scribal idiosyncrasy) the external support for συγκληρονόμοις appears to be slightly stronger (𝔓⁷² אᶜ‎ (א*‎ συγκληρονόμους) Bᶜ (B* συνκληρονόμοις) 33 1739 itᵃʳ, ᵗ vg syrᵖ arm eth (Speculum)) than that for συγκληρονόμοι (A C K P Ψ 81 614 Byz Lect syrʰ). If one adopts the dative, the reference of the clause ὡς ... ζωῆς is to the wives; if the nominative, the reference is to the husbands.[1] The transition in sense from the singular τῷ γυναικείῳ σκεύει to the plural συγκληρονόμοις may have seemed harsh to copyists, who therefore preferred the nominative. Actually, however, the transition is not unnatural, and the dative is more in harmony with the structure of the sentence and the thought (for the presence of καί seems to favor taking the two clauses as co-ordinate).

3.7   χάριτος ζωῆς {A}

Several witnesses (including ℵ A C² al) have added ποικίλης from 4.10, where the epithet is natural and appropriate.

3.8   ταπεινόφρονες {A}

Instead of ταπεινόφρονες, the Textus Receptus, following later manuscripts, reads φιλόφρονες ("courteous"). In a few witnesses (including L and some editions of the Vulgate) both words stand side by side – obviously a growing text.

3.14   μηδὲ ταραχθῆτε {A}

A few witnesses (𝔓⁷² B L) lack μηδὲ ταραχθῆτε because the eye of the copyist passed from φοβηΘΗΤΕ to ταραχΘΗΤΕ, omitting what lies between.

3.15   τὸν Χριστόν {A}

In place of Χριστόν the Textus Receptus substitutes θεόν, with the later uncials (K L P) and most minuscules. The reading Χριστόν, however, is strongly supported by early and diversified external evidence (𝔓⁷² ℵ A B C Ψ 33 614 1739 itᵃʳ vg syrᵖ, ʰ copˢᵃ, ᵇᵒ arm Clement), as well as by transcriptional probability, the more

---

[1] The substantive συγκληρονόμος, being derived from an adjective of two termi-nations, is both masculine and feminine.

familiar expression (κύριον τὸν θεόν) replacing the less usual expression (κύριον τὸν Χριστόν). The omission of τὸν Χριστόν in the patristic treatise *de Promissionibus* attributed to Quodvultdeus must be due to accidental oversight on the part of either translator or copyist.

3.16 καταλαλεῖσθε {A}

Although the shorter reading καταλαλεῖσθε is supported chiefly by Egyptian (Alexandrian) witnesses, including 𝔓⁷² B Ψ 614 cop^sa Clement, it is to be preferred on transcriptional grounds, for recollection of the writer's earlier statement ἐν ᾧ καταλαλοῦσιν ὑμῶν ὡς κακοποιῶν (2.12) undoubtedly prompted copyists to modify the shorter reading by adding ὡς κακοποιῶν (syr^h with * cop^bo?) or by altering the person of the verb and adding ὑμῶν (vg arm (Speculum)) or ὑμῶν ὡς κακοποιῶν (ℵ A C K P 049 33 81 *Lect* it⁶⁵ syr^p, hmg cop^bo? eth *al*).

3.18 περὶ ἁμαρτιῶν ἔπαθεν {B}

The bewildering diversity of readings can be listed in connection with the variation involving the accompanying verb. Followed by ἔπαθεν the variants are:

(*a*) περὶ ἁμαρτιῶν B K P 049 056 0142 326* 330 451 1877 2127 *Byz Lect* Ps-Oecumenius.

(*b*) ὑπὲρ ἡμῶν ἁμαρτιῶν 326^c.

(*c*) ὑπὲρ ἁμαρτιῶν 2 241 242 325 337 460 489 2492.

Followed by ἀπέθανεν the variants are:

(*d*) περὶ ἁμαρτιῶν ὑπὲρ ὑμῶν 𝔓⁷² A 206 429 441 1241 arm.

(*e*) περὶ ἁμαρτιῶν ὑπὲρ ἡμῶν ℵ^c (ℵ* τῶν ἁμαρτιῶν) C^2vid 33 88 322 323 436 614 630 945 1739 1881 2412 *l*⁶ cop^bo eth Didymus.

(*f*) περὶ ὑμῶν ὑπὲρ ἁμαρτιῶν Ψ.

(*g*) περὶ ἁμαρτιῶν ἡμῶν C*vid 5 629 2298 it⁶⁵ syr^p cop^sa Cyprian.

(*h*) ὑπὲρ ἁμαρτωλῶν Didymus.

While acknowledging the difficulty of ascertaining the original text, a majority of the Committee preferred the reading περὶ ἁμαρτιῶν ἔπαθεν because (a) this verb, which is a favorite of the author (it occurs elsewhere in 1 Peter eleven times), carries on the thought of ver. 17, whereas ἀποθνῄσκειν (which occurs nowhere else in the epistle) abruptly introduces a new idea; (b) in view of the presence of the expression περὶ ἁμαρτιῶν scribes would be more likely to substitute ἀπέθανεν for ἔπαθεν than vice versa; and (c) the readings with ἡμῶν or ὑμῶν (which in later Greek had the same pronunciation) are natural and, indeed, expected scribal expansions.

3.18 ὑμᾶς {C}

The Committee was inclined to prefer ὑμᾶς (𝔓⁷² B P Ψ it⁶⁵ syrᵖˑʰ arm) to ἡμᾶς (ℵᶜ (ℵ* accidentally omits the pronoun) A C K 81 614 1739 vg syrʰᵐᵍ copˢᵃˑ ᵇᵒ Clement), because copyists would have been more likely to alter the second person to the first person (as more inclusive) than vice versa.

3.19 ἐν ᾧ καί

Several scholars have advocated the conjectural emendation that introduces the subject "Enoch" (ⲈⲚⲰⲔⲀⲒⲈⲚⲰⲬ). Instead of improving the intelligibility of the passage (as a conjectural reading ought to do), the word Ἐνώχ breaks the continuity of the argument by introducing an abrupt and unexpected change of subject from that of ver. 18.[2]

3.21 ὅ {A}

Despite the difficulty of construing ὅ, the Committee felt obliged to accept it as the text, (a) because it is strongly and widely supported

---

[2] See Metzger, *Journal of Religion,* xxxii (1952), pp. 256 f. or, more briefly, *The Text of the New Testament,* p. 185, n. 1, and the discussion of William J. Dalton, S.J., in his monograph, *Christ's Proclamation to the Spirits; a Study of 1 Peter 3:18–4:6* (Rome, 1965), pp. 135 ff.

by אᶜ A B C K P Ψ 33 81 614 1739 *Byz* it⁶⁵ vg arm Cyprian Origen^lat *al*, and (*b*) because the other readings are obvious ameliorations of the difficulty, some witnesses (𝔓⁷² א* 255 436 eth) having omitted the word, and others having substituted for it either ᾧ (69 206 216 241 630 1518) or ὡς (cop^bo vid Augustine^vid).

3.22 θεοῦ

After θεοῦ most manuscripts of the Vulgate insert *deglutiens mortem ut vitae aeternae haeredes efficeremur* ("swallowing up death that we might be made heirs of eternal life"). As is suggested by the use of the present participle *deglutiens* in the sense of the past tense, it is probable that the addition is a translation of a Greek gloss, which, according to Harnack's reconstruction, may have read καταπιὼν (τὸν) θάνατον, ἵνα ζωῆς αἰωνίου κληρονόμοι γενηθῶμεν (A. von Harnack, *Beiträge zur Einleitung in das Neue Testament,* VII [Leipzig, 1916], p. 83).

4.1 παθόντος {A}

The reading that best explains the origin of the others is παθόντος, which is strongly supported by 𝔓⁷² B C Ψ 330 1739 it⁶⁵ vg cop^sa *al*. In order to express the idea more fully some copyists added ὑπὲρ ἡμῶν (so the Textus Receptus, following אᶜ A K P 33 81 614 *Byz Lect* syr^h cop^bo arm eth *al*) while others added ὑπὲρ ὑμῶν (א 1505 2495 syr^p *al*). Had either of the latter readings been the original, no adequate reason can account for the absence of the prepositional phrase from the best representatives of both the Alexandrian and the Western types of text.

4.14 δόξης καὶ τὸ τοῦ θεοῦ {A}

After δόξης a considerable number of witnesses, some of them early, read καὶ δυνάμεως. The words are suitable to the context, but their absence in such diversified witnesses as 𝔓⁷² B K Ψ 049 330 Tertullian Ephraem Cyril Fulgentius *al,* and the fact that those that have the addition present it in somewhat different forms, sufficiently condemn all of them as homiletic supplements to the original text.

4.14 ἀναπαύεται {A}

At the close of the verse the Textus Receptus adds the clause κατὰ μὲν αὐτοὺς βλασφημεῖται, κατὰ δὲ ὑμᾶς δοξάζεται, with the support of K L P (Ψ) most minuscules it$^{r, 65}$ vg syr$^{h \ with \ *}$ cop$^{sa, (bo^{ms})}$ Cyprian. Although it is possible that the words may have been accidentally omitted because of parablepsis (-εται … -εται), the Committee thought it far more probable that they were added as an explanatory gloss on the preceding reference to the spirit of glory. Of the several forms of the verb, the perfect tense and the forms compounded with ἐπ- appear to be secondary developments, arising from a desire to strengthen and clarify the form ἀναπαύεται (א* B 056 0142 1739 al).

5.2 [ἐπισκοποῦντες] μὴ ἀναγκαστῶς ἀλλὰ ἑκουσίως κατὰ θεόν {C}

It is difficult to decide whether one should follow the authority of such important witnesses as א* B al and regard the inclusion of ἐπισκοποῦντες in 𝔓^{72} א^2 A and most other witnesses as an exegetical expansion (made perhaps in accordance with 2.25), or whether the shorter text is the result of deliberate excision, prompted either by stylistic considerations (namely, that after ποιμάνατε the word is redundant) or by ecclesiastical conviction (namely, that Peter could never have admonished presbyters [ver. 1] to exercise the function of bishops). In order to represent the balance of external evidence and of transcriptional probabilities, the Committee decided to include the word (which tallies very well with the author's fondness for participles), but to enclose it within square brackets to indicate a certain doubt that it belongs in the text. The phrase κατὰ θεόν, which is read by a variety of witnesses representing several text types (𝔓^{72} א A P Ψ 33 81 1739 it$^{h, r}$ vg syr^h cop$^{sa, bo}$ arm eth (Speculum)), is omitted by B K L most minuscules syr^p, perhaps because copyists found difficulty in understanding its precise import (i. e. "according to [the will of] God").

5.3 μηδ᾽ ὡς κατακυριεύοντες τῶν κλήρων ἀλλὰ τύποι γινόμενοι τοῦ ποιμνίου {A}

Because of some unaccountable quirk in transmission, this verse is lacking in codex Vaticanus.

5.6 καιρῷ {A}

After καιρῷ the Textus Receptus adds ἐπισκοπῆς, with A P (Ψ) 5 28ᶜ 33 104 181 326 436 623 913 1827 1898 vg syrʰ ʷⁱᵗʰ * copᵇᵒ eth Ephraem Bede. The word, which is absent from 𝔓⁷² ℵ B K L 0206 most minuscules syrᵖ·ʰᵗˣᵗ copˢᵃ Origen, appears to be a scribal addition derived from 2.12.

5.8 [τινα] καταπιεῖν {C}

After ζητῶν there are three main variant readings: (a) τινα καταπιεῖν "[seeking] someone to devour"; (b) τίνα καταπίῃ "[seeking] whom he may devour"; and (c) καταπιεῖν "[seeking] to devour." (The reading τίνα καταπίει is a transcriptional error either for the infinitive, written ΚΑΤΑΠΙΕΙ, or, by itacism, for the subjunctive.) On the one hand, it can be argued that (c), which is supported by B Ψ Origenˡᵃᵗ, is the original reading, and that the others are scribal attempts to alleviate the difficulty of the absolute use of καταπιεῖν. On the other hand, it can be argued that the constancy of position of τινα (however accented) in the overwhelming bulk of the manuscripts makes it probable that it is original and that its absence from a few witnesses is the result of accidental oversight. In either case reading (b), which is supported by 𝔓⁷² A 614 *Byz* most early versions (whose evidence, however, may count for little, being merely idiomatic), appears to be a secondary development, arising when the colorless indefinite τινα was taken as the interrogative τίνα. In the light of such considerations a majority of the Committee voted to represent the divergent textual evidence by adopting the reading (*a*), which is supported by ℵ^c (K P 049) 81 181 326 1739 cop^{bo} Origen, but to enclose τινα within square brackets.

5.10   ὑμᾶς {A}

The Textus Receptus, following later Greek manuscripts, reads ἡμᾶς instead of ὑμᾶς, the latter of which is supported by the over-whelming preponderance of evidence. In later Greek, the vowels η and υ were pronounced alike, and it is altogether possible that some copyists who wrote ἡμᾶς intended to write ὑμᾶς.

5.10   ἐν Χριστῷ ['Ιησοῦ] {C}

A majority of the Committee was impressed by the support of 𝔓⁷² and many other Greek, versional, and patristic witnesses reading Χριστῷ 'Ιησοῦ, yet because 'Ιησοῦ is absent from several important manuscripts (including ℵ B 614), it was decided to enclose the word within square brackets, indicating doubt that it belongs in the text.

[In view of the tendency of scribes to add rather than omit sacred names, the shorter text is to be preferred. B.M.M.]

5.10   καταρτίσει, στηρίξει, σθενώσει, θεμελιώσει {B}

Similarity of ending of the successive verbs accounts for the ac-cidental omission of σθενώσει by 𝔓⁷² 81 and the ancestor of it^r and of θεμελιώσει by A B Ψ *al*. The replacement with optative forms (σθενώσαι, θεμελιώσαι) in several later witnesses (614 630 1505 2412 *al*) reflects scribal or editorial modification.

5.11   τὸ κράτος {B}

The variation of position of ἡ δόξα (before κράτος in ℵ K P 049 056 0142 88 104 181 326 330 *al*; after κράτος in 33 81 614 630 945 1241 1505 1739 1881 *al*), as well as its absence from such witnesses as 𝔓⁷² A B Ψ vg eth^{ro}, can be explained best on the assumption that it is a later intrusion into the text, derived from 4.11. Other singular and sub-singular variants occur, derived from traditional doxologies.

5.11 αἰῶνας {B}

Considering the almost universal tendency to expansion in doxologies, a majority of the Committee preferred the shorter reading, supported by 𝔓⁷² B 36 307 *l*¹³⁶⁵ᵐ cop^bo arm.

5.13 Βαβυλῶνι {A}

Instead of Βαβυλῶνι a few minuscules (4ᵐᵍ 1518 2138) read Ῥώμῃ.

5.14 ἀγάπης {A}

Instead of ἀγάπης, the scribes of several minuscule manuscripts (436 1735 2464 *al*) read ἁγίῳ, thus imitating the familiar Pauline expression φίλημα ἅγιον (Ro 16.16; 1 Cor 16.20; 2 Cor 13.12; 1 Th 5.26); lectionary 422 combines both expressions, φιλήματι ἁγίῳ καὶ ἀγάπης.

5.14 Χριστῷ {A}

The Textus Receptus, along with ℵ K P 81 614 1739 it^h syr^h cop^bo arm *al*, adds Ἰησοῦ, and 629 substitutes κυρίῳ Ἰησοῦ. In view of the tendency of copyists to expand the sacred name, the Committee preferred to adopt the shorter text, supported by representatives of several types of text, including A B Ψ 33^vid 307 *l*¹³⁶⁵ᵐˑ ¹⁴⁴¹ᵐ it^r vg syr^p cop^sa, bomss eth (𝔓⁷² lacks the entire final clause).

5.14 *omit* ἀμήν. {A}

Although most witnesses, as might be expected, conclude the epistle with ἀμήν (including ℵ K P 614 1739 *Byz* it^h, r vg syr^p, h cop^bomss arm), what must have been a strong liturgical temptation to add the word was resisted by the copyists of A B Ψ 81 629 945 1241 1881 cop^sa, bo geo.

THE SECOND LETTER OF PETER

1.1 Συμεών {B}

The weight of external support for the two readings is almost equally divided (Συμεών ℵ A K P 049 056 0142 1739 syr^ph, h arm *al*; Σίμων 𝔓^72 B Ψ 81 614 it^h, r vg syr^pal cop^sa, bo eth *al*). The Committee was agreed that transcriptionally it is more likely that Σίμων is a correction of Συμεών than vice versa, since Συμεών is used of Peter in only one other passage in the New Testament (Ac 15.14).

1.2 τοῦ θεοῦ καὶ Ἰησοῦ τοῦ κυρίου ἡμῶν {A}

Amid the variety of readings here, the Committee chose what it regarded as the earliest and the origin of the other readings. The absence of τοῦ θεοῦ καὶ Ἰησοῦ in P Ψ and other witnesses can be accounted for by parablepsis, when the scribe's eye passed from τοῦ to τοῦ. Other readings incorporate various amplifications reflecting the piety of copyists.

1.3 ἰδίᾳ δόξῃ καὶ ἀρετῇ {B}

Although the reading of the Textus Receptus διὰ δόξης καὶ ἀρετῆς is an exceedingly ancient reading (𝔓^72 B, and K L most minuscules), a majority of the Committee preferred ἰδίᾳ δόξῃ καὶ ἀρετῇ (ℵ A C P Ψ 33 81 614 1739 it^h, r vg syr^ph, h, pal cop^sa, bo arm (Speculum)) on the strength of the following considerations: (*a*) it is attested by a broad spectrum of witnesses, including all ancient versions; (*b*) the presence of several other instances of διά in the context makes it more likely that διά would have been written by mistake for ἰδίᾳ than vice versa; and (*c*) ἴδιος is a favorite word with the author of 2 Peter, occurring six other times in three chapters.

1.4   *τίμια καὶ μέγιστα ἡμῖν ἐπαγγέλματα*

The order of words varies greatly:

(*a*) *τίμια καὶ μέγιστα ἐπαγγέλματα ἡμῖν*	$\mathfrak{P}^{72}$.
(*b*) *τίμια καὶ μέγιστα ἡμῖν ἐπ.*	B 1 206 255 429 489 614 1611 1898 2143.
(*c*) *τίμια ἡμῖν καὶ μέγιστα ἐπ.*	ℵ K L 0142 many minuscules.
(*d*) *μέγιστα καὶ τίμια ἡμῖν ἐπ.*	C P (*ὑμῖν* A; *ὑμῶν* Ψ) 5 33 69 81 88 104 218 307 326 441 623 1175 1739 2298 vg syr[ph, h] cop[sa, bo].
(*e*) *μέγιστα ἡμῖν καὶ τίμια ἐπ.*	several minuscules and Textus Receptus.

The reading that best explains the origin of the others appears to be (*b*). A desire to relate the pronoun more closely either to the verb or to *τίμια* resulted in reading (*a*) on the one hand, and readings (*c*) and (*d*) on the other. The sequence of *μέγιστα* and *τίμια* in (*d*) and (*e*) may have originated in an accidental or deliberate omission of *τίμια καί* and its later insertion from the margin. The readings *ὑμῖν* of A and *ὑμῶν* of Ψ have been conformed to the following *γένησθε*.

1.4   *τῆς ἐν τῷ κόσμῳ ἐν ἐπιθυμίᾳ φθορᾶς* {B}

The earliest form of text appears to be that supported by A B *al.* Inasmuch as the verb *ἀποφεύγειν*, which is not used by any other New Testament author, properly takes the accusative case (as in 2.20 below), several witnesses read *τὴν ἐν τῷ κόσμῳ ἐπιθυμίαν* ($\mathfrak{P}^{72}$ ℵ cop[sa, bo]), while $\mathfrak{P}^{72}$ also reads *φθοράν*.

1.5   *αὐτὸ τοῦτο δέ* {B}

By moving *δέ* from following *τοῦτο* ($\mathfrak{P}^{72}$ B C* P *al*) to precede *τοῦτο* (ℵ C² Ψ 33 81 1739 *al*), the adverbial expression *αὐτὸ τοῦτο* is divided in two. This reading, obviously faulty, is probably the origin of the reading in A (αὐτοὶ δέ).

1.10 σπουδάσατε βεβαίαν ... ποιεῖσθαι {A}

After σπουδάσατε several witnesses, including ℵ A Ψ 81 630 and the Latin, Syriac, and Coptic versions, replace the complementary infinitive construction (which occurs regularly in the New Testament after σπουδάζειν) with the ἵνα construction; by a *lapsus calami,* however, at the close of the clause ℵ A and a few other witnesses absentmindedly retain the infinitive instead of the subjunctive ποιῆσθε (which, by itacism, was pronounced like ποιεῖσθαι and ποιεῖσθε). At the same time these witnesses introduce an edifying explanation, διὰ τῶν καλῶν (ὑμῶν) ἔργων. In view of the several variations among these expansions, the Committee regarded the shorter reading of 𝔓⁷² B C K P 614 1739 *al* as original.

1.17 ὁ υἱός μου ὁ ἀγαπητός μου οὗτός ἐστιν {B}

The original text appears to have been preserved only in 𝔓⁷² B (the Coptic and Ethiopic are ambiguous), all the other witnesses having conformed the reading to the traditional text in Matthew, οὗτός ἐστιν ὁ υἱός μου ὁ ἀγαπητός (Mt 3.17; 17.5). The expanded reading of P 1175 *(οὗτός ἐστιν ὁ υἱός μου ὁ ἀγαπητὸς οὗτός ἐστιν)* suggests that an ancestor of each read as 𝔓⁷² and B, but that when the assimilated reading was adopted the copyist overlooked deleting the words οὗτός ἐστιν at the close.

1.20 πᾶσα προφητεία γραφῆς

Instead of πᾶσα προφητεία γραφῆς the copyists of several minuscules (206 378 429 522 614 1108 1758 2138), recollecting the statement about scripture in 2 Tm 3.16, wrote πᾶσα γραφὴ προφητείας. The scribe of 𝔓⁷² introduced a different conflation, πᾶσα προφητεία καὶ γραφή.

1.21 ἀπὸ θεοῦ {A}

The reading that best accounts for the origin of the others is ἀπὸ θεοῦ, which is read by 𝔓⁷² B P 614 1739 syrʰ copᵇᵒ arm *al*. The reading ἅγιοι θεοῦ (ℵ K Ψ 33 *Byz al*) appears to be secondary, being either (*a*) an emendation that commended itself to copyists because it gives greater prominence to the idea of holiness, or (*b*) the result of palaeographical confusion, ΑΠΟΘΥ having been taken for ΑΓΙΟΙΘΥ. The two readings are combined in differing conflations in C 81 *l*⁸⁰⁹ *al*.

2.4 σειραῖς {C}

The textual evidence is singularly evenly balanced between σειραῖς and σιροῖς. The latter reading, despite its being supported by ℵ A B C 81ᵛⁱᵈ copˢᵃ *al*, was regarded by the Committee as a correction (made, perhaps, in Egypt where σιρός was current) of the original reading σειραῖς. If, as is generally supposed, 2 Peter depends in part upon Jude, the author of the former appears to have substituted the more elegant word σειραῖς for the commonplace δεσμοῖς of Jude 6. In any case, the reading adopted for the text is both the oldest (it is read by 𝔓⁷²) and the most widespread, being supported by many versional and patristic witnesses, as well as by almost all minuscules.

2.6 [καταστροφῇ] κατέκρινεν {C}

It is difficult to decide whether καταστροφῇ, read by ℵ A C² K Ψ 049 056 0142 33 81 614 *al*, was added by scribes, or whether it was original and accidentally fell out of the text of 𝔓⁷² ᵗˣᵗ B C* 945 1241 1243 1739 1881 *al*. Since the shorter reading might well have arisen by transcriptional oversight (note the sequence ΚΑΤαστροφῇ ΚΑΤέκρινεν), and since, if the word had been added by copyists, one would expect to find it (or a synonym) at various places in various witnesses, the Committee thought it best to include καταστροφῇ in the text, but to enclose it within square brackets in order to reflect the weight of several important witnesses that lack the word (𝔓⁷² ᵗˣᵗ B C* 1739).

2.6 ἀσεβέ[σ]ιν {C}

External evidence is rather evenly divided between ἀσεβέσιν, supported by 𝔓⁷² B P 614 syr^{ph, h} (cop^{sa, bo} τοῖς ἀσεβέσιν) arm, and ἀσεβεῖν, supported by ℵ A C K Ψ 33 81 1739 *Byz* (it^h) vg. From the point of view of transcriptional probability, after μελλόντων copyists would be more likely to change the noun to the infinitive than the reverse. From the point of view of intrinsic probability, the noun gives better sense ("an example [or warning] to ungodly persons of things in store for them") than the verb ("an example [or warning] to those about to do wrong [act impiously]"). In order to represent the balance of probabilities, it was decided to enclose the sigma within square brackets.

2.11 παρὰ κυρίου {C}

As between παρὰ κυρίῳ, read by ℵ B C K P 88 1739 arm *al,* and παρὰ κυρίου, read by 𝔓⁷² 056 0142 330 *al,* a majority of the Committee preferred the latter as the more difficult reading. In order to avoid attributing βλάσφημον κρίσιν to God, scribes altered κυρίου to κυρίῳ or omitted the prepositional phrase entirely (as in A Ψ 33 81 614 vg cop^{sa, bo} eth). The omission may also reflect scribal recollection of the parallel account in Jude 9, which lacks any mention of the presence of the Lord.

[In view of the absence of the prepositional phrase from a wide variety of Greek, versional, and patristic witnesses, one suspects that scribes added it either in the form παρὰ κυρίου or παρὰ κυρίῳ.[1] If such a phrase is to be included in the text at all, the least unsatisfactory decision is to adopt the reading of the great uncials (ℵ B C), but to enclose the words παρὰ κυρίῳ within square brackets. B.M.M.]

---

[1] The genitive is used with παρά 78 times in the New Testament, as compared with 50 times with the dative and 60 times with accusative (J. H. Moulton, *Prolegomena,* p. 106).

2.13 ἀδικούμενοι {B}

The reading ἀδικούμενοι, which is supported by early and diversified witnesses (𝔓⁷² ℵ* B P Ψ 1175 1852 syrᵖʰ arm), involves a very rare construction with μισθόν, and therefore copyists introduced the less objectionable κομιούμενοι (ℵᶜ A C K 049 most minuscules vg syrʰ copˢᵃ, ᵇᵒ eth Speculum). The author seems to have tolerated the unusual grammatical construction in the interest of contriving a play on the words ἀδικούμενοι ... ἀδικίας ("defrauded of the hire of fraud," J. B. Mayor, *Com.*, p. cxcvi; see also Schrenk in Kittel's *Theological Dictionary of the New Testament*, I, pp. 156 f. and Bauer-Arndt-Gingrich-Danker, *s.v.* ἀδικέω, at end).

2.13 τρυφήν {A}

Instead of τρυφήν, K reads τροφήν ("nourishment") and 𝔓⁷² ungrammatically reads τρυφῆς.

2.13 ἀπάταις {B}

In view of the probability that the original reading of Jude ver. 12 is ἐν ταῖς ἀγάπαις ὑμῶν (see comment on that passage), a majority of the Committee was of the opinion that the author of 2 Peter consciously altered Jude's expression, substituting (as he does elsewhere) a more generalized expression, ἐν ταῖς ἀπάταις αὐτῶν, which is strongly supported by 𝔓⁷² ℵ A* C K P 33 81 614 syrʰ copᵇᵒ arm *al,* and for which the presence of αὐτῶν is a supporting argument. The reading ἀγάπαις (Aᶜ B Ψ 424ᶜ 623 1827 vg syrᵖʰ, ʰᵐᵍ copˢᵃ eth Speculum *al*) is then a scribal assimilation to the prevailing text of Jude.

2.14 μοιχαλίδος {A}

Instead of μοιχαλίδος ("an adulteress"), which is strongly supported by 𝔓⁷² B C 81 and most minuscules, Ψ *al* read μοιχείας ("adultery"), while ℵ A 33 *al* read μοιχαλίας, a word not known elsewhere.

2.15 Βοσόρ {A}

The reading Βοσόρ, a name not found elsewhere, is strongly supported by almost all Greek manuscripts, and by most early versions. The reading Βεώρ, found in B 453 vg^mss syr^ph cop^sa arm, is the prevailing spelling of the Septuagint. The singular reading of ℵ* *(Βεωρσόρ)* is no doubt due to the conflation of Βοσόρ with a marginal correction -εωρ.

2.18 ὀλίγως {A}

Among the palaeographically similar readings (ολιγωc: οντωc: οντΑc), ὀλίγως, a rare word that occurs nowhere else in the New Testament or the Septuagint (although Aquila has it in Is 10.7), appears to be original. As regards external evidence, ὀλίγως is supported by representatives of both the Alexandrian and the Western types of text (𝔓^72 A B Ψ 33 vg syr^ph, h cop^sa, bo Jerome Augustine Bede). As regards transcriptional probability, since copyists were more likely to substitute the familiar word for the unfamiliar than the reverse, ὄντως is far more likely to be secondary than ὀλίγως. Finally, as regards intrinsic probability, ὄντως seems to involve a self-contradiction after δελεάζουσιν, and ὄντας (read by several minuscules, including 181 489 1241 1881) is utterly inappropriate with ἀποφεύγοντας.

2.20 κυρίου [ἡμῶν] καὶ σωτῆρος Ἰησοῦ Χριστοῦ {C}

On the one hand, the variation in position of ἡμῶν (after κυρίου and/or after σωτῆρος) seems to condemn the word as a scribal addition in both instances. On the other hand, the full form of the expression appears to be a favorite of the author (1.11; 3.18), and scribes could occasionally omit elements from the full form – as is shown here by the absence of καὶ σωτῆρος from L 38 309 425 483 629 1881 cop^bo eth *al*. On balance it seemed best to include ἡμῶν after κυρίου (following 𝔓^72 ℵ A C P Ψ 614 1739 *al*), but to enclose it within square brackets in order to reflect the weight of the testimony of B K 049 *al.*

3.9 εἰς ὑμᾶς {A}

Although the preposition διά is widely supported (it is read by ℵ A Ψ 33 630 vg syr^ph, h cop^sa, bo^mss eth Speculum *al*), the Committee preferred εἰς, which is supported by 𝔓^72 B C K L P most minuscules cop^bo arm, and regarded διά as an exegetical correction. Instead of ὑμᾶς the Textus Receptus, following secondary textual authorities (including K 049 *Byz Lect*), reads ἡμᾶς.

3.10 εὑρεθήσεται {D}

At the close of ver. 10 the extant witnesses present a wide variety of readings, none of which seems to be original. The oldest reading, and the one which best explains the origin of the others that have been preserved, is εὑρεθήσεται, which is attested by ℵ B K P 424^c 1175 1739^txt 1852 syr^ph, hmg arm Origen. In view of the difficulty of extracting any acceptable sense from the passage, it is not strange that copyists and translators introduced a variety of modifications. Thus, several witnesses retain εὑρεθήσεται but qualify it with other words: (*a*) the Sahidic version and one manuscript of the Harclean Syriac version insert the negative, and (*b*) the Bodmer Papyrus (𝔓^72) adds λυόμενα ("the earth and the things in it will be found *dissolved*") – an expedient, however, that overloads the context with three instances of the same verb. Other witnesses either (*c*) omit εὑρεθήσεται and the accompanying clause (so Ψ vg Pelagius *al*), or substitute another verb that gives more or less good sense. Thus (*d*) C reads ἀφανισθήσονται ("will disappear"), and (*e*) A 048 049 056 0142 33 614 *Byz Lect* syr^h cop^bo eth *al* read κατακαήσεται ("will be burned up").

Because εὑρεθήσεται, though the oldest of the extant readings, seems to be devoid of meaning in the context (even the expedient of punctuating as a question, "Will the earth and the things in it be found?" fails to commend itself), various conjectural emendations have been proposed: (*a*) after ἔργα the word ἀργά has fallen out

(Bradshaw), "the earth and the things in it will be found *useless*"; (*b*) εὑρεθήσεται is a scribal corruption of ῥυήσεται or ῥεύσεται (Hort),[1] "the earth and the things in it *will flow*"; (*c*) συρρυήσεται (Naber), "... will flow together"; (*d*) ἐκπυρωθήσεται (Olivier), "... will be burnt to ashes"; (*e*) ἀρθήσεται (J. B. Mayor), "... will be taken away"; (*f*) κριθήσεται (Eb. Nestle), "... will be judged"; (*g*) ἰαθήσεται (or ἐξιαθήσεται) (Chase), "... will be healed (thoroughly)"; (*h*) πυρωθήσεται (Vansittart), "... will be burned."

3.11　τούτων οὕτως　{B}

Although the reading τούτων οὖν is supported by representatives of both the Alexandrian and the Western types of text, the Committee was inclined to prefer the reading τούτων οὕτως because of the weight of the combination of $\mathfrak{P}^{72}$ B 614 1739 syr^h *al,* and because οὖν may have been introduced to provide a smoother connection with the previous statements. The readings τούτων δὲ οὕτως (C P *al*) and τούτων οὖν οὕτως (81 *al*) are obviously secondary.

3.11　*[ὑμᾶς]*　{C}

In place of ὑμᾶς, which is read by a wide variety of Greek and versional witnesses (including A (C*) K P Ψ 33 81 614 1739 vg syr^ph, h cop^sa arm), several witnesses read (by itacism) ἡμᾶς, which appears to be less suitable to the context (ℵ* 104 209 241 630 *al*). Although the absence of any pronoun in $\mathfrak{P}^{72*, 74vid}$ B 1175 *al* may be either accidental or the result of deliberate scribal pruning of an apparently superfluous word, in view of the age and importance of $\mathfrak{P}^{72}$ and B a majority of the Committee considered it advisable to enclose ὑμᾶς within square brackets.

3.18　*[ἀμήν.]*　{C}

On the one hand, the external testimony supporting the presence of ἀμήν at the close of the doxology is almost overwhelming in scope

---

[1] In support of Hort's conjecture, cf. I Enoch 1.6 where, in a similar context, some witnesses read τοῦ δια<ρ>ρυῆναι ὄρη ("so that the mountains shall waste away").

and weight, including $\mathfrak{P}^{72}$ ℵ A C 33 81 614 vg syr[ph, h] cop[sa, bo] arm eth. On the other hand, if the word were present originally, it is difficult to account for its absence in such notable Eastern and Western witnesses as B 1739* Augustine Bede, as well as several other minuscules (82 440 522 1175 1241 1881). In order to reflect this conflict between external and internal considerations, the Committee thought it best to include ἀμήν but to enclose it within square brackets, suggesting a considerable measure of doubt as to its right to stand in the text.

THE FIRST LETTER OF JOHN

1.4 ἡμεῖς {B}

Although the reading ὑμῖν is widely supported (Aᶜ C K L almost all minuscules vg syrᵖˑ ʰˑ ᵖᵃˡ copˢᵃˑ ᵇᵒ arm eth), a majority of the Committee preferred ἡμεῖς because of the quality of its support (it is read by the Alexandrian text and one Old Latin manuscript: ℵ A* B P Ψ 33 it⁶⁵ copˢᵃᵐˢ), and because copyists were more likely to alter γράφομεν ἡμεῖς to the expected γράφομεν ὑμῖν (compare ὑμῖν after ἀπαγγέλλομεν in verses 2 and 3) than vice versa.

1.4 ἡμῶν {A}

Instead of ἡμῶν (read by ℵ B L Ψ 049 88 326 it⁶⁵ vg copˢᵃ al), the Textus Receptus, following A C²ᵛⁱᵈ K P 33 81 614 1739 most minuscules vgᵐˢˢ syrʰˑ ᵖᵃˡ copᵇᵒ arm al, reads ὑμῶν. As regards transcriptional probability, copyists who recollected Jn 16.24 (ἵνα ἡ χαρὰ ὑμῶν ᾖ πεπληρωμένη) would have been likely to alter ἡμῶν to ὑμῶν. As regards intrinsic probability, ἡμῶν seems to suit best the generous solicitude of the author, whose own joy would be incomplete unless his readers shared it; whereas copyists, insensitive to such a nuance, would have been likely to alter ἡμῶν to the more expected second person ὑμῶν.

2.4 ἡ ἀλήθεια {A}

Instead of "the truth," several witnesses (Ψ 436 945 1505 al) weaken the statement by reading "truth"; on the other hand, ℵ and a few other witnesses strengthen it by expanding to read "the truth of God."

2.6 [οὕτως] {C}

The external evidence for and against the presence of οὕτως is rather evenly divided (ℵ C Ψ 81 al for; A B 33 2464* al against).

From a transcriptional point of view, the word might have been accidentally omitted following αὐτός. On the other hand, it might have been added as an emphatic correlative with the preceding καθώς. In light of such considerations, the Committee considered it best to include the word but to enclose it within square brackets.

2.7 ἀγαπητοί

Instead of ἀγαπητοί (strongly supported by ℵ A B C P vg syr^{p, h} cop^{sa, bo} arm *al*) the Textus Receptus, following K L and most minuscules, reads ἀδελφοί. The latter word, which the author of 1 John almost never uses in the vocative (only in 3.13), crept into the Byzantine text of the present passage because of its customary usage as the introductory word in lectionary pericopes derived from the apostolos.

2.7 ἠκούσατε

The Textus Receptus, again following K L and most minuscules, reads ἀπ’ ἀρχῆς after ἠκούσατε. The phrase is an intrusion (cf. ver. 24 and 3.11), added by copyists in order to balance εἴχετε ἀπ’ ἀρχῆς earlier in the verse. The shorter text is decisively supported by ℵ A B C P 33 181 218 322 323 431 453 642 643 vg syr^{p, h} cop^{sa, bo} arm eth Augustine Theophylact.

2.14 ἔγραψα (1) {A}

Scribes of many of the later manuscripts (followed by the Textus Receptus) absent-mindedly wrote γράφω in accord with the three previous instances of the present tense.

2.17 αἰῶνα

At the close of the verse several versional and patristic witnesses expand the text by adding the gloss "just as God [or, that (one), cop^{sa}] abides for ever" (vg^{mss} (cop^{sa}) Cyprian Lucifer Augustine). There is no Greek authority for the expansion (cf. 5.7-8a).

2.18 ὅτι (1) {B}

The reading that best explains the origin of the other readings appears to be ὅτι, which is strongly supported by ℵ* B C Ψ 1739 *al*. The conjunction is lacking in a few witnesses (A L 1881 *al*), thus making a more direct statement. The definite article, which is not present in ℵ* B C Ψ 1739 *al* (showing that the word was understood as a proper name), was supplied by scribes in a number of witnesses, including ℵ² A L 1881 *al*, in order to identify Antichrist more forcefully.

2.20 πάντες {B}

A majority of the Committee, understanding the passage to be directed against the claims of a few to possess esoteric knowledge, adopted the reading πάντες, read by ℵ B P 398 1838 1852 cop^sa Jerome Hesychius. The reading πάντα, which is widely supported by A C K 33 614 1739 *Byz Lect* it^h, 65 vg syr^h cop^bo arm eth *al*, was regarded as a correction introduced by copyists who felt the need of an object after οἴδαμεν.

Westcott and Hort punctuate with a dash after πάντες.

2.23 ὁ ὁμολογῶν ... ἔχει

Because of homoeoteleuton *(τὸν πατέρα ἔχει ... τὸν πατέρα ἔχει)*, K L and most minuscules, followed by the Textus Receptus, have accidentally omitted the second part of the verse *(ὁ ὁμολογῶν ... ἔχει)*. The words, however, belong to the original text, being strongly supported by ℵ A B C P many minuscules vg syr^p, h cop^sa, bo arm eth *al*.

2.25 ἡμῖν {A}

The external evidence supporting ἡμῖν is extensive and diversified, including ℵ A C 81 614 1739 *Byz Lect* it^65 vg syr^p, h cop^sa, bo arm. A few witnesses (B 69* 241 451 1241 1881 2127 it^h) read ὑμῖν, which is either the result of scribal confusion between η and υ, or a deliberate accommodation to the expression ἀπαγγέλλομεν ὑμῖν in 1.2 and 3.

2.27 τὸ αὐτοῦ

Instead of τὸ αὐτοῦ, which is strongly supported by ℵ B C P about twenty minuscules vg syrʰ copˢᵃ arm eth Athanasius Augustine *al*, the Textus Receptus, following A K L most minuscules copᵇᵒ Theophylact *al*, reads τὸ αὐτό. The latter construction (ὁ αὐτός), which has the appearance of a scribal emendation, occurs nowhere else in either the Fourth Gospel or the three Johannine Epistles.

3.1 καὶ ἐσμέν {A}

Although it can be argued that the words καὶ ἐσμέν are an explanatory gloss introduced by copyists in order to affirm the reality of the state previously described, it is much more likely that they are genuine, being supported by representatives of both the Alexandrian and the Western types of text (𝔓⁷⁴ᵛⁱᵈ ℵ A B C 33 81 614 1739 itʰ·⁶⁵ vg *al*). The absence of the words in several of the later witnesses (K L most minuscules), followed by the Textus Receptus, is due either to scribal oversight, perhaps occasioned by graphical similarity with the preceding word (ΚΛΗΘΩΜΕΝΚΑΙΕϹΜΕΝ), or to deliberate editorial pruning of an awkward parenthetical clause.

3.5 ἁμαρτίας {A}

A majority of the Committee preferred the reading ἁμαρτίας, supported by A B 33 1739 itʰ·⁶⁵ syrʰ copᵇᵒ arm, and regarded the reading with ἡμῶν (ℵ C K L Ψ most minuscules vg syrᵖ copˢᵃ·ᶠᵃʸ *al*) to be the result of scribal assimilation to such passages as 2.2 and 4.10.

3.13 [καὶ] μή {C}

It is difficult to decide whether καί (which is read by ℵ Cᵛⁱᵈ P Ψ 1739 itʳ·⁶⁵ syrᵖ arm eth) was added by copyists in order to provide a closer connection with what goes before; or whether, because of the preceding word *(δίκαια),* copyists accidentally omitted καί (A B K L 33 81 614 *Byz Lect* it[h] vg syr[h] cop[sa, bo, fay] *al*). A majority of the Committee preferred to retain the word in the text, but to enclose it within square brackets in order to indicate considerable doubt that it belongs there.

3.14   *ἀγαπῶν* {A}

After *ἀγαπῶν* a variety of witnesses add *τὸν ἀδελφόν* (C K L Ψ 81 *Byz Lect al*) or *τὸν ἀδελφὸν αὐτοῦ* (P 056 614 syr[p, h] *al*). In the opinion of a majority of the Committee, the shorter reading is to be preferred *(a)* because it is attested by superior witnesses (ℵ A B 33 1739 it[h, r, 65] vg cop[bo, fay] arm) and *(b)* because copyists were more likely to add than to delete an object that completes the thought of the participle.

3.19   *[καὶ] ἐν τούτῳ* {C}

As in the case of 3.13, the balance of external evidence and of internal probabilities warrants the use of square brackets around καί.

3.19   *γνωσόμεθα* {A}

The Textus Receptus, following K L and a great number of minuscules, has assimilated the future tense to the present tense so as to accord with the frequently occurring formula *ἐν τούτῳ γινώσκομεν* (2.3; 3.24; 4.2,13; 5.2).

3.21   *ἡ καρδία [ἡμῶν] μὴ καταγινώσκῃ* {C}

In the following tabular arrangement the eleven different readings are subsumed under four principal readings:

(1) *ἡ καρδία   μὴ καταγινώσκῃ*   B Origen
(2) *ἡ καρδία ἡμῶν μὴ καταγινώσκῃ*   C[1] 1852 2464
                                            Origen

(3) ἡ καρδία   μὴ καταγινώσκῃ ἡμῶν   (A) Ψ (33) 322 436
945 (1241) 1739
John-Damascus

     ἡ καρδία   μὴ καταγινώσκει ἡμῶν   A 33

     ἡ καρδία   μὴ καταγινώσκει ὑμῶν   1241

(4) ἡ καρδία ἡμῶν μὴ καταγινώσκῃ ἡμῶν   (ℵ*) K (049) 056
0142 81 104 181 326 330 451 614 623 629 630 (1243) (1505)
1844 1877 1881 (2127) 2412 2492 (2495) *Byz Lect* it[r] vg syr[ph]
arm eth Origen Didymus Ps-Athanasius (John-Damascus)

     ἡ καρδία ὑμῶν μὴ καταγινώσκῃ ἡμῶν   2127

     ἡ καρδία ὑμῶν μὴ καταγινώσκῃ ὑμῶν   2495

     ἡ καρδία ἡμῶν μὴ καταγινώσκῃ ὑμῶν   1505

     ἡ καρδία ἡμῶν μὴ καταγινώσκω ἡμῶν   ℵ*

     ἡ καρδία ἡμῶν μὴ καταγινώσκει ἡμῶν   049   1243   John-
Damascus

On the one hand, it can be argued that reading (1) is original and that ἡμῶν is a natural addition supplied by copyists in accord with the usage of the preceding verses. On the other hand, a majority of the Committee was unwilling to adopt a reading that may be the result of Alexandrian pruning (B Origen), and preferred to follow those witnesses that read ἡμῶν after καρδία, in which position the pronoun can serve also as the object of the verb. In view, however, of the general excellence of codex Vaticanus, it was thought best to enclose the pronoun within square brackets. (The reading καταγινώσκω of ℵ* is, of course, a scribal blunder, and the replacement of ἡμῶν by ὑμῶν in a variety of witnesses arises from the circumstance that in later Greek both words were pronounced alike.)

4.3 μὴ ὁμολογεῖ {A}

In place of μὴ ὁμολογεῖ several versional and patristic witnesses substitute the remarkable reading λύει ("Every spirit that *annuls* Jesus is not of God") or *solvit* ("severs"). Although several scholars (including Zahn, Harnack, Büchsel [in Kittel], Preisker) have argued that λύει is the original reading, the Committee preferred μὴ ὁμολογεῖ because of overwhelming external support. The origin of λύει is probably to be sought in second century polemic against Gnostics who made a distinction between the earthly Jesus and the heavenly Christ.

4.3 τὸν Ἰησοῦν {A}

A majority of the Committee considered it probable that the shortest reading τὸν Ἰησοῦν, which is supported by good representatives of both Alexandrian and Western types of text (A B 1739 itʳ vg copᵇᵒ Irenaeusˡᵃᵗ Clement *al*), was expanded by copyists with additions derived from the previous verse *(Ἰησοῦν Χριστὸν ἐν σαρκὶ ἐληλυθότα)*. The variety of the supplements is a further indication that they are secondary modifications of the original text.

4.10 ἠγαπήκαμεν {B}

As concerns the weight of external evidence, the two readings are more or less equally supported. From a transcriptional point of view, scribes would be likely to assimilate the perfect tense to the following verbs, which are aorist.

4.19 ἀγαπῶμεν {A}

The reading that best explains the origin of the others is ἀγαπῶμεν, which is adequately supported by A B 5 322 323 424ᶜ 945 1241 1739 1881 itʳ ᵛⁱᵈ vg *al*. Feeling the need of an accusative object after the verb, especially when it was (wrongly) taken to be the hortatory subjunctive, some copyists added τὸν θεόν (ℵ 33 81 614 syrᵖ· ʰ copᵇᵒ *al*) and others αὐτόν (K L Ψ most minuscules).

4.20 οὐ δύναται ἀγαπᾶν. {A}

Instead of the negative οὐ, which is strongly supported by the Alexandrian text as well as by other witnesses (ℵ B Ψ 1739 syrʰ cop^{sa} Cyprian Lucifer), the Textus Receptus, following A K L most minuscules it^r vg syr^p cop^{bo} arm eth *al*, substitutes the interrogative πῶς. The latter appears to be an improvement introduced by copyists in order to heighten the rhetorical style.

5.1 *[καὶ] τόν* {C}

On the one hand, the absence of καί in B Ψ 048 33 62 326 2298 it^r vg cop^{sa} Speculum *al* may be the result of accidental oversight; on the other hand, the presence of καί in ℵ A K P 049 81 614 1739 most minuscules syr^{p, h} cop^{bo} arm eth *al* may well be a scribal emendation suggested by the similar καί in the preceding sentence. In order to represent the balance of probabilities, the Committee enclosed the word within square brackets.

5.2 *ποιῶμεν* {B}

The expression τὰς ἐντολὰς αὐτοῦ ποιῶμεν (B Ψ (33 ποι-οῦμεν) 81 614 1739 it^r vg syr^{p, h} cop^{sa, bo} arm eth *al*) is extremely rare in the New Testament (elsewhere only in the inferior text of Re 22.14). In ℵ K L P and most minuscules the verb is replaced by the much more usual τηρῶμεν, thus harmonizing with ver. 3 and other passages in 1 John (2.3, 4, 5; 3.22, 24).

5.6 *αἵματος* {A}

The original reading appears to be αἵματος, which is well supported by a variety of witnesses, including representatives of both the Alexandrian and the Western types of text (B Ψ 1739* it^r vg syr^p Tertullian *al*). Copyists who recalled Jn 3.5 (ἐξ ὕδατος καὶ πνεύματος) introduced πνεύματος either (*a*) as a substitution for αἵματος (43 241 463 945 1241 1831 1877* 1891) or as an addition (*b*) before αἵματος (P 81 88 442 630 915 2492 arm eth) or (*c*) after αἵματος (ℵ A 104 424^c 614 1739^c 2412 syr^h cop^{sa, bo} Origen), occasionally appending ἁγίου after πνεύματος (39 61 326 1837).

5.6 ὅτι τὸ πνεῦμα

Instead of ὅτι τὸ πνεῦμα the Latin Vulgate, followed by one Greek manuscript copied in the sixteenth century (61), reads ὅτι Χριστός ("And it is the Spirit that bears witness that *Christ* is the truth"). According to Westcott (*Com., ad loc.*), the substitution may have arisen from confusion between x̄p̄c̄ (*Χριστός*) and S̄P̄S̄ (*Spiritus*). Within the Latin tradition there is variation, some witnesses adding *Iesus* either before or after *Christus,* and some replacing *Christus* with *Iesus.*[1]

5.7-8 μαρτυροῦντες, **8** τὸ πνεῦμα καὶ τὸ ὕδωρ καὶ τὸ αἷμα {A}

After μαρτυροῦντες the Textus Receptus adds the following: ἐν τῷ οὐρανῷ, ὁ Πατήρ, ὁ Λόγος, καὶ τὸ Ἅγιον Πνεῦμα· καὶ οὗτοι οἱ τρεῖς ἕν εἰσι. (8) καὶ τρεῖς εἰσιν οἱ μαρτυροῦντες ἐν τῇ γῇ. That these words are spurious and have no right to stand in the New Testament is certain in the light of the following considerations.

(A) EXTERNAL EVIDENCE. (1) The passage is absent from every known Greek manuscript except eight, and these contain the passage in what appears to be a translation from a late recension of the Latin Vulgate. Four of the eight manuscripts contain the passage as a variant reading written in the margin as a later addition to the manuscript. The eight manuscripts are as follows:

61:     codex Montfortianus, dating from the early sixteenth century.

88[v.r.]: a variant reading in a sixteenth century hand, added to the fourteenth-century codex Regius of Naples.

221[v.r.]: a variant reading added to a tenth-century manuscript in the Bodleian Library at Oxford.

429[v.r.]: a variant reading added to a sixteenth-century manuscript at Wolfenbüttel.

---

[1] For the evidence see *Vetus Latina; Die Reste der altlateinischen Bibel;* XXVI, *Epistulae Catholicae* (Freiburg, 1966), p. 361.

636[v.r.]: a variant reading added to a sixteenth-century manuscript at Naples.

918: a sixteenth-century manuscript at the Escorial, Spain.

2318: an eighteenth-century manuscript, influenced by the Clementine Vulgate, at Bucharest, Rumania.

(2) The passage is quoted by none of the Greek Fathers, who, had they known it, would most certainly have employed it in the Trinitarian controversies (Sabellian and Arian). Its first appearance in Greek is in a Greek version of the (Latin) Acts of the Lateran Council in 1215.

(3) The passage is absent from the manuscripts of all ancient versions (Syriac, Coptic, Armenian, Ethiopic, Arabic, Slavonic), except the Latin; and it is not found (*a*) in the Old Latin in its early form (Tertullian Cyprian Augustine), or in the Vulgate (*b*) as issued by Jerome (codex Fuldensis [copied A.D. 541–46] and codex Amiatinus [copied before A.D. 716]) or (*c*) as revised by Alcuin (first hand of codex Vallicellianus [ninth century]).

The earliest instance of the passage being quoted as a part of the actual text of the Epistle is in a fourth century Latin treatise entitled *Liber Apologeticus* (chap. 4), attributed either to the Spanish heretic Priscillian (died about 385) or to his follower Bishop Instantius. Apparently the gloss arose when the original passage was understood to symbolize the Trinity (through the mention of three witnesses: the Spirit, the water, and the blood), an interpretation that may have been written first as a marginal note that afterwards found its way into the text. In the fifth century the gloss was quoted by Latin Fathers in North Africa and Italy as part of the text of the Epistle, and from the sixth century onwards it is found more and more frequently in manuscripts of the Old Latin and of the Vulgate. In these various witnesses the wording of the passage differs in several particulars. (For examples of other intrusions into the Latin text of 1 John, see 2.17; 4.3; 5.6, and 20.)

(B) INTERNAL PROBABILITIES. (1) As regards transcriptional probability, if the passage were original, no good reason can be found to account for its omission, either accidentally or intentionally, by copyists of hundreds of Greek manuscripts, and by translators of ancient versions.

(2) As regards intrinsic probability, the passage makes an awkward break in the sense.

For the story of how the spurious words came to be included in the Textus Receptus, see any critical commentary on 1 John, or Metzger, *The Text of the New Testament,* pp. 101 f.; cf. also Ezra Abbot, "I. John v. 7 and Luther's German Bible," in *The Authorship of the Fourth Gospel and Other Critical Essays* (Boston, 1888), pp. 458–463.

5.10   ἐν ἑαυτῷ {B}

On the basis of ℵ Ψ 049 88 1739 *al* a majority of the Committee preferred ἑαυτῷ, a reading that the minority regarded as a secondary development from αὐτῷ understood in a reflexive sense.

5.10   τῷ θεῷ {A}

Among the several readings, τῷ θεῷ, which is well supported by representatives of a variety of types of text (ℵ B K P Ψ 614 it‍ syr[p, h] *al*), is to be preferred. The other readings (except the accidental omission by the first hand of the Vulgate codex Amiatinus) arose from a desire to make the negative clause correspond more exactly to the preceding positive clause.

5.13   ὑμῖν

After ὑμῖν the Textus Receptus, following K L P most minuscules, reads τοῖς πιστεύουσιν εἰς τὸ ὄνομα τοῦ υἱοῦ τοῦ θεοῦ, ἵνα εἰδῆτε ὅτι ζωὴν ἔχετε αἰώνιον, καὶ ἵνα πιστεύητε εἰς τὸ ὄνομα τοῦ υἱοῦ τοῦ θεοῦ. Although one could argue that the shorter reading arose in order to remove the redundancy of τοῖς πιστεύουσιν ... ἵνα πιστεύητε, it is more likely that the reading of the earlier witnesses (ℵ* B syr) is original, especially since ἵνα πιστεύητε seems to have arisen as a scribal assimilation to the statement in Jn 20.31.

5.17 οὐ {A}

The negative οὐ, which is strongly attested, is lacking in several Greek and versional witnesses, probably for dogmatic reasons.

5.18 ὁ γεννηθεὶς ἐκ {A}

The ambiguity of reference intended by the words ὁ γεννηθεὶς ἐκ τοῦ θεοῦ (a reading strongly attested by witnesses of all textual types) prompted copyists to introduce one or another change in the interest of clarification of meaning. (See also the following comment.)

5.18 αὐτόν {B}

The Committee understood ὁ γεννηθεὶς to refer to Christ, and therefore adopted the reading αὐτόν, which is supported by A* B 330 614 it^r vg syr^h cop^bo al. Copyists who took ὁ γεννηθεὶς to refer to the Christian believer (although elsewhere John always uses ὁ γεγεννημένος, never ὁ γεννηθεὶς, of the believer) naturally preferred the reflexive ἑαυτόν (ℵ A^c K P Ψ 33 81 1739 al).

5.20 ἥκει

After ὁ υἱὸς τοῦ θεοῦ ἥκει several Latin witnesses (vg^mss Julianus of Toledo) add, without Greek authority, the following doctrinal expansion: *et carnum induit nostri causa et passus est et resurrexit a mortuis; adsumpsit nos et dedit* … ("[The Son of God has come] and was clothed with flesh for our sake, and suffered, and arose from the dead; he has received us and given …").

5.20 τὸν ἀληθινόν {A}

The reading that best explains the origin of the others is τὸν ἀληθινόν, which is supported by representatives of several early types of text (B 81 syr^p, h cop^bomss arm Speculum). In order to clarify the reference of the adjective, copyists added θεόν, either before τὸν ἀληθινόν (629) or after (A Ψ 33 614 1739 vg cop^bomss eth). Several other copyists preferred the neuter τὸ ἀληθινόν (ℵ* it^r cop^sa, bomss).

5.21 εἰδώλων. {A}

After εἰδώλων the Textus Receptus, following K L P 81 614 *Byz Lect*, reads ἀμήν, a common liturgical addition. The earlier text, without ἀμήν, is strongly supported by the best Alexandrian and Western witnesses (ℵ A B 33 it^r vg Speculum *al*).

THE SECOND LETTER OF JOHN

ver. 1 ἐκλεκτῇ κυρίᾳ

Although either or both nouns may be taken as proper names, and hence capitalized according to modern usage ("to the elect Kyria [or, Cyria]," or "to the lady [or, the dear] Electa," or "to Electa Kyria [or, Cyria]"), the Committee understood the words to be used metaphorically of a local congregation.

ver. 3 παρὰ Ἰησοῦ Χριστοῦ {A}

Before Ἰησοῦ the Textus Receptus, in accord with ℵ K L P most minuscules syr[h] cop[bo] arm *al,* reads κυρίου. Since it is more likely that copyists would have added rather than deleted such a word, the Committee preferred the shorter text, which is supported by good representatives of early types of text (A B 81 1739 vg cop[sa]).

ver. 5 κυρίᾳ

It is possible to take κυρίᾳ as a proper name (see the comment on ver. 1).

ver. 8 ἀπολέσητε ... ἀπολάβητε {A}

Superior manuscript evidence supports the second person verbs, which are also congruent with βλέπετε ἑαυτούς. See also the following comment.

ver. 8 εἰργασάμεθα {B}

Despite the relatively meager external evidence supporting the reading εἰργασάμεθα, on internal considerations the Committee was persuaded that the delicate nuance ("... that you do not destroy the things which we, apostles and teachers, wrought in you") is more likely to be due to the author than to copyists. On transcriptional grounds also this reading best explains the origin of the second person verb, which arose through a levelling process.

ver. 9 $\delta\iota\delta\alpha\chi\hat{\eta}$ (2) {A}

After the second $\delta\iota\delta\alpha\chi\hat{\eta}$ the Textus Receptus, following K L P most minuscules cop[bo] eth, adds $\tauο\hat{υ}$ $Χρισ\tauο\hat{υ}$. This reading is obviously secondary, the result of scribal assimilation to the first part of the sentence. Likewise $\delta\iota\delta\alpha\chi\hat{\eta}$ $αὐ\tauο\hat{υ}$, read by certain versional and patristic witnesses (syr[ph, h with *] Lucifer), originated from a similar desire to relate the two clauses more closely. The shorter reading is strongly supported by ℵ A B Ψ 33 81 1739 vg cop[sa] al.

ver. 11 $πονηρο\hat{ι}ς$

The Sixtine edition of the Vulgate, following several Latin manuscripts that differ slightly among themselves, adds *Ecce prae-dixi vobis, ut in die Domini non confundamini* ("Behold, I have forewarned you, that in the day of the Lord you may not be con-founded").

ver. 12 $ἡμ\hat{ω}ν$ {B}

In the opinion of a majority of the Committee, the reading $ἡμ\hat{ω}ν$, which is supported by ℵ K L P Ψ 614 *Byz Lect* syr[ph, h] arm *al,* is quite in harmony with the author's generous spirit in associating himself with his readers (cf. $ἡμ\hat{ω}ν$ in 1 Jn 1.4). The reading $ὑμ\hat{ω}ν$, which is widely supported by several generally superior witnesses (A B 33 81 1739 vg cop[bo]), appears to have arisen by scribal assimilation to $ὑμ\hat{ι}ν$ and $ὑμ\hat{α}ς$ earlier in the sentence. Other singular and sub-singular readings ($ἐμο\hat{υ}$, cop[sa], and the omission of the pronoun, 309 327 378) also occur.

654 A TEXTUAL COMMENTARY

ver. 13 τῆς ἐκλεκτῆς. {A}

After ἐκλεκτῆς the Textus Receptus, following K L 049 056 0142 most minuscules syr^(ph, h), reads ἀμήν, a common liturgical addition. The shorter text, without ἀμήν, is strongly supported by ℵ A B P Ψ 33 81 1739 vg cop^(sa, bo). Other witnesses present a variety of readings, the most widespread being the addition of ἡ χάρις μετὰ σοῦ (or μεθ᾽ ὑμῶν). ἀμήν.

THE THIRD LETTER OF JOHN

ver. 4   οὐκ ἔχω χαράν {A}

Although the reading χάριν (B 5 57 1891 2143 2298 2492 vg cop^{bo} Hilary) may seem to be intrinsically superior, expressing "the divine favour in a concrete form" (Westcott, *Commentary, ad loc.*), the Committee considered it to be a transcriptional modification and preferred the more Johannine χαράν, which is strongly supported by ℵ A C K L P 81 614 1739 syr^{ph, h} cop^{sa} arm eth.

ver. 9   ἔγραψά τι {B}

The reading that best explains the origin of the others appears to be ἔγραψά τι, read by ℵ* A (B) 048 1241 1739 (cop^{sa, bo}) arm. In order to prevent the reader from drawing the conclusion that an apostolic letter was lost, the reading ἔγραψα ἄν ("I would have written …") was introduced into ℵ^c 33 81 181 614 vg *al*. Other copyists, to avoid undue deprecation of apostolic authority, omitted τι (C K L P Ψ most minuscules, followed by the Textus Receptus). The readings ἔγραψάς τι (B cop^{sa, bo}) and ἔγραψα αὐτῇ (326^c) are obviously transcriptional errors.

ver. 15   ὄνομα.

After ὄνομα several of the later witnesses (L 307 321 378 467 614 1836 1837 1838 vg^{mss}) append the liturgical ἀμήν.

THE LETTER OF JUDE

ver. 1 τοῖς ἐν θεῷ πατρὶ ἠγαπημένοις {A}

Instead of ἠγαπημένοις, which is decisively supported by 𝔓⁷²
ℵ A B Ψ 81 1739 vg syr^{ph, h} cop^{sa, bo} arm eth Origen Lucifer *al,*
the Textus Receptus, following K L P and most minuscules, reads
ἡγιασμένοις. The latter reading, which is modeled upon 1 Cor 1.2,
was introduced by copyists in order to avoid the difficult and unusual
combination ἐν θεῷ πατρὶ ἠγαπημένοις.

ver. 1 καὶ Ἰησοῦ Χριστῷ τετηρημένοις {A}

The omission of these words in a few witnesses was occasioned
by parablepsis, owing to homoeoteleuton *(ηγαπHMENOIΣ ...
τετηρHMENOIΣ).*

ver. 3 ἡμῶν {A}

As between ἡμῶν and ὑμῶν, the former is strongly supported
by such excellent witnesses as 𝔓⁷² ℵ A B Ψ 81 614 1739 syr^{ph, h}
cop^{sa} arm *al,* whereas the latter is read by only a few minuscules and
by vg cop^{bo} Hilary Ephraem. The omission of the pronoun in K L P
049 *Byz Lect* probably reflects a desire to give the idea a universal
character.

ver. 4 δεσπότην {A}

Since δεσπότης was sometimes used by Greek writers to refer
to God (in the New Testament at Lk 2.29; Acts 4.24; Re 6.10), the
Textus Receptus, following K L P Ψ and many minuscules, added
θεόν in order more clearly to distinguish δεσπότην from the following κύριον ἡμῶν Ἰησοῦν Χριστόν. In later manuscripts many
other variant readings are found (see also the following comment).

ver. 4   ἡμῶν Ἰησοῦν Χριστόν {A}

Despite many occasional variant readings,[1] the wording of the text is strongly supported by (𝔓⁷²) 𝔓⁷⁸ ℵ A B C Ψ 33 81 1739 *al*.

ver. 5   πάντα ὅτι [ὁ] κύριος ἅπαξ {D}

Despite the weighty attestation supporting Ἰησοῦς (A B 33 81 322 323 424ᶜ 665 1241 1739 1881 2298 2344 vg copˢᵃ, ᵇᵒ eth Origen Cyril Jerome Bede; ὁ Ἰησοῦς 88 915), a majority of the Committee was of the opinion that the reading was difficult to the point of impossibility, and explained its origin in terms of transcriptional oversight (κ̅ς̅ being taken for ι̅ς̅). It was also observed that nowhere else does the author employ Ἰησοῦς alone, but always Ἰησοῦς Χριστός. The unique collocation θεὸς Χριστός read by 𝔓⁷² (did the scribe intend to write θεοῦ χριστός, "God's anointed one"?) is probably a scribal blunder; otherwise one would expect that Χριστός would be represented also in other witnesses.

The great majority of witnesses read ὁ before κύριος, but on the strength of its absence from ℵ Ψ and the tendency of scribes to add the article, it was thought best to enclose ὁ within square brackets.

[Critical principles seem to require the adoption of Ἰησοῦς, which admittedly is the best attested reading among Greek and versional witnesses (see above). Struck by the strange and unparalleled mention of Jesus in a statement about the redemption out of Egypt (yet compare Paul's reference to Χριστός in 1 Cor 10.4), copyists would have substituted (ὁ) κύριος or ὁ θεός. It is possible, however, that (as Hort conjectured) "the original text had only ὁ, and that ΟΤΙΟ was read as ΟΤΙΙ̅C̅ and perhaps as ΟΤΙΚ̅C̅" ("Notes on Select Readings," *ad loc.*).

The origin of the variations in the position of ἅπαξ is best explained by assuming that it originally stood after εἰδότας (as in 𝔓⁷² A B C² L 049 33 81 104 181 326 330 436 451 629 945 1877 2127

---

[1] For a full conspectus of variant readings here (and elsewhere in Jude), see C. A. Albin, *Judasbrevet, traditionen texten tolkningen* (Stockholm, 1962), pp. 596–631.

al); because, however, the word did not seem to suit εἰδότας, and because the following τὸ δεύτερον appeared to call for a word like πρῶτον, ἅπαξ was moved within the ὅτι-clause so as to qualify σώσας.[2] B.M.M. and A.W.]

ver. 8 κυριότητα {A}

Instead of the more abstract κυριότητα, a few witnesses read the plural κυριότητας.

ver. 12 ἀγάπαις ὑμῶν {A}

Instead of ἀγάπαις, which is strongly attested by ℵ B K L most minuscules vg cop[sa, bo] syr[h, hgr] arm eth Ephraem Lucifer Augustine Palladius *al,* several witnesses, influenced by the prevailing text of 2 Pe 2.13, read ἀπάταις (82 378 460) and two read εὐωχίαις (6 224[c]).

ver. 19 ἀποδιορίζοντες {A}

In order to clarify the sense of the verb, C and a number of minuscules, followed by the Textus Receptus, add ἑαυτούς.

verses 22-23 {C}

The text of verses 22 and 23 has been transmitted in quite diverse forms. Some of the witnesses refer to three classes of people, while other witnesses refer to only two classes; and there are other variations as well.

I. The following witnesses distinguish between three classes of people, and differ as to the verb in the first clause:

---

[2] For further discussion see Allen Wikgren, "Some Problems in Jude 5," in *Studies in the History and Text of the New Testament in Honor of Kenneth Willis Clark,* edited by Boyd L. Daniels and M. Jack Suggs (= *Studies and Documents,* vol. xxix; Salt Lake City, 1967), pp. 147–152.

(a) ℵ reads   καὶ οὓς μὲν ἐλεᾶτε διακρινομένους, οὓς δὲ σῴζετε ἐκ πυρὸς ἁρπάζοντες, οὓς δὲ ἐλεᾶτε ἐν φόβῳ.

(b) A reads   καὶ οὓς μὲν ἐλέγχετε διακρινομένους, οὓς δὲ σῴζετε ἐκ πυρὸς ἁρπάζοντες, οὓς δὲ ἐλεεῖτε ἐν φόβῳ.

II. The following witnesses distinguish between only two classes of people, and involve several other variations as well:

(c) B reads   καὶ οὓς μὲν ἐλεᾶτε διακρινομένους σῴζετε ἐκ πυρὸς ἁρπάζοντες, οὓς δὲ ἐλεᾶτε ἐν φόβῳ.

(d) C* reads   καὶ οὓς μὲν ἐλέγχετε διακρινομένους, οὓς δὲ σῴζετε ἐκ πυρὸς ἁρπάζοντες ἐν φόβῳ.

(e) K L P read   καὶ οὓς μὲν ἐλεεῖτε διακρινόμενοι, οὓς δὲ ἐν φόβῳ σῴζετε ἐκ πυρὸς ἁρπάζοντες.

III. Still more condensed is the reading of 𝔓⁷²: οὓς μὲν ἐκ πυρὸς ἁρπάσατε, διακρινομένους δὲ ἐλεεῖτε ἐν φόβῳ. Somewhat similar to this reading are also those of syr^ph and Clement^lat.

In view of the author's predilection for arranging his material in groups of three (as in verses 2, 4, 8, in the examples of judgment in verses 5-7, and of sin in ver. 11), a majority of the Committee was disposed to prefer as original the triple arrangement of the passage, and to regard the other forms as aberrations that arose partly from scribal inattentiveness, partly from indecision concerning the sense of διακρίνεσθαι in ver. 22 (in ver. 9 it means "to contend" with someone; here, however, it must mean "to doubt"), and partly from concern to provide a main clause after three (or two) relative clauses. (See also the following comments.)

ver. 22   ἐλεᾶτε διακρινομένους {C}

Instead of the verb "to have mercy on" (whether spelled ἐλεᾶτε, as in ℵ B C² Ψ 88, or ἐλεεῖτε, as in K L P 049 056 0142 *Byz Lect*), several witnesses read ἐλέγχετε, meaning "convince" or "refute" (A C* 33 81 1739 vg cop^bo arm Ephraem Cassiodorus). Although the latter reading was widely known in the ancient church (cf. the versions and fathers that support it), a majority of the Committee preferred to follow the testimony of the Alexandrian text (ℵ B) and regarded ἐλέγχετε as a scribal modification introduced in order to differentiate the statement from that in the clause οὓς δὲ ἐλεᾶτε in ver. 23, thus producing a sequence progressing from severity ("reprove") to compassion ("show mercy").

Instead of διακρινομένους (𝔓^72 ℵ A B C 33 81 1739 al), the Textus Receptus, following most of the later witnesses (K P most minuscules), reads διακρινόμενοι. The latter reading is obviously a secondary development, introduced by copyists in order to conform the participle to the nominative case in agreement with the following two participles in ver. 23 (ἁρπάζοντες and μισοῦντες).

ver. 23   οὓς δὲ σῴζετε ἐκ πυρὸς ἁρπάζοντες {C}

Besides the highly condensed form of text in 𝔓^72 (see comment on verses 22-23), other witnesses (syr^ph cop^sa Clement^lat al) omit οὓς δὲ σῴζετε and replace ἁρπάζοντες with ἁρπάζετε, thus providing a suitable main clause after the relative clause(s). Still other witnesses transpose the phrase ἐν φόβῳ from the third relative clause to a position either after ἁρπάζοντες (C 630 syr^h al) or before σῴζετε (K L P 056 Byz Lect). The phrase, however, clearly belongs to the third clause, in which it supplies the reason for the addition of the explanatory phrase μισοῦντες ... χιτῶνα. The singular reading of B καὶ οὓς μὲν ἐλεᾶτε διακρινομένους σῴζετε ἐκ πυρὸς ἁρπάζοντες, οὓς δὲ ἐλεᾶτε ἐν φόβῳ ("and those, whom you pity when they contend [or doubt], save and snatch from the fire, but some pity in fear"), can scarcely be correct, for it involves, as Hort admits, "the incongruity that the first οὓς must be taken as a relative, and the first ἐλεᾶτε as indicative."[3] It is probable that the scribe of B accidentally omitted οὓς δέ before σῴζετε, in which case his archetype would

---

[3] "Notes on Select Readings," p. 107. In Hort's opinion, "Some primitive error evidently affects the passage."

have agreed with the text preserved in ℵᶜ A Ψ 33 81 1739 vg cop^{bo} arm Ephraem.

ver. 23   οὓς δὲ ἐλεᾶτε ἐν φόβῳ {C}

In accord with the decisions made on the preceding sets of variant readings in verses 22 and 23, the reading οὓς δὲ ἐλεᾶτε ἐν φόβῳ, which is strongly supported by a variety of early types of text (ℵ A B Ψ 33 81 1739 vg cop^{bo} arm Ephraem), appears to be superior to any of the other readings.

ver. 25   μόνῳ {A}

After μόνῳ, K L P and many minuscules, followed by the Textus Receptus, add σοφῷ, thus assimilating the doxology to Ro 16.27. (See also comment on 1 Tm. 1.17.)

ver. 25   πρὸ παντὸς τοῦ αἰῶνος

Several of the later uncials, as well as most minuscules (followed by the Textus Receptus), omit πρὸ παντὸς τοῦ αἰῶνος, perhaps because the expression did not seem to be appropriate in a doxology. The words are strongly supported by ℵ A B C L 5 378 436 467 623 808 1827 1837 1845 1852 vg syr^h cop$^{sa, bo}$ arm (eth) Ephraem.

THE REVELATION TO JOHN

The title of the book in the earliest manuscripts (ℵ C) is simply
Ἀποκάλυψις Ἰωάννου (-άνου ℵ). In later witnesses this brief title
is modified in a great variety of expansions (sixty different wordings
of the title are cited by Hoskier[1]). What is probably the longest and
most fulsome title is that of a manuscript at Mount Athos (no. 1775,
copied A.D. 1847): Ἡ ἀποκάλυψις τοῦ πανενδόξου εὐαγγε-
λιστοῦ, ἐπιστηθίου φίλου, παρθένου, ἠγαπημένου τῷ Χριστῷ,
Ἰωάννου τοῦ θεολόγου, υἱοῦ Σαλώμης καὶ Ζεβεδαίου, θετοῦ
δὲ υἱοῦ τῆς θεοτόκου Μαρίας, καὶ υἱοῦ βροντῆς ("The Revelation of the all-glorious Evangelist, bosom-friend [of Jesus], virgin,
beloved to Christ, John the theologian, son of Salome and Zebedee,
but adopted son of Mary the Mother of God, and Son of Thunder").

1.5 λύσαντι ἡμᾶς ἐκ {A}

Instead of λύσαντι the Textus Receptus, following the later
uncials (P 046), most of the minuscules, and several early versions
(it[gig] vg cop[bo] eth), reads λούσαντι. The reading λύσαντι is to be
preferred because it has superior manuscript support ($\mathfrak{P}^{18}$ ℵ A C
1611 it[h] syr[ph, h] arm *al*); because it is in accord with Old Testament
imagery (e. g. Is 40.2 LXX); and because it suits better the idea
expressed in ver. 6a. The reading λούσαντι, which sometimes may
have been pronounced like λύσαντι, seems to have arisen "due
to failure to understand the Hebraic use of ἐν to denote a price ... and
a natural misapplication of 7.14" (Hort, "Notes on Select Readings,"
ad loc.).

With the verb λούειν the preposition ἀπό is naturally more appropriate than ἐκ; the early versions cannot discriminate between the
two prepositions.

---

[1] H. C. Hoskier, *Concerning the Text of the Apocalypse; Collations of all Existing
Greek Documents ...*, II (London, 1929), pp. 25–27.

1.6 εἰς τοὺς αἰῶνας [τῶν αἰώνων] {C}

The words τῶν αἰώνων are absent from 𝔓[18] A P about thirty minuscules cop[bo] Andrew[a], but are present in ℵ C 046 1 1006 1611 1854 2053 it[gig, h, ar] vg syr[ph, h] arm eth Andrew[bav, c, p] Arethas. It is difficult to decide whether the shorter text arose accidentally through scribal oversight, or whether the words were added by copyists in accord with the customary liturgical formula. Since the fuller form occurs eleven other times in Revelation (1.18; 4.9, 10; 5.13; 7.12; 10.6; 11.15; 15.7; 19.3; 20.10; 22.5), the Committee was reluctant to drop τῶν αἰώνων from the text here. At the same time, however, since copyists tended to expand such doxological formulas, it seemed best to enclose the words within square brackets, thus indicating doubt concerning their right to stand in the text.

1.8 Ὠ {A}

After Ὠ[2] the Textus Receptus, following ℵ* 1 (2344) it[gig, ar] vg *al*, adds ἀρχὴ καὶ τέλος, and twenty other minuscules add ἡ ἀρχὴ καὶ τὸ τέλος. If the longer text were original no good reason can be found to account for the shorter text, whereas the presence of the longer expression in 21.6 obviously prompted some copyists to expand the text here.

1.15 πεπυρωμένης {C}

Although πεπυρωμένης is without syntactical concord in the sentence, it was preferred by the Committee not only because it is rather well attested (A C Primasius) but chiefly because it best explains the origin of the other readings. In order to remove the grammatical difficulty some copyists read πεπυρωμένῳ (ℵ 2053 the ancient versions

---

[2] It will be noticed that in the Greek text alpha is spelled out, whereas omega is represented by the letter. The reason for this difference arises from the fact that Greek grammarians did not invent the name ὦ μέγα (in distinction from ὸ μικρόν) until long after the Apocalypse had been written (see Metzger, *Manuscripts of the Greek Bible* [Oxford, 1981], p. 6, note 13).

al), which qualifies καμίνῳ, and other copyists read πεπυρωμένοι (P 046 most minuscules), which qualifies οἱ πόδες.

2.7 θεοῦ {A}

A number of minuscules, influenced by the recollection of θεοῦ μου in 3.2 and four instances of the expression in 3.12, have added μου to θεοῦ in 2.7.

2.13 Ἀντιπᾶς

Since the context seems to demand the genitive Ἀντιπᾶ, several modern exegetes (including Swete, Charles, Zahn) adopt Lachmann's conjecture that, after accidental dittography of the definite article (ΑΝΤΙΠΑΟΟΜΑΡΤΥϹ), the first omicron was taken as a sigma. The Committee, however, regarded the conjecture as more ingenious than compelling.

2.16 οὖν

The Textus Receptus, following ℵ P 1 2053 vg syr^h *al*, omits οὖν. A majority of the Committee preferred the reading with οὖν, which is supported by A C 046 1006 1611 1854 syr^ph cop^sa, bo, and explained its absence in other witnesses as due either to transcriptional oversight (after -σον) or to taking μετανόησον with the preceding ὁμοίως.

2.20 γυναῖκα {B}

On the basis of what was regarded as preponderant testimony, a majority of the Committee preferred the reading γυναῖκα without σου (ℵ C P 1 1611 2053 2344 Old Latin vg cop^sa, bo arm eth Tertullian *al*). The reading with σου ("your wife Jezebel"), which requires ἄγγελος in ver. 18 to be taken as the bishop or leader of the church at Thyatira, is supported by (A) 046 1006 1854 syr^ph, h Cyprian *al*, and appears to be the result of scribal confusion arising from the presence of several instances of σου in verses 19 and 20.

2.22 κλίνην {A}

Instead of κλίνην, which is decisively supported by ℵ C P 046 1 1006 1611 1854 2053 2344 it^{gig, ar} vg syr^{ph, h} cop^{bo} *al*, several witnesses, wishing to increase the punishment threatened to Jezebel, have introduced various glosses. Thus, A reads φυλακήν, probably derived from ver. 10; 2071 and arm read κλίβανον ("an oven, furnace"); 1597 and cop^{sa} read ἀσθένειαν; and several (Latin) manuscripts known to Primasius read *luctum* ("sorrow, affliction").

2.22 ἔργων αὐτῆς {A}

Instead of αὐτῆς (which is strongly supported by ℵ C P 1006 1611 2053 it^{gig} vg syr^h cop^{sa, bo} Tertullian *al*), the Textus Receptus, following A 1 1854 2081 2344 it^{ar} syr^{ph} arm eth Cyprian *al*, reads αὐτῶν. The latter reading appears to be secondary, having been introduced either unwittingly (a mechanical repetition of the preceding termination) or deliberately (so that the repentance should be for their own works rather than for another's). Several singular readings reflect scribal eccentricities.

3.5 οὕτως {B}

Instead of οὕτως the Textus Receptus, following ℵ^c P 046 and most minuscules, reads οὗτος. A majority of the Committee preferred οὕτως, partly because of superior manuscript evidence (ℵ* (A) C 1006 2344 it^{gig, ar} vg syr^{ph, h} cop^{sa, bo} arm eth *al*), and partly because οὕτως, seeming to be superfluous, may have therefore been corrected by copyists to οὗτος.

4.11 ἦσαν {A}

The difficulty of the text (where we might have expected the sequence ἐκτίσθησαν καὶ ἦσαν) was alleviated in several witnesses either by reading οὐκ ἦσαν or by omitting ἦσαν καί.

5.6 τὰ [ἑπτά] {C}

The evidence for the presence of ἑπτά before πνεύματα (𝔓²⁴ ℵ 046 1854 2053 2344 2432 it^gig syr^ph, h cop^sa, bo arm Hippolytus *al*) is fairly evenly balanced against the evidence for its absence (A P^vid 1 1006 1611 it^ar vg eth Irenaeus^arm *al*). From the transcriptional point of view, through confusion with the two previous instances of ἑπτά in the preceding line, the word may have been accidentally omitted. On the other hand, copyists may have inserted the numeral in imitation of 1.4; 3.1; 4.5. In order to represent the ambiguities of external and internal considerations, the Committee decided to print the word, but to enclose it within square brackets, thus indicating doubt whether it belongs in the text.

5.9 τῷ θεῷ {A}

Although the evidence for τῷ θεῷ is slight (A eth), this reading best accounts for the origin of the others. Wishing to provide ἠγόρασας with a more exactly determined object than is found in the words ἐκ πάσης φυλῆς κ.τ.λ., some scribes introduced ἡμᾶς either before τῷ θεῷ (94 2344 *al*) or after τῷ θεῷ (ℵ 046 1006 1611 2053 *al*), while others replaced τῷ θεῷ with ἡμᾶς (1 2065* Cyprian *al*). Those who made the emendations, however, overlooked the unsuitability of ἡμᾶς with αὐτούς in the following verse (where, indeed, the Textus Receptus reads ἡμᾶς, but with quite inadequate authority). See also the following comment.

5.10 αὐτούς {A}

The third person pronoun, which is overwhelmingly supported, was replaced by ἡμᾶς in several versional and patristic witnesses, followed by the Textus Receptus.

5.10 βασιλεύσουσιν {A}

Of the three variant readings, it is obvious that βασιλεύσομεν (2432 *al*) is a secondary development, arising from the introduction of ἡμᾶς in the preceding verse (see the comment on ver. 9). It is more difficult to choose between βασιλεύσουσιν, supported by ℵ P 1 94 1854 2053 2344 it^{gig} vg syr^{ph} cop^{sa, bo} arm *al*, and βασιλεύουσιν, supported by A 046 1006 1611 it⁶¹ syr^h *al*. A majority of the Committee, noting that in 20.6 codex Alexandrinus mistakenly reads βασιλεύουσιν for the future tense, preferred βασιλεύσουσιν here, as more suited to the meaning of the context.

5.13 καί (5) {B}

In order to provide a verb for the relative clause (with or without an additional relative pronoun), after θαλάσσης some witnesses read ἐστίν, καί (A 1006 1611^c 1854 2344 *al*), others read ἅ ἐστιν, καί (P 046 1 2073 2081 *al*, followed by the Textus Receptus), and still others read ὅσα ἐστίν, καί (1828 2053 *al*). The text that seems to have given rise to these modifications is simply καί, supported by ℵ 1611* 2020 2065 2432 *al*.

6.1 ἔρχου {B}

After ἔρχου, which is well supported by A C P 1 1006 1611 1854 2053 vg cop^{sa, bo} *al*, several witnesses add (as though the verb "Come!"[1] were addressed to the Seer) καὶ ἴδε (ℵ 046 about 120 minuscules it^{gig} syr^{ph, h} eth *al*) or καὶ βλέπε (296 2049 and Textus Receptus). The singular readings ὅτι ἔρχομαι (arm) and *et veni* (it^{ar}) are due to freedom in translation.

6.2 καὶ εἶδον {B}

The words καὶ εἶδον are absent from 046 about 100 minuscules (most of which add καὶ ἴδε in ver. 1; see previous comment) *al*. The Committee preferred to include the words (*a*) because of preponderant testimony, including ℵ (A C ἴδον) P 1 1006 1611 2053 2344 it^{gig} vg syr^h cop^{bo} arm *al*, and (*b*) because the omission can be either accidental (ΚΑΙΕΙΔΟΝΚΑΙΙΔΟΥ), or deliberate on the part of copyists

---

[1] It is also possible to translate (as Zahn prefers), "Go!"

of the manuscripts that read καὶ ἴδε at the close of ver. 1 (who therefore would naturally have regarded καὶ εἶδον as superfluous). The singular readings εἶδον (cop^sa) and καὶ ἤκουσα καὶ εἶδον (syr^ph) are due to freedom in translation.

6.3-4   ἔρχου. καί {B}

As in ver. 1, after ἔρχου, which is here well supported by A C P 046 1006 1611 1854 2053 vg syr^ph, h cop^sa, bo *al*, several witnesses (including ℵ 1828 2073 2344 it^gig, ar cop^boms *al*) add καὶ ἴδε, while a few others (296 2049 followed by the Textus Receptus) add καὶ βλέπε. (See also the comment on ἔρχου in ver. 1.)

6.5   ἔρχου {B}

See the comment on ver. 1.

6.5   καὶ εἶδον {B}

See the comment on ver. 2.

6.7   ἔρχου {B}

See the comment on ver. 1.

6.8   καὶ εἶδον {B}

See the comment on ver. 2.

6.17   αὐτῶν {A}

Although the reading αὐτοῦ is supported by A P 046 almost all minuscules cop^sa, bo arm eth *al*, it appears to be the easier reading, having been introduced to avoid the ambiguity of αὐτῶν (which is strongly supported by ℵ C 1611 1854 2053 2344 it^gig, ar vg syr^ph, h *al*) and to carry on the reference to τῆς ὀργῆς τοῦ ἀρνίου of the preceding verse.

8.1 ὅταν

Although ℵ P and almost all minuscules, followed by the Textus Receptus, read ὅτε, the Committee preferred ὅταν, which is supported by A C 1006 1611 1841. The reading ὅτε seems to be an assimilation to the six instances of ὅτε ἤνοιξεν in chap. 6. (For another example of ὅταν with the indicative in the book of Revelation, see 4.9.)

8.8 πυρί

The word πυρί is absent from 046, about 125 minuscules, syr^ph *al*. A majority of the Committee preferred to include the word on the basis of its presence in such diversified witnesses as ℵ A P 052 1006 1854 2053 2344 it^gig. (h), ar vg syr^h cop^sa, bo *al*. The word may have been omitted because it seemed redundant with καιόμενον.

8.13 ἀετοῦ

Instead of ἀετοῦ (which is decisively supported by ℵ A 046 most minuscules it^gig, h vg syr^ph, h cop^sa,bo eth) the Textus Receptus, following P 1 680 2059 2060 2081 2186 2286 2302 arm *al*, reads ἀγγέλου. The substitution may have been accidental (a scribe misread ΑΕΤΟΥ as ΑΓΓΕΛΟΥ), but more likely it was deliberate, since the function ascribed to the eagle seems more appropriate to an angel (cf. 14.6). Furthermore, "had the Apocalyptist written ἀγγέλου, ἄλλου would probably have taken the place of ἑνός; cf. 7.2; 8.3" (H. B. Swete, *The Apocalypse of St. John, ad loc.*). The two readings are conflated by 42 *al* into ἀγγέλου ὡς ἀετοῦ.

9.12-13 οὐαὶ μετὰ ταῦτα. Καί

Since μετὰ ταῦτα (or μετὰ τοῦτο) almost always begins a sentence or clause (elsewhere in Revelation the phrase occurs at the close of a sentence only in 1.19 and 4.1), many witnesses (0207, more than 100 minuscules, syr^ph) join μετὰ ταῦτα to ver. 13. In order to smooth the juncture several witnesses either move the initial καί of ver. 13 so as to precede μετὰ ταῦτα (046) or omit it altogether (𝔓⁴⁷ ℵ 61 69 456 469 664 2058 2344 syrᵖʰ copˢᵃ, ᵇᵒ arab). The text adopted is adequately supported (A P 1 172 2015 2023 it vg syrʰ *al* Tyconius Andrew Haymo Arethas) and is in accord with the author's manner of introducing previously mentioned angels (8.1, 8, 10, 12; 9.1).

9.13 μίαν ἐκ τῶν [τεσσάρων] κεράτων {C}

The weight of the external evidence for the presence and for the absence of τεσσάρων is almost evenly balanced. Among internal considerations, on the one hand it is possible that the word was added in order to make an antithesis to φωνὴν μίαν and a parallelism with τοὺς τέσσαρας ἀγγέλους of ver. 14; on the other hand it is possible that the word was accidentally omitted in transcription when the eye of the scribe passed from τῶν to the last letters of τεσσάρων. In view of such considerations a majority of the Committee thought it best to include the word in the text, but to enclose it within square brackets. Among the singular readings the omission of μίαν ... κεράτων in ℵ* is noteworthy.

9.21 φαρμάκων

The Committee preferred φαρμάκων, which occurs nowhere else in the New Testament, partly on the basis of external support (𝔓⁴⁷ ℵ C 1006 1611 1854 *al*) and partly because copyists would have been more likely to alter it to the more specific φαρμακ(ε)ιῶν (A P 046 2053 2344 *al*), which occurs in 18.23 and Ga 5.20, than vice versa.

10.4 ὅτε ἐλάλησαν αἱ ἑπτὰ βρονταί, ἤμελλον γράφειν {B}

Instead of ὅτε (which is read by A C P 046 1006 1611 1854 2053 2344 vg syrᵖʰ, ʰ arm) several witnesses, including 𝔓⁴⁷ ℵ several minuscules copˢᵃ, ᵇᵒ *al*, substitute ὅσα. A majority of the Committee, impressed by the external evidence, preferred ὅτε, and considered ὅσα to be an exegetical modification, similar to other interpretative rewritings of the text found in sporadic witnesses.

10.6 καὶ τὴν θάλασσαν καὶ τὰ ἐν αὐτῇ {A}

The omission of καὶ τὴν θάλασσαν ... αὐτῇ by a number of witnesses (including ℵ* A 1611 2344 it^gig syr^ph cop^sa *al*) is probably accidental, arising from homoeoarcton and homoeoteleuton. The predominant weight of the external evidence (𝔓⁴⁷ C P 1006 1854 2053 it⁶¹ vg (syr^h) cop^sams, bo *al*) favors the originality of the words, as does also the impression that they are appropriate to the completeness of the formal discourse of the author.

10.10 βιβλαρίδιον

In view of the variation between βιβλαρίδιον in verses 2 and 9 and βιβλίον in ver. 8, it is not easy to decide in ver. 10 between βιβλαρίδιον (A C P *al*) and βιβλίον (ℵ 046 1854 *al*). A third reading, βιβλιδάριον, has only minuscule support, including 1006 1611 2053. On the basis chiefly of the weight of external evidence the Committee preferred βιβλαρίδιον, to which also 𝔓⁴⁷ seems to point with βιβλίδιον.

11.1 ῥάβδῳ {A}

The unusual construction of ἐδόθη μοι ... λέγων, calling for adjustment, was relieved in some witnesses (ℵ² 046 1854 2329 2351 *al*), followed by the Textus Receptus, by the insertion of καὶ εἱστήκει ὁ ἄγγελος before λέγων.

11.2 ἔξωθεν (1) {A}

The reading ἔξωθεν is to be preferred on both external and internal grounds: (*a*) it is strongly supported by 𝔓⁴⁷ A P 046 1006 1611 1854 2053 it^ar vg syr^h cop^sa, bo arm *al*; and (*b*) copyists who understood the αὐλή to be the inner courtyard were puzzled by the expression τὴν αὐλὴν τὴν ἔξωθεν, and therefore changed the adverb to ἔσωθεν (ℵ about thirty-five minuscules syr^ph *al*).

11.12 ἤκουσαν {B}

Instead of ἤκουσαν 𝔓⁴⁷ ℵᶜ 046 many minuscules cop^bo arm *al* read ἤκουσα. Not only does the weight of external evidence favor ἤκουσαν, but since the Seer constantly uses ἤκουσα throughout the book (24 times), copyists were more likely to substitute ἤκουσα for ἤκουσαν than vice versa.

11.17 ὅτι {B}

The reading ὅτι, in the view of a majority of the Committee, is to be preferred because of superior external evidence (ℵᶜ A P 046 1 1611 1854 2053 it^gig, h vg syr^ph, h cop^sa *al*) and because it best explains the origin of the readings. The addition of ὁ ἐρχόμενος ὅτι (051 1006 sixteen minuscules vg^mss and the Textus Receptus) is a typical Byzantine accretion, in imitation of the tripartite expression in 1.4, 8; cf. 4.8. The reading καὶ ὅτι, although supported by 𝔓⁴⁷ ℵ* C 2344 cop^boms arm, strains the syntax and appears to be a scribal blunder.

11.18 τοὺς μικροὺς καὶ τοὺς μεγάλους

The reading τοὺς μικροὺς καὶ τοὺς μεγάλους, which is strongly supported by 𝔓⁴⁷ ℵ* A C 2321 2322 2329 2344 2351, is to be preferred to the easier reading τοῖς μικροῖς καὶ τοῖς μεγάλοις (ℵᶜ P 046 almost all minsucules).

11.19 ὁ ἐν τῷ οὐρανῷ

On the one hand, the reading with the article is supported by superior external evidence (A C about 30 minuscules including 1006 1828 2020 2073 it^gig, h cop^bo arm eth *al*); on the other hand, however, since it has the appearance of being a grammatical correction, the reading ἐν τῷ οὐρανῷ (𝔓⁴⁷ ℵ P 046 051 most minuscules *al*) may seem to be preferred. In view of the weight of the external evidence, a majority of the Committee preferred the reading with the definite article, and explained its absence in other witnesses as the result of transcriptional oversight.

12.10 κατήγωρ

Codex Alexandrinus reads κατήγωρ, a hapax legomenon in the New Testament, whereas all other witnesses (including 𝔓⁴⁷ ℵ C P 046) read the more usual Greek word κατήγορος. A majority of the Committee preferred κατήγωρ, which, it was judged, was more likely to be altered to κατήγορος than vice versa. A minority of the Committee, while acknowledging that for the book of Revelation codex Alexandrinus is a remarkably good witness, preferred κατήγορος, agreeing with Tasker that in the present instance "it may well be that the fifth-century scribe of A is [merely] reflecting the usage of his day and not copying from a manuscript which retained the original reading κατήγωρ."[1]

12.18 καὶ ἐστάθη {B}

Instead of καὶ ἐστάθη, which is well supported by 𝔓⁴⁷ ℵ A C about 25 minuscules (including 1854 2344) and it^{gig, ar} vg syr^h arm eth al, the Textus Receptus, following P 046 051 most minuscules syr^{ph} cop^{sa, bo} al, reads Καὶ ἐστάθην (preceded by a full stop). The latter reading appears to have arisen when copyists accommodated ἐστάθη to the first person of the following εἶδον.

13.1 ὀνόμα[τα] {C}

On the one hand, the reading ὄνομα may have arisen from ὀνόματα through the accidental omission of ΤΑ after ΜΑ; on the other hand, however, after the plural κεφαλάς copyists may have tended to alter ὄνομα to ὀνόματα. On the strength of the two most important witnesses (A 2053) a majority of the Committee preferred to print ὀνόματα in the text, but to enclose the last two letters within square brackets in order to represent the opposing evidence.

---

[1] R. V. G. Tasker, *Journal of Theological Studies*, L (1949), p. 65.

13.6 τοὺς ἐν τῷ οὐρανῷ σκηνοῦντας {B}

Among the several readings a majority of the Committee preferred τοὺς ... σκηνοῦντας on the grounds of its superior external support (it is read by (ℵ*) A C (1006) 1611 2053ᶜᵒᵐᵐ 2344 *al*) and its being the more difficult reading. The presence of καί before τοὺς (in ℵᶜ P 046* 051 most minuscules and early versions) appears to be due to copyists who wished to alleviate the strained syntax. In view of occasional omissions in 𝔓⁴⁷ the Committee regarded its reading ἐν τῷ οὐρανῷ as a secondary modification, introduced probably because of the syntactical difficulty. The singular reading of syrᵖʰ is probably due to the freedom of the translator.

13.7 καὶ ἐδόθη αὐτῷ ποιῆσαι πόλεμον μετὰ τῶν ἁγίων καὶ νικῆσαι αὐτούς {A}

The absence of the clause καὶ ἐδόθη ... αὐτούς in a variety of witnesses (𝔓⁴⁷ A C P about 50 minuscules (including 2053) syrʰ copˢᵃ arm) is no doubt due to oversight in transcription, the eye of the scribe passing from the first to the second instance of καὶ ἐδόθη αὐτῷ. Several minuscules (1859 2020 2065 2432) introduce ἐξουσία from the following clause, while other secondary witnesses modify the order of words (1611 1854 *al*).

13.10 εἰς αἰχμαλωσίαν, εἰς αἰχμαλωσίαν ὑπάγει {B}

The epigrammatic style of the saying has perplexed the scribes (and interpreters!). The reading εἰς αἰχμαλωσίαν, εἰς αἰχμαλωσίαν ὑπάγει (A vg Ps-Ambrose) best accounts for the origin of the others. The absence of one of the two instances of εἰς αἰχμαλωσίαν, although rather widespread (𝔓⁴⁷ ℵ C P 046 1006 1611 2053 *al*), appears to be the result of accidental oversight in transcription. The absence of a verb with the first clause prompted various copyists to attempt to improve the text by adding either ἀπάγει (616 1828 1854 1862 1888 2322 itᵍⁱᵍ, ⁽ᵃʳ⁾ vgᵐˢˢ syrᵖʰ, ʰ *al*) or συνάγει (2059 2081 Arethas, followed by the Textus Receptus), or by altering the construction to αἰχμαλωτίζει (94 104 459 2019).

The reading ἔχει αἰχμαλωσίαν ὑπάγει (051 and about 130 minuscules), which can scarcely be translated, must be regarded as a scribal blunder (ἔχει being written instead of εἰς); it is thus a further development of the second reading mentioned above (𝔓⁴⁷ al).

13.10 ἀποκτανθῆναι, αὐτόν {B}

Among a dozen variant readings, the least unsatisfactory appears to be ἀποκτανθῆναι, αὐτόν, supported by codex Alexandrinus. As in the first two lines of the verse, the third and fourth lines teach fulfillment of the will of God. Perhaps under the influence of such sayings as Mt 26.52 (πάντες γὰρ οἱ λαβόντες μάχαιραν ἐν μαχαίρῃ ἀπολοῦνται), copyists modified in various ways the difficult Greek construction (which, as Charles points out, seems to be a literal rendering of a distinctively Hebrew idiom, אֲשֶׁר בַּחֶרֶב לָמוּת הוּא בַחֶרֶב לָמוּת "if anyone is to be slain with the sword, he is to be slain with the sword") and introduced the idea of retribution (persecutors will be requited in strict accord with the *lex talionis*) – an idea that is contrary to the reading of Alexandrinus, where the subject throughout the verse remains the Christians themselves.[1]

13.15 ποιήσῃ [ἵνα] ὅσοι {C}

The word ἵνα, which seems to be indispensable with ἀποκτανθῶσιν, stands after ποιήσῃ in A P 1006 2065 al, and before ἀποκτανθῶσιν in 051 1 1854 2073 and the Textus Receptus. The latter reading, which is supported by inferior external witnesses, is an obvious scribal amelioration of the difficulty occasioned by ἵνα ... ἐάν followed by two verbs in the subjunctive. The omission of ἵνα in א 046 1611 1859 al appears to be accidental, resulting in a shift of subject ("that even the image of the beast should speak; and he

---

[1] For discussions of the textual problems of this verse, see Josef Schmid, *Studien zur Geschichte des griechischen Apokalypse-Textes;* II. Teil, *Die alten Stämme* (Munich, 1955), pp. 138–141, and Joël Delobel in *L'Apocalypse johannique et l'Apocalyptique dans le Nouveau Testament,* ed. by J. Lambrecht (Louvain, 1980), pp. 162–165.

shall cause that as many as ... should be killed" ASV^{mg}). In view of the multiplicity of readings, no one of which clearly explains the origin of the others, a majority of the Committee thought it best to include ἵνα in the text, but to enclose the word within square brackets.

13.17 καί {A}

The absence of καί in ℵ* C about 25 minuscules (including 1611) syr^{ph, h} cop^{sa, bo} *al* appears to be a secondary modification arising from misunderstanding the relationship between verses 16 and 17. When the ἵνα μή clause was taken to be dependent upon δῶσιν, καί was naturally regarded as superfluous, whereas the clause is no doubt to be taken as dependent upon ποιεῖ and therefore coordinate with the ἵνα δῶσιν clause. The text is supported by 𝔓⁴⁷ ℵ^c A^{vid} P 046 051 1006 1854 2344 it^{gig, ar} vg arm eth *al*.

13.18 ἑξήκοντα ἕξ {A}

Instead of ἑξήκοντα, which is strongly supported by 𝔓⁴⁷ ℵ A P 046 051 all extant minuscules it^{gig} vg syr^{ph, h} cop^{sa, bo} arm *al*, δέκα is read by C some manuscripts known to Irenaeus (who, however, says that 666 is found "in all good and ancient copies," and is "attested by those who had themselves seen John face to face") and Tyconius^{pt}. According to Tischendorf's 8th ed., the numeral 616 was also read by two minuscule manuscripts that unfortunately are no longer extant (nos. 5 and 11; cf. C. R. Gregory, *Prolegomena*, p. 676).[2] When Greek letters are used as numerals the difference between 666 and 616 is merely a change from ξ to ι (666 = χξϛ and 616 = χιϛ). Perhaps the change was intentional, seeing that the Greek form Neron Caesar written in Hebrew characters (נרון קסר) is equivalent to 666, whereas the Latin form Nero Caesar (נרו קסר) is equivalent to 616.

---

[2] For a variety of other numerals in several minuscules and in Armenian witnesses, see H. C. Hoskier, *Concerning the Text of the Apocalypse,* II (London, 1929), pp. 364 f.

14.1 τό (1) {A}

The presence of τό before ἀρνίον is strongly supported by ℵ A C *al*; it is lacking in 𝔓⁴⁷ P 051 and a number of minuscules, followed by the Textus Receptus.

14.3 [ὡς] {C}

The weight of the external evidence supporting the presence of ὡς (A C 1006 1841 2042 itᵃʳ vg syrᵖʰ *al*) is about equal to that supporting its absence (𝔓⁴⁷ ℵ P 046 1611 1854 2053 (2344) itᵍⁱᵍ syrʰ copˢᵃ, ᵇᵒ arm eth *al*). It is difficult to decide whether the word was mechanically introduced by copyists as an echo of ver. 2, where it appears three times, or whether it was dropped, either accidentally or in imitation of 5.9, where the expression ᾄδουσιν ᾠδὴν καινήν occurs without ὡς. In order to represent the even balance of external evidence and transcriptional probabilities, the word was retained but enclosed within square brackets.

14.5 ἄμωμοι

The introduction of the connective γάρ (𝔓⁴⁷ ℵ 046 1006 1611 2344 itᵃʳ vgᵐˢˢ syrᵖʰ, ʰ copˢᵃ, ᵇᵒ *al,* followed by the Textus Receptus) is a natural addition for copyists to make, especially in view of the expression παρθένοι γάρ εἰσιν in the previous verse; whereas there is no reason why the word should have been deleted. The reading without γάρ (A C P 1854 2053 2081 itᵍⁱᵍ vg *al*) is more solemn, and entirely appropriate for the author (cf. 16.6). The reading ὅτι ἄμωμοι (051 2056 2131 2254) is obviously secondary.

14.5 εἰσιν

After εἰσιν two minuscule manuscripts (296 2049) and several Latin witnesses, followed by the Clementine Vulgate and the Textus Receptus, add ἐνώπιον τοῦ θρόνου τοῦ θεοῦ. Eleven other minuscules (including 424 617 1888 2018 2084) add after εἰσιν the clause οὗτοί εἰσιν οἱ ἀκολουθοῦντες τῷ ἀρνίῳ, a gloss derived from ver. 4.

14.6 ἄλλον ἄγγελον {B}

The more difficult reading, which is strongly supported by A C 1006 1611 2053 2344 it^{gig. ar} vg syr^{ph, h} cop^{bo} arm Cyprian *al*, is to be preferred. The absence of ἄλλον (𝔓⁴⁷ ℵ* 046 most minuscules cop^{sa} Origen *al*) is either an accidental omission (due to the similarity of the first letters, ΑΛΛΟΝ and ΑΓΓΕΛΟΝ) or, more probably, a deliberate excision owing to its seeming lack of relevancy (for no individual angel has been mentioned since 11.15).

14.8 ἄλλος ἄγγελος δεύτερος {B}

The reading that seems to explain best the origin of the others is ἄλλος ἄγγελος δεύτερος, which is supported by ℵ^c (C δεύτερον) P 051 1611 2053 *al* (the versional evidence is without much force) and by the sequence of ἄλλος ἄγγελος τρίτος in ver. 9. This sequence, which agrees with the author's style in 6.4; 10.1; 15.1 (where an adjective used in addition to ἄλλος is placed after the noun), is altered in A 046 more than one hundred minuscules Primasius *al* to ἄλλος δεύτερος ἄγγελος, while other witnesses, followed by the Textus Receptus, eliminate the tautological δεύτερος (61 69 296 598 2039 2049 2066 2286 it^{ar} vg eth *al*). Likewise the reading ἄλλος δεύτερος (𝔓⁴⁷ ℵ* 1006 1841 1854 2040 syr^{ph}) appears to presuppose the reading ἄλλος ἄγγελος δεύτερος, from which ἄγγελος was accidentally omitted in transcription because of the similarity of letters in ἄλλος and ἄγγελος[1]. (See also the comment on 14.6.)

14.13 ναί, λέγει {A}

Although the shorter reading λέγει (𝔓⁴⁷ ℵ* 336 582 620 628 1918 cop^{bo} eth) may be thought to be primitive, and the other readings scribal expansions, it is perhaps more probable that ναί, λέγει is original, for it is strongly supported (ℵ^c A C P 051 1006 1611 1854 2344 it^{ar, (gig)} vg syr^{ph, h} cop^{sa} arm Speculum *al*) and is in the style of the

---

[1] See Josef Schmid, *Studien zur Geschichte des griechischen Apokalypse-Textes;* II. Teil, *Die alten Stämme* (Munich, 1955), pp. 104 f.

Apocalypse (1.7; 16.7; 22.20). The readings λέγει ναί (046 and ninety minuscules), καὶ λέγει (205 2018 2019 2053), and λέγει καί (218 522) are obviously secondary.

14.18 ἄγγελος [ἐξῆλθεν] ἐκ τοῦ θυσιαστηρίου {C}

On the one hand, it can be argued that ἐξῆλθεν was inserted by scribes from ver. 17, sometimes after ἄγγελος (ℵ C P 046 most minuscules it[h] syr[ph, h] cop[sa, bo] arm *al*) and sometimes after θυσιαστηρίου (051 1854 2073). On the other hand, repetition is characteristic of the author of the Apocalypse, and the absence of the verb in 𝔓[47] A 1611 2053 *al* may be due to either accidental omission or deliberate excision by scribes who considered it unnecessary in view of its presence in the preceding verse. Because of the balance of such considerations, a majority of the Committee preferred to follow ℵ C 1006 *al* and to include the word in the text, but to enclose it within square brackets, thus reflecting considerable doubt that it belongs there.

14.20 χιλίων ἑξακοσίων

Instead of 1600 stadia, a reading well supported by ℵ[c] A C P 046 most minuscules, versions, and patristic references, several inferior witnesses read 1606 stadia (χιλίων ἑξακοσίων ἕξ, 1876 2014 2036 2037 2042 2043 2046 2047 2074 2082 Andrew[a]); a few other witnesses read 1200 stadia (χιλίων διακοσίων, ℵ* 203 506 syr[ph]), probably because this numeral lends itself better to symbolic interpretation. One Old Latin manuscript (it[gig]) reads *mille quingentis* ("1500"), and χιλίων has been accidentally omitted in 2065 and by the first hand of codex Amiatinus.

15.3 ἐθνῶν {B}

The weight of external evidence supporting the reading ἐθνῶν (ℵ[a] A P 046 051 most minuscules it[gig, h] cop[bo] arm eth Cyprian *al*) is nearly the same as that supporting αἰώνων (𝔓[47] ℵ*, c C 94 469 1006

1611 1841 2040 2065 2073^{mg} 2076 2254 2258 2344^{vid} 2432 it^{61} vg
syr$^{ph, h}$ cop^{sa} *al*). The former reading was preferred by a majority of
the Committee on the grounds that (*a*) αἰώνων was introduced by
copyists who recollected 1 Tm 1.17 (cf. Enoch 9.4 and Tobit 13.4),
and (*b*) the reading ἐθνῶν is more in accord with the context (ver. 4).
In order to enhance the meaning a few witnesses add πάντων (it^h arm
eth Primasius). The reading of the Textus Receptus *(ἁγίων)*, which
has only the slenderest support in Greek witnesses (296 2049, neither
of which was available when the Textus Receptus was formed),
appears to have arisen from confusion of the Latin compendia for
sanctorum (sctorum) and *saeculorum (sclorum [= αἰώνων])*; "saint"
is also read by several Latin writers, including Victorinus-Pettau,
Tyconius, Apringius, and Cassiodorus.

15.6   λίνον {B}

Although the reading λίθον is strongly attested (A C 2053 vg *al*)
and was widely circulated at an early date, in the opinion of the Committee it is a transcriptional error that, despite a superficial parallel
with Eze 28.13, makes no sense; it is particularly inapposite with the
adjective καθαρόν, which, on the contrary, is altogether appropriate
with λίνον (P 051 1 1006 1611 1859 2081 it$^{gig, h, ar}$ syr$^{ph, h}$ arm *al*). The
reading λινοῦν (𝔓^{47} 046 94 1828; cf. λινους *[sic]*, ℵ), though a
secondary improvement ("made of linen") for a rare use of λίνον,
indirectly strengthens the external support for the latter. The omission
of the noun (cop^{sa} eth Cassiodorus) is probably due to translational
freedom.

16.1   ἐκ τοῦ ναοῦ

The words ἐκ τοῦ ναοῦ, which are adequately supported by ℵ A
C P 1 2020 2057 2329 vg arm Andrew and Primasius, are omitted
(perhaps because they were regarded as somehow inappropriate
in the context) in 046 about ninety minuscules arm^{pt} Arethas. The
reading ἐκ τοῦ οὐρανοῦ (42 367 468 2196 vg^{mss} cop$^{sa, bo}$ arm^{pt}
Tyconius Beatus) arose when ναοῦ was taken to be the contraction
of οὐρανοῦ (οὐνοῦ).

16.4 ἐγένετο {B}

Instead of ἐγένετο several important witnesses, including 𝔓⁴⁷ A 1006 1854 2053 it^{gig, h} syr^{ph,h} cop^{sa,bo} *al*, mechanically conform the verb to the preceding plurals and read ἐγένοντο. The more difficult reading, ἐγένετο, is adequately supported by ℵ C P 046 051 most minuscules it^{ar} vg arm *al*.

16.16 Ἁρμαγεδών

The mystic place-name, usually spelled in English "Armageddon" (based on one form of the late Byzantine text), is spelled Ἁρμαγεδών in ℵ A E and about 95 minuscules. Another form of the word, lacking the first syllable, is spelled either Μαγεδδών (046 1611 2053 2063) or Μαγεδών (about 80 minuscules). Other orthographic variations occur in one or more witnesses, including the following (information concerning the breathing and accentuation is not available for most readings): Αρμεγηδων (2054), Αρμαγεδδων (2049 2081^c), Αρμεγεδδων (2029), Ἀρμεγεδων (ℵ^a 2028 2033 2044 2054 2069 2083 2186), Ἀρμαγεδῶ (2091), Αρμαγεδον (2065), Αρμαγεδωμ (205 206 209 2045), Μαγεδωδ (1828), Μαγιδων (2015), and Μακεδδων (61 69). Still other spellings occur in the early versions.

16.17 ναοῦ ἀπὸ τοῦ θρόνου {A}

The phrase ναοῦ ἀπὸ τοῦ θρόνου, which is supported by the preponderant weight of witnesses, has undergone a variety of modifications in various manuscripts: it is replaced by ναοῦ τοῦ θεοῦ in ℵ; by ἀπὸ τοῦ οὐρανοῦ in 051*; and is expanded by the addition of τοῦ οὐρανοῦ and/or τοῦ θεοῦ in still other witnesses.

17.4 πορνείας αὐτῆς {B}

Among the several readings πορνείας αὐτῆς appears to be best attested, being supported by A 1006 2344 vg syr^{ph} *al*. The substitution of τῆς γῆς for αὐτῆς seems to be due to a copyist's blunder. Codex

Sinaiticus presents the conflate reading πορνείας αὐτῆς καὶ τῆς γῆς (cf. the Sahidic "of her fornication with those of the earth" and the Bohairic "... with all the earth").

17.8 ὑπάγει {B}

Orthographically ὑπάγει (A 1611 2053 *al*) differs very little from ὑπάγειν (ℵ P 046 051 1006 1854 *al*), for in Greek manuscripts final ν is often represented merely by a horizontal stroke over the preceding letter. In the context the present indicative is the more difficult reading, which copyists would have been prone to alter to the infinitive after μέλλει.

18.2 [καὶ φυλακὴ παντὸς θηρίου ἀκαθάρτου] {C}

The multiplicity of variations among the witnesses, though complicated, is set forth clearly in the following tabular arrangement (drawn up for the Committee by Dr. Klaus Junack), where the three main elements are represented by 1, 2, and 3, and the five groups of readings are represented by A, B, C, D, and E.

1 καὶ φυλακὴ παντὸς πνεύματος ἀκαθάρτου

2 καὶ φυλακὴ παντὸς ὀρνέου ἀκαθάρτου

3 καὶ φυλακὴ παντὸς θηρίου ἀκαθάρτου

    3*a* add καὶ μεμισημένου

A:	1 — 2 — 3 3*a*	2329 cop^{sa} Oecumenius	
	1 3*a* 2 3*a* 3 3*a*	it^{gig}	
	1 — 3 3*a* 2 —	Primasius	
B:	1 — 2 3*a* –	ℵ 2053 *Byz* vg	
	1 3*a* 2 3*a* –	2080 *al*	
C:	1 3*a* – — 3 3*a*	A P	
D:	– — 2 — 3 3*a*	1611 *al*	
E:	1 3*a* – — –	Andrew	

It will be observed that amid the variety of readings each concludes with καὶ μεμισημένου, except that quoted by Primasius, who transposes the second and third elements. The similarities of the beginning and ending of the three main elements gave ample occasion for accidental omission. The Committee was of the opinion that all three elements (each of which involves an allusion to Is 13.21; 34.11) probably belonged to the original text of Revelation; since, however, καὶ φυλακὴ παντὸς θηρίου ἀκαθάρτου is absent from such important witnesses as ℵ 2053 2080 vg *al*, it was decided to enclose these words within square brackets.

18.3   τοῦ οἴνου τοῦ θυμοῦ τῆς πορνείας {B}

The reading that seems to explain best the origin of the others is τοῦ οἴνου τοῦ θυμοῦ τῆς πορνείας, read by ℵ 046 1006 1859 2138 cop[sa, boms] *al*. The difficulty of understanding the expression, as well as carelessness on the part of copyists, led to such modifications as τοῦ θυμοῦ τοῦ οἴνου τῆς πορνείας (P 051 about 90 minuscules it[gig] cop[bo] arm eth[pp] *al*), τοῦ θυμοῦ τῆς πορνείας (A 1611 2053 it[ar] vg eth[ro] *al*), τοῦ οἴνου τῆς πορνείας (792 1854 2070[comm] syr[ph] *al*), τῆς πορνείας τοῦ θυμοῦ (C), and τοῦ οἴνου τοῦ θυμοῦ (syr[h] Ps-Ambrose).

18.3   πέπωκαν {D}

On the one hand, the most strongly supported readings, πέπτωκαν (A C 69 2031) and πεπτώκασιν (ℵ 046 about 50 minuscules including 1006[c vid] 1611 cop[sa, bo] *al*), are scarcely suitable in the context and seem to have arisen from a mechanical conformation to ἔπεσεν in ver. 2. On the other hand, the sense of the passage, as well as prophetic imagery (Jr 25.15 [= LXX 32.15] f.; 51.7, 39 [= LXX 28.7, 39]), seems to demand some form of the verb "to drink," or "to make drunken" (compare Re 14.8). Among such readings a majority of the Committee preferred πέπωκαν (1828 2321), which can also be said to be supported by a variety of versional and patristic evidence, as well as by the Greek witnesses that read πεπώκασιν or πέπωκεν (which are morphological or grammatical improvements of πέπωκαν).

18.12 ξύλου {A}

To the scribes of several witnesses (A 1006 1841 *al*) the mention of vessels made of wood did not seem to be congruent with the materials that followed, and therefore they substituted λίθου for ξύλου.

18.17 ὁ ἐπὶ τόπον πλέων {B}

The reading ὁ ἐπὶ τόπον πλέων ("he who sails for (any) part") is strongly supported by A C about 100 minuscules, including 1006 1854, it⁶¹ vg, as well as by ℵ 046 0229 *al*, which insert τόν before τόπον. The unusual expression with τόπον (though one similar to it occurs in Ac 27.2) prompted copyists to substitute one or another interpretation, as (*a*) ἐπὶ τῶν πλοίων πλέων (P 051 about 100 minuscules *al*), (*b*) ὁ ἐπὶ πόντον πλέων (469 582 2076* 2254 cop^bo), (*c*) ὁ ἐπὶ τῶν πλοίων ἐπὶ τόπον πλέων (syr^ph), (*d*) ὁ ἐπὶ τὸν ποταμὸν πλέων (2053 2062, cf. cop^sa "who sail in the rivers"), (*e*) "those who sail from a distance" (Ps-Ambrose), and (*f*) ἐπὶ τῶν πλοίων ὁ ὅμιλος (1 296 2049 2186 Hippolytus), which passed into the Textus Receptus ("the company in ships" AV).

18.22 καὶ πᾶς τεχνίτης πάσης τέχνης {B}

The absence of πάσης τέχνης in ℵ A cop^bo is probably accidental; the words are adequately attested by C P 046 051 most minuscules it^gig vg syr^h cop^sa *al*, and are in harmony with the author's style, but would scarcely have been inserted by copyists. The addition of καί before πάσης (2053 2138 Ps-Ambrose) is probably a mechanical blunder in transcription, suggested by the repeated use of καί in the first half of the verse. Because of homoeoteleuton several witnesses accidentally omit one or another of the clauses that end in ἐν σοὶ ἔτι.

19.5 [καὶ] οἱ φοβούμενοι {C}

The presence of καί is attested by A 046 051 and almost all other witnesses; on the other hand the word is absent from ℵ C P cop^sa, boms. Was the word added by copyists to avoid the asyndetic construction, or was it deleted lest the unwary reader, not seeing that it means "even," imagine that "those who fear God" constitute a different group from "all of his servants"? In the opinion of the Committee the external evidence and the transcriptional probabilities are so evenly balanced as to suggest the advisability of using square brackets around καί.

19.6 κύριος ὁ θεὸς *[ἡμῶν]* {C}

It is difficult to decide whether ἡμῶν was omitted in some witnesses (A 1 254 792 1006 2023 2040 2065 2070 2186 syr^phc cop^sa, bo eth) because it was felt to be inappropriate with the expression κύριος ὁ θεὸς ὁ παντοκράτωρ (none of the other instances of the expression in Revelation has the possessive pronoun, 1.8; 4.8; 11.17; 15.3; 16.7; 21.22); or whether, on the other hand, copyists introduced the pronoun after ὁ θεός in accord with the usage in verses 1 and 5. In view of the weight of evidence supporting the pronoun (ℵ^a P 046 1611 1854 2053 2344 it^ar, (gig) vg syr^h cop^sams *al*) ἡμῶν was retained in the text, but enclosed within square brackets in order to express doubt whether it belongs there.

19.7 δώσωμεν {C}

If δῶμεν (ℵ* 046 051 most minuscules) were original, it is not easy to account for the origin of the other readings. The future tense δώσομεν, though attested by ℵ^a A 2053 *al*, is intolerable Greek after two hortatory subjunctive verbs, and must be judged to be a scribal blunder. The least unsatisfactory reading appears to be δώσωμεν (P and 25 minuscules), which, being the irregular aorist subjunctive and used only rarely (4.9 in ℵ and six minuscules; Mk 6.37 in ℵ and D), seems to have been intentionally or unintentionally altered in the other witnesses to one or another of the other readings.

19.11 *[καλούμενος]* πιστὸς καὶ ἀληθινός {C}

Although it might be supposed that the reading πιστὸς καὶ ἀληθινός (A P 051 1 2042 2081 *al*) is original, and that καλούμενος was added by various transcribers either before or after the phrase, or after πιστός, a majority of the Committee considered the omission of the word to be either accidental (καλούμενος καί) or deliberate (lest it be imagined that the Rider is merely *called* Faithful and True), and preferred to adopt the reading attested by 046 94 1006 1611 1841 1854 2020 2053 2062 2065 2073 2138 2329 *al.* The reading of ℵ arose after a scribe, following the short reading represented by A P *al,* replaced καλούμενος, but inserted it at an incorrect position. In view, however, of the divergent positions of καλούμενος, it was thought best to enclose the word within square brackets.

[The reading of ℵ *(πιστὸς καλούμενος καὶ ἀληθινός)* seems to explain best the origin of the other readings. The word καλούμενος was transferred to a position either before πιστός or after ἀληθινός so as to permit the customary connection of the two adjectives πιστὸς καὶ ἀληθινός (as in 3.14; 21.5; 22.6). The preferred sequence of text, therefore, is πιστὸς [καλούμενος] καὶ ἀληθινός. B.M.M.]

19.12 *[ὡς]* {C}

The ὡς before φλόξ is attested by A, about 20 minuscules, most ancient versions, and several important patristic witnesses. Furthermore, the use of the word is a characteristic of the author of the Apocalypse. On the other hand, however, it is lacking in four uncials (ℵ P 046 051) and about 170 minuscules, as well as the Armenian version and Hippolytus. Its presence can be explained as due to scribal assimilation to the similar expression in 1.14. So indecisive is the evenly balanced evidence that the Committee considered it best to retain the word enclosed within square brackets.

19.13 *βεβαμμένον* {B}

Among the many variant readings βεβαμμένον appears to be both the best supported (A 046 051 most minuscules cop^sa arm *al*) and most likely to provoke change. Either the absence of ἐν with the following αἵματι or, more probably, the feeling that the context (and perhaps also the recollection of Is 63.3) made βάπτω less appropriate to express the sense than ῥαίνω or its collateral ῥαντίζω, prompted copyists to substitute ἐρραντισμένον (172 256 792 1006 1341 1778 1862 2017 2018 2040 2065 2070 Origen), or ῥεραντισμένον (P 2019 2321 2329 Origen), or ἐρραμμένον (2053 2062 Origen), or ῥεραμμένον (105 1611 Origen), or, in order to heighten the description, περιρεραμμένον (ℵ* Irenaeus), later corrected to περιρεραντισμένον (ℵᶜ). (The versional and non-Greek patristic evidence often cited for the several forms of ῥαίνω and ῥαντίζω tends to be ambiguous.)

20.2 ὁ ὄφις ὁ ἀρχαῖος

After τὸν δράκοντα the Textus Receptus, following most witnesses (ℵ 046 P most minuscules), reads τὸν ὄφιν τὸν ἀρχαῖον, thus avoiding the inconcinnity of the nominative ὁ ὄφις ὁ ἀρχαῖος (A 1678 1778 2080). The latter reading is in accord with the linguistic usage of the book of Revelation, which employs the nominative case for a title or proper name that stands in apposition to a noun in an oblique case. Eleven minuscules accidentally omit τὸν ὄφιν and read only τὸν ἀρχαῖον.

20.6 [τά] {C}

The external evidence for the presence of the article τά before χίλια ἔτη (ℵ 046 about thirty minuscules copˢᵃ, ᵇᵒ) is almost evenly balanced by the evidence for its absence (A 051 most minuscules copᵇᵒᵐˢ arm Andrew Arethas). Likewise, transcriptional and intrinsic probabilities are so indecisive that a majority of the Committee thought it best to include the word but to enclose it within square brackets.

20.9 ἐκ τοῦ οὐρανοῦ {A}

Among the seven variant readings ἐκ τοῦ οὐρανοῦ has in its favor the preponderant weight of external evidence (A about 25 minuscules copᵇᵒᵐˢˢ Tyconius Augustine Primasius al). The reading ἐκ τοῦ οὐρανοῦ ἀπὸ τοῦ θεοῦ (046 and about 120 minuscules) appears to be an expansion introduced by copyists in imitation of 21.2 and 10. The other variants involve deliberate or accidental modifications of the preposition(s) or of the sequence of clauses in the expanded reading. In codex Sinaiticus the words from πῦρ to λίμνην of ver. 10 are supplied by ℵª, the lines having been accidentally omitted by ℵ*.

21.3 θρόνου

Instead of θρόνου, which is attested by ℵ A 94 vg Irenaeus^lat Tyconius Ambrose Augustine Haymo, the Textus Receptus, following P 046 almost all minuscules and most versions, reads οὐρανοῦ. The latter appears to be an assimilation to ἐκ τοῦ οὐρανοῦ of ver. 2.

21.3 λαοί {B}

It is difficult to decide between the reading λαοί, which is supported by ℵ A 046 2053 and twelve other minuscules it^ar Irenaeus^lat, and the reading λαός, which is supported by E P almost all minuscules and versions and many Fathers. Has the author followed the prophetic Scriptures that consistently speak of the one people of God (e. g. Jr 31.33 [= LXX 38.33]; Eze 37.27; Zch 8.8)? In that case, λαοί was introduced by copyists who pedantically conformed the word to the preceding αὐτοί. Or, did the author deliberately modify the traditional concept, substituting "the many peoples of redeemed humanity for the single elect nation, the world for Israel" (Swete)? In that case, λαός betrays the hand of the emendator who conformed the reading to the imagery of the Old Testament. Chiefly on the basis of what was taken to be slightly superior manuscript evidence a majority of the Committee preferred λαοί.

21.3 μετ᾽ αὐτῶν ἔσται [αὐτῶν θεός], {C}

Once again it is singularly difficult to determine the original reading. Was the expression αὐτῶν θεός (or θεὸς αὐτῶν) omitted (ℵ 046 most minuscules) because it seemed to be totally superfluous, or was it added as a marginal gloss, derived from Is 7.14 and 8.8? If it be argued that the preceding clause ($\kappa\alpha\grave{\iota}$ $\alpha\mathring{\upsilon}\tau o\grave{\iota}$ $\lambda\alpha o\grave{\iota}$ $\alpha\mathring{\upsilon}\tau o\hat{\upsilon}$ $\check{\varepsilon}\sigma o\nu\tau\alpha\iota$) requires some such parallelism as provided by $\alpha\mathring{\upsilon}\tau\hat{\omega}\nu$ $\theta\varepsilon\acute{o}\varsigma$ or $\theta\varepsilon\grave{o}\varsigma$ $\alpha\mathring{\upsilon}\tau\hat{\omega}\nu$, the question arises whether these words are the author's or were supplied by a perceptive copyist. Moreover, in choosing between $\alpha\mathring{\upsilon}\tau\hat{\omega}\nu$ $\theta\varepsilon\acute{o}\varsigma$ and $\theta\varepsilon\grave{o}\varsigma$ $\alpha\mathring{\upsilon}\tau\hat{\omega}\nu$, one is faced with conflicting considerations. The former order, involving the unemphatic position of $\alpha\mathring{\upsilon}\tau\hat{\omega}\nu$, seems to be contrary to the author's usage elsewhere (only in 18.5a does such an order appear). The latter order, however, may have arisen as an attempt to avoid the sequence $\alpha\mathring{\upsilon}\tau\hat{\omega}\nu$ $\check{\varepsilon}\sigma\tau\alpha\iota$ $\alpha\mathring{\upsilon}\tau\hat{\omega}\nu$. After considerable discussion the Committee concluded that the least unsatisfactory procedure was to print the text of A, but to enclose the words $\alpha\mathring{\upsilon}\tau\hat{\omega}\nu$ $\theta\varepsilon\acute{o}\varsigma$ within square brackets.

21.4 $[\check{o}\tau\iota]$ $\tau\grave{\alpha}$ $\pi\rho\hat{\omega}\tau\alpha$ {C}

On the one hand it can be argued that the reading $\tau\grave{\alpha}$ $\pi\rho\hat{\omega}\tau\alpha$, which is strongly supported by A P 051 1006 1611 2053 *al,* is original and that copyists sought to avoid asyndeton by inserting $\check{o}\tau\iota$ or $\gamma\acute{\alpha}\rho$. On the other hand, however, it is altogether possible that the shorter reading originated through an accident in transcription[1] when, because of the preceding $\check{\varepsilon}\tau\iota$, copyists overlooked $\check{o}\tau\iota$. In order to represent the balance of probabilities the Committee decided to include $\check{o}\tau\iota$ enclosed within square brackets.

21.12 $[\tau\grave{\alpha}$ $\mathring{o}\nu\acute{o}\mu\alpha\tau\alpha]$ {C}

Whether scribes considered that the words $\tau\grave{\alpha}$ $\mathring{o}\nu\acute{o}\mu\alpha\tau\alpha$ were superfluous in the context, and therefore omitted them ($\aleph$ P 051 *al*), or that they were needed for the sense, and therefore added them (A 1611 1841 1854 *al*), it is difficult to decide; consequently, the Committee preferred to retain the words, but to enclose them within square brackets.

---

[1] As an example of what nonsense scribes can produce, cf. the absurd reading of $\aleph$* ($\tau\grave{\alpha}$ $\pi\rho\acute{o}\beta\alpha\tau\alpha$ instead of $\tau\grave{\alpha}$ $\pi\rho\hat{\omega}\tau\alpha$!).

22.14   πλύνοντες τὰς στολὰς αὐτῶν {A}

Instead of πλύνοντες τὰς στολὰς αὐτῶν, supported by ℵ A about 15 minuscules (including 1006 2020 2053) it[ar] vg cop[sa] *al,* the Textus Receptus, following 046 most minuscules it[gig] syr[ph, h] cop[bo] *al,* reads the somewhat similar sounding words ποιοῦντες τὰς ἐντολὰς αὐτοῦ. The latter reading appears to be a scribal emendation, for elsewhere the author uses the expression τηρεῖν τὰς ἐντολάς (12.17; 14.12). "Moreover, the prepossessions of the scribes would have favoured ποιοῦντες τὰς ἐντολάς rather than πλύνοντες τὰς στολάς" (H. B. Swete, *in loc.*).

22.19   ἀπὸ τοῦ ξύλου

Instead of ἀπὸ τοῦ ξύλου, the Textus Receptus (followed by the King James Version) reads ἀπὸ βίβλου, a reading that occurs in no Greek manuscript. The error arose when Erasmus, in order to provide copy for the last six verses of Revelation (which were lacking in the only Greek manuscript of Revelation available to him), translated the verses from the Latin Vulgate into Greek (see p. 8* above). The corruption of "tree" into "book" had occurred earlier in the transmission of the Latin text when a scribe accidentally miscopied the correct word *ligno* ("tree") as *libro* ("book").

22.21   κυρίου Ἰησοῦ {A}

The reading κυρίου Ἰησοῦ, which is well supported by ℵ A and about 15 minuscules (including 1611 2053), was expanded by pious scribes by adding Χριστοῦ after Ἰησοῦ (046 051 most minuscules) and ἡμῶν after κυρίου (about 15 minuscules it[ar, gig] vg syr[ph, h] arm *al*). The omission of ἡ χάρις τοῦ κυρίου Ἰησοῦ (2329 cop[bo]) arose by accident when the eye of the copyist or translator passed from Ἰησοῦ (ver. 20) to Ἰησοῦ (ver. 21). Likewise, the singular reading of 1859 *(κυρίου)* is a transcriptional blunder.

22.21   μετὰ πάντων {B}

The concluding words of the book have been transmitted in curiously diverse forms. Apringius and Primasius omit ver. 21

entirely, and the Bohairic version unites verses 20 and 21 to read, "Come, our Lord Jesus Christ, upon all the saints unto age of the age (or ages). Amen." The Greek witnesses present seven different endings (not counting those that append "Amen"):

(1) μετὰ πάντων

(2) μετὰ πάντων ὑμῶν

(3) μετὰ πάντων ἡμῶν

(4) μετὰ τῶν ἁγίων

(5) μετὰ τῶν ἁγίων σου

(6) μετὰ πάντων τῶν ἁγίων

(7) μετὰ πάντων τῶν ἁγίων αὐτοῦ

In favor of (4), which is read by ℵ it^gig, is the fact that elsewhere in the book of Revelation ἅγιος is used twelve times (in 8.3 with πάντων) to designate the Christian believers. Reading (2), adopted by the Textus Receptus, is attested by only one Greek manuscript (296) and shows the influence of 2 Cor 13.13 and 2 Th 3.18. Reading (6), which has the most extensive testimony (046 051 about 180 minuscules syr^h cop^sa, bo arm Andrew Arethas), appears to be a conflation of (1) and (4). Readings (3), (5), and (7) are supported by quite insignificant evidence. On the basis of the weight of codex Alexandrinus (4th century), which is joined by manuscripts of the Latin Vulgate and by Tyconius (A.D. 380) and Beatus (A.D. 786), a majority of the Committee preferred the shortest reading, μετὰ πάντων.

22.21 *omit* ἀμήν. {B}

The Textus Receptus, following ℵ 046 051 almost all minuscules vg syr^ph, h cop^sa, bo arm eth *al,* concludes the book with ἀμήν. If, however, this word were present originally, it is difficult to account for its omission in such witnesses as A 1006 2065^txt 2432 it^gig several mss. of the Vulgate (including codex Fuldensis) Tyconius *al.*

APPENDIX

Here and there in the commentary occasional reference is made to a variety of witnesses, chiefly Greek minuscule manuscripts, which are not cited in the text-volume. The following list of 246 such witnesses supplies the kind of information that is given for Greek manuscripts in the Introduction of the text-volume, namely, an indication of the contents and date of each manuscript. In the column headed "Content," the letter "e" refers to one or more of the Gospels; the letter "a" to the Acts and/or the Catholic Epistles; "p" to one or all of the Pauline Epistles; and "r" to Revelation. For more extensive information (i. e. whether a manuscript is fragmentary; whether it is a palimpsest; whether it contains a commentary; the dimensions and layout of its pages; its present location), one may consult the reference volumes compiled by Gregory and by Aland, mentioned above on p. xiii.

Number	Content	Date	Number	Content	Date
R	e	VI	51	eap	XIII
Ω	e	IX	55	e	XIII
0151	p	IX	59	e	XIII
0211	e	IX	60	er	1297
3	eap	XII	62	ap	XIV
8	e	XI	68	e	XI
10	e	XIII	72	e	XI
16	e	XIV	74	e	1292?
21	e	XII	75	e	XI
23	e	XI	82	apr	X
25	e	XI	89	e	1006
29	e	X	90	eap	XVI
39	e	XI	98	e	XI
43	eap	XII	101	ap	XI
47	e	XV	105	eap	XII

Number	Content	Date	Number	Content	Date
106	e	X	385	apr	1407
111	e	XII	390	eap	1282
114	e	XI	398	ap	XI
123	e	XI	399	e	IX/X
134	e	XII	404	ap	XIV
151	e	X	418	e	XV
172	apr	XIII/XIV	437	a	XI
177	apr	XI	442	ap	XIII
201	eapr	1357	450	ap	X
203	apr	1111	455	ap	XIII/XIV
213	e	XI	456	apr	X
218	eapr	XIII	463	ap	XII
221	ap	X	464	ap	XI
223	ap	XIV	466	ap	XI
224	e	XII	471	e	XII
226	eap	XII	476	e	XI
236	e	XI	478	e	X
243	e	XIV	481	e	X
257	ap	XIII/XIV	484	e	1292
258	e	XIII	506	eapr	XI
262	e	X	536	ea	XIII
265	e	XII	566	e	IX
267	e	XII	571	e	XII
270	e	XII	573	e	XIII
304	e	XII	582	eapr	1334
317	e	XII	598	e	XIII
319	ap	XII	602	ap	X
321	ap	XII	603	ap	XIV
331	e	XI	606	ap	XI
337	apr	XII	611	ap	XII
339	eapr	XIII	616	apr	1434
349	e	1322	617	apr	XI
356	ap	XII	620	apr	XII
364	e	X	628	apr	XIV
367	eapr	1331	642	ap	XV
383	ap	XIII	659	e	XII

Number	Content	Date	Number	Content	Date
660	e	XI/XII	1295	e	IX
661	e	XI	1341	e	XII/XIII
664	eapr	XV	1346	e	X/XI
665	ap	XIII	1354	eap	XIV
680	eapr	XIV	1355	e	XII
697	e	XIII	1375	e	XII
726	e	XIII	1402	e	XII
743	ear	XIV	1405	ap	XV
782	e	XII	1521	eap	XI
794	eap	XIV	1555	e	XIII
807	e	XIV	1570	e	XI
823	eap	XIII	1579	e	XI
850	e	XII	1592	e	1445
876	ap	XII	1604	e	XIII
913	ap	XIV	1610	ap	1364
919	apr	XI	1642	eap	1278
920	apr	X	1704	eapr	1541
941	eap	XIII	1738	ap	XI
990	e	XIV	1753	ap	XIII
999	eap	XIII	1765	ap	XIV
1043	e	XIV	1773	r	XIV
1070	ap	XIII	1799	ap	XII/XIII
1076	e	X	1819	e	XV
1099	ap	XIV	1820	e	XV
1108	ap	XIII	1827	ap	1295
1149	eap	XIII	1829	a	XI
1178	e	XIII	1831	ap	XIV
1188	e	XI/XII	1845	ap	X
1194	e	XI	1849	apr	1069
1200	e	XII	1862	apr	IX
1219	e	XI	1872	apr	XII
1223	e	X	1874	ap	X
1245	ap	XII	1875	ap	XI
1270	ap	XI	1876	apr	XV
1279	e	XI	1884	a	XVI
1288	e	XII	1888	apr	XI

Number	Content	Date	Number	Content	Date
1893	apr	XII	2057	r	XV
1895	a	IX	2059	r	XI
1896	ap	XIV/XV	2060	r	1331
1911	p	XVI	2063	r	XVI
1918	pr	XIV	2064	r	XVI
1924	p	XI	2066	r	1574
1927	p	X	2070	r	1356
1930	p	XVI	2076	r	XVI
1932	p	XI	2078	r	XVI
1944	p	XV	2080	apr	XIV
1952	p	1324	2082	r	XVI
1961	p	XIV	2084	r	XV
1964	p	XV	2104	p	XII
1977	p	XIV	2125	ap	X
1978	p	XV	2131	eap	XIV
1992	p	1232	2143	ap	XII
1994	p	XVI	2145	e	1145
2000	p	XIV	2147	eap	XI
2004	pr	XII	2180	ap	XIV
2005	ap	XIV	2183	p	1042
2014	r	XV	2186	ar	XII
2015	r	XV	2196	r	XVI
2017	r	XV	2248	p	XIV
2018	r	XIV	2254	r	XVI
2019	r	XIII	2256	eap	XVI
2023	r	XV	2258	r	XVII
2031	r	1301	2286	r	XII
2036	r	XIV	2321	e	XI
2037	r	XIV	2322	e	XII/XIII
2039	r	XII	2386	e	XII
2045	r	XIII	2401	ap	XII
2046	r	XVI	2430	e	XI
2047	r	1543	2576	ap	1287
2051	r	XVI	2685	ep	XV
2055	r	XV	2690	p	XVI
2056	r	XIV	2739	p	XIV